ROYAL HISTORICAL SOCIETY
STUDIES IN HISTORY 60

BERTIE OF THAME
EDWARDIAN AMBASSADOR

BERTIE OF THAME
EDWARDIAN AMBASSADOR

Keith Hamilton

THE ROYAL HISTORICAL SOCIETY
THE BOYDELL PRESS

© Keith Hamilton 1990

All Rights Reserved. Except as permitted under current legislation no part of this work may be photocopied, stored in a retrieval system, published, performed in public, adapted, broadcast, transmitted, recorded or reproduced in any form or by any means, without the prior permission of the copyright owner.

First published 1990

A Royal Historical Society publication
Published by The Boydell Press
an imprint of Boydell & Brewer Ltd
PO Box 9   Woodbridge   Suffolk IP12 3DF
and of Boydell & Brewer Inc.
PO Box 41026   Rochester   NY 14604   USA

ISBN 0 86193 217 X

ISSN 0269-2244

British Library Cataloguing in Publication Data
Hamilton, Keith A.
    Bertie of Thame : Edwardian ambassador. - (Royal Historical Society studies in history, ISSN 0269-2244; 60).
    1. Great Britain. Foreign relations. Diplomacy - Biographies
    I. Title   II. Series
    327.2'0924
    ISBN 0-86193-217-X

Library of Congress Cataloging-in-Publication Data
Hamilton, Keith A., 1942-
    Bertie of Thame : Edwardian ambassador / Keith A. Hamilton.
        p.   cm. – (Royal Historical Society studies in history, ISSN 0269-2244 ; 60)
    Includes bibliographical references.
    ISBN 0-86193-217-X (alk. paper)
    1. Bertie, Francis, Sir, 1844-1919. 2. Ambassadors – Great Britain – Biography. 3. Great Britain – Foreign relations – 1901-1936. 4. Great Britain – Foreign relations – 1837-1901. I. Title. II. Series: Royal Historical Society studies in history ; no. 60.
DA568.B47H36   1990
327.2'092 – dc20
[B]   89-70002
                                                                       CIP

This publication is printed on acid-free paper

Printed in Great Britain by
Woolnough Bookbinding Ltd, Irthlingborough, Northants.

TO MY PARENTS
ALEXANDER AND IRENE HAMILTON

Contents

	Page
Acknowledgements	
Introduction	1
1 A master in the art of quarrelling	3
2 *Ein ausgesprochener Gegner Deutschlands*	16
3 His heart's desire	38
4 An open sore	64
5 New masters and old diplomacy	101
6 The *entente* and the *status quo*	125
7 The industrial *entente*	166
8 A purely negative position	194
9 Agadir	214
10 The partition of Morocco	248
11 The clarification of the *entente*	270
12 Sick at heart	298
13 *Quelle fin de carrière*	328
14 The end of an embassy	343
15 Conclusion	388
Bibliography	398
Index	423

The Society records its gratitude to the following whose generosity made possible the initiation of this series: The British Academy; The Pilgrim Trust; The Twenty-Seven Foundation; The United States Embassy's Bicentennial funds; The Wolfson Trust; several private donors.

Publication of this volume was further aided by a generous grant from the Advisory Board of the Woodrow Wilson Chair of International Politics, University College of Wales, Aberystwyth.

Acknowledgements

The final draft of this book was accepted for publication in the summer of 1985. Since then several works bearing upon Bertie's embassies at Rome and Paris have appeared in print. Other academic commitments have, however, deterred me from attempting any fresh revision of a manuscript which has already been far too long in preparation. It began as a doctoral thesis, which I completed under the supervision of the late Professor W. N. Medlicott — a scholar from whose knowledge of nineteenth and twentieth century diplomacy I derived enormous benefit. It was born again as a research project when in 1980 the prospect of a sabbatical term happily coincided with the British Library's acquisition of a fresh collection of Bertie papers.

My access to these and other documents in London and in Paris was assisted by grants kindly awarded by the British Academy, the University College of Wales, and the Advisory Board of the Wilson Chair of International Politics. Correspondence in the Royal Archives is cited with the gracious permission of Her Majesty the Queen, and Crown-copyright material in the Public Record Office is reproduced by permission of the Controller of Her Majesty's Stationery Office. The Ministère des Affaires Étrangères, the Bibliothèque Nationale, the Archives Nationales, and the Bibliothèque de l'Institut de France, have likewise sanctioned my use of documents in their custody.

I am also grateful to the Trustees of the British Library for permission to quote from the Austin Lee, A. J. Balfour, Bertie, Campbell-Bannerman, Charles Scott, C. P. Scott and J. Spender papers; and, in the same way, to the Syndics of Cambridge University Library in respect of the Hardinge papers; to the University of Birmingham in respect of the Joseph Chamberlain papers; to the National Library of Scotland in respect of the Haldane and Murray of Elibank papers; to the Bodleian Library, Oxford, in respect of the Monson, Ponsonby and Sandars papers; to the Syndics of the Fitzwilliam Museum, Cambridge, in respect of the Wilfrid Scawen Blunt papers; to the National Maritime Museum, Greenwich, in respect of the Howard Kelly papers; to Times Newspapers Ltd. in respect of material in *The Times* Archives; to the Clerk of the

Records of the House of Lords and the Trustees of the Beaverbrook Foundation in respect of the Lloyd George papers; to the Master, Fellows and Scholars of Churchill College in the University of Cambridge in respect of the Hankey and Phipps papers; to the Master and Fellows of Balliol College, Oxford, in respect of the Morier papers; to the Trustees of the Liddell Hart Centre for Military Archives at King's College, London, in respect of the Robertson papers; to the Yorkshire Archaeological Society in respect of the Bradfer Lawrence collection; to Lord Salisbury in respect of the Cecil papers at Hatfield House; to Lord Rosebery in respect of the Rosebery papers; to Lord Esher in respect of the Esher papers; to Lord Derby in respect of the Derby papers; to Lady Arthur in respect of the Spring Rice papers; to Lady Salisbury-Jones in respect of the de Bunsen papers; to Mr Mark Bonham Carter in respect of the Asquith papers; to Sir Henry Rumbold in respect of the Rumbold papers; and to the Hon. Mrs Juliette Boobbyer in respect of the Rennell Rodd papers.

Amongst the many individuals whom I would like to thank for their assistance and advice are Mr Peter Barber, Mr Richard Brinkley, Professor David Dilks, Dr M. L. Dockrill, Professor J. C. Garnett, Dr Christopher Howard, Professor I. G. John, Professor Ian Nish, Dr Ritchie Ovendale, Mr Gordon Phillips, Dr Zara Steiner and Dr Moorhead Wright. But I am especially indebted to Dr F. V. Parsons, who encouraged and enlightened me, to Dr Brian Porter, who distracted and informed me, and to Mr Peter D. Thornton, a good friend, who sheltered and entertained me during my frequent research trips to London. Finally, I should like to thank my wife, Kathryn, for her forbearance, good humour and support.

Keith Hamilton
November, 1989

Introduction

Sir Francis Bertie (from 1915 Lord Bertie of Thame) was a British diplomat of the late Victorian and Edwardian eras. Entering the Foreign Office in 1863 as a junior clerk, he rose to become an assistant under-secretary of state in 1894, and in 1903 was appointed ambassador at Rome. Two years later he succeeded Sir Edmund Monson as British ambassador to France, a post which he continued to hold until April 1918. In his time he was noted for his industry and his bullish temper, and his name was, and still is, associated with the rise of what has been labelled 'anti-Germanism' in the British foreign service. He impressed colleagues and subordinates alike with the resolution with which he pursued his ends and the forthright manner in which he expressed his views. Some of those who served under him, and who were later themselves to occupy important diplomatic positions, thought him a 'great ambassador'. Others found him self-centred, short-sighted, tetchy and tyrannical. But to both friends and foes he was the epitome of what in the aftermath of the first world war was dubbed the 'Old Diplomacy'. King Edward VII's choice for Paris, he adopted regal styles and was a jealous guardian of the privileges he thought due to his age and rank. In the words of another British ambassador to France, he 'succeeded in making himself part of the Paris landscape without surrendering a particle of his essentially English characteristics'.[1]

This is in large part a study of Bertie's career, and more especially of the thirteen years which he spent in France: a period which is almost coterminous with the evolution of the Anglo-French *entente* from a political understanding on matters imperial to a war-winning military alliance. Ambassadors do not, however, invariably make good subjects for biography. Their recollections may provide fascinating reading, but their prime concern as diplomats is with the conduct rather than the making of foreign policy, and although they may record their activities in detail, the full extent of their achievements is often difficult to discern. A diplomat may distinguish

---

[1] Sir Eric Phipps, *Diplomatic Light and Shade in Paris and Elsewhere* (unpublished memoir), p.66, Phipps MSS. (Churchill College, Cambridge), PHIPP 9/1.

himself through the accuracy of his information, the quality of his advice, his skill as a negotiator and the confidence which he inspires in foreign governments. But in an age of rapid communication his duties are in the main likely to be those of an intermediary, and such independent judgement as he can exercise may be confined to deciding how best to carry out the instructions of his political superiors. Even an ambassador with as robust a personality as that possessed by Bertie may in the end leave the researcher with little more than a collection of amusing anecdotes. Indeed, what makes Bertie worthy of detailed consideration is not so much his character as the positions which he occupied, and the significance which others attached to his opinions at a time of Foreign Office reform and international crisis.

1

A master in the art of quarrelling

Edwardian diplomats regarded the British embassy at Paris as the greatest prize of their country's diplomatic service. Sir Francis Leveson Bertie, its occupant in the vital years between 1905 and 1918, asserted that it was his by hereditary title. One of his ancestors, Lord Norreys of Rycote, had been an envoy of Elizabeth I to the French court and his father-in-law, the first Earl Cowley, had been ambassador at Paris during the reign of Napoleon III. But Bertie's purpose in conjuring up this claim was probably to humour rather than to impress the politicians of a republic in which deference to aristocratic rank was in theory, if not always in practice, out of fashion.[1] He had in any case no need of it, for at the time of his appointment to Paris he could look back on a career of forty-one years in the public service. True only two of these had been spent abroad. Nevertheless, the position which he had occupied in the Foreign Office during the last years of the Victorian era had been by no means undistinguished. And although his pedigree had assured him his place in society, it was not birthright but industry and the careful cultivation of kingly favour that secured for him his embassy.

Frank Bertie, as he was generally known to his family and friends, was born on 17 August 1844 in the parish of Wytham, which lies to the west of Oxford in what was then Berkshire. His birthplace, the manor house of Wytham Abbey, had been built by the Harcourt family in the early part of the sixteenth century. It and the adjoining estates had subsequently been purchased by Lord Williams of Thame, through whose descendants they had passed to James Bertie who in 1662 was rewarded for his services to the king with the earldom of Abingdon.[2] Lord Montagu Norreys, the future sixth Earl of Abingdon, was Francis's father. He had entered parliament in

---

[1] Bertie set forth his hereditary claim to the Paris embassy in a draft statement which he evidently intended to use when he presented his letters of credence to the president of the republic. In the event, however, he seems not to have used this draft. Draft declaration by Bertie, Jan. 1905, Bertie MSS. (hereafter cited as B.P.), B, F.O.800/183. *Rémise des lettres de l'ambassadeur de l'Angleterre*, Jan. 1905, Delcassé MSS. (Ministère des Affaires Étrangères), 14.
[2] For a history of the Bertie family see: Lady Georgina Bertie, *Five Generations of a Loyal House* (London, 1845).

1830 as a Tory member for Oxfordshire, and he had taken as his wife Elizabeth Lavinia Harcourt, the daughter of the county's other sitting member.[3] Before her early death in 1858 she bore him six sons and three daughters. They, like their ancestors, exhibited a disposition for serving church and state. Three of them, George, Charles, and Reginald, obtained commissions in the army, another, Alberic took holy orders, and the youngest, Evelyn, eventually entered the Convent of the Visitation at Harrow-on-the-Hill. Francis, the second son, having neither inclination towards soldiering, nor much respect for religion, set his sights upon a clerkship in the Foreign Office.

This was a sensible choice for a young man in Bertie's position. During the 1850s his father had found himself in serious financial difficulties. The family estates had incurred heavy debt charges, and he had been forced to let his London house in Grosvenor Street. Francis Bertie was therefore probably in need of an occupation that would provide him with an early and steady remuneration.[4] Moreover, despite the introduction in 1857 of competitive examinations for admission to the Foreign Office, the prevailing system whereby candidates had to be nominated by the secretary of state helped to ensure that there was still a bias towards social class rather than intellectual ability in the selection of clerks.[5] Since, however, the examinations did eliminate weaker applicants, some preparation had to be made for them. Evidently with a view to improving his languages Bertie travelled abroad, and after leaving Eton in 1860 he spent two years in Bonn.[6] In the meantime Lord Abingdon sought the support of the foreign secretary, Lord John Russell, for his son's

---

[3] Lord Montagu Norreys sat as an MP for Oxfordshire in 1830, and between 1832 and 1852. He was subsequently MP for Abingdon until 1854 when he succeeded to his father's title. He died in 1884. George Granville Venables Harcourt (the name was changed in 1840 to Vernon-Harcourt) was the eldest son the of the Most Rev. E.V. Harcourt, the Archbishop of York. He sat as MP for Lichfield from 1806 to 1830, and for Oxfordshire from 1831 to 1861.
[4] Lady Lavinia Abingdon to Lord Granville, Jan. 1856, Granville MSS. (Public Record Office), P.R.O.30/29/23/6. Townley to Norreys, 5 May 1858. B.P. (Bodleian Library), MS., DD Bertie, C7/14/24. The fortunes of the Bertie family appear to have improved somewhat during the next thirty years. Notes which were probably written by his elder brother at the time of his father's death indicate that Bertie was then receiving from his father an allowance of £150 p.a., and that he was living in Lord Abingdon's London house which was worth a rental of £500 p.a. Bertie inherited from his father the family's Oxfordshire estates which provided an income of £6,925 p.a. Undated notes, B.P. (Bodleian Library), MS. Top. Oxon. C389.
[5] Ray Jones, *The Nineteenth Century Foreign Office. An Adminstrative History* (London, 1971), pp.49 – 50.
[6] Lady Algernon Gordon Lennox (ed.), *The Diary of Lord Bertie of Thame, 1914 – 1918* (2 vols., London, 1924), II, p.431.

nomination. 'All the time that you were Premier', he reminded Russell in August 1862, 'I gave your Government a good support in the House of Commons, & rendered them a good assistance besides, on one or two occasions when they were in difficulty.' Russell was happy to oblige, but Bertie still had to wait another year for his nomination.[7] When finally at the age of nineteen he sat the Foreign Office examination he passed with flying colours. The first of three candidates, Bertie scored 813 out of a possible 930 marks, and in the autumn of 1863 he was appointed to a junior clerkship with the salary of £100 per annum.[8]

The Foreign Office in which Bertie served his apprenticeship was still primarily concerned with the administration rather than the determination of policy. For more than ten years his duties were confined to those mundane but necessary tasks that the office required its functionaries to fulfill. He copied despatches in his bold clear handwriting, cyphered and decyphered telegrams, helped keep the registers, and provided such abstracts of communications as his superiors demanded. In 1874 he acquired more responsibility when he was appointed private secretary to Robert Bourke, the parliamentary under-secretary of state for foreign affairs in Disraeli's administration. But a volume of papers entitled 'Memoranda on Political and Other Questions by Mr F. L. Bertie' which dates from 1874 consists almost entirely of summaries of reports and views expressed in official correspondence, and it provides no insight into Bertie's opinions upon policy and its application.[9]

Bertie had his first opportunity to travel abroad in an offical capacity when in the spring of 1878 he accompanied Lords Beaconsfield and Salisbury to the congress of Berlin. Much of his time there was occupied by his secretarial duties. But such letters as he found time to write to Lord Tenterden, the permanent under-secretary at the Foreign Office, were characterized by a sardonic humour and abrasive comments which were to be common features of his later correspondence. Thus he agreed with the Berliners that William Waddington, the French foreign minister, was 'so Bürgerlich'. 'He looks', Bertie wrote to Tenterden, 'the cheesemonger all over.' On the other hand he thought Count Julius Andràssy, the senior Austro-Hungarian delegate, 'a clean looking

---

[7] Abingdon to Russell, 5 Aug. 1862, and minute by Russell, Russell MSS. (Public Record Office), P.R.O.30/22/116. Note by Russell, F.O.366/675.
[8] Jones, *Foreign Office*, p.167.
[9] *Memoranda on Political and Other Questions by Mr F.L. Bertie, 1874-75*, F.O.97/452 (Except where otherwise stated all Foreign Office material cited in this work is to be found in the Public Record Office).

knock'm down man at a fair on the Epsom Downs'. He was also amused by the social life of the conference, especially when on one Saturday evening the entire congress was united in the zoological gardens 'to show themselves gratis and to listen to a military band'. 'There were', he noted, '20,000 tickets sold at the door so that the entertainment was a paying speculation.'[10]

It was another three years before Bertie again visited the continent on Foreign Office business. Then, however, it was only a matter of accompanying the Earl of Fife on a mission to invest the King of Saxony with the order of the garter. Bertie was in the meantime appointed to the rank of assistant clerk, and from December 1882 until August 1885 he was acting senior clerk with charge of the Eastern department: the division of the Foreign Office which handled issues relating to Russia, the Near and Middle East, and central Asia.[11] In a troublesome period during which the department had to deal with the problems resulting from the British military occupation of Egypt, and the threat of war with Russia over the frontiers of Afghanistan, Bertie had every opportunity to display his talents.[12] Julian Pauncefote, the then permanent under-secretary, was very impressed by his industry, and he duly recorded that he could not 'speak too highly of his services'. Salisbury, who had recently returned to the Foreign Office, agreed with this judgement, and four years later, after a brief spell in the American and Asiatic department, Bertie was made chief clerk in charge of the Eastern.[13] There he remained until the end of 1893 when at the age of forty-nine he was appointed by Lord Rosebery to be, along with Percy Anderson, one of the two assistant under-secretaries of state. For the next four years he superintended, first on his own, and then after 1896 with Anderson's successor, Francis Villiers, the American and Asiatic department. A further redistribution of work within the office, which involved the appointment of Martin Gosselin as a third assistant under-secretary, left Bertie by the end of the century with the superintendance of the Far Eastern, or China, department, and matters concerning the east African protectorates and south-east Africa.[14]

To his contemporaries Bertie had appeared to be a rather timid youth, too shy even to announce his first arrival at the Foreign

---

[10] Bertie to Tenterden, 23 June 1878, Tenterden MSS., F.O.363/1, pt.i.
[11] Jones, *Foreign Office*, pp.73 – 4.
[12] C.J. Lowe, *The Reluctant Imperialists. British Foreign Policy, 1878 – 1902* (2 vols., London, 1967), I, 52 – 120.
[13] Pauncefote to Salisbury, 15 May 1885, and minute by Salisbury, F.O.366/760.
[14] Jones, *Foreign Office*, p.81.

Office.[15] Yet by the time of his elevation to the rank of assistant under-secretary Bertie had already earned a reputation for hard work, firm resolve, and strong language. A man of near boundless energy, he was a strict task-master. He required and admired efficiency in his subordinates and peers alike, and to fail to meet his standards was to risk an explosion of his violent temper.[16] Typical of him was the Scrooge-like protest which he made on 26 December 1896 against the laxity of the Office of Works, whose employee, a stoker, had treated Christmas as a holiday and failed to maintain the furnaces which heated the passages of the Foreign Office.[17] According to James Rennell Rodd, a diplomat who first served under Bertie in the Eastern department, he was a 'master in the art of quarrelling'. He seemed, Rodd complained on one occasion, 'to take a malign pleasure in making everyone miserable'.[18] Later at Paris his blunt frankness and caustic tongue were to lead the junior staff of the embassy to baptize him 'The Bull'.[19] Many a raw recruit to his department was shattered by the crudity and license of his expression, and even the charladies of Whitehall blushed and made haste to erase the obscenities which he was wont to scrawl upon the otherwise grimy windows of the Foreign Office.[20]

Some found in Bertie's aversion to conventional propriety a flavour of the *ancien régime*.[21] 'A dying world', wrote Lord Vansittart, 'breathed through his dilated nostrils.'[22] Less poetically and with much less sympathy, the French premier, Joseph Caillaux, maintained that he was 'as reactionary as thirty-six gendarmes'.[23] But those who could withstand his bullying and condone his Rabelaisian

---

[15] Reginald, 12th Earl of Meath, *Memories of the Nineteenth Century* (London, 1923), p.45.
[16] E. Howard to Spring Rice, 17 Sept. 1885, Spring Rice MSS. (Churchill College, Cambridge), CASR 1/44. J. Tilley and S. Gaselee, *The Foreign Office* (London, 1935), p.130. J. Tilley, *London to Tokyo* (London, 1942), pp.21 – 3. Lord Vansittart, *The Mist Procession* (London, 1958), pp.53 – 4. Zara Steiner, *The Foreign Office and Foreign Policy, 1898 – 1914* (Cambridge, 1969), pp. 37 – 8 and 180 – 2.
[17] Note by Bertie, 26 Dec. 1896, F.O.366/760. Bertie appears to have insisted on working on days which other departments of state treated as holidays. Tyrrell to Bertie, 29 March 1907, B.P., B, F.O.800/185.
[18] James Rennell Rodd, *Social and Diplomatic Memories* (3 vols., London, 1922 – 5), III, p.41. Diary, IV, 7 May 1904, Rennell Rodd MSS. (Bodleian Library).
[19] Vansittart, p.54. E. Phipps, *Diplomatic Light and Shade in Paris and Elsewhere* (unpublished memoir), pp.51 – 2, Phipps MSS. (Churchill College), PHIPP 9/1.
[20] Rennell Rodd, I, 41. G.P. Antrobus, *King's Messenger. Memories of a Silver Greyhound* (London, 1941), p.91. The windows of the Foreign Office were cleaned once every quarter. Minute by Alston, 20 Jan. 1882, F.O.366/678.
[21] Viscount Esher, *The Tragedy of Lord Kitchener* (London, 1921), p.96.
[22] Vansittart, p.54.
[23] Joseph Caillaux, *Mes Mémoires* (3 vols., Paris, 1942 – 7), II, 136.

rebukes, found beneath Bertie's gruff exterior a far gentler soul. His joviality and impish pranks were the delight of his colleagues at home and abroad. Esmé Howard, who later became British ambassador at Washington, recalled in his memoirs how on one occasion Bertie, on discovering a lady whom he particularly disliked in the private secretary's room in the Foreign Office, tip-toed up behind her, executed in complete silence an Indian war dance, and having successfully scalped her, pranced triumphantly out of the door.[24] And if he abandoned and discouraged the playing of stump cricket in the corridors of the Foreign Office, he was none the less always prepared to enliven the slack hours of the day by demonstrating how high he could kick, and his ability to cut candles in two with a sword.[25]

Such antics betray a certain immaturity in Bertie's personality. There was, indeed, always something of the overgrown schoolboy about him. His humour was coarse and his conversation spiced with the lewdest of tales, and he revelled in the scandal and gossip of what passed for high society. Music and literature were of little or no interest to him, and he had no taste for the visual arts beyond a devotion to collecting pornographic prints. Some of these, which, as Lady Gladwyn has suggested, he probably valued more for their sheer vulgarity than for their erotic content, he later hung on the reverse sides of perfectly respectable pictures in his study at the Paris embassy. Their revelation seems to have been reserved for the amusement of visiting compatriots.[26] Other visitors were less liberally entertained. Captain Howard Kelly, who was for some time the naval *attaché* at Paris, commented that invitations to embassy functions 'were more sought for the social prestige they conferred than for the ritual pleasure they brought to the favoured recipient'.[27] In truth Bertie had little patience with such events and formal entertainments as were likely to upset his daily routine. His treatment during January 1906 of a visiting choir and orchestra from the Royal College of Music led their conductor, Sir Charles Stanford, to complain bitterly to the Foreign Office after his return to London. Not only had the ambassador left his box in the middle of the performance, but,

[24] Esmé Howard, *Theatre of Life* (2 vols., London, 1935), pp.325–6.
[25] Tilley and Gaselee.
[26] C. Pearl, *Morrison of Peking* (London, 1967), p.161. Diary, 2 Nov. 1917, Hankey MSS. (Churchill College, Cambridge), HNKY 1/4. Cynthia Gladwyn, *The Paris Embassy* (London, 1976), p.165.
[27] *Journal as Naval Attaché*, p.3, Howard Kelly MSS. (National Maritime Museum), KEL/3.

THE ART OF QUARRELLING

according to Stanford, he had addressed him as if he were a 'crossing sweeper'.[28]

Bertie's rather ungracious behaviour may have been due to a failure on his part to overcome his early shyness. Acutely sensitive with regard to his own position, and rarely at ease in the company of strangers, he was in the words of Rodd 'genial but not social'.[29] He was, nevertheless, punctilious of etiquette, and he maintained great state at the Paris embassy. Nearly one-fifth of his allowance for the post was spent on the stables, and on full dress occasions he would drive from the embassy in the rue du Faubourg St-Honoré to the neighbouring Elysée palace in a sumptious coach, hung on C springs, upholstered in white satin, ornamented with silver fittings and embroideries, and bearing his arms written large upon its panels.[30] The impression which he sought to create at Paris was matched by his own picturesque appearance. His white curly hair and moustache offset a rosy complexion, and though short in stature he usually made up for this by wearing an exceptionally high top hat, the 'only one', noted Howard Kelly, 'to call forth a salute from the democratic police of Paris'.[31] To Caillaux he seemed like a character who had stepped out of a novel by Dickens or Thackeray, 'stick en bataille, la moustache au vent . . . saucissoné dans des jaquettes ou dans des vestons trops ajustés, portant la large cravate lavallière bleue à pois blancs'.[32] 'He made one feel', Vansittart wrote, 'that the finest thing in the world was to be His Britannic Majesty's Ambassador at Paris.'[33]

By contrast Bertie's wife did not cut a fine figure in French society. The great-niece of the Duke of Wellington and the daughter of a former British ambassador to France, Feodorowna Wellesley had not been noted either for her looks or for her social graces. Prospective suitors had been few in number, and she was already in her thirties when she married Bertie, her junior, in 1874. Four years later she gave birth to their only child, a son, Vere. To all outward appearances the marriage was a happy one. Nevertheless, for a man who in his youth had enjoyed the company of pretty and amusing young women, and who during his years at Paris delighted in the friendship of the beautiful Lady Algernon Gordon Lennox, Bertie's

---

[28] Stanford to Parrott, enclosed in Knollys to Bertie, 27 Jan. 1906, B.P., F.O. 800/184.
[29] Diary, IV, 21 Sept. 1904, Rennell, MSS.
[30] *The Times*, 27 Sept. 1919, p.8.
[31] *Journal as Naval Attaché*, p.3.
[32] Caillaux, II, 134.
[33] Vansittart, p.54.

choice of partner was odd.³⁴ Those who knew Lady Feo well found her to be kind and good humoured, and her knitting between August 1914 and February 1915 of seventy woollen comforters and scarves for Belgian refugees attest both to her charity and to her devotion to the allied cause.³⁵ But in her manner she was retiring and inclined to be rather vague, and perhaps because of this, she was, despite her long association with diplomacy, a poor hostess. Embassy receptions bored her, and much to the discomfort of her guests she made no effort to disguise her feelings.³⁶ Her one consuming passion was the card table, and she would readily play bridge or poker until the early hours of the morning. Monte Carlo and its casino was a temptation which she found difficult to resist, and in later years she was to spend a good deal of her time there.³⁷ Sir Frederick Ponsonby, who dined at the embassy during the royal visit to Paris in the spring of 1914, found that she knew hardly any of the diplomatic corps by sight. She was, he concluded, 'quite impossible as Ambassadress'.³⁸

Such an eccentric pair were bound to attract criticism and Bertie was rarely without enemies. These included not only past victims of his verbal assaults, but also those whose words and deeds he would not suffer. He had no time for either prigs or prudes, and although he expected others to tolerate his truculence, he was easily incensed when he failed to have his way.³⁹ A man of great likes and even greater dislikes, he was slow to forgive those who dared to resist his will.⁴⁰ One individual for whom he had but little love was Thomas Sanderson. Better known to his colleagues as 'Lamps' or 'Giglamps' because of the spectacles which he invariably wore, Sanderson was

---

³⁴ One very attractive young lady whom Bertie befriended was Jennie Jerome. It was Bertie who during Cowes week 1873 introduced her to her future husband, Lord Randolph Churchill. Bertie was thus in part responsible for Sir Winston Churchill, a politician whom he thoroughly disliked. R.G. Martin, *Lady Randolph Churchill* (London, 1969), p.46. Gladwyn, pp.162 and 165.
³⁵ Diary, 9 Nov. 1915, Austin Lee MSS. (British Library), Add. MS. 46774. E. Cadogan, *Before the Deluge. Memories and Reflections, 1880 – 1914* (London, 1961), p.142. Nevile Henderson, *Water Under the Bridges* (London, 1945), p.83.
³⁶ *Journal as Naval Attaché*, p.3 Boni de Castellane, *L'art d'être pauvre* (Paris, 1925), p.186. Wilfred Scawen Blunt, who had once seemed to engage in the courtship of Feo Wellesley, later described her as having 'acquired a character of almost rudeness in her father's house by the little pains she took to do the honours'. But, he added that with himself 'she was from the first gay & unreserved and uniformly kind'. Autograph Diaries, pt.2, pp.6 – 7, Blunt MSS. (Fitzwilliam Museum, Cambridge), MS. 296 – 1975.
³⁷ Diary, 11 Feb. 1916, Austin Lee MSS., Add. MS. 46775A. Viscount Mersey, *A Picture of Life*, 1872 – 1940 (London, 1941), p.282.
³⁸ Ponsonby to Hardinge, 28 April 1914, Hardinge MSS. (University Library, Cambridge), 105. Gladwyn.
³⁹ Diary, 1890 – 97, p.8, Rumbold MSS. (Bodleian Library), dep.I/1.
⁴⁰ E. Howard, I, p.325.

just three years older than Bertie.[41] Of Yorkshire yeoman stock, he had been forced by his father's failure in business to leave Eton, and he had entered the Foreign Office in 1859.[42] There for five years during Gladstone's second administration he was private secretary to Lord Granville, the Liberal foreign secretary. The latter was impressed by his ability, and only fear of the disruption that might be caused by Sanderson passing over the heads of his more senior colleagues seems to have withheld Granville from supporting his promotion after the death of Tenterden in 1882.[43] Bertie may have been jealous of Sanderson's success. And the fact that in the summer of 1885 Sanderson was made chief clerk in charge of the Eastern department, and thereby became Bertie's superior in a department which he had probably come to regard as his own can hardly have helped relations between the two men. Moreover, Bertie's prospects for promotion were effectively blocked when in January 1894 Sanderson succeeded Sir Philip Currie as permanent undersecretary. Unless Sanderson were to decide upon an early retirement, the most that Bertie could henceforth hope for was the possibility of three years as his immediate successor.

Bertie's animosity towards Sanderson was also connected with changes which were being forced upon the Foreign Office in the latter part of the 1890s. Pressure of business during these years allowed the permanent officials a much greater opportunity for taking initiatives. In these circumstances Bertie freely volunteered his advice, and by the turn of the century an increasing number of memoranda and minutes bear witness to what Sir Edward Grey later called his 'clear, crisp opinions'.[44] Their significance was enhanced by the fact that Britain's interests seemed so often to be menaced in those areas which fell within Bertie's administrative purview. He was to become entangled with the problems of southern Africa, and he was able to play an important part in helping to formulate Britain's policies in the Far East in the first years of this century. But in this same period Bertie and some of his associates were to become impatient with the apparent reluctance of Sanderson to countenance any early reform of the manner in which the Foreign Office conducted its affairs.

A methodical and painstaking bureaucrat, Sanderson was altogether more cautious and discreet than Bertie in the advice which

---

[41] Meath, p.65.
[42] B.J.R.H. Weaver (ed.), *Dictionary of National Biography. Twentieth Century, 1922–1930* (London, 1933), pp.739–40.
[43] Jones, *Foreign Office*, p.76.
[44] Gordon Lennox, I, p.vii. G.W. Monger, *The End of Isolation. British Foreign Policy, 1900–1907* (London, 1963), pp.99–100.

he proffered to the secretaries of state he served. And although his sharp wit and cultured intellect seem to have appealed to Rosebery and Salisbury, he never enjoyed that popularity which Bertie had amongst some of the junior staff of the office and diplomatic service. According to Horace Rumbold, who joined the Eastern department in 1891, Bertie was 'always turning Sanderson into ridicule in front of us'.[45] Yet for Bertie Sanderson was more than just a figure of fun. In his eyes he represented the 'red tapeism' of the office. He was in Bertie's estimate too tied to established and out-moded procedures for policy-making and promotion. This opinion was borne out by aspiring young diplomats like Frank Rattigan who later described Sanderson as a 'martinet of the old order', and likened his relations with the junior clerks to that of 'headmaster and pupils at a private school'.[46] According to Maurice Baring many of the clerks 'lived in terror of him', and his 'minute eye for detail used constantly to discern a slight inaccuracy in the mode of address or the terminology'.[47] More damning still was the condemnation of Sanderson's administration by Cecil Spring Rice, another young diplomat who had come to know Bertie in the Eastern department. In a letter to Rosebery of 8 January 1903 he complained:

> Sanderson never listens to anyone: has no personal knowledge of Europe and no general ideas: is an ideal official for drafting despatches and emptying boxes: but this is not the business of the head of an office: he should have time to think and the art to make other people do the current work. And as you know, and Lord Salisbury knew, he has the faculty of carrying out his master's orders but not of independent suggestion or intelligent understanding. And his influence on the office and the diplomatic service is paralysing. As long as he is there the officials at home & abroad are simply useful as machines and the Foreign Office is like Johnson's definition of fishing: a line with a fool at one end and a worm at the other.[48]

Spring Rice's view of Sanderson's régime was probably influenced by Bertie. Only four months before on 29 August 1902 he had confessed to Spring Rice his dissatisfaction with the situation in the Foreign Office. 'So long as Sanderson rules', he wrote, 'there will be

---

[45] Diary, 1890–97, p.14, Rumbold MSS, dep.I/1.
[46] F. Rattigan, *Diversions of a Diplomat* (London, 1924), p.31.
[47] M. Baring, *the Puppet Show of Memory* (London, 1930), p.233.
[48] Spring Rice to Rosebery, 8 Jan. 1903, Rosebery MSS. (National Library of Scotland), 10116.

no reform and it will get worse & worse.'[49] This judgement was neither just nor wholly accurate. One of the principal causes for complaint within the Foreign Office was the fact that the bright, and sometimes not-so-bright, young men whom it recruited were for many years employed in work which they felt to be below their intellectual capacities. Sanderson, who was by his own admission 'an official and narrow-minded', was extremely cautious about devolving work from under-secretaries and heads of department downwards.[50] His first concern was with the proper transaction of business in an office in which a blunder could have far more serious consequences than any other department of state, and he believed, not without good reason, that 'constant practice . . . [was] . . . necessary to ensure methodical attention to matters of detail'.[51] But he was prepared to consider and to inculcate such changes as he conceived practicable. Moreover, some of the criticisms which Spring Rice and his colleagues made of Sanderson might equally well have been levelled at Bertie. He could certainly be every bit as fastidious, and there are no grounds for supposing that his political superiors valued his work any more highly than that of Sanderson.[52] In 1897 Salisbury considered Bertie and Horace Walpole of the India Office as possible candidates for the permanent under-secretaryship of the Colonial Office, but finally dismissed the idea because although both men had been trained in a variety of work and would discharge their duties unimpeachably, there was 'not much original power in either'.[53]

It is equally doubtful whether Bertie was as effective a force for radical change within the Foreign Office as he liked to imagine himself. He may well have helped to foster the career of Charles Hardinge, who as Sanderson's successor was responsible for

---

[49] Bertie to Spring Rice, 29 Aug. 1902, Spring Rice MSS., CASR 1/2.
[50] Sanderson to Morier, 23 March 1886, Morier MSS. (Balliol College, Oxford), Mission to Russia: correspondence with English Court and Foreign Office, 1885 – 86. Valerie Cromwell and Zara Steiner, 'The Foreign Office before 1914: a study in resistance', in Gillian Sutherland (ed.), *Studies in the Growth of Nineteenth Century Government* (London, 1972), pp.167 – 94.
[51] Jones, *Foreign Office*, pp.115 – 16. Villiers to Sanderson, 27 April 1903; minute by Sanderson, 2 May 1903; F.O. General Librarian's Dept. Correspondence and Memoranda 1845 – 1905, vol.3A (Foreign and Commonwealth Office Library), Sanderson to Ponsonby, 30 Aug. 1902, Ponsonby MSS. (Bodleian Library), MS. Eng. Hist. C652.
[52] See for example: Minute by Sanderson on Bertie to Sanderson, 29 March 1904, F.O. 45/889, *private*.
[53] J. Chamberlain to Salisbury, 8 Jan. 1897, Salisbury MSS. (Hatfield House, Herts.). Salisbury to J. Chamberlain, 10 Jan. 1897, Joseph Chamberlain MSS. (University of Birmingham), J.C. 5/67/76. Bertie was also a somewhat less efficient administrator than he imagined himself to be. Sanderson to Scott, 19 Dec. 1900, Charles Scott MSS. (B.L.), Add. MS. 5298.

overseeing the introduction of the Foreign Office reforms of 1906.[54] He may also have befriended and encouraged younger men like Maurice de Bunsen, Louis Mallet, William Tyrrell and Spring Rice. Yet in later years as ambassador at Paris, he was indignant when youthful advice ran counter to his own opinions. One former member of his staff was later to complain that Bertie found 'a certain enjoyment in trampling on anyone with spirit at all, whom he may have power over'.[55] It was in any case Sanderson and Villiers who, after Bertie's departure, were to initiate the processes which were finally to lead to a greater devolution of business within the office.[56] Moreover, there is but scanty documentary evidence to indicate the sort of reforms that Bertie would like to have seen implemented. He favoured drawing into the upper echelons of the Foreign Office men who had experience in posts abroad, and he probably agreed with Hardinge's desire to relieve the junior clerks of some of the drudgery of their work.[57] He was not, however, enthusiastic about such measures as seemed likely to attain this end. Thus he was critical of the idea of establishing a cypher room which might employ men lower in social status than the present clerks. That, he thought, would increase the 'chance of leakage because in the higher social scale there is a feeling of the honour of the name to a larger extent than in a lower stratum'. Besides which, he felt that accurate decyphering required a knowledge of the subject in discussion. For the same reason he was opposed to the establishment of a parliamentary or blue book department.[58] All that exists by way of a Bertie programme for reform is a memorandum which he drafted for the perusal of Rosebery in September 1899. This was primarily intended to demonstrate 'how a Prime Minister might possibly have his Foreign Secretary in the House of Commons without killing him, and without having another Cabinet Minister, other than the Prime Minister, with a finger in the Foreign Office pie'. And only towards the end of this paper did Bertie propose that the foreign secretary's energies might be spared if, instead of receiving all incoming despatches, he were in the first place

---

[54] B.C. Busch, *Hardinge of Penshurst. A Study in Old Diplomacy* (Hamden, 1980), pp. 60–4. For an excellent summary of the Foreign Office reforms of 1906 and their impact on the administration of policy see: Zara Steiner, 'The Foreign Office under Sir Edward Grey, 1905–1914', in F.H. Hinsley (ed.), *British Foreign Policy under Sir Edward Grey* (Cambridge, 1977), pp.22–69.
[55] Bridgeman to Loraine, 17 May 1916, Loraine MSS., F.O.1011/116.
[56] Jones, *Foreign Office*, pp.111–35.
[57] Busch.
[58] Bertie to Cranborne, 1 June 1903, Cecil MSS. (Hatfield House, Herts.), S(4) 52/116. Bertie's view that the lower classes could not be trusted was but an echo of opinions expressed by other British diplomats on previous occasions. See: R.A. Jones, *The British Diplomatic Service, 1815–1914* (Ontario, 1983), pp.112–13.

simply provided with summaries of information received by mail and any 'very important despatches'.[59]

Such expressions of opinion as these hardly accord with the notion of Bertie as an ageing Young Turk urging modernization upon an antiquated Foreign Office. Not that there can be any denying his dissatisfaction with the prevailing state of affairs in Downing Street. It is however probable that Bertie found in criticizing Sanderson's conservatism a means of giving vent to his personal frustration and his dislike of a man who seemed to stand in the way of his obtaining the permanent under-secretaryship. He was thereby able to identify his own grievances with opposition to a system which some felt to offer little scope to the development of individual talent. Ultimately, Bertie sought satisfaction for himself in a post abroad. By then he had already made a significant contribution to a shift in British foreign policy in at least one part of the globe.

---

[59] Memo. enclosed in Bertie to Rosebery, 20 Sept. 1899, Rosebery MSS., 10112.

2

Ein ausgesprochener Gegner Deutschlands

The antipathy which Bertie and some of his younger friends felt towards Sanderson has been linked with differences not only over the manner in which policy was formulated, but also over policy itself. In his study of the nineteenth-century Foreign Office Ray Jones has thus suggested that the 'bad press' that Sanderson received from the so-called Bertie-Hardinge faction 'can be at least partly explained by their desire to be rid of an opponent of their anti-German ideas'.[1] Some support is lent to this contention by the way in which in later years Sanderson attempted to portray German policy in a more favourable light to that in which it was interpreted by his former critics. Moreover, it hardly seems accidental that much of the letter which Spring Rice wrote to Rosebery on 8 January 1903, in which he derided Sanderson, was devoted to expressing its author's fears about the threat which he believed Germany to pose to Britain and the rest of western Europe. His charge was that the Foreign Office was inefficient and therefore not fully able to appreciate the dangers to which Britain was exposed. It was not, however, Sanderson's views on foreign policy as such, but the shortcomings of the system with which he was associated, that Spring Rice singled out for attack.[2] This was equally true of Bertie's criticisms of Sanderson's *régime*. Indeed, in the period prior to Bertie's departure from the Foreign Office it is far from easy to draw any clear distinction between Bertie and Sanderson in their attitudes towards Britain's continental neighbours. Bertie was more inclined to advocate a firm line in the handling of imperial disputes, and Sanderson was less outspoken in his counsels. Yet Sanderson could be just as critical as Bertie of German diplomacy, and both men were at one in supporting Salisbury in his opposition to Britain becoming entangled in an alliance with a continental great power.

Bertie's name is none the less frequently linked with the rise of an anti-German sentiment in the British Foreign Office and diplomatic service, and some of his contemporaries certainly regarded him as

---

[1] Jones, *Foreign Office*, p.114.
[2] Spring Rice to Rosebury, 8 Jan. 1903, Rosebury MSS., 10116.

hostile towards Germany.³ In April 1905 Prince Hugo von Radolin, the Silesian aristocrat who was Germany's ambassador at Paris, wrote home to Berlin that according to a reliable source, whereas in England the prime minister was not regarded as Germany's friend, and the foreign secretary was not regarded as her enemy, Bertie passed for 'einen ausgesprochenen Gegner Deutschlands' (an outspoken opponent of Germany).⁴ And during the ten years which preceded the outbreak of the first world war distrust of Germany, and support for the Anglo-French *entente*, were to be two of the most consistent elements in Bertie's thinking about international affairs. He himself denied that he was a Germanophobe. He was, he told the Baron von Stumm in December 1911, an Anglomane.⁵ The defence of what Bertie defined as British interests did, however, lead him to give overriding support to such lines of policy as might contain what he conceived to be Germany's ambitions.

It may seem hardly surprising that one whose career in the British foreign service commenced in the year following Bismarck's appointment as minister-president of Prussia, and ended four weeks after the conclusion of the treaty of Brest-Litovsk, should have exhibited some apprehension about the growth in Germany's power. During the forty years that Bertie spent in the Foreign Office British governments had to accommodate themselves to the creation of the Prusso-German state, its evolution as the foremost industrial and military power of the continent, and its emergence alongside Britain's older rivals as a competitor for empire in Africa and the Pacific. Shortly before his death in 1919 Bertie claimed that his stay in Bonn after leaving Eton had enabled him to learn the 'real German character'.⁶ This may have been so. But such correspondence of Bertie's as dates from the 1870s does not reveal any ill-feeling on his part towards the Germans. Nor for that matter is there any reason to suppose that during the next decade Bertie considered Germany to be any more dangerous or potentially more hostile towards Britain than any of the other great powers of Europe. Bismarck's bid for colonies would

---

³ Monger, pp.100 – 1. Paul M. Kennedy, *The Rise of Anglo-German Antagonism 1860 – 1914* (London, 1982), p.253. For an alternative new see: K.M. Wilson, 'The Question of Anti-Germanism at the British Foreign Office before the First World War', *Canadian Journal of History*, XVIII (1983), 23 – 42.
⁴ *Die Grosse Politik der europäischen Kabinette* (hereafter cited as *G.P.*), vol.XX, pt.2, no.6847. Prince von Radolin's career is briefly considered in Maurice Baumont, 'Le Prince Radolin', in *Mélanges Pierre Renouvin. Études d'histoire des Relations Internationales* (Paris, 1966), pp.169 – 76.
⁵ *British Documents on the Origins of the War 1898 – 1914* (hereafter cited as *B.D.*), vol.X, pt.2, no.265.
⁶ Gordon Lennox, II, 431.

appear to have disturbed him, and in retrospect he blamed Granville for having been 'rather weak' in his dealings with the German chancellor.[7] It was, however, Germany's methods rather than her objectives that initially gave him most cause for concern. Above all, he was irritated by the brusqueness both of Bismarckian and post-Bismarckian diplomacy. 'Much more', Bertie explained to the German state secretary in November 1899, 'could be got from England by calm discussion than by bringing out heavy artillery on every occasion and stating that the non-solution of a question in a particular way would have a disastrous effect on the relations of the two countries.'[8]

Bertie's attitude towards Germany was in part determined by the problems which beset Britain in her so-called 'splendid isolation'. Bertie's appointment as an assistant under-secretary coincided with the ratification of the military convention which completed the Dual Alliance between France and Russia. During the next seven years first Lord Kimberley, who replaced Rosebery as Liberal foreign secretary in March 1894, and then Salisbury, were compelled to cope with the menaces to which those two countries repeatedly subjected British interests in Africa and Asia. The understandings that Salisbury had established with Germany's allies, Austria-Hungary and Italy, through the Mediterranean agreements of 1887, lapsed, and the German leadership, as it shifted towards the pursuit of *Weltpolitik*, appeared only too ready to take advantage of Britain's exposed position. Bismarck's earlier exploitation of Gladstone's difficulties in Egypt in order to win for Germany benefits elsewhere in Africa had been considered blackmail in the Foreign Office. The opposition of his successors to the Anglo-Congolese agreement of 1894, by which the British government had hoped to block French access to the upper Nile, and their meddling in relations between Britain and the Transvaal, also helped to breed fear and resentment there.[9] Bertie's own experience in dealing with both these matters and the negotiations which settled the boundaries of the Gold Coast and German Togoland did nothing to enhance his affection for the Germans.[10] And when in the spring of 1898, after their seizure of

---

[7] J.M. Goudswaard, *Some Aspects of the End of Britain's 'Splendid Isolation', 1898 – 1904* (Rotterdam, 1952), pp.39 – 41.
[8] *Ibid.* In the following year Bertie told Alfred de Rothschild that the 'real reason' why Britain and Germany found it difficult to make any arrangement was that 'the Germans always wanted a good deal, and offered little or nothing in return'. Memo. by Bertie, 5 Sept. 1900, B.P., A, F.O.800/170.
[9] Kennedy, *The Rise of Anglo-German Antagonism*, pp.205 – 88.
[10] Bertie to Spring Rice, 4 Aug. 1897, Spring Rice MSS., CASR1/2. Anglo-German differences in west Africa are referred to in a memorandum by J.A.C. Tilley published in *B.D.*, .i, 322 – 337.

Kiaochow, the Germans induced the Chinese to grant them a railway concession in Shantung by offering the unfounded assurance that the British government had been consulted, he was scathing in his condemnation of their mendacity. The Germans, he claimed, had 'lied with their customary awkwardness'. 'I live in hope', he added, 'that we may succeed in putting them into the cart.'[11]

Bertie soon grew accustomed to thinking of the Germans more as rivals than as potential partners in the Far East.[12] It was, however, German policies towards southern Africa that continued to give him most cause for concern. There Britain's local paramountcy was threatened by the pretensions of the gold-rich Transvaalers, and with the object of containing the Boer republic the British government sought to control its rail link with Delagoa bay in the Portuguese colony of Mozambique.[13] Already in March 1897 Bertie had proposed to Salisbury and to Joseph Chamberlain, the colonial secretary, that the near-bankrupt Portuguese government might yield to British wishes if it were offered a new guarantee of its African possessions as the means to raising a loan in London.[14] Indeed, Bertie's subsequent involvement with this and other schemes which aimed at salvaging the Portuguese economy and safeguarding Britian's strategic interests in Mozambique help to explain the irritation which he felt when in June 1898 the Germans signalled their opposition to such a plan. Count von Hatzfeldt, the German ambassador at London, urged Salisbury to accept instead an Anglo-German accord which envisaged a joint loan to Portugal, and, in the event of the Portuguese having to dispose of their colonial empire, a division of the spoils.[15] The proposition was not unattractive from the British point of view. If accepted, it would mean the removal of German opposition to the acquisition by Britain of the Delagoa bay railway, and it opened up the prospect of Anglo-German co-operation elsewhere in the world at a time when the situation in the Far East was anything but bright, and when a crisis with France in the Nile valley seemed ever more likely.[16]

---

[11] Bertie to Lascelles, 16 March 1898, F.O.64/1437, *private*.
[12] Bertie to Salisbury, 6 July 1898, F.O.17/1360. On the scramble for concessions in China which followed the occupation of Kiaochow and Port Arthur see: L.K. Young, *British Policy in China, 1895 – 1902* (Oxford, 1970), pp.77 – 99.
[13] J.A.S. Grenville, *Lord Salisbury and Foreign Policy. The close of the Nineteenth Century* (London, 1964), pp.181 – 4.
[14] Bertie to Salisbury, 1 March 1897, F.O.63/1359. Memo. by Salisbury, 15 March 1897, J. Chamberlain MSS., JC7/3/2D/12.
[15] Memo. by Bertie, 20 June 1898, F.O.63/1359.
[16] A.N. Porter, *The Origins of the South African War. Joseph Chamberlain and the Diplomacy of Imperialism* (Manchester, 1980), pp.152 – 60. Lowe, *Reluctant Imperialists*. I, 219 – 21. *B.D.*, I, nos.70 to 74. Memo. by Bertie, 16 Aug. 1898, F.O.63/1159.

Bertie regarded Hatzfeldt's intervention as another example of German *chantage*. Germany, he noted, 'makes the usual more or less covert threats that . . . she will join Russia or France or both of them to our detriment all the world over.' He also rejected the idea that an accord with Germany on the Portuguese colonies would win her support for Britain on other issues. On the contrary, he though that Germany's ambitions would be far from satisfied by the acquisition of a reversionary claim on some of Portugal's possessions. Moreover, he believed the Germans unlikely to 'risk a quarrel or even an estrangement with Russia' unless Britain guaranteed them against France and Russia. That, he observed, evidently with Franco-German differences over Alsace-Lorraine in mind, 'would involve a permanent quarrel between England and France'. But quite apart from these arguments, Bertie insisted that Britain still had an obligation under her ancient treaties to defend Portugal and her empire, and that it would be in Britain's interests to prevent the Germans from acquiring any of Portugal's insular possessions, or such territories as would permit them to encircle British central Africa.[17] On this occasion, however, his arguments did not carry the day, and during Salisbury's absence from England in August 1898 the cabinet under the guidance of Arthur Balfour, the first lord of the Treasury, sanctioned an agreement with Germany.[18]

Portugal eventually succeeded in raising the money that she required in France. Nevertheless, it remained Bertie's conviction that the Germans were determined to make the most of Britain's embarrassment in southern Africa, and he readily blamed them for Portugal's reluctance to prevent the passage of arms to the Transvaal.[19] 'The German Government', he wrote to Salisbury on 2 October 1899, 'want to make our job in the Transvaal as long & as tough as they can and they want to create a sore here against Portugal so as to make us more willing than we have hitherto shown ourselves to cut up the Portuguese African cake.'[20] Even after Salisbury had succeeded in circumventing the Anglo-German accord by securing a Portuguese promise to close Delagoa bay to the trade in munitions in return for a guarantee of Portugal's possessions, Bertie continued to harp upon this theme. After a visit by the German emperor and his state secretary, Bernhard von Bülow, to England Bertie wrote to the queen's private secretary that he hoped Chamberlain had given no encouragement to the idea of 'killing the Portuguese goose'. 'She

---

[17] *B.D.*, I, nos 74 and 81.
[18] Grenville, *Lord Salisbury*, pp.190–8.
[19] Bertie to Salisbury, 1 Sept 1899, Salisbury MSS.
[20] Bertie to Salisbury, 2 Oct 1899, B.P., A, F.O.800/170.

does not', he added, 'lay golden eggs, but she would be of great use to us in the event of a war in which we had to operate in the Mediterranean & S. Atlantic, & we do not want her islands to pass into other hands than our own.'[21]

The essence of Bertie's complaints against the Germans was that their supposed territorial ambitions tended to undermine the *status quo* in those areas where he considered it to be in Britain's interests to preserve it, and that they were all too ready to threaten to combine with France and Russia to achieve their objectives. It should not, however, be assumed that he considered these latter powers to pose any less of a menace to Britain than did Germany, or that he considered the authorities in Paris and St Petersburg to be any more trustworthy than those in Berlin. He may have criticized the Germans 'for continually making difficulties for us in Zanzibar', but he also considered the French to be 'so shifty' that it was advisable 'to have all communications from them in writing if possible'.[22] Moreover, it was not so much the German acquisition of the lease of Kiaochow that worried him as their apparent determination to monopolize all concessions in Shantung.[23] Almost two years before the German move he had confidently predicted that if the Germans were to obtain a coaling station in China it would 'be a place for us to take or destroy in the event of a war with Germany'.[24] The great danger was that if Germany were to carve out a sphere of influence for herself in China, France and Russia might be tempted to follow her example. Likewise, one of Bertie's criticisms of the idea of an accord with Germany on the future of Portugal's colonies was that France and Russia would be led to demand a share in any loan to Portugal, and that the end result would be the internationalization of the Delagoa bay railway, and the Transvaal's assertion of its full independence.[25]

There was in Bertie's eyes one vital difference between the powers of the Dual Alliance and Germany. The former were established adversaries of Britain, while the latter was a professedly friendly power which was regarded by an influential section of the cabinet as a potential ally. When William II visited Sandringham in November

---

[21] Bertie to Bigge, 28 Nov. 1899, B.P., A, F.O.800/176.
[22] Memo. by Bertie, 28 March 1898, F.O.64/1454. Memo. by Bertie, 31 Jan. 1898, F.O.27/3436.
[23] Memo. by Bertie, 14 Jan. 1898, F.O.17/1357. Memo. by Bertie, 15 April 1898, F.O.17/1358.
[24] Memo. by Bertie, 28 Jan. 1896, F.O.17/1287.
[25] *B.D.*, I, no.72.

1899 Bertie had at the emperor's behest 'a rather snatchy conversation' with Bülow, and whilst they were being shown over the gardens, the farm animals and the stables, he took the opportunity to assure the state secretary 'that Englishmen generally, regarded the bickerings between Germany and England in the press and elsewhere as in the nature of family squabbles which are carried on with great heat, but disappear in face of common danger'. Whether Bertie shared the view that he so readily attributed to his compatriots is a different matter. Implicit in much of what he found to write about German diplomacy during the next few years was the opinion that German behaviour was not such as to justify their being regarded as particularly friendly. On the other hand it might also be argued that Bertie like many of his fellow countrymen was inclined to judge German conduct more harshly than that of other powers because it did not befit that of a member of a family. He was already beginning to think that the notion of bargaining with France and Russia might be more profitable than paying Germany for her non-association with them. Moreover, Bertie considered there to be underlying causes of friction between Britain and Germany that were not necessarily connected with the actions of diplomats and statesmen. When pressed by Bülow to account for the ill feeling in British commercial circles towards Germany, Bertie answered that Germany was a 'very pushing and successful rival', whose merchants had successfully challenged Britain's commercial preeminence in the world, and that the German government subsidised German shipping lines and German railways charged lower rates to exporters. He also added that:

> Englishmen are bad at learning languages, whereas Germans are not, & young Germans for the sake of learning English and getting on commercially come to England & work as clerks at salaries on which an Englishman cannot live, & the young Englishmen are consequently at a disadvantage & the German commercial traveller being a good linguist has the advantage over his English rival.

These remarks were perhaps not uninfluenced by the fact that Bertie's own German was in need of 'renovating', and he had found other members of the imperial suite less easy to understand than Bülow. Not that he had been greatly impressed by what the latter had said. Bülow was, he subsequently noted, 'very coulant & most agreeable, but I should say a great humbug'.[26] Bertie could, however,

---

[26] Goudswaard, pp.39–41. Bertie to Bigge, 28 Nov. 1899,B.P., A, F.O.800/176.

treat the British political leadership with equal disdain, especially when it seemed reluctant to take any resolute stand in the defence of Britain's interests. He was, for example, furious when in the midst of the controversy that developed over Russia's seizure of Port Arthur he learned that Sanderson had assured the Russian ambassador that the two British warships which were then at the port would be withdrawn. 'Lord Salisbury', he later protested, 'never does put his foot down now — or if he does — he takes it up again directly.'[27] His own conviction was that if Britain showed sufficient resolution in defending her interests, she would have very little trouble with her 'big European friends'. 'Unfortunately', he wrote to Sir Frank Lascelles, the British ambassador at Berlin, 'France, Russia & Germany have got it into their heads that we shall never stand up to one First Class Power, much less to two or three even if we had with us little Japan.'[28] Thus when during the summer of 1898 the arrival of Marchand's mission at Fashoda, and Kitchener's victories over the Dervishes, made probable an Anglo-French crisis, Bertie wasted no time in letting Balfour know the course that he would like to see pursued. 'I hope', he wrote on 14 September, 'that if the French are there Kitchener will squeeze them out, salute the Tricolore and lower it with all honour and send it in a silver box to Cairo to be handed over to the French Representative.'[29] Salisbury's resistance to French claims therefore met with Bertie's approval. Fourteen years later he was to tell the French premier, Raymond Poincaré, that Fashoda had removed the impression then prevalent on the continent that England would accept anything rather than fight, and that it had led to the Anglo-French *entente*.[30]

An equally firm stand by the government in southern Africa was to end less favourably. Quite apart from revealing the weaknesses of the British military machine, the Anglo-Boer war exposed Britain to pressures from the continental powers and to a fresh rash of difficulties with Germany. Bertie, who was largely responsible for handling complaints over the arrest and search for contraband on vessels bound for southern Africa, found good reason to grouse at the tone of German protests. His recent homily to Bülow on the need for more caution in communications with the British government seemed, he supposed, to have gone no further than the state

---

[27] C.H.D. Howard, (ed.), *The Diary of Edward Goschen 1900 – 1914* (London, 1980), p.17.
[28] Bertie to Lascelles, 16 March 1898, F.O.64/1437, *private*.
[29] Bertie to Balfour, 14 Sept. 1898, Balfour MSS. (British Library), Add. MS. 49746.
[30] Bertie to Grey, 22 Jan,1912, B.P., A, F.O.800/181.

secretary.[31] And even Sanderson was moved to pronounce in January 1900 that the latest notes from Hatzfeldt were of 'a nature not usual except in cases of Admirals addressing South American Republics'.[32] Nevertheless, events in the Far East, the Boxer rising, the siege and relief of the legations at Peking, and moves by the Russians to consolidate their position in northern China, were regarded by Chamberlain and some of his colleagues in the cabinet as providing good reason for renewing their efforts to secure German collaboration.[33]

Ever since his appointment as an assistant under-secretary the fate of China and British interests in that country had been one of Bertie's principal preoccupations. Not that he had any first hand knowledge of the Far East. Constantinople was about as far east as he ever ventured, and such assessments as he made of the situation in China were based upon reports from Britain's representatives in the region, the press and views expressed by British merchants and financiers.[34] These he interpreted almost entirely in terms of the relations between the European great powers. The structure of Asian societies and their cultures meant nothing to him. As with Europe he thought of the Far East largely in terms of checks and balances, and of rights and interests. This was logical enough in an age of imperialism, but it was perhaps this attitude of mind that led George Morrison, *The Times* correspondent in China, to comment after a conversation with Bertie that his views were 'so ignorant, so vulgarly expressed and so ill-considered that he wasn't worth listening to'.[35] Nevertheless, Bertie's mastery of the political geography of the area, and his ability to draw simple and straightforward conclusions from a mass of detailed information, placed him in a position of advantage when it came to dealing with less knowledgeable politicians and members of the cabinet. His appreciation of the changing power structure in the Far East and his determination to press his views upon Lord Lansdowne, who in October 1900 succeeded Salisbury at the Foreign Office, also enabled him to play a key role in the making of the Anglo-Japanese alliance.

---

[31] Memo. by Bertie, 6 Jan. 1900, F.O.2/434. Bertie to Lascelles, 6 and 10 Jan. 1900, Lascelles MSS., F.O.800/9.
[32] Sanderson to Lascelles, 6 Jan. 1900, *ibid*. Bülow blamed Hatzfeldt's poor state of health for the notes. Lascelles to Salisbury, 26 Jan. 1900, Salisbury MSS., A/131/37.
[33] Young, pp.202 – 3.
[34] In the autumn of 1897 Bertie and his son travelled to Constantinople where they stayed as the guests of Bertie's former chief, Sir Philip Currie, who was then ambassador there. E.T.S. Dugdale, *Maurice de Bunsen. Diplomat and Friend* (London, 1934), pp.147 – 8.
[35] C. Pearl, p.170.

That alliance was essentially the result of the apprehensions felt in both Britain and Japan about the activities of the Russians in Manchuria and their ambitions in neighbouring lands. Russia's reluctance to withdraw from Manchuria the forces which she had sent to the province at the time of the Boxer rising appeared in British eyes to pose a threat to the independence and integrity of China.[36] For Bertie the alliance was also a more satisfactory way of coping with this menace than that supported by the proponents of an accommodation with Germany. The Germans might be, as Bülow maintained, free traders in China, but in Bertie's estimate an understanding with them would probably mean conceding to their commerce and industry a special position in the lands between the Yangtze valley, where British trade predominated, and the Yellow river. Even then he thought that the Germans were unlikely to constitute an effective barrier against a Russian advance towards the south, and that they would be reluctant to put cooperation with Britain in Asia before their desire to remain on good terms with their Russian neighbours in Europe.[37] Such suspicions seemed only to be borne out when barely six months after the conclusion in October 1900 of a somewhat obscurely worded Anglo-German accord on the maintenance of the open door and the 'territorial condition of the Chinese Empire', Bülow publicly proclaimed his indifference towards demands by the Russians for what amounted to political and economic control of Manchuria.[38] 'A reliable understanding with Germany in opposition to Russian designs in the Far East is', Bertie wrote a few months later, 'not obtainable'.[39]

Bertie was probably confirmed in his view that British and German interests were too divergent to permit a satisfactory agreement by Dr Stuebel, the director of the colonial department of the German foreign office. The latter was sent to London in March 1901 in order to try to reach agreement with Britain on a number of outstanding issues. These included: the raising of the Chinese tariffs in order to provide security for a loan to indemnify the powers for the cost of

---

[36] From the very start of the Boxer troubles Bertie was apprehensive about the future of China. See: Journal, 31 May 1900, Satow MSS. (Public Record Office), P.R.O.30/33/16/3. Bertie's role in the making of the Anglo-Japanese alliance is considered in detail in Ian H. Nish, *The Anglo-Japanese. The Diplomacy of Two Island Empires, 1894–1907* (London, 1966), pp.153–7, and 370–1.

[37] Goudswaard, pp.39–41. Bertie to Lascelles, 12 Sept 1900, Lascelles MSS., F.O.800/6.

[38] Bertie characteristically placed some of the blame for such errors as had occurred in the drafting of the German translation of this agreement upon Sanderson. Bertie to Lascelles, 20 March 1901, Lascelles MSS., F.O.800/6. Young, pp.193–213 and 281–94.

[39] Memo. by Bertie, 22 July 1901, F.O.46/547.

their recent military intervention in China; and matters relating to German nationals, imprisoned in, and expelled from, southern Africa. But Bertie, with whom Stuebel had a series of lengthy interviews, was in no mood to encourage such special missions, and he neither pulled punches, nor offered concessions.[40] His 'logic' may, as Lansdowne suspected, have been 'too unsparing for the Doctor's taste', for Stuebel returned to Germany disappointed at his own lack of achievement and apparently offended by Bertie's tone of address.[41] Indeed, in later years Bertie was to claim that his handling of Stuebel had led the Wilhelmstrasse to conclude that he was anti-German.[42] Whether or not this was the case remains uncertain. By the spring of 1901 Bertie had, however, begun to think that where the Far East was concerned Britain might derive more advantage from cooperation with Japan than from further attempts to work with Germany.

One of Bertie's first tasks as an assistant under-secretary had been to arrange negotiations for a new Anglo-Japanese commercial treaty. But it was Japan's military victory in her war with China which brought home to him the desirability of keeping on good terms with 'the Rising Power in the Far East'.[43] As the danger from Russia became more apparent, the idea of an accord of some kind with Japan gained wider currency in England. The events of the summer of 1900 offered the two countries the practical experience of cooperation, and in October that year Japan adhered to the Anglo-German agreement on the maintenance of the open door.[44] Yet Bertie was wary of what he conceived to be German efforts to push Britain into an understanding with Japan. Such an arrangement, he thought, would help to safeguard Germany's own interests in the Far East, and, in so far as it would help maintain ill-feeling between Britain and Russia, it would ease Germany's situation in Europe. Germany's object was, he suspected, to push Britain and Japan into a war with Russia, while she looked on 'as honest broker ready to mediate at any time on terms, and meanwhile helping herself to all the good things she could safely lay hands on'.[45] Bertie was, however, equally apprehensive

---

[40] Memo. by Bertie, 29 and 30 March, and 5 April, 1901, F.O.17/1502. Bertie to Lascelles, 27 March and 2 April 1901, Lascelles MSS., F.O.800/6.
[41] Lansdowne to Lascelles, 13 April 1901, F.O.64/1655, *private*. Lascelles to Lansdowne, 18 and 20 April 1901, Lascelles MSS., F.O.800/18. *G.P.*, XVI, no. 4892.
[42] Bertie to Mallet, 11 June 1904, B.P., F.O.800/170.
[43] Kimberley to Bertie, 26 June 1895, B.P., Add MS. 63013. Memo. by Bertie, 1 Dec. 1895, F.O.46/460. Peter Lowe, *Britain in the Far East. A survey from 1819* (London, 1981), p.60.
[44] Nish, pp.91–5, and 107–11.
[45] On learning from the Japanese minister in London that von Mühlberg, the German under state-secretary for Foreign affairs, had assured the Japanese minister at Berlin that in the event of a crisis in the Far East England would 'probably support Japan',

lest, if the Japanese were not encouraged to look towards Britain as a friend and possible ally, they should, through fear of an eventual Russian intervention in Korea, 'come to some sort of terms with Russia'.[46] Thus, after putting aside the idea of a tripartite agreement, such as the Germans had seemed to recoil from in March 1901, Bertie drafted a memorandum in the following June in which he proposed a consultative accord with Japan. To this, he thought, could be added a secret agreement by which Britain would offer Japan naval assistance in defence of Korea, in return for a Japanese commitment to aid Britain in the defence of the Yangtze region and southern China against foreign encroachment.[47]

This memorandum, the first written statement by a British official in favour of an exclusive arrangement with Japan, contained some of the essential elements of what was to become the Anglo-Japanese alliance. It was a cause which Bertie took up with enthusiasm, and during the summer and autumn of 1901 he continued to impress upon Lansdowne the importance of indicating to Japan that Britain was interested in an understanding.[48] He urged that the Japanese should be offered assistance to enable them to overcome their financial problems, and while he remained alert to the possibility of Britain being drawn by a Japanese alliance into a war with France and Russia, he also argued that 'to have an alliance with anyone would be dangerous'. A reliable arrangement with Germany could not in his opinion be had, and Russia, he claimed, 'would probably not adhere to the spirit of any agreement with England, even if one were attainable'. Besides which, he reasoned, a commitment to aid Japan would not compel Britain to make any sacrifice. Russia, he asserted, was 'in reality as much afraid of our strength as we are of the largeness of her forces', and if she were to advance into Korea Britain would be obliged by her own interests to resist her. An Anglo-Japanese alliance might also, as Bertie understood, reduce the strains placed upon the Admiralty's resources by the growth of French and Russian naval strength in Far Eastern waters.[49]

It was with such considerations in view that the cabinet, after preliminary discussions between Lansdowne and the Japanese minister in London, agreed on 16 August 1901 to the pursuit of an

---

Bertie commented: 'The Germans want to push us into the water and steal our clothes.' Bertie to Salisbury, 9 March 1901, F.O.46/545. Memo. by Bertie, 22 July 1901, F.O.46/547.
[46] Memo. by Bertie, 11 March 1901, F.O.17/1501. Memo. by Bertie, 22 July 1901, F.O.17/1507.
[47] Memo. by Bertie, 20 June 1901, F.O.46/547.
[48] Bertie to Lansdowne, 2 July 1901, and enclosed memo., F.O.17/1506.
[49] Memo. by Bertie, 22 July 1901, F.O.46/547.

alliance.⁵⁰ Bertie was requested by Lansdowne, who spent the latter part of the summer in Ireland, to 'agitate over the question of an understanding with Japan',⁵¹ and when negotiations commenced in October the foreign secretary spoke in terms which seemed to reflect Bertie's thinking on the subject. In fact, however, the draft treaty which the cabinet sanctioned on 5 November went beyond that originally envisaged by Bertie in so far as it provided for the observance by each power of neutrality in the event of the other engaging in a war in defence of its Far Eastern interests, and participation in the conflict if a fourth power became involved. There were some in the cabinet who would have preferred to have had an alliance which would also cover India and south-east Asia.⁵² Bertie would certainly have welcomed cabinet approval for a general alliance with Japan, if for no other reason than that he felt that it would not please Germany. To Sir Francis Knollys, an old friend and private secretary to King Edward VII, he wrote on 23 November that Germany 'would feel that with a general alliance with Japan we could more easily than now dispose with German offers of alliance'. And when the Japanese failed to make an early response to the British proposals, Bertie began to wonder whether the Germans were meddling in the negotiations.⁵³

Bertie's suspicions were ill-founded. The Japanese simply wished to give fuller consideration to the project, and after the Foreign Office received Japan's counter-proposals on 12 December there followed a month of hard bargaining before the alliance was concluded on 30 January 1902. In so far as this treaty was a full alliance, made specific reference to the right of the contracting parties to safeguard their interests in China and Korea, and was accompanied by an exchange of notes which referred to the size of the naval forces that each power would keep in the Far East, it exceeded the sort of arrangment that Bertie had proposed. Nevertheless, in the ends which it sought to attain it clearly bore the imprint of his thinking.⁵⁴

An alliance with Japan had not been regarded by the British government as an alternative to an understanding with Germany. It had, as Professor Nish has argued, been considered complementary to anything that might have emerged from negotiations with Berlin.⁵⁵ Even Bertie was prepared to admit that there might be scope for a

---

⁵⁰ Nish, pp.143 – 63.
⁵¹ Lansdowne to Bertie, 27 Aug. 1901, B.P., A, F.O.800/163.
⁵² Nish, pp.177 – 82.
⁵³ Goudswaard, pp.82 – 3.
⁵⁴ Nish, pp.185 – 228.
⁵⁵ *Ibid*, pp.232 and 370 – 1.

regional agreement with Germany. In a memorandum of 7 November 1901 he indicated that Britain and Germany might find advantage in a joint declaration of policy, which would be limited to Europe and the Mediterranean, and which would cite the interests that they would jointly defend. This was not, however, a course which Bertie advocated. It was offered as an alternative to the Anglo-German alliance that Lansdowne still seemed ready to contemplate, and to which Bertie made plain his opposition. Thus, although he readily admitted that it would be a great relief for Britain to have a 'powerful and *sure* ally' for the contingency of an attack by a Franco-Russian combination, he again insisted on the deceitful nature of German diplomacy. He also stressed the weak position which Germany occupied in Europe.

Bertie saw Germany 'surrounded by Governments who distrust her and peoples who dislike or at all events do not like her'. She was, he wrote, in a constant state of tariff war with Russia, she had 'beaten and robbed Denmark', she had taken money and territory from France, she coveted the Dutch seaboard, and she had designs upon the Congo Free State. Pan-German agitation and commercial issues might, he suggested, soon bring about complications in her relations with Austria-Hungary. Besides which, the latter power, and Germany's other ally, Italy, both had serious domestic problems. If in these circumstances Britain were to arrive at 'general understandings' with France and Russia, or with either of them, Germany's position would, Bertie concluded, become 'critical', and it was therefore an object of her policy to foster friction between Britain and the powers of the Dual Alliance. On the other hand, he reasoned, as he had done so often before, no effective aid would be forthcoming from Germany in opposition to Russia unless she were obliged by European considerations to take part in a war. Moreover, for all Germany's protestations of friendship, Bertie noted that she had not shown herself particularly cooperative of late. What then, he asked, 'would her attitude towards this country be if she held England bound by a defensive alliance'?

Bertie also wondered how such an alliance might function when British and German interests were so different and, in some cases he felt, irreconcilable. In this context he cited Germany's desire to become a great naval power. She would, he supposed, need coaling stations to fortify. Yet, he explained:

> Good ones on the highways of trade can only be got in the great seas by purchase from Spain; by force from Holland — for she would not sell —; by the spoilation of Portugal, which we would be bound to resist; from Siam whose integrity within certain limits we

have guaranteed; or from France as the outcome of a successful war.

If Germany seek a station in the Mediterranean it must be obtained from Morocco, Spain, Greece or Turkey, and to the detriment of our naval position.

He likewise suggested that Germany might find herself at loggerheads with the British dominions, who, having played a prominent part in the south African war, would in the future expect the imperial government to take their interests more into account. And in the last resort Bertie considered that the defence requirements of Britain and her empire were so different from those of Germany and her continental allies that there was bound to be bickering and friction between them, which 'might lead to estrangement and end in an open quarrel'.

Bertie was above all anxious that closer ties with Germany should not be allowed to jeopardize what he evidently regarded as Britain's strong diplomatic position. Her 'isolation' was, he argued, not nearly as dangerous as the Germans claimed, and the best proof of this was the fact that despite her considerable commitment of men and money to the south African war, and the hostility of a large section of foreign opinion towards her, the continental powers had been unable to force her to accept arbitration. In fact, Bertie asserted, Britain now held the balance of power between the Triple and the Dual Alliances, and her position as a great and strong power was necessary to all in order to preserve that balance. But were Britain to bind herself in a formal defensive alliance with Germany and practically join the Triple Alliance, he declared 'we shall never be on decent terms with France our neighbour in Europe and in many parts of the world, or with Russia whose frontiers are coterminous with ours or nearly so over a large portion of Asia'. If in any event there were a danger of Britain's destruction or defeat by France and Russia, then Bertie reckoned that Germany would be bound in order to avoid a similar fate to come to Britain's assistance. 'She might', he observed, 'ask a high price for such aid, but could it be higher than what we should lose by the sacrifice of our liberty to pursue a British world policy, which would be the result of a formal defensive alliance with the German Empire.'[56]

This memorandum constituted the most comprehensive statement of Bertie's views on Britain's relations with Germany and the other continental powers that he was to commit to paper before his

[56] *B.D.*, II, no.91.

departure from the Foreign Office. It once more exhibited his profound mistrust of the practitioners of German foreign policy. Yet it was not so much motivated by hostility towards Germany as by a desire to steer Lansdowne and his colleagues away from any entangling alliance with her. It was in essence a defence of what Bertie understood as 'isolation': a term which he here interpreted as Britain's non-association with either of the great continental alliances. In this respect Bertie's views were not dissimilar to those which Salisbury had expressed six months before when he maintained that Britain's supposed isolation was *'a danger in whose existence we have no historical reason for believing'*.[57] Bertie's analysis was, however, novel in the emphasis which he placed upon Germany's aspirations to become a great naval power and her concomitant need for coaling stations as a factor in Anglo-German relations. In later years Bertie was time and again to interpret German actions in terms of what he assumed to be her desire for a network of naval bases and coaling stations, and he was repeatedly to advise the government in London to take measures to prevent their acquisition.[58]

One other aspect of his paper which deserves attention is its recognition of the unfavourable political position which Germany occupied in Europe, and the dilemma with which her statesmen and diplomats would have to grapple if Britain were ever to succeed in settling her differences with France and Russia. Indeed, one reason for Bertie's opposition to an alliance with Germany was that it would hamper any improvement in relations between Britain and her two foremost imperial rivals. The same might also have been said about the Anglo-Japanese alliance and future relations with Russia. But in the case of Japan Bertie claimed to perceive a clearer identity of interest between her and Britain. Besides which, since he thought Russia's Far Eastern policy to be 'bluff' and that she would give way once she realized that her adversary was 'in earnest as well as strong', he may well have felt that alliance with Japan would aid rather than hamper Britain in achieving an eventual settlement with Russia.[59]

With the signing of the Anglo-Japanese alliance and the successful conclusion of the south African war Bertie's confidence in Britain's global position increased. There remained the perennial problem of the threat posed by Russia to Britain in central Asia and Persia. But

---

[57] *B.D.*, II, no. 86.
[58] During 1902 Bertie was to grow inceasingly apprehensive about Germany's intentions with regard to Siam where he thought she would probably seek a coaling station. Bertie to Lansdowne, 26 May 1902; and Memo. by Bertie, 3 Aug. 1902, F.O.69/237.
[59] Memo. by Bertie, 22 July 1901, F.O.46/547.

Bertie felt that there was little reason to worry about Russia's partner in the Dual Alliance. In a letter which he addressed to Spring Rice on Boxing day 1902 he observed he believed the French government realised the ruin that a war with England would entail for them, and thus they would do almost anything to avoid one. They could, he thought, not resist the opportunity to squeeze Britain with the help of Russia or another power, but the only danger that he feared was that they might miscalculate matters and be pushed into a position where a repetition of Fashoda would be made impossible by parliamentary opinion. As to what objects Britain should pursue, Bertie considered that it would be wise to cultivate the best terms with the United States, and, at a time when it seemed likely that the prospect of a north African empire might tempt Spain to incline towards the Dual Alliance, to get on good terms with Spain to prevent her throwing in her lot with France. 'We can then', Bertie reasserted, 'remain the Country holding the balance between the Dual and Triple Alliances.' Germany remained, however, 'the element of mischief'. The German government, Bertie claimed:

> go to the Russian Govt. with stories of our designs and duplicity; they come to us with reports of Russian and French intrigues and intentions and they probably feed France with the same stuff as to what we have done & are doing. They also do all they can to make bad blood between us & the Americans and they sow distrust of us in the minds of the Spanish Government telling them that we have designs on Morocco.[60]

The irritation felt by Bertie with the tortuous ways of German diplomacy was shared by many of his fellow countrymen. To this was added resentment at the manner in which Germany's leaders and her press had proved so ready to criticize England's conduct in south Africa. Better treatment had been expected from a supposedly friendly power. Valentine Chirol, the foreign editor of *The Times*, observed in a letter to Lascelles of 21 January 1902 that he had gathered at the Foreign Office that the Germans would 'be made to realise that we can no longer treat them as a nation with whom our relations are in any way different from the relations of technical friendship & "correctitude" we entertain with other nations'.[61] Some

---

[60] Bertie to Spring Rice, 26 Dec. 1902, Spring Rice MSS., CASR 1/2.
[61] Chirol to Lascelles, 21 Jan. 1902, Spring Rice MSS., CASR 1/14. Shortly after the commencement of the Anglo-Boer war Chirol had written to Lascelles with regard to German conduct: 'The ill-will of France & Russia was to be expected & to a certain extent excusable. But that Germany should have displayed such rancorous hatred had come as a surprise even to those who were under no illusions as to the

six weeks later Sanderson, who regretted this 'inconvenient state of things', admitted to Lascelles that he had whenever the German government were mentioned to show that their conduct had 'in some respects been friendly'. 'There is', he wrote, 'a settled dislike of them, and an impression that they are ready and anxious to play on us any shabby trick they can.'[62]

The Admiralty in the meanwhile began to concern itself with Germany's growing naval strength, and the question of whether or not she should be regarded as a potential enemy. Such fears were associated with suspicions about German attitudes towards the Netherlands.[63] Salisbury had predicted in 1897 that William II would, with the object of securing a maritime population to man his fleet, seek to lay hold of the country, and in April 1902 news reached the Foreign Office of a German inquiry about the likely reaction of the United States government towards Germany's acquisition of the Dutch colonies in the event of her annexation of the Netherlands.[64] Spring Rice, who was responsible for this report, also feared that Britain might be lulled into a false sense of security, and that she, like Austria and France before her, would one day fall victim to Prussian aggression. Shortly after receiving Bertie's letter of 26 December 1902, he wrote to Rosebery to remind him that Britain's 'most dangerous enemy' was 'not in Asia and Africa but in Europe and at our doors'. He forecasted that in the not too distant future Germany would absorb the Netherlands and the German-speaking provinces of Austria, and he recommended that in order to forestall her ambitions Britain should arrive at an understanding with France, Spain and Italy, 'on the grounds of common danger to Western Europe'.[65]

Spring Rice's proposal, which went some way beyond Bertie's notion of Britain holding the balance between the continental alliance blocs, was no more than an opinion expressed by a relatively junior diplomat to a former prime minister. It was none the less symptomatic of a growing suspicion of the purposes of Wilhelmine Germany which during the next few years was to characterize the thinking of some of Bertie's closest associates. These included Louis Mallet, who as an assistant clerk had worked under Bertie in the American and Asiatic department, and Bertie's second cousin,

---

unscrupulousness of her policy.' Chirol to Lascelles, 6 March 1900. Spring Rice MSS., CASR 1/14.
[62] Sanderson to Lascelles, 5 March 1902, Lascelles MSS., F.O.800/10.
[63] Lansdowne to Lascelles, 2 April 102, Lascelles MSS., F.O.800/11.
[64] Salisbury to Lansdowne, 21 April 1897, Lansdowne MSS., F.O.800/145. Pauncefote to Sanderson, 28 April 1902, Lansdowne MSS., F.O.800/115.
[65] Spring Rice to Rosebery, 8 Jan. 1903, Spring Rice MSS., CASR 1/2.

Charles Hardinge, who since 1898 had been first secretary of the British embassy at St Petersburg. With Hardinge Bertie was to correspond on a fairly regular basis for the best part of twenty years. The two men were also able to assist each other in securing the promotions and diplomatic translations that they both desired.

Hardinge was a very able, clear-sighted and determined diplomat. But his near meteoric rise within the foreign service was aided by his close connexions with the royal family. His father-in-law, Lord Alington, was, besides being another of Bertie's cousins, a well-known figure in the sporting world and a companion of King Edward VII, and Hardinge's wife, Winifred, was a lady-in-waiting to Queen Alexandra.[66] Bertie too was on good terms with the king. He and Edward VII shared a common interest in field sports, and the king probably enjoyed Bertie's coarse conviviality. For his part Bertie may have taken advantage of the king's wish to play a more active part in the making of foreign policy, and he certainly sought his sovereign's patronage for his various schemes for changing the personnel of the Foreign Office. One such plan which he began to nurture in the spring of 1902 was to have Hardinge transferred from St Petersburg to London. He had already made sure that such of Hardinge's letters as contained political information were seen by the king and Lansdowne.[67] When, however, it became known that Gosselin was planning to give up his assistant under-secretaryship in order to spend the remainder of his years in the service as British minister at Lisbon, Bertie began to work for Hardinge's appointment in his stead. He supported Hardinge's candidature on the grounds that it would improve the office's efficiency to have a diplomat of his experience in a senior position.[68] But Bertie's efforts were not at first rewarded with success. The king, as Bertie explained to Hardinge, could not well intervene in what was 'really only a Departmental matter', and towards the end of July Francis Campbell, Sanderson's choice for the post, was appointed as Gosselin's successor.[69]

---

[66] Busch, *Hardinge*, pp.27–9 and 32–3.
[67] See for example: Bertie to Knollys, 4 June 1902 and enclosure, R(oyal) A(rchives) W42 82 and 83. Bertie to Hardinge, 6 Nov. 1901, Hardinge MSS., 3. Hardinge to Bertie, 14 Nov. 1901, B.P., A, F.O.800/176. Lady Feodorowna may also have provided Bertie with a royal connexion for she had been a bridesmaid to Princess Alexandra at her marriage to the Prince of Wales. Seymour Fortescue, *Looking Back* (London, 1920), p.327.
[68] Bertie to Hardinge, 4 and 9 June, and 3 July, 1902, Hardinge MSS., 3.
[69] Bertie to Hardinge, 25 July 1902, *ibid*.

Bertie was depressed by this news.⁷⁰ Indeed, Campbell's promotion shattered any illusion he might have entertained that Lansdowne, whom he had known since his schooldays, would be more susceptible to his influence than Salisbury. Hardinge could afford to muse about whether Sanderson might 'be made a Duke for the coronation' and his services be transferred from Downing street to the House of Lords.⁷¹ Bertie had, however, to reckon with the likelihood of Sanderson remaining at the Foreign Office until he was sixty-five. He might even seek an extension of his appointment. One suggestion which seems again to have been made was that Bertie should go to the Colonial Office as permanent under-secretary. But Rosebery advised him against this course, and Bertie recognized that it would probably mean his being 'shelved'.⁷² A better alternative appeared to be a mission abroad. The prospects of a lighter workload and a warmer climate were no doubt appealing. There were also good precedents for senior officials accepting such postings. Not only had Bertie's colleague, Gosselin, gone to Lisbon, but his former chief, Philip Currie, had been appointed ambassador firstly at Constantinople and then at Rome. Moreover, Currie's ill-health made it more than likely that a new ambassador to Italy, a country which Bertie had visited in the spring, would soon be required.⁷³

In the week following the announcement of Campbell's appointment, Bertie had the opportunity to discuss his career prospects with the king. He had been granted a knighthood in the coronation honours list, and on 3 August he travelled to Cowes to be invested by the king upon the royal yacht, *Victoria and Albert*. Edward VII knew by then that Bertie wanted the embassy at Rome, and prior to his investiture, first the Marquis de Soveral, the Portuguese minister in London, and then Knollys impressed upon him the king's wish that he should remain at the Foreign Office. The king, Soveral said, wanted Sanderson to be appointed to Rome, and Bertie to succeed him as permanent under-secretary. But Bertie was not convinced that Lansdowne would part with Sanderson. In any case, Bertie subsequently told the king, he did 'not think that he [Sanderson] would feel himself fit or that the Italians would find him acceptable and that Lansdowne found him so useful in inventing reasons for not doing anything that he wished to keep him at the Foreign Office'.

---

⁷⁰ *ibid.*
⁷¹ Lansdowne to Pansa, 30 Dec. 1902, Lansdowne MSS., F.O.800/132. Bertie to Spring Rice, 29 Aug. 1902, Spring Rice MSS., CASR 1/2. Hardinge to Bertie, 29 May 1902, B.P. A, F.O.800/164.
⁷² Bertie to Rosebery, 13 Jan. 1903, Rosebery, MSS., 10116.
⁷³ Hardinge to Bertie, 29 May 1902, B.P. A, F.O.800/164.

Bertie also added that Sanderson 'was quite devoid of tact and was very excitable particularly after dinner'. He was, nevertheless, ready to agree, at this stage albeit reluctantly, that if he obtained Rome, he would, if required, return to the Foreign Office on Sanderson's retirement.[74]

His meeting with the king left Bertie in a more optimistic mood. 'The general result of my visit to the Royal Yacht is', he noted, 'I feel pretty confident that I shall succeed Bossy [Sanderson] or get an Embassy.'[75] All, however, was still far from settled. Lansdowne was reluctant to lose either Sanderson or Bertie, and evidently with a view to deterring Bertie from persisting in his quest for an appointment abroad, he suggested that he might take the legation at Stockholm. But Bertie simply responded by threatening that if he were not given Rome, he would retire when he reached a pensionable age in two years time.[76] Knollys in the meanwhile kept Bertie's case before the king, who in his turn urged Lansdowne to let Bertie have his way.[77] Finally, when in mid-December 1902 Bertie learned that Currie had on his doctor's advice decided not to return to Rome, Bertie wrote to Lansdowne to ask him if he might have the embassy. 'I am', he observed, 'no longer young and I see no prospect of obtaining advancement in the Foreign Office before I become entitled to a pension.'[78] There were other candidates in the field. Lascelles was tiring of Berlin and would have preferred translation to Rome, and the names of Arthur Nicolson and Edwin Egerton, the British ministers at Tangier and Athens respectively, were mentioned in connexion with the post. It was, nevertheless, unlikely that the king would agree to the removal from Berlin of an ambassador who was on such good terms with the German emperor as was Lascelles, and neither Nicolson nor Egerton seem to have been serious competitors for Rome.[79] Thus, on 22 December Lansdowne gave way and wrote to Balfour, who in July had succeeded Salisbury as prime minister, recommending Bertie as successor to Currie.[80] Four days later he sent for Bertie to inform him of his decision. Bertie for his part felt sure

---

[74] Bertie to 'My Darling' (presumably Lady Feodorowna), 3 Aug. 1902, B.P., Add. MS. 63011.
[75] *Ibid.*
[76] Knollys to Bertie, 10 Nov. 1902, B.P., A, F.O.800/163. Georges Louis, *Les carnets de Georges Louis* (2 vols, Paris, 1926), I, p.135.
[77] Knollys to Bertie, 14 Oct., 5 Nov., 19 and 21 Dec., 1902, B.P., A, F.O.800/163.
[78] Bertie to Lansdowne, 19 Dec. 1902, B.P., A, F.O.800/163.
[79] Bertie to 'My Darling', 2 Aug. 1902, B.P., Add, MS.63011, Bertie to Knollys, 22 Dec. 1902, B.P., A, F.O.800/163. Bertie to Lascelles, 31 Dec. 1902, Lascelles MSS., F.O.800/11.
[80] Lansdowne to Balfour, 22 Dec. 1902, Balfour, MSS., Add. MS.49727.

that he owed his embassy to the support given to his cause by the king and Knollys, both of whom were to aid him in persuading Lansdowne to appoint Hardinge to the newly vacant assistant under-secretaryship.[81]

The choice of Hardinge as his successor was regarded by Bertie as a fresh challenge to Sanderson's regime. 'I am glad', he wrote to his cousin, 'that I could do something to obtain recognition of merit and ability . . . . You must be prepared to meet with obstruction from guts of red tape & elastic bands.'[82] Sanderson naturally viewed things in a somewhat different light, and he had sincere doubts about Bertie's suitability for Rome. He was, Sanderson observed to Lascelles, 'not to my mind an ideal selection, but we must hope that in the Italian climate and with much less work some of the asperities from which we have suffered will disappear'.[83] Lansdowne also foresaw difficulties arising from Bertie's transfer, for he thought that the new ambassador would not be popular with British residents at Rome. Nevertheless, he believed Bertie to be the 'best man' for the post. 'He is', he assured Balfour, 'shrewd enough to keep his temper in control when he is transacting international affairs', and, he added, the 'foreigners here all like him.'[84] Others were prepared to predict even greater rewards ahead for Bertie. Shortly after the announcement of his appointment to Rome, Lord George Hamilton, the secretary of state for India, wrote to his permanent under-secretary: 'I am very sorry we are to lose Bertie. He will make a good Ambassador as his practicability, courage and decision never fail him. I should like to see him afterwards at Paris.'[85] This thought may perhaps have occurred to Bertie. But at fifty-eight years of age he could hardly have surmised that his career in diplomacy had another fifteen years to run.

---

[81] Bertie to Knollys, 27 Dec. 1902, B.P., A, F.O.800/163.
[82] Bertie to Hardinge, 14 Jan. 1903, Hardinge MSS., 3. Lansdowne also recognized the value of having a diplomat like Hardinge in the Foreign Office. He would, Lansdowne noted, 'be much handier with foreigners than men of the Campbell type'. Lansdowne to Cranborne, 31 Dec. 1902, Cecil MSS., S(4) 50/141.
[83] Sanderson to Lascelles, 31 Dec. 1902, Lascelles MSS., F.O.800/11.
[84] Lansdowne to Balfour, 22 Dec. 1902, Balfour MSS., Add. MS49727.
[85] Hamilton to Godley, 1 Jan. 1903, Kilbracken MSS., 6B. I am grateful to Professor David Dilks of the University of Leeds for having provided me with this quotation.

3

His heart's desire

'Frank Bertie has his heart's desire', wrote one member of the royal household on 10 January 1903.[1] Bertie did not, however, match the energy which he had expended in securing his new post with an equivalent display of enthusiasm for his new responsibilities. His first official visit to Rome lasted barely a fortnight. He arrived at the embassy house, which was situated near the Porta Pia, on 31 January, and made his debut in Roman society at a ball given by the Princess Radziwill.[2] He subsequently presented his credentials to King Victor Emmanuel III, paid courtesy calls upon the other ambassadors, and was received by the president of the council of ministers, Giuseppe Zanardelli, and the navy minister, Enrico Morin. Finally, after an audience with the queen mother on 14 February, he boarded the night train for Paris, from whence he travelled to London to complete his packing and arrange his affairs. Five weeks later on 19 March he returned to Rome to resume his duties as ambassador.[3]

During his absence Bertie left the embassy in the care of his first secretary, Sir James Rennell Rodd. An ambitious and talented diplomat with literary predilections, Rodd had been *chargé d'affaires* at Rome since Currie's departure in April 1902.[4] He had in that time succeeded in ingratiating himself with the Italian foreign minister, Giulio Prinetti, and the latter had in his turn tried to use his influence to have Rodd appointed as ambassador.[5] Anglo-Italian relations had in Prinetti's estimate suffered from the failure of recent British ambassadors to keep in touch with the Consulta. 'You have', he had complained to Rodd in July 1902, 'had a long series of ambassadors here who have been charming men, but they have generally been out of health or for some reason or other little able to come forward.'[6] The

---

[1] Arthur Ellis to Lascelles, 10 Jan. 1903, Lascelles MSS., F.O.800/11.
[2] Bertie to Lansdowne, 4 Feb. 1903, Lansdowne MSS., F.O.800/132.
[3] Bertie to Lansdowne, 15 Feb. 1903, F.O.45/872, despt.28. Bertie to Lansdowne, 19 March 1903, F.O.45/872, despt. 49. Bertie to Knollys, 14 Feb. 1903; Bertie to Lansdowne, 14 Feb. 1903; B.P., A, F.O.800/173.
[4] Rennell Rodd, III, 42 – 3.
[5] *Ibid*, 23.
[6] Rodd to Barrington, 29 July 1902, Lansdowne MSS., F.O.800/132.

charge was not without foundation. Rosebery may have regarded the British embassy at Rome as the 'only pleasant post left' in the diplomatic service.[7] But in spite of, or perhaps because of this, it had also become what Chirol termed 'a 'place of embalming' for our decrepit diplomats'.[8] Sir Francis Ford, Currie's immediate predecessor, had been a noted drunkard, and Currie, whose previous embassy at Constantinople had been generally regarded as a failure, had suffered from heart trouble and had been a virtual invalid for much of his time at Rome.[9] Even Rodd, who was reluctant to criticize his former chief, could hardly ignore the contrast between the conspicuous efforts of the French ambassador, Camille Barrère, to win popularity for himself and his country, and the implastic and sometimes tactless behaviour of Currie.[10] Rodd also had some misgivings about the choice of Bertie for the post. He wondered whether the new ambassador, 'a first-class-fighting man, would get on with Prinetti, who carried his head very high'.[11] As fate would have it, he need not have worried. On 20 January Prinetti was laid low by a syphilitic stroke, and, although he tried to hold on to office, Italy's foreign policy was for the remaining months of Zanardelli's administration supervised by his colleague Morin at the ministry of marine.[12]

Shortly before he was taken ill, Prinetti had broached with Rodd the subject of an accord with Britain. Irritated by the readiness of Austria-Hungary to cooperate with Russia in matters relating to the troubled Ottoman province of Macedonia, and evidently desirous of strengthening Italy's international standing, he suggested to Rodd an Anglo-Italian exchange of views on the Near Eastern *status quo*. Rodd was optimistic about what he regarded as evidence of a sincere desire in Italy 'to fall into line with ourselves'. There was, he wrote to Lansdowne, 'now an excellent opportunity with the advent of a new Ambassador to inaugurate, if it be in comformity with the views of the Government, a return to the old policy of intimate relations with

---

[7] Rosebery to Bertie, 1 Jan. 1903, B.P., Add, MS 63015.
[8] Chirol to Spring Rice, (?) 1904, Spring Rice MSS., CASR 1/10.
[9] H. Wickham steed to Moberly Bell, 28 March and 17 April 1902, Wickham Steed MSS. (*The Times* archives). Chirol to Wickham Steed, 22 Jan. 1902, Chirol MSS., (*The Times* archives). Spring Rice to Rosebery, 8 Jan. 1903, Rosebery MSS., 10116. Rennell Rodd, III, 4.
[10] Rodd described Barrère as having Prinetti 'quite in his pocket'. Rennell Rodd, III, 4. Rodd to Lansdowne, 12 May 1902, Lansdowne MSS., F.O.800/132.
[11] Rennell Rodd, III, 24.
[12] Rodd to Lansdowne, 20 Jan. 1903, F.O.45/875, tel.13. Bertie to Lansdowne, 6 April and 22 June 1903, B.P., A, F.O.800/173. Bertie to Lansdowne, 15 March 1904, Lansdowne MSS., F.O.800/133.

Italy.'[13] Lansdowne was more cautious. He was uncertain about the precise role that Prinetti would like Britain to assume, and when Bertie had his first audience with King Victor Emmanuel he could offer no more by way of assurance than the platitude that he 'did not think that the interests — the essential ones — of Italy and England clashed anywhere'.[14] In truth the intimacy that had once prevailed between London and Rome, and which had found expression in the Mediterranean agreements of 1887, had owed much to Salisbury's desire to work with the powers of the Triple Alliance in containing the threat of Russian expansion in the Near East.[15] Since then, however, the British had lost much of their former interest in the *régime* of the straits between the Black sea and the Aegean, and those in the government who still favoured an understanding with Germany preferred to deal directly with Berlin. In consequence the Foreign Office had regarded with equanimity Italy's recent *rapprochement* with France, and little or no support had been offered to Italian aspirations in Tripolitania.[16] Only in the horn of Africa, where both powers had to reckon with a widespread Somali revolt and the menace posed to their interests by France's economic penetration of Abyssinia did there seem in 1903 to be any scope for effective cooperation between Britain and Italy.[17] Nevertheless, in one quarter at least Prinetti's overture was greeted with enthusiasm.

Edward VII thought that Rodd's suggestion was 'an admirable one', and that it should place Bertie in good standing with Prinetti.[18] It also seemed likely to furnish the king with the chance of appearing to score a diplomatic success if a new era of Anglo-Italian amity could be inaugurated with the visit which he was hoping to make to Rome that spring. The original plan for this visit, which was revealed to Bertie after his return to England in February, was for the king, who was to be accompanied by Hardinge, to embark on a cruise which would take him first to Lisbon and then, if a meeting could be arranged with the president of the republic, to the French Riviera. After this, in the latter half of April the *Victoria and Albert* would sail to Naples, whence the king could proceed to Rome for a stay of two or

---

[13] Rodd to Lansdowne, 13 Jan. 1903, Lansdowne MSS., F.O.800/132.
[14] Lansdowne to Rodd, 5 Feb. 1903, Lansdowne MSS., F.O.800/132. Bertie to Lansdowne, 5 Feb. 1903, B.P., A, F.O.800/173.
[15] C.J. Lowe, *Salisbury and the Mediterranean* (London, 1965).
[16] C.J. Lowe and F. Marzari, *Italian Foreign Policy, 1870–1940* (London, 1975), pp.82–90. Memo. by Bertie, 22 Dec. 1901, B.P., A, F.O.800/173.
[17] R. Bosworth, *Italy and the Approach of the First World War* (London, 1983), pp.52–4.
[18] Minutes by Edward VII on Rodd to Lansdowne, 13 Jan. 1903, Lansdowne MSS., F.O.800/132.

three days.¹⁹ The royal visit was, however, fraught with difficulties for Bertie. Hardly had the ambassador left England for Italy than King Edward learned that the German emperor and empress were intending to visit Rome in May. Perturbed lest his own private and more modest visit should be overshadowed by that of his imperial nephew, the king began to think in terms of limiting himself to a visit to Naples and a day trip to Rome. He would then at a later date pay an official visit to Rome in the company of the queen, which, as Knollys put it, 'would be a great compliment . . . and would enable the visit to be a larger affair'.²⁰ But there was another reason for adopting this course. The king had been hoping to meet the pope during his stay in Rome. Indeed, he felt obliged to honour the ninety-three year old Leo XIII with a visit in this the twenty-fifth year of his pontificate.²¹ In the first instance such a meeting was opposed by the cabinet. It was feared that protestant opinion in Britain would see the visit as part of an attempt to conciliate the Irish and to ensure the success of the forthcoming visit of the king to Ireland.²² Knollys too was unhappy about the king's wish to see the pope, and he thought that it might be better to abandon the idea of Edward VII staying in Rome.²³

At a time when the results of the *Risorgimento* continued to divide church from state in Italy, Bertie was only too well aware of the need to tread carefully. Currie had raised a storm in the Italian press by attending a party given in Rome by the Duke of Norfolk at which had been present several members of the Vatican hierarchy. And Bertie had been glad to be in England when in February 1903 the same duke led a pilgrimage of English Roman Catholic notables to Rome to celebrate the papal jubilee.²⁴ It was, however, less easy for him to escape the consequences of a proposed royal audience with the pope. Moreover, the situation was complicated by the fact that it was not until after he had communicated King Edward's original plan to King Victor Emmanuel that Bertie learned from Knollys that Buckingham Palace was having second thoughts about the visit. As a

---

¹⁹ Bertie to Knollys, 22 March 1903; Bertie to Sandars, 20 April 1903; B.P., B, F.O.800/183. On the details of Edward VII's peregrinations in 1907 see: Gordon Brook-Shepherd, *Uncle of Europe. The Social and Diplomatic Life of Edward VII* (London, 1975), pp.153 – 207.
²⁰ Knollys to Bertie, 21 March 1903, B.P., B, F.O.800/183.
²¹ Hardinge to the Duke of Norfolk, 18 April 1903, B.P., B, F.O.800/183.
²² *Ibid*. Hardinge to Bertie, 13 April 1903, B.P., B, F.O.800/183.
²³ Knollys to Balfour, 16 and 19 March 1903, Sandars MSS., (Bodleian Library), Eng. hist. c719. Knollys to Hardinge, 23 April 1903, Hardinge MSS., 4.
²⁴ Rennell Rodd, III, 2. Bertie to Lansdowne, 4 Feb. 1903, Lansdowne MSS., F.O.800/132.

result, Bertie was faced with the disagreeable task of explaining to Zanardelli and Morin, who had already begun to think in terms of converting the proposed private visit into a full state occasion, that the king no longer wished to stay in Rome. This in the opinion of Victor Emmanuel and his ministers seemed likely to lead to domestic political difficulties in Italy. They had no serious objection to Edward VII meeting the pope. But they explained that if the English king were to pay an official visit to Lisbon, and were then to decline to stay at the Quirinal palace at Rome, it would be misunderstood by Italian public opinion. The Emperor Francis Joseph had demonstrated his disapproval of the enforced surrender of the temporal powers of the papacy by refusing to visit Italy's new capital, and King Edward's latest proposals could well be represented as a similar snub to the Italian state. In any event since news of the proposed visit seemed bound to leak out, Bertie considered that if it did not take place the effect was sure to be bad 'notwithstanding any explanation'. The best that he could suggest was that King Edward should travel from Naples to Rome and spend a night at the Quirinal. Desirous also of overcoming any doubts that the king might still have about the proximity of the German emperor's visit to his own, Bertie tried to impress upon Knollys the excellent effect that the royal visit would have on Anglo-Italian relations, and the good reception that he would receive in Rome. It would be much better, Victor Emmanuel had assured him, than that which would be given to the emperor.[25]

Towards the end of March the king gave way. On the 26th, just five days before the *Victoria and Albert* sailed from Portsmouth, Knollys wrote to Bertie to inform him that the king would arrive in Rome on 26 or 27 April, and that he would be prepared to stay for two nights at the Quirinal. He would then leave Rome by train for Paris. This was now to be regarded as an official visit, and there was to be no meeting with the pope.[26] If, however, the king felt himself compelled to abandon his proposed papal audience, the Vatican and its partisans did not. On 3 April a report appeared in the Italian press that discussions were going on between the Vatican and the English court with regard to preparations for an audience, and two days later Monsignor Stonor, the resident English prelate at Rome, tackled Bertie on this subject.[27] In the meanwhile, the Duke of Norfolk and Lord Edmond Talbot, prominent Roman Catholics, had succeeded in working themselves into a mood which bordered on hysteria.

---

[25] Bertie to Knollys, 22, 23 and 24 March 1903; Knollys to Bertie, 22 March 1903; Bertie to Lansdowne, 23 March 1903; B.P., B, F.O.800/183.
[26] Knollys to Bertie, 26 March 1903, B.P., B, F.O.800/183.
[27] Bertie to Hardinge, 3 and 6 April 1903, B.P., B, F.O.800/183.

During a meeting with Balfour on 8 April they claimed that if the king did not see the pope at Rome, it would be regarded by 'the Roman Catholic world as a deliberate slight upon an old and venerable man'.[28]

The prime minister was left in something of a quandary. Neither he nor Lansdowne was personally opposed to the king meeting the pope, but they were loath to alienate protestant sentiment by recommending such a course.[29] The news of the Duke of Norfolk's intervention provided the king with an opportunity to once more press his case for a visit to the Vatican.[30] There thus followed a flurry of less than cordial messages between Downing Street and the *Victoria and Albert*, which culminated in Balfour telegraphing to the king on 12 April that if the proposed visit to the pope could really be made privately and unofficially, he would 'think it an impertinence to offer any observation on it'. He further explained:

> If the whole stress could be laid on the fact that Your Majesty had visited the Pope before, that he was very aged and in the course of nature could live but a short time, that he had expressed a personal desire to see Your Majesty and that as a matter of courtesy between gentlemen you could not pass his door without acceding to his wishes, it is possible that object might be attained. But it would require skilful handling both in Italy and here.[31]

It was up to Bertie and his staff to ensure that these requirements were met.

Bertie may not have welcomed this task, but he was wholly in favour of a meeting between the king and the pope. Indeed, he sympathized with the desire of the Vatican to have a British agent appointed to the holy see.[32] As he reminded Knollys, the government 'may think that the Irish Catholics are past praying for and the English and Scotch Catholic influence is not worth considering', but there were many catholics in the overseas dominions, and the Vatican would always have its revenge for any supposed slight 'by encouraging opposition where they (the Priests) would not naturally

---

[28] Lansdowne to Bertie, 10 April 1903; Cranborne to Bertie, 11 April 1903; B.P., A, F.O.800/181. Barrington to Bertie, 10 April 1903, B.P., B, F.O.800/183. Balfour to Edward VII, 9 April 1903, Hardinge MSS., 4.
[29] Barrington to Hardinge, 10 April 1903, Hardinge MSS., 4. Barrington to Bertie, 18 April 1903, B.P., B, F.O.800/183.
[30] Hardinge to Balfour, 10 April 1903, Hardinge MSS., 4.
[31] Hardinge to Bertie, 13 April 1903, B.P., B, F.O.800/183. Frederick Ponsonby, *Recollections of Three Reigns* (London, 1951), pp.162–4.
[32] Bertie to Cranborne, 6 April and 5 May 1903, Cecil MSS., S(4) 52/72.

oppose'.³³ It was therefore with some satisfaction that he learned from Hardinge that he should see Stonor in order to elicit from the pope some expression of his desire to receive a visit from King Edward.³⁴ This, however, was easier said than done, for although the papal entourage was eager to have a royal visit, it was equally insistent that the pope could not take the initiative in issuing an invitation. The most that Cardinal Rampolla, the papal secretary of state, was prepared to concede was a statement to Stonor that if the king were to pay the pope a visit, 'the courtesy of His Majesty would be acceptable and duly appreciated by His Holiness'.³⁵ Bertie was thus placed in an unenviable position. He knew full well that the king would be upset if his proposed audience with the pope were to fall through at this stage. Yet he was also aware that Balfour's conditions could not be set aside. Moreover, a telegram from the secretary of the Church Assocation, which arrived at the embassy on 20 April, and which expressed the 'grave anxiety' felt in England over the rumour of a royal visit to the Vatican, was a salutary reminder of the feelings of some protestants on the subject.³⁶

There was no time for protracted negotiations for Bertie was required to be in Naples on 23 April in order to greet the royal yacht there. But Stonor, whom Bertie thought might be after a cardinal's hat, seemed only to encourage Rampolla in the belief that the king would eventually accept the Vatican's terms.³⁷ In desperation Bertie turned to Esmé Howard, a distant cousin of the Duke of Norfolk, whom he had only recently persuaded to accept the post of honorary second secretary at the embassy. A convert to Roman Catholicism, Howard was able to ask his religious instructor, the papal secretary, Monsignor Merry del Val, to intercede directly with the pope.³⁸ Not, however, until the evening of 24 April was Howard able to extract from the Vatican the message that the pope had 'personally expressed his concurrence with what the Duke of Norfolk conveyed as to the pleasure which His Holiness would derive from a visit from His Majesty': an ingenious formula which satisfied the demands of both papal and royal etiquette.³⁹ Bertie was no doubt relieved to learn from Rodd of Howard's achievement. He had all along felt that in the end

---

³³ Bertie to Knollys, 25 March 1903, R.A. W43 66.
³⁴ Hardinge to Bertie, 13 April 1903, Hardinge MSS., 4.
³⁵ Bertie to Hardinge, 18 April 1903, B.P., B, F.O.800/183.
³⁶ Bertie to Cranborne, 5 May 1903, Cecil MSS., S(4) 52/72.
³⁷ Bertie to Hardinge, 14 April 1903; Hardinge to Bertie, 20 April 1903; B.P., B, F.O.800/183.
³⁸ Memos. by E. Howard, 21 April 1903; Bertie to Sandars, 26 April 1903; Sandars MSS., Eng. hist. c719.
³⁹ Rodd to Hardinge, 25 April 1903, Hardinge MSS., 4.

the Vatican would give way, but he had also feared that the king might in his eagerness to see the pope be prepared to accept terms which would be objectionable to the cabinet. In consequence, since joining the *Victoria and Albert* he had been trying to impress upon the king that this was a 'matter of dignity', and that he should 'stand out for his own conditions'.[40] This demanded a good deal of nervous energy, and in spite of the company of old friends and the entertainments offered by Neapolitan society, Bertie seems to have derived little pleasure from his stay aboard the royal yacht. 'Since I have been here', he wrote from Naples on 26 April, 'I have lived in a continual state of motion without exercise.'[41]

Once back in Rome Bertie had some respite from his labours. The final arrangements for the papal audience were settled by Hardinge and Rampolla, and although Bertie had to ward off an attempt by the Italian minister of the interior to foist a military escort on the king, all he personally had to provide were two carriages and suitable entertainments at the embassy.[42] Nevertheless, when King Edward left Rome for Paris on 30 April, Bertie was glad that the affair was over. Accustomed to the routine work of the Foreign Office, Bertie had found the seemingly interminable discussions with papal emissaries and court officials to be wearisome and often unrewarding. 'I have', he wrote to Lansdowne shortly after the king's departure, 'been very busy for the past fortnight doing nothing and never finding time in which to do it.'[43] Moreover, no sooner had one royal visit ended than another began, for on 2 May the German emperor descended on Rome and treated its citizens and the pope to an ostentacious display of regal splendour. Bertie, who was able to relax and draw comparisons, concluded that of the two visits that of the king had been the more popular.[44] Certainly in the Foreign Office it was regarded as a great success, 'greater even', noted Lord Cranborne, the parliamentary under-secretary of state, 'than the French sequel'.[45] Yet in retrospect, Edward VII's visit to Rome, like that to Lisbon, appears as no more than a prelude to the politically more significant one to Paris. Interesting though the king's presence in Rome may have been from the point of view of relations between protestant England and the papacy, it made no contribution, either

---

[40] Bertie to Cranborne, 5 May 1903, Cecil MSS., S(4) 52/72.
[41] Bertie to Sandars, 26 April 1903, Sandars MSS., Eng. hist. c719.
[42] Hardinge to Balfour, 29 April 1903, Hardinge MSS., 3. Bertie to Cranborne, 5 May 1903, Cecil MSS., S(4) 52/72.
[43] Bertie to Lansdowne, 30 April 1903, Lansdowne MSS., F.O.800/132.
[44] Bertie to Lansdowne, 5 May 1903; Bertie to Knollys, 16 May 1903; B.P., B, F.O.800/183. Bertie to Lansdowne, 17 May 1903, B.P., A, F.O.800/170.
[45] Cranborne to Bertie, 22 May 1903, B.P., A, F.O.800/174.

real or symbolic, to the realignment of the European powers. No-one would write of it, as Barrère wrote of the Paris visit, that it was proof of a new orientation in British foreign policy and 'l'indice grave de l'isolement de l'Allemagne'.[46] It was, however, by no means evident to Bertie that the royal visit to Paris would be associated with any new departure in British foreign policy. Indeed although Bertie was pleased with the idea of an Anglo-French *rapprochement*, he seems in the spring of 1903 to have seen little scope for an accommodation on Egypt and Morocco such as was achieved in April 1904.[47] When, for instance, Barrère, with whom he was on quite friendly terms, suggested to him at the end of May that Britain might agree to acquiesce in France being the 'predominant Power in Morocco', he received from Bertie a distinctly cool response.

Bertie explained to Barrère that Britain's interests in Morocco were not limited to the seaboard, and that her desire was to maintain the *status quo*. 'The possession or practical hold of Morocco by France' would, Bertie observed, 'change the balance of power in the Western Mediterranean and outside it.' Moreover, he warned his French colleague that if they began 'cutting up' Morocco, 'other Powers including Germany might want slices'. Barrère 'pooh, poohed' the idea of Germany having any claim.[48] But Germany was rarely far from Bertie's thoughts. After all, one of the great advantages, in his opinion, of an Anglo-French accord was that it would limit the ability of Germany to join her continental neighbours in applying pressure upon Britain. 'What we have got to do', he observed to Cranborne on 30 June, 'is to prevent Germany from obtaining coaling stations and so becoming a Great Naval Power for war purposes beyond the immediate neighbourhood of her own coasts, and to encourage differences between France & Germany so as to make a naval combination between them improbable.' There could, however, be no question of an Anglo-French alliance. That, Bertie told Barrère, would be 'impossible', and, he added, 'it would be much more likely that peace would be preserved in Europe if we joined neither the Triples nor the Duals'.[49] At a time when feelers were being put out for a broad-based Anglo-French colonial understanding, Bertie remained wedded to the notion that Britain's interests might best be served by her maintaining a free hand and a divided Europe.

[46] Barrère to Delcassé, 11 May 1903, Delcassé MSS., 1.
[47] Bertie to Cranborne, 6 April 1903, Cecil MSS., S(4) 52/72.
[48] Bertie to Cranborne, 1 June 1903, Cecil MSS., S(4) 52/116.
[49] Bertie to Cranborne, 30 June 1903, Cecil MSS., S(4) 52/162.

The Italians were in the meanwhile encouraged by the prevailing mood of Anglo-Italian amity to propose an agreement with Britain in the horn of Africa. There the British had already benefited from Italian cooperation in their efforts to quell a revolt amongst their Somali subjects. Both Britain and Italy were also concerned about the future of Abyssinia.[50] Forced by their defeat at Adowa in 1896 to abandon their pretensions to exercise a protectorate over that empire, the Italians were none the less anxious to prevent any other European power from obstructing the chances of their acquiring a territorial link between their colony of Eritrea and their protectorate on the Benadir coast. They therefore wished to ensure that the British, Abyssinia's neighbours on three sides, respected Italian aspirations.[51] The danger was that the death of Abyssinia's present ruler, the Negus Menelik II, might be followed by internecine strife and foreign intervention. The British authorities in Egypt and the Sudan would have preferred the maintenance of the *status quo*.[52] That, however, was also threatened by the construction with the financial assistance of the French government of a railway between Jibuti in French Somaliland and the interior: a line which when completed could leave France preeminent at Addis Ababa.[53] It was evidently with this in view that the Consulta presented Bertie on 23 May 1903 with a rather obscurely worded memorandum. It contained an offer of Italian support for British opposition to the French railway company's claim to have the exclusive right to link Addis Ababa to the sea, and a recommendation that Britain and Italy should arrive at a general understanding for the safeguarding of their interests in Abyssinia.[54]

Bertie, who never fully appreciated the extent to which the Italians were perturbed about possible British ambitions in the area, wrongly assumed that what the Consulta wanted was mutual guarantee by Britain and Italy of their respective possessions in east Africa. It was not an idea that appealed to him. Nor did he suppose it would 'smile' to Lansdowne. Britain, he admitted, could not afford to see Italy replaced in her possessions by another European power, but given the

---

[50] Bosworth, *Italy and the Approach of the First World War*, pp.52 – 4. Rennell Rodd, III, 22 – 3. Lansdowne to Bertie, 10 April 1903, B.P., A, F.O.800/181.
[51] Rodd to Lansdowne, 13 Dec. 1902, Lansdowne MSS., F.O.800/132.
[52] H.G. Marcus, *The Life and Times of Menelik II. Ethiopia 1844 – 1913* (Oxford, 1975), p.206; and by the same author 'A Preliminary History of the Tripartite Treaty of December 13, 1906', *Journal of Ethiopian Studies*, II (1964), 21 – 40.
[53] Marcus, *Menelik II*, pp.152 – 3 and 201 – 3. Memo. by Bertie by Harrington, 4 Jan. 1904, F.O.1/50. K.V. Ram, 'The British Government, Finance Capitalists and the French Jubuti-Addis Ababa Railway 1898 – 1915', *Journal of Imperial and Commonwealth History*, IX (1981), 146 – 68.
[54] Bertie to Lansdowne, 25 May 1903, and enclosures, F.O.1/43, despt. 103.

general lack of administrative capacity displayed by the Italians, he feared that through such an arrangement Britain would soon find herself at loggerheads with the Abyssinians. 'I think', he wrote to Lansdowne, 'that the Italians would trade on any obligations taken by us to do rash things', and the most that he could suggest was that 'a mutual understanding to resist foreign (European) aggression might satisfy the Italian government.'[55]

As Bertie anticipated, Lansdowne was reluctant to commit Britain to a guarantee of Italy's territories in Africa. Thus, while he agreed to the idea of cooperating with Italy on the railway question, he insisted that any further scheme for safeguarding British and Italian interests would have to await the result of recent operations against the Somali tribesmen.[56] The Italians none the less continued in their efforts to achieve an agreement, and on 29 August Rodd, who was again acting as *chargé d'affaires*, received a further memorandum from Morin. It called for 'a practical definition of reciprocal interests in the sphere of activity assigned to each of the Powers', and proposed that Britain and Italy should come to an understanding if the *status quo* in Abyssinia should for any reason be disturbed.[57] Bertie did not learn of this communication until the end of September. He and Lady Feo, who had been taken seriously ill in June, had spent most of the summer at Elm House in Windsor forest, and after their return to Italy on 14 September they decided to take a cure at Salso di Maggiore.[58] There had, after all, appeared to be no important business requiring ambassadorial attention. Lansdowne preferred to adopt a dilatory approach towards the Italian overtures for an Abyssinian agreement, and the Consulta displayed no haste in its handling of the issue. But the news that in October Morin was intending to accompany King Victor Emmanuel on an official visit to Paris led Bertie to introduce a new sense of urgency into the discussions. Not that he had any illusions about the likely outcome of this visit. He did not, for instance, share Barrère's view that this was another move towards severing Italy's ties with her partners in the Triple Alliance. Bertie did, however, think that Victor Emmanuel might seek advantage in a 'flirtation' with France, and he was

---

[55] Bertie to Lansdowne, 26 May 1903, B.P., A, F.O.800/160.
[56] Bertie to Lansdowne, 12 June 1903, F.O.1/43 despt.132.
[57] Memo. by Bertie by Morin enclosed in Rodd to Lansdowne, 6 Sept. 1903, F.O.45/871, despt.184. *B.D.*, I, 315 – 19.
[58] Bertie to Cranborne, 30 June 1903, Cecil MSS., S(4) 52/162. Bertie to Knollys, 5 June 1903, B.P. (British Library). Bertie to Lansdowne, 15 Sept. 1903, B.P., B, F.O.800/183.

apprehensive lest the French should try to inveigle Morin into giving assurances that could be contrary to British interests in Abyssinia.[59]

On 28 September, before he had had time in which to digest the details of the latest Italian proposals, Bertie wrote privately to Lansdowne to urge him to 'do something without delay to prevent the Italians coming to some arrangement with the French'. 'The French', he observed, 'are a danger to our Nile interests in Abyssinia and it seems to me to be worth some risk to keep the Italians from throwing in their lot with them.'[60] He therefore pressed Lansdowne to give Morin some confidence in Britain's intention to meet Italy's wishes in Abyssinia. What he had in mind was an arrangement by which Britain and Italy would agree that after Menelik's death, they would recognize as his successor the person who on gaining power declared himself ready to abide by existing agreements with them. If the new negus were to decline to accept the validity of such engagements, then, Bertie later explained to Lansdowne, discussions between Britain and Italy on the defence of their respective interests might 'possibly lead to dissuading France from taking any part unfriendly to England and Italy and the ring being kept for a true fight in Abyssinia'. He also recommended that the two governments should give each other's nationals diplomatic support in applying for concessions. The important point in Bertie's opinion was to deny the French the opportunity for making mischief in the country.[61]

Lansdowne was quite ready to accept the idea of a consultative agreement on Abyssinia, so long as it did not bind Britain to armed intervention.[62] Nevertheless, he found the kind of language that Bertie proposed to use with the Italians 'rather more precise' than was necessary.[63] The Italian overture had been made at an awkward moment for the British government. Lansdowne was just on the point of commencing negotiations with Paul Cambon, the French ambassador at London, for an Anglo-French agreement on Egypt, Morocco and other imperial issues, and it was hardly the most convenient time for proceeding towards an accord with Italy, one of whose objects was the containment of French influence on the upper Nile.[64] He was likewise reluctant to see Britain pledged to supporting

---

[59] Bertie to Hardinge, 11 Oct. 1903, B.P., A, F.O.800/164.
[60] Bertie to Lansdowne 28 Sept. 1903, F.O.45/871, *private*.
[61] *Ibid*. Bertie to Lansdowne, 14 Oct. 1903, Lansdowne MSS., F.O.800/133.
[62] Minute by Lansdowne on Rodd to Lansdowne, 6 Sept 1903, F.O.45/871, despt.184.
[63] Sanderson to Bertie, 2 Oct. 1903, and enclosed draft by Lansdowne, B.P., A, F.O.800/160.
[64] P.J.V. Rolo, *Entente Cordiale. The Origins and Negotiation of the Anglo-French Agreements of 8 April 1904* (London, 1969), pp.205 – 3.

Italian concession-seekers, a course which, as Lansdowne noted, could scarcely be undertaken 'without falling foul of the French'.⁶⁵ But Bertie felt no such concern over possible French reactions. His purpose in recommending support for prospective Italian concessionaires had been that Britain might thereby secure Italian 'assistance for British applications'. 'Italians may not', he wrote to Lansdowne, 'be desirable concessionaires, but as concerns British interests would not Italians be more acceptable to us than Frenchmen, Germans, or Russians.'⁶⁶ Morin was, however, quite pleased with such assurances as Bertie was able to give him, and there the matter rested. It was not raised again for another two months, and by then Italy had a new government.⁶⁷

Ever since Bertie's arrival in Rome it had seemed likely that the eloquent, but aged, Zanardelli would soon have to relinquish office. Somewhat surprisingly, he managed to survive the departure of Prinetti, who had once been the strong man of his administration, a general strike in Rome and a ministerial crisis in the spring.⁶⁸ But by the autumn of 1903 Bertie was convinced that ill-health and physical exhaustion would compel him to resign. In a letter to Lansdowne of 28 September, he observed:

> The President of the Council, Zanardelli, is said to be serving two Mistresses and to have cancer on the Rectum. This is, however, a country of exaggerations and it is possible that there may be only one Mistress and a fistula, but at his age, 76, it is more than enough and it is very likely that he will give up office.⁶⁹

The diagnosis was largely speculation. The forecast was correct. Late in October 1903 Zanardelli resigned, and a new government was constituted under the leadership of a former minister of the interior, Giovanni Giolitti, with Tommaso Tittoni, a southern Catholic, as foreign minister.⁷⁰ These changes were not unwelcome to Bertie, for although he had liked Morin's calm northern temperament, he had found him prone to indecision and invariably poorly informed on

---

⁶⁵ Sanderson to Bertie, 9 Oct. 1903; Cromer to Bertie, 23 Oct. 1903; B.P., A, F.O.800/160. Minute by Lansdowne on Rodd to Lansdowne, 6 Sept. 1903, F.O.45/871, despt.184.
⁶⁶ Bertie to Lansdowne, 14 Oct. 1903, Lansdowne MSS., F.O.800/133.
⁶⁷ *Ibid.* Bertie to Lansdowne, 10 Oct. 1903, Lansdowne MSS., F.O.800/133.
⁶⁸ Bertie to Lansdowne, 17 June 1903, B.P., A, F.O.800/173.
⁶⁹ Bertie to Lansdowne, 28 Sept. 1903, *Ibid.*
⁷⁰ Bertie to Lansdowne, 24 Oct. 1903, B.P. (British Library). Bertie to Lansdowne, 3 and 7 Nov. 1903, F.O.45/875, tels.80 and 81.

matters of foreign policy. On the other hand, his first impression of Tittoni was a good one. After his appointment in 1910 as Italian ambassador at Paris, Bertie was to find harsher things to say about him, but in 1903 he found him 'moderate and sensible'.[71]

During the week following the formation of the new government Bertie left Italy again for England. There he was to stay with the king at Windsor and to participate in the celebrations connected with the return visit of Victor Emmanuel. As with King Edward's visit in the spring, this royal journey was to give rise to wrangles over etiquette and protocol. On this occasion the main issue at stake was that of court dress. Victor Emmanuel, a sovereign of distinctly diminutive dimensions, felt that his appearance would not be enhanced by the black knee breeches customarily required by the English court.[72] In order to satisfy his vanity Bertie succeeded in wringing from Edward VII the concession that the king of Italy might be permitted to wear trousers when others assumed breeches.[73] Even this was insufficient for Victor Emmanuel, who wished that both he and his suite should be allowed to wear military uniforms after the fashion of the Austrian and German courts. Bertie protested that it was usual for guests to conform to the usages of their host, and finally on the eve of the ambassador's departure for London Victor Emmanuel gave way and instructed his tailor to run him up some breeches.[74] The result was far from edifying, and Bertie 'quite appreciated' the king's objection when he saw 'his poor little legs dangling from his seat'.[75]

The settlement of such tiresome issues as those relating to the proper attire of princes did not appeal to Bertie. Indeed, it is possible that by the summer of 1903 he was already, as at least one of his friends suspected, beginning to regret his decision to leave London.[76] At the Foreign Office he had 'felt infernally irritated at the insensate red tapeism that went on in the same rotten way from day to day & year to year'. He had also at times felt overburdened by the work. But after less than six months at Rome he had to admit to Cranborne that he was sometimes 'infernally bored at having so little to do'.[77] Since then matters had not improved. The only business of any great import with which he had become involved was that which concerned the proposed accord on Abyssinia, and even then he had

---

[71] Bertie to Cranborne, 12 June 1903; Bertie to Lansdowne, 10 and 31 Oct. 1903; Bertie to Knollys, 31 Oct. 1903, B.P., A, F.O.800/173.
[72] Bertie to Knollys, 2 Nov. 1903, B.P., B, F.O.800/183.
[73] Bertie to Granotti, 4 and 5 Nov. 1903, *Ibid.*
[74] Bertie to Knollys, 9 and 10 Nov 1903, *Ibid.*
[75] Bertie to Ponsonby, 16 April 1914, B.P., B, F.O.800/188.
[76] Hardinge to Bertie, 26 June 1903, B.P., A, F.O.800/174.
[77] Bertie to Cranborne, 30 June 1903, Cecil MSS., S(4) 52/162.

not been able to make his views prevail upon the foreign secretary. Moreover, Bertie missed the companionship of men of his own age. He had little in common with Rodd, and although he took to going with some of his staff for short constitutional walks and motor excursions in the country, their company was no substitute for the convivial banter in which he had for so long engaged with his colleagues in Whitehall. In these circumstances he began to think about seeking another post. Sir Edmund Monson, the British ambassador at Paris, was due to retire in 1904, and in November 1903 Bertie indicated his desire to succeed him.[78]

Quite apart from the prestige which was attached to the Paris embassy, the post offered a number of personal advantages to the Berties. At Paris they would be nearer to their family and friends, and Lady Feo, who had been far from well in Rome, wanted to return to a more temperate climate. But above all, Bertie as ambassador to France would once more have a say in arranging some of the more important matters relating to Britain's position in the world. According to one of Bertie's contemporaries, 'the Paris embassy was looked upon as a sort of branch of Foreign Office'.[79] Indeed, even if the negotiations on which Lansdowne had embarked were to come to nothing, Britain's relations with France, her neighbour in Africa, America, Asia and Europe, would remain central in the determination of British foreign policy.

Bertie hoped once more to obtain the king's backing for his ambitions, and he made use of his stay at Windsor during the Italian royal visit to seek out the aid of Knollys. The king, however, had different plans in mind. Sir Charles Scott, his ambassador at St Petersburg, was due to retire in the near future, and Edward VII considered Bertie to be a suitable successor. This was the last thing that Bertie wanted, and Knollys was quick to point out that Hardinge would be a better choice.[80] Hardinge's recent experience of Russia fitted him for the post, and at a time when the government was contemplating a fresh attempt at settling Anglo-Russian differences in Asia, St Petersburg seemed bound to become a key position. Spring Rice might then, Bertie thought, replace Hardinge in London. Knollys was unenthusiastic about this last suggestion, but he appears to have had no difficulty in persuading the king that

---

[78] Bertie to Cranborne, 18 May and 1 June 1903, Cecil MSS., S(4) 52/100 and 116.
[79] Lord Redesdale, *Memories* (2 vols, London, 1915), I, 115. Bertie to Lascelles, 28 Sept. 1904, Lascelles MSS., F.O.800/12.
[80] Knollys to Bertie, 28 Nov. 1903; Hardinge to Bertie, 4 Dec. 1903; B.P., A, F.O.800/163.

Hardinge was the right man for St Petersburg.⁸¹ The idea appealed to Hardinge himself, and he for his part endeavoured to promote Bertie's candidature for Paris. In this he seemed at first to be successful, and in a letter which he wrote to Bertie on Christmas eve 1903 he felt able to assure him that if Paris and St Petersburg were at that moment to fall vacant; 'I think there is no doubt that you & I would get them.'⁸²

Hardinge was less certain about the way in which matters might develop, and he suspected that there was a cabal in the upper ranks of the Foreign Office against Bertie having Paris. Eric Barrington, Lansdowne's private secretary, had suggested to him that Lascelles might go to Paris, and that in that event he, Hardinge, might have a 'very good chance of Berlin'. But the king was no more likely to approve the removal of Lascelles from Berlin in 1904 than he had been in 1902. Knollys, who according to Hardinge was Bertie's 'greatest ally', had 'very decided views' on Lascelles staying where he was and Bertie succeeding Monson.⁸³ Moreover, on 13 February 1904, just six days after the news reached London of the outbreak of war between Russia and Japan, Lansdowne offered to Hardinge the embassy at St Petersburg. On the next day Hardinge wrote to thank Bertie for his help, and to assure him that although he feared that there was 'a certain amount of obstruction at the top of the FO' to his going to Paris, there was 'absolutely no other candidate in the field'.⁸⁴ Hardinge also found the king 'as strong as ever' on Bertie going to Paris, and Lord Esher, the only outsider whom he thought might gain royal backing, had, it seemed, already succeeded in thoroughly alienating Lansdowne by proposing reforms in the War Office which involved the removal of the latter's friends. Nevertheless, there did seem to be a danger that Bertie's chances of obtaining Paris might be prejudiced by political changes. The split which had emerged in the ranks of the Conservative party over fiscal policy, Joseph Chamberlain's resignation from the administration, and Balfour's ill-health, did not bode well for the future of the government. If Rosebery were to succeed Lansdowne in a Liberal administration, then Hardinge judged that Bertie would 'probably be all right'.⁸⁵ But on 23 February Monson wrote to warn Bertie of a report that Asquith, the future

---

⁸¹ *Ibid*. Knollys to Bertie, 23 Dec. 1903, B.P., A, F.O.800/176. Edward VII to Hardinge, 15 Feb. 1904, Hardinge MSS., 7.
⁸² Hardinge to Bertie, 24 Dec. 1903, B.P., A, F.O.800/163.
⁸³ *Ibid*. Hardinge to Bertie, 2 Jan. 1904, B.P., B, F.O.800/183. According to one account the king refused to appoint Lascelles, a widower, to Paris 'on the ground that he was not married'. W.S. Blunt, *My Diaries* (2 vols, London, 1919–20), II, 213.
⁸⁴ Hardinge to Bertie, 14 Feb. 1904, B.P., A, F.O.800/176.
⁸⁵ Hardinge to Bertie, (?) Feb., 14 March, and 4 April, 1904, B.P., B, F.O.800/183.

Liberal prime minister, had recently told Rodd's wife, Lilias, that if the Liberals came to power Bertie would not be their choice for Paris.[86]

It is difficult to say how seriously Bertie regarded such tales. The 'Black Lily' had a reputation for gossip-mongering, and Bertie's relations with her husband were not especially good.[87] This may in part have been due to Bertie's own unfamiliarity with embassy life. He had for instance been astounded at the state of affairs which he had found prevailing in the embassy at Rome at the time of his arrival there. Convinced that it 'ought to be the duty of every Secretary & Attaché to read all the print so far as more pressing duties permitted', he had been shocked to find that the confidential print, the printed Foreign Office correspondence, was seldom read by the younger men of the embassy, who spent much of their time driving about 'to pay visits & attend tea fights to the detriment of their inbibing knowledge of diplomatic correspondence'.[88] Rodd, on the other hand, soon came to resent Bertie's attempts to impose a more rigid *régime* upon the chancery and what he termed the ambassador's 'still prevailing under-secretarial state of mind'. He was irritated by Bertie's insistence on amending all drafts of correspondence which were sent up to him, even when it seemed impossible to improve upon them.[89] And he evidently felt that more credit was due to himself for the thirteen months during which he had had charge of the embassy after Currie's departure, and for the way in which he had acted for Bertie during his frequent absences from Rome. He had been particularly irked by the ambassador's refusal to allow him leave in October 1903 because it would interfere with Bertie's own wish to go to Salso di Maggiore, and a curt ambassadorial reminder that life was 'full of disappointments' was no compensation for being denied the chance to see his children in England.[90] Nevertheless, Bertie considered Rodd to have an all too high opinion of himself. He disliked the way in which he tried to court royal favour, and he did his best to thwart the schemes of Lilias Rodd to secure early promotion for her husband.[91] During his stay in England in the autumn of 1903 Bertie insisted to Knollys that Rodd simply would not be 'stiff' enough to be

---

[86] Monson to Bertie, 23 Feb. 1904, *Ibid*.
[87] Monson to de Bunsen, 19 Jan. 1904, de Bunsen MSS. (In the possession of Lady Salisbury-Jones), MB/IV/e. Hardinge to Bertie, 21 July 1904, B.P., B, F.O.800/176.
[88] Bertie to Cranborne, 22 May 1903, Cecil MSS., S(4) 52/110.
[89] Rennell Rodd, III, 41–2.
[90] *Ibid*. Bertie to Lansdowne, 4 Dec. 1903, F.O.45/874, despt.244. Rodd to Bertie, 20 Aug., 3, 6 and 11 Sept. 1903; Bertie to Rodd, 3 and 7 Sept. 1903; B.P., Add. MS.163015.
[91] Bertie to Hardinge, 28 Nov. 1904, Hardinge MSS., 7.

appointed Hardinge's successor at the Foreign Office.[92] It was, however, Rodd who in December 1903 was left with the task of resuming discussions with the Italians on the future of Abyssinia.[93]

Rodd was an old hand in matters relating to Abyssinia. In 1897 he had, as one of Cromer's lieutenants, led a mission there with the object of keeping Menelik neutral in the impending Anglo-French confrontation in the Sudan.[94] The talks which he and John Harrington, the British agent at Addis Ababa, began with the officials of the Consulta on 12 December were similarly concerned with containing the possible expansion of French influence towards the headwaters of the Nile. Thus while the accord which they drafted attempted to define the rights and interests of Britain and Italy in Abyssinia, and to provide for their joint action in the event of the country's disintegration, it also referred to their opposing any other powers which might threaten their designs. Bertie readily endorsed the idea of such an agreement. The negotiations which had recently commenced in London for what was to be dubbed the *entente cordiale*, had done nothing to ease Bertie's fears about French ambitions in Africa, and he urged upon Lansdowne the importance of the proposed accord with Italy as a means of deterring France. Although it did not bind Britain to armed intervention, it would, he thought, be difficult 'to conceive of what argument short of force or the fear of its use would restrain France . . . from occupying derelict Abyssinian territory if it suited her to do so'.[95] More cautious advice was proffered by Lord Cromer, Britain's consul-general at Cairo.. He now doubted if it would be necessary to have resort to arms to keep the French out of the Nile valley, and he deprecated even a covert reference to France in an accord with Italy. Instead, he recommended that the British government threaten the French with the prospect of the construction of a competing railway from the Somali coast, and thereby persuade them of the advantages of an agreement which would place the whole of their projected line from Jibuti under Anglo-French control, constitute Jibuti a free port, and place Abyssinia's independence under a three power guarantee.[96]

Cromer's proposal was welcomed by Lansdowne.[97] Prior to his visit to Rome, Harrington had been able to explore with the French

[92] Knollys to Hardinge, 1 Dec. 1903, *ibid*.
[93] Bertie to Lansdowne, 16 Dec. 1903, F.O.45/874, despt.254.
[94] H.G. Marcus, 'The Rodd Mission of 1897', *Journal of Ethiopian Studies*, III (1965), 25 – 35.
[95] Bertie to Lansdowne, 19 Dec. 1903, and enclosures, F.O.1/56, despt.264.
[96] Cromer to Lansdowne, 8 Jan. 1904, F.O.1/56, despt.6. Cromer to Sanderson, 14 Jan. 1904, F.O.1/50, *private*.
[97] Minute by Lansdowne on Cromer to Sanderson, 14 Jan. 1904, *ibid*.

minister at Addis Ababa the possibility of an Anglo-French agreement on the Jibuti railway, and Lansdowne had contemplated introducing the subject into the negotiations with Paul Cambon.[98] Yet for the moment he was determined to subordinate any arrangement on Abyssinia to the achievement of agreements on Egypt and Morocco. Besides which, his pursuit of an understanding with France provided Lansdowne with an additional motive for postponing further talks with the Italians. If Britain were to reach an agreement with France on the eventual abolition of the international control of Egypt's finances, then it would still be necessary to come to terms with those other European powers whose citizens were bondholders of the Egyptian debt, and Lansdowne anticipated that they would all resort to 'blackmail'. He therefore thought it wise to keep in reserve for an eventual understanding with Italy on Egypt a number of related east African issues on which Britain could make concessions.[99] This, however, was no excuse for Lansdowne's failure to reply to Bertie's communication to him of the draft Anglo-Italian agreement.

Bertie was for nearly three months left in the dark with regard to the foreign secretary's intentions, and he, like the Italians, soon began to wonder whether Abyssinia might not be a subject of Lansdowne's negotiations with Paul Cambon.[100] Hardinge assured Bertie that it formed no part of the projected Anglo-French agreement.[101] But Bertie was justly aggrieved at the way in which he was being treated, and he made this clear to Lansdowne when the latter enquired about the views of the Italians on the Egyptian negotiations.[102] He informed Lansdowne on 7 April that he did not know 'except from stray allusions in the confidential print' the terms of the arrangements to be settled with the French, and that consequently he could not advise him on how Italy 'might be bought off'. Not that there was any doubt in Bertie's mind that the Italians would require something. They were, he warned Lansdowne, 'individually and collectively . . . beggars', and even if they had no good reason for claiming payment, he thought that their German allies would urge them not to hurry their adherence.[103]

---

[98] Ram, pp.157–8. Memo. by Bertie by Sanderson, 12 Dec. 1903, and minute by Lansdowne, F.O.1/43.
[99] Lansdowne to Bertie, 30 March 1904, Lansdowne MSS., F.O.800/133. Balfour to Edward VII, 4 May 1904, CAB 41/29/14.
[100] Bertie to Lansdowne, 15 March 1904, B.P., A, F.O.800/160.
[101] Hardinge to Bertie, 20 March 1904, B.P., B, F.O.800/183.
[102] Lansdowne to Bertie, 30 March 1904, Lansdowne MSS., F.O.800/133.
[103] Bertie to Lansdowne, 7 April 1904, Lansdowne MSS., F.O.800/133. Bertie to Lansdowne, 20 April 1904, B.P., A, F.O.800/164.

If the Italians were to procrastinate on Egypt, then Lansdowne was equally prepared to bide his time on Abyssinia.[104] Both he and the French foreign minister, Théophile Delcassé, hoped that the conclusion on 8 April 1904 of those accords which were to form the basis of the *entente cordiale* would have favourable repercussions throughout the Nile basin, and enable Britain and France to settle their differences over the Jibuti-Addis Ababa railway. There therefore seemed to be no reason for haste in arranging matters with the Italians.[105] Of this Tittoni was probably aware. He had already tried to persuade Barrère of Italy's desire to work with France in Abyssinia, and in April the Italian ambassador in London proposed to Lansdowne that Britain and Italy should conclude a preliminary arrangement on Abyssinia to which the French might be invited to subscribe.[106] But Lansdowne rejected the notion of doing anything behind the backs of the French, and following representations from Paul Cambon in May, he suggested that negotiations on Abyssinia should proceed *pari passu* with France and Italy.[107] Bertie, who, despite his previous predictions, had in the meanwhile succeeded in winning Italy's unconditional assent to the recently promulgated khedival decree on Egypt's finances, recommended that Lansdowne 'should quickly do something pleasing to the Italian Government' in regard to east Africa.[108] While, however, Lansdowne was prepared to resume discussions with the Italians on Abyssinia, he insisted that no commitment could be given until the French had been consulted. Having only just disposed of what he assumed to be the main causes of Anglo-French misunderstanding, Lansdowne was reluctant to risk giving fresh umbrage to Delcassé.[109]

Lansdowne's response to Italy's proposals was indicative of the limitations which *entente* diplomacy had already begun to place upon the conduct of British foreign policy. Yet within the Foreign Office there were amongst Bertie's friends those who anticipated a much tighter relationship with France. Louis Mallet, who after working under Bertie in the Far Eastern department, had become précis

---

[104] Lansdowne to Bertie, 14 April 1904, F.O.1.56, tel. 61.
[105] Delcassé to Lagarde, 16 April 1904, N.S. (Ministère des Affaires Étrangères) Éthiopie 11, tel.13. *Les Documents Diplomatiques Français, 2e série* (hereafter cited as *D.D.F.2*), vol. V, no.148.
[106] Pansa to Lansdowne, 18 April 1904, Lansdowne MSS., F.O.800/133. *D.D.F.2*, IV, nos. 161 and 175.
[107] Lansdowne to Bertie, 4 and 18 May 1904, F.O.1/56, despts. 79 and 86. Lansdowne to Monson, 16 and 18 May 1904, F.O.1/56, despts.259 and 263.
[108] Bertie to Lansdowne, 22 May 1904, Lansdowne MSS., F.O.800/133.
[109] Lansdowne to Pansa, 24 May 1904, Lansdowne MSS., F.O.800/133. Lansdowne to Bertie, 30 May 1904, B.P., A, F.O.800/170. Lansdowne to Bertie, 1 June 1904, F.O.1/56, despt. 96.

writer to Lansdowne, had forecasted in February that the proposed understanding with France 'would have a very marked effect internationally . . . & might be the prelude to a closer understanding'.[110] He, like Spring Rice, was one of those younger men who seem to have taken seriously pan-German designs upon Austria and the Netherlands, and he regarded the Anglo-French *entente* as a means of limiting Germany's ambitions. In a private letter to Bertie of 2 June, in which he reflected upon the fact that despite the German government's request for the prior settlement of certain outstanding claims on Britain, the Austrians and the Italians had consented to the khedival decree, he observed:

> Entre nous, I do not think that Mr Balfour at all realizes what may be expected from the Anglo-French understanding and would be ready to make an agreement with Germany tomorrow. It seems to me that a close understanding with France is a great safeguard to us — & that our object ought to be to keep Germany isolated in view of her nefarious projects with regard to the Austrian Empire & Holland, to say nothing of this island . . . The next Ambassador to Paris will have a great role to play. It has never been so necessary to have someone there with his eyes open & above all to German designs. I hope it will be you.[111]

With these sentiments Bertie heartily agreed. Germany, he replied 'has never done anything but bleed us. She is false and grasping and our real enemy commercially and politically'. So long, however, as Britain remained on good terms with the French, he thought that there was nothing to fear from the Germans. Without the active support of a naval power like France, he did not think that Germany could injure Britain. Britain ought, he declared, to resist German attempts to acquire ports and coaling stations from minor powers 'even at the risk of war'. 'Subject to this', he concluded, 'I would be very civil to Germany but not be bluffed into anything and bear in mind that whatever Germany's profession may be she is in terror of Russia and will never risk her displeasure.'[112]

Bertie thus welcomed the Anglo-French *entente* as a means of denying to the Germans the prospect of future opportunities for exploiting Britain's differences with France. Germany, he told Tittoni, was now 'isolated and no longer a great factor in Europe'.[113]

---

[110] Mallet to Spring Rice, 29 Feb. 1904, Spring Rice MSS., CASR 1/49.
[111] Mallet to Bertie, 2 June 1904, B.P., A, F.O.800/170.
[112] Bertie to Mallet, 11 June 1904, *ibid.*
[113] Bertie to Lansdowne, 16 June 1904, F.O.45/889, despt.89.

But there is no indication that at this stage Bertie favoured a closer alignment with the French. Indeed, he displayed little or no affection for Britain's new found friends. He had, after all, until recently been seeking to persuade Lansdowne of the value of collaborating with Italy in order to exclude the French from Abyssinia, and he continued to regard Barrère's efforts to wean the Italians away from the Triple Alliance with a sort of bemused resignation. There was no doubt in his mind that such nervousness as Tittoni exhibited with regard to the possibility of Austria-Hungary taking independent action in Macedonia was due to 'information' from the French ambassador. 'However', Bertie noted, 'the latter has rather overstuffed the former and Tittoni is inclined to have indigestion.'[114] He was equally droll in his reporting of the celebrations in connexion with the visit of Émile Loubet, the president of the French republic, to Italy at the end of April 1904. Not only did the dense crowd which greeted the president on the evening of his arrival in Rome smell 'very bad', but a procession which was subsequently trailed before him, and which consisted of illuminated pictures of various beasts, birds and vegetables, was in Bertie's estimation a wholly grotesque affair. 'The animal part', he recorded 'looked like a réclame for a menagerie.'[115]

There could, nevertheless, be no disguising the fact that Loubet had received a far more enthusiastic reception than that which had been accorded to either the British or the German sovereign. This Bertie attributed to pressure applied by Barrère to ensure that the preparations were more costly and elaborate than those for the royal visitors; to the noisy enthusiasm of the 'socialist part of the population' for the president of a republic; and the relief felt by many Italians at the achievement of a reconciliation with France. Yet Bertie did not consider the Italians ready to give up their membership of the Triple Alliance. He thought that the king and his government were only interested in a working understanding with Britain and France such as would enable them to feel more independent of Germany.[116] In any case the Triple Alliance did not in his opinion constitute a threat to peace. 'Bülow', he reminded Barrère, 'was not a

---

[114] Bertie to Lansdowne, 30 Jan. 1904, B.P., A, F.O.800/173. Bertie to Knollys, 26 Feb. 1904, B.P., A, F.O.800/176. Bertie to Lansdowne, 10 Feb. 1904, F.O.45/889, despt.17. Bertie to Lansdowne, 20 and 25 Feb. 1904, Lansdowne MSS., F.O.800/133. Bertie to Lansdowne, 6 March 1904, B.P., Add. MS.63016. Barrère to Delcassé, 20 Feb. 1904, Delcassé MSS., 1.
[115] Bertie to Sanderson, 25 April 1904, B.P., A, F.O.800/173. For a somewhat more complementary account of Loubet's visit see: J. Laroche, *Quinze ans à Rome avec Camille Barrère (1898–1913)* (Paris, 1948), pp.129–37.
[116] Bertie to Lansdowne, 1 May 1904, B.P., A, F.O.800/173.

Bismarck.'[117] Perhaps if he had been the peace of Europe might more easily have been preserved.

Loubet's visit to Rome provided Bertie with his first opportunity to meet Delcassé, whose conversion to a bargain on Egypt and Morocco had helped make possible the conclusion of the *entente cordiale*.[118] In the following year Bertie was, as ambassador to France, to have a significant part to play in the events which led to his resignation. But in the spring of 1904 Bertie did not know whether he could count on the Paris embassy. Although Austin Lee, the British commercial *attaché* there, considered him the 'hot favourite', Bertie was aware that he was not the 'so-called "Foreign Office candidate" '.[119] Sanderson was now said to favour Sir Nicholas O'Conor, the ambassador at Constantinople, and there were rumours that Lord Cadogan was hankering after the appointment. Bertie also suspected that Lansdowne was opposed to his having Paris, and he fancied that the Germans would not like him to be there. He believed the Count von Metternich, Hatzfeldt's successor at London, to consider him to be anti-German, and he recalled to Mallet that his handling of Stuebel had not been 'at all pleasing to the German Govt.'.[120]

Fate was to smile upon him however, for when Sanderson was taken seriously ill in July 1904, Bertie was summoned from Rome to replace him temporarily at the Foreign Office. This placed Bertie in a much better position from which to press his claim to Paris. It may also have led him to speculate on the possibility of returning permanently to the Foreign Office. A former colleague, who met him shortly after his return to England, subsequently told Chirol that he thought Bertie 'might not be unwilling to come back to the FO when Lamps returns if he does not get Paris — so sick does he profess to be of being abroad'. 'In Downing St.', Bertie maintained, 'one can at least pull the wires whereas an Ambassador is only a d—d marionette.'[121] He had, however, not long to await the achievement of his goal. The king was resolved that he should have Paris, and on 11 August he was asked to Lansdowne House where the foreign secretary offered him the embassy. 'I well know', Bertie wrote later to

---

[117] Bertie to Lansdowne, 20 May 1904, B.P., A, F.O.800/170.
[118] Bertie to Lansdowne, 2 May 1904, B.P., A, F.O.800/164. On Delcassé and the part which he played in negotiating the *entente cordiale* see: Christopher Andrew, *Théophile Delcassé and the Making of the Entente Cordiale. A Reappraisal of French Foreign Policy 1898–1905* (London, 1968), especially pp. 180–215.
[119] Austin Lee to Bertie, 16 May 1904, B.P., Add. MS.63016.
[120] Bertie to Mallet, 11 June 1904, B.P., A, F.O.800/170. Hardinge to Bertie, 9 Aug. 1904, B.P., A, F.O.800/176. Chirol to Hardinge, 10 Aug. 1904, Hardinge MSS., 7.
[121] Chirol to Hardinge, 10 Aug. 1904, *ibid*.

the king, 'that it is entirely due to YM's gracious advocacy that I have been offered the appointment and I beg leave to submit by humble and most grateful thanks to YM.'[122]

For the time being, as Monson was not due to leave Paris until the end of the year and Sanderson was still not well enough to return to work, Bertie remained at the Foreign Office.[123] There the prospect of Sanderson deciding to take the full pension that he had earned and retiring led to speculation about who should be the next permanent under-secretary. Even before he left Rome, Bertie had been thinking about a suitable successor. The trouble was that Hardinge, whom Bertie had favoured, was now ambassador at St Petersburg, and Lansdowne hardly seemed likely to agree to his early return to London.[124] With this in mind, Bertie devised a scheme, which he put to Balfour in November, for the transfer of Arthur Godley, the permanent under-secretary at the India Office, to the Foreign Office, and the designation of Hardinge as his eventual successor.[125] But the plan was premature for Sanderson had no intention of being forced into retirement. He recommenced work at the office in mid-November, and in spite of the opposition of his medical advisers, he insisted on resuming his full duties when Bertie left on 13 December. Bertie expected that his health would break down. 'His temper', he noted on 28 November, 'has not been improved by his illness, and he passes his time writing offensive minutes and letters about the re-organisation of the office.'[126] Nevertheless, Bertie had to wait for more than a year before his efforts were rewarded with the appointment of Hardinge as permanent under-secretary.

During the five months which Bertie spent in the Foreign Office in the summer and autumn of 1904 relations between Britain and Germany steadily deteriorated. The conditions set by the Germans for their acceptance of the khedival decree generated fresh friction and caused considerable resentment in England. And although a visit by the king to Kiel in June was apparently successful, British suspicions about Germany's intentions were further roused by reports that the authorities in Berlin were seeking a closer understanding with those in St Petersburg. By the end of September, Bertie was himself exercised over the question of what Britain should do if

---

[122] Bertie to Edward VII, 11 Aug. 1904, B.P., A, F.O.800/164.
[123] Lansdowne to Edward VII, 1 Sept. 1904, R.A. W44 1986.
[124] Bertie to Knollys, 29 March 1904, B.P., B, F.O.800/183. Bertie to Lascelles, 28 Sept. 1904.
[125] Hardinge to Bertie, 12 Oct. 1904, B.P., A, F.O.800/176. Chirol to Hardinge, 18 Oct. 1904; Bertie to Hardinge, 28 Nov. 1904; Hardinge MSS., 7.
[126] *Ibid.* Knollys to Hardinge, 15 Nov. 1904; Maxwell to Hardinge, 28 Nov. 1904; Hardinge MSS., 7.

the Germans offered to coal Russian warships at Kiaochow.[127] He had, however, reservations about British press attacks upon Germany. 'The "Times" ', Bertie wrote to Lascelles on 28 September, 'certainly loses no opportunity for digging its knife into the Germans. It is a pity that it does it so relentlessly.' But he also thought that if the occasion served, the German press would probably not spare England, and he readily accepted and repeated all sorts of tales of German intrigue and conspiracy.[128] He told Paul Cambon that the German emperor had encouraged the Japanese to attack Russia, and he held the same sovereign in part responsible for the massacre that occurred when on the night of 21 October the Russian Baltic fleet, *en route* for the Far East, opened fire on a flotilla of Hull trawlers fishing off the Dogger bank.[129] The attack, Bertie suggested to Hardinge, was an act of 'funk due partly to the warnings of danger transmitted by the German Emperor and possibly in part to drink taken to get Dutch courage'.[130] Mallet was of much the same opinion. There was, he informed Spring Rice, no doubt in his mind that 'repeated warnings given to Russia of the chances of an attack on them in the North Sea came from Germany directly and indirectly'.[131]

The effect of the Dogger bank incident was to bring Britain and Russia almost to the verge of war: a war which Mallet feared 'would leave Germany supreme in Europe with a large part of our carrying trade and general commerce'.[132] Bertie, who had already urged caution upon Lansdowne in the government's reaction to interference by the Russians with British merchant shipping, strove to calm this crisis.[133] Nevertheless, Paul Cambon found the Foreign Office wanting in its handling of this affair. He placed much of the blame for public agitation in Britain against Russia upon the office's failure to keep the press properly informed of the government's intentions, and in a despatch to Delcassé of 6 November he expressed his regret at the absence from the Foreign Office of Sanderson and Barrington. They, he claimed, knew how to give precise instructions to those journalists who were admitted to the Foreign Office. Indeed, despite all the abuse that Bertie and his friends heaped upon

---

[127] Monger, pp.164–6. A.J.A Morris, *The Scaremongers. The Advocacy of War and Rearmament 1896–1914* (London, 1984), pp.60–5. Chirol to Lascelles, 27 Sept. 1904, Lascelles MSS., F.O.800/12.
[128] Bertie to Lascelles, 28 Sept. 1904.
[129] *D.D.F.2*, VI, no.22, Monger, pp.172–4.
[130] Bertie to Hardinge, 28 Nov. 1904; Hardinge MSS., 7.
[131] Mallet to Spring Rice, 29 Oct. 1904, Spring Rice MSS., CASR 1/49.
[132] *Ibid*.
[133] Bertie to Hardinge, 21 Sept. and 11 Nov. 1904, Hardinge MSS., 7. Bertie to Lansdowne, 6 Nov. 1904, F.O.65/1730, tel. *private*.

Sanderson's *régime*, Cambon, an outsider, could still find something to say in its favour.[134]

At the end of his term at the Foreign Office Bertie returned to Rome. But absence had not made his heart grow fonder, and his final official visit there lasted no longer than his first. On the evening of 28 December he bade farewell to Tittoni, and on the next day he left for London.[135] His Roman embassy was over. It could hardly be hailed a diplomatic triumph. In the fifteen months during which he had actually graced Rome with his presence he had made few friends and shown no interest in getting to know any Italians of rank or distinction.[136] He had helped to ease the way for the king's visit to the pope, and he had succeeded in securing Italy's acceptance of the new order in Egypt. Nevertheless, he had been unable to respond to Italian pleas for British support against supposed Austrian designs in the Balkans with anything more than fair words and sympathy, and the negotiations for an agreement of Abyssinia seemed unlikely to come to any early fruition. They had in the first place been subordinated to those with France for a colonial *entente*, and since its conclusion had proceeded fitfully on a tripartite basis. Yet this was hardly Bertie's fault. The truth was that valuable though Italy's friendship was to Britain, British governments found it unnecessary to make any great efforts to retain it. In consequence the embassy at Rome offered little scope for the exercise of such talents as Bertie possessed. At Paris matters might be different. Chirol, who had misgivings about Bertie's performance at Rome, considered him the best candidate in the service for Paris. He was, however, reluctant to prophesy how he would fare there. Of Bertie, he wrote to William Lavino, *The Times* correspondent at Paris: 'He may be a great success: he may also be a complete failure. He is a man of moods. If he takes a liking to Paris, all right. If he takes it *en grippe* all wrong.'[137] Much was also to depend upon the way in which events in the Far East and north Africa were to impinge upon the European equilibrium, and the manner in which they were to occupy the attention of King Edward's ambassador to France.

---

[134] *D.D.F.2*, V, no.432.
[135] Bertie to Lansdowne, 30 Dec. 1904, F.O.45/899, tel. *private*.
[136] Diary, IV, 21 Sept. 1904, Rennell Rodd MSS.
[137] Chirol to Lavino, 26 May 1904, Foreign Dept. Letter Book, vol.IV, *The Times* MSS. (*The Times* archives).

4

An open sore

The British embassy at Paris is housed in a handsome and imposing building whose courtyard opens on to the fashionable rue du Faubourg St-Honoré. Constructed during the first half of the eighteenth century for the Duc de Béthune, it was the home of the Princess Pauline Borghese, Napoleon's beautiful sister, until in October 1814 it was acquired by the British government for 500,000 francs. A near equivalent sum was spent on the purchase of the house's furniture and a building for stabling in the rue d'Anjou.[1] But those to whose charge its upkeep was entrusted were rarely so generous in their expenditure of public funds, and although electric lighting and a more efficient system of central heating were installed at the turn of the century, the house was by 1904 in a poor state of repair.[2] Its timbers were full of dry rot, its gutters and flats required attention, and its interior was sorely in need of painting and decoration.[3] There had even been a move afoot to transfer to the Foreign Office some of the house's more valuable furnishings and works of art: a project which had drawn from Lansdowne the protest that he was 'not at all sure that fine pieces of French furniture would harmony with the hideous Victorian decoration of the F.O.'[4] Moreover, much to Bertie's disgust and future discomfort, the Treasury refused to meet the cost of having the house gutted.[5] The Office of Works did, however, heed Monson's complaints, and it sanctioned a programme of extensive renovation. This meant that Bertie, who arrived at Paris on 12 January 1905, was unable to take up residence at the embassy. He moved, instead, into a suite of rooms at the Hotel Bristol, where he remained until the work of redecoration and repair was completed in the spring.[6]

---

[1] Enclosure in Nicolson to Bertie, 4 April 1912, B.P., B, F.O.800/187. S. Fortescue, *Looking Back*, (London, 1920), pp.325 – 7.
[2] Monson to Lansdowne, 27 Dec. 1901, and 2 Sept. 1902, F.O.27/3695, *private*.
[3] Monson to Bertie, 25 Oct. 1901, B.P., Add. MS.63014. Monson to Sanderson, 29 Feb. 1904, Monson MSS. (Bodleian Library), Eng. hist. c595.
[4] Esher to F.O., 20 June 1902, and minute by Lansdowne, F.O.27/3695.
[5] Bertie to Nicolson, 23 Aug. 1912, B.P., B, F.O.800/187.
[6] *Vanity Fair*, 23 Feb. 1905, p.252; and 11 May, p.652.

AN OPEN SORE

For a while Bertie lived in a sort of diplomatic limbo. The death of Loubet's mother meant that he had to postpone his official visit to the Élysée palace, and in consequence he was unable to present his letters of credence until 23 January.[7] Moreover, within a fortnight of his arrival at Paris there was a change of government. French politics in the early years of the twentieth century were dominated by the passions released by the Dreyfus affair and the efforts of the parties of the left and centre to impose their republican philosophy on the army and the church. But on 18 January, after nearly three years in office during which support for his largely radical administration had dwindled in parliament, Émile Combes resigned the presidency of the council of ministers. Eight days later he was succeeded by Maurice Rouvier, a former minister of finance, whose involvement in the Panama scandal in the early 1890s had left him with a somewhat tarnished reputation.[8] So Bertie had plenty of time in which to make his calls upon other members of the diplomatic body. Amongst these were to be numbered the German ambassador, Hugo von Radolin, the only person in Paris besides Loubet and Delcassé to whom Bertie was required to convey the compliments of King Edward. Other friends of the king offered their hospitality to the new ambassador. These were mostly members of the nobility, who, though they counted for little in the politics of the republic, counted for much in the entertainment of visiting British royalty.[9]

Bertie was fortunate in having as minister plenipotentiary at Paris a friend of long-standing in the person of Maurice de Bunsen. The latter had known Bertie for the best part of eleven years, and the two men had enjoyed each other's company when in the autumn of 1897 Bertie had spent a holiday with Currie at Constantinople.[10] De Bunsen also had the distinction, unusual amongst Bertie's staff, of having a wife of whom the ambassador approved. She was, Bertie informed Mallet, 'peaceful and straightforward and a nice woman'.[11] But de Bunsen, like Rodd before him, soon found cause to grouse over Bertie's methods, which, he claimed, were 'those of the F.O.'[12]

---

[7] De Bunsen to wife, 16 Jan. 1905, de Bunsen MSS., MB/I/gg. Mollard to Bertie, 16 and 18 Jan, 1905, F.O.146/3858. Bertie to Lansdowne, 18 Jan. 1905, F.O.27/3705, despt.22.
[8] M. Larkin, *Church and State after the Dreyfus Affair. The Separation Issue in France* (London, 1974), especially pp.133 – 42. D. Porch, *The March to the Marne. The French Army 1871-1914* (Cambridge, 1981), pp.73 – 104.
[9] De Bunsen to wife, 21 Jan. 1905, de Bunsen MSS., MB/I/gg. Bertie to Knollys, 23 Jan. 1905, B.P., Add MS.63011.
[10] De Bunsen to mother, 4 and 8 Oct.1897, de Bunsen MSS., MB/I/y.
[11] Bertie to Mallet, 10 Feb. 1905, B.P., B, F.O.800/183.
[12] De Bunsen to wife, 11 Feb. 1905, de Bunsen MSS., MB/I/gg.

Moreover, an impending reshuffle in the diplomatic service made it probable that de Bunsen would not have long to wait before being rewarded with a legation. And it seemed possible that in his stead Bertie would receive Alan Johnstone, who was then councillor at Vienna. The prospect did not please Bertie, who considered Johnstone to be pompous, and his American wife far from suitable for the embassy.[13] Bertie had in any case begun in the summer of 1904 to work for the appointment of Reginald Lister as a successor to de Bunsen. The youngest son of the third Lord Ribblesdale, Lister had previously served at Paris and was anxious to return there.[14] According to Bertie, he 'knew everybody official and non-official', was 'universally liked', and was 'full of tact'.[15] He was also an engaging conversationalist and a close acquaintance of the king, and had in Bertie's eyes the additional virtue of being a bachelor.[16] With such qualities and qualifications he seemed destined for rapid promotion, and when de Bunsen was appointed minister at Lisbon in March Lister was transferred from Rome, where he had recently succeeded Rodd, to Paris with the rank of councillor. Johnstone, who was Lister's senior in the service, was, like Rodd, eventually compensated with a Scandinavian legation.

The affairs of the embassy, and especially the efficient running of the chancery, were to occupy a good deal of Bertie's attention during the course of 1905.[17] In the first instance he had also to establish relations with the political leadership in France. This involved reacquainting himself with Delcassé, whose continued presence at the Quai d'Orsay was reassuring for those who hoped to retain France's new-found friendship with England. It was, however, far from obvious in January 1905 that Anglo-French cooperation would be extended beyond the scope of that foreseen in the previous April. Lansdowne had hoped that the *entente* might lead the French to make common cause with Britain in the Near East, where he anticipated that the spring would bring fresh troubles in the Macedonia.[18] But Delcassé was more concerned about the consequences of the war in

---

[13] Bertie to Mallet, 5 Feb. 1905; Bertie to Hardinge, 14 Feb. 1905; Bertie to Lansdowne, 28 Feb, 1905; B.P., B, F.O.800/183.
[14] Bertie had known Lister for the best part of ten years. Lister to Lady Ribblesdale, 27 March 1897, and (undated) 1904, Bradfer Lawrence MSS. (Yorkshire Archaeological Society), M.D.335, box 101. Mallet to Bertie, 24 June 1904; Bertie to Mallet, 29 June 1904; B.P., B, F.O.800/183.
[15] Bertie to Mallet, 10 Feb. 1905, B.P., B, F.O.800/183.
[16] Knollys to Hardinge, 15 Nov. 1904, Hardinge MSS., 7. Rattigan, p.57. Baring, pp.245 – 7.
[17] Bertie to Sanderson, 4 Oct. 1905, B.P., B, F.O.800/184.
[18] Lansdowne to Balfour, 23 Dec. 1904 and 6 Jan. 1905, Balfour MSS., Add. MS. 49729. Lansdowne to Bertie, 11 Jan 1905, F.O.27/3703.

Asia than about the prospects for peace in the Balkans. When he visited Bertie on 16 January he made it plain that France's attitude towards Lansdowne's proposals for reform in Macedonia would depend upon the views of the Russian government, and that his own desire was to foster a *rapprochement* between England and Russia. If these two powers were brought together, then, he predicted, 'peace would have a long reign'. Bertie did not dispute this contention. Yet, he gave no encouragement to the hope expressed by Delcassé of his being able to reduce the distrust then prevailing between London and St Petersburg, and he emphasised how little faith the British felt they could place in Russian assurances.[19] His answer pleased Lansdowne. While the foreign secretary did not consider an Anglo-Russian understanding to be impossible, he thought that the Russian 'diplomatic currency' had 'become debased and discredited', and that it would 'not be easy to restore its face value'.[20]

The attitude of both Bertie and Lansdowne towards Russia was no doubt influenced by the crisis that had resulted from the Dogger bank incident. There remained, however, the possibility that Japan's successes and the consequent weakening of Russia might lead to a diplomatic realignment in Europe. Reports that the Germans were trying to improve their relations with Russia had already contributed to the estrangement of Britain and Germany in the autumn.[21] Then, during January 1905, a rumour about an impending German peace initiative caused Lansdowne to wonder if the French might be a party to such a move.[22] Bertie doubted if the French would again willingly enter a German-sponsored combination. But he warned Lansdowne that the 'Yellow Peril' was the 'order of the day' in Paris.[23] Several people, including Barrère and Paul Cambon, had recently professed to fear a Japanese descent upon France's possessions in Indo-China, and evidently with the object of depriving the French of a pretext for joining with Germany to apply pressure upon Japan, Bertie proposed to Lansdowne that they might be offered a 'reinsurance à la Bismarck'. He thought that Britain might guarantee the French

---

[19] Bertie to Lansdowne, 17 Jan 1905, B.P., A, F.O.800/176.
[20] Lansdowne to Bertie, 19 Jan. 1905, *Ibid*.
[21] In Berlin the Dogger Bank incident was certainly seen as offering an opportunity for winning Russia's friendship and obstructing progress towards an Anglo-Russian *rapprochement*. N. Rich, *Friedrich von Holstein. Politics and Diplomacy in the Era of Bismarck and Wilhelm II* (2 vols, Cambridge, 1965), II, 688 – 91. Mallet to Sandars, 11 Nov. 1904, Balfour MSS., Add. MS. 49747.
[22] Lansdowne to Bertie, 13 Jan. 1905; Mallet to Bertie, 17 Jan. 1905; B.P., A, F.O.800/170. Lansdowne to Bertie, 19 Jan. 1905, B.P., A, F.O.800/176.
[23] Bertie to Lansdowne, 16 and 17 Jan. 1905, B.P., A, F.O.800/176. Bertie to Lansdowne, 13 and 17 Jan. 1905, F.O.27/3705, despts.16 and 22a.

against a Japanese attack, and that Japan could be informed of, or even brought into, the arrangement. Lansdowne was not, however, tempted to take up the idea. He dismissed the 'Yellow Peril' as absurd, and the matter was allowed to drop.[24]

Bertie was similarly unimpressed by French fears of the menace that would be posed to European interests in the Far East by a China 'organised by, or according to Japanese methods'. He suggested to Paul Doumer, the president of the chamber of deputies, that the Japanese were unlikely to educate the Chinese up to their level, and that if Russia were to defeat Japan and to take in hand the organization of China 'Europe might find a nearer and more serious danger from the resulting combination'. This was hardly a surprising conclusion for Bertie to have reached. After all, just four years before he had argued that a Japanese victory over Russia would lead to a new balance of power in Asia. 'The Yellow Danger', he had predicted in March 1901, 'would be kept in check by Russia and the Russian danger by Japan.'[25] Where the European equilibrium was concerned, Bertie had less cause for optimism since any decline in Russia's power seemed bound to enhance that of Germany. Viewed, however, from Bertie's standpoint, Germany was a country with which Britain could successfully cope so long as she was not united with another great naval power, and the bottling up of the Russian fleet in Port Arthur seemed to lessen the chances for such an alignment. This may explain his cautious response to Delcassé, when, following his receipt of the news of Russia's defeat at Mukden, he put it to Bertie that it was in the 'interests of England as well as France that Russia should remain a great European Power', and that the war should be terminated for otherwise 'another state might become too powerful'. Although Bertie assented to Delcassé's conclusions, he warned him that it was not in the interests of England that 'Russia should be the Dictator in the Far East or the Possessor of Constantinople'.[26]

All that Bertie had to suggest as a means of achieving an early settlement of the war was that Britain should utilize the vanity of the German emperor in order to persuade him to sound out both sides as to whether they had not had enough.[27] At the same time, however, he wanted to ensure that the British government should have no dealings

[24] Bertie to Lansdowne, 17 Jan. 1905, despt.22a, *ibid*. Bertie to Lansdowne, 20 Jan. 1905, B.P., B, F.O.800/183. Lansdowne to Bertie, 19 Jan. 1905, B.P., A, F.O.800/176.
[25] Bertie to Lansdowne, 27 Jan. 1905, B.P., A, F.O.800/164. *B.D.*, II, no.54.
[26] Bertie to Lansdowne, 15 March 1905, Lansdowne MSS., F.O.800/126.
[27] *Ibid*.

with Berlin that might be taken amiss in Paris. The news which reached his naval *attaché* in March that the Admiralty were planning visits by British warships to Brest and Kiel, led Bertie to urge Lansdowne that the visit to Brest should not only precede that to Kiel, but that it should be more numerous as well. 'The French', he observed, 'might otherwise be disappointed and make comparisons.' Yet, even Delcassé could sometimes be sensitive to German susceptibilities. While, therefore, he was delighted with the British proposal for a visit to Brest and an invitation to the French navy to pay a complementary visit to Spithead in August, he was very reluctant to advertise the news of this exchange. Having only recently learnt that the German emperor intended to visit Tangier in the near future, Delcassé told Bertie on 24 March that any announcement about the British fleet going to Brest might be interpreted in some quarters as a *contre-coup* to German policy.[28]

The German government's decision to demonstrate its interest in Morocco and thus to challenge French colonialist aspirations there, was of obvious significance to Anglo-French relations. By the accords of 8 April 1904 the British government had, in return for a promise of French backing for British policies in Egypt, committed itself to giving diplomatic support to France for the achievement of what would amount to a protectorate over the greater part of the Shereefian empire. An agreement concluded by France with Spain on 3 October 1904, the text of which had been communicated to the British government, had also provided for the eventual division of Morocco into French and Spanish zones of influence.[29] Thus assured of the assistance of London and acquiescence of Madrid, and having already settled with Rome, the French had lost no time in settling how Morocco's administration, armed forces and finances might best be put in order. And in January 1905 Georges Saint-René Taillandier, the French minister at Tangier, had departed for Fez, bearing a programme of reforms which seemed destined to reduce the lands of the Sultan Abdul Aziz to the status of a French protectorate.[30]

---

[28] Bertie to Lansdowne, 13 and 24 March 1905, B.P., A, F.O.800/164. Alston to Bertie, 21 March 1905; Bertie to Lansdowne, 28 March 1905; F.O.27/37/5, despt.126. *D.D.F.2*, VI, no.200. G.M. Paléologue, *The Turning Point. Three critical years 1904-1906* (London, 1935), p.210.

[29] Lyle A. Mcgoech. 'British Foreign Policy and the Spanish corollary to the Anglo-French Agreement of 1904', in N. Barker and M.L. Brown Jnr. (eds.), *Diplomacy in the Age of Nationalism. Essays in Honor of Lynn Marschall Case* (The Hague, 1971), pp.208-22. Andrew, *Delcassé*, pp.216-28.

[30] *Ibid*, pp.264-7. The only comprehensive study of the Morocco crisis of 1905 remains E.N. Anderson, *The First Moroccan Crisis, 1904-1906* (Chicago, 1930). See also: F.V. Parsons, *The Origins of the Morocco Question 1880-1900* (London, 1976); and

This course of events was viewed with displeasure in Berlin. The authorities in the Wilhelmstrasse had been disturbed by the implications of the Anglo-French understanding for Germany's diplomatic position, and in the autumn of 1904 they had revived their efforts to better their relations with Russia.[31] In the meanwhile they had awaited an approach from Delcassé on the subject of Morocco. Germany was after all a European great power with established economic interests in Morocco, and might not unreasonably have claimed a right to be consulted on the future of that country. But just as an alliance with Russia eluded the Germans, so Delcassé chose to ignore them. Irritated by this apparent affront to Germany's dignity, and aware of the diplomatic advantage that might be drawn from denying to the French the fruits of their *entente* with England, Bülow was persuaded to launch a counter-offensive against French efforts to impose their will upon the sultan. He and Friedrich von Holstein, the head of the political section of the German foreign office, decided to make use of the Emperor William's forthcoming cruise in the Mediterranean to demonstrate their country's interest in Morocco. As a result the emperor landed at Tangier on 31 March, and in an address to his compatriots at the German legation announced that his government considered Morocco to be an independent state and that it would not tolerate another power establishing its supremacy there.[32]

That Germany should have claimed the right to be consulted on Morocco's future could hardly have come as a surprise to Bertie. Just two years before he had warned Barrère that Germany might want a share in any partition of the country. Contrary, however, to what Bertie and some of his colleagues in Whitehall assumed, the Wilhelmstrasse seems not to have been motivated by any desire to acquire for Germany a territorial stake in Morocco. Although von Tirpitz, the German navy secretary, had long since recognized that Germany might find advantage in obtaining a coaling depot for its ships on the north-west corner of Africa, Bülow's diplomacy had in this respect been effectively circumscribed by an assurance offered by William II to the king of Spain that he had no territorial aspirations in

---

Heiner Raulff, *Zwischen Machtpolitik und Imperialismus. Die deutsche Frankreichpolitik, 1904–1905* (Düsseldorff, 1976).
[31] I.N. Lambi, *The Navy and German Power Politics, 1862–1914* (London, 1984), pp.245–7. Rich, II, pp.689–91. Raulff, pp.85–8.
[32] Rich, II, pp.692–5. Pierre Guillen, *L'Allemagne et le Maroc de 1870 à 1905* (Paris, 1967), especially pp.813–81. Lambi, pp.257–61.

the lands of the Sultan Abdul Aziz.[33] But in Holstein's view the legal and diplomatic position which Germany occupied was strong enough to allow her to press that Morocco should be made the subject of an international conference. He hoped that Germany's insistence on the maintenance of the 'open door' in Morocco would win for her the support of the United States, that this would restrain Britain, and that Italy and Spain could be kept in line. Germany might thereby frustrate France's designs, discredit her *entente* with England, and perhaps even secure in Morocco some kind of European mandate for a Franco-German programme of reform.[34]

Walter Harris, *The Times* correspondent at Tangier, would have agreed with Holstein on the soundness of the German case. In an article which appeared in *The Times* on 20 March he argued that however much Germany's acquiescence in France's action might be desirable 'it must be acknowledged that she is strictly within her rights in pursuing a policy of her own'. France, he claimed, had been unwise not to approach Germany on the subject for as a consequence of German opposition to French policies German influence was 'predominant all over Morocco today'.[35] Bertie, an avid reader of *The Times*, was disturbed by the tone of Harris's report. 'Is it wise', he wrote to ask Chirol on 21 March, 'for Mr Harris to write and the 'Times' to publish the . . . communication from Tangier?' 'Moreover', he added, 'do you think the information is correct?'[36] Chirol, whose own confidence in Harris was 'by no means unbounded', had to admit that there was 'a strong anti-French party at Fez'. But that, he informed Bertie, was no reason 'why Harris should make himself its mouthpiece'. On the contrary, he assured the ambassador that he would see what he could do 'to keep him in order', and he telegraphed to Harris to remind him 'that the policy of the *Times* is to support the French in Morocco'. 'The French', Chirol observed, 'may not have acted in every way wisely & they will probably commit many blunders before they have done, but that is their business, not ours.'[37] Bertie in the meanwhile received Delcassé's somewhat lame excuses for his failure to treat with Germany. Radolin, he claimed, had appeared quite satisfied when in March 1904 he had explained to him that the object of his negotiations with England was the

---

[33] Guillen, pp.553–7, 583–6 and 692–3. P.M. Kennedy, 'The Development of German Naval Operations Plans against England, 1896–1914', *English Historical Review*, LXXXIX (1974), 48–76. Raulff, pp.54–5.
[34] Rich, II, pp.696–702.
[35] *The Times*, 20 March 1905, p.2.
[36] Bertie to Chirol, 21 March 1905, B.P., Add. MS. 63017.
[37] Chirol to Bertie, 22 March 1905, B.P., Add. MS. 63017. Chirol to Harris, 27 March 1905, The Foreign Dept. Letter Book, vol. V, *The Times* MSS.

reformation of Morocco with French assistance, and that the commercial interests of other powers would be safeguarded.[38] Even Paul Cambon thought that Delcassé had been mistaken not to treat with Germany, and Geoffray, his councillor at London, said as much to Lansdowne.[39] But Bertie simply passed on Delcassé's words to Lansdowne with neither criticism nor protest.

Bertie had none the less little to offer Delcassé by way of comfort. He from the first assumed that the Germans were seeking to use the opportunity offered to them by the weakening of France's eastern ally in order to secure some concession in Morocco. The German intervention was, Bertie thought, 'bluff', and William II a 'good Commis Voyageur', trading on the sultan's hopes of support in return for some commercial and other advantage. He suggested to Delcassé that the German government might perhaps be hoping for some 'price' for their recognition of France's arrangement with Britain.[40] What he thought that price might be, he made clear in a letter to Mallet of 31 March. 'Of course', he wrote, 'the Germans would like a coaling station on the Atlantic coast. That would not suit us.'[41] This may have been a misjudgement of the purposes of German diplomacy, but Bertie was not alone in arriving at this conclusion. In a letter of 4 April Sanderson wrote to remind him that Hatzfeldt had once tried to persuade Salisbury to admit that Britain would not object to Germany acquiring such a port. And in Sanderson's estimate the Germans would not be satisfied until they were promised some reversion.[42]

Bertie could personally see no reason for encouraging the French to offer the Germans anything in Morocco or elsewhere. Indeed, he thought that Britain might derive some benefit from this turn of events. He wrote in his letter to Mallet: 'I hope that we shall not do anything to smooth matters between the French and German Governments. If we advised the French to make concessions they would be furious . . . Let Morocco be an open sore between France and Germany as Egypt was between France and ourselves.' For the moment he assumed that the French would not be prepared to go beyond their previous assurances to respect the commercial rights of other powers in Morocco.[43] Yet he was also aware that Delcassé was

[38] Bertie to Lansdowne, 22 and 26 March 1905, B.P., A, F.O.800/170.
[39] Henri Cambon (ed.), *Paul Cambon: Correspondance, 1870–1924* (3 vols., Paris, 1940–6), II, 181. Lansdowne to Bertie, 26 April 1905, B.P., A, F.O.800/160.
[40] Bertie to Mallet, 12 April 1905, B.P., A, F.O.800/160. Bertie to Lansdowne, 22, 24 and 31 March 1905, B.P., A, F.O.800/170. *B.D.*, III, no.67.
[41] Bertie to Mallet, 31 March 1905, B.P., A, F.O.800/170.
[42] Sanderson to Bertie, 4 April 1905, B.P., A, F.O.800/160.
[43] Bertie to Mallet, 31 March 1905, B.P., A, F.O.800/170.

uneasy about the German action, and he attributed a request from Loubet for a meeting with King Edward, who was due to pass through Paris on 6 April, to a desire to 'emphasise the entente'.[44] The king, who was on his way to Marseilles, was pleased to oblige. He had been 'much put out' by the antics of his nephew, and thought that an interview with the president would 'in some degree act as a sort of counterblast to the Emperor's visit to Tangiers'.[45] Yet Bertie, who accompanied Loubet when he boarded the royal train, was evidently nervous about the British government's intentions, and one member of the king's suite subsequently reported to London that both the ambassador and Lister were anxious about the possibility of Lansdowne recommending Delcassé to make concessions to the Germans.[46] Mallet was quick to assure Bertie that no such thought had entered Lansdowne's head. Echoing Bertie's own assertion, Mallet observed of the *entente*: 'It has put us in the position which the Germans held for so many years & we must do everything in our power to keep it.'[47]

The danger, which Mallet well understood, was that if the French were uncertain about how far they could rely upon British support, they might settle with the Germans on terms detrimental to Britain's interests.[48] From the start, however, Lansdowne seems to have considered the 'Tangier escapade' as far more than just an attempt on the part of the Germans to squeeze material concessions from the French. 'There can', he wrote to Lascelles on 9 April, 'be no doubt that the Emperor was much annoyed by the Anglo-French Agreement and probably even more so by our refusal to vamp up some Agreement of the same kind with Germany over the Egyptian question.' He insisted tha the emperor's action could hardly be regarded as an 'isolated incident'. 'We shall', Lansdowne predicted, 'find the Emperor avails himself of every opportunity he can make to put spokes in our wheels and convince those who are watching the progress of the game that he means to take part in it.' In the spring of 1905 this was apparent to Lansdowne and his officials not only in Morocco, but also in Abyssinia.[49]

---

[44] Bertie to Knollys, 4 April 1905, B.P., A, F.O.800/164, Bertie to Lansdowne, 4 April 1905, B.P., Add. MS. 63017.
[45] Knollys to Bertie, 5 April 1905, B.P., Add. MS. 63017.
[46] Bertie to Mallet, 7 April 1905, B.P., A, F.O.800/164. Lansdowne to Cranborne, 11 April 1905, Cecil MSS., S(4) 56/32.
[47] Mallet to Bertie, 10 April 1905, B.P., A, F.O.800/160.
[48] *Ibid.*
[49] Lansdowne to Lascelles, 9 April 1905, Lansdowne MSS., F.O.800/130, cited in part in lord Newton, *Lord Lansdowne, a biography* (London, 1929), p.334.

Progress towards the achievement of a tripartite agreement on Abyssinia such as had been envisaged in May 1904 had been conspicuously slow. When Paul Cambon had taken up the subject of France adhering to the projected Anglo-Italian accord, he had urged Delcassé to erect a protective dyke around Abyssinia in order to prevent its being submerged by a flood of British influence on the Nile.[50] But after negotiations began in October the French were less concerned with defending Abyssinia against the rapacity of its other European neighbours, than with preparing for possible partition.[51] Even Lansdowne, for all his experience of bargaining with the French, was shocked by the immoderation of Paul Cambon's reversionary claims.[52] Moreover, although Delcassé was prepared both to forego the extension of the Jibuti railway to the White Nile and to renounce the application of discriminatory tariffs, he was determined to retain France's exclusive control of the line. He also insisted that Menelik, who had originally granted the railway concession, not to the French government, but to a private individual, and who now favoured its internationalization, should cease to obstruct the line's continuation from its present terminus at Diré Dowa.[53] Lansdowne was, however, reluctant to agree to any course that might precipitate the disintegration of Menelik's empire,[54] and it was presumably with the aim of overcoming the foreign secretary's qualms about applying pressure upon a hitherto friendly monarch that Paul Cambon tried to link developments in Abyssinia and Morocco. He advised Lansdowne on 27 March that it was necessary to respond to the Tangier visit by 'l'arrangement à trois en Éthiopie'.[55] The remark was made all the more pertinent by the news that a German mission had arrived in Abyssinia and was engaged in commercial negotiations.[56] German involvement in Abyssinia might of course compel the French to relinquish their monopoly railway rights. Yet, as Mallet observed to Bertie in a letter of 10 April, Britain wanted neither German intrigues nor German competition in that part of the world. The moral for the French,

[50] *D.D.F.2*, V, no.148.
[51] Lansdowne to Monson, 19 Oct. 1904, F.O.1/56, despt.544.
[52] Lansdowne to Bertie, 11 Jan. 1905, F.O.1/56, despt.29. Lansdowne to P. Cambon, 13 Jan. 1905, with annotations by Delcassé, N.S. Éthiopie 1.
[53] P. Cambon to Lansdowne, 9 Jan. 1905, F.O.1/56. Lansdowne to Bertie, 11 Jan. 1905, F.O.1/56, despt. 29.
[54] Lansdowne to P. Cambon, 16 Dec. 1904, F.O.1/56. Geoffray to Delcassé. 27 April 1905, N.S. Éthiopie 11.
[55] *D.D.F.2*, VI, no.196.
[56] Marcus, 'Tripartite Treaty', 33, n47. Lagarde to Delcassé, 20 March 1905, N.S. Ethiopie 11. Lansdowne to Bertie, 19 April 1905, F.O.1/56, despt.228. Lansdowne to Cromer, 3 April 1905, Cromer MSS., F.O.633/56.

Mallet added, was to come to terms with the British and 'slam the door in their faces'.[57]

Bertie did not need reminding of the dangers of German meddling. He was already an expert on the subject, and on 12 April he warned Delcassé that 'there would be a German push in Abyssinia' if something were not done quickly about the railway question. He also wrote to ask Mallet if a British and an Italian director could not be appointed to the railway board in order to 'smooth down' Menelik?[58] Lansdowne, to whom Mallet conveyed Bertie's views, was seemingly impressed by this idea, and on 19 April he suggested to Léon Geoffray, the French *chargé d'affaires* in London, an arrangement similar to that which Bertie had recommended.[59] Nevertheless, he was still insistent that the French could not expect Britain 'to ride roughshod over Menelik in order to get them their precious railway'.[60]

Bertie may have hoped for the opportunity to discuss this matter with Lansdowne when he placed the embassy in Lister's charge on 16 April and left for a spell of leave in London. He was, however, forced to cut short his holiday by developments in Paris. There Radolin had thus far remained silent on the subject of Morocco and the emperor's visit. Holstein had insisted that there should be no separate deal with France, but that Germany must negotiate as a cosignatory of the Madrid convention of 1880: an act by which the European powers had sought to regulate the practice of protection in Morocco.[61] Count Tattenbach, the German minister at Lisbon, had therefore been sent on a special mission to Fez, and efforts were made to drum up support for an international conference. All this was unnerving for those in France who feared lest the confrontation with Germany should lead to war. Delcassé was subjected to increasing criticism for his neglect of Germany, and there were signs of a growing rift between the foreign minister and his colleagues in the government. Rouvier, who wanted to open up a dialogue with the Germans had but little liking for Delcassé. Moreover, Eugène Étienne, the minister for the interior, had long favoured a Franco-German understanding on Morocco, and as one of the leading figures in the *parti colonial*, the French colonialist movement, he was a potential candidate for the

---

[57] Mallet to Bertie, 10 April 1905, B.P., A, F.O.800/160.
[58] Bertie to Mallet, 12 April 1905, B.P., A, F.O.800/160.
[59] Mallet to Bertie, 15 April 1905, B.P. Add. MS. 63017.
[60] Lansdowne to Bertie, 26 April 1905, B.P., A, F.O.800/160.
[61] Parsons, p.86.

foreign ministry.⁶² But it was in the chamber of deputies, which had grown impatient with Delcassé's reserve and his method of defending himself by reciting his past achievements, that matters came to a head on 19 April. First Jean Jaurès, the socialist leader and then Paul Deschanel of the centre, lunged into an attack upon Delcassé's diplomacy and demanded that he should enter immediately into negotiations with the Germans. Rouvier defended the foreign minister. Nevertheless, he only declared himself 'solidaire' with the policy pursued by Delcassé since the formation of the present government, and in the assurances that he offered to the chamber he implied that henceforth the council of ministers would exercise greater supervision over foreign policy. Dissatisfied by Rouvier's speech, and no doubt troubled by the criticisms of his former supporters in parliament, Delcassé offered his resignation on 20 April. When two days later he withdrew his offer, he did so only on condition that a *communiqué* be issued making clear that he had the backing of all his colleagues in the government.⁶³ The news of Delcassé's decision to resign caused Bertie to hurry back to France on 21 April. And although there is no documentary evidence with which to substantiate the claim of Count Khevenhüller, the Austro-Hungarian ambassador at Paris, that Bertie had been sent back in order to intercede with Loubet in Delcassé's favour,⁶⁴ it is apparent that the prospect of a change at the Quai d'Orsay was regarded with disquiet in London. Both Balfour and Lansdowne had already decided that England's understanding with France obliged them to support the French government in opposition to a German-sponsored conference on Morocco.⁶⁵ Moreover, Delcassé's removal seemed likely to discredit the *entente*, especially as it might result in the appointment of a successor who would be more amenable to German pressure. During a meeting with Delcassé on 22 April Bertie warned him that in the present situation his resignation would be disastrous. But Bertie knew that there were differences within the French cabinet. In a private letter to Lansdowne he explained that he thought

---

⁶² *Ibid*, pp.522 – 4. On Étienne and the French colonialist movement see: C.M. Andrew and A.S. Kanya-Forstner, *France Overseas. The Great War and the Climax of French Imperial Expansion* (London, 1981), pp.24 – 5.
⁶³ Lister to Lansdowne, 19 April 1905, F.O.27/3705, tel.19. Lister to Lansdowne, 20 and 21 April 1905, F.O.27/3705, despt.142 and 145. Andrew, *Delcassé*, pp.276 – 7. For a thorough examination of the pressures brought to bear upon Delcassé by his colleagues, see: P. Muret, 'La politique personelle de Rouvier et la chute de Delcassé (31 mars – 6 juin 1905)', *Revue de l'histoire de la guerre mondiale*, XVII (1939), 209 – 31 and 305 – 52.
⁶⁴ *G.P.*, XX, pt.2, no.6847.
⁶⁵ Nicolson to Lansdowne, 11 April 1905, and minutes by Lansdowne and Balfour, F.O.99/434, tel.19.

Delcassé's insistence on a declaration of ministerial solidarity was 'not only for foreign consumption but because one or more of his colleagues were thought not to be with him in the Moroccan question policy'. Étienne, he noted, was 'credited with a desire to step into his shoes'.[66] Darker forces were also assumed to be at work. Delcassé claimed that he had 'proof' that 'the intrigue to get him out of office was started by the German Emperor', and Bertie himself had it from a 'reliable source' that Count Monts, the German ambassador at Rome, had recently declared that once Germany had got rid of Delcassé it would not be difficult to destroy his arrangements.[67] It is possible that in these circumstances Bertie may have encouraged Delcassé to believe that he could rely on more than diplomatic support from Britain. In any event, Maurice Paléologue, a *sous-directeur* of the foreign ministry, whom Delcassé saw on the evening of the 22nd, and who was subsequently despatched on a special mission to Berlin, informed the French ambassador there that the British government had told Delcassé 'that in the present crisis Germany's success would mean nothing less than the admission of her supremacy and it is determined to oppose it'.[68]

In the meanwhile Mallet acted on his own initiative and tried to secure from Lansdowne a further pledge of support for France. On 20 April he had warned J. S. Sandars, Balfour's private secretary, that the Germans would probably demand a Moroccan port, and that if Britain did not support France they would succeed in demonstrating the *entente* was valueless.[69] On learning of Delcassé's proffered resignation, he wrote to the foreign secretary to say that 'things looked serious for the Entente', and he asked him 'what we should do supposing Germany pressed home her victory and asked for a port'? 'I urged him', Mallet informed Bertie, 'to tell the French that we should see them through.' Lansdowne advised Mallet to consult the Admiralty, and as a result he visited Sir John Fisher, the first sea lord. According to a private letter which Mallet wrote to Bertie on 24 April, Fisher said 'of course the Germans will ask for Mogador and I

---

[66] Bertie to Lansdowne, 22 April 1905, B.P., A, F.O.800/164. Lister had already warned Lansdowne that Delcassé's position in the French cabinet was rendered more cirtical by the presence in it of a powerful rival in the person of Étienne. Lister to Lansdowne, 21 April 1905, F.O.27/3405, despt.145. On the development of the French colonial party and its ideas see: Andrew and A.S. Kanya-Forstner, 'The French "Colonial Party": its composition, aims, and influence, 1885 – 1914', *Historical Journal*. XIV (1971), 99 – 128.
[67] Bertie to Edward VII, 22 April 1905; Bertie to Lansdowne, 2 April 1905; B.P., A, F.O.800/164.
[68] Andrew, *Delcassé*, pp.285 – 6. Paléologue, pp.229 – 30.
[69] Mallet to Sandars, 20 April 1905, Balfour MSS., Add. MS. 49747.

shall tell Lord L. that if they do we must *at least* have Tangier — of course it's all rot and it would not matter to us whether the Germans got Mogador or not but I'm going to say so all the same'.[70] Moreover, in a letter to Lansdowne on 22 April Fisher claimed that 'without any question the Germans would like a port on the coast of Morocco'. He added: 'This seems a golden opportunity for fighting the Germans in alliance with the French, so I earnestly hope you will bring this about.'[71]

Lansdowne did not take seriously the bellicose tone of Fisher's note.[72] But the harping of Bertie, Mallet and others in the Foreign Office on the theme of Germany's designs upon the Moroccan coast may already have had its effect. In any event on the 19th Lansdowne had written to Arthur Nicolson, who after serving as minister at Tangier was now ambassador at Madrid, that he would not be surprised if the Germans were 'to seek compensation in the shape of a coaling station'.[73] And although he was as yet undecided as to the circumstances in which Britain should 'help' France, he was sufficiently worried about the future standing of the *entente* to inform Balfour by telegram on the morning of the 23rd of the Admiralty's views, and to request permission to advise the French not to accede to German pressure for a port without giving Britain a full opportunity for conferring with them 'as to the manner in which demand might be met'.[74] That same day, Easter Sunday, Lansdowne, who was staying at his country seat of Bowood, had an unexpected opportunity to discuss this matter with the prime minister, and late in the evening the following telegram was sent to Bertie:

It seems not unlikely that the German Government may ask for a port on the Moorish coast.

You are authorised to inform Minister for Foreign Affairs that we should be prepared to join French Government in offering strong opposition to such a proposal and to beg that if the question is raised French Government will afford us a full opportunity of conferring with them as to steps which might be taken in order to meet it.

---

[70] Mallet to Bertie, 24 April 1905, B.P., A, F.O.800/170.
[71] A.J. Marder(ed.), *Fear God and Dread Nought. The Correspondence of Admiral of the Fleet Lord Fisher of Kilverstone* (3 vols., London, 1952–9), I, 55.
[72] Lansdowne to Balfour, 23 April 1905 (incomplete draft of letter), Balfour MSS., Add. MS. 49729.
[73] Lansdowne to Nicolson, 19 April 1905, Nicolson MSS., F.O.800/356.
[74] Lansdowne to Balfour, 23 April 1905, tel. Balfour MSS., Add. MS. 49729.

German attitude in this dispute seems to be most unreasonable having regard to M. Delcassé's attitude and we desire to give him all the support we can.[75]

This arrived at the embassy on the following morning. As, however, the Monday after Easter was a public holiday in France, and Delcassé was away in the country, Bertie could do no more than write to the foreign minister that he had received an important communication and would like to meet him.[76] A quarter of a century later Eugene Anderson contended in his book, *The First Moroccan Crisis*, that when on 25 April Bertie finally delivered Lansdowne's message to Delcassé, he gave to it a 'form and meaning which was originally lacking'. This claim Anderson based upon the difference in composition between the *aide mémoire* which Bertie drafted and gave to the French foreign minister, and the already cited copy of Lansdowne's telegram, both of which were published in the *British Documents on the Origins of the War*. The telegram limited the British offer to join France in 'strong opposition' to Germany to the specific case where she might demand a Moroccan port, and it emphasized the importance of conferring beforehand. But Bertie's *aide mémoire* appeared to reverse the order of this document, and began with the declaration that the British government 'trouve que les procédés de l'Allemagne dans la question du Maroc sont des plus déraisonnables vu l'attitude de Monsieur Delcassé et il desire accorder à Son Excellence tout l'appui en son pouvoir'. Thus, Anderson maintained, Delcassé was given what appeared to be a blanket offer of British support in which the assumed German desire for a Moroccan port appeared as an example of when that offer might be applicable. Moreover, while Lansdowne had in his telegram sought only the opportunity to 'confer' with the French government, Bertie's *aide mémoire* asked Delcassé to give the British government 'toute occasion de concerter avec le Gouvernement Français'. The implication was that the French might expect some agreement to act together to result from the consultations which Lansdowne requested.[77]

Bertie's assurances to Delcassé would seem then to have had a wider scope than those contained in Lansdowne's instructions.

---

[75] Lansdowne to Balfour, 23 April 1905 (draft letter), Balfour MSS., Add. MS. 49729.
[76] Bertie to Delcassé, 24 April 1905, Delcassé MSS., 14. Bertie to Lansdowne, 25 April 1905, F.O.146/3842, despt.156 (the latter part of this despatch is published in *B.D.*, III, no.93.
[77] *D.D.F.2*, VI, no.347. Anderson, pp.21–11. The *British Documents* also contain a copy of a rough draft in Bertie's handwriting which would appear to have formed the basis of this *aide-mémoire*. It is evident from this that Bertie considered and then

Nevertheless, the accusation made by Anderson, and since echoed by other historians, that Bertie's *aide mémoire* was 'so colored by his own very pro-French feeling that it did not accurately reproduce his chief's proposal' is not entirely justified.[78] The copy of Lansdowne's telegram upon which Anderson relied was found by the editors of the *British Documents* in the archives of the Paris embassy. As they pointed out, no copy of it is to be found in the general correspondence of the Foreign Office. There is, however, in this collection a paraphrase of the telegram. Unlike the document in the embassy papers, which was dated 22 April, this bears what would seem to be the correct date of despatch (i.e. 23 April). Of more interest though is the fact that its composition is very similar to that employed by Bertie in his *aide mémoire*. It, for instance, begins: 'German attitude in dispute with regard to Morocco seems to us most unreasonable having regard to the attitude of M. Delcassé, to whom we desire to give all possible support. It is not improbable that German Govt. may ask for a Moorish port'. Indeed, it is just possible that this may have formed the basis of Bertie's communication to Delcassé.[79]

This is not to say that Bertie failed to recognize the different interpretation that could be placed upon his *aide mémoire*. But the existence of the two versions of Lansdowne's message does lend credence to the suggestion made by Bernadotte Schmitt in 1930 that Bertie changed the order of the sentences 'probably with the object of guarding the cipher'.[80] After all, it is hardly likely that Bertie would have risked giving the very able code-breakers of the Quai d'Orsay the key to a Foreign Office cypher by delivering Lansdowne's

---

discarded the use of the verbs 'conférer' and 'discuter' before deciding on 'concerter'. B.D., III, no.91.

[78] Anderson, *ibid*. Andrew, *Delcassé*, p.281. D.C. Watt, 'The First Moroccan Crisis', in J.M. Robertson (ed.), *Europe in the Twentieth Century* (4 vols., London, 1970 – 1), I, 91.

[79] Lansdowne to Bertie, 23 April 1905, F.O.27/3708, tel.61P. It is interesting to note that in the draft of the despatch in which Bertie recorded his interview with Delcassé on 25 April he at first referred to 'Your Lordship's tel. no.61 dated the night of the 22nd'. He subsequently altered this to the 'night of the 23rd'. The editors of the *British Documents*, who only summarised this portion of the despatch did not mention this alteration, but suggested that Bertie was referring to the date of the embassy's reception of Lansdowne's telegram. Bertie to Lansdowne, 25 April 1905. Paraphrases, which were sent by the Foreign Office to embassies through the normal channels of communication, were intended to permit the recipient to check on decypherment. They were meant to convey the substance of telegrams without repeating the wording and thus not compromising the cypher if they were intercepted. Public Record Office Handbooks, No.13, *The Records of the Foreign Office 1782–1939* (London, 1969), pp.46 – 7.

[80] B.E. Schmitt, *The Coming of the War 1914* (2 vols., New York, 1930), I, 32 – 3.

message in its original form.[81] It seems in any case evident from an incomplete letter, drafted by Lansdowne for Balfour on 23 April, that the foreign secretary was as much concerned with the political situation in France and the menace posed by Germany to the *entente* as he was with the prospect of a German coaling station in Morocco.[82] On 24 April Mallet wrote to Bertie on the subject of Lansdowne's telegram: 'If the French are wise they will read between the lines and see that if we undertake as we are doing to back them up, we shall not be able to leave them in the lurch if Germany resorts to force.'[83] There were, however, considerable differences between Bertie's view of German diplomacy and those expressed by Mallet and Fisher. Unlike them, he displayed no desire for a preventive war with Germany. Moreover, the prospect of Germany acquiring a Moroccan port was not for him simply a means by which to persuade Lansdowne to commit himself to further support of France. He wanted to keep Delcassé in office, and to maintain the *entente* in order to bar the way to just such a concession to Germany.

Delcassé, whom Bertie found 'much calmer' than before the debate in the chamber, was grateful for Lansdowne's offer of support. During his interview with Bertie on 25 April he said that he believed everything should be done to show that the *entente* was a 'living force', and that same day he telegraphed to the French minister at Tangier that he and the British ambassador had recognized 'l'utilité de rendre bien apparente en toute occasion l'union étroite et ferme de la France et l'Angleterre'.[84] He seems, however, to have been surprised by Bertie's reference to a possible German demand for a Moroccan port, and he doubted if the sultan would be prepared to grant one. All that Bertie could tell him was that he supposed the British government 'must have received reliable information that a port was the aim of the German Emperor'.[85] This was nonsense. Although Lansdowne himself had in the past found reason to suppose that the Germans might desire a point on the Moroccan coast, the only recent

[81] Bertie knew full well that all 'telegrams having the appearance of being important which pass over the wires in France' were communicated to the ministry of the interior, and he was justly irritated when messages which were intended for communication to the Quai d'Orsay were sent in new cyphers. Bertie to Nicolson, 20 July 1911, B.P. B, F.O.800/186. Bertie to Grey, 22 May 1913, B.P., Add. MS. 63031. On the code-breakers of the Quai d'Orsay see: C.M. Andrew, 'Dechiffrement et diplomatie: le cabinet noir du Quai d'Orsay sous la Troisième République', *Relations internationales*, V (1976), 37 – 64.
[82] Lansdowne to Balfour, 23 April 1905, F.O.27/3708, tel.61P.
[83] Mallet to Bertie, 24 April 1905, B.P., A, F.O.800/170.
[84] Bertie to Lansdowne, 25 April 1905, Lansdowne MSS., F.O.800/127. *D.D.F.2*, VI, no.350.
[85] *B.D.*, III, nos.92 and 93.

information that he had on the subject was that which had been concocted in the fertile imaginations of Bertie and others of his officials. Indeed, Lansdowne was still uncertain as to what German intentions might be. In a letter to Bertie of 26 April he expressed the hope that there was 'nothing in the rumour as to the demand for a Moorish port'. 'I doubt', he added, 'whether Mogador or Mogazhem are worth much, but the establishment of a German station no matter how unimportant at either of these places would have a very bad effect.'[86] Paul Cambon was equally puzzled about the purpose of Germany's Moroccan policy. It might, he suggested to Lansdowne on 3 May, be the outcome of a *mouvement irréfléchi* on the part of William II, or more probably of an attempt to get rid of Delcassé. A Moroccan port, he speculated, could also be Germany's objective.[87] His attempt, however, to secure from Lansdowne some clarification of Bertie's *aide mémoire* met with little success. Lansdowne evaded Cambon's request to know what measures he envisaged in the event of Germany acquiring a port, and in reply he advised him that they would have to wait until Germany uncovered herself.[88]

Britain's position was not made any clearer to the French by the king, whose return from the Mediterranean took him to Paris on 29 April. Again this was intended to be a private visit.[89] Again Loubet was bent upon using it to demonstrate the solidarity of the *entente*. Edward VII had, however, his priorities in the right order. He was determined that politics should not interfere with pleasure, even if, much to the disgust of Bertie, this meant disregarding republican mores and driving from one of the most legitimist houses in France to a reception at the Élysée palace.[90] Moreover, at a banquet at the Élysée on the evening of the 30th, the king closeted himself with Radolin and engaged in a long and animated conversation. What passed between king and prince was, as Lansdowne later indicated to Bertie, of little consequence. Nevertheless, Bertie, who had not previously had the opportunity 'to deprecate to His Majesty a sermon to Radolin', was worried lest the conversation 'however innocent in intention . . . be magnified here and at Berlin, and cause further irritation against us with the Emperor and the German Anglophobes'.[91] Indeed, the Baron von Eckhardstein, a German diplomat

---

[86] Lansdowne to Bertie, 26 April 1905, B.P. A, F.O.800/160.
[87] *B.D.*, III, no.86.
[88] *D.D.F.2*, VI, no.390.
[89] Ponsonby to Bertie, 18 April 1905, B.P. Add. MS. 6301.
[90] Bertie to Lansdowne, 30 April 1905, B.P. Add. MS. 63017.
[91] Bertie to Lansdowne, 1 May 1905, B.P., A, F.O.800/170. Lansdowne to Bertie, 11 May 1905, Lansdowne MSS., F.O.800/127. *G.P.*, XX, pt.2, no.6848.

who was in Paris at the time, reported to Bülow that King Edward had shown himself very Germanophobe during his private meetings, and had left no doubt in Paris that in the event of war England would range herself alongside France.[92] He certainly seems to have inspired Delcassé with greater confidence in the *entente*. But to judge from the record of Paléologue, who was prone to exaggeration, the substance of what the king said in society was that the French should seek to settle the Moroccan business quickly. 'Sponge it off', he told the veteran French diplomat, the Baron de Courcel, 'Schwamm darüber! . . . Schwamm darüber!'[93]

In Bertie's eyes a Franco-German deal on Morocco seemed likely to lead to further complications, especially if the French were to appear to yield to German pressure. Not only might the *entente* suffer, but such an accord might also create problems for the future security of the British empire. Paul Cambon, who was paying one of his not infrequent visits to Paris, suggested to him on 29 April that there were 'contiguous frontiers between France & Germany in Africa where compensation might have been found for Germany'.[94] Perhaps it was with this in mind that Bertie warned Lansdowne on 1 May:

> If there are any points in Africa other than Morocco and Egypt where the French might throw bones to the German watch dog to gnaw to our detriment you ought to indicate I think to Cambon what concessions which we know the Germans want we should particularly object to, otherwise we might discover too late for remedy that our interests have been sacrificed.[95]

Bertie might have been a good deal more concerned about a Franco-German settlement if he had known that on the evening of 26 April Rouvier had assured Radolin that the French people leaned more towards the German people than towards the English. Moreover, according to Radolin, a confidant of Rouvier had indicated to him that France and Germany might be able to conclude a bargain on the German sponsored Baghdad railway project, central Africa and Morocco.[96]

After his conversation with Delcassé on 25 April, Bertie had informed Lansdowne that the French public 'realizing that the Emperor's wrath is against England for enabling France to carry out

---

[92] *G.P.*, XX, pt.2, no.6652.
[93] Paléologue, *Turning Point*, pp.239 – 40 and 242.
[94] Bertie to Lansdowne, 30 April 1905, B.P. Add. MS. 63017. Keith Eubank, *Paul Cambon. Master Diplomatist* (Norman, Oklahoma, 1960), pp.97 – 9.
[95] Bertie to Lansdowne, 1 May 1905, B.P. A, F.O.800/170.
[96] *G.P.*, XX, pt.2, nos.6635 and 6645.

her Morocco policy and not against France for taking advantage of her agreement with England feel that if they keep their heads nothing really serious will come of His Majesty's ill-temper'.[97] This view may also have been shared by Delcassé and his three staunch supporters, Barrère, and the brothers Paul and Jules Cambon, the latter French ambassador at Madrid. Fortified by the assistance offered by Britain, and confident that his diplomatic position was strong, Delcassé felt that he could withstand German blandishments and eventually achieve a negotiated settlement. But Rouvier and some of his other colleagues were not inclined to believe that Germany was bluffing. They feared that any tightening of the *entente* with England would simply be regarded in Berlin as an act of provocation and expose an unprepared France to the risk of a German surprise attack, against which the British would be incapable of providing any effective military aid. So disturbed was Rouvier by the course being pursued by Delcassé that he endeavoured in conversation with Radolin, and through the agency of his friends in the world of high finance, such as Wilhelm Betzold, the representative of Bleichroeder's bank at Paris, to circumvent the foreign minister and to sound out Berlin on the possibility of an understanding. He even permitted it to be known that he would not be unhappy to see Delcassé removed from office. The effect of these initiatives was firstly to weaken Delcassé's negotiating position and to encourage the Wilhelmstrasse to work for his removal; and secondly, since the Quai d'Orsay soon knew of what was afoot from decyphered German telegrams, to reopen divisions within the council of ministers.[98] Moreover, Delcassé's relations with his colleagues were worsened as a result of his evident reluctance to follow their wishes and to require the Russian Baltic fleet to quit French waters in the Far East.[99]

Bertie may not have known at this stage of Rouvier's dealings with the Germans, but he was aware of the mounting opposition to Delcassé within the French cabinet. On 8 May he wrote privately to Lansdowne to warn him that Delcassé's position was again 'very shaky'. There was also some talk of his being succeeded by Barrère or Paul Cambon.[100] Bertie personally hoped that Delcassé would survive at least until matters were settled. He still believed that one of the German emperor's objects was to break the *entente*, for, as he observed to de Bunsen, so long as Britain and France held together, he would

---

[97] Bertie to Lansdowne, 25 April 1905, Lansdowne MSS., F.O.800/127.
[98] Muret.
[99] Bertie to Lansdowne, 8 May 1905, B.P., A, F.O.800/179.
[100] *Ibid.*

'find it difficult to exercise the influence he desires to possess'.[101] Germany, he thought, was determined to take the first opportunity of any difficulty Britain might be in to humiliate her. 'We shall not conciliate her', he observed to Lansdowne on 12 May, 'unless we break with France and facilitate her preparations to become a really Great Naval Power to our detriment.'[102] Mallet shared Bertie's conviction that the Germans were determined to drive a wedge into the *entente*. Their ultimate diplomatic objective was, he thought, the achievement of an alliance with France and Russia 'the spectre of which we thought was dead'. But Mallet, despite his sympathy for a closer relationship between England and France, could hardly contain his disappointment with the recent behaviour of the French. Frightened lest they should 'through funk' settle with Germany and leave Britain in the lurch, he complained to Balfour's secretary on 13 May that the French had 'shown no sign of taking us into their confidence over Morocco . . . they have never so much as approached the question of what we should do if Germany attacked them'.[103] Seen from this standpoint it appeared possible that Delcassé might be forced out of office, and, without the British government ever having been consulted, his successor be prepared to enter into an accord with Germany which might both involve territorial changes inimical to British interests, and constitute a preliminary to future Franco-German cooperation. Indeed, this attitude of mind helps to explain the language used by Lansdowne when on 17 May Paul Cambon called at the Foreign Office to discuss in the first place, not Morocco, but Abyssinia.[104]

The Quai d'Orsay had only recently learnt from Rome that the Italians suspected the British and French governments of preparing a separate agreement on Abyssinia. This story, which Delcassé attributed to German machinations, allowed Cambon to complain to Lansdowne that the German government was 'engaged all over the world in attempts to sow discord between us'. German officials were, he claimed, 'wooden-faced' when they were approached on the subject of Morocco, and he maintained that according to information which he had received a German force had occupied Haichow in China. Lansdowne thought this last report to be exaggerated. Nevertheless, he impressed upon Cambon that the 'moral of all these

---

[101] Dugdale, *Maurice de Bunsen*, p.205.
[102] Bertie to Lansdowne, 12 May 1905, Bertie MSS., F.O.800/170.
[103] Mallet to Sandars, 13 May 1905, Balfour MSS., Add. MS. 49747. Mallet to Spring Rice, 16 May 1905, Spring Rice MSS., CASR 1/49.
[104] Lansdowne to Bertie, 17 May 1905, F.O.1/53, despt.307 (the latter part of this despatch is pubished in *B.D.*, III, n.94).

incidents' was that the British and French governments should keep each other fully informed of everything that came to their knowledge. They should, he observed, 'so far as possible discuss in advance any contingencies by which they might in the course of events find themselves confronted'. To illustrate this point, he reminded Cambon of Bertie's communication to Delcassé of 25 April with regard to a Moroccan port for Germany. He had heard fears expressed, he said, 'that ... the French might be induced to purchase the acquiescence of Germany by concessions of a kind which we were not likely to regard with favour in other parts of the world'.[105]

This plea for consultations appeared to Paul Cambon to be nothing less than an extension of the assurances contained in Bertie's *aide-mémoire*. Moreover, according to a despatch which Cambon subsequently sent to Delcassé, when he had asked Lansdowne if for example the French had serious reason to believe in an unjustified aggression the British government 'serait tout prêt à se concerter avec le gouvernement français sur les mesures à prendre', the foreign secretary had agreed.[106] There is, however, no record of this in Lansdowne's account of the conversation. He may, perhaps, have regarded it as simply a clarification of a point that was not worth recording. It may also be that the French ambassador had misunderstood what had been said to him. But Cambon, who had been authorized by Delcassé to sound out Lansdowne on a possible British military commitment to assist France in the event of a German attack, evidently felt that both Lansdowne's answer and his previous spontaneous declaration met this requirement.[107] In any event Lansdowne's language could hardly have discouraged Delcassé and his senior officials from thinking in terms of tighter links with England.

Bertie had in the meanwhile concluded that Delcassé's position had improved. Barrère and Paul Cambon had been hard at work trying to foster a *rapprochement* between Delcassé and Rouvier, and on 18 May Barrère assured Bertie that Delcassé had 'weathered the storm'. And at a dinner that evening Bertie found both the foreign minister and the president of the council to be on good terms. This led him to

---

[105] *Ibid.*
[106] *D.D.F.2*, VI, no.443.
[107] Muret, p.332. This would not have been the first occasion on which Paul Cambon had seemed to misconstrue what Lansdowne had said to him. In January 1905 Lansdowne had found it necessary to correct Cambon's account of what had passed between them with regard to Abyssinia. 'There are', Lansdowne had then objected, 'one or two points at which your recollection of our earlier discussions does not entirely agree with mine.' Lansdowne to Cambon, 13 Jan. 1905, F.O.1/56.

completely misjudge the situation, and he wrote on the next day to assure Mallet that unless Germany succeeded in detaching Italy and Spain, the French government, 'so long as we stick to France will not believe in a German attack on France'. He similarly deprecated Mallet's idea that the French might be persuaded to accept an arrangement between themselves and the Germans and the Russians. Any such agreement that might satisfy Germany would, he argued, 'be detrimental to French interests'. Nevertheless, he recommended to Mallet that Britain should come to an agreement with France for the defence of 'certain Anglo-French interests viz. the non-acquisition by Germany of any political position in Holland or her colonies, or any port on the coast (Atlantic) of Morocco'.[108] This proposal for a very limited commitment to France, which in form resembled the arrangement which four years before he had suggested that Britain might make with Germany, was the nearest that Bertie was to come during 1905 to advocating in a written document an alliance with the French. Indeed, it was probably no more than an engagement such as this that Bertie had in mind when on 20 May at a dinner given by the Marquise de Breteuil, he raised the subject of the *entente* with de Courcel and Paléologue. According to the latter, he asserted: 'It is not enough to have created the *entente cordiale*; we must give it muscles and the wherewithal to show its strength. We shall never serve the cause of peace until the brawlers and troublemakers in Berlin are afraid of us.'[109]

Language such as this was doubtless pleasing to the ears of one like Paléologue who favoured a firm stand by France against Germany on Morocco. Yet Bertie may have unwittingly encouraged Delcassé's opponents to unseat him. His *aide mémoire* of 24 April, the cautious assurances that King Edward had offered to Delcassé, and Lansdowne's declaration of 17 May had all allowed the foreign minister and those officials who were closest to him to think in terms of a possible Anglo-French defensive alliance. Already on 30 April Barrère had written to Delcassé that implicit in the latest British overtures was a proposal on Britain's part 'd'aller jusqu'au bout'.[110] Such a course remained, however, anathema to Rouvier and those of Delcassé's colleagues who were apprehensive lest France should, as some agents of the Wilhelmstrasse predicted, become a battlefield in

---

[108] Bertie to Lansdowne, 18 May 1905; Bertie to Mallet, 19 May 1905; B.P. A, F.O.800/164.
[109] Paleologue, *Turning Point*, p.249.
[110] *Ibid*, pp.239 and 249 – 50. Barrère to Delcassé, 30 April 1905, Delcassé MSS., 14.

an Anglo-German war.[111] So great was their fear of offering further provocation to Germany that they also called into question the idea of a tripartite agreement on Abyssinia. France might, they contended, appear to have concluded yet another engagement from which Germany was excluded, and to have taken a further step towards the seduction of Germany's ally, Italy.[112]

Paul Cambon quite naturally had a different view upon this subject. For France now to withdraw from the discussions on Abyssinia would, he reasoned, mean the end of her railway project, the rupture of her good relations with Italy, and 'à bref delai l'écroulement de l'entente cordiale avec l'Angleterre qui n'aura plus pour nous que les sentiments du plus parfait mépris'.[113] He was quite able to state his case on this matter at a meeting which took place at the Élysée palace on 21 May at which were present Loubet, Delcassé, Étienne, Rouvier and Barrère. More, however, was at stake than the fate of proposed agreement on Abyssinia, for during the course of the conference Rouvier made clear his opposition to any further entanglements with Britain. Thus, after Paul Cambon had communicated his interpretation of what Lansdowne had said to him five days before, Rouvier demanded that there should be no new negotiations with the British government for 'ce serait trop dangereux'.[114]

It was unfortunate for Delcassé that in these circumstances Lansdowne should have chosen to try to correct Cambon's misapprehension of what he had said on 17 May. After receiving on 24 May a copy of that part of Cambon's account of their conversation which related to closer cooperation, Lansdowne wrote to him that he was not sure that he had 'succeeded in making quite clear . . . our desire that there should be full and confidential discussions between the two Governments, not so much in consequence of some act of unprovoked aggression on the part of another Power, as in anticipation of any complications to be apprehended.'[115] To Cambon this appeared less like a tactful attempt to put right his own misinterpretation of Britain's position than an amplification of Lansdowne's original proposals. 'Ce n'est plus', he observed to Delcassé, 'à une entente en cas d'agression qu'il nous convie c'est à une discussion immédiate et

---

[111] *G.P.*, XX, nos.6635, 6646, 6657 and 6658. Paléologue, *Turning Point*, p.248. Andrew, *Delcassé*, pp.288 – 9.
[112] Delcassé to P. Cambon, 17 May 1905, Delcassé MSS., 14.
[113] P. Cambon to Delcassé, 18 May 1905, *ibid*.
[114] Abel Combarieu, *Sept ans à l'Elysée avec le President Émile Loubet* (Paris, 1932), pp.309 – 11. Combarieu incorrectly cites the date of this meeting. Muret, p.332.
[115] *B.D.*, III, no.95. *D.D.F.2*, VI, no.455.

à un examen de la situation générale.' For the French government to accept this would, he thought, be to enter in 'la voie d'une entente générale qui constituerait en réalité une alliance'.[116]

Delcassé likewise regarded Lansdowne's letter as an offer of an alliance. As such, however, it was not welcomed by either Rouvier or the majority of his other colleagues. The Germans had of late stepped up their campaign against Delcassé, and by the beginning of June Rouvier felt politically strong enough to risk a confrontation with the foreign minister. Thus when on the morning of 6 June Delcassé insisted at a meeting of the council of ministers on the need for France to conclude an alliance with Britain, Rouvier responded by rallying the rest of the council behind him in opposition to the idea. In consequence Delcassé resigned, and later that day Rouvier provisionally took his post at the Quai d'Orsay.[117] News of these events came as a surprise to Bertie, who despite his earlier reports on the precariousness of Delcassé's position, appears to have had no inkling of his impending clash with Rouvier. He had left Paris on 5 June for Dieppe from which resort he did not return until the evening of the 8th.[118] When he did meet Delcassé on 10 June, the ex-minister attributed his fall to the 'manoeuvres of the German Government who had spent a good deal of money for the purpose'. The Germans had, he claimed, wanted his head because they regarded him as an obstacle to their schemes. He further said that he would have been ready to make commercial concessions, but not political or territorial ones, if the Germans had been willing to discuss Morocco with him. Bertie found this far from reassuring for if Delcassé's colleagues had disapproved his policy, 'it would', he warned Lansdowne, 'seem probable that they might be ready to yield something more than commercial advantages'.[119]

Far more was, however, at stake than the question of what concessions France might now be prepared to make to Germany for, as Lansdowne pointed out to Bertie, Delcassé's removal had produced 'a very painful impression' in England. He further explained that people said that if a British minister had had 'a dead set' made against him by a foreign power, the country and government would not only have stood by him, but would probably have supported him more vigorously than ever, whereas France had 'apparently thrown over Delcassé in a mere fit of panic'. The result, he estimated, was that the ' "entente" is quoted at a much lower

---

[116] *D.D.F.2*, VI, no.465.
[117] *D.D.F.2*, VI, 601–7; VIII, 560–1. Andrew, *Delcassé*, pp.289–98.
[118] Bertie to Delcassé, 9 June 1905, B.P., Add. MS. 63017.
[119] *B.D.*, III, no.96.

price than it was a fortnight ago'. He had gathered from what Cambon had told him that Rouvier would not accept a conference, but, he commented, if the French 'really are on the run, we might not extract an unsatisfactory settlement out of such a Conference'. Metternich had recently represented Germany as the upholder of the legal status of Morocco, and Lansdowne considered that attitude to 'scarcely be reconcilable with a proposal to steal territory from the Sultan'.[120]

Bertie, who evidently wished to maintain his government's confidence in the *entente*, did not judge France so harshly for the fall of Delcassé. Nor did he place the blame for it entirely on German intrigues. He assured Lansdowne on 15 June that Delcassé 'would have fallen even if Germany had not been menacing; but he might not have fallen so soon'. Delcassé's departure, he thought, was in great part due to his treatment of his colleagues, whom he had not kept fully informed of his intentions. Whilst Combes had been preoccupied with matters affecting relations between church and state, Bertie thought that things had gone well for Delcassé. But, Bertie claimed, he had come to consider himself indispensable, had 'avoided carrying out to the letter the decisions of the Cabinet especially with regard to relations with Russia, and some ministers were jealous of him'. Germany, Bertie suspected, had taken advantage of the feeling that a scapegoat was needed, and had 'spent money, and spread it about' that Delcassé's mismanagement of foreign policy was the sole cause of the misunderstanding. His resignation, he concluded, had 'the appearance of being a sacrifice to a German menace but it was not entirely so'.[121]

As a result of Delcassé's fall both the future and the value of the *entente* were called into question in London.[122] In May Mallet had recommended that one way of checking a possible realignment of France with Germany might be through the extension of Britain's Far Eastern alliance, which, he thought, would 'immensely increase our value to France as an ally, & our offensive Power as an enemy'.[123] But Japan's subsequent acceptance of British proposals for a new alliance treaty, and the annihilation of the Russian battlefleet in the

---

[120] Newton, pp.341 – 2.
[121] Fresh confirmation was given to Bertie's analysis by Willaim Lavino, *The Times* correspondent at Paris, who maintained that Rouvier had been bent upon getting rid of Delcassé of whom he was 'violently jealous'. Bertie to Lansdowne, 15 June and 7 Sept. 1905, B.P., A, F.O.800/164.
[122] Lansdowne to Egerton, 12 June 1905, Lansdowne MSS., F.O.800/133.
[123] Mallet to Spring Rice, 16 May 1905, Spring Rice, 16 May 1905, Spring Rice MSS., CASR 1/49.

Tshushima strait on 28 May, hardly contributed to a strengthening of France's position in Europe in the spring of 1905. Balfour was in any case concerned with a more immediate danger when on 8 June he warned the cabinet that France would no longer be trusted 'not to yield to threats at the critical moment of negotiation'. If, he observed, 'Germany is really desirous of obtaining a port on the coast of Morocco, and if such a proceeding be a menace to our interests, it must be to other means than French assistance that we must look for our protection'.[124] He may have had in mind the possibility of a separate Anglo-Spanish agreement such as Bertie had suggested to Lansdowne some four weeks before.

The idea of an Anglo-Spanish understanding had been mooted in the Foreign Office during the latter stages of the Spanish-American war of 1898. At that time work on gun emplacements in the hills behind Gibraltar had seriously disturbed the British military authorities and produced a minor crisis in Anglo-Spanish relations. Worried at the threat to the security of the harbour at Gibraltar, Salisbury had sought in the autumn of 1898 to persuade the Spaniards to discontinue this work by offering to use British forces to defend the coast of the bay of Algeciras and the Balearic and Canary islands against hostile attack.[125] Desultory negotiations on this subject had led to a secret exchange of notes in March 1899 between the Spanish foreign minister and the British ambassador at Madrid in which the former explained that the work on the batteries would not be continued, and the latter disclaimed on the part of his government any designs on Spanish territory, and promised British military and naval assistance to Spain in the defence of her coasts in the vicinity of Gibraltar.[126] This helped to ease British fears with regard to the role that Spain might play in the event of a conflict between Britain and France. Five years later the British tried to guard themselves against French acquisition of the coast opposite Gibraltar by backing Spanish claims to the reversion of the northern littoral of Morocco. However, neither the exchange of notes of 1899, nor the Franco-Spanish accord on Morocco of October 1904, offered any guarantee against either a future combination between France and Spain, or in the event of a

---

[124] Balfour to Edward VII, 8 June 1905 CAB 41/30/21 (P.R.O.).
[125] R.G. Neale, *Britain and American Imperialism, 1898–1900* (Brisbane, 1965), pp.58–74. C.H.D.Howard, *Britain and the Casus Belli, 1822–1902* (London, 1974), pp.115–16. Balfour to Salisbury, 30 Aug. 1898; Salisbury to Balfour, 31 Aug. 1898; Balfour MSS., Add. MS. 49691. Salisbury to Drummond Wolff, 6 Aug 1898, F.O.72/2100, despt.194. Drummond Wolff to Balfour, 31 Aug. 1898, F.O.72/2100, tel.388. Drummond Wolff to Balfour, 14 Sept. 1898, F.O.72/2099.
[126] Drummond Wolff to Salisbury, 4 Feb. and 17 March 1899, F.O.425/242, despts.21 and 64.

war between them, a cession by Spain of any of her actual or prospective territories to another country.[127] Moreover, the expansion of the German navy, and Germany's purchase of the Caroline and Mariana islands from Spain awakened British fears about possible German designs upon Spain's other overseas possessions.

With a view to acquiring additional security for Britain's maritime interests Sanderson had in January 1905 suggested to Nicolson, who was about to take up his new post at Madrid, that there might be advantage in obtaining from Spain a promise not to alienate to any other power a portion of its promised sphere of influence in Morocco.[128] Nicolson had considered it 'more prudent to feel the way' before broaching a secret convention.[129] But the potential advantage of some kind of arrangement with Spain was given a new poignancy by reports which reached the Foreign Office at the beginning of May that a German syndicate was negotiating with a Spanish merchant from the Canaries for a coaling depot there.[130] Besides which, the efforts of the German ambassador at Madrid to dissuade the Spanish government from despatching its minister at Tangier to Fez appeared in Bertie's eyes to provide Britain with the occasion to retake the initiative with Spain. He had long considered it possible that Germany might seek to acquire coaling facilities or a naval station in Spain's insular possessions, and in a letter of 12 May he asked Lansdowne if the government could not 'take advantage of the menacing attitude of Germany towards Spain in order to offer to assist Spain in meeting any attack on the Balearic Isles, the Canaries and Fernando Po', in return for Spanish assurances on the future safety of Gibraltar. He suggested that the government might declare to Spain that it had no territorial desires for any of the Spanish mainland or islands, and that if she would undertake not to 'cede, sell, let or otherwise alienate in whole or part any of her islands, or allow them to be used by a foreign power as coaling stations or depots', Britain would assist her in defending them. The Spaniards, he thought, should promise that 'no works or gun emplacements' should be 'created or laid down that would affect the safety of Gibraltar, its works, harbour or anchorage'. He was well aware that in other circumstances the French could have been expected to

---

[127] Mcgeoch.
[128] Nicolson to Sanderson, 4 Feb. 1905, Nicolson MSS., F.O.800/337. Sanderson to Nicolson, 15 Feb. 1905, Nicolson MSS., F.O.800/336.
[129] Nicolson to Sanderson, 25 Feb. 1905, Nicolson MSS., F.O.800/337.
[130] Lansdowne to Nicolson, 2 May 1905, F.O.185/994, tel.22P. Nicolson to Lansdowne, 5 May 1905, F.O.72/2209, despt.86.

oppose such an exclusive arrangement between Britain and Spain, but, he contended, they could not at the moment feel it to be aimed at them.[131]

The opportunity for Lansdowne to raise this matter with the Spanish government was presented by the visit to London in June of the young King of Spain, Alfonso XIII, and his minister of state, de Villa-Urrutia. In a conversation with the latter Lansdowne put to him a proposal for an Anglo-Spanish agreement which was broadly similar to that which Bertie had recommended.[132] But Bertie had little sympathy with the manner in which the project was thereafter handled. Even at this stage obtaining new pledges on Gibraltar from Spain appears to have been for Bertie essentially a pretext for an arrangement whose main purpose would be to 'keep out from Spanish Islands Germans whether as possessors or concession holders'.[133] Nevertheless, he did not lose sight of the fact that the interests of the two *entente* powers in the Mediterranean were far from identical, and that Britain might one day have to defend Spain's territories against the French. When, therefore, he learned that Nicolson had suggested that he might inform Jules Cambon of the proposed agreement, Bertie immediately protested to the Foreign Office. 'Security for Gibraltar', he claimed, 'is not a *permanent* French interest and its protection from danger on the land side might not always suit the policy of France.' He thought that if the French were informed of the British project they would, if they objected, try to persuade the Spanish not to accept it in its entirety. Besides which, he reasoned that if the Germans were to learn of the scheme they would have another grievance against England and France for it would appear to be aimed at excluding them from the Spanish islands. Much to Bertie's annoyance, Lansdowne was unable to restrain Nicolson from communicating the British proposals to his French colleague.[134] A change of government at Madrid was, however, to inhibit any further progress towards an understanding, and another thirteen months were to pass before the project was revived in somewhat different circumstances.

---

[131] Nicolson to Lansdowne, 6 April and 5 May 1905, F.O.72/2209, despts. 58 and 85. *B.D.*, III, no.87. Lansdowne to Bertie, 8 May 1905, F.O.27/3703, despt.279. Bertie to Lansdowne, 12 May 1905, B.P., A, F.O.800/179.
[132] Lansdowne to Nicolson, 3 June 1905, Nicolson MSS., F.O.800/336. *B.D.*, VII, no.1.
[133] Bertie to Hardinge, 23 Nov. 1905, B.P., A, F.O.800/179.
[134] Nicolson to Lansdowne, 4 July 1905, F.O.72/2211, tel.49. Bertie to Lansdowne, 8 July 1905; Barrington to Bertie, 11 July 1905; B.P., A, F.O.800/179. Bertie to Barrington, 13 July 1905, Lansdowne MSS., F.O.800/127. J. Cambon to Rouvier, 6 July 1905, N.S. Espagne 40, despt.110.

While Bertie busied himself with projects to shore up the *status quo* against supposed German designs upon the Spanish islands, Radolin continued to insist on the need to defend the *status quo* against manifest French ambitions in Morocco. Rouvier had hoped that Delcassé's resignation would leave the way open to a Franco-German agreement on Morocco, but the German government had already committed itself to an international solution, and to Rouvier's dismay Radolin required France's acceptance of the sultan's invitation to a conference.[135] Bülow was similarly disappointed by Rouvier's insistance on a preliminary arrangement on what was to be settled at such a gathering. On 14 June Radolin indicated to Rouvier that Germany would be prepared to take into account France's wishes with regard to the future administration of Morocco, but the Germans continued to insist that there could be no *pourparlers* until the French accepted the idea of a conference.[136] In this situation war was increasingly regarded as a possible outcome of the crisis, and Paul Cambon, fearing lest his countrymen be stampeded into an agreement with Germany, scurried back and forth between London and Paris in an effort to ensure that Rouvier stand firm.[137]

For his part Bertie remained convinced that the Germans were bluffing.[138] He was not, however, aware of how the conversations between Rouvier and Radolin were progressing, and it was perhaps this combination of optimism and ignorance that led him to propose to Lansdowne on 20 June that the applicability of article xvii (the most favoured nation provision) of the Madrid convention, upon which the Germans based their demand for an international conference, should be submitted to arbitration. Moreover, without his having received any instructions on the matter, he also mentioned to Rouvier the possibility of taking the question to the International Court of Justice at the Hague. This course, he argued, would not settle the Franco-German quarrel, but if arbitration were to declare the article's non-applicability to the present dispute, 'the German Emperor need no longer insist on a conference as a point of dignity, and the two governments could negotiate without other parties being drawn into the question'.[139] Although Bertie was probably correct in

---

[135] Combarieu, p.317. Paléologue, *Turning Point*, pp.271 – 2. *G.P.*, X, pt.2, nos.6694, 6700, 6702, 6705 and 6710. *B.D.*, III, no.52.
[136] *D.D.F.2*, VII, nos.54, 55 and 71.
[137] Paléologue, *Turning Point*, pp.272 – 5. H. Cambon, II, 197 – 204. Chirol to Hardinge, 26 June 1905; Bertie to Hardinge, 25 July 1905; Hardinge MSS., 7.
[138] Bertie to Lansdowne, 15 June 1905, B.P., A, F.O.800/170.
[139] Parsons, pp.63 – 86. Bertie to Lansdowne, 14 June 1905, F.O.99/434, tel.114. Bertie to Lansdowne, 20 June 1905, Lansdowne MSS., F.O.800/127. *B.D.*, III, no.116. *D.D.F.2*, VII, no.102.

assuming that the German demand for a conference was largely a matter of saving face, neither in London nor in Paris did he find any support for his idea. Sanderson not only doubted if the Germans would accept this course, but thought that the result of arbitration would 'not probably be what Bertie anticipated unless the terms of reference worded the question in a very restricted manner'. And to Cambon Lansdowne indicated that the French need not bother with a reply. Bertie's suggestion, he said, was 'intempestive', and he felt it wrong to complicate the conversations with Germany with useless legal discussion.[140]

In the meanwhile on 21 June Rouvier delivered a note to Radolin in which he reiterated the French desire to know Germany's views on the precise points to be discussed at a conference, and the solution which she foresaw.[141] This refusal on the part of Rouvier to accept unconditionally a conference was with some justice attributed by Bülow and Radolin to pressure put upon Rouvier by those officials who had been closest to Delcassé. They were also inclined to blame the British government and its representatives for aggravating the situation. A report had reached Berlin from Paris that Britain had offered a defensive and offensive alliance to France, and at the end of June stories began to circulate about a row between Bertie and Radolin.[142] This was supposed to have taken place at a party given by the Prince de Murat on 23 June. In a despatch which Bertie wrote to Lansdowne on the 24th he merely stated that during a conversation with Radolin he had said to the German ambassador that 'unless some settlement were arrived at beforehand, a conference would be likely to complicate matters'.[143] Other accounts, however, indicated that Bertie had, in the presence of the Crown Prince of Greece, chosen to remonstrate with Radolin on Germany's recent conduct, and that in an excited tone of voice he had maintained that France could not and must not accept a conference.[144] Indeed, some six

---

[140] Minute by Sanderson on Bertie to Lansdowne, 20 June 1905, *ibid. D.D.F.2*, VII, no.108.
[141] *G.P.*, XX, pt.2, no.6720.
[142] *Ibid*, nos.6708, 6710, 6723, 6724, 6726 and 6853. *D.D.F.2*, VII, no.69. N. Rich and M.H. Fischer (eds.), *The Holstein Papers* (4 vols., Cambridge, 1963), IV, 345–6. Rich, II, 710–11. Paléologue, *Turning Point*, pp.263–4 and 272–3.
[143] Bertie to Lansdowne, 24 June 1905, F.O.99/434, despt.228.
[144] There appears to be some discrepancy amongst those who recorded Bertie's conversation about the date upon which it took place. But if Bertie's reports are correct the only party which he attended at the Prince de Murat's during this period was on 23 June. Prince Albert of Monaco to Reinach, 26 June 1905, tel. and letter Reinach MSS. (Bibliothèque Nationale, Paris), N.A.Fr. 13550. R. Whyte (ed.), *Letters of Prince von Bülow* (London, 1930), p.139. De Stuers, the Dutch minister at Paris, reported that Bertie had introduced hiself to von Radolin with the words ' "Why the devil do you

months later William II told the financier, Alfred Beit, that Bertie's language had been so bad 'that Prince Radolin would have been justified in challenging him to a duel'.[145]

Some exaggeration must be allowed for on the emperor's part. But available evidence suggests that Bertie had addressed himself to Radolin in terms that were a good deal less guarded than those which he reported to Lansdowne.[146] Not that the German ambassador, who, according to Bülow, had chosen to ignore Bertie's remarks, appears to have borne any personal grudge against him.[147] Radolin had, however, by then come to accept that Bertie was no friend of Germany. On 29 June Radolin informed Holstein that Paul Cambon was doing everything he could to prevent the conclusion of a Franco-German accord, and that Bertie was going to London to act in a similar sense.[148] From Jean Dupuy, a former minister who had acted as an intermediary between Rouvier and the German embassy, he had also learnt that Bertie was endeavouring to bring about an Anglo-French alliance.[149] And although Holstein did not believe this, he did think that Bertie and possibly Lansdowne would like to see a war between France and Germany from which England would draw profit.[150] This was a mistaken judgement, for much as Bertie saw advantage for Britain in continuing friction between France and Germany, he did nothing to encourage the French to resort to arms. A report which had appeared in the nationalist newpaper, *La Patrie*, that Bertie had tried to persuade Rouvier to resist German demands by making known to him that the British government could transfer to the continent 250,000 soldiers during the first month of war and 500,000 within six months, was pure fabrication.[151] Bertie does appear, however, to have been less than cautious in the language which he employed, and there was probably some truth in the obtuse claim of his private secretary at Paris,

---

want to go to that conference"?' C. Smit(ed.), *Bescheiden Betreffende Buitenlandse Politiek van Nederland*, 3rd. period, vol. II (The Hague, 1958), no.459.

[145] M.V. Brett and Oliver, Viscount Esher (eds.), *Journal and Letters of Reginald Viscount Esher* (4 vols., London, 1934 – 8), II, 138. Beit to Grey, 29 Dec. 1905, Lascelles MSS., F.O.800/13.

[146] Lascelles to Lansdowne, 3 Aug. and 27 Oct. 1905, Lascelles MSS., F.O.800/18.

[147] Lascelles to Grey, 6 Sept. 1906, F.O.371/79, despt.273. Lascelles to Grey, 11 April 1907, Lascelles MSS., F.O.800/19.

[148] *G.P.*, XX, pt.2, no.6751.

[149] *G.P.*, XX, pt.2, no.6752.

[150] Rich and Fischer, IV, 348.

[151] The article also asserted that the ambassador knew what he had said was untrue, but that he had lied 'par ordre et avec affronterie'. Extract from *La Patrie* enclosed in Bertie to Barrington, 25 June 1905, Lansdowne MSS., F.O.800/127.

Wilfrid Athelstan Johnson, that Bertie was 'quite as pacific' as the German emperor.[152]

Talk about a British offer of an alliance to France probably had its origins in Cambon's accounts of Lansdowne's earlier attempts to explain the British government's position and his wish for consultations. Garbled reports of these exchanges may have emanated from the Quai d'Orsay, an institution which according to Athelstan Johnson had 'been chattering as usual like a monkey house', and have thereby served to increase the misapprehension of those in France who feared lest they be pushed into a war with Germany[153] Yet within the British embassy the idea of a broader Anglo-French agreement did find an advocate in Lister. Whilst Bertie was absent from Paris at the end of June he wrote privately to Lansdowne of French fears that even after the settlement of the Moroccan question the Germans might continue to threaten them, and of their concern about how far Britain would be prepared to support them against Germany 'in the event of the point at issue being one not so closely connected with the Anglo-French Agreement'. It might, he concluded, be in British and French interests for Britain to make some declaration extending the scope of the existing understanding. The only doubt in Lister's mind concerned the timing of such a proposal and whether or not it might in the present circumstances be embarrassing to the French government.[154] But Lansdowne was in no mood to sanction a fresh approach to France. Although he admitted that a 'good deal of thought' had been given to this matter, the French had not yet given any hint of what aid they might want against Germany, and the moment was in his opinion not opportune for suggesting an extension of the *entente* to the cabinet and the country. 'Recent events', he explained to Lister, 'have undoubtedly shaken people's confidence in the steadfastness of the French nation.'[155]

The diplomatic support which Lansdowne continued to give to France, the probability that she would have on her side a majority of the powers, and the readiness of the Germans to concede that France had a special interest in the maintenance of order in Morocco, finally

---

[152] Athelstan Johnson to Bertie, 29 June 1905, B.P., A, F.O.800/170. W. Athelstan Johnson was appointed honorary *attaché* at Paris on 2 January 1905, and he was employed there as Bertie's private secretary until 14 January 1909. He returned to Paris as a temporary secretary in May 1916.
[153] *Ibid. G.P.*, XX, pt.2, no.6853. *B.D.*, III, nos.97, 98, 101, 102 and 103.
[154] Lister to Lansdowne, 30 June and 3 July 1905, Lansdowne MSS., F.O.800/127.
[155] Lansdowne to Lister, 10 July 1905, Lansdowne MSS., F.O.800/127.

allowed the French government to drop its objections to a conference.[156] An exchange of notes between Rouvier and Radolin on 8 July thus established that France and Germany would settle the agenda for the projected international gathering. This provided the basis for further squabbling between Paris and Berlin, and it was 28 September before agreement was finally reached. Nevertheless, Bülow was encouraged by a meeting of the German and Russian emperors at Björkö in July to think once more in terms of a continental coalition embracing France and Russia.[157] By then, however, Bertie felt confident that the French would not willingly sacrifice their understanding with England for the sake of some other combination. William II's 'evident fear of the Anglo-French Entente has', he wrote to Hardinge on 25 July, 'opened their eyes to its importance & its protective force for France and has . . . shown our loyalty to France'. During conversations which he had with Betzold on 30 July, and Radolin on the 31st, Bertie also placed the blame for the poor state of Anglo-German relations upon the architects of Germany's naval policy.[158]

Superficial though Bertie's comments upon the German navy were, they were taken in Berlin as evidence of his continuing hostility towards Germany. This may in part have been due to a misinterpretation of what he had actually said, According, for instance, to Bertie's own account, he had told Betzold that in a war with Germany Britain might act as she had done against France at the time of Napoleon.[159] But in a letter to Bülow of 10 August Otto von Mühlberg, an under-secretary at the Wilhelmstrasse, reported that Bertie had, amongst other violent invectives against Germany, warned Betzold that at Berlin they seemed to nourish Napoleonic tendencies and that Britain must counter them as before.[160] German officals would have had an additional reason for complaint if they had known of the efforts made by Bertie in early August to dissuade King Edward from including any visit to the Emperor William in the holiday which he was planning to take at Marienbad. Such a meeting had been mentioned in the German press, and Bertie took advantage of the celebrations in connexion with the visit of a French naval squadron to Cowes to impress upon the king that it would be

---

[156] *B.D.*, III, nos.146, 147, 150 and 152. *D.D.F.2*, VII, no.209. Rich, II, 712–13.
[157] Rich, II, 714–29. On the prospects for a Russo-German agreement in the summer of 1905 see; Beryl Williams, 'The Revolution of 1905 and Russian Foreign Policy', in C. Abramsky (ed.), *Essays in Honour of E.H. Carr* (London, 1974), pp.101–18.
[158] Bertie to Hardinge, 25 Sept. 1905, B.P., A, F.O.800/163.
[159] Bertie to Lansdowne, 31 July and 1 Aug. 1905, F.O.27/3705, despts.285 and 286.
[160] *G.P.*, XX, pt.2, no.6236.

regarded in France as a *léger oubli* of Britain's obligations.¹⁶¹ The king appears to have heeded Bertie's advice for he eventually decided against a visit to the emperor, and to Lansdowne's distress the outcome was a personal quarrel between the two monarchs that did nothing to ease the troubled course of Anglo-German relations.¹⁶² Bertie, in the meanwhile, took himself off to Boulogne, where, much to the irritation of those responsible for distributing the Foreign Office print, he remained until the early autumn.¹⁶³

The events of the previous six months had seemed to confirm Bertie in the assumptions which he had previously made with regard both to Germany's intentions and to the courses which British policy-makers ought to pursue. Germany's intervention in Morocco had in his eyes been a manifestation of her imperial designs. But, in so far as it had also been a challenge to the Anglo-French *entente*, it had seemed to emphasize the significance and value of that relationship to Britain.¹⁶⁴ Moreover, the reestablishment of peace in the Far East had raised the prospect of Britain being able to further limit Germany's room for diplomatic manoeuvre through an understanding with Russia. Japan's victories had checked Russian expansion and the conclusion of a new treaty of alliance between Britain and Japan had appeared to strengthen Britain's position in Asia.¹⁶⁵ This led Bertie to look with more sympathy upon the idea of an Anglo-Russian *rapprochement*. 'If it could be effected', he observed to Hardinge, 'German Bill might amuse himself as much as he liked within his own German circle, he could hurt nobody.' For Bertie this was not as yet a matter of restoring any theoretical balance of power in Europe. It was, however, a means of denying to the Germans the opportunities that they had once known for taking advantage of Anglo-Russian rivalry in Asia.¹⁶⁶

By the end of September Bertie believed that the French had 'regained their equanimity and courage'.¹⁶⁷ But the survival of the *entente cordiale* had been due much less to Bertie's diplomacy, than to the misjudgement of Bülow and Holstein. Nothing had come of either

---

¹⁶¹ *D.D.F.*, VII, no330.
¹⁶² Knollys to Lascelles, 8 and 14 Aug. 1905; Lansdowne to Lascelles, 12 Sept. 1905; Lascelles MSS., F.O.800/12. Lansdowne to Lascelles, 25 Sept. 1905, Lansdowne MSS., F.O.800/130. Lansdowne to Balfour, 23 Aug.1905, Balfour MSS., Add. MS. 49729.
¹⁶³ Bertie to Hardinge, 27 Aug. 1905, Hardinge MSS., 7. Sanderson to Bertie, 19 Sept. 1905, B.P. B, F.O.800/184.
¹⁶⁴ Bertie to Hardinge, 25 July 1905, Hardinge MSS., 7.
¹⁶⁵ Nish, *The Anglo-Japanese Alliance*, pp.298 – 344.
¹⁶⁶ Bertie to Hardinge, 25 Sept. 1905, B.P., A, F.O.800/163.
¹⁶⁷ *Ibid.*

Bertie's or Lister's suggestions for extending the scope of the *entente*. Such encouragement as Lansdowne had offered to the French to think in terms of a closer relationship with Britain had probably only helped to nurture the false impression that he was seeking an alliance. Moreover, after Delcassé's resignation Bertie had not succeeded in fully reassuring Lansdowne that Britain could rely upon the steadfastness of the French. Nor in the first instance had he been able to counter the view held by Rouvier and other Frenchmen that the *entente* with England had exposed France to the menace of war with Germany without providing her with any corresponding advantage or protection. Indeed, in a letter of 14 June to the manager of *The Times*, its correspondent in Paris expressed his regret that 'we have not an active, popular, and well informed Ambassador here just now'.[168] Had the Germans at that stage acted in a less maladroit fashion, and had they put aside their demand for a conference and been prepared to negotiate a bilateral accord with Rouvier, the alignment of the European powers might have been very different in the autumm of 1905. Lansdowne himself admitted in August that Germany had had 'a very fine opportunity if she had known how to use it for driving a wedge into the entente'.[169] As it was, the *entente* remained in tact. Yet, as Bertie was quite aware, its future would depend upon the attitude assumed by Lansdowne's successor, and the outcome of the forthcoming international conference on Morocco.

---

[168] Lavino to Bell, 14 June 1905, Lavino MSS. (*The Times* archives).
[169] Lansdowne to Lister, 29 Aug. 1905, Lansdowne MSS., F.O.800/127.

5

New masters and old diplomacy

The collapse of the Conservative government in December 1905 came as no great surprise to Bertie and his colleagues. Ever since the spring of 1903, when Joseph Chamberlain had pronounced himself publicly in favour of tariff reform and imperial preference, they had had cause to speculate about the outcome of the rift within the Unionist ranks in parliament and the likely impact of a Liberal administration upon the conduct of British foreign policy.[1] The prospect was not a pleasing one, especially as it seemed possible that the Foreign Office might fall into inexperienced hands, and that a radical government might be prepared to abandon the alliance with Japan and the *entente* with France. This in their eyes made it all the more urgent to find as a successor to Sanderson someone 'to keep the Liberals straight'. 'What an awful combination Lamps and Campbell-Bannerman', Mallet had exclaimed on learning in January 1905 that the Liberal leader might take the Foreign Office.[2] Yet in Bertie's opinion there could be no question as to who should be the next permanent under-secretary. Contemptuous of Francis Villiers, whom Sanderson had hoped to make his heir, Bertie had long backed Hardinge as his candidate for the post. And when in July 1905 it seemed probable that Hardinge would be offered the appointment, Bertie intervened with his cousin in order to urge him to put aside his fears about the financial problems in which his acceptance might involve him.[3] Hardinge finally followed Bertie's advice. He had in any case already realized 'that the only way to get on in the service was to disregard material advantages and to seek only for power', and with some encouragement from the king he agreed in October to return to London[4]

---

[1] Mallet to Bertie, (?) Oct. 1905, B.P. B, F.O.800/183.
[2] Mallet to Bertie, 27 Jan. 1905, B.P., A, F.O.800/174. Zara Steiner, *Britain and the Origins of the First World War* (London, 1977), p.179.
[3] Bertie to Hardinge, 5 and 25 July 1905, Hardinge MSS., 7. Hardinge to Bertie, 16 July 1905, B.P., A, F.O.800/163. Hardinge to Bertie, 21 July 1905; Mallet to Bertie, (?) Oct. 1905; B.P. B, F.O.800/183.
[4] Hardinge, *Old Diplomacy* pp.118 – 19. Busch, *Hardinge*, pp.93 – 7.

By the time that Hardinge took up his new appointment in February 1906 the Liberal administration of Sir Henry Campbell-Bannerman had been in office for more than six weeks. Moreover, much to the relief of Mallet and the satisfaction of Bertie, Campbell-Bannerman had chosen Sir Edward Grey as his foreign secretary.[5] A former parliamentary under-secretary at the Foreign Office, and one of that band of Liberal imperialists who had supported the war in South Africa, Grey had a view of Britain's foreign relations which was not far removed from that of Bertie. By 1903 he had concluded 'that Germany is our worst enemy & greatest danger', and he had sympathized with Lansdowne's efforts to renew the Anglo-Japanese alliance.[6] But of more immediate significance to Bertie was the fact that Grey seemed likely to reassure the French of Britain's continuing friendship and support. The press and government circles in France had, he informed the new foreign secretary, feared the appointment of a minister with German leanings, and were pleased to have one who had 'made a speech favourable to France'.[7]

The speech to which Bertie referred had been delivered by Grey to the electors of the City of London on 20 October. In it he had outlined the basis of the foreign policy of a future Liberal government: the alliance with Japan, friendship with the United States, and the understanding with France. At the same time he had spoken of his hopes for an improvement in relations with Russia, and also with Germany, so long as this was not at the expense of good relations with France.[8] The address helped to reassure Paul Cambon that the *entente* would survive a change of government in England, and in a letter to Rouvier of 12 December he pointed out that while the Liberals were traditionally inclined towards Germany, they were above all pacifists and would therefore give their approbation to the *entente* as a guarantee of peace.[9] Nevertheless, Cambon had his doubts about the attitude of some of Grey's colleagues, and the possibility

---

[5] Mallet to Spring Rice, 17 Oct., 28 Nov., and 12 Dec. 1905, Spring Rice MSS., CASR 1/49. Mallet to Bertie, 5 Dec. 1905; Bertie to Knollys, 5 Dec. 1905; B.P. (British Library), Mallet to Nicolson, 21 Dec. 1905, Nicolson MSS., F.O.800/336.
[6] H.C.G. Matthew, *The Liberal Imperialists. The ideas and politics of a post-Gladstonian élite* (Oxford, 1973), especially pp.203 – 10. Keith Robbins, *Sir Edward Grey. A biography of Lord Grey of Fallodon* (London, 1971), pp.128 – 32.
[7] Bertie to Grey, 12 Dec. 1905, B.P., A, F.O.800/164.
[8] Robbins, p.133. *D.D.F.2*, VIII, no.79. In making the speech Grey had been anxious to combat the view that a Liberal government would unsettle the *entente* with France in order to improve relations with Germany. Grey to Spender, 19 Oct. 1905, Spender MSS. (British Library), Add. MS. 46389. See also: K.M. Wilson, *The Policy of the Entente. Essays on the Determinants of British Foreign Policy, 1904 – 1914* (Cambridge, 1984), pp.17 – 23.
[9] *D.D.F.2*, VIII, no.219.

that the prime minister might make a bid for the Irish vote and thereby alienate the Liberal imperialists had seemed to worry him.[10] Even at the end of January 1906 Bertie was still having to reassure Rouvier about the security of Grey's position.[11]

The general theme of Grey's pronouncement of 20 October had been to emphasize his endorsement of the broad lines of Lansdowne's foreign policy. But Grey was more inclined than his predecessor to regard the *entente* as a fundamental and permanent element in Britain's relations with the continental powers. In this he differed from Bertie for whom close relations with France always remained essentially a matter of political expediency. Moreover, Bertie could hardly have countenanced the degree of equanimity with which Grey at first appeared to be ready to view the expansion of the German navy. Certainly he would not have agreed with the opinion expressed by Grey in a letter to Lascelles of 1 January that if only Britain could be sure that the Germans did not regard her public engagements as incompatible with their interests, and if they would believe that Britain did not mean badly to them, 'recent friction would disappear'.[12] The poor state of Anglo-German relations could not in Bertie's estimate be divorced from what he assumed to be the threat posed by Germany's might and global ambitions to the security of the British empire. He frowned upon any notion of encouraging the French to give way to German demands in Morocco both because he feared that Britain would risk sacrificing the favourable position that she had achieved as a result of the *entente*, and because he anticipated that Germany's imperial and naval power would thereby be enhanced. The new foreign secretary was, however, prepared to seek the advice of his officials, and the replacement of Sanderson by Hardinge, and the appointment of Mallet as Grey's private secretary, helped to create in the Foreign Office a climate of opinion which was more receptive to Bertie's views.[13]

The forthcoming conference on Morocco, which was due to assemble at the Spanish port of Algeciras, heightened Grey's interest

---

[10] *Ibid.* no.196.
[11] Bertie to Knollys, 31 Jan. 1906, B.P., A, F.O.800/174.
[12] Grey to Lascelles. 1 Jan. 1906, Lascelles MSS., F.O.800/8. Such was Grey's personal attachment to the *entente* that after only nine months in office he wrote to his friend and colleague, R.B. Haldane, 'I want to preserve the entente, but it isn't easy, and if it is broken up I must go.' Grey to Haldane, 7 Sept. 1906, Haldane MSS. (National Library of Scotland), 5907. A year later he noted: 'Good relations with other countries must still be dependent upon the maintenance in letter and spirit of our agreement with France'. Grey to Rowland, 1 Sept. 1907, Grey MSS., F.O.800/110.
[13] In the following year Mallet succeeded Eldon Gorst as an assistant under-secretary, and his place as Grey's private secretary was taken by William Tyrrell. According to

in the future of the *entente*. Determined to support France within the terms of the 1904 agreement, he, like Lansdowne, sought from the French full information about their aims and intentions.[14] At the same time Paul Cambon, who was still under the impression that in the previous spring Lansdowne had wanted closer ties with France, tried to regain the opportunity that he thought his government had missed. Rouvier continued to regard an English alliance as a risky business.[15] Nevertheless, neither he nor Grey could afford to neglect the possibility of Britain and France finding themselves engaged in a war with Germany. On 3 January Grey warned Metternich that if Germany forced a war on France 'public feeling in England would be so strong that it would be impossible to be neutral'.[16] Some five days later he counselled Haldane, the secretary of state for war, that 'popular feeling' might compel the government to aid France, and that he, Haldane, might suddenly be asked what he could do.[17] It was with a view to easing the problems that might arise in such a situation that Sir George Clarke, the secretary of the Committee of Imperial Defence (C.I.D.), had already established contact with Major Huguet, the French military *attaché* in London.[18] Grey, who saw Clarke on 9 January, accepted that it would be impossible to approach the French through official channels to ascertain their views on cooperation 'as this would give the idea of an offensive and defensive alliance which does not exist'.[19] When, however, on the next day Cambon suggested to him that unofficial military and naval communications should continue, Grey 'did not dissent'.[20]

Bertie had no part in these first tentative discussions about joint contingency planning. Indeed, he probably had no knowledge of them until he received from Grey an account of his interview with

---

Lister, Hardinge intended Mallet to be trained as his successor as permanent undersecretary. Lister to Bertie, 12 Dec. 1905, B.P., A, F.O.800/163.
[14] *B.D.*, III, nos.200 and 204. Grey to Bertie, 13 Dec. 1905, B.P., A, F.O.800/164. Grey to Bertie, 21 Dec. 1905, B.P. Add. MS. 63018. Grey to Nicolson, 13 Dec 1905, Grey MSS., F.O.800/37. Grey to Lascelles, 16 Jan. 1906, Grey MSS., F.O.800/61.
[15] *D.D.F.2*, VIII, nos.262 and 265.
[16] *B.D.*, III, no.229.
[17] D. Sommer, *Haldane of Cloan. His Life and Times, 1856-1928* (London, 1960), p.159.
[18] The opening of the Anglo-French military conversations is considered in detail in S.R. Williamson, *The Politics of Grand Strategy. Britain and France Prepare for War, 1904-1914* (Cambridge. Mass., 1969), pp.59-98; and in Monger, pp.236-56. The significance of the conversations for British defence policy is discussed in N. d'Ombrain, *War Machinery and High Policy. Defence Administration in Peacetime Britain, 1902-1914* (London, 1973), pp.81-90; and in J. Gooch, *The Plans of War. The General Staff and British Military Strategy, c.1900-1916* (London, 1974), pp.280-2.
[19] Monger, p.248.
[20] *B.D.*, III, nos.210 and 212.

Paul Cambon of 10 January. On that day Cambon, who had recently talked over the matter with Rouvier, also put to Grey the 'great question' as to whether in the event of German aggression against France 'Great Britain would be prepared to render to France armed assistance'? Grey was upset at being asked this. With a general election impending and the cabinet dispersed, he told Cambon that he felt unable 'to pledge the country to more than neutrality — a benevolent neutrality if such a thing existed'. Nevertheless, he did express his personal opinion that if Germany attacked France in consequence of a question arising from the 1904 agreement, 'public opinion in England would be strongly moved in favour of France'. This answer did not satisfy Cambon who promised to repeat the question after the elections.[21] Nor did it meet with the approval of Mallet, who was convinced that for the sake of preserving the balance of power in Europe it was Britain's 'duty now to lead a peaceful & defensive coalition agst. Germany'.[22] He had already informed the French *chargé d'affaires* of Grey's warning to Metternich of 3 January, and on the 11th he wrote to Bertie to implore his assistance. 'There is', he observed, 'of course only one possible answer and that is that if aggression arises out of the Entente with us and we are given an equal voice with the French in the negotiations which result in the attack, we will take our share in the fighting.' Mallet thought that no risk would be involved in giving such an undertaking as there 'would certainly be no war and we stand to gain heavily in France and everywhere by pursuing a logical course'. But, he cautioned Bertie, 'if we refuse . . . we lose at once all the Entente had given us — be looked upon as traitors by the French and needs be despised by the Germans'. Finally, he requested Bertie to write a 'very strong personal letter to Grey', and to 'prime C. Hardinge', who must 'supposing he agrees, do everything he can to buck up these miserable creatures'.[23]

Before Bertie could fulfil this request he learned of Holstein's latest prediction to Lascelles that if the conference were to fail, the French, relying upon British support, would attempt to create a *fait accompli* by

---

[21] *B.D.*, III, nos.210 and 216. Mallet to Bertie, 11 Jan. B.P., A, F.O.800/164. *D.D.F.2*, VIII, no.385.
[22] Three months later Mallet wrote to Spring Rice of relations with France: 'I shall never be a happy until we have a defensive alliance with that country.' Mallet to Spring Rice, 23 Jan. and 2 May 1906, Spring Rice MSS., CASR 1/49.
[23] Mallet to Bertie, 11 Jan. 1906, B.P., A, F.O.800/164. Mallet also told the French *chargé d'affaires* that in his opinion it would not be necessary for the Liberal cabinet to submit to public opinion in order to march with France. Geoffray to Rouvier, 7 Jan. 1906, N.S. Grande-Bretagne 20, tel.10.

invading Morocco.[24] It was a contention that Bertie thought necessary to refute. In a despatch of 13 January he insisted on the peaceful intentions of the French, and he suggested that the Germans might themselves attempt to promote an incident on the borders of Morocco in order to have an excuse for resorting to 'extreme measures'. If the French were forced to take defensive action against a Moorish tribe, and Germany treated this as provocation, then Bertie concluded, 'it would only mean that she was seeking a pretext for a war'. This rather jaundiced interpretation of German diplomacy overlooked the degree to which the Wilhelmstrasse may have been genuinely concerned lest the French, emboldened by British assurances of friendship and support, should prove unamenable to argument at the conference. Bertie wished, however, to dispel any idea that a pledge of British assistance would lead the French to adopt a more aggressive attitude. The French, he pointed out, were already confident that England would for her own sake give France armed support in a Franco-German war. He contended that it was felt in France that if diplomacy failed to remove German opposition in Morocco, the natural sequence would be that France would receive from her partner 'more than the diplomatic support that had proved insufficient for the purpose of the agreement'. If Grey could not ensure them of this, there would, Bertie thought, be a 'serious danger of a complete revulsion of feeling on the part of the French Government and public opinion in France'.[25]

Bertie also thought the moment right to warn Grey that if he were not prepared to go beyond the assurances that he had offered to Paul Cambon, the French might, in order to secure their objectives in Morocco, make concessions there which would be inimical to British interests.[26] It is doubtful, however, whether this argument could have carried much weight with Grey. Anxious though he was that British interests in Morocco should not he ignored, he was not overwhelmingly opposed to Germany making gains there or elsewhere. He was prepared to give sympathetic consideration to the German acquisition of a port on Morocco's Atlantic coast, and he doubted if it were important for Britain to prevent Germany from obtaining coaling stations. The moment might come, he informed the prime minister, 'when a timely admission that it is not a cardinal object of Britain's policy to prevent her having such a port may be of great value'.[27]

[24] *B.D.*, III, no.241.
[25] *B.D.*, III, no.213.
[26] *Ibid.*
[27] G.M. Trevelyan, *Grey of Fallodon, being the life of Sir Edward Grey, afterwards Viscount Grey of Fallodon* (London, 1937), pp.117 – 18.

What probably mattered more to Grey was the avoidance of a military conflict in Europe, and it was upon this point that Eyre Crowe, who was still at this time a clerk in the newly-founded registry, concentrated his attention. In a minute on Bertie's despatch, he claimed that the dominant factor in the situation was whether Germany was in a position at the moment to go to war with Britain and France. 'If she is not', he concluded, 'but is not, on the other hand disinclined to try conclusions with France alone, then clearly a promise of armed assistance from this country would be the means to preserve peace'.[28]

Bertie's despatch did not in fact reach the foreign secretary until 18 January, and by then Grey had already written to Bertie to ask for his advice. His own views, Grey claimed, were 'still in solution'. And although he rejected the notion of giving France a promise in advance committing Britain to participation in a continental war, for that would transform the *entente* into an alliance, he did state the sort of terms that Britain would require if such a pledge were offered.[29] This and Grey's assent to the military conversations, the purpose of which was to provide the British government with the option, if it so decided, of sending an army to the continent, may have encouraged Bertie to think that Paul Cambon might yet obtain the assurances he wanted. He was in any case able to tell Cambon of the contents of his despatch of 13 January when a few days later the two ambassadors were guests of the king at Windsor. According to Cambon's account, Bertie then said that the conclusions that he had reached were that a Franco-German war would lead to the collapse of France and German hegemony in Europe. Belgium and Holland would fall under German influence, and England would sooner or later have to fight Germany, but without the benefit of French support.[30]

These remarks would seem to indicate a growing concern on Bertie's part with the threat that Germany might pose to the continental balance of power. Yet what Cambon described as Bertie's conclusions were views which Bertie had himself attributed to the French. This may have been due to the inaccuracy of Cambon's reporting. It may also have reflected Bertie's desire to impress upon Cambon the importance for Britain of maintaining an independent France. Bertie was, however, quite frank in his assessment of Cambon's chances of gaining any further commitment from the British government. To him he expressed his doubts as to whether

---

[28] Minutes by Crowe on Bertie to Grey, 13 Jan. 1906, F.O.371/70, despt.13. On Crowe and the quality of his advice see: Steiner, *Britain and the Origins*, pp.183 – 5.
[29] B.D., III, no.216.
[30] D.D.F.2, IX, pt.1, no.55.

Campbell-Bannerman, supported by those of his colleagues who represented 'les traditions gladstoniennes', would be prepared to commit Britain to participation in a future conflict. In any event, Bertie warned Cambon he would obtain nothing in writing. Cambon asserted that he did not want that. All he wished to know was 'si dans le cas d'une agression dont le Maroc pourrait être le prétexte, mais dont le vrai motif serait notre entente avec l'Angleterre, l'Angleterre nous abandonnerait'. Given the tone of Grey's recent communications, Bertie was perhaps not too over-optimistic in replying that it did not seem possible that 'on ne reponde pas affirmativement si vous posez la question dans ces termes'.[31] Cambon was none the less to be disappointed.

In order to facilitate early and effective cooperation in a war in which Britain and France were allies, Grey had approved the opening of joint military conversations. To deter German aggression he had delivered his warning to Metternich on 3 January. Beyond this he felt he could not go. A plea made by Cambon on 31 January that in the event of a war resulting from German meddling in Morocco, British aid might be too late if it were necessary for the government to consult and wait for public opinion to manifest itself, did not cause Grey to change his stance. He deprecated a verbal pledge as he would have to submit it to the cabinet, and he felt sure that his colleagues would require it in writing. As such, he reasoned, it would amount to an alliance, and, he explained to Cambon, he did not think that people in England would be prepared to risk a war in order to put France in possession of Morocco. If, however, it appeared that Germany was forcing a war on France in order to break up the *entente*, then, he observed, 'public opinion would undoubtedly be very strong on the side of France'. Even so, he could not give a decided opinion as to whether this would be sufficient to overcome the 'great reluctance which existed amongst us now to find ourselves involved in a war'.[32] Such language Hardinge thought Bertie would find 'fairly satisfactory so far as it goes'. Anything of a more definite nature would, he suggested, 'have been at once rejected by the Govt'.[33]

On 28 January Bertie had returned to Paris where he found the attention of the French concentrated upon the negotiations which had commenced on 16th at Algeciras. There Franco-German differences soon crystallized on two issues: the future policing of the Moroccan ports, and the establishment with international finance of a state bank

---

[31] *Ibid.*
[32] *B.D.*, III, no.219.
[33] Hardinge to Bertie, 2 Feb. 1906, B.P. Add. MS. 63018.

for Morocco.[34] Rather than concede to France and Spain the mandate which they desired for the organization of the police, Holstein would probably have preferred to see the conference fail.[35] But the seemingly contradictory statements of German diplomats did not allow foreign observers to arrive at any clear understanding of Germany's policies and intentions.[36] When on 19 February Metternich informed Grey that his government had turned down the latest French proposal, the foreign secretary feared that he was about to witness the early termination of the conference. In a memorandum which he drafted on the next day he ruminated on the possibility that the Germans might then try to establish their influence in Morocco, that the French would counter them, and that the Germans might make that a *casus belli*. Horrible though he thought Britain's involvement in a Franco-German war would be, he nevertheless emphasized that if she failed to support France in a conflict over Morocco, her honour and international standing would be seriously compromised.[37]

Whilst Grey was attempting to come to terms with the diplomatic problems arising from the *entente*, Bertie had to attend to the needs of those who wished to celebrate its existence. As ambassador he could hardly ignore the endeavours of those individuals and institutions who sought thereby either to promote their own interests, or to enjoy the pleasures of foreign travel. Thus a visit to Paris in January 1906 by a choir and orchestra from the Royal College of Music necessitated Bertie's presence at the opera house, and a subsequent visit by a group of London county councillors required his attendance at a number of functions laid on by their hosts.[38] But rarely enthusiastic about the social niceties of diplomacy, Bertie grew irritated at the prospect of more such visitors from Britain. News therefore of a forthcoming visit by the lord mayor and sheriffs of the City of London, and an enquiry from the lord provost of Edinburgh with regard to a journey that he and his corporation were planning to make to France, produced a predictable effusion of protests from

---

[34] S.L. Mayer, 'Anglo-German Rivalry at the Algeciras Conference', in Prosser Gifford and Wm. Roger Louis (eds.), *Britain and Germany in Africa. Imperial Rivalry and Colonial Rule* (London, 1967), pp.315 – 22.
[35] Rich, II, 734 – 5.
[36] Crowe thought that the German government intended 'to maintain as long as possible an ambiguous atitude'. Minute by Crowe on Nicolson to Grey, 6 Feb. 1906, F.O.3371/71, despt.31.
[37] *B.D.*, III, no.299.
[38] Bertie to Tyrrell, 29 Jan. 1906; Bertie to Mallet, 30 Jan. 1906; Stanford to Parrot, enclosed in Knollys to Bertie, 27 Jan. 1906; memo. by Bertie, enclosed in Bertie to Knollys, 29 Jan. 1906; B.P. B, F.O.800/184.

Bertie against overdoing these municipal peregrinations. He warned the Foreign Office that other cities might wish to follow Edinburgh's example, and that the French might soon begin to jib at the cost of offering entertainments.[39] In the end Grey was able to obtain from the lord provost an assurance that he and his colleagues intended to make only a private visit to Paris to see the 'Abattoirs and other municipal things', and Bertie managed to ward off a proposed visit by the mayors of the London boroughs.[40] He also succeeded in quashing an attempt by Walter Behrens, a prominent member of the British business community in Paris, and according to Bertie 'a pushing musical Jew who [wanted] to be made Sir Walter', to bring a guards band over to France. There had, Bertie concluded, 'been too much of the musical entente'.[41]

There was, however, one old gentleman whose visits to Paris Bertie clearly had to tolerate. King Edward VII had been upset by the attention which had been paid by French journalists to his stay in Paris in May 1905, but he continued to insist on sampling the city's delights.[42] Unfortunately, his presence there was rarely convenient to Bertie. Thus his desire to break his journey to Biarritz in March 1906 and to pass a few days in Paris gave rise to difficulties of a diplomatic kind. The trouble was that Edward VII, whose role in the making of British foreign policy was generally exaggerated in France, had recently adopted a friendlier attitude towards the German emperor. Indeed, he had even agreed to arrange a meeting between himself and William II during the cruise that he was planning to take in the Mediterranean in the spring.[43] This and the possible effect of the news of the king's intentions upon the French caused some consternation in the Foreign Office, and Grey sought to enlist Bertie's assistance to restrain the king from acting on his own initiative.

Pessimistic about the future of the conference, Grey wrote to Bertie on 2 March predicting that a meeting of the king and emperor so soon after its possible dissolution would have a very bad effect. The problem, Grey explained, was that the king thought that he could prepare the French for it on his way through Paris. But he personally

---

[39] Bertie to Hardinge, 11 Feb. 1906, B.P. B, F.O.800/184.
[40] Grey to Bertie, 12 March 1906; Bertie to Grey, 26 April 1906; B.P. B, F.O.800/184.
[41] Bertie to Mallet, 25 March 1906; Mallet to Bertie, 27 March 1906; Bertie to Gorst, 23 March 1906; B.P. B, F.O.800/184.
[42] Bertie to Lansdowne, 3 May 1905, B.P. B, F.O.800/183.
[43] Barrère had assured Combarieu in December 1905 that the Liberal government in Britain would continue to maintain the *entente cordiale* intact because 'King Edward VII directed personally the foreign policy of Great Britain'. Combarieu, pp.325–6.

thought that they were more likely to be alarmed than prepared, and he asked Bertie to use his influence with the king in order to prevent him from making a bad impression in France. 'If the Germans give way', he concluded, 'and the Conference comes to an agreement the meeting in the Mediterranean would be alright, but otherwise I dread the effect of it.'[44] In similar terms Hardinge, Mallet and Tyrrell, who was to succeed Mallet in the following year, implored Bertie to do what he could to change King Edward's mind.[45] Bertie responded with a memorandum, which he presented to the king on 4 March. It recalled that the Germans were working in Paris to make the French believe that England desired a Franco-German war in which France would be left in the lurch, and that press reports emanating from Germany were being used to indicate that a rapprochement was being prepared between England and Germany without regard to France. The French government, press and public, were, Bertie claimed, coming to the conclusion that William II's objective was not only to oust France from her special position in Morocco, but to humble her, and prove that she could not in any circumstances rely on England for anything more than 'platonic diplomatic support'. It would, Bertie warned the king, 'very much alarm the French Government if they are allowed to believe that His Majesty intends to have a meeting with the Emperor irrespective of the results of the Algeciras Conference'. He thought that if either Armand Fallières, who had recently succeeded Loubet as president of the republic, or Rouvier raised the subject, then the king should say that no date had been fixed, nor would be until the questions in discussion at Algeciras had been settled.[46]

Bertie deliberately based his recommendations on the assumption that the king would not possibly think of broaching with French statemen the subject of his proposed meeting with the emperor. Instead, in his memorandum he contemplated the contingency where the French themselves might raise the subject with the king. This he thought was the best way of influencing the king, and he made no attempt to extract from him a promise that he would accept his advice. This would seem to have been a wise decision for when the king subseqently received Fallières and Rouvier at an embassy dinner

---

Sidney Lee, *King Edward VII, biography* (2 vols., London, 1925), II, pp.524–8. Bertie to Grey, 4 March 1906, B.P., A, F.O.800/170.
[44] Grey to Bertie, 2 March 1906, B.P., A, F.O.800/170.
[45] Tyrrell to Bertie, 2 March 1906, B.P. B, F.O.800/184. Hardinge to Bertie, 2 March 1906; Mallet to Bertie, 2 March 1906; B.P., A, F.O.800/170. Knollys to Hardinge, 4 March 1906, Hardinge MSS., 9.
[46] The recommendations made by Bertie in his memorandum were first put by him to the king on the evening of 3 March. Memo. given by Bertie to the king, 4 March 1906, B.P. B, F.O.800/184. Bertie to Grey, 4 March 1906, B.P., A, F.O.800/170.

he made no allusion to a meeting with the emperor, but chose rather to pour scorn upon tales that Britain desired to bring about a war between Germany and France and that she was not a country to be relied upon. Bertie was also able to scotch a plan by Radolin and his friends to arrange a meeting with the king. He was, however, probably relieved when on 6 March Edward VII left Paris for the south of France.[47]

Bertie was to have joined the king at Biarritz on 10 March, but events at Algeciras and Paris compelled him to change his plans.[48] It was evident to the German government by the end of February that they had miscalculated in hoping for the support of the neutral powers at the conference. With the exception of the backing from the delegates of Austria-Hungary, they were diplomatically isolated, and to Bülow a compromise agreement with France seemed to be the only credible alternative to political defeat. Thus after Holstein failed to obtain direct talks with the French, Bülow on 6 March authorized the Austrians to put forward a project which conceded to the French almost everything for which they had asked with regard to the police. French and Spanish officers were according to these proposals to have control of the police at seven of the Moroccan ports, while at Casablanca the police force was to be under the command of a superior officer or inspector who would be a national of a minor power.[49]

Although this was widely represented as a major concession, Rouvier was not ready to accept even this small element of internationalization. He was prepared to agree to the appointment of a Danish or a Swiss inspector, but only on the condition that he should not have an independent command at any of the ports.[50] The Quai d'Orsay was in any case already in possession of a report from the prince of Monaco, who had recently visited Germany, which indicated that the Wilhelmstrasse had more to offer.[51] But Arthur

---

[47] *B.D.*, III, no.327. Bertie to Grey, 5 and 9 March 1906, B.P., A, F.O.800/170.
[48] Bertie to Grey, 6 March 1906, F.O.371/71, despt.95. Bertie to Grey, 9 March 1906, tel.; Grey to Bertie, 9 March 1906, tel.; Grey MSS., F.O.800/49. Mallet to Bertie, 9 March 1906, B.P., A, F.O.800/160.
[49] Rich, II, pp.739–40.
[50] *B.D.*, III, nos.336 and 340.
[51] *D.D.F.2*, IX, pt.2, no.392. A telegram of 6 March from the prince of Monaco's secretary warned Reinach 'on fera bien à prendre aucune resolution importante avant notre retour demain car notre voyageur parait satisfait du resultat'. When the Germans appeared to be less ready to pursue the conciliatory line that the prince had predicted, he attributed this to the change of government in France. This, he thought, had led the Germans to believe that the French would be less fixed in their ideas 'car j'apportais de Berlin une certitude totale en faveur d'un arrangement'. Lamotte to Reinach, 6 March 1906, tel.; note by Reinach, 8 March 1906 (on foreign ministry notepaper); Prince Albert of Monaco to Reinach, 14 March 1906; Reinach MSS., N.A. Fr. 13550.

Nicolson, the British delegate at Algeciras, was less optimistic.⁵² Moreover, to him and to Grey it seemed evident that if a French refusal to accept the Austrian project led to the collapse of the negotiations, this would be blamed by the other powers upon France and her associates.⁵³ Grey might then have to reckon with a cabinet and a public reluctant to give further support to France. In these circumstances Nicolson advised his French colleague, Paul Révoil, that it would be unfortunate if Britain, France and Spain, were left isolated, and Hardinge urged Grey to repeat this advice to Paul Cambon.⁵⁴ With this Grey agreed. It did not seem to him that any real sacrifice of principle was involved in accepting the proposal, and on 9 March he informed the French ambassador that they represented 'a real concession on the part of Germany, and had brought agreement so near that it would not do to let the Conference break up without a settlement'. In a telegram of the same date he also instructed Bertie to communicate these views to Rouvier.⁵⁵

Bertie was far more cautious than either Grey or Hardinge in his reaction to the news from Algeciras, and he was much less inclined than they were to regard the Germans as having conceded anything of value. Moreover, when on 10 March he put Grey's views to Rouvier, he found him confident that he could modify the Austrian scheme so as to suit the needs of France. To Grey Bertie endeavoured to explain that the view generally held in Paris was that all the concessions had been made by the French side, for 'after Oriental fashion' Germany had begun by making 'impossible demands, and their reduction in view of the almost universal disapproval of them to something less offensive to France [was] not real moderation'.⁵⁶ Crowe was sympathetic to these objections. Yet he, like Hardinge and Nicolson, feared that the Germans would not be prepared to give way again.⁵⁷ And although Grey assured Cambon that Nicolson would continue to support Révoil, he also urged the French to accept

---

⁵² *B.D.*, III, no.339. Nicolson to Grey, 12 March 1906, Nicolson MSS., F.O.800/357. Bertie appears to have had no knowledge of the Prince of Monaco's intervention. When Rouvier seemed confident that the Germans would yield further Bertie assumed that perhaps some promise had been conveyed to Paris. Bertie to Grey, 11 March 1906, B.P., A, F.O.800/160.
⁵³ Grey to Campbell-Bannerman, 10 March 1906, Campbell-Bannerman MSS. (British Library), Add. MS. 41218. *B.D.*, III, no.335.
⁵⁴ *B.D.*, III, no.332. Minute by Hardinge on Nicolson to Grey, 8 March 1906, F.O.371/173, tel.89.
⁵⁵ *B.D.*, III, no.333.
⁵⁶ Bertie to Mallet, 10 March 1906; Bertie to Grey, 1 March 1906; B.P., A, F.O.800/160.
⁵⁷ Minutes by Crowe and Hardinge on Nicolson to Grey, 9 March 1906, F.O.371/173, tel.90. *B.D.*, III, nos.336, 339 and 340.

a Swiss police command at Casablanca rather than let the conference fail.[58] This brought forth an immediate protest from the Paris embassy. In a letter of 12 March Bertie warned Grey of the unfortunate impression that would be created in France once the public learned that he had urged their government to give way on Casablanca. He observed to Grey that if the French government were to follow his advice, they would say that they were doing so because of English pressure. It would then, Bertie predicted, become a cry encouraged by the Germans of 'save us from our friends.'.[59]

The situation was complicated by France's domestic politics. Much of 1905 had been occupied by the passage through the French parliament of a bill to effect the separation of the church and state. But the application of the measure was resisted in some parishes, and on 7 March during a debate on the government's handling of the matter elements of the centre joined with the right in the chamber to defeat Rouvier's administration. As a result, though Rouvier remained at the Quai d'Orsay for another five days, he resigned as premier, and on the 14th a new government was formed with Jean Sarrien as president of the council and Léon Bourgeois as foreign minister. The ministry appeared from the start to be an unstable combination.[60] Its formation had, according to Bertie, been hampered by Bourgeois's objection to the inclusion in it, as minister of the interior, of Georges Clemenceau, the sixty-four year old warrior of the left.[61] Besides which, Bourgeois, a former delegate at the Hague peace conference of 1899, had, in marked contrast to Clemenceau, distinctly internationalist inclinations. Bertie thought that Clemenceau would check any disposition of Bourgeois towards conciliation.[62] Of more immediate importance to Bertie, however, was the fact that the uncertain state of French politics helped to reinforce his objections to any British intervention in favour of the Austrian proposals. He pointed out in a despatch of 11 March that since Rouvier would soon be out of office, it was natural that he should not wish to make concessions and thereby 'incur reproaches in the Chamber from his successors and the odium of the country'.[63]

Révoil also raised with Nicolson the spectre of nationalists and others declaring against the *entente* at the forthcoming parliamentary

---

[58] *B.D.*, III, no.336.
[59] Bertie to Grey, 8 and 14 March 1906, F.O.371/71, despt.98 and 101. Bertie to Grey, 9 and 10 March 1906, F.O.371/71, tels.15, 16, 18 and 21. Bertie to Grey, 12 March 1906, B.P., A, F.O.800/160.
[60] J-B. Duroselle, *La France et les français, 1900–1914* (Paris, 1972), pp.273–4.
[61] Bertie to Grey, 12 March 1906, F.O.371/71, despt.103.
[62] *Ibid.*
[63] *B.D.*, III, no.340.

elections, and Crowe agreed that the British government 'ought to be most careful on the eve of a general election in France not to appear as prime movers in persuading France to accept an arrangement which will meet with strong opposition in France'. He suggested instead that the British should simply put to the French the necessity of choosing between the Austrian project and no arrangement at all.[64] In the meanwhile Nicolson was confirmed in his opinion that the Germans would not yield further by a conversation which, at Révoil's request, he had with von Radowitz, the senior German delegate.[65] Yet neither Nicolson nor Grey made their support for France dependent upon the French adopting a particular course. Indeed, Grey, who remained convinced that the French were mistaken in not settling on the basis of the Austrian proposals, was perturbed by a claim made by Metternich that all the delegates, 'including Nicolson', had told Radowitz that the French ought to 'concede the small points still outstanding'.[66] On 14 March, after the publication in *Le Temps* of what was purported to be Rouvier's final instructions to Révoil not to give way on Casablanca, Grey affirmed to Bertie his continuing support for France.[67]

Grey's pledge, which Bertie delivered to Georges Louis, the *directeur politique* at the Quai d'Orsay, on the afternoon of 14 March, relieved Bourgeois of the anxiety which he and his colleagues had evidently felt over the attitude of the British government and its representatives at Algeciras.[68] Since Nicolson had so far appeared to stand aloof from Révoil, and his support for the French cause had been formal rather than enthusiastic, all the more importance had been attached to such sympathy as he had exhibited for the Austrian project.[69] And even after Nicolson rallied to Revoil's side, French diplomats found cause to complain that he followed 'd'un pas boiteuse'.[70] Reports emanating from Berlin had also seemed to indicate that the British and German governments were in accord, and when Bourgeois learned from Révoil that Nicolson believed himself to be in a position to negotiate an understanding with the

---

[64] *B.D.*, III, no.342.
[65] Nicolson to Hardinge, 12 March 1906, Nicolson MSS., F.O.800/337. *B.D.*, III, nos.341 and 345.
[66] *B.D.*, III, nos.348 and 351. Minutes by Crowe, Barrington and Hardinge on Bertie Grey, 11 March 1906, F.O.371/173, despt.140.
[67] *B.D.*, III, nos.350 and 352. *D.D.F.2*, IX, pt.2, no.443. On Grey's disappointment at the failure of the French to settle on the Austrian proposal see: Grey to Cromer, 15 March 1906, Grey MSS., F.O.800/46.
[68] *D.D.F.2*, IX, pt.2, no.440. Bertie to Grey, 15 March 1906, F.O.371/174, tel.27.
[69] Memo. initialled by Bertie, 24 April 1906, B.P. Add. MS. 63019.
[70] De Margerie to J. Cambon, 12 March 1906, Jules Cambon MSS. (Ministère des Affaires Étrangères), 11.

German delegate, he began to wonder whether or not Nicolson had already reached an agreement with Radowitz.[71] Apparently with Bourgeois's approval, Crozier, the French minister at Copenhagen, told Lister of the foreign minister's fears. He maintained that several influential and competent French parliamentarians had in the past few days tried to persuade Bourgeois that the policy of the British government was to withdraw from continental politics into an isolation favoured by Campbell-Bannerman.[72]

Bourgeois's misgivings were shared by others inside the French cabinet. When Étienne, who was now the minister for war, met Bertie at a party at the German embassy on 14 March, he practically accused Britain of intending to abandon France at Algeciras. Moreover, according to Clemenceau, who visited Bertie on the following day, he alone had combatted the supposition which had been raised in the council of ministers that England had made a separate agreement with Germany.[73] Even Paul Cambon, who felt sure that Grey would continue to back France, warned Bourgeois that the British foreign secretary would be obliged to take into account the views of his cabinet colleagues, who might disinterest themselves in France if she appeared to endanger the success of the conference.[74] But the French reaction to the advice proffered by himself and Nicolson was resented by Grey. After verifying that his views had been correctly transmitted by Cambon to the Quai d'Orsay, he objected to Bertie: 'It is too bad of the French to run off the rails like this'. 'A nation', he observed, 'which is always suspecting her friend will never be able to keep her friend.' Grey admitted to Bertie that French suspicions of Britain might be due to France's 'bad luck' during the past thirty-five years, but he estimated that as a result of Russia recovering her strength, and the betterment of Anglo-Russian relations, France would in two or three years be in the strongest position she had been in for several generations. Nevertheless, he concluded:

> to bring all this about people must be content to go slow and not to get jumpy and throw over the Foreign Minister and change their Government every few months and talk nonsense at the German Embassy and send their Minister at Copenhagen to make nervous

---

[71] *D.D.F.2*, IX, pt.2, nos.439, 440 and 450, and pp.930–40. *B.D.*, III, no.358.
[72] *B.D.*, III, no.355. Grey of Fallodon, *Twenty-five Years, 1892–1916* (2 vols., London, 1925), I, pp.105–10.
[73] Bertie to Grey, 15 March 1906, tel., B.P., A, F.O.800/160. Bertie to Edward VII, 16 March 1906, B.P., A, F.O.800/164. *B.D.*, III, no.356.
[74] *D.D.F.2*, IX, pt.2, no.449.

enquiries at the Embassy in Paris before they have consulted their ambassador in London.[75]

Bertie did not share Grey's exasperation. Frequently prejudiced in his attitude towards Germany, and dogmatic in his defence of Britain's imperial interests, he was usually prepared to make a real effort to understand the workings of the French political mind. On 17 March he responded to Grey's protests with a sermon on toleration.

> One must take the French as they are and not as one would wish them to be. They have an instinctive dread of Germany and an hereditary distrust of England, and with these characteristics they are easily led to believe that they may be deserted by England and fallen upon by Germany.

Bertie regretted that 'Frenchmen of education and position should be found ready to believe imputations against England of bad faith'. Their mistrust, he thought, had been played upon by those working in the interests of Germany. Besides which, he assumed that Bourgeois had sent Crozier to Lister in order to gain assurances with which to combat the views of his colleagues who were unfamiliar with the details of recent diplomacy. As to the alarm felt by the French cabinet, that he attributed to Révoil having reported that he supposed Nicolson's advice to denote a change in policy. Some members of the government, he suggested, had been inclined to believe in the existence of an Anglo-German arrangement because of the apparent inconsistency between Britain's willingness to acquiesce in the Austrian project as it affected Casablanca and the message which he himself had delivered to Delcassé on 25 April 1905.[76]

The net outcome of this episode was in the end a fresh reaffirmation by Grey of his intention to stand by France. 'Cordial cooperation with France in all parts of the world', Grey wrote to Bertie on 15 March, 'remains a cardinal point of British policy and in some respects we have carried it further than the late Government were required to do.'[77] Grey certainly showed no sign of deviating from this principle during the remaining sessions of the conference, and in the face of a firm Anglo-French stand on the police issue the Germans eventually ceased to insist on a neutral command at

---

[75] Grey to Bertie, 15 March 1906, B.P., A, F.O.800/160 (part of this letter is published in *B.D.*, III, no.358). Bertie to Edward VII, 16 March 1906, *op cit*.
[76] *B.D.*, III, no.357.
[77] *Ibid*, no.358.

Casablanca.⁷⁸ True the general act of Algeciras of 7 April 1906 placed barriers in the way of the establishment of French and Spanish protectorates in Morocco. It thus proclaimed the independence and territorial integrity of Morocco, and required the submission to adjudication of applications for public works concessions. But it also granted to France and Spain a five year mandate for the command and instruction of the police at the eight open ports of Morocco, under the condition that the sultan should appoint a Swiss officer as inspector, and it provided for the creation of a state bank in which French capital would predominate.⁷⁹ In these respects France and Spain acquired duties and privileges in Morocco which French colonialists learned quickly how to utilize for the advantage of the republic.

During the Algeciras conference the maintenance of the Anglo-French *entente* had tended to coincide with what Bertie judged to be Britain's interests in Morocco. But when elsewhere in Africa French policies seemed to augment rather than diminish what he considered to be the menace of German intervention, Bertie was less inclined to rush to the defence of France. This helps to explain his attitude towards the negotiations which were still proceeding between the British, French and Italian governments, for the delimitation of their interests in Abyssinia. By November 1905 the Foreign Office and the Quai d'Orsay had already reached agreement on the contents of a draft convention, and only Italy's insistence on an arrangement which would give clear recognition to her hopes of acquiring a territorial link between Eritrea and the Benadir coast seemed likely to hinder its conclusion.⁸⁰ Yet in both London and Paris it was suspected that the Italians were reluctant to risk alienating their German allies by entering into any accord with the *entente* powers, and that they were deliberately seeking to delay a settlement.⁸¹ Bertie shared these suspicions, and during his conversation with Paul Cambon at Windsor in January he had suggested that Britain and France should sign the draft convention. The idea appealed to Cambon who saw in

---

78 Nicolson to Grey, 17 March 1906, F.O.371/174, tel.104, with minute by Crowe, (published without minute in *B.D.*, III, no.359).
79 Anderson, pp.392 – 6.
80 *Note sur les négociations relatives aux affaires d'Abyssinie*, 9 Oct. 1905, N.S. Éthiopie 12. *B.D.*, VIII, no.9. Eubank, pp.117 – 20. Cromer to Grey, 1 Jan. 1906, F.O.371/1, despt.1. Harrington to Grey, 20 Jan. 1906, F.O.371/1, tel.1.
81 *Négociation concernant l'Abyssinie-question des chemins de fer*, note for the minister, 17 March 1906, N.S. Éthiopie 11. Grey to Harrington, 23 Jan. 1906,F.O.371/1, tel.3. Minutes by Gorst, Hardinge, and Grey, on Egerton to Grey, 3 March 1906, F.O.371/1. Tittoni to Grey, 12 and 19 April 1906, F.O.371/1. Grey to Cromer, 25 May 1906, F.O.371/1, despt.86. Grey to Cromer, 17 Jan. 1906, Grey MSS., F.O.800/46.

the threat of a separate Anglo-French accord a means of inducing the Italians to cease their prevaricating.[82]

Grey likewise favoured this course.[83] Reports from Abyssinia indicated that the Germans were preparing to send another mission there, and that Menelik might seek their assistance in the completion of the final section of the railway from Jibuti to Addis Ababa. There were even fears in Cairo that Germany, thought to be behind recent Turkish claims in Sinai, intended to 'bring pressure to bear on Egypt from both flanks'.[84] Barrère was, however, perturbed lest Britain and France should by their action forfeit Italy's support at Algeciras.[85] And in spite of the disturbing news that Menelik had suffered an apoplectic stroke, Bourgeois was less than enthusiastic about proceeding with the draft convention. He told Bertie on 29 May that what he wanted to settle at once was the future of the French railway concession, and that he wished to leave an understanding on other matters to a later date. To do otherwise, he argued, would be to risk German intervention, and France could not afford another confrontation with Berlin. Germany, he thought, would appear in the same guise in Abyssinia as she had done in Morocco, and she would claim that the projected tripartite agreement was a preliminary to the partition of Menelik's empire.[86]

Neither Grey not Bertie was impressed by Bourgeois's case. Grey might at one stage have been prepared to adhere to a limited understanding with France on the railway question, but he could see little advantage in an agreement that made no reference either to the integrity of Abyssinia, or to Britain's interest in the headwaters of the Nile. It would leave the French with a free hand to proceed with their railway, but deny Britain a *quid pro quo*. Besides which, Grey thought that such a agreement would not disarm German hostility since they were bound to suspect that there was something behind it, or that it was the first step towards a larger scheme. If fear of Germany were Bourgeois's main objection to a tripartite agreement, then he thought that it might be overcome by explaining to her that she was not a power limitrophe of Abyssinia, and that the arrangement contained provisions safeguarding the freedom of commerce. The 'bold course', Grey observed to Bertie in a letter of 1 June, would be to make a clean

---

[82] *D.D.F.2*, IX, pt.1, no.99.
[83] Grey to Egerton, 23 May 1906, F.O.371/1, despt.78. Grey to Cromer, 25 May 1906, F.O.371/1, tel.86. *D.D.F.2*, IX, pt.1, no.295.
[84] Findlay to Hardinge, 24 March 1906; Cromer to Grey, 13 April 1906; Grey MSS., F.O.800/46. Cromer to Grey, 5 April 1906, F.O.371/1, tel.85.
[85] *D.D.F.2*, IX, pt.1, no.319.
[86] Bertie to Bourgeois, 28 May 1906, N.S. Éthiopie 14. Bertie to Grey, 29 May 1906, B.P., A, F.O.800/160. *D.D.F.2*, X, no.81.

job of the whole matter by signing without consulting Germany. Yet as Bourgeois was reluctant to do that, Grey proposed that there should be a complete change of policy, and that Britain and France should at once take Germany into their confidence.[87]

This proposal drew an immediate protest from Bertie. If it suited Germany's purpose then Bertie did not think that any amount of explanation would satisfy her. To sign without consulting Germany, he explained, 'would not only be the bold course but the wisest course to adopt'. The idea of offering an explanation to her would, he reckoned, 'be almost tantamount to an admission that she is to be consulted by us in regard to matters which in no way concern her'. He fulminated: 'It would encourage her to consider herself the arbiter of the world. France may be moved by fear of Germany to not doing anything of any importance in any part of the globe without German acquiescence, but there is no reason why we should at present occupy this position.' He was equally opposed to allowing the French to delay further the conclusion of the agreement. Indeed, faced with Bourgeois's reservations and the risk of German intrigues, Bertie's solution was unequivocal and expedient. He recommended to Grey that the same line be pursued towards the French as had previously been used towards the Italians. Italy, which had indicated its readiness to complete the convention, should, Bertie thought, be brought to signing point, and the French then informed that 'we cannot wait any longer and that we shall initial the draft with the Italians and leave the agreement open to French adherence'. In such circumstances, he believed the French would sign.[88]

Grey agreed that the course suggested by Bertie with regard to informing Germany and the other powers was the best one. He maintained, however, that Britain's policy must be dependent upon the course chosen by Bourgeois, and he completely ignored Bertie's proposal on bringing pressure to bear on France.[89] In the meanwhile Italy's conditional acceptance of the draft convention on 7 June did little to change Bourgeois's mind and Bertie seems to have resolved to act on his own initiative.[90] On 21 June he warned Bourgeois that it might be necessary for England and Italy to sign the agreement and for them to leave it to France to join later. Bertie had certainly exceeded his instructions and the news of his action was not favourably received in London. Grey thought that it 'was going too

---

[87] Grey to Bertie, 1 June 1906, B.P., A, F.O.800/160.
[88] Bertie to Grey, 3 June 1906, Grey MSS., F.O.800/51.
[89] Minute by Grey on *ibid*. Grey to Bertie, 8 and 19 June 1906, F.O.371/1, despt.311 and tel.87.
[90] Grey to Egerton, 7 June 1906, F.O.371/1, despt.89.

far', and Hardinge considered it a dangerous move which 'might have been resented'.[91] It probably served well, however, to reinforce the advice which Bourgeois had already received from Paul Cambon that if France failed to sign it would strike 'un coup sensible' to the *entente cordiale*. In any event visits to Paris by Tittoni on 22 June and Paul Cambon on 25 June clinched the affair.[92] After textual modifications largely to Italy's benefit and at Britain's expense, the convention was initialled on 6 July and signed some five months later.[93]

Both the concern that Bertie had evinced in March over Grey's reaction to the Austrian proposals, and the warning which he had given to Bourgeois on 21 June, were consistent with his belief that it was neither wise nor necessary for Britain or France to seek to placate Germany. He thus greeted with a distinct lack of enthusiasm, and at times outright hostility, the various official and unoffical attempts which were made during the remainder of 1906 to improve relations between London and Berlin. Not that Grey's conduct gave him any reason to complain. Whatever hopes the foreign secretary may have entertained for securing a better relationship with Germany, it seems clear that he was embarrassed by such manifestations of Anglo-German amity as were provided by visiting German burgomasters and journalists. In private and in public Grey and his officials were profuse in their assurances of continuing British support for the *entente* with France.[94] But Bertie, Mallet and Tyrrell were disturbed by Hardinge's apparent sympathy for a more conciliatory approach towards Berlin. Anxious to see an end to the 'continual back-biting' between Britain and Germany, Hardinge supported the idea of a meeting between the king and German emperor, and in August 1906 he accompanied Edward VII on a journey to Cronberg. There he was favourably impressed by the attitude of von Tschirschky, the German state secretary, who confided his wish that England should assist Germany in diminishing the mistrust then prevalent in her relations

---

[91] Bertie to Grey, 21 June 1906, F.O.371/1, despt.249, and minutes by Grey and Hardinge.
[92] *D.D.F.2*, X, nos.93 and 136. Cambon, II, pp.219–20.
[93] Grey to Lister, 4 July 1906, F.O.371/1, despt. 354. Grey to Bertie, 6 July 1906, F.O.371/1, despt.362. The tripartite convention was finally signed on 13 December 1906. *British and Foreign State Papers*, IC, pp.486–9.
[94] Grey, I, pp.113–16. *B.D.*, III, nos.414, 416, 419, 420, 421 and 422. *B.D.*, III, X, nos.144 and 158. D.W. Sweet, 'Great Britain and Germany, 1905–1906'. Hinsley, p.217.

with France.⁹⁵ Mallet, however, considered German protestations of friendship to be aimed at undermining the unity of the *entente*, and Bertie was scathing in his criticism of Hardinge. From the resort of Bagnoles-de-l'Orne in Normandy he wrote to Mallet on 25 August: ' "Quem William vult perdere prius dementat". Whenever the anaesthetic takes effect we shall be operated on. When we wake up we shall find we were fools to believe what the surgeon said and that we are crippled.' Shocked by Hardinge, of whose intelligence he 'would have thought better', Bertie proposed that Grey should 'send him to Berlin, vice Lascelles promoted to Rome, and appoint Egerton to Hardinge's present post'.⁹⁶

Bertie viewed with no less apprehension the decision of Haldane, who visited Berlin at the end of August, to attend a military review and dinner there on 1 September. The date was sufficiently close to the anniversary of Sedan on the 2nd to cause Bourgeois to suspect that a British cabinet minister was to be present at the celebration of the French defeat.⁹⁷ On 28 August Paul Cambon warned Grey that it would lead to a campaign in the French press backed by German agents against Haldane and the British government.⁹⁸ Under the misapprehension that Bertie's friendship with the king would enable him to influence Haldane, Bourgeois had his officials inform Bertie of his fears. It was fortunate that he did so, for as the result of an error in the Foreign Office Bertie had received no warning of Cambon's protest. When on the 30th he did learn from the Quai d'Orsay of the French objections, he lost no time in protesting to Grey.⁹⁹ A week later, on 6 September, he reminded Grey that there were nationalists and many royalists in France who had been in favour of an understanding with Germany, and that an agitation for such a policy might easily be started again if the French public were led to suspect that the British government contemplated an Anglo-German agreement on general policy.¹⁰⁰ But in this instance Bertie was unable to influence events. The French objections were in Grey's opinion 'too wholesale', especially as this was the 'time of the year apparently for

---

⁹⁵ *B.D.*, III, no.425. Lee, *Edward VII*, II, pp.329 – 31. Hardinge to Nicolson, 21 Aug. 1906, Nicolson MSS., F.O.800/338. Mallet to Bertie, 24 Aug. 1906,B.P., A, F.O.800/170. Fitzmaurice, to Lascelles, 21 Sept. 1906, Lascelles MSS., F.O.800/13.
⁹⁶ Bertie to Mallet, 25 Aug. 1906, B.P., A, F.O.800/170.
⁹⁷ *D.D.F.2*, X, no.190.
⁹⁸ Grey to Haldane, 28 Aug. 1906, Grey MSS., F.O.800/101. *D.D.F.2*, X, no.191.
⁹⁹ Bertie to Grey, 30 Aug 1906; Bertie to Tyrrell, 6 Sept. 1906; B.P., A, F.O.800/170. Bertie to Grey, 30 and 31 Aug. 1906, F.O.371/78, tels.76 and 78.
¹⁰⁰ *B.D.*, III, no.437.

manoeuvres and reviews'.[101] Moreover, although he had suggested to Haldane that if he could not change his plans his visit had better be abandoned, Haldane had claimed that there was no connexion between the functions that he was to attend and Sedan, and he had proceeded with his programme.[102]

During Haldane's stay in Berlin the idea was once more put forward that England should through the *entente* help to facilitate a Franco-German *rapprochement*. The September edition of the *Deutsche Revue* went further, and in an article which Bertie attributed to official inspiration, denounced the policy of 'counterpoises' represented by the *entente*. It suggested instead that Germany should be included in the circle of friendship. But Bertie could see nothing but danger in attempting to persuade the French to come to terms with Germany, for, he contended, 'it would be taken as an attempt to persuade the mouse to make friends with the cat, and be regarded as covering some secret designs arranged with Germany'. He concluded:

> It appears to me that our policy as regards relations between France and Germany should not be to create friction as was Prince Bismarck's practice in regard to relations between France and England; but to do nothing to facilitate an understanding between Germany and France; for it is difficult to conceive how an understanding of any real importance between these two countries could be satisfactory without being detrimental to our interests.[103]

Bertie was thus no longer recommending, as he had done three years before, that Britain should encourage differences between France and Germany. The important point, however, was that in Bertie's estimate the political constellation in Europe which the *entente* and the Moroccan crisis had helped bring into being was one which it was in Britain's interest to preserve.

It was Hardinge's apparent readiness to accept German assurances of goodwill at their face value that set him apart from Bertie during the summer of 1906. That autumn the two friends also differed over an administrative issue. Their quarrel arose out of Hardinge's irritation at Bertie's persistent complaints about the delays and errors which occurred in the Foreign Office's handling of communications

---

[101] Minute by Grey on Bertie to Grey, 30 Aug. 1906, F.O.371/78, tel.76. Sommer, p.180. Granville to Lascelles, 5 Oct. 1906, Lascelles MSS., F.O.800/15.
[102] Grey to Haldane, 28 Aug. 1906; Ponsonby to Lascelles, 2 Sept. 1906; Lascelles MSS., F.O.800/15.
[103] *B.D.*, III, no.437.

with the Paris embassy.[104] Matters came to a head at the beginning of October when Bertie wrote privately to Hardinge objecting to the repetition to Paris of a telegram meant for Rome. It was a trivial issue, and Hardinge resented the tone of the letter in which Bertie dispensed with his usual 'My dear Charlie', and used the less familiar 'My dear Hardinge'.[105] It drew from Hardinge a reply whose sarcasm matched Bertie's petulance. 'I know', Hardinge observed, 'that you are a model of perfection and never made a mistake when you first joined the F.O., but . . . the very excellent and hard-working attachés in the Eastern Department have not yet arrived at the same pitch of perfection.' The question was anyway one which Hardinge thought should have been dealt with by a letter from the head of chancery at Paris to the Foreign Office department concerned.[106] But the bonds of friendship which united Bertie and Hardinge were strong enough to survive this reprimand, and after October the only serious threat to their relationship resulted from the king's desire to have Hardinge appointed ambassador to Washington. The proposal was, however, successfully resisted by Grey, who insisted that Hardinge was 'invaluable' and must therefore remain in London.[107]

Hardinge was not the only official whom Grey valued. In December 1906 he volunteered to Mallet some 'very flattering remarks' about Bertie, who, he said, impressed him with the accuracy of his information and the soundness of his judgements.[108] It would be difficult, however, to assess the extent to which Bertie had actually influenced Grey during his first year as foreign secretary. Other officials with whom Grey had closer contact held views on relations with France and Germany which were similar to those expressed by Bertie. Moreover, on no occasion either during the Algeciras conference or the discussions which followed it, does his advice appear to have been decisive in determining the courses which Grey pursued. But given the importance which Grey attached to the understanding with France, and the esteem in which he held the ambassador's opinions, Bertie was in a powerful position to affect the formulation and execution of Liberal foreign policy.

[104] Bertie to Hardinge, 31 Jan., 10 and 14 March, 27 Oct., and 12 Dec. 1906; Bertie to Crowe, 2 July 1906; Hardinge to Bertie, 12 and 15 March 1906; B.P. B, F.O.800/184.
[105] Hardinge to Bertie, 12 Oct. 1906, *ibid*.
[106] Hardinge to Bertie, 6 Oct. 1906, *ibid*.
[107] Edward VII to Campbell-Bannerman, 20 Nov.1906; Campbell-Bannerman to Knollys, 23 Nov. 1906; Knollys to Hardinge, 24 Nov. 1906; minute by Edward VII, 24 Nov. 1906; Hardinge MSS., 9. Bertie to Hardinge, 12 Dec. 1906; Hardinge to Bertie, 13 Dec. 1906; B.P., A,F.O.800/181/ Hardinge, *Old Diplomacy*, pp.130 – 1.
[108] Mallet to Bertie, 14 Dec. 1906, B.P., A, F.O.800/180.

6

The entente and the status quo

On 1 January 1907 Eyre Crowe submitted to Grey his celebrated memorandum on Britain's relations with France and Germany. Therein he identified Britain's foreign policy interests with the 'maintenance of the independence of nations', the protection of the 'weaker communities'and the preservation of the balance of power. And after seeking to examine Anglo-German relations in the light of this last 'general law', he concluded that while, so long as they did not conflict with its interests and international obligations, the British government should not attempt to thwart the expansion of Germany's overseas commerce and investment and the development of her naval strength, it should resist any one-sided bargains and show the 'most unbending determination to uphold British rights and interests in every part of the globe'.[1] Bertie was inclined to regard any growth in German naval power as contrary to British interests. But he could hardly have disagreed with the substance of Crowe's advice. Indeed, only two days later he wrote privately to Grey: 'We used to regard isolation as splendid but in view of the growing strength of Germany can we afford to do so? Does it not become necessary to take every precaution for the maintenance of the *status quo* and the preservation of the Balance of Power in the European System?'[2] This was not a plea for a closer understanding with France. It was, however, a further indication of the extent to which Bertie had departed from his previous support for the idea of an uncommitted Britain holding the balance between the continental alliances. He now looked increasingly towards the Anglo-French *entente* as a means of limiting Germany's ambitions.

The formation of Clemenceau's first government in October 1906 may have encouraged Bertie to think in these terms.[3] Although his relations with Clemenceau were not always cordial, they were closer than those which he enjoyed with any other French premier during

---

[1] *B.D.*, III, pp.397 – 420. See also: K.M. Wilson, 'Sir Eyre Crowe on the Origin of the Crowe Memorandum of 1 January 1907', *Bulletin of the Institute of Historical Research*, LVI (1983), 38 – 241.
[2] *B.D.*, III, no.8.
[3] D.R. Watson, *George Clemenceau. A Political Biography* (London, 1974), p.183.

his thirteen years in Paris. This was in part due to a certain affinity of temperament between the two men. It was also a measure of the dominating influence exercised by Clemenceau over his colleagues, and of his determination to have his say in the shaping of France's foreign relations.[4] Reputedly an Anglophile, Clemenceau had long been an advocate of an alignment with England. But unlike Delcassé, his personal and political opponent, he had originally conceived of such an understanding almost entirely in terms of bettering France's continental, rather than her imperial, position. Thus, as early as 1891, he had argued in favour of France offering concessions to Britain in Egypt and on the Newfoundland fisheries, in order to entice her away from her association with the Triple Alliance and to win her moral support for France's recovery of Alsace-Lorraine.[5] He had eventually welcomed the agreement of April 1904, and Mallet, whom Clemenceau met in July 1905, found him 'strongly of the opinion' that Britain and France 'should act side by side as if they were allied and consult each other about everything and be prepared to back each other up'. Clemenceau was, however, cautious about the notion of entering a military alliance with Britain. He told Mallet in 1905 that the time was not right for one. And although in subsequent years he sought to maintain the impression in public that the *entente* was more than just a friendly understanding, he was concerned less with securing a pledge of military assistance from Britain, than with trying to ensure that she possessed an army of sufficient strength to aid France in a European war.[6]

Bertie always assumed that the French would have liked a more tangible assurance of British support, but that they realized the difficulties which stood in the way of their achieving this, and therefore contented themselves with the conviction that Britain's interests would compel her to support France in a war with Germany. Yet it is probable that Clemenceau, who professed to believe in the inevitability of an Anglo-German war, may simply have preferred to avoid the strictures of an alliance with a power whose military strength he doubted. It is also likely that during the summer of 1905

---

[4] On Clemenceau's views on France's foreign relations see: D.R. Watson, 'The making of French Foreign Policy under the First Clemenceau Government, 1906 – 9', *English Historical Review*, LXXXVI (1971), 774 – 82.
[5] *Occasional Diary*, 26 June 1891, J. Chamberlain MSS., JC8/1/5. *Memorandum of Events, 1880 – 1892*, July 1891, J. Chamberlain MSS., JC 8/1/1. Clemenceau had felt that the French government should have joined Britain in the negotiations which led to the Anglo-Japanese alliance. The 'great danger in the future', he told one British minister in December 1902, 'was pan-Germanism'. Cranborne to Lansdowne, 20 Dec. 1902, Cecil MSS., S(4) 50/133.
[6] Memo. by Mallet, 13 July 1905, Lansdowne MSS., F.O.800/145.

he had shared the view then prevalent in some circles in Paris that Germany's 'bullying' of France was really aimed at England, and that France might be forced to fight England's 'battles with Germany'. This opinion had certainly been expressed to Bertie by Stephen Pichon, the former diplomat whom Clemenceau chose to replace Bourgeois at the Quai d'Orsay.[7] Once French minister at Peking, and more recently resident general at Tunis, Pichon was, according to one member of Bertie's staff, favourably regarded by public opinion as an 'enlightened and laborious official well-suited for his post by direct acquaintance with diplomacy and the administration of an important protectorate'.[8] Nevertheless, during the next four years Bertie was to complain frequently of Pichon's indolence. His habit of disappearing into the country for long intervals delayed negotiations and left the permanent officials of the foreign ministry with more influence than Bertie liked. Not that in Bertie's estimate Pichon was without an excuse for his misconduct. He felt that Clemenceau left Pichon with few opportunities for taking personal initiatives. 'I suppose', Bertie wrote in October 1908, 'that he feels that as his function is to register Clemenceau's decisions he may as well draw his pay and enjoy himself out shooting.'[9]

Unlike Bertie, who was a good shot, Pichon did not kill much. He did, however, preside over one of the few formal extensions of the geographical limits of the *entente* which took place in the decade before 1914. This was effected by the so-called Mediterranean agreements of 1907 — arrangements which seemed also to respond to the proposals that Bertie had made two years earlier for a British guarantee of Spain's possessions. His idea had not been forgotten in the Foreign Office.[10] It had been considered by Grey and Hardinge at the time of the Algeciras conference, and Nicolson even suggested to Révoil that the marriage of Alfonso XIII to an English princess in May 1906

---

[7] Bertie to Lansdowne, 15 June 1905, B.P., A, F.O.800/164. Watson, *Clemenceau*, pp.220 – 1.
[8] Memo. by Grahame enclosed in Bertie to Grey, 25 Oct. 1906, F.O.371/71, despt.404. Paul Cambon gave Pichon his seal of approval. Pichon seemed, he observed, to have 'l'esprit net et sensé'. P. Cambon to Barrère, 4 Nov. 1906, Barrère MSS. (Ministère des Affaires Étrangères), 1.
[9] Bertie to Hardinge, 26 Dec. 1907, B.P., A, F.O.800/164. Bertie to Hardinge, 26 June and 5 Oct. 1908, B.P., A, F.O.800/165. Bertie to Grey, 8, 21 and 30 Oct. 1909, Grey MSS., F.O.800/51. Bertie to Grey, 3 Jan. 1910, Grey MSS., F.O.800/52.
[10] The relations between the *entente* powers and Spain are considered in more detail in K.A. Hamilton, 'Great Britain, France, and the Origins of the Mediterranean Agreements of 16 May 1907', in B.J.C. McKercher and D.J. Moss (eds.), *Shadow and Substance in British Foreign Policy. Memorial Essays Honouring C.J. Lowe* (Edmonton, Alberta, 1984), pp.115 – 50.

might provide the occasion for taking up the subject.[11] But of more immediate concern to the British government in the aftermath of the conference had been the efforts of a German cable company, *Feltern und Guilleaume* of Cologne, to obtain from the Spanish government the right to extend the existing telegraph cable between Emden and Vigo to the Canaries with a view to the eventual achievement of an all-German cable link with South America and southern Africa. The scheme, which was backed by the German embassy at Madrid, offered Spain the benefits of improved domestic communications. Yet at the same time it presented a new challenge to the early pre-eminence which British companies had achieved in submarine telegraphy.[12] Once completed the German cable would compete for business with those operated by the *Eastern Telegraph Company*, and in an age in which governments were dependent upon cable telegraphy for the rapid transmission of information from one continent to another, it would, as the Admiralty maintained, have the undesirable effect of greatly strengthening German telegraph communications for war purposes.[13]

The French were equally apprehensive about the German project. They had for some time suspected the Germans of wanting to acquire a contract for a cable network in Morocco, and they feared that the granting to them of cable landing rights in the Canaries would hasten the achievement of this end.[14] Besides which, France had discreetly purchased a majority shareholding in the *South American Cable Company*, which, with the aid of a state subsidy, operated a cable between Senegal and Brazil.[15] But in seeking to persuade Spain to reject the German request, the French made no mention of this

---

[11] *Negotiations with the Spanish Government respecting a proposal that H.M. Govt. should undertake the defence of the Canary and Balearic Islands*, 9 March 1906, with minutes by Grey and Hardinge, F.O.371/135. On 31 May 1906 King Alfonso XIII married Princess Victoria Eugenia of Battenberg. De Margerie to J. Cambon, 12 March 1906, J. Cambon MSS., 11. *D.D.F.2*, IX, pt.2, no.453 and p.934.

[12] P.M. Kennedy, 'Imperial Cable Communications and Strategy, 1870–1914', *English Historical Review*, LXXXVI (1971), 728–52. J-C. Allain, *Agadir 1911. Une crise impérialiste en Europe pour la conquête du Maroc* (Paris, 1976), pp.133–5. Cartwright to Grey, 24 May 1906, F.O.368/51, despt.78c(ommercial). *Memo. respecting Cable Communications with the Canaries in relation to English, French, Spanish and German Interests*, by G. Young, 5 Nov. 1906, F.O.368/51. *General Report on Spain for the Year 1906*, F.O.371/366.

[13] Admiralty to F.O., 30 June 1906, F.O.368/51.

[14] Berard to M(inistère des) A(ffaires) É(trangères), 22 Dec. 1904; Berard to Rouvier, 10 July 1905; N.S. Maroc 394. The German delegation at the Algeciras conference had reserved for Germany the right to land a cable on the Moorish coast. *D.D.F.2*, X, no.166.

[15] Berard to M.A.E., 7 July 1906; Barthou to Pichon, 27 Feb. 1907; N.S. Maroc 394. Bourgeois to P. Cambon, 21 July 1906, N.S. Maroc 394, tel.28.

pecuniary interest and chose instead to give prominence to the threat which the concession would pose to Franco-Spanish aspirations in Morocco. Both Bourgeois and Pichon also wished to avoid taking a too overtly anti-German stance by relying on what they assumed to be Britain's superior strategic interest in opposing the laying of the cable.[16] At first, the British appeared ready to oblige. The Foreign Office persuaded a hesitant *Eastern Telegraph Company* to participate in the formation of what was in essence an Anglo-French consortium, but in name a Spanish cable company. This, in its turn, proposed to the Spanish government a project for the laying of a new cable between the Canaries and the Spanish mainland, in return for which it requested monopoly landing rights in the islands.[17]

Unfortunately for the British and French promoters of this venture it emerged during the autumn of 1906 that the Spanish authorities had already gone far towards committing themselves to acceptance of the German scheme. Moreover, *Feltern und Guilleaume* was ready to meet such objections as were made by the Spaniards, and von Radowitz, the German ambassador at Madrid, did all that he could to ensure a speedy settlement of the contract.[18] Grey was thus presented with the problem of trying to find a satisfactory basis upon which to oppose German diplomacy in Spain. He was evidently reluctant to seem to act simply in defence of a British commercial interest, and, as he explained to Bertie in a telegram of 22 December, he did not feel that Britain could 'on ground of Eastern Telegraph monopoly alone urge Spain to refuse German concession and make consequent sacrifice'. Nor did he regard the German wish to have a direct telegraphic communication with South America and southern Africa 'as an object which we could permanently oppose on its merits'.[19] Opposition to a German-controlled transatlantic cable would, Grey feared, 'give unnecessary provocation'.[20] Nevertheless, the foreign secretary was very much aware of Britain's obligation to support French designs upon Morocco, and he was reluctant to do anything that might harm the *entente*. If the French were sure that the

---

[16] Barthou to Pichon, 27 Feb. 1907, *ibid*. Bourgeois to J. Cambon, 10 July 1906, N.S. Maroc 394, tel.228. J. Cambon to Bourgeois, 11 and 12 July 1906, N.S. Maroc 394, tels.266 and 268. *D.D.F.2*, X, no.380. De Bunsen to Grey, 17 and 26 July 1906, F.O.368/51, despts.19c and 116c.
[17] Note to Hardinge, 25 July 1906, F.O.368/51. Grey to de Bunsen, 25 July 1906, F.O.368/51, tel.25c. Bourgeois to P. Cambon, 24 July 1906, N.S. Maroc, tel.228. Denison Pender to F.O., 27 Aug. 1906, F.O.368/51.
[18] De Bunsen to Grey, 18 and 28 Dec. 1906, F.O.368/51, despt.197c. and 204c.; *Further memo. respecting Cable Communications with the Canaries in relation to English, French, German and Spanish Interests*, by G. Young, 10 Jan. 1907, F.O.368/127.
[19] Grey to Bertie, 22 Dec. 1906, F.O.368/51, tel.9c.
[20] Grey to de Bunsen, 28 Dec. 1906, Grey MSS., F.O.800/77.

object of the German concession was to secure a communication to Morocco which could not otherwise be obtained, then, he informed Bertie, Britain would continue to support France's objections.[21] 'I should', he wrote to the prime minister, 'like to give a graceful concession to the Germans, but I do not like to do it in a matter which the French think will affect Morocco'.[22]

Bertie faithfully communicated Grey's views to the Quai d'Orsay.[23] Yet he was far from satisfied with what they implied. After all, it had long been the policy of the Foreign Office to protect the British telegraph companies against competition 'not merely out of consideration for British commercial interests, but also for strategical reasons'.[24] And just as Crowe cautioned the government against trying to conciliate Germany with 'graceful British concessions', so Bertie insisted on the need to resist what he considered to be German 'bluff'. Bertie feared that to do otherwise would be to sacrifice the happy results of the stand taken against the French at Fashoda, and mean a return to the days when Britain had been a country which other powers felt they could squeeze *ad libertum*.[25] In a private letter to Grey of 3 January 1907 he claimed that the *Eastern Telegraph Company* and the investment of British and French capital in the proposed Spanish cable were 'quite sufficient' to justify British opposition to the German cable. Starting from this premise, Bertie went on to warn Grey that it would not be advisable to let the French think, or give them grounds for saying, that in order to protect British interests 'we are using French interests in Morocco and our obligation to support them as a lever wherewith to oppose the laying of the German Cable to the Canaries'.[26]

Pichon did indeed arrive at just this conclusion, and in consequence he instructed Jules Cambon on 29 December that it was above all necessary that France should not appear as 'soulevant une opposition contre une entreprise allemande dans une intérêt purement et principalement française'. France, he thought, should simply seek to associate and concert her efforts with those of England.[27]

---

[21] Grey to Bertie, 22 Dec. 1906, F.O.368/51, tel.9c.
[22] Grey to Campbell-Bannerman, 27 Dec. 1906, Campbell-Bannerman MSS., Add. MS. 53514.
[23] *Aide-mémoire* enclosed in Bertie to Grey, 24 Dec. 1906, F.O.368/51, despt.318c. Oddly enough, Jules Cambon suspected that Bertie had exceeded his instructions, and that it was he, rather than Grey, who wished to persuade the French government to take the lead in opposing Germany on the cable question. J. Cambon to P. Cambon, 2 Jan. 1907, P. Cambon MSS., 11.
[24] Minute by Law on de Bunsen to Grey, 29 Dec. 1906, F.O.368/51, tel.83c.
[25] *B.D.*, III, pp.387–420. Bertie to Hardinge, 19 Jan. 1907, B.P., A, F.O.800/179.
[26] *B.D.*, VII, no.8.
[27] *D.D.F.2*, X, no.383.

Much as Jules Cambon may have agreed with the object of this message, he was disturbed by its tone. Had the British learnt of its contents, it would, he protested to his brother, Paul, have seemed like treachery, and it would have been 'un coup droit à l'entente cordiale'.[28] Nevertheless, he made it plain to de Bunsen, who had succeeded Nicolson at Madrid, and to Perez Caballero, the Spanish minister of state, that France intended to act with, 'mais derrière l'Angleterre'.[29] The impression left in London by this warning was somewhat modified by Arsène Henry, the *directeur commercial* at the Quai d'Orsay, who told Bertie on 5 January that notwithstanding a German undertaking not to connect their cable with Morocco, France was still 'strongly opposed' to it.[30] Moreover, Grey continued to insist that but for French interests he would offer no further opposition to the German cable. A reminder from the Foreign Office's commercial department that it had been at the government's behest that the *Eastern Telegraph Company* had entered the Anglo-French consortium, did lead Grey to show some belated concern for the company's position.[31] All effective British opposition to the German scheme was, however, to collapse after Grey learned of a German assurance that their cable would be laid direct from Emden to the Canaries and that it would not be extended to Morocco.[32]

Grey's attitude disappointed those in France who had deliberately understated their country's involvement in the transatlantic cable business.[33] But the prospect of Spain yielding to German solicitations, and the tardy response of the Spaniards to French requests for their military collaboration in Morocco, had already led to consideration being given in Paris to the idea of drawing the peninsular monarchy into a closer association with Britain and France. Jules Cambon, who had previously advocated a French guarantee of Spain as a means of safeguarding the Balearic and the Canaries against the threat of an American or British occupation, had become convinced of the virtues of such a tripartite accord. In any event, he thought that Spain should not be encouraged to lean towards England alone, and that France must be a party to any political understanding that the British might

[28] J. Cambon to P. Cambon, 2 Jan. 1907, P. Cambon MSS., 11.
[29] *D.D.F.2*, X, no.383.
[30] Bertie to Grey, 5 Jan. 1907, and minute by Villiers, F.O.368/127, tel.35c. Bertie to Grey, 5 Jan. 1907, despt.5c.
[31] Minute by Law on de Bunsen to Grey, 29 Dec. 1906, F.O.368/51, tel.83c. Grey to de Bunsen, 7 Jan. 1907, F.O.368/127, tel.3c.
[32] De Bunsen to Grey, 18 Jan. F.O.368/127, depst.9c., and minutes by Campbell, Hardinge and Grey. The concession was finally granted by royal decree to *Feltern und Guilleaume* in June 1907.
[33] Barthou to Pichon, 27 Feb. 1907; N.S. Maroc 394.

arange with Madrid.³⁴ During a visit to Paris in December 1906 he was able to examine these points with Paul Cambon, and as a result of their deliberations Bertie was broached upon this subject. Thus, on 22 December Paul Cambon took advantage of a conversation with Bertie about the cable concession and posssible German designs upon Spanish territory to suggest 'that it would perhaps be as well to make some arrangement between France, England, and Spain for the preservation of the *status quo* in the Mediterranean'. Two days later Pichon mentioned to Bertie a 'recollection in the Quai d'Orsay of some pourparlers or communications of some kind about Spanish Islands'.³⁵

Bertie deduced from these approaches that Jules Cambon had informed his brother of what Nicolson had said in 1905, and that the French now saw a tripartite accord as the best means of blocking German ambitions. It was not in itself a proposition for which he felt able to display much enthusiasm. He was doubtful about the way in which the cabinet would view such an extension of the *entente*, and he told Paul Cambon that although Grey would favour the proposal, he would have to reckon with the opposition of colleagues who were 'paralysés par les craintes de responsabilités'. But Bertie also recognized that the alarm expressed by the French over Germany's pretensions might furnish Britain with a good opportunity to achieve a politically more acceptable bilateral agreement with Spain. In a letter to Grey of 25 December he repeated the proposal that he had made to Lansdowne for an Anglo-Spanish understanding on Gibraltar and the Spanish islands. Again he emphasized that Gibraltar was a 'solid British interest', and that a sacrifice to secure it would be justified in 'public opinion in England, and foreign Powers would have no just cause for complaint'. Once more he explained that if Britain were to get on bad terms with the French they would instigate the Spaniards to put up works threatening Gibraltar, and that an Anglo-Spanish agreement on the rock might in 'ordinary circumstances' meet with French opposition. To this he added a warning to Grey about heeding the advice of 'experts'. Some, he observed, might think that a German occupation of the islands would not be harmful since it would necessitate a distribution of German

³⁴ J. Cambon to de Margerie, 15 March 1906, de Margerie MSS. (Ministère de Affaires Étrangères). De Margerie to de Billy, 30 June 1906, de Billy MSS. (Ministère des Affaires Étrangères) 63. Geneviève Tabouis, *The Life of Jules Cambon* (Oxford, 1938), p.152. Andrew, *Delcassé*, pp.149–51. 191–4 and 217. *D.D.F.2*, III, nos.144 and 195; VI, no.403; VIII, nos.223 and 295. J. Cambon to Bourgeois, 19 May 1906, N.S. Espagne 41, despt.74.
³⁵ J. Cambon to P. Cambon, 2 Jan. 1907, P. Cambon MSS., 11. *D.D.F.2*, X, nos.384 and 390. *B.D.*, VII, nos.6 and 7.

naval forces which would be advantageous to Britain in the event of a war. Yet, as his long stay at the Foreign Office had taught him, experts could often differ in their opinions.[36]

What Bertie may not have been aware of was that the whole subject of an arrangement with Spain had already come under the scrutiny of military and naval experts in Whitehall. At a time when a Franco-Spanish military intervention in the area around Tangier had seemed imminent Hardinge had reminded Grey that Spain was under no obligation towards Britain not to alienate any of the zone of influence that she had been promised in northern Morocco. To remedy this 'serious flaw' in the arrangements of 1904, he suggested to Grey on 8 December that he should recall the attention of de Villa Urrutia, who was now Spanish ambassador in London, to the proposal that Lansdowne had put to him in June 1905.[37] Grey recognized the value of such an accord, but he, like Bertie, raised the subject of Gibraltar. Reluctant to multiply the country's treaty obligations, he minuted on 12 December that what would exert a 'determining influence' on his decision was the 'question of the necessity of making further provision for the security of Gibraltar, and of the possibility of attaining this object by the means proposed'.[38] But by 1906 Britain's service chiefs had doubts about whether any assurance from Spain covering the absence or presence of gun emplacements in the vicinity of Gibraltar would be of advantage to Britain. At a meeting on 20 December of the Committee of Imperial Defence (C.I.D.) the chief of the general staff argued that guns using indirect fire could always be hidden in the folds of the ground behind Gibraltar, and that they 'would be more effective than if mounted in permanent works'.[39] Given this assumption, the only effective solution to the problem of Gibraltar's security was in the view of Sir George Clarke, the secretary of the committee, to maintain good relations with Spain.[40]

Informed of this military advice, Bertie carefully amended his argument. 'As Gibraltar appears to be at the mercy of mortars placed in Spanish ground invisible from Gibraltar is it not of vital importance', he asked Grey, 'to make sacrifices to retain the permanent friendship of Spain and therefore to guarantee her island property?'[41] This was a somewhat different view from that which he

---

[36] *B.D.*, *ibid.*
[37] *B.D.*, VII, no.3.
[38] Minute by Grey, 12 Dec. 1906, CAB.38/12/58. *B.D.*, VII, nos.4 and 5.
[39] Minutes of the 94th. meeting of the C.I.D., 20 Dec. 1906, CAB.38/12/59.
[40] *Note on the Spanish Territory adjacent to Gibraltar* by Clarke, 16 Dec. 1906, F.O.371/364. *Spanish territory which British interests required to be secured against alienation to another Power*, note by Clarke, 28 Dec., 1906, CAB.38/12/62.
[41] *B.D.*, VII, no.8. Grey to Bertie, 30 Dec. 1906, B.P., A, F.O.800/177.

had expressed during the confrontation over gun emplacements in 1898. Then Bertie had advised Balfour that if Gibraltar were 'useless to us without Spain as a reliable friend . . . we had better remove our guns &c. to some more eligible situation, and blow up as much as we can at Gibraltar'.[42] But whatever may have been his original concern for the future of the rock, this was now relegated to a secondary role in the case which he presented to the foreign secretary. 'The safety of Gibraltar might', he suggested, 'be used as an ostensible reason for an agreement with Spain though the maintenance of the integrity of Spain in the interests of the balance of power is really quite sufficient justification for a guarantee by us.' He also made it clear that the primary purpose of such a guarantee would be to deter Germany. In the existing circumstances, he reasoned, the German government could always establish interests in Spain's possessions, provoke a quarrel between its nationals and the local authorities, and then take the opportunity to seize an island. If, however, Britain were bound to defend the Spanish islands, then, Bertie claimed, the Germans would 'take good care not to push matters unless they desired war with us'.[43]

The likelihood of Britain achieving a bilateral accord with Spain was in the meanwhile diminished by Jules Cambon. Possibly spurred on by the knowledge that he was soon to be appointed French ambassador at Berlin, he began shortly after his return to Madrid to explore with Perez Caballero the basis of a tripartite agreement. He thought de Bunsen favourable to the idea, and he proceeded to draft a *projet de note*. This was intended to commit Britain, France and Spain to the preservation of the territorial *status quo* in their respective possessions in the Mediterranean and eastern Atlantic, and to provide for mutual consultations and diplomatic assistance.[44] As such, even without any specific reference to Gibraltar, it did not conflict in principle with the requirements set by the C.I.D. for an Anglo-Spanish agreement. Nevertheless, the news which reached London on 8 January 1907 that Jules Cambon had made a verbal communication of its terms to Alfonso XIII and Perez Caballero was resented in the Foreign Office. With the exception of what Paul Cambon and Pichon had said to Bertie before Christmas, there had been no recent exchange of views between the British and French governments on this issue. True, Jules Cambon had acted on his own initiative. His intervention had, however, circumscribed British diplomacy at Madrid. De Bunsen had deliberately refrained from broaching the subject with Perez Caballero because of the uncertain

---

[42] Bertie to Balfour, 14 Sept. 1898, Balfour MSS., Add. MS. 49746.
[43] *B.D.*, VII, no.8.
[44] *D.D.F.2*, X, no.384.

state of Spanish politics. He was, in any case, under the impression that the Spaniards would prefer a bilateral accord, or that the proposal should at least be a British one.[45] Bertie too was upset by an intervention which seemed more likely to obstruct than facilitate the offer of a British pledge to Spain. He still considered Lansdowne to have been mistaken in taking the French into his confidence in a matter which was purely Anglo-Spanish, and, like Tyrrell, he thought that it would be better if Britain were to conclude an agreement with Spain and invite France to join later.[46]

Grey seems to have favoured just such a course. He had already been persuaded of the advantages of a British guarantee of Spain as a means of deterring the Germans from transforming a cable landing place into a territorial occupation.[47] In terms which echoed Bertie's earlier appeal he thus advised the prime minister that Britain should counter German endeavours 'to get an ascendancy over Spain', and give her confidence by offering to protect her possessions in return for guarantees which would increase the security of Gibraltar.[48] Campbell-Bannerman assented to an approach to Spain along these lines.[49] Nevertheless, as became apparent during the next two months, the British were mistaken in thinking that the Spaniards could thus be satisfied. Despite reports of the desire of Alfonso XIII for an Anglo-Spanish accord, the conservative administration which he appointed at the end of January was averse to any explicit endorsement of Britain's possession of Gibraltar, and preferred a tripartite agreement which would preserve for Spain 'a place in the concert of Europe'.[50] Antonio Maura, the new Spanish premier, was clearly impressed by the arguments of Jules Cambon, and the draft treaty which Villa Urrutia finally delivered to the Foreign Office on 25 March bore a marked resemblance to the French ambassador's proposals.[51]

The Spanish project was regarded with some scepticism in London.[52] There the government's principal naval advisers persisted in thinking that the advantages to be derived from an Anglo-Spanish

---

[45] B.D., VII, no.9.
[46] Bertie to Hardinge, 19 Jan. 1907, B.P., A, F.O.800/179.
[47] Grey to de Bunsen, 9 Jan. 1907, F.O.368/127, despt.4c.
[48] Grey to Campbell-Bannerman, 11 Jan. 1907, Campbell-Bannerman MSS., Add. MS. 52514.
[49] Campbell-Bannerman to Grey, 14 Jan. 1907, Grey MSS., F.O.800/100.
[50] De Bunsen to Grey, 26 Jan. 1907, F.O.371/334, despt.27. J. Cambon to Pichon, 9 Feb. 1907, N.S. Espagne 41. J. Cambon to Pichon, 24 Feb. 1907, N.S. Espagne 41. tel. 4. Memo. P. Cambon MSS., 11. B.D., VII, no.16.
[51] D.D.F.2, X, nos.423 and 428. De Bunsen to Grey, 23 Feb. 1907, Grey MSS., F.O.800/77. B.D., VII, nos.17 and 18.
[52] D.D.F.2, X, no.412.

agreement 'would be much greater in the case of a war with France than they would be in the case of a war with Germany'.⁵³ Grey's chief objection to a tripartite agreement stemmed, however, from his concern about its reception in Britain and abroad. He had been hoping to fend off criticism of his diplomacy by giving prominence to the additional security that an arrangement with Spain would provide for Gibraltar, and he probably shared Hardinge's fear that unless an Anglo-Franco-Spanish accord were kept secret it would be 'seriously resented' in Germany, where it would 'appear as a tightening of the net around German political activity'.⁵⁴ In order to overcome this problem Hardinge recommended, and Grey accepted, the idea of reducing the projected agreement to an exchange of notes between Britain and Spain. These, which Hardinge drafted, established that the two governments were resolved to maintain their respective rights over their maritime and insular possessions in the Mediterranean and the eastern Atlantic, and provided for joint consultations in the event of a threat to the *status quo*. Grey assumed that the notes would be published. He also thought that France might supplement her existing agreement with Spain with a similar note, or that Britain might assure the French that she would consult with them at the same time as with Madrid.⁵⁵

An exchange of notes was hardly compatible with the tripartite agreement that the Cambon brothers had envisaged. Nevertheless, at the beginning of April 1907, when Grey was preparing to have Hardinge convey his latest ideas to Spain, they were poorly placed to influence events, Jules had already left Madrid for Berlin, Paul was about to embark on a visit to Italy, and Pichon was on the point of leaving Paris for his Easter holiday. Besides which, Clemenceau, the political future of whose government was in question, appears to have been as anxious as Grey to avoid offering further provocation to the Germans. Neither he nor Pichon was therefore in any mood to quibble over what was essentially a matter of form, and on 6 April Bertie gained their consent to a parallel British and French exchange of notes with Spain.⁵⁶ This enabled Hardinge, who from 8 to 10 April accompanied Edward VII on a semi-official visit to Alfonso XIII at Cartagena, to persuade Maura to forego a tripartite treaty.⁵⁷ But from Berlin Jules Cambon persisted in pressing upon the Quai

---

⁵³ Note by Admiralty, 25 Feb. 1907, CAB.38/13/11.
⁵⁴ *B.D.*, VII, nos.11, 14 and 19.
⁵⁵ *Ibid.* nos.20. 21 and 23.
⁵⁶ *Ibid.* nos.22 and 24. Bertie to Grey, 30 March 1907, B.P., A, F.O.800/164.
⁵⁷ Hardinge to Bertie, 10 April 1907, B.P., A, F.O.800/179. Diary, 1907 – 9, pp.26 – 9. Rumbold MSS., Dep.I/3. *B.D.*, VII, nos. 25 and 26. P. Cambon to Pichon, 25 April 1907, N.S. Espagne 41, despt. 147.

d'Orsay the importance of uniting the three powers by a single instrument, and, after consultations with Paul Cambon and Clemenceau, Pichon sought British acceptance of what would have amounted to a complementary Anglo-French exchange of notes.[58] Bertie alone amongst Grey's officials saw some advantage in what others regarded as an attempt to resuscitate the notion of an accord à trois.[59] Reconciled to France being a party to an understanding with Spain, he advised Grey in a despatch of 26 April that a separate agreement with France would be useful as if France were defeated by Germany in a war in which Britain was not engaged, 'it would give us a locus standi to object to the transfer to Germany of any of the French possessions covered by the engagement between France and England'. Grey recognized that such a *locus standi* would make it easier for the government to put its case before the public.[60] He restricted himself, however, to telling Paul Cambon that it would be 'much better to make a simple communication to each other of the text of the Notes which we had exchanged with Spain, and to express our views in conversation'.[61]

In the end it was this procedure that was followed when on 16 May 1907 near identical notes on a basis similar to that proposed by Hardinge were exchanged by Britain and France with Spain.[62] Thus on the same day Grey, in a declaration which he recorded in an *aide-mémoire*, assured Paul Cambon that if in the circumstances alluded to in the notes it should be necessary for the British and Spanish governments to communicate with each other, both would be able to communicate with the French government, 'knowing that France takes the same view, and is firmly resolved to preserve intact her rights over her insular and maritime possessions in the regions referred to'. Cambon likewise informed Grey of his goverment's readiness to concert with the British government at the same time as with Spain.[63] Pichon had hoped that the notes would remain a secret, and Grey was prepared to delay their publication until the matter was raised in parliament.[64] But the royal visit to Cartagena had already

---

[58] Pichon to Daeschner, 16 April 1907, N.S. Espagne 41, despt.323. Pichon to P. Cambon, 20 April 1907, N.S. Espagne 41. Bertie to Grey, 21 April 1907, F.O.371/364, despt.201. *B.D.*, VII, nos. 29, 30 and 31. *D.D.F.2*, X, no.458.
[59] Note by Grey and minute by Hardinge (registered 24 April 1907); Grey to Bertie, 25 and 26 April 1907; F.O.371/364, despt.249 and 252. P. Cambon to Pichon, 24 April 1907, N.S. Espagne 41, despt.43.
[60] Bertie to Grey, 27 April 1907, F.O.371/364, despt.217, and minutes by Hardinge and Grey.
[61] Grey to Bertie, 26 April 1907, F.O.371/364, despt.252.
[62] Campbell-Bannerman to Edward VII, 1 May 1907, CAB.41/31/17. *B.D.*, VII, nos.39, 40, 41 and 46.
[63] *B.D.*, VII, nos.42 and 43.
[64] *Ibid.* nos.35, 37 and 38. *D.D.F.2*, X, no.489.

led to rumours of an impending Anglo-Spanish naval alliance, and when towards the end of May it became apparent that the French press might know the contents of the notes, Pichon consulted with France's ambassadors at London, Madrid and Rome. Always the opportunist, Barrère suggested that they might profit from the occasion 'pour revenir sur certains engagements moraux et les faire renouveler'.[65] What this amounted to was made clear by Paul Cambon when on 6 June he reminded Grey that the Moroccan crisis had turned the Anglo-French agreement into 'something like an alliance', and enquired 'whether if Germany brought pressure to bear on France or Spain in consequence of the Spanish Notes, English support would be forthcoming'. In reply, Grey, without questioning Cambon's assertion, offered the assurance that he would 'regard the spirit of the Agreement of 1904' as applying to the provisions of the notes: a phrase which, given Britain's stance in 1905, could be interpreted as meaning that he would be prepared to contemplate giving more than just diplomatic assistance to France and Spain.[66]

Bertie, who gave Pichon a similar assurance on 22 June, was no doubt satisfied with these arrangements.[67] Although he had originally advocated a bilateral agreement with Spain which would appear to provide Gibraltar with additional security, he could hardly complain at an exchange of notes which committed Spain to consultations and the preservation of the *status quo*. Moreover, while the notes did not in themselves tighten the Anglo-French *entente*, Grey's declaration did seem to extend the area within which Britain was bound to cooperate with France. But Bertie was unsympathetic to the idea, much favoured by Barrère and other French diplomats, of including Italy in a sort of quadruple Mediterranean agreement. When on 1 November 1907 Barrère put it to him that Italy should be encouraged to make an agreement with England analogous to the Anglo-Spanish exchange of notes, he was curtly informed that that would be an 'unnecessary offence to Germany'. Spain, Bertie explained, had possessions with which she might be persuaded to part, but there was no likelihood of Italy behaving in that fashion, and 'if she required to be protected from the rapacity of others we could always defend her without an

---

[65] P. Cambon to Pichon, 26 April, 9 May and 6 June 1907, N.S. Espagne 41, despt.149, and tels.48 and 71. Pichon to P. Cambon, 27 May 1907, N.S. Espagne 41, tel.71. Bertie to Grey, 31 May and 1 June 1907, F.O.371/364, tels.20 and 21. *B.D.*, VII, no.45. Lee, *Edward VII*, II, p.450.
[66] *B.D.*, VII, no.50.
[67] Bertie to Grey, 22 June 1907, F.O.371/364 despt.320.

agreement'.⁶⁸ What Bertie had encouraged Grey to pursue was not a realignment of the Mediterranean powers, but a limited local accord whose main purpose was to deter Germany from seeking, and to discourage the Spaniards from conceding, a port or coaling station in their territories.

The Mediterranean agreements were portrayed in both the Austrian and the German press as yet another example of a policy designed in London with the purpose of containing and further isolating Germany.⁶⁹ The news of their conclusion had an equally cool reception in St Petersburg. Alexandre Izvolsky, the Russian foreign minister, complained to the French ambassador, Maurice Bompard, that the notes would have a deplorable effect upon the government in Berlin, which was only 'trop disposé prendre pour diriger contre lui tout ce qui est fait sans lui'.⁷⁰ Indeed, he seemed prepared to encourage just such inclinations. He told the German ambassador at St Petersburg that the notes had introduced a 'third western power into the entente cordiale' and constituted a 'link in a chain which England was forging around Germany'.⁷¹ Izvolsky's intention was to dissociate Russia from a move which might incur German ill-will. At a time when Russia had still not recovered from her defeat in the Far East, and when he was engaged in negotiations with Britain for the removal of outstanding causes of Anglo-Russian friction in Persia and central Asia, Izvolsky wanted to maintain good relations with Germany in Europe. Yet wise though this may have been, further efforts on his part to reassure Germany of 'Russia's amicable intentions were disconcerting for France, and disturbing for those, who, like Bertie, were attached to the maintenance of the balance of power.

The convention which the British and Russian governments eventually concluded on 31 August 1907 appeared to complement the *entente cordiale*. Bertie had favoured such an understanding.⁷² But he did not share the enthusiasm of either Hardinge or Nicolson, his successor at St Petersburg, for a closer relationship with Russia. Nor

---

⁶⁸ *B.D.*, VII, no.14; VIII, no.20. J. Cambon, to Pichon, 5 Feb. 1907, N.S. Espagne 41. Barrère to Pichon, 19 April 1907, N.S. Espagne 41, tel.130.
⁶⁹ Memo. by Lord Granley enclosed in de Salis to Grey, 21 June 1907, F.O.371/364, despt.300.
⁷⁰ Bompard to J. Cambon, 15 June 1907, J. Cambon MSS., 14. G. Chklaver (ed.), *Au Service de la Russie: Alexandre Isvolsky correspondance diplomatique, 1906–1911* (Paris, 1937), pp, 161–2.
⁷¹ *G.P.*, XXV, pt.1, no.8544.
⁷² Monger, pp.281–5. Beryl Williams, 'Great Britain and Russia, 1905 to the 1907 Convention', Hinsley, pp.133–47.

did Bertie exhibit much faith in Russian protestations of friendship and goodwill. In this respect he was particularly suspicious of Izvolsky. The latter, a devious and self-centred career diplomat, certainly left a poor impression upon Bertie when the two men met for the first time in the autumn of 1906. Then, as later, Izvolsky had wanted to avoid offending the Germans through his negotiations with the British, and with this in mind he had set out in October on a private journey across Europe which took him first to Paris, and then to Berlin. He had not intended to go to London, and Count Benckendorff, the Russian ambassador there, was asked to join him in Paris.[73] There was no just reason why the British should have been upset by this itinerary, and all might have been well had not Edward VII happened to remark to Poklewsky, the Russian *chargé d'affaires* at London, that he would welcome a visit from Izvolsky. Hardinge was pleased with this suggestion. But after having heard Poklewsky's objections with regard to the ill-effects that such a visit could have upon the susceptibilities of other powers, he persuaded Grey not to send an official invitation.[74] Unfortunately, Bertie was not informed of these proceedings, and hence his surprise when on 22 October Izvolsky, who had already been warned by Benckendorff that Bertie was not 'un bon intermédiare', presented himself at the embassy in order to explain why he had declined the king's proffered hospitality. He told Bertie that he could not go to London as the press would make out that the negotiations with Britain had gone further than they had, and because he would have to discuss matters for which he was not prepared. Furthermore, he said that he wanted to ascertain at Berlin what interests Germany had in Persia so as to avoid the sort of crisis that France had had to contend with over Morocco[75]

Grey and Hardinge accepted Izvolsky's explanations in good faith. Bertie did not. Like Clemenceau, he suspected that in deciding not to go to London, Izvolsky had changed his plans in deference to Berlin. Moreover, he was annoyed at Izvolsky consulting with the Germans on what he considered to be an Anglo-Russian matter. As Germany had stated that her interests in Persia were 'purely commercial', Bertie thought that it would be sufficient for Britain and Russia to accept this and act accordingly. This was not, however, the opinion of

---

[73] For a fuller discussion of the international problems confronting Izvolsky in 1906 see: P. Luntinen, *The Baltic Question* (Helsinki, 1975), pp.75–81; and D.C.B. Lieven, *Russia and the Origins of the First World War* (London, 1983). pp.31–3. Chklaver, pp.365–7. Bertie to Grey, 21 Oct. 1906, F.O.371/74, despt.394.
[74] Hardinge to Nicolson, 21 Oct. 1906, Nicolson MSS., F.O.800/335. Chklaver, pp.379–82.
[75] Chklaver, pp.374–6 and 382–5. *B.D.*, IV, nos.230 and 233. Bertie to Grey, 26 Oct. 1906, B.P., A, F.O.800/177.

the Russians, and Benckendorff's observation to Bertie that Russia 'was under great obligations to Germany and was bound to conciliate her as much as possible' would hardly have allayed Bertie's fears. It seemed to him that Russia would not go far without German permission, and in a letter to Mallet of 23 October he predicted that Izvolsky would 'make use of German pretensions in negotiating with us and will use us in coming to terms with Germany'.[76] Even after Grey had explained to him that it was the 'King's verbal invitation and not any change in his own plans which was the origin of M. Iswolsky's explanation for not coming', Bertie clung to the view that he had originally meant to go to London. 'Iswolsky's face', he wrote, 'reminded me very much of Ignatieff [the former Russian ambassador at Constantinople] who was known as the grandfather of lies. Absit omen'.[77]

Bertie's opinion of Izvolsky was not improved by Russia's attitude towards recent political developments in Scandinavia. There the separation of Norway from Sweden in 1905 had led to the search for some kind of international agreement with which to replace the guarantee that Britain and France had given to the twin kingdoms just fifty years before. The danger for Britain was that without a new accord the Scandinavian states might through weakness and isolation gravitate towards their stronger continental neighbours.[78] Another possibility was that the Germans would try to neutralize Denmark, and thereby seek to close the Baltic to the warships of non-riverain powers. This, Bertie believed, could well form the basis of a Russo-German deal, and in November 1906 he said as much to Pichon.[79] It was not, however, clear that the neutralization of Denmark would shut the approaches to the Baltic, and a more worrying prospect for Britain's defence experts was an international agreement, which, in the event of an Anglo-German war, would leave the Germans free to occupy Jutland, but oblige France and Russia to oppose Britain's seizure of a Norwegian port.[80] This seemed likely to materialize when in June 1907 Norway yielded to pressure, and accepted a Russian

---

[76] *B.D.*, IV, nos.231 and 232. Bertie to Grey, 4 Nov. 1906, Grey MSS., F.O.800/49. Bertie to Mallet, 23 Oct. 1906, B.P., A, F.O.800/177. Barrère told Bertie that he 'knew for certain that Isvolsky had been dissuaded from going to England by the German Government'. *B.D.*, VIII, no.109.
[77] *B.D.*, IV, no.237. Bertie to Grey, 10 Nov. 1906, Grey MSS., F.O.800/49.
[78] Luntinen, pp.43–9 and 91–100. Folke Lindberg, *Scandinavia in Great Power Politics, 1905–1908* (Stockholm, 1958), pp.3–48. D.W. Sweet, 'The Baltic in British Diplomacy before the First World War', *Historical Journal*, XIII (1970), 451–90.
[79] Bertie to Grey, 2, 20 and 23 Dec. 1906, F.O.371/98, despts.482, 531 and 536.
[80] Luntinen, pp.97–100, 114–19 and 127–31. *D.D.F.2*, X, no.318. Minutes of the 95th meeting of the C.I.D., 21 Feb. 1907, CAB.38/13/10. Sweet, 'The Baltic', 461–3.

draft treaty which provided for a great power guarantee of her neutrality. Sweden's security was also brought into question by the request made by Izvolsky on 25 June for the abrogation of the convention of 1856 which forbade Russia's fortificaion of the Aland islands.[81]

Izvolsky's proposal provided Grey with the occasion to reject outright the neutralization of Norway.[82] It also reawakened Bertie's fears about the dangers inherent in Russia's ambitions. On 9 July Bertie observed to Clemenceau that it was a 'curious coincidence' that Russia should introduce her demand for the abrogation of the Aland islands convention, which 'would reduce Sweden to the position of a Russian Grand Duchy', at the same time as she proposed, and Norway accepted, a treaty which would deprive the Norwegians and the Swedes of the opportunity to make arrangements for their common defence. He put it to Clemenceau that 'he not having Russian predilections could not be in favour of making the Baltic a Russo-German lake', and that given the intimacy between the Russian and German emperors, Russia might not continue to be France's ally. There might, Bertie implied, be a renewal of the *Dreikaiserbund*. For the moment Clemenceau thought that unlikely. Yet the speed with which the Germans adhered to Russia's latest proposals for Norway's neutralization led Bertie to suspect that the Germans and the Russians had already arrived at a preliminary agreement.[83] Bompard reached much the same conclusion.[84] Indeed, Izvolsky seems to have been set upon the pursuit of what Bompard defined as a 'politique d'équilibre entre toutes les Puissances'. He wanted to balance his projected convention with the British with an equivalent understanding with the Germans, and during a meeting of Nicholas II and William II at Swinemünde in early August he suggested an agreement whose effect would have been to exclude non-riverain powers from the affairs of the Baltic.[85]

The Germans responded with caution. They were reluctant to subscribe to an arrangement which seemed to be so clearly anti-British, and they preferred the notion of a Baltic agreement on the model of the Mediterranean accords. As a result, on 29 October

---

[81] Sweet, 'The Baltic'. 463 – 4. *B.D.*, VIII, no.95.
[82] Luntinen, pp.136 – 40.
[83] *B.D.*, VIII, no.106.
[84] *D.D.F.2*, XI, no.30. Nicolson to Grey, 18 June 1907, F.O.371/358, despt.328. Nicolson to Hardinge, 19 June 1907, Hardinge MSS., 10.
[85] Luntinen, pp.20 – 4, 131 – 3 and 156 – 71. Lindberg, pp.94 – 104 and 156 – 66. Bompard initially believed that Izvolsky had gone to Swinemünde in order to prevent Nicholas I from falling prey to the intrigues of William II. Bompard to Pichon, 10 Aug.

Germany and Russia concluded a secret protocol which expressed the desire of the two powers to maintain the Baltic *status quo*, and their willingness to sign similar accords with Denmark and Sweden. The Germans also declared that they would not regard the abrogation of the Aland islands convention as contrary to these provisions.[86] In the meantime, however, the Swinemünde meeting had helped generate fresh speculation in London and Paris about what was going on between Germany and Russia.

Bertie was both more prepared than were his friends in the Foreign Office to endorse French suspicions of the existence of a Russo-German understanding, and less disposed than was Pichon to attribute the initiative for such an accommodation to Germany.[87] He was also doubtful about the extent to which Britain could rely on French support in opposing any attempt to convert the Baltic into a closed sea. 'In questions such as that of the Baltic', he noted, 'where French and British interests are identical but not in accordance with those of Russia or of Germany, the French Government are inclined to leave the defence of them to His Majesty's Government.'[88] On 1 November he admonished Barrère on this point, and when, after the signing of an international guarantee of Norway's integrity, the French began to show some concern over the future of Sweden, Bertie spared few words in reminding Pichon that Britain could not be expected to defend French interests without her assistance.[89] But it was not long before reports of Izvolsky's dealings with the Germans were to cause the French to complain loudly over the conduct of their ally. Bertie wrote to Grey on 13 November that the French possessed 'reliable information' about a Franco-German understanding, and a fortnight later he informed the foreign secretary that he knew for certain that an agreement had been concluded. He had no idea about what its terms were, or whether Sweden was a party to it. Nor for that matter did he tell Grey from whence he had received this intelligence, save to say that it had not come from the Quai d'Orsay — an

---

1907, Pichon MSS. (Bibliothèque de l'Institut de France), 4395. Bompard to Louis, 16 Nov. 1907, Louis MSS. (Ministère des Affaires Étrangères) 1.
[86] Luntinen and Lindberg, *ibid.*
[87] *B.D.*, VIII, nos.107 and 111. *D.D.F.2*, XI, no.196. Minute by Spicer on Bertie to Grey, 1 Nov. 1907, F.O.371/358, despt.525. Minute by Hardinge on Bertie to Grey, 1 Nov. 1907, F.O.371/358, despt.526. Bompard to Pichon, 16 Nov. 1907, Pichon, MSS. (B.I.F.), 4395. Lindberg, pp.166 – 9. Sweet, 'The Baltic', 467 – 8.
[88] Bertie to Grey, 13 Nov. 1907, F.O.371/358, despt.544.
[89] *B.D.*, VIII, no.109. Bertie to Grey, 7 Nov. 1907, F.O.371/338, despt.534. Sweet, 'The Baltic', 466 – 7.

intimation which suggests that Clemenceau may have been the source.[90]

Hardinge was very reluctant to believe that the Russians had settled anything with the Germans[91] Moreover, the endeavours of the German government to forestall a British intervention in its negotiations with Russia by proposing a *status quo* agreement for the countries of the North Sea, reinforced the tendency in the Foreign Office to regard Berlin as the prime-mover in the pursuit of a Baltic accord.[92] The fact that France was not invited to join in the proposed North Sea arrangement seemed once more to demonstrate Germany's desire to split the *entente*.[93] Neither Pichon nor his officials were, however, especially worried by this German move, and the eventual communication of the proposal to Paris removed any serious difficulty with regard to it.[94] On the other hand, Russian attempts to explain the object of their diplomacy did nothing to mollify the French, who grew increasingly angry over what they perceived as Izvolsky's duplicity. Clemenceau was particularly vociferous in his denunciation of the Russians.[95] On 12 December he warned Lister, temporarily left in charge of the embassy, that he had learnt that the Russo-German agreement was not yet signed, and that he intended to 'brouiller' the cards between Russia and Germany by taking a stand on France's treaty obligations in the Baltic, and by exercising financial pressure on the Russians. 'If', Lister observed in a private letter to Hardinge, 'he succeeds in upsetting the Russo-German agreement, the Germans will be furious and they will seek to vent their ill-humour elsewhere; probably in Morocco. He believes that one guarantee more of peace has disppeared, and that these negotiations have brought France and Germany a step nearer to War.'[96]

---

[90] Bertie to Grey, 13 Nov. 1907, F.O.371/358, despt.544. Bertie to Grey, 28 Nov. 1907, B.P., A, F.O.800/177. Bompard seems to have had no very specific information with regard to a Russo-German agreement. Such an arrangement might, he thought, relate to the Aland islands. Bompard to Pichon, 30 Nov. 1907, Pichon MSS. (B.I.F.), 4395. Bompard to Louis, 30 Nov. 1907, Louis MSS., 1.
[91] Minutes by Hardinge on Bertie to Grey, 1 and 13 Nov. 1907, F.O.371/338, despts.526 and 544.
[92] Luntinen, pp.183–4. *B.D.*, VIII, no.113.
[93] Tyrrell to Grey, 5 Dec. 1907, Grey MSS., F.O.800/92. Grey to Bertie, 6 Dec. 1907, Grey MSS., F.O.800/51. Minute by Hardinge on Nicolson to Grey, 4 Dec. 1907, F.O.371/338, tel.255. *B.D.*, VIII, nos.117 and 121.
[94] *D.D.F.2*, XI, nos.222, 224 and 225. *B.D.*, VIII, no.120. Lister to Hardinge, 17 Dec. 1907, B.P., A, F.O.800/177.
[95] M. Bompard, *Mon Ambassade en Russie, 1903–1908* (Paris, 1937), pp.281–2. Nicolson to Grey, 15 Dec. 1907, B.P., A, F.O.800/177. *B.D.*, VIII, nos.123, 126, 128 and 130.
[96] Lister to Hardinge, 12 Dec. 1907, B.P., A, F.O.800/77. *B.D.*, VIII, no.121.

Clemenceau's anger was, as Lister understood, directed against Izvolsky. But Grey, to whom Hardinge showed Lister's letter, was upset by what he regarded as a threat by Clemenceau to provoke a quarrel with the Germans over what was assumed in London to be no more than a question of *amour propre*. The Foreign Office held the view that Russia and Germany had taken the Mediterranean accords as their model, that Izvolsky had done nothing more than consult the Germans on what should be settled with the Swedes, and that an agreement on the Baltic *status quo* was in any case a relatively insignificant matter.[97] Even Lister, who thought that Clemenceau was right to want France to be associated with the proposed arrangements, feared that he could be playing Germany's game, and that Germany might reemerge in her old position of *tertius gaudens*.[98] When, however, Clemenceau met Bertie on 23 December he assured the ambassador that he had no intention of 'quarrelling with Germany or breaking with Russia'. What, he said, he could not tolerate was that Russia should secretly enter into a compact with Germany in which French interests were involved. Besides which, he insisted to Bertie that he had positive German written proof that the negotiations for a Russo-German agreement had been initiated by Russia, that the terms were arranged, and that it went beyond the mere maintenance of the *status quo*. Then, after roundly abusing Izvolsky, he added that 'means must be found for getting rid of him'.[99]

Bertie did his best to explain Clemenceau's attitude to the Foreign Office. He wrote to Hardinge that he did not think that Clemenceau would 'do anything rash, though he may talk of what he could do to punish Russia for her treason if he chose to do so'.[100] Hardinge was far from reassured. On 24 December he complained to Nicolson that the French were 'stupid and would, to satisfy their amour propre, like Izvolsky to fall'.[101] Hardinge may have expressed similar sentiments to Léon Geoffray, the French *chargé d'affaires* in London. In any event, a report by Geoffray on Hardinge's observations to him was sufficient to cause Clemenceau to summon Bertie to his presence on Christmas day.[102] Hardinge later claimed that Geoffray must have

---

[97] *B.D.*, VIII, no.124. Grey to Lister, 16 Dec. 1907, B.P., A, F.O.800/177. Grey to Lister, 17 Dec. 1907, F.O.371/338, despt.711. Minute by Grey on Bertie to Grey, 6 Dec. 1907, F.O.371/338, despt.586.
[98] Lister to Grey, 18 Dec. 1907; Lister to Hardinge, 18 Dec. 1907; B.P., A, F.O.800/177.
[99] Bertie to Grey, 23 Dec. 1907, *ibid. B.D.*, VIII, nos.115 and 157.
[100] Bertie to Hardinge, 23 Dec. 1907, B.P. Add. MS. 63021.
[101] Hardinge to Lister, 17 Dec. 1907, B.P., A, F.O.800/177. *B.D.*, VIII, no.134.
[102] *B.D.*, VIII, nos.115 and 134.

exaggerated what he had said. Clemenceau was, nevertheless, worried by the British reactions to his complaints, and he insisted that Lister must have misunderstood him for he had never meant to convey the idea that the French would become 'guerriers'.[103] What is more likely is that Clemenceau had said just what Lister had reported, and that he had only realized what Grey might infer from his language when he was reminded of it by Bertie. The Foreign Office's reaction to Clemenceau's protests had, on the other hand, been governed by Grey's impression that Germany had been bent upon demonstrating that she was not isolated, and Hardinge's unwillingness, despite mounting evidence to the contrary, to attribute any deception to Izvolsky. It was then natural that they should have regarded Clemenceau's threats to intervene in the Baltic negotiations as directed towards the frustration of Germany, rather than the chastisement of Russia.[104]

Bertie's efforts to restrain Clemenceau were assisted by an eloquent plea from Jules Cambon to the Quai d'Orsay to avoid turning this affair into a fiasco. Already struck by Grey's philosophic acceptance of a political combination which he considered to be aimed 'toute entière contre l'Angleterre', he urged upon Louis the need for France to be prudent and discreet.[105] But while there might have been some scope for France to play what Jules Cambon termed the part of 'courtier honnête', there was little foundation in Clemenceau's claim to Bertie that the result of the French representations at St Petersburg had been 'to knock on the head the proposed agreement between Russia and Germany'.[106] That agreement had been in existence since 29 October in the form of the Russo-German protocol. If it did not, as Izvolsky had originally proposed, provide for the exclusion of the western powers from the affairs of the Baltic, that was due not to French diplomacy, but to German caution. Moreover, it was the German proposal for a North Sea agreement which robbed the Russo-German accord of its exclusive nature, and Sweden's opposition to the abrogation of the Aland islands convention which denied Izvolsky the one material concession that he had hoped to achieve. Disillusioned with Germany's conduct, he had in the end to reserve the right to return to the Aland islands question in the future, and to acquiesce in the conclusion on 23 April 1908 of two rather innocuous

---

[103] Hardinge to Bertie, 29 Dec. 1907, B.P., A, F.O.800/177. *B.D.*, VIII, no.134.
[104] Lister to Tyrrell, 27 Dec. 1907, Grey MSS., F.O.800/51. Memo. by Bertie, 10 May 1908, F.O.371/529.
[105] J. Cambon to Louis, 20 Dec. 1907, Louis MSS., 1.
[106] J. Cambon to Louis, 23 Dec. 1907, *ibid.* Bertie to Grey, 2 Jan. 1908, B.P., A, F.O.800/177.

agreements on the maintenance of the territorial *status quo* in the lands bordering the North Sea and the Baltic.[107]

Bertie did not play a prominent part in the discussions which preceded the signing of these agreements. They had resulted from decisions taken in the first instance by the German and Russian governments, and Bertie's task had rarely amounted to more than helping to chart the course of Izvolsky's diplomacy. Yet Russia's readiness to concert with Germany came as no great surprise to Bertie. He had doubted Izvolsky's word in October 1906, and his subsequent suspicions about a possible *rapprochement* between Berlin and St Petersburg had pre-dated the French revelations of November 1907. Unlike Hardinge, who at times displayed an almost naive faith in Izvolsky's honesty of purpose, Bertie readily assumed that Russia might revert to her former alignment with Germany. He also recognized that the *entente cordiale* could prove to be a purely transient feature of international politics. That, after all, had been evident in his advocacy of an Anglo-Spanish accord. Thus, just as Jules Cambon had been determined to ensure that France should be associated with any such arrangement in order to guard against Britain securing any political advantage at Madrid, so Bertie had considered France to be a potential threat to Britain's position at Gibraltar. At the same time Hardinge had stressed the importance of having an agreement with Spain which would prevent her from ceding any of her zone of influence in Morocco to another power such as France. In this sense the shape and form which was given to the Mediterranean agreements reflected British and French diplomats' awareness of that flexibility of the European system which Russia's subsequent flirtation with Germany in the Baltic made manifest.[108] The degree to which Bertie found it necessary to take this into account was equally apparent in the time and energy which he devoted in these years to the maintenance of the *entente*.

Bertie had judged the impact of the Moroccan crisis upon France to have been so profound as to leave little scope for any early Franco-German *rapprochement*. He thought that while the French might once have been prepared to make great concessions to obtain German goodwill, the events of 1905 had made it plain to them that Germany aimed to separate France from England in order to have France at her

---

[107] Luntinen, pp. 199–237.
[108] Izvolsky's conduct confirmed Jules Cambon in the views which he had previously expressed on the importance of France being party to any arrangement that Britain might make with Spain. 'Nous voyons aujourd'hui', he observed, 'combien il est

beck and call. 'Since then', he wrote in March 1907, 'it had become more and more evident to them that short of France being in the tow of Germany, there are no means of coming to an understanding with the German Emperor, for to them he is the embodiment of all that is threatening to France in the policy of the German Empire.'[109] This was not just wishful thinking. Jules Cambon, who hoped that in time he would be able to find the basis of an agreement with the Wilhelmstrasse on Morocco, warned Pichon on 22 April 1907 that the Germans wanted at all costs to neutralize France, and that France's strength *vis-à-vis* Germany resulted from her being England's friend. It was, he subsequently observed, necessary to surround the peace of Europe and France's integrity with as many guarantees as possible.[110] Nevertheless, the *entente* had its critics in the press and parliament in France, and so long as Bertie had to deal with governments in Paris which were dependent upon fluctuating parliamentary majorities, he could not afford to ignore their opponents and possible successors.

The insufficiency of the military aid which Britain could render to France in the event of a continental war, the danger of France becoming both a battlefield and a hostage in an Anglo-German conflict, and the gains to be had from political and economic cooperation with Germany, had to be weighed by Frenchmen against the advantages to be derived from close association with England. Certainly the idea of an accommodation with Germany had its attractions for those who were anxious to see France consolidate her position in north Africa and the Middle East. Crowe minuted in November 1906 that there was 'still observable in France, even in ministerial circles, a desire to find a "working arrangement" with Germany'. And after recalling the support given by Bismarck to Jules Ferry on colonial matters in the early 1880s, he pointed to the menace of Germany thus trying to recreate friction between Britain and France. Such fears were discounted by Hardinge, who, like Bertie, believed that the French experience at the hands of the Germans had been too bitter to allow any friendly understanding between them. The French, he noted, would require 'something more than smiles'.[111] Yet, as Bertie himself opined: 'Germany would probably

---

utile d'avoir des gages et des secretes même contre ses alliés.' J. Cambon to Louis, 16 Dec. 1907, Louis, MSS., 1.
[109] *Annual Report for France, 1906*, F.O.371/255.
[110] *D.D.F.2*, X, no.481.
[111] Minutes by Crowe and Hardinge on Bertie to Grey, 19 Nov. 1906, F.O.371/74, despt.453.

be ready to make great sacrifices to obtain French support in pursuit of her world policy and the British Empire would be the sufferer.'[112]

From the French point of view one of the chief drawbacks to collaboration with Britain in any future European crisis stemmed from the small size of the British military establishment. Bertie was well aware of French fears that the British would be of little use in helping to halt a German invasion of France, and that the Royal Navy's contribution to any joint war effort wuld be limited to defending France's coasts and cutting off supplies to Germany.[113] For Clemenceau this problem was to become almost an obsession. Even before his entry into Sarrien's government he had suggested to Lister that France might attempt to secure the aid of the Italian army for France and during the next three years he rarely missed an opportunity to enlighten British ministers on the virtues of conscription.[114] Clear expression of the concern felt in France over the value of Britain as a friend and potential ally was also given by André Tardieu, the foreign editor of *Le Temps*. In an address which he delivered at the École libre des sciences politiques on 22 February 1907 he argued that while the friendship of England was a 'precious guarantee of peace', it would not in time of war avail to halt a German advance. Moreover, in marked contrast to the hostile attitude which he had previously assumed towards Germany, Tardieu went on to refer to the possibility of an arrangement with Berlin.[115] Bertie did not, however, attach undue importance to such expressions of sympathy for a Franco-German understanding. The chief promoters of the idea were, he claimed, the German subsidised press, a limited number of office-seeking politicians, and those nationalists and royalists who considered Germany to be more antagonistic to the republican system than England. 'Other partisans of such an understanding', he observed, 'are those who for financial reasons desire closer relations with a country which requires capital and where profitable business might be done.'[116]

When he wrote this Bertie was probably thinking about the favourable attitude of some French financiers towards the German-sponsored Baghdad railway: a project which was intended to link the Bosphorus with Baghdad and ultimately the Persian gulf. In his address at the École libre Tardieu outlined an arrangement whereby

---

[112] *Annual Report for France, 1906*, F.O.371/255.
[113] *Ibid.*
[114] Memo. by Lister enclosed in Bertie to Grey, 2 Jan. 1906, B.P., A, F.O.800/164.
[115] Lister to Grey, 27 Feb. 1907; Bertie to Grey, 25 March 1907; F.O.371/255, despts. 109 and 146.
[116] *Annual Report for France, 1907*, F.O.371/456.

Germany might be persuaded to accept the French acquisition of Morocco in return for French financial assistance in the construction of the railway. This proposal gained some popularity in banking, diplomatic, and political circles in France. As the result of an agreement concluded with the *Deutsche Bank* in 1903 the French-controlled *Imperial Ottoman Bank* had already been allotted a thirty per cent share in the financing of the railway. But with a view to protecting France's interests in Syria and to ensuring that her financiers had at least an equal stake to that of the Germans in the undertaking, Delcassé had persuaded his colleagues in the council of ministers not to sanction the involvement of French capital on these terms. The *Ottoman Bank* was thus denied the opportunity for floating its railway shares upon the Paris *bourse*.[117] This was a policy which suited the British Foreign Office. Grey, like his predecessor, wanted to protect British commercial and strategic interests in Mesopotamia and the Persian gulf, and for this purpose he hoped to work with France and Russia in ensuring that the railway should only be completed on conditions acceptable to themselves.[118] Clemenceau seemed ready to make use of the leverage which he possessed in the French government's control over the quotation of securities on the *bourse*, and both he and Pichon assured Bertie of their readiness to restrain French bankers from assisting the project.[119] Bertie could not, however, be certain that future French governments would maintain this stance. Rouvier had, as minister of finance, opposed Delcassé on the question of French participation in the railway, and there was no reason to suppose that he might not return to power. Bertie was also aware that quite apart from the *bourse* there were other less direct channels by which French capital might pass into German hands.[120]

Even more problematic for the British was the attitude towards them of Jean Constans, the French ambassador to Turkey. He had long favoured French participation in the railway, and he was unenthusiastic about France's association with a power like Britain

---

[117] Jacques Thobie, *Intérêts et impérialismes français dans l'Empire Ottoman (1895 – 1914)* (Paris, 1977), pp.718 – 9. L. Bruce Fulton, 'France and the End of the Ottoman Empire', in Marian Kent (ed.), *The Great Powers and the End of the Ottoman Empire* (London, 1984), pp.143 – 150.
[118] *B.D.*, VI, no.222. Grey to Cromer, 15 April 1906, Grey MSS., F.O.800/46. Stuart A, Cohen, *British Policy in Mesopotamia, 1903 – 1914* (London, 1976), pp.1 – 89.
[119] Bertie to Mallet, 10, 11 and 21 Nov. 1906; Bertie to Hardinge, 2 Dec. 1906; B.P., A, F.O.800/174. *B.D.*, VI, nos.239 and 242.
[120] W.I. Shorrock, *French Imperialism in the Middle East. The failure of policy in Syria and Lebanon, 1900 – 1914.* (London, 1976), pp.138 – 46. D.C.M. Platt, *Finance, Trade and Politics in British Foreign Policy, 1815 – 1914* (Oxford, 1968), p.8.

which persisted in alienating the Porte.[121] In consequence Britain's representatives in Constantinople received little or no support from the French embassy when during the autumn of 1906 they attempted to apply such conditions to the granting of a three per cent rise in Turkish customs dues as would prevent any surplus revenues being employed as security for the financing of the railway.[122] At the same time a French group of financiers, with the tacit support of the *Ottoman Bank*, appeared to be acting in collusion with the Germans. Neither an attempt by Bertie to persuade Pichon of the pro-German sympathies of Gaston Auboyneau, the director general of the *Ottoman Bank* at Paris, nor the efforts of the Foreign Office to secure French assistance at Constantinople, met with any real success.[123] During December Pichon tried to ensure that Commandant Berger, the representative of the French bondholders on the council of the Ottoman Public Debt, would cooperate with Sir Adam Block, his British colleague. But Constans was reluctant to follow Pichon's instructions, and to the annoyance of the French cabinet and the distress of Block, Berger refused to abandon the German cause.[124]

Grey felt that the French government had done its best for Britain in this matter. Mallet disagreed. He considered that Pichon's action had been worse than useless because Constans was in the 'financial ring' at Constantinople.[125] On 21 November Bertie had warned Mallet that there seemed to be an inclination on the part of French financiers to revert to their former scheme for obtaining a substantial share in the Baghdad railway, and the explanation which he subsequently received from Auboyneau of events at Constantinople did little to dispel his misgivings about the French financial world.[126] In the meantime the *Ottoman Bank* kept open its option on participating in the railway, and at the end of March 1907 the idea of a Franco-German understanding on the basis suggested by Tardieu was taken up by the French and German press.[127] Such speculation does not seem to have worried Bertie. So long as the French

---

[121] J.B. Wolf, *The Diplomatic History of the Baghdad Railroad* (Columbia, Miss., 1936), p.34. *B.D.*, V, p.169. Block to Hardinge, 24 Jan. and 14 May 1907, F.O.371/344. Hardinge to Goschen, 9 March 1908; Hardinge to Nicolson, 1 April 1908; Hardinge MSS., 13.
[122] This subject is considered in more detail in K.A. Hamilton, 'An attempt to form an Anglo-French "Industrial Entente" ', *Middle Eastern Studies*, XI (1975), 47 – 73.
[123] *Ibid*.
[124] *Ibid*.
[125] Minute by Grey with Grey to Bertie, 29 Dec. 1906, F.O.371/144, despt.722.
[126] Bertie to Mallet, 21 Nov. 1906, B.P., A, F.O.800/174. Bertie to Hardinge, 19 Jan. 1907, B.P., A, F.O.800/180.
[127] *Passim*. F.O.371/253. Minute by Crowe on Bertie to Grey, 13 April 1907, F.O.371/257.

government remained confident of Britain's friendship, Bertie thought that nothing would come of it. But in the spring of 1907, at a time when Clemenceau was embroiled in a struggle with the trade union movement, there were indications that his government might not survive. A small group of radicals was intriguing against him and Clemenceau seems to have been anxious to emphasize to Bertie that if they attained power they would move towards a closer relationship with Germany.[128] First Pichon on 30 March, and then Clemenceau on 3 April, warned Bertie that a change of government might bring to power Alexandre Millerand, a prominent and talented deputy, whom Clemenceau accused of having consorted with Radolin to bring about a Franco-German *rapprochement*.[129] Clemenceau's government was of course to survive. Nevertheless, Bertie warned Grey on 18 April that if the government were to fall the Germans would no doubt 'squeeze' an agreement out of the next ministry.[130]

It was in these apparently precarious circumstances that Campbell-Bannerman made a brief, but for Bertie, unfortunate, incursion into *entente* diplomacy. The occasion was a meeting at the British embassy on 9 April of Campbell-Bannerman, who was on a private visit to France, and Clemenceau. Once in conversation with his opposite number Clemenceau reverted to his usual patter about Britain's military unpreparedness for a continental war, and after having stressed what he saw as the danger posed by Germany to the European *status quo*, he expressed his regret at the reductions being made in the size of the army by the Liberal government. Campbell-Bannerman's reply was, to say the least, a shock for Clemenceau, for, according to the latter's account, he said that he 'did not think that English public opinion would allow of British troops being employed on the continent'. Disturbed lest this should mean some change in British policy, Clemenceau subsequently put it to Bertie that the effect on his colleagues of such an exposition would be disastrous.[131] Campbell-Bannerman denied the accuracy of Clemenceau's charges. He claimed that although he had dwelt upon the reluctance of the British people to undertake obligations which would commit them to a continental war, he had not said that in no circumstances would they allow troops to be employed on the continent. And Grey, who was irritated by Clemenceau's handling of Campbell-Bannerman, was at pains to assure Bertie that the prime minister had said nothing

---

[128] Watson, *Clemenceau*, pp.186–7.
[129] Bertie to Grey, 31 March and 3 April 1907, B.P., A, F.O.800/164.
[130] Bertie to Grey, 17 April 1907, F.O.371/253, despt.197. *B.D.*, VII, no.31.
[131] J. Wilson, *C-B. A Life of Sir Henry Campbell-Bannerman* (London, 1973), pp.540–4.

new. In the event of Britain being involved in a continental war, he maintained that her armed forces would be used in the way in which they were most effective.[132]

Others found reason to doubt both the veracity of Clemenceau's account, and the wisdom of his decision to raise the topic with Campbell-Bannerman. After all, as Hardinge pointed out, the prime minister had in the previous year contemplated sending a British army to France.[133] Mallet, who personally believed that Britain would intervene in the event of an unprovoked German attack upon France, wrote to Bertie that he thought that Clemenceau had been 'very stupid to raise this question again now, à propos of nothing and with C-B of all people'.[134] Bertie could hardly having disagreed. Yet while the ambassador took the opportunity to deliver another homily to Grey on the necessity of Britain continuing to back France, his reaction was in all fairly calm. The prime minister's statement to Clemenceau had, he thought, been 'intended as a douche to cool any martial ardour that he might feel in reliance on any military support from us'.[135] He suspected that Clemenceau had put the case 'too straight', and that Campbell-Bannerman, in order to avoid giving a distinct answer, or making a definite statement, had 'shied at it and run into the ditch on the opposite side of the road laying too much stress on the unwillingness of the British public to land men on the continent'. 'The danger for us to avoid', he reminded Mallet, 'will be to make the French lose confidence in our support and drive them into some arrangement with Germany harmful to us while not being harmful to France.' At the same time he thought that the French should not be encouraged to 'rely on our material land support to the extent of making them beard the Germans'.[136]

Bertie was also determined, if possible, to avoid any repetition of this incident. When in the following January he learned that Campbell-Bannerman, who was about to return from a holiday at Biarritz, had been invited by Sir Thomas Barclay, an early exponent of the *entente*, and, according to Bertie, 'a self-advertiser with no authority whatever', to attend a dinner at which some of Clemenceau's political opponents would be present, he intervened to persuade the prime minister not to accept. Campbell-Bannerman,

---

[132] Campbell-Bannerman to Grey, 12 April 1907, Grey MSS., F.O.800/100. F.O.800/100. *B.D.*, VI, nos.10, 11, 14 and 15.
[133] Hardinge to Edward VII, 24 April 1907, Hardinge MSS., 9.
[134] Mallet to Bertie, 13 April 1907, B.P., A, F.O.800/164.
[135] *B.D.*, VI, no.11.
[136] Bertie to Mallet, 15 April 1907, B.P., A, F.O.800/164.

who all along had suspected that the proposed entertainment was 'ad majoram gloriam Barclayi', was amenable to Bertie's arguments.[137] But Clemenceau was not to be dissuaded from his efforts to convert the British to a continental strategy, and Campbell-Bannerman's death in April 1908 provided him both with a pretext to go to England for the funeral, and the chance to quiz Grey on what England would do if the Germans were to invade France by way of Belgium. Grey could tell Clemenceau no more than if Belgium were overrun 'it would make a great stir in England'.[138] Reports had, however, already reached Paris of remarks recently made by the German state secretary to the effect that in a war with England, Germany would, if defeated at sea, take her compensation in France.[139] This was a familiar refrain. It was also a timely reminder of the exposed position which France occupied, and when in May Fallières visited London for the Anglo-French exhibition at Shepherd's Bush the Paris press returned to the subject of the importance of Britain having a conscript army.[140] The matter was raised again by Clemenceau in August 1908. Thus during a holiday in Bohemia, he urged first *The Times* correspondent, Wickham Steed, and then King Edward, on the necessity of Britain possessing a 'national army worthy of the name'. On 29 August he reinforced his argument with a warning to Sir Edward Goschen, the British ambassador at Vienna, that as soon as the French public realized the price that it would have to pay for England's friendship, it would be the end of the *entente* and its supporters.[141]

Bertie seems to have been unruffled by such talk. Constant repetition doubtless dulled the impact of Clemenceau's protestations. In any case, Bertie still held to his view that a realignment of France and Germany was unlikely since it would mean the former subordinating its interests and diplomacy to the latter.[142] Of more immediate concern to him in the summer of 1908 were the public statements of Winston Churchill, who had recently been appointed

---

[137] Bertie to Grey, 6 Jan. 1908; Grey to Bertie, 6 and 8 Jan. 1908; Campbell-Bannerman to Bertie, 7 and 8 Jan. 1908; Bertie to Campbell-Bannerman, 7 Jan. 1908; Bertie to Hardinge, 9 Jan, 1908; B.P., A, F.O.800/166.
[138] Pichon to *chargé d'affaires* (London), 29 April 1908, N.S. Grande-Bretagne 21, despt.201. Grey of Fallodon, II, pp.289–93. Wickham Steed to Bell, 22 Aug. 19(), Wickham Steed MSS. (*The Times* archives).
[139] Bertie to Grey, 2 April 1908, B.P., A, F.O.800/177. *D.D.F.2*, XI, no.317.
[140] E.M. Carroll, *French Public Opinion and Foreign Affairs, 1870–1914* (London, 1931), pp.214–15.
[141] Notes by Wickham Steed, Aug.1908, Wickham Steed MSS. H. Wickham Steed, *Through Thirty Years, 1892–1922* (2 vols., London, 1924), I, pp.283–8. *D.D.F.2*, XI, no.434. *B.D.*, VI, no.100.
[142] *B.D.*, VI, no.98.

president of the Board of Trade, and David Lloyd George, the new chancellor of the exchequer, in favour of better relations between Britain and Germany and an agreement on arms limitation.[143] Neither minister really went much beyond what had been said in private by Grey and Hardinge, but Bertie did not disguise his disgust with these 'Very silly young men'.[144] And he reacted strongly against the news sent to him by Tyrrell, who had succeeded Mallet as Grey's private secretary, that Churchill might visit Paris in January 1909 if there were a chance of seeing 'any of the important people'.[145] The prospect of having to receive a young radical minister, who was considered in Paris to have German proclivities, was hardly pleasing. In a letter to Grey Bertie tried to explain that people of real importance would not speak their minds to Churchill, and others, whom he might believe to be influential, would simply mislead him. Such a visit, he predicted, would lead to some confusion in France, and might also set a precedent. Indeed, faced with the possibility that other members of the government might also seek interviews with French ministers, Bertie advised Grey to 'throw buckets of cold water on the project'. Otherwise, he added, 'you would probably have to explain away all sorts of statements perhaps attributed to him, and to seek explanations of statements which he believed to have been made to him but which the interviewed would deny'.[146] Grey appears to have been impressed by Bertie's case, for not only on this occasion, but also in March 1909, when Churchill was invited to Paris by the British chamber of commerce there, he intervened to discourage him from going.[147]

Bertie could generally rely upon the assistance of Grey in warding off potentially embarrassing visits from ministers and other undesirables. But the foreign secretary was of little help when it came to handling King Edward, who persisted in disrupting the smooth running of the embassy with his travels to and from the south of France. On one occasion, during February 1907 Bertie had to vacate the embassy and take rooms once more in the Hotel Bristol in order to allow the king and queen to stay privately in the Faubourg St

---

[143] M.G. Fry, *David Lloyd George and Foreign Policy. Vol. I, The Education of a Statesman* (London, 1977), pp. 96–103. R.S. Churchill, *Winston S. Churchill* (2 vols., London, 1966–7), II, pp.511–14.
[144] Bertie to Tyrrell, 20 Aug. 1908, F.O.800/170.
[145] Marsh to Montgomery, 15 Dec. 1908, Grey MSS., F.O.800/89. Tyrrell to Bertie, 18 Dec. 1908, F.O.800/165.
[146] Bertie to Tyrrell, 18 and 19 Dec. 1908; Bertie to Grey, 19 Dec. 1908; B.P., A, F.O.800/165.
[147] Tyrrell to Marsh, 22 Dec. 1908; Grey to Churchill, 26 Dec. 1908; Grey to Churchill, 22 April 1909; Grey MSS., F.O.800/89.

Honoré. Bertie, who was confined to bed with a bout of influenza, was rewarded for his troubles with a clock and candlesticks.[148] The king was, however, in no mood to accept Bertie's advice when that spring he planned a return journey from his Mediterranean cruise which involved his arrival at Paris on 1 May. The date was inconvenient for the French government, which was already coping with a wave of strikes, and which feared that May Day would be marred by labour demonstrations and possibly riots in the capital. At Clemenceau's request Bertie therefore urged the king to rearrange his itinerary. He warned Frederick Ponsonby, who was accompanying the king, that the king could not cross Paris from the Gare de Lyon on 1 May, that he would have to go around the city by the Ceinture railway and alight at the Porte Dauphine station near the Bois de Boulogne, and that since the French goverment would be responsible for his safety he would have to be met there by the prefect of police, who ought properly to be elsewhere. The king was not to be persuaded. Annoyed by the fussiness of the French authorities, he refused to alter his arrangements. It would, he told Ponsonby, 'interest him to see a revolution'.[149] Events conspired to deny him this spectacle, but his visit was still not without a diplomatic upset, for when he arrived at the Porte Dauphine he was so monopolized by the prefect of police that he took virtually no notice of Pichon who was also there to greet him. For the sake of propriety Bertie had therefore to exercise further pressure upon the king in order to have him grant the foreign minister a private audience.[150]

This visit was but a minor episode in the history of the *entente*. It provided some criticism from the pen of Ernest Judet in *L'Éclair*, a nationalist newspaper which habitually took a hostile attitude towards England and the *entente cordiale*, but there were few other repercussions.[151] There were, nevertheless, signs at this time that Bertie's relations with the king were not as warm as they had once been. This may have been due to Bertie having fallen foul of that coterie of socialites and expatriate sycophants that invariably flocked to the king's side whenever he was in Paris. One of the chief

---

[148] Hardinge to Bertie, 20 Jan. 1907, B.P., A, F.O.800/164. Bertie to Hardinge, 22 Jan. and 11 Feb. 1907; Bertie to Knollys, 29 Jan. 1907; B.P. B, F.O.800/185. Edward VII to Bertie, 9 Feb, 1907, Add. MS. 63011.
[149] Lee, *Edward VII*, II, pp.544–5. Bertie to Ponsonby, 25 and 26 April 1907, RA X32 303 and 304. Ponsonby to Bertie, 27 April 1907, and minute by Ponsonby, RA X32 306. Ponsonby to Bertie, 25 April 1907; Bertie to Hardinge, 27 April 1907; Hardinge to Bertie, 27 April 2907; B.P. B, F.O.800/185.
[150] Mollard to Ponsonby, 2 May 1907; Ponsonby to Bertie, 2 May 1907; Bertie to Grey, 3 May 1907; B.P. B, F.O.800/185.
[151] Bertie to Hardinge, 29 April 1907, B.P. Add. MS. 63020.

complaints of this so-called 'gang', of which Lady Colebrooke was a leading light, was that Bertie did not entertain enough. In the ambassador's defence Hardinge informed the king at the end of April 1907 that the embassy had only recently issued a thousand invitations to a party, and that it was about to issue a further two thousand to another in May. The king seems to have been satisfied by this report.[152] Yet Bertie did not enjoy hosting such functions, and as one of his contemporaries commented, 'with the exception of a good cook and a stately *train de maison*, he had few of the superficial qualities expected of an ambassador'.[153] A jealous man, Bertie also suspected Lister of consorting with Lady Colebrooke and of trying to usurp his position as the king's representative at Paris.[154] His suspicions were not wholly misplaced, for Lister, who, like Rodd, had begun to resent the way in which the ambassador's absences interfered with his own plans, had taken advantage of Bertie's illness in February to cultivate his own relations with King Edward and Queen Alexandra.[155] Moreover, when the king visited Paris in March 1908 he chose to use Lister and Lady Colebrooke to help him make the arrangements for his stay.[156]

Neither the king's use of Lister as a channel of communication, nor Lady Colebrooke's intrigues, ought really to have been of great concern to Bertie. As Hardinge observed to Knollys, 'the position of an Ambassador should be unassailable & beyond the range of competition by any member of his staff'.[157] Bertie could, however, exhibit a touchiness and small-mindedness over comparatively insignificant matters which at times seemed to border on paranoia. It was one of his greatest failings, and it was in later years to weaken his position at Paris. Yet in so far as he identified himself with the maintenance of the *entente*, it may also have heightened his appreciation of the sensibilities of the French. Thus, although in his personal relationships he could be as insensitive towards the feelings of others as he was mindful of his own, where Anglo-French relations

---

[152] Hardinge to Edward VII, 24 April 1907, Hardinge MSS., 9. Hardinge to Bertie, 9 May 1907, B.P. B, F.O.800/185.
[153] V. Corbett, *Reminiscences autobiographical and diplomatic* (London, 1927), p.47.
[154] Hardinge to Knollys, 1 March 1908, RA W53 16. Bertie to Hardinge, 7 March 1908, B.P. B, F.O.800/185.
[155] Beatrix Lister (ed.), *Emma Lady Ribblesdale. Letters and Diaries* (London, 1930), p.197. Lister to Lady Ribblesdale, (?) 1907; Lister to Lady Ribblesdale, 1 and 5 March 1907; Bradfer-Lawrence MSS., M.D.355 Box 101. Diary, 1907–9, p.142, Rumbold MSS., Dep.I/3.
[156] Hardinge to Knollys, 1 March 1908, RA W5316. Bertie to Hardinge, 2 March 1908, B.P. B, F.O.800/185.
[157] *Ibid.*

were concerned he was always aware of the need to safeguard what he himself termed 'the tender susceptibilities of the French'.[158] Thus he made every effort to obviate any actions by the British government which might cause unnecessary offence in Paris. Even a proposal, which was first made by the Portuguese government in August 1908, that Britain should send representatives to participate in the celebration of the centenary of the Peninsular war was frowned upon by Bertie. Within the Foreign Office it was not thought that the French could take umbrage over Britain's participation, and Clemenceau assured Bertie that he and his colleagues were indifferent.[159] But Bertie insisted that the 'Royalist, nationalist, and German subventioned press would make capital out of it', and he advised Grey to 'choke off the Portuguese': a course which the foreign secretary was apparently ready to follow.[160]

Bertie's desire to maintain French confidence in England's friendship did not blind him to the fact that Frenchmen were quite capable of using the menace of a Franco-German *rapprochement* for their own advantage. Clemenceau seemed to be doing just this when during the summer of 1907 he attempted to counter Grey's efforts to free Britain from the obligations placed upon her by the Brussels sugar convention of 1902 to levy countervailing duties on imports of bounty-fed sugar.[161] The Liberal government's wish to abandon a convention which conflicted with its free trade principles threatened to harm French sugar producers, and at a time when Clemenceau was having to cope with serious disturbances in the wine-producing regions of the south, he was anxious to avoid troubles amongst the beet growers of the north.[162] Nevertheless, the situation hardly warranted his warning Bertie that France would be led to cooperate with Austria and Germany on this issue, and that the French government 'might be forced by public opinion into an economic combination which would lead to important political results in the near future'. As Bertie recognized, there was no reason why a quarrel over imported sugar should lead to France being 'dragged . . . into a political combination of an anti-English tendency'. The

---

[158] Bertie to Tyrrell, 1 March 1909, B.P., A, F.O.800/186.
[159] Memo. by Mallet, 25 Aug. 1908, and minutes by Spicer, Crowe, Langley and Grey, F.O.371/510, *private*. Campbell to Bertie, 31 Aug. 1908, B.P., A, F.O.800/176.
[160] Bertie to Grey, 13 Sept. 1908, *ibid.*, and minute by Grey.
[161] *The Sugar Convention*, memo. by Lloyd George, 16 April 1907, CAB.37/88/46. Grey to P. Cambon, 12 June 1907, B.P., A, F.O.800/174. Grey to Bertie, 11 July 1907, Grey MSS., F.O.800/51.
[162] Watson, *Clemenceau*, pp.192–4.

entente, he reckoned, 'ought to be able to survive such tea-cup storms'.[163]

Bertie could not, however, neglect the extent to which the notion of a Franco-German bargain on Morocco and other extra-European issues continued to find favour in France. The involvement of French forces in coercive action in Morocco, and the declining authority of the Sultan Abdul Aziz, made such an agreement particularly attractive to those who wished to avoid the risk of another German intervention there.[164] Clemenceau himself had told Radolin in March 1907 of his desire for better relations with Germany, and from Berlin Jules Cambon pressed upon Louis his belief in the importance of France being prepared to negotiate with the Germans.[165] Bertie thus had good reason to speculate about the motives of Étienne when the latter accepted an invitation from the prince of Monaco to join him on his yacht during Kiel regatta week in July 1907. True Étienne attempted to assure Bertie on 19 June that his object was neither to intrigue, nor 'faire de la politique'. But Bertie rightly predicted that Étienne would not confine himself to exchanging pleasantries with Bülow and the German emperor.[166] The subject of a German recognition of France's preponderant position in Morocco was raised at Kiel, and Etienne seems to have shown himself ready to support the idea of a broader Franco-German *rapprochement*.[167] Indeed, after his return to Paris in August, he published an article in *La Dépêche Coloniale* in which he questioned the value for France of the *entente* with England.[168]

Étienne's activities did not greatly disturb Bertie. He had none too high an opinion of Étienne either before or after his excursion to Kiel, and he suspected that the prince of Monaco was serving German interests. The acceptance of his invitation by Étienne was, he concluded, 'probably prompted by the desire to do a little profitable business by holding out to influential Germans whom he might meet the prospect of obtaining French financial assistance for German

---

[163] Bertie to Grey, 20 June 1907, F.O.371/254, despt.314. Bertie to Grey, 21 June 1907, F.O.371/254, tel.29. Bertie to Grey, 21 Oct. 1907, F.O.371/256, despt. 507. Bertie to Grey, 10 and 12 July 1907, Grey MSS., F.O.800/51.
[164] I.C. Barlow, *The Agadir Crisis* (Chapel Hill, N.C., 1940), pp.64–7. J.Ganiage *L'expansion coloniale de la France sous la Troisième République* (Paris, 1968), pp.265–8.
[165] *G.P.*, XXI, pt.2, no.7317. J.Cambon to Louis, 4 Feb. and 29 July 1908, Louis MSS., 2.
[166] Peter Grupp, 'Eugène Étienne et la tentative de rapprochement franco-allemand en 1907', *Cahiers d'Études africaines*, LVIII (1975), 303–11. Bertie to Grey, 19 June 1907, F.O.371/255, despt.311.
[167] Whyte, pp.214–20. *B.D.*, VI, no.36.
[168] Extract from *La Dépêche Coloniale* enclosed in Bertie to Grey, 12 Sept. 1907, F.O.371/255, despt.442.

enterprise'.¹⁶⁹ And despite the fact that Pichon had told Radolin that he had encouraged Étienne's visit, there is no evidence to suggest that Bertie was inclined to disbelieve the disclaimer of Pichon and Clemenceau of any official support for the mission.¹⁷⁰ Besides which, the reports which he received about Étienne's discussions were to the effect that they had foundered on the subject of the existing territorial *status quo* in Europe. According to Delcassé, who spoke to Bertie about the visit in February 1908, William II had dropped the question of a Franco-German understanding when Étienne had informed him that for such an arrangement to be feasible 'it would be necessary that "la France fut reconstituée" or words to that effect'.¹⁷¹ This and the apparently inconclusive results of Étienne's talks helped to confirm Bertie in his view that there was little likelihood of a general political arrangement between France and Germany. 'So long', he observed in his annual report for 1907, 'as Alsace-Lorraine remains part of the German Empire there cannot in my opinion be any real political understanding of any consequence between France and Germany.'¹⁷²

Subsequent events would seem to suggest that Bertie was correct. Nevertheless, there was still scope for Franco-German cooperation and agreement on a number of particular issues. During the summer of 1907 there were discussions between Bülow and Jules Cambon on collaboration in the economic development and exploitation of Morocco, and unofficial talks on the same subject proceeded between the French and German legations at Tangier. Had Bülow not been so reluctant at this stage to abandon Germany's political interests in Morocco, more progress might indeed have been made towards the achievement of some kind of accord.¹⁷³ Bertie had, however, also to reckon with doubts amongst his compatriots about France's ability to stand up to German pressure. Hardinge confessed to Bertie in a letter of 16 July 1908 that he was 'always afraid that if the French became really frightened there may be a general stampede'.¹⁷⁴ But French

---

¹⁶⁹ Lister to Mallet, 27 Jan. 1907, Grey MSS., F.O.800/51.
¹⁷⁰ *G.P.*, XXI, pt.2, nos.7257 and 7263. Cambon, II, pp.232 – 233. J.J. Cooke, *New French Imperialism, 1880 – 1910. The Third Republic and Colonial Expansion* (Newton Abbot, 1973), pp.148-52. Lister to Grey, 6 July 1907, F.O.371/255, despt.337. Bertie to Grey, 9 July, B.P., A, F.O.800/170.
¹⁷¹ Bertie to Grey, 9 July 1907, F.O.371/256, tel.140. *B.D.*, VI, no.79.
¹⁷² *Annual Report for France, 1907*, F.O.371/456.
¹⁷³ E.W. Edwards, 'The Franco-German Agreement on Morocco, 1909', *English Historical Review*, LXXVIII (1963), 483 – 513. R. Poidevin, *Les relations economiques et financières entre la France et l'Allemagne de 1898 à 1914* (Paris, 1969), pp.413 – 57.
¹⁷⁴ Hardinge to Bertie, 16 July 1908, B.P., A, F.O.800/170. Very similar doubts about the steadfastness of France had been expressed by Jules Cambon. See: J. Cambon to Louis, 4 Feb. 1908, Louis MSS., 2.

conduct during the following autumn lent little credence to such fears. In September 1908 a French officer intervened in an attempt by the German consul at Casablanca to help a group of Austrian and German nationals deserting from the foreign legion. A quarrel between Paris and Berlin ensued, and the Quai d'Orsay firmly insisted on arbitration on its terms.[175] Grey was favourably impressed by the attitude, tone and temper of the French government, and felt compelled to envisage the possibility of a British military intervention on the side of France.[176] Morocco, it seemed, could just as well serve as the catalyst for an Anglo-French alliance, as it could offer the basis for a future Franco-German accommodation.

The Casablanca deserters affair, and the problems posed by the overthrow of Abdul Aziz by his half-brother and successor, Moulai Hafid, probably encouraged the French and Germans to seek a settlement of their differences over Morocco. But Bertie remained confident about the future of the *entente*. In March 1908 he had recommended to Grey that France was so dependent upon Britain in matters of foreign policy that 'pressure might be brought to bear upon the French Government to show a more accommodating spirit in some of the questions in which the two countries are not entirely agreed'.[177] What Bertie had in mind was a variety of issues, mostly of a colonial or extra-European kind, which continued to bedevil Anglo-French relations in these years. Some of these related to the interpretation of the agreements of 1904. But they were exacerbated by a sense of rivalry between British and French representatives in Africa and Asia which those accords had failed to extinguish. Moreover, other ministries and other departments of state proved less willing than the Foreign Office and the Quai d'Orsay to endorse a policy of cooperation, and tended at times to put immediate and local interests before the supposed wider aspects of the *entente*.

Bertie's role in the handling of such issues was in some cases limited to no more than conveying to, and confirming with, the foreign ministry the results of discussions carried on elsewhere. Very often he was faced with the problem of overcoming the seemingly endless delays which attended the settlement of any question in which the *bureaux* of the Quai d'Orsay did not perceive the prospect of solid economic or political advantage. Frustrated by this work, and

---

[175] G.E. Silberstein, 'Germany, France and the Casablanca incident, 1908 – 1909; an investigation of a forgotten crisis', *Canadian Journal of History*, XI (1976), 331 – 54.
[176] *B.D.*, VII, no.132; VI, nos.135 and 106. Hardinge to Bertie, 5 Nov. 1908, B.P., A, F.O.800/180. Grey to Nicolson, 10 Nov. 1908, Nicolson MSS., F.O.800/341.
[177] *Annual Report for France*, 1907, F.O.371/456.

dissatisfied by his want of success, Bertie registered his disenchantment in his annual report for 1907. Therein he reminded Grey that the French were ready to accept all the British support which was ungrudgingly given them. Yet, he claimed;

> they have not met our reasonable requests on the question of the Newfoundland fisheries; they did not act with us at the Hague Conference to the extent which they might have done without detriment to the interests of France; they do not accept our views with regard to the Baghdad Railway; they want to go back on the loss of what they have given in Egypt for valuable consideration under the convention of 1904; they do not act loyally with us in matters Abyssinian, and it is doubtful what their attitude will be in questions affecting the Persian Gulf.[178]

To Barrère, whom he met during a visit to Italy in the spring of 1909, he protested that in some cases 'the persons who made their views prevail with Pichon appeared not to realise the existence of the Entente & to act as they would have been expected to twenty years ago'.[179]

Bertie's complaints were similar to those of other British officials.[180] Crowe was particularly critical of what he stigmatized as the 'well-known French method of dealing with unpleasant questions . . . which may be characterised as "pigeon-hole and no answer" '.[181] And when in March 1908 Paul Cambon protested over the fining of a French fishing boat which had been operating in Newfoundland waters, Crowe minuted that the French 'permit themselves in addressing us a latitude which borders on the impertinent'.[182] In similar terms Eldon Gorst, who was now British consul general in Egypt, complained persistently over the way in which the French agent and colony there continued to obstruct his administration.[183] The French, Hardinge lamented to Bertie in July 1908, were exceedingly tiresome in Egypt and had not really observed the letter and the spirit of the *entente*.[184] Yet Grey was rarely prepared to take as firm a line towards them as his officials would have liked. His

[178] *Ibid.*
[179] Bertie to Tyrrell, 20 May 1909, B.P. Add. MS. 63024.
[180] See for example: minute by hardinge on Bertie to Grey, 1 July 1910. F.O.371/898.
[181] Minute by Crowe on communication from the French embassy, 16 Jan. 1908, F.O.371/454.
[182] Minute by Crowe on P. Cambon to Grey, 23 March 1908, F.O.371/453. *Note sur l'état des négotiations franco-britanniques relatives à Terre Neuve*, 21 May 1908, N.S. Grande-Bretagne 21.
[183] Gorst to Grey, 17 May 1908, Grey MSS., F.O.800/47. *Passim.* F.O.371/895.
[184] Hardinge to Bertie, 30 July 1908, B.P., A, F.O.800/180.

response to French complaints over the enforcement of the provisions of the 1904 accord on the Newfoundland fisheries was more conciliatory than Crowe had hoped for, and Grey was reluctant to follow the suggestion made by Gorst in May 1908 that he should give the French a 'rap over the knuckles about their attitude' in Eygpt.[185] The difficulty, he thought, about complaining to the French over conduct there was that they had got 'such a bad bargain in Morocco that one doesn't like to set off one against the other'.[186]

That Bertie had few such qualms was evident in his attitude towards a tedious, and at times acrimonious, dispute which developed between Britain and France over arms trafficking in the Red sea and the Persian gulf. What angered the British government was the ease with which munitions passed from Jibuti to neighbouring British possessions, and the participation of French firms in the arms trade conducted between the sultanate of Muscat and the tribesmen of the north-western frontier of India. In order to curtail this traffic the British sought, firstly through direct negotiations, to persuade the French to agree to measures which would effectively suppress the trade at Jibuti and to secure some modification of the rights enjoyed by French citizens to import into Muscat arms intended for reexport across the gulf. Since, however, the arms trade was not only profitable, but also made Jibuti virtually self-supporting, any attempt by the French authorities to restrict it was bound to meet with the opposition of colonial and commercial interests in France. Besides which, the officials of the foreign ministry were not slow to realize that negotiations on this matter might enable France to obtain concessions from Britain in other parts of the world.[187] Their efforts to make an agreement on the arms trade part of a comprehensive colonial settlement were, nevertheless, to come to nought. Thus while they asked for the Gambia, they were reluctant to concede anything of substance to Britain other than their trading rights in Muscat.[188] When in October 1909 Bertie returned to the subject with Pichon, he indicated that France's attitude would bring people in England to question the value of the *entente*. Yet Bertie's plea

---

[185] Gorst to Grey, 17 May 1908, Grey MSS., F.O.800/47.
[186] Grey to Gorst, 25 May 1908, Grey MSS., F.O.800/47.
[187] Agnes Picquart, 'Le commerce des armes à Djibouti de 1888 à 1914', *Revue français d'Histoire d'Outre Mer*, LVIII (1971), 407 – 32. B.C. Busch, *Britain and the Persian Gulf, 1894 – 1914* (Berkley and Los Angeles, 1967), pp.270 – 82. *Note sur le régime des armes et des munitions en Afrique*, 22 May 1908, N.S. Grande-Bretagne 21. Bertie to Hardinge, 31 Oct. 1908, B.P., A, F.O.800/160.
[188] Aide-memoire enclosed in Bertie to Pichon, 12 June 1908, F.O.146/4041. Bertie to Grey, 12 and 14 June 1908, F.O.146/4041, despt.34 (Africa) and tel.7 (Africa).

that compensation was not due to France for putting a stop to a trade which 'enabled wild tribes to kill the friends of France', failed to produce from Pichon anything more than a promise to reexamine the issue.[189]

In Bertie's opinion the French were determined 'to squeeze us if they can'. He suggested that the Foreign Office should therefore go further in putting pressure upon them. 'Would it not', he enquired of Grey on 8 October 1909, 'be a good thing that the "Times" should be moved to publish an article not too harshly worded, but hinting at more later on, on the subject of France being the obstructive Power and the consequent injury to our interests which is difficult to understand considering the Entente &c?' If this failed to make the French more pliable, then Bertie thought that a question in the Commons might move them.[190] But while Grey was inclined to regard French demands for 'proper compensation' as 'blackmail', he and his officials in London were reluctant to risk damaging the *entente* by a public pillorying of France.[191] This was a pity since if Bertie's suggestion had been acted upon Pichon might at least have been in a better position to combat the objections of his colleagues to concessions on this subject.[192] As it was, no real progress was made towards an agreement, and when, as during 1910, the Royal Navy began to demonstrate its ability to deal effectively with the trade in the Persian gulf, the Foreign Office became less interested in responding to French proposals for a settlement.[193]

Matters were again brought to a head when in September 1912 the British succeeded in persuading the sultan of Muscat to establish a bonded warehouse in order to regulate the passage of arms though his dominions. The French protested that this was contrary to their treaty rights, and they threatened to send a warship to the gulf.[194] This moved even Grey to contemplate responding with the despatch of an armoured cruiser there,[195] and Bertie complained at the iniquity of French conduct. They are, he noted, 'almost invariably

---

Asquith to Edward VII, 29 July 1908, CAB.41/31/65. Note for the minister, 25 March 1911, N.S. Grande-Bretagne 24.
[189] Bertie to Grey, 7 Oct. 1909, Grey MSS., F.O.800/51.
[190] Bertie to Grey, 8 Oct. 1909, *ibid*.
[191] Minute by Grey on Bertie to Grey, 7 Oct. 1909, Grey MSS., F.O.800/51. Minutes by Montgomery and Grey on Bertie to Grey, 8 Oct. 1909, *ibid*. Minute by Hardinge on Bertie to Grey, 30 Oct. 1909, F.O.367/172, despt.34 (Africa).
[192] Bertie to Grey, 30 Oct. 1909, Grey MSS., F.O.800/51.
[193] Busch, *Britain and the Persian Gulf*, pp.282–92.
[194] *Ibid*., pp.292–8. Note for the minister, 24 Aug. 1912, N.S. Grande-Bretagne 24. Grey to Bertie 16 Oct. 1912, B.P., A, F.O.800/174.
[195] Busch, *Britain and the Persian Gulf*, pp.289–99.

blackmailers in such matters'.[196] Ultimately, the British decision to stand by the sultan, and perhaps the desire of both London and Paris to avoid a confrontation at a critical juncture in European politics, led to a compromise solution. In May 1913 the Quai d'Orsay indicated its readiness to adhere to the sultan's regulations, and, in return for the British government's indemnification of the arms dealers, undertook to prevent French firms participating in the trade. On this basis an accord was established, and notes confirming it were exchanged by the two governments on 14 March 1914.[197]

The Muscat arms trade affair was typical of the several Anglo-French misunderstandings which Bertie had to deal with in the ten years that preceded the outbreak of the first world war. But until the autumn of 1911, when a quarrel over the future of Morocco brought into question one of the most fundamental elements of the agreements of 1904, Bertie does not appear to have considered any of them to have been of sufficient magnitude to threaten the future of the *entente*. Indeed, for some of his colleagues the very persistence of these rivalries, along with the failure of the conventions of August 1907 to end friction between Britain and Russia in Asia, provided in itself a good reason for retaining the ties established with the powers of the Dual Alliance. Nicolson, for whom the difficulties encountered with France were 'merely family squabbles which must be borne and dealt with in a friendly manner', was to observe in February 1913 'an unfriendly France and Russia would give us infinite trouble, especially the former, in localities where we should find it extremely difficult to maintain our own'.[198] It is, however, worth recalling that Bertie had once regarded the bickering between England and Germany as being in 'the nature of family squabbles', and Germany as one of the chief practitioners of the ignoble art of *chantage*. The *entente* had clearly not freed the British from the exactions of their European neighbours. Moreover, it was also a disappointment to those who had hoped that the achievement of a political reconciliation would lead to Anglo-French cooperation in matters of finance and investment in the extra-European world. Nowhere was this more apparent than in the Near and Middle East.

---

[196] Bertie to Nicolson, 16 Sept. 1912, B.P., A, F.O.800/174.
[197] Busch, *Britain and the Persian Gulf*, pp.299 – 302. But French arms trading in east Africa continued to anger Grey. Memo. by Bertie, 27 June 1914, B.P., A, F.O.800/171.
[198] Nicolson to Cartwright, 19 Feb. 1913, Nicolson MSS., F.O.800/363.

7

The industrial entente

Throughout the forty years that Bertie had spent in the Foreign Office the political problems which beset the Ottoman empire and its neighbours had been matters of near constant concern to British diplomats and statesmen. The area was one of obvious commercial and strategic interest to Britain. The sultan's dominions lay in close proximity to the main lines of Britain's imperial communications and Britain remained Turkey's principal trading partner.[1] Yet, as Adam Block made clear in a gloomy memorandum of 18 June 1906, one of the salient features of Anglo-Ottoman relations in the previous quarter of a century had been the progressive decline in the British share in capital investment and state finance in Turkey. French financiers had by contrast maintained their position as the chief creditors of the Porte, and had, through their association with the agents of German capital, established what Block termed a 'Franco-German entente in Turkish finance'. The 'prime mover in French financial operations' was, according to Block, the *Imperial Ottoman Bank*: an institution which was Anglo-French in origin, but whose policies were by 1906 effectively controlled by the representatives of its French shareholders. Moreover, at Constantinople it had in collaboration with German bankers succeeded in creating a virtual monopoly of Turkish state finance whose predatory methods, Block feared, would drive the Porte into eventual bankruptcy. In that event, Block predicted, the powers interested would in the defence of the Turkish stock and railways that they controlled be obliged to take measures for creating order out of financial chaos. But, he contended; 'English houses . . . have no interest to speak of to protect in comparison with the French and Germans who are laying the economic foundation on which they will be able to build a political edifice.' If there were a financial crisis in Turkey, Britain, unlike

---

[1] *B.D.*, V, No.147. On the relative decline in British investment in the Ottoman empire see: H. Feis, *Europe, the World's Banker, 1870–1914* (New Haven, Conn., 1930), pp. 318–20; and Marian Kent, 'Great Britain and the End of the Ottoman Empire 1900–1923', in Kent, p.179. Relations between the *Ottoman Bank* and German financial institutions are surveyed in Poidevin, pp.267–76.

France and Germany, would not possess the economic basis with which to justify a political intervention.²

None of this might have warranted Bertie's personal attention if Grey had not attempted to utilize the *entente cordiale* in order to change the situation in Turkey to Britain's advantage. Such a course was recommended by Block to Hardinge in October 1906. He suggested that some reform of the *Ottoman Bank* might thus be attempted in order to give to the bank's London committee of directors greater influence in determining policy. Much, however, as Grey was pleased with this advice, the business of the surplus revenues seemed only to demonstrate that diplomatic pressure upon the French government was insufficient to prevent the representatives of French interests at Constantinople from acting in sympathy with their German colleagues. Mallet wrote to Bertie on 18 November 1906 that any financial *entente* with France in the Near East would mean a financial *entente* with Germany.³ Yet when faced during that same autumn with the prospect of the Constantinople quays company falling into German hands, the British and French governments did succeed in combining to give official encouragement to the purchase of the majority of its shares by the *Bank of England* and a French group headed by the *Ottoman Bank*.⁴

The purchase of the quays company shares, which Chirol characterized as a 'little *coup*, quite à la Beaconsfield', gave additional fillip to the pursuit of further Anglo-French ventures in Turkey.⁵ It would, Hardinge hoped, be the first step towards a more systematic commercial cooperation between Britain and France in the Near and Middle East.⁶ In fact Sir Arthur Vere, the agent of *Armstrong, Whitworth and Company* at Constantinople was already preparing a scheme for collaboration between British and French contractors and financiers in Turkey. His plan was for the formation of separate British and French syndicates which would seek out and share concessions in the Ottoman empire. It was clearly attractive from the point of view of the Foreign Office for if successful it might replace Anglo-French rivalry in Turkey with cooperation, stem the relative decline in Britain's investment in the area, and check the growth of German influence over the Porte. But in spite of assurances which

---

² Block to Hardinge, 20 Oct. 1906, F.O.371/155, and minute by Grey.
³ Mallet to Bertie, 18 Nov. 1906, B.P., A, F.O.800/174.
⁴ *Passim*, F.O.368/58. Hardinge to Grey, 28 Dec. 1906, Grey MSS.. F.O.800/92. P. Cambon to Pichon, 7 Jan. 1907, N.S. Grande-Bretagne 20, tel.1. Grey to Bertie, 28 and 29 Jan. 1907, F.O.368/132, *private*.
⁵ Chirol to Spring Rice, 18 Feb. 1907, Spring Rice MSS., CASR 1/12.
⁶ Hardinge to Bertie, 17 Jan. 1907, B.P., A, F.O.800/180.

Auboyneau gave to Lister in January 1907 of the *Ottoman Bank*'s desire to work with British capital, its support for the project soon proved to be more apparent than real, and the obstructive tactics employed by its committees in London and Paris did much to hinder progress towards the establishment of the consortium.[7]

The trouble was that while cooperation with British capital might enable the *Ottoman Bank* to surmount those limitations upon its conduct which seemed to result from France's political association with Britain, it could gain little from the emergence of a consortium over which it did not exercise a preponderant influence.[8] At the same time French diplomats were unlikely to encourage any arrangement which would weaken the position of the bank, and therefore France's influence, in Turkish affairs. It was thus hardly surprising that the support which Bertie gave to Vere at Paris yielded no early results. There were indeed some amongst the banking fraternity in France who favoured involving German capital in the proposed combination. Even de Verneuil, the syndic of the *Société des Agents de Change*, who was an enthusiastic exponent of Vere's plan,[9] was moved to suggest to Bertie on 23 May 1907 that the Germans should be offered a share in the consortium in order to overcome the opposition which he anticipated from them at Constantinople. This drew angry retorts from Bertie's friends in London. 'The whole object of forming an Anglo-French combination', observed Mallet, 'would be defeated if we admitted the Germans to a share in it.'[10] Hardinge protested to Bertie that Britain did not want 'an Anglo-Franco-German combine at all', and he added that if 'the French Govt and French houses do not wish the Anglo-French combine to assume a definite form it would be better to say so at once so that we may push our concerns on different lines'.[11]

---

[7] Only two days after assuring Lister of the *Ottoman Bank's* wish to co-operate with British institutions Auboyneau informed the *directeur commercial* of the Quai d'Orsay with regard to Vere's proposed consortium that he foresaw 'des inconvénients à l'entrée officiele de la Banque Ottomane dans les arrangements de cette nature, portant sur les affaires indeterminées'. Departmental note, *Visite de M. Auboyneau*, 29 Jan. 1907, N.S. Turquie 360. Lister to Mallet, 27 Jan. 1907, Grey MSS., F.O.800/51. The subsequent history of Vere's project is examined in more detail in K.A. Hamilton, 'An attempt to form an Anglo-French "Industrial Entente" ', 47–73.

[8] Bertie to Vere, 2 March 1907; Hardinge to Bertie, 9 May 1907; B.P., B, F.O.800/185. Bertie to Mallet, 18 April 1907; Bertie to Hardinge, 4 May 1907; B.P., A, F.O.800/180. Block to Hardinge, 2 April 1907, F.O.371/340. Vere to Bertie, 2 May 1907, enclosed in Bertie to Hardinge, 2 May 1907; Vere to Hardinge, 8 May 1907; F.O.371/350.

[9] Bertie to Mallet, 18 April 1907, *ibid*.

[10] Bertie to Hardinge, 23 May 1907, F.O.371/350, and minutes by Hardinge and Mallet. Hardinge to Bertie, 28 May 1907, B.P., A, F.O.800/180.

[11] Hardinge to Bertie, 30 May 1907, B.P., A, F.O.800/180.

Pichon also deprecated de Verneuil's suggestion. Much as he appreciated the importance of the financial considerations involved, he insisted that the Anglo-French project 'was political and must be considered in that light'.[12] But when Pichon displayed more than his usual lack of application in the handling of this matter, Bertie began to wonder whether Joseph Caillaux, the minister of finances could be against the scheme. The French government might, he thought, 'feel some hesitation about doing another deal in opposition to Germany'.[13] His suspicions were not wholly misplaced. Ever since January Henry, the *directeur commercial*, had been worried about arousing further German hostility towards France, and he was also concerned about the possible ill-effects of the projected consortium on present and prospective French interests in Turkey.[14] Pichon had himself written to Paul Cambon on 14 May of his fears lest the scheme should cause difficulties and complications for France's 'politique générale'.[15] And when on 11 July Vere requested Henry's support for what he now termed an 'Anglo-French Industrial Entente', he received a very frosty answer. Henry declared that he disapproved of the formation ' "with beating of drums and blowing of trumpets" of allied Anglo-French companies, as he was of the opinion that this would cause trouble [with Germany, Vere presumed] . . . and could only do harm'. Nevertheless, Vere remained optimistic, and on 13 July Pichon informed him that he was instructing Henry to tell Bertie that a French syndicate had been formed which would have the same support from the Quai d'Orsay as the British one would have from the Foreign Office.[16]

Pichon's expressed desire to promote cooperation between British and French institutions may have been genuine. It soon emerged, however, that the proposed French group was to consist of no more than a slightly enlarged version of the *Société Mirabaud*, a syndicate that Auboyneau had helped to form in close association with the *Ottoman Bank*. This meant that the French part of the consortium would be dominated by the bank and other establishments belonging to what Bertie called the 'protestant Germanophile faction'. To overcome this danger Bertie enlisted the aid of Clemenceau, and after frank discussions on 17 July the premier agreed to entrust de

---

[12] Bertie to Hardinge, 30 May 1907, B.P., A, F.O.800/180.
[13] Bertie to Hardinge, 5, 12, 16 and 17 June, 10 and 11 July, 1907 B.P., A, F.O.800/180
[14] *Visite de M. Auboyneau*, 29 Jan. 1907, N.S. Turquie 360.
[15] Pichon to P. Cambon, 14 May 1907, N.S. Turquie 360, despt.139.
[16] Bertie to Hardinge, 10 July 1907; Vere to Bertie, 11 July 1907; B.P., A, F.O.800/180. Vere to Hardinge, 11 July 1907; Bertie to Hardinge, 12 July 1907; F.O.371/350.

Verneuil with the formation of a French syndicate. The *Ottoman Bank* was to be allowed a thirty per cent share in this group, Vere was to be director general of the combination at Constantinople, and he was to have a Frenchman as his partner.[17] But Bertie had achieved only a tactical, and in some respects a rather superficial, victory over the *Ottoman Bank* and its allies in the foreign ministry. A Quai d'Orsay memorandum of 22 July, which was probably drafted by Henry, stipulated that Clemenceau had agreed that everything should be avoided which would give to 'cette union un caractère sensational', and that de Verneuil was to seek an extension of the *Société Mirabaud*, 'étant bien entendu d'ailleurs que si la situation de la Banque Ottomane n'était pas dominante elle resterait néamoins spéciale'.[18] Moreover, neither Bertie, Vere, nor the Foreign Office had reckoned with the opposition of the London committee of the *Ottoman Bank*. Until September 1907 they remained confident that it would be content with a substantial share in a British syndicate. They were wrong. Having failed to obtain a controlling interest in the French group, the bank appears to have been in no mood to accept a subordinate position in the British one, and for the remainder of 1907 its London committee procrastinated over the part that it would play in such an enterprise.[19]

The consequent delay in the formation of a British syndicate prompted de Verneuil to complain to Clemenceau over the tardiness of the British, and on 2 December he reminded Pichon that it had been on the insistence of Bertie that the French group had been constituted. Two months later on 7 February 1908 the French financiers, Bardac and de Gunzburg, called at the embassy to press for more haste on the part of the Foreign Office. A banker of Russian origin, the Baron Jacques de Gunzburg was a close friend of the ambassador. Bertie had known him for the best part of three years, and he sometimes spent weekends with him at his house at Dieppe, near to which town Bertie possessed a stretch of a trout stream. De Gunzburg was also a useful source of information on matters financial and political. Now, however, in conversation with Lister, he claimed that the French government had to a considerable extent been actuated by a desire to meet British wishes in a financial scheme which seemed to benefit Britain more than France. This was all very

---

[17] Bertie to Hardinge, 17 and 19 July 1907, B.P., A, F.O.800/180.
[18] Departmental notes, 19 and 22 July, N.S. Turquie 360.
[19] Bertie to Hardinge, 9 Sept. 1907; Hardinge to Bertie, 25 Sept. 1907; B.P., A, F.O.800/180. Bertie to Hardinge, 18 Sept. 1907, B.P., B, F.O.800/185. Mallet to Grey, 8 Sept. 1907; Hardinge to *Ottoman Bank*, 11 Oct. 1907; F.O.371/350. Bertie to Hardinge, 18 and 19 Sept. 1907, F.O.371/350.

embarrassing from the British point of view. But it did not incline Grey's officials to welcome the announcement on 13 February by Ernest Barry, the manager of the *Ottoman Bank* in London, of the formation of a British group called the *Ottoman Society*.[20]

It was from the start quite apparent that this group was to be dominated by the *Ottoman Bank*, and Grey admitted as much to Bertie. Moreover, the possibility that other British financiers might eventually support the *Ottoman Society* was of little comfort to those at Paris who had struggled to put together the French syndicate.[21] Bertie, after hearing the complaints of de Gunzburg and de Verneuil, suggested to Mallet that he should go to Somerset House to find out if the British group had been registered, and, if so, who its members were. The result, he rightly suspected, would show that the society was the 'Ottoman Bank in other clothing'.[22] Mallet's investigations in fact revealed that the *Ottoman Society* had not even been registered, and in these circumstances the Foreign Office refused to endorse it as the British part of the consortium. They had not, Mallet protested, gone to all this trouble to persuade the *Ottoman Bank* to turn itself into a company. 'Our whole object', he wrote to Bertie on 24 April, 'was to get some good British firms to work with French Houses and get concessions in competition with the international financial ring of which the O.B. is part.'[23] Bertie in his turn envisaged the possibility of trying to make things difficult for the bank at Constantinople if its London committee were not more accommodating.[24] 'The great object', he observed to Mallet, 'being to put an end to the preponderance of the Bank.'[25]

Nobody within the Quai d'Orsay regarded this as the 'great object' of the projected consortium. Nevertheless, it still seemed possible that

---

[20] De Verneuil to Pichon, 2 Dec. 1907, N.S. Turquie 383. Bertie to Hardinge, 6 Sept. 1907, F.O.371/350. Memo. by Lister, 7 Feb. 1908 F.O.371/538. Draft letter by Mallet to the *Ottoman Bank*, Feb. 1908, F.O.371/538 (cancelled). Bertie to Hardinge, 8 Feb. 1908 B.P., A, F.O.800/180.
[21] Hardinge to Barry, 19 Feb. 1908, F.O.371/538. Grey to Bertie, 24 Feb. 1908, F.O. 371/538, despt.82.
[22] Bertie to Hardinge, 2 April 1908, tel.; Bertie to Mallet, 23 April 1908; B.P., A, F.O.800/180.
[23] Mallet to Bertie, 24 April 1908, B.P., A, F.O.800/180. A subsequent telephone call to the Registrar of Joint Stock Companies revealed that the *Ottoman Society* had been registered at Somerset House on 15 April 1908. But no return was available as to the amount of share capital issued, and no list of directors had yet been filed. Record of telephone communication of 5 May 1908; Hardinge to the Registrar of Joint Stock Companies, 5 May 1908; F.O.371/538.
[24] Bertie to Mallet, 26 April 1908, B.P., A, F.O.800/180.
[25] According to figures which de Verneuil supplied to Bertie the *Ottoman Bank* in France was to have effectively a 25% share in the capital of the French group. Bertie to Mallet, 5 May 1908, F.O.371/538.

Vere's scheme could be brought to fruition. On 1 May Barry indicated to Mallet that he had approached other British firms, and that they would be prepared to enter a British group once a draft agreement had been settled between the French and British syndicates.[26] Unfortunately this was easier said than done. Indeed it was the elaboration of such an accord which further obstructed the formation of a consortium during the spring of 1908.[27] Appeals from Bertie to the Foreign Office to ensure that an understanding was arrived at before the French holidays commenced were without effect,[28] and it was the end of July before Hardinge finally approved an agreement. By then Sir Ernest Cassel, a financier of German-Jewish extraction whom the Foreign Office had expected to work with the *Ottoman Bank*, had left London without yet engaging himself in writing. De Verneuil was also on the point of leaving Paris, and the annual exodus of ministers and officials from the French capital had begun.[29] Besides which, the political situation in Turkey and Britain's standing at Constantinople was undergoing a fundamental transformation.

Within the Foreign Office there had been a tendency to attribute the subordinate position occupied by British capital and enterprise in Turkey to the maladministration of the Porte and the consequent reluctance of British bankers and businessmen to invest there.[30] The Young Turk revolution of July 1908 and the emergence at Constantinople of a *régime* which was reformist in its aspirations and pro-British in its sympathies, therefore seemed bound to affect any attempt to associate British and French interests there.[31] The full significance of this for Vere's project was not, however, appreciated by Bertie until the autumn when discussions were resumed on the form of the proposed combination. In the meanwhile the prospect of Turkey's new rulers seeking to exercise their authority throughout the Ottoman empire raised the question of the future status of Bosnia

---

[26] Mallet to Bertie, 24 April and 1 May 1908, B.P., A, F.O.800/180. Hardinge to Barry, 6 May 1908; Barry to Hardinge, 2 June 1908; F.O.371/538.
[27] *Passim*, F.O.371/538. Mallet to Bertie, 27 June 1908, B.P., A, F.O.800/180.
[28] Bertie to Mallet, 13 June 1908, B.P., A, F.O.800/180. Minute by Norman, 29 June 1908, F.O.371/538.
[29] Draft contract schedule C submitted to the F.O. by Vere, 21 July 1908, and minutes by Norman and Hardinge; F.O.371/538. Mallet to Lowther, 5 Aug. 1908, F.O.371/547.
[30] See for example: Hardinge to Block, 19 May and 2 June 1908, Hardinge MSS., 13.
[31] Feroz Ahmad, *The Young Turks. The Committee of Union and Progress in Turkish Politics, 1908 – 1914* (Oxford, 1969), pp.1 – 13. M.B. Cooper, 'British Policy in the Balkans, 1908 – 1909', *Historical Journal*, VII (1964), 263. Block to Hardinge, 25 July 1908,

and Herzegovina, lands which, though nominally under the sovereignty of the sultan, had since the congress of Berlin been administered by Austria-Hungary. To meet the challenge posed by developments at Constantinople Lexa von Aehrenthal, the Austrian foreign minister, decided upon the annexation of the two provinces. Even before the revolution Izvolsky had suggested this course to Aehrenthal as part of a package whereby the straits between the Black Sea and the Aegean might be opened to Russian warships. Talks between the two foreign ministers at Buchlau on 15 and 16 September produced a verbal agreement that they would not oppose each other's plans. But Aehrenthal seems to have avoided making his move dependent upon the opening of the straits, and on 3 October, before Izvolsky had had the opportunity to confer with either the British or French government upon the matter, Khevenhüller, the Austrian ambassador at Paris, informed Fallières and Pichon that his government intended to proceed with the annexation. Moreover, according to the French account, Khevenhüller said that the Austrian action would be preceded by a Bulgarian declaration of independence.[32]

Within a few hours of Khevenhüller making his communication to the Quai d'Orsay Louis informed Bertie of its substance, and later that day Pichon indicated to him that Aehrenthal had the concurrence of the Russian, German and Italian governments.[33] As a former participant at the congress of Berlin, and an ambassador accredited to a country with substantial interests in Turkey and an alliance with Russia, Bertie could have been expected to interest himself in the ensuing troubles. He was also personally involved in that he was one of the first representatives of the *entente* powers to meet Izvolsky in the aftermath of the 'Austrian bombshell'. This was because when Izvolsky, already on his way to Paris, arrived there on Sunday 4 October, he was unable to contact Pichon who was away shooting. Bertie, had, however, decided to abandon the leave that he had been planning to take in England and in consequence was able to receive the now repentant Russian at the embassy. Once in the ambassador's presence, Izvolsky attempted to justify his policies and actions. Aehrenthal, he claimed, had broached the subject of the annexation,

---

Hardinge MSS., 11. Hardinge to Block, 31 July 1908, Hardinge MSS., 13. Joseph Heller, *British Policy towards the Ottoman Empire, 1908 – 1914* (London, 1983), pp.9 – 16.
[32] F.R. Bridge, *From Sadowa to Sarajevo. The foreign policy of Austria-Hungary, 1866 – 1914* (London, 1972), pp.300 – 05; and 'Izvolsky, Aehrenthal, and the End of the Austro-Russian Entente, 1906 – 8', *Mitteilungen des österreichischen Staatsarchivs*, XXIX (1976), 315 – 62. B.D.., V, no.294. Bertie to Hardinge, 7 Oct. 1908, B.P., A, F.O.800/161. Bertie to Hardinge, 29 Oct. 1908, B.P., A, F.O.800/170.
[33] B.D., V, nos.281 and 285. D.D.F.2., XI, no.74.

but he had not said that the Austrian decision was either definitive or imminent. On the other hand, he asserted that he, Izvolsky, had warned Aehrenthal that such a course would be contrary to the Berlin treaty, and that Russia would therefore require a change in the *régime* of the straits in a sense favourable to the Black Sea powers. Moreover, while he maintained that Russia would support Bulgarian independence, he denied ever having mentioned this at Buchlau.

Bertie was no more favourably impressed by Izvolsky on this occasion than he had been during his first meeting with him in 1906. Of the Russian foreign minister he wrote to Grey: 'I have the impression, I may say the conviction that he did not tell me the truth, the whole truth and nothing but the truth.' It was no doubt with this in mind that he persuaded Izvolsky to commit his statement to paper in the form of a memorandum. Not that Bertie was convinced of the innocence of any of the parties to the affair. He supposed that Germany had promised Austria moral support for her annexation of Bosnia; that Izvolsky had probably received assurances from Rome and Vienna with regard to the straits; that he had hoped to prepare the ground for British and French acquiescence during visits to London and Paris; and that although matters had been discussed in detail at Buchlau, Izvolsky had been 'mistaken and deceived' in thinking that the Austrians would not act without first consulting Russia. For the moment, however, the task facing Bertie was that of dealing with French reactions to the new situation in the Balkans, and in this respect he was distinctly unenthusiastic about Clemenceau's suggestion that a conference should be summoned. Without a preliminary agreement between the majority of the powers, Bertie thought that such a gathering would be liable to end in discord, and he feared that if Austria had the concurrence of the other powers, Britain and France would find themselves in a minority and possibly in disagreement with Russia.[34] Nevertheless, this argument carried little weight with the French ministers. Pichon told Bertie on 5 October that Izvolsky favoured a conference, and that he was ready to try to reach a preliminary understanding with Britain, France and Italy. In Pichon's view, Austria would stand as the party accused with Germany as her 'brilliant second'.[35] From this, Bertie inferred that Izvolsky was trying to 'drag along the French Government and rush

---

[34] B.D., V, nos.293 and 294. Bertie to Tyrrell, 5 Oct. 1908, Tel.; Grey to Bertie, 5 Oct. 1908, tel.; Grey MSS., F.O.800/51. Bertie to Hardinge, 4 and 7 Oct. 1908, B.P., A, F.O.800/161.
[35] *B.D.*, V, nos.297 and 304.

us'. The French, he suspected, were so afraid of losing their ally that they would accept the Russian version of the transaction.[36]

The attitude of Grey and Hardinge did not differ substantially from that assumed by Bertie. They agreed that before any conference the powers would first have to agree that Turkey should not be required to make further concessions, and that nothing should be done to endanger the new administration at Constantinople.[37] When, however, on 6 October Clemenceau and Pichon warned Bertie that Izvolsky intended to propose a conference, Grey was compelled to act with some haste. That afternoon he telegraphed to Bertie to ask if the French could not induce the Russians to postpone such a proposal.[38] This did not please Clemenceau, who protested that if a conference did not meet without delay a war would break out. None the less, Bertie succeeded in overcoming his opposition and finally won French agreement to the course which Grey recommended.[39] This and Bertie's other recent diplomatic achievements won him the felicitations of his colleagues in London. Tyrrell, who 'chuckled' at Bertie's account of his 'cross-examination of the vain old fox as to what passed with Aehrenthal', thought his handling of Clemenceau was 'admirable' and was sure that Grey would think so too.[40] On the 12th Hardinge also expressed the Foreign Office's pleasure at the information which Bertie had been sending from Paris, and the manner in which he had dealt with Izvolsky, Clemenceau and Pichon. 'It was very clever of you', Hardinge commented, 'to have got Izvolsky to write down his views so fully. We have been congratulating ourselves that you were still there and had not gone away on leave.'[41] Pleased with such praise, Bertie thanked Tyrrell for his approval. It had been 'well worth a mass', and he appreciated it more.[42]

Bertie was a good deal less happy about Grey's apparent willingness to acquiesce in Izvolsky's demands with regard to the straits. After leaving Paris, the Russian minister visited London where he made it clear to Grey that while he was prepared to accept the exclusion of the subject of the straits from the agenda of an international conference, he nevertheless intended to raise it with the Turks. He pressed Grey not to oppose Russia, and if possible to

---

[36] Bertie to Hardinge, 7 Oct. 1908, B.P., A, F.O.800/161.
[37] Grey to Asquith, 5 Oct. 1908, Grey MSS., F.O.800/100, Hardinge to Bertie, 5 Oct. 1908, B.P., A, F.O.800/161. *B.D.*, V, nos.301, 303, 306, 311, and 321.
[38] *B.D.*, V, no.314.
[39] *B.D.*, V, Nos.333 and 335.
[40] Tyrrell to Bertie, 5 Oct. 1908, B.P., A, F.O.800/180.
[41] Hardinge to Bertie, 12 Oct. 1908, *ibid.*
[42] Bertie to Tyrrell, 12 Oct. 1908, *ibid.*

support her claim for the Black Sea states to have the exclusive right of passage for their warships though the straits. Without such compensation, he pointed out, both his own position in Russia and the Anglo-Russian understanding would be in danger. The prospect of the opening of the straits did not personally worry Grey, and both Hardinge and Nicolson sympathized with Izvolsky's cause.[43] It had since 1896 been a settled principle of British naval policy that a British fleet would not enter the straits unless Britain were in alliance with Turkey, and that the containment of Russia in the Black Sea could no longer therefore be regarded as strategically feasible. And although no reference had been made to the question in the Anglo-Russian convention of 1907, Grey had intimated to Benckendorff that the old policy of keeping the straits closed would have to be abandoned.[44] It was not, however, a concession which seemed likely to be easily accepted by either Grey's cabinet colleagues or the British public.[45]

Bertie himself made much of the probable public reaction to such a concession, which he believed could be damaging to Britain's international standing and prestige. For him the strategic assumptions of the Admiralty counted for little. After a remark made to him by the Russian ambassador in Paris on 12 October about the importance of Russia being able to maintain her fleet in the Black Sea, Bertie appealed to Tyrrell:

Are we going to give away the Straits? What will the public think and perhaps say, if and when they learn that the non-opposition to the ambitions of Russia in the matter of the Straits was part of the price but not declared for the Anglo-Russian understanding? If Russia is to be allowed to go in and out of the Mediterranean through the Straits to her unapproachable haven, shall we not look foolish?

If there were to be changes in the *régime* of the straits then Bertie considered that the Black Sea should be open to the ships of all nations with limits upon the number passing through the straits at

---

[43] Grey of Fallodon, I, pp.178–80. *B.D.*, V, no.372.
[44] A.J. Marder, *The Anatomy of British Sea Power. A History of British Naval Policy in the pre-Dreadnought Era, 1880–1905* (New York, 1964), pp.578–80. Beryl Williams, 'Great Britain and Russia', Hinsley, p.146.
[45] Cooper, 266–9. *B.D.*, V, no. 358. Hardinge to Bertie, 12 Oct. 1908, B.P., A, F.O.800/180.

any one moment.⁴⁶ He need not have worried. On 12 October Grey and Asquith failed to persuade the cabinet to agree to Izvolsky's request.⁴⁷ A second Russian proposal that in the event of Russia being involved in a war, Turkey should give equal rights to other belligerents, did contain an element of reciprocity and was accepted by the cabinet on the 14th.⁴⁸ Nevertheless, Grey's policy was still limited by the susceptibilities of the Young Turks, and in a private letter of 15 October he would go no further than to promise Izvolsky that at a 'favourable time' he would support Russia's views at Constantinople.⁴⁹

The crisis in the Near East also drew Bertie's attention to the long standing problem of Crete. Fierce inter-communal strife between the island's christian and muslim populations in the mid-1890s had resulted in a Greco-Turkish war, and since 1897, when it was granted a semi-autonomous status within the Ottoman empire, it had been under the protection of Britain, France, Italy and Russia, powers which were pledged to maintain the suzerainty of the sultan and which provided forces of occupation.⁵⁰ The desire of the Cretan christians for union with Greece, and the evident lack of enthusiasm displayed by the protecting powers for maintaining their occupation, had, however, made the existing order ever less tenable. In May 1908 the four powers agreed to begin the withdrawal of their forces on 28 July and to complete it within a year. This still left open the question of what they should do if the Cretans were themselves to seek to alter their relationship with the Porte.⁵¹ Moreover, in the aftermath of the Young Turk revolution Grey's policy towards Crete was conditioned by his desire to retain the goodwill of the new government at Constantinople. He tried therefore to exclude the issue of Crete from the agenda of the proposed conference, and when on 6 October the

---

⁴⁶ Bertie to Tyrrell, 12 Oct. 1908, B.P., A, F.O.800/180. Bertie had never had much faith in the views expressed by naval experts, and he had long opposed the notion of allowing the Russians access to the Mediterranean. According to a story related by the Austro-Hungarian ambassador at London, Bertie, when approached on this subject in 1902, had torn a map from the wall, and holding it in his hand, had declared that 'England would never permit the route to India to be endangered by the abandonment to the Russians of the free passage of the Dardanelles'. *G.P.*, XIX, pt.1, no.6075.
⁴⁷ Asquith to Edward VII, 12 Oct. 1908, CAB.41/31/66. *B.D.*, V, nos.364 and 372.
⁴⁸ Asquith to Edward VII, 14 Oct. 1908, CAB.41/31/67.
⁴⁹ *B.D.*, V, no.387.
⁵⁰ J. Garniage, 'Les affaires de Crète (1895 – 1899)', *Revue d'histoire diplomatique* (1974), 86 – 111. E. Driault and M. Lhéritier, *Histoire diplomatique de la Grèce de 1821 à nos jours* (5 vols., Paris, 1926), IV, pp.301 – 469. D. Dakin, *The Unification of Greece, 1830 – 1923* (London, 1972), pp.149 – 54.
⁵¹ Dakin, pp.170 – 7. While Grey accepted that Crete would eventually be united with Greece, he insisted that union 'must come decently and in order, and in such a way as

Cretan assembly declared the island's union with Greece, he despatched a naval squadron to the eastern Mediterranean. Through the British consul at Canea he warned the Cretans that Britain could neither allow nor admit their union with Greece without the consent of the protecting powers.[52]

At Paris Bertie tried with little success to ensure the cooperation of the French government on this issue. He had to reckon with the philhellenic sentiments of Clemenceau and the reluctance of the Quai d'Orsay to countenance any action that might risk France losing such influence as she possessed at Athens or interfere with Greek orders for French armaments. When on 7 October Pichon explained to Bertie that the Russian government would be prepared to agree that apart from that resulting from the actions of Austria and Bulgaria there should be no diminution in Ottoman territory, Clemenceau protested that he must make a reservation with regard to Crete. In this instance Bertie found an ally in Pichon, and faced with objections from both his foreign minister and the British ambassador, Clemenceau waived the point. Pichon was none the less reluctant to take any prominent stand on the matter. He objected to Grey's proposal that Britain and France should encourage the Greeks to negotiate directly with the Turks, and to the British suggestion that there should be no reduction in the foreign contingents on the island whilst the illegal situation continued.[53] Then on 21 October he intimated to Bertie that the French government was opposed to any manifestation that might be considered anti-Greek. Bertie responded with a predictable warning to Pichon about the advantages that the Austrians and the Germans might derive from being able to insinuate at Constantinople that the Turks would gain more from being able to lean towards them. For Britain and France not to take precautions to prevent Crete's union with Greece would, he argued, be to play into the hands of the enemies of reform in Turkey. Pichon was not impressed. Confident that the Porte would not be so short-sighted as to follow German advice, he assured Bertie that Germany would not succeed in reestablishing her influence at Constantinople if Britain and France supported the Turks in financial matters.[54]

---

not to constitute an inexcusable breach of our promise to the Turkish Government'. Grey to Howard, 3 April 1906, Grey MSS., F.O.800/108.
[52] Driault and Lhéritier, V, p.21. Cooper, 267. Grey to Bertie, 29 Oct. 1908, B.P., A, F.O.800/172.
[53] *B.D.*, V, no.333. Grey to Wylbore-Smith, 8 Oct. 1908, F.O.371/444, tel.26. Bertie to Grey, 9 Oct. 1908, F.O.371/444, tel.62. Bertie to Grey, 10 Oct. 1908 F.O.371/444, despt.396. Grey to Bertie, 17 Oct. 1908, F.O.371/444, despt.202. Bertie to Grey, 31 Oct. 1908, B.P., A, F.O.800/172
[54] Bertie to Grey, 21 Oct. 1908, F.O.371/444, despt.417.

Pichon in the meanwhile offered to Bertie two possible solutions to the Cretan question which he thought might satisfy both Greek and Turkish aspirations. The first, which he put to him on 13 October, was that the Greeks should compensate the Turks for the loss of Crete by ceding to them certain territories in Epirus: a suggestion which, although it was supposed to relate to the Greco-Turkish frontier changes of 1881, was vague and confusing and met with an unenthusiastic response in London.[55] His second proposal proved no more acceptable to the Foreign Office. It was made at the close of his interview with Bertie on 21 October when Pichon, speaking 'non pas ministre, mais comme ami', remarked that if England wished to 'counteract the intrigues of Germany at Constantinople, to show her disinterestedness and to well-establish her influence in Turkey, let her give back to the Sultan Cyprus'. This idea Bertie at first attributed to Clemenceau and the Greek king, but three days later he learned that it had originated with Izvolsky. He was not very surprised. Izvolsky, Bertie thought, was using Pichon to do what he did not like to do himself.[56] And although neither Grey nor Hardinge considered Cyprus to be of any further value to Britain, Grey was of the opinion that since three-quarters of its population were Greek, its return to Turkey would simply create more trouble for the Porte. 'For these reasons', Grey wrote to Bertie, ' "l'affaire ne marchera" or as we say "this cock won't fight".'[57]

Grey was not, however, irreconcilably opposed to the idea of seeking some arrangement with the Turkish government on Crete. On 20 November he informed Bertie by telegram that the British government proposed to express the hope to the Turks that as soon as the projected conference had met, they would 'lose no time in communicating to the Protecting Powers their views as to the solution of the Cretan question'.[58] Unfortunately for Bertie, both Pichon and Clemenceau were busy entertaining the Swedish royal family, who were then visiting Paris, and he was unable personally to communicate Grey's views to them until 23 November. By then Clemenceau had already learnt from Rome of Grey's intentions. Moreover, Tittoni, who was still Italian foreign minister, and who had recently received the King of Greece at Rome, thought that negotiations to

---

[55] Bertie to Hardinge, 13 and 18 Oct. 1908; Hardinge to Bertie, 16 Oct, 1908; B.P., A, F.O.800/180. Hardinge to Bertie, 29 Oct. 1908; Bertie to Hardinge, 31 Oct. 1908; B.P., A, F.O.800/172.
[56] Bertie to Grey, 21 Oct. 1908, F.O.371/444, despt.417. Bertie to Hardinge, 26 Oct. 1908 B.P., A, F.O.800/172.
[57] Hardinge to Nicolson, 28 Oct. 1908, Nicolson MSS., F.O.800/341. Grey to Bertie, 29 Oct. 1908; Hardinge to Bertie, 29 Oct. 1908; B.P., A, F.O.800/172.
[58] B.D., V, no.456.

solve the problem should take place between the protecting powers and the Turks 'prior to and independent of the Conference'. In this respect Tittoni seems to have succeeded in encouraging Clemenceau to take a firm stand in favour of an early settlement. At any rate when on the 23rd Bertie attended a dinner at the Élysée palace, he was forewarned by Pichon that Clemenceau had been 'got at again by the King of Greece' through Tittoni, and had returned to his former philhellenic stance on Crete. As a result Bertie was brought into a direct and open confrontation with Clemenceau.

During the course of the evening's entertainment Clemenceau told Bertie that he entirely concurred in Tittoni's view that the matter should be settled without delay, and he described as extraordinary a communication made to Tittoni by Egerton, the British ambassador at Rome. This had been based upon the same instructions as Grey had sent to Paris on 20 November, but Bertie was quite unaware of what Egerton had said, and Clemenceau refused to enlighten him. Indeed, when Bertie ridiculed his view that the British government was harbouring some *arrière pensée*, he suggested that this had been held back from the ambassador's knowledge. The British government, he claimed, was more Turkish than the Turks themselves. For his part what Clemenceau appears to have desired was that the protecting powers should decide the fate of Crete, press the solution upon the Porte, and submit it to a conference for confirmation. 'France', he impressed on Bertie, 'was not prepared to risk losing her influence in Greece.' Bertie was no less uncompromising. Britain, he insisted, did not intend to lose her influence at Constantinople to please the Greeks and the Cretans, and if Clemenceau 'adhered to his present attitude it would mean a separation of France and England in the matter of Crete, for we could not give way'. This brought the discussion to an abrupt close, and although, according to Bertie's account, Clemenceau had by then calmed down, the premier left the dinner, shirked the *représentation-théatrale*, and retired to bed.[59]

In Bertie's opinion Clemenceau had hoped that by using Italian support he could return to the reservations which he had made earlier with regard to Crete being excepted from the provision that no territorial compensation should be demanded of Turkey for the Austrian and Bulgarian actions. Nevertheless, he did not take Clemenceau's language too seriously, and he advised Grey not to pay any attention to his display of temper as he was very excitable by nature and had had an attack of 'remittent Philhellenism'. 'I would',

---

[59] Bertie to Grey, 24 Nov. 1908, B.P., A, 800/172. Bertie to Grey, 25 Nov. 1908, F.O.371/445, despt.480.

Bertie concluded, 'take no notice of it, and treat it as not having been reported to you'.[60] Evidently he anticipated that a night's rest would dissipate Clemenceau's suspicions, and, as he wrote to the foreign minister, Pichon would be able to tell him 'que la France marchera d'accord avec l'Angleterre'.[61] Grey was again pleased with Bertie's conduct. 'Sir F. Bertie', he minuted on Bertie's report of his conversation with Clemenceau, 'upheld our view excellently.'[62] There was, however, no radical change in French policy, and despite Bertie's efforts to discourage such a proposal, Pichon persisted in pressing for Britain's agreement to a plan whereby the protecting powers should try to reach an understanding with the Porte which would be submitted to a conference.[63] Convinced that it was the 'height of folly' to throw away British influence at Constantinople for the goodwill of Greece, which could be easily won in the future, Grey urged Bertie to press this view on Clemenceau.[64] If Clemenceau were a card player, then Grey thought that Bertie might indicate to him that 'it is a bad policy to make small tricks, of which you can be sure at any time, at a moment when it may mean losing all the other tricks in the game'. But the metaphor was not one which recommended itself to Bertie. He did not know whether Clemenceau was a card player, but he admitted that he himself was not, and that 'never having taken a hand at whist or bridge', he would be in 'helpless confusion' if he attempted to argue about tricks. By December he had in any case reached the conclusion that there was little point in persisting with this issue.[65]

Bertie assumed that France's policy towards developments in the eastern Mediterranean was in large part governed by the Quai d'Orsay's desire to protect French commercial and financial interests in the region. A remark by Pichon to one of the embassy staff to the effect that France was not going to sacrifice her 'Greek clientèle' was thus taken by Bertie to mean that Pichon was hoping that Athens would reward a friendly France with orders for arms and ships.[66] His diagnosis seems not to have been ill-founded, and Clemenceau's subsequent readiness to postpone any decision on Crete may have

---

[60] *Ibid.*
[61] Bertie to Pichon, 24 Nov. 1908, F.O.146/2043.
[62] Minute by Grey on Bertie to Grey, 25 Nov. 1908, F.O.371/445, despt.480.
[63] Grahame to Grey, 27 Nov. 1908, F.O.371/445, tel.102. P. Cambon to Grey, 3 Dec. 1908, F.O.371/445.
[64] Grey to Bertie, 7 Dec. 1908, Grey MSS., F.O.800/51.
[65] Grey to Bertie, 4 Dec. 1908, tel.; Bertie to Grey, 5 Dec. 1908, and 10 and 14 Jan. 1909; B.P., A, F.O.800/172.
[66] Grahame to Grey, 27 Nov. 1908, F.O.371/445, tel.102. Bertie to Grey, 5 Dec. 1908, *ibid.*

been due to warnings from Constans that France's pro-Greek policy could lead to a Turkish boycott of French imports. There was also the danger that France might find herself isolated on the Cretan question, for, as Louis pointed out in a minute of 2 January 1909, if the British were not prepared to withdraw their forces from the island, the Italians and the Russians would also be reluctant to do so.[67] But despite the fact that by the beginning of 1909 the prospects for an international conference on the Near East had already begun to fade, Pichon and his officials seemed incapable of pursuing a consistent policy towards Crete. Symptomatic of this was the French government's agreement to a British proposal that after July the Ottoman flag should be maintained on Suda island outside the harbour at Canea under the guardianship of one of the protecting powers,[68] and Pichon's indication to Bertie on 27 May that Clemenceau no longer favoured ending the occupation before an agreement had been reached with the Turkish government.[69]

This change of front may, as Bertie supposed, have been attributable to German meddling in the affair. According to the Turkish ambassador at Paris, the German emperor had not only promised to support an Italian *démarche* favouring the Greek annexation of Crete, but had also whilst staying on Corfu given formal assurances to the king of Greece. From this information Bertie deduced that Clemenceau was afraid lest the union of Crete with Greece under German auspices should mean 'the appearance of Germany in the Mediterranean by some agreement with Greece'.[70] It is certainly true that when an Italian initiative failed to materialize, Pichon beat a speedy retreat from his statement of the 27th. He told Bertie on 4 June that his personal opinion was that the troops had better leave. Clemenceau also began to have his doubts about the idea of keeping a *stationnaire* in Suda bay.[71] Yet at the end of June the British embassy got wind of reports emanating from the foreign

---

[67] Bertie to Hardinge, 22 Oct. 1908; Bertie to Grey, 10 Jan. 1909; B.P., A, F.O.800/172. Bertie to Grey, 10 Jan. 1909, F.O.371/647, despt.18. *D.D.F.2*, nos.592, 594 and 597. Constans to Pichon, 5 Jan. 1909, N.S. Crète 56, tel.2. Delcassé attributed Clemenceau's change of mind to parliamentary pressure. Bertie to Grey, 29 Jan. 1909, B.P., A, F.O.800/165.

[68] Grey to Bertie, 24 May 1909, F.O.371/648, despt.234. In view of the threat of a Greco-Turkish war, Hardinge considered the protection of the flag on Suda island to be the only possible solution. Hardinge to Lowther, 28 May 1909, Lowther MSS., F.O.800/193A.

[69] Bertie to Grey, 27 May 1909, F.O.371/648, despt.208.

[70] *Ibid*. Bertie to Grey, 27 May 1909, Grey MSS., F.O.800/51. *D.D.F.2*, XII nos.201 and 211. Touchard to Pichon, 25 May 1909, N.S. Crète 56, despt.165.

[71] Bertie to Grey, 4 June 1909, F.O.371/648, despt.220. Daeschner to Pichon, 3 June 1909, N.S. Crète, 56 despt.198.

ministry that it was Britain which had instigated plans for the withdrawal of the international forces from Crete. 'The French', Bertie reminded Hardinge, 'want to stand well with the Turks, but they are afraid of losing their Greek clientèle'.[72] It was a perilous course. Indeed, the withdrawal of the forces of the protecting powers at the end of July was followed by a bitter dispute over the flying of flags which brought Greece and Turkey to the brink of war, and only after the landing of a fresh contingent of troops did the crisis recede.[73]

The revival of British political influence at Constantinople, Grey's defence of which had been largely responsible for Anglo-French differences over Crete, also had an adverse effect upon the pursuit of an 'industrial entente'. Grey and those in the Foreign Office who were concerned with the project had anticipated that the collapse of the Hamidian regime would lead to an expansion of British investment in Turkey, and that this would provide the basis for a more satisfactory collaboration with the French. In particular Grey had hoped to strengthen British influence in the *Ottoman Bank* in order to make it an instrument of, rather than an obstacle to, effective Anglo-French cooperation.[74] Both the French government and French bankers likewise seemed prepared to welcome any sign of a revival of British investment in the Ottoman empire, so long as it did not threaten established French interests there.[75] But the apparent improvement in the political situation at Constantinople was not in the first instance matched by any corresponding increase in the confidence of British firms in Turkish finance, and in spite of the representations of the Foreign Office neither Rothschilds nor Barings were ready to launch a Turkish loan on the London market in September 1908. This helps to explain the warm response which British officials gave to the news that the Young Turks, who wished to circumvent the strictures placed upon their finances by the *Ottoman Bank*, were seeking to establish a new state bank under the title of the *National Bank of Turkey*. The proposed bank, which Block told Hardinge about on 3 November, was intended to promote commerce and industry in the empire. It was also to be an essentially Anglo-

---

[72] Memo. by Grahame, 30 June 1909; Bertie to Hardinge, 30 June 1909; B.P., Add. MS. 63024. Heller, pp.43–4.
[73] Peel to Grey, 4 June 1909, Grey MSS., F.O.800/110. Grey to Bertie, 7 Aug. 1909, F.O.371/650, despt.493. Hardinge to Lowther, 9 Aug. 1909, Lowther MSS., F.O.800/193A. Driault and Lhéritier, V, pp.29–32.
[74] *B.D.*, V, no.28. Hardinge to Block, 31 July and 21 Sept. 1908, Hardinge MSS., 13. Hardinge to Bertie, 30 July 1908, B.P., A, F.O.800/180. Hardinge to Grey, 25 Sept. 1908, F.O.371/549. Chirol to Tyrrell, 21 Nov. 1908, Grey MSS., F.O.800/106.
[75] Bertie to Grey, 10 Sept. 1908, F.O.371/549, despts.341 and 343.

Turkish venture, for its capital was to be provided by Cassel and his associates, and the Foreign Office was to be permitted a say in the appointment of its directors. This, Hardinge assumed, 'would naturally commend itself to Sir E. Grey', and during the following months he and his colleagues gave to it their enthusiastic support.[76]

With the attention of the Foreign Office focussed upon Cassel's *National Bank*, its interest in Vere's proposed consortium languished. The *Ottoman Society* had still not been reorganized on the lines foreseen in July, and as Vere had counted upon having the assistance of Cassel, the possibility of this being achieved was rendered somewhat remote.[77] Nevertheless, the French syndicate was in being, and its sponsors regarded the *National Bank* project with trepidation. On 19 November de Gunzburg wrote to Bertie that the *National Bank* was for the *Ottoman Bank* 'un gros échec'.[78] Yet for the Foreign Office this was as good a reason as any for favouring Cassel's project. 'It is sufficiently clear', noted Hardinge, 'that the Bank scheme is a far more important undertaking than the Ottoman Society and would serve British interests better.'[79] Only the possible effects of the failure of the consortium plan upon opinion in France caused British officials to have any serious misgivings about the *National Bank*.[80]

Bertie knew nothing about the *National Bank* until 18 November, and he was not aware of the details of the scheme until he received de Gunzburg's letter of the 19th. But even had he so desired, there was little that he could have done to check Hardinge's enthusiasm for Cassel's proposals. Hardinge was unmoved by French complaints about the *National Bank*, and when on 14 December Paul Cambon told him that there was a need to reorganize the *Ottoman Bank* on an equal Anglo-French basis, he was quick to point out that the Quai d'Orsay had ignored repeated British requests on this matter. Besides which, he argued that the institution of the *National Bank* should not be an obstacle to the reform of the *Ottoman Bank*.[81] In these circumstances the *Ottoman Bank* was no longer prepared to participate

---

[76] Block to Hardinge, 3 Nov. 1908; Hardinge to Block, 13 Nov. 1908; Hardinge to Cassel, 3 Nov. 1908; Hardinge to Jackson, 13 Nov. 1908; F.O.371/549. Hardinge to Block, 17 Nov. 1908; Hardinge to Gorst, 4 Dec. 1908; Hardinge MSS., 13. Marian Kent, 'Agent of Empire? The National Bank of Turkey and British Foreign Policy', *Historical Journal*, XVIII(1975), 367 – 89.
[77] Vere to Mallet, 16 June 1908, and minute by Hardinge, F.O.371/547.
[78] Bertie to Hardinge, 18 Nov. 1908, F.O.371/538. De Gunzburg to Bertie, 19 Nov. 1908, B.P., A, F.O.800/180. De Verneuil to Clemenceau, 5 Jan. 1909, N.S. Turquie 362.
[79] Hardinge to Bertie, Nov. 1908, (cancelled draft), F.O.371/538.
[80] Minute by Normal on Vere to Mallet, 16 Nov. 1908, F.O.371/538.
[81] Hardinge to Lowther, 15 Dec. 1908, Hardinge MSS., 13. P. Cambon to Pichon, 16 Dec. 1908, N.S. Turquie 361, despt.483.

in any British syndicate, and it seemed probable that the French government would proceed with the business alone. It was also apparent that it might through its control over the Paris *bourse*, attempt to bring pressure to bear upon the Turkish government in the matter of the *National Bank*. Bertie had learnt that the *Société Générale*, a French house which Cassel had induced to leave the French syndicate, had been informed that it would not be granted a quotation for any securities which it might issue in combination with Cassel. This in Bertie's view had significant implications. It was important to bear in mind, he reminded Hardinge, that the Turks could not afford to forego a quotation on the Paris *bourse*, and that such quotations depended upon the goodwill of the French finance minister.[82]

One solution was offered by de Verneuil to Bertie. He suggested that Cassel's group should be substituted for the *Ottoman Society* as the British part of the Anglo-French consortium.[83] There was, however, little support of the idea in London. Hardinge had grown indifferent towards the fate of the original project, and he informed Bertie that the French could do what they liked with regard to Cassel's bank, but that he thought that Cassel could look after himself. If Cassel wanted it, then Hardinge thought the Foreign Office would give him support.[84] And during a visit to Paris in January 1909 Cassel certainly showed himself to Bertie to be very confident that he had satisfied Clemenceau and Caillaux with promises that he would give the French a share in any concessions that he might obtain at Constantinople. Bertie doubted whether Cassel had derived a true impression of the feelings of French ministers. He was personally disinclined to broach the subject with either Clemenceau or Pichon, for he felt that the part that Britain had played, 'however blameless in reality', would 'not seem to the French quite straightforward'. Moreover, he was worried by Hardinge's evident readiness to abandon wholesale the idea of an Anglo-French consortium. The French, he feared, might think that under the old régime in Turkey, Britain felt that she could obtain nothing without French cooperation, but that 'now we feel confident of getting by our own efforts of the Young Party ... the concessions we may desire, and that we consequently drop the Anglo-French Combination scheme and instigate Sir Ernest Cassel to start another and will support him against the French Group'. If Clemenceau, Pichon and Caillaux were not satisfied with Cassel's assurances, then, Bertie predicted,

---

[82] Bertie to Hardinge, 9 Jan. 1909, B.P., F.O.800/180.
[83] *Ibid.*
[84] Hardinge to Bertie, 14 Jan. 1909, B.P., A, F.O.800/180.

there would be strong opposition to his scheme from the French at Constantinople, and threats to make things difficult for the Turks on the Paris money market.[85]

Bertie had probably come closer than he thought to gauging the change of mood in England concerning Anglo-French cooperation in Turkish finance. His predictions with regard to the likely French reaction also proved correct. When on 20 January 1909 Vere protested to Mallet that the *National Bank* would be bitterly opposed by the French, Mallet replied that 'we were top dogs at Constantinople nowadays and it was more likely that the French would wish to make terms with us'. Mallet was still prepared to welcome cooperation with the French in Turkey, but he was reluctant to give any further official backing to that end. He told Vere 'we must now leave the matter to the financiers and could do nothing more ourselves'.[86] But as de Verneuil informed Bertie, the French syndicate were not inclined to accept 'such gifts of charity' as Cassel was prepared to offer to them. Faced also with the charges of indifference which de Verneuil brought against the Foreign Office, Bertie protested that the *Ottoman Bank* had long stood in the way of the fulfillment of Vere's plans, and that the British government had had nothing to do with Cassel's withdrawal from the English group. They could not, he insisted, have prevented it as they had no control over quotations on the stock exchange, and no such influence in commercial and financial matters as the French government possessed in France.[87]

This last contention, which was used by both Hardinge and Mallet to justify Britain's attitude, was diplomatic, but facile.[88] While the Foreign Office had not been responsible for either instigating the *National Bank* project or Cassel's decision not to participate in the *Ottoman Society*, it had discouraged neither. Moreover, although the British government may have lacked the formal instruments possessed by Clemenceau and Caillaux for controlling financial establishments, this had not prevented Bertie from assisting Vere and

---

[85] Bertie to Grey, 31 Jan. 1909, Grey MSS., F.O.800/51. De Verneuil told Bertie that Cassel must have derived a very false impression if he thought that Clemenceau was satisfied with his assurances. Bertie to Grey, 1 Feb. 1909, F.O.800/51.
[86] Minute by Mallet, 20 Jan. 1909, F.O.371/766. P. Cambon to Pichon, 28 Jan. 1909, N.S. Turquie 362, despt.25. The prospect of renewed Anglo-French rivalry at Constantinople did not greatly worry Hardinge. 'I have no doubt', he observed to Bertie, 'that there will be war at first, but as it will be war amongst the Jews there is little doubt that all the Jews will come to terms.' Hardinge to Bertie, 4 Feb. 1909, Hardinge MSS., 17.
[87] Bertie to Grey, 1 Feb. 1909, F.O.800/51.
[88] Hardinge to Lowther, 15 Dec. 1908, Hardinge MSS., 13. Minute by Mallet, 20 Jan. 1909, F.O.371/766.

his associates during the previous two years. Indeed, by the beginning of 1909 attempts to maintain cordial economic relations with the French, not only in Turkey, but also in China and Morocco, were proving so tiresome that there were signs that Grey's officials positively welcomed the failure of Vere's scheme. In a letter to Bertie of 21 January, in which he criticized the activities of the French and Germans in Morocco and the way in which they seemed able to work together there to the disadvantage of British enterprise, Hardinge concluded: 'It is very unfortunate that the French are so unreliable in all financial matters. It makes me think that on the whole it is a good thing for our commercial and industrial people that we failed to get an Anglo-French group.'[89]

Criticism of the financial aspects of French foreign policy was not limited to the officials of the Foreign Office. George Saunders, who had recently been transferred from Berlin to replace Lavino as *The Times* correspondent at Paris, was struck by the 'prevailing desire of pecuniary gain' in France. He told Lancelot Carnegie, Lister's successor at the Paris embassy, that he thought French policy to be 'largely if not wholly influenced by the idea of gain'.[90] And although Bertie could not completely endorse Hardinge's views, he was evidently uneasy about this situation. He believed French financiers supported by Caillaux to be among the chief obstacles in the way of a settlement of the sum which Bulgaria should pay to Turkey to indemnify her for her losses.[91]

The French complained in their turn about Britain's conduct at Constantinople.[92] When on 19 January Bertie criticized the part being played by the French in the Bulgarian indemnity question, Pichon warned him that the British government 'ought not by pressing Turkish claims too strongly to endeavour to monopolize the goodwill of Turkey'. There was widespread suspicion in France, Pichon explained, that the British government had far-reaching designs, and that the boycott system of the Young Turks had been

---

[89] Hardinge to Bertie, 21 Jan. 1909; Hardinge to Nicolson, 2 Feb. 1909; Hardinge MSS., 17.
[90] *B.D.*, VII, no.148.
[91] Bertie to Grey, 3 Dec. 1908, F.O.371/445, tel.105. Bertie to Grey, 20 Jan. 1909, F.O.371/745, tel.12. Bertie to Grey, 8 Jan. 1909, F.O.371/747, despt.12. Bertie to Grey, 12 Jan. 1909, F.O.371/747, tel.6. Bertie to Grey, 17 Jan. 1909, F.O.371/748, tel.11 and despt.33.
[92] Constans conplained to Pichon that the British wanted to 'confiscate Young Turkey to their profit'. Constans to Pichon, 23 Jan. 1909, N.S. Turquie 362, despt.33. P. Cambon to Pichon, 28 Jan, 1909, N.S. Turquie 362, despt.25.

adopted on its advice, or at all events with its encouragement.[93] Some ten days later de Verneuil told Bertie that Clemenceau would not allow Cassel a quotation on the *bourse*, and from another 'financial friend' Bertie learned that Caillaux was putting it around that 'les Anglais commencent à nous embêter à Constantinople'.[94] Clemenceau, who was clearly annoyed over the failure of the consortium business and reports such as that from Constans of the British seeming 'to want to confiscate Young Turkey to their profit', vented his ill-humour on Saunders. 'The English', he exclaimed on 1 February, 'want to get everything in Turkey for themselves.' His resentment was certainly not softened by a British suggestion that Germany be brought into a projected Anglo-French railway loan in China. Astonished at this proposition, and angry at Britain's behaviour, he told Saunders: 'There is a cleft in the *entente*, and care must be taken that it does not widen.'[95]

Saunders, who recounted his interview to Carnegie, doubted if France wanted a strong Turkey, and he hinted that in this respect French and German interests were alike. 'There seemed', he observed, 'to be a danger that France and Germany might come to an understanding on the subject to the detriment of English interests in Turkey and of Turkey herself.'[96] In London too there were indications that some of the foremost supporters of the *entente* were beginning to worry about the state of Anglo-French relations. Chirol, for instance, claimed that he had noticed 'for some little time past, a curious disposition in Paris to listen to those whose interest it is to place an evil construction upon everthing we do or leave undone'.[97] Likewise, Tyrrell, who was impressed by Clemenceau's 'état d'âme', was upset by the way in which he seemed to accept every criticism of Britain, but almost to resent being set right in his facts. In a letter to Bertie of 3 February he observed that several people lately in Paris had told him that everybody they met there had said that of course England wanted war to result from the Near Eastern crisis on the off chance of France being dragged into a conflict with Germany, which would relieve Britain of any further shipbuilding against Germany. He concluded:

---

[93] Bertie to Grey, 20 Jan. 1909, F.O.371/745, tel.12. Annual Report for France, 1909.
[94] Bertie to Grey, 1 Feb. 1909, F.O.800/51. Caillaux was particularly perturbed about Block's desire to have the Turkish tobacco *régie*, which had served as security for certain foreign loans, absorbed by the Ottoman debt council, D.D.F.2, XI, no.643.
[95] B.D., VII, no.148. Bertie to Tyrrell, 1 Feb. 1909, B.P., B, F.O.800/186.
[96] Ibid.
[97] Chirol to Saunders, 3 Feb. 1909, Chirol MSS (*The Times* archives).

Of course they are wholly misinformed people who say this, but it takes one back to the days before the entente when every lie was swallowed which told against us, but even people who should be better informed appear to have swallowed the favourite insinuation put about by interested parties to the effect that England had always required an army on the Continent and that at present it is France who is 'soldat de l'Angleterre en Europe'.[98]

Bertie seems not, however, to have considered French criticisms of British diplomacy to pose any serious threat to Britain's friendship with France. Unperturbed by Clemenceau's outburst to Saunders, he tried to reassure Tyrrell. 'What Clemenceau may say on occasions', he explained, 'must not always be taken quite literally.' Besides which, he observed, there were plenty of people not only in France, but all the world over, who said that England wanted a continental war for the opportunity of destroying the German navy. 'The French', he added, 'are not always pleasant bedfellows but we might go further (viz. Berlin) and fare worse.'[99] Bertie also suggested that one reason for Clemenceau's opposition to bringing Germany into the Chinese railway loan project was that the French themselves would like to have proposed this course.[100] This may not have been far from the truth, for in the past month there had been a marked improvement in Franco-German relations. Indeed, on 6 February Bertie was informed by Pichon that an agreement had been arrived at between the French and German governments on Morocco. Just twelve days later he also learned that the French group which had been intended to participate in the Anglo-French consortium had come to terms with a German financial group:[101] information which appeared to be confirmed by a subsequent report from Block that the *Ottoman Bank* had reemerged at Constantinople in open alignment with German finance.[102] Within little more than a month Bertie had then to witness not only the achievement by Germany of a *rapprochement* with France in Morocco, but also signs of a renewal of Franco-German cooperation in Turkish finance.

Prior to 6 February 1909 the Foreign Office had received few indications of an impending Franco-German accord. Lister, who had recently been appointed British minister at Tangier, had warned

---

[98] Tyrrell to Bertie, 3 Feb. 1909, B.P., A, F.O.800/163.
[99] Bertie to Tyrrell, 14 Feb. 1909, ibid.
[100] Bertie to Grey, 3 Feb. 1909, Grey MSS., F.O.8000/51.
[101] *B.D.*, V, no.579; VII, no.149. Bertie to Grey, 8 Feb. 1909, F.O.371/695, despt.62.
[102] Block to Hardinge, 2 March 1909, F.O.371/762.

Grey on 11 January of enquiries which *The Times* correspondent there had been making about a Franco-German *détente*.[103] There had been some speculation about what might be the contents of such an arrangement, and at least one of Grey's officials had been led to conclude that it would 'probably not be such as would commend itself to us'.[104] In the event, however, the Franco-German declaration which was signed on 9 February, and the explanatory notes that accompanied it, contained nothing to which the British government could fairly object. The German government simply stated its political disinterest in Morocco, the French government committed itself to respecting the principles of the Algeciras act, and they both agreed to seek to associate their nationals in those affairs in Morocco for which they were able to obtain the concession.[105] It was the sort of arrangement that had already been envisaged in the discussions which had taken place between the representatives of France and Germany in the summer of 1907, and which had continued to attract sympathy and support from diplomats, politicians and publicists on both sides of the Vosges.[106] Jules Cambon had thought that the reopening of the Near Eastern question would provide the occasion for removing the last obstacles to the completion of France's north African empire, and late in October the German state secretary, von Schoen, had indicated his readiness to conclude a bargain on Morocco.[107] But in sanctioning an agreement with Germany at a time of international tension in the Balkans, and when Anglo-German relations were hardly at their best, Clemenceau appeared willing to risk causing disharmony in France's alliance with Russia and *entente* with Britain.

Caillaux later claimed that Clemenceau had not been a party to the negotiations with Germany, that Pichon had presented him with a *fait accompli*, and that he had been compelled to accept it by his fellow ministers.[108] There is indeed no evidence to suggest that Clemenceau had any hand in the discussions between Jules Cambon and Schoen, and Bertie had noted on 3 January that Pichon was 'kicking' against Clemenceau's interference in the administration of the foreign

---

[103] *B.D.*, VII, no.146.
[104] Goschen to Hardinge, 19 Jan. 1909, Hardinge MSS., 15. *B.D.*, VII, nos.147 and 148.
[105] *D.D.F.2.* XI, no.642; XII, no.2. Edwards, 'The Franco-German agreement'. Watson, *'The Making of French Foreign Policy'*.
[106] Freiherr von der Lancken, *Mémoires* (Paris, 1932), pp.58–68.
[107] Jules Cambon had reminded Pichon in October that a second congress of Berlin might complete 'ce qu'il fait le premier auquel après tout nous devons la Tunisie'. J. Cambon to Pichon, 5 Oct. 1908; J. Cambon to Louis, 29 Oct. 1908; Louis MSS., 2.
[108] Caillaux, *Mes Mémoires*, I, pp.274–7.

ministry.[109] Moreover, on 8 February Paul Cambon wrote to a friend that he did not think Clemenceau was yet aware of the accord.[110] The Franco-German agreement would, however, seem to have been consistent with Clemenceau's desire to avoid a fresh quarrel over Morocco.[111] It may also have been made all the more acceptable to him by the way in which the British and Russian governments had appeared ready to neglect France's interests in their efforts to profit from the Young Turk revolution.[112]

Bertie seems to have had little or no foreknowledge of the negotiations which had led to the conclusion of the Franco-German agreement. He also seems not to have regarded it as signifying any serious shift in France's foreign policy. His correspondence is more remarkable for the sparcity of its references to the arrangement than for any warnings of the threat that it might pose to British interests. Moreover, unlike the Russians, he did not connect it with the apparently accommodating stance assumed by Pichon towards Austria's demands that Serbia desist from claiming compensation for the annexation of Bosnia. On 6 March Edward VII, who was on a private visit to Paris, gave Bertie to understand that the Russian embassy at London was anxious that he should tell the French not to carry on their 'flirtation' with Germany. But Bertie, who well knew the sort of reaction that this might provoke suggested to the king that he had better confine his discussions with Clemenceau to the state of the drains at Biarritz.[113] His colleagues in London were more sceptical about France's intentions. Hardinge may have regarded the Moroccan accord as a 'complete vindication of the Anglo-French "entente" ' and have looked forward to a further improvement in Franco-German relations, but others within the Foreign Office were concerned lest concessions had been made to Germany of which they did not know. Even Grey appears to have felt some disquiet over whether or not Britain might suffer commercially as a result of it.[114] He warned Paul Cambon that it was not necessary to renounce the

---

[109] Bertie to Grey, 3 Jan. 1909, B.P., A, F.O.800/165.
[110] Cambon, II, pp.273-6.
[111] Paul Cambon thought it unlikely that Pichon would experience any difficulty in persuading Clemenceau to accept the agreement with Germany. P. Cambon to Louis, 8 Feb. 1909, Louis MSS., 2.
[112] One of Clemenceau's biographers has even suggested that Clemenceau's acceptance of the agreement can be explained by his annoyance with the British over Crete. G. Bruun, *Clemenceau* (Cambridge, Mass., 1943), pp.101-2.
[113] Bertie to Grey, 6 March 1909, B.P., A, F.O.800/165.
[114] *B.D.*, VII, nos.149 and 157, note 1. Hardinge to Cassel, 6 Feb. 1909, HardingeMSS., 17. Minute by Mallet on Bertie to Grey, 18 Feb. 1909, F.O.371/750, tel.31.

entente 'aujourd'hui que le ciel éclairci, car il peut s'obscurcir de nouveau. C'est maintenant qu'il faut réserrer notre entente'.[115]

Three years later, after the implications of the Franco-German agreement for British enterprise in Morocco had become much clearer, the head of the Foreign Office's commercial department was to complain that the French had shown 'an extraordinary impudence' in communicating it to London.[116] There was also a certain irony in the fact that at a time when it was becoming apparent that the attempt to form an Anglo-French consortium in Turkey had failed, France and Germany should have succeeded in concluding an agreement which envisaged their cooperation in the economic exploitation of Morocco. Yet neither of these events was to disturb Bertie's confidence in the *entente*. Indeed, to judge from his papers, he would seem to have attached far more importance to the defeat of Clemenceau's government and the resignation of the premier on 20 July 1909, than he ever did to the agreement of 9 February. 'Clemenceau is', he lamented, 'a great loss from an English point of view as regards the Foreign Policy of France.' Though at times impulsive and over hasty in his judgements, Bertie had found him to be open to persuasion, and ready to temper his actions to meet the needs of the *entente*.[117] His successor, the former minister of justice, Aristide Briand, brought into his administration Jean Dupuy, who was credited with pro-German sympathies, and Millerand, whom Bertie expected to work for a closer understanding with Germany.[118] But Pichon remained at the Quai d'Orsay, and so long as he stayed there Bertie felt convinced that there would be no important change in the attitude of the French government towards Britain.[119]

Events were to prove Bertie correct. That the Anglo-French understanding had its limits, and that it could not easily be translated into economic cooperation at Constantinople was again demonstrated in the autumn of 1910 by the failure of an attempt to effect a merger

---

[115] *D.D.F.2.*, XII, no.58. Paul Cambon suggested that a new Anglo-French commercial treaty might serve as a means of counterbalancing the Franco-German agreement, and help overcome some of the harm that seemed likely to be done to Anglo-French relations by France's adoption of new protective tariffs. P. Cambon to Pichon, 11 and 20 Feb. 1909, N.S. Grande-Bretagne 90, despts.46 and 63. P. Cambon to Pichon, 6 Feb. 1909, Pichon MSS. (B.I.F.), 4396.
[116] Minute by Law on Bertie to Grey, 2 Feb. 1912, F.O.371/1402, despt.60.
[117] Watson, *Clemenceau*, pp.211–14. J. Cambon to Pichon, 25 July 1909, Pichon MSS. (B.I.F.), 4396. Bertie to Grey, 22 and 26 July 1909, F.O.371/668, despts.289 and 296.
[118] Bertie to Grey, 3 Aug. 1909, Grey MSS., F.O.800/51. Bertie to Grey, 4 Aug. 1909, F.O.371/669, despt.316.
[119] *B.D.*, IX, pt.1, no.28.

between the *National Bank* and the *Ottoman Bank*.[120] Yet, on the other hand, the collaboration of French and German banking institutions was not sufficient to form the basis of a real political *rapprochement* between their governments in Europe. And in Morocco it was ultimately to prove impossible to reconcile Franco-German cooperation in the development of the country with French political preeminence there. In truth such negotiations as those to form Vere's projected consortium were peripheral to the politics of the *entente*. French and German nationals, with or without the encouragement of their governments, might from time to time collaborate to the detriment of Britain's interests. So long, however, as France remained unreconciled to the existing *status quo* in Europe, and Germany was unwilling to contemplate change in France's favour, there was, as Bertie recognized, little chance of the French deserting Britain for a wider Franco-German combination.

---

[120] *Memo. on recent Ottoman Loan Negotiations* communicated by Babington-Smith to the F.O., 4 Oct. 1910, F.O.371/993.

8

A purely negative position

Bertie's views on German policies and objectives changed very little between 1906 and 1912. Germany, and the ambitions which he attributed to her, remained in his opinion the principal threat to the continental equilibrium and the security of the British empire, and he saw no scope for agreement on any matter of substance between London and Berlin. Both on the high seas and in Africa and Asia Germany remained a power with which Bertie felt Britain could not afford to compromise. And the readiness of the Germans to step up their naval construction programme to keep in line with that of Britain, and their reluctance to accept any limitations on their armaments, served only to confirm him in these views.[1] 'The only chance of doing any good', he observed in August 1908, 'is for the Emperor to be told that we will go on building up to the proportion of the Two Power standard, and that consequently the question of the heavy expenditure rests with him'.[2] It was not an approach to relations with Germany that could easily be reconciled with the accommodation on naval matters which was pursued by the British government during the summer of 1908. But naval rivalry was for Bertie essentially a reflection of more fundamental differences between Britain and Germany, which resulted from the acquisitive nature of the latter's policies. He thus greeted with derision suggestions which some of Grey's radical colleagues made for an Anglo-German *rapprochement*, and he dismissed as worthless assurances given by Bülow and William II of their peaceful intentions. It was unlikely, he thought, that the German emperor would ever accept a naval limitations agreement, and if he did, then Bertie doubted if he or his government would respect its terms.[3]

---

[1] Anglo-German relations in these years are surveyed in Steiner, *Britain and the Origins*, pp.42–78; Hinsley, pp.193–235; and P. Kennedy, *The Rise of Anglo-German Antagonism*, pp.441–7. *B.D.*, VI, no.69. Bertie to Grey, 25 Nov. 1907, B.P., A, F.O.800/170.
[2] Bertie to Tyrrell, 20 Aug. 1908, B.P., A, F.O.800/170.
[3] *Ibid.* Bertie told Pichon in February 1909 with reference to Anglo-German relations that he did not think 'the question of the ships' was one 'capable of solution'. Bertie to Grey, 8 Feb. 1909, F.O.371/675, despt.26.

Where colonial and extra-European questions were concerned, Bertie was equally critical of those who favoured bargaining with the Germans, and he sought to discourage deals with third powers which might permit Germany to make territorial gains. This largely explains his opposition to Grey's readiness to accept French claims to possess preemptive rights upon the territories of the Congo Free State. These claims, which were based on agreements previously concluded by France with the International Association of the Congo and the Belgian government, had not been officially recognized by the British government.[4] But on 18 January 1907, when he was contemplating the summoning of an international conference to supervise the transfer of the lands of the Free State, the maladministration of which had for some time been a matter of mounting public concern in Britain, to the Belgian government, Grey referred in a conversation with Paul Cambon to the French having 'a special interest in the matter owing to their right of preemption'.[5] This drew an immediate protest from Bertie. Such a right, he declared in a letter to Grey, had not been recognized by any power other than Belgium, and Germany, he feared, 'would certainly resist any attempt on the part of France to act on the claim unless in agreement with her'. The result, he thought, would be a compromise arrangement which would allow Germany to acquire a continuous band of territory stretching from the Atlantic to the Indian Ocean: in his opinion, a longstanding German objective. It was with that in view, he reasoned, that they had opposed the Anglo-Congolese agreement of 1894, and staked out their reversionary claims on Portugal's colonies in the Anglo-German agreement of 1898.[6]

Grey did not heed Bertie's objections. Indeed, he even told Paul Cambon in April that if France did not desire to exercise her right in its entirety, 'it might be very easy for her to make a satisfactory deal

---

[4] On the origins of the rights claimed by French government with regard to the Congo Free State see: Jean Stengers, 'King Leopold and Anglo-French rivalry, 1882 – 1884', in P. Gifford and Wm.R. Louis (eds.), *France and Britain in Africa. Imperial Rivalry and Colonial Rule* (London, 1971), pp.158 – 61. In 1895 at a time when Belgium was contemplating the annexation of the free state, the French and Belgian governments concluded a convention which gave France a preemptive claim to the territory if the Belgians were to relinquish their hold upon it. This convention was not, however, ratified. S.J.S. Cookey, *Britain and the Congo Question, 1885 – 1914* (London, 1968), p.199.
[5] Cookey, pp.170 – 189. Grey to Bertie, 18 Jan. 1907, F.O.367/68, despt.9(Africa). Already in an address to the Congo Reform Association on 20 November 1906 Grey had referred to France having a pre-emptive claim upon the free state. *D.D.F.2.*, X, no.302.
[6] Bertie to Grey, 23 Jan. 1907, F.O.367/68, *private*. On the Anglo-Congolese agreement of 1894 see: J. Willequet, 'Anglo-German Rivalry in Belgian and Portuguese Africa', Gifford and Louis, *Britain and Germany in Africa*, pp.246 – 7.

with Germany, and she would certainly not find that we should be in any way difficult to deal with'.[7] It would, he later asserted, be difficult to challenge the terms of a treaty that had lain before the world without protest for twelve years, and he had no desire to see Britain assume responsibility for more territory in Africa. If there were a Franco-German agreement on the Congo, then he considered that Britain would have to put her word in according to what her interests were.[8] His views were in this respect wholly contrary to those of Bertie, and when the subject of a conference was again raised in the autumn the latter vigorously protested against the idea of the Foreign Office leaving the Congo 'cake to be cut up between France and Germany'. Germany, he speculated in a memorandum of 25 November, might ultimately have a common frontier with the British empire from the Orange river to the southern Sudan, and neither she nor France, he argued, would show any respect for such stipulations on the maintenance of free trade that Grey might require.[9] In the meanwhile the prospects for a Franco-German agreement on the Congo were considered in the Quai d'Orsay. Phillipe Berthelot, who was then a *sous-directeur* in the foreign ministry, suggested in a paper of 5 December that France could in virtue of her rights be mistress of the situation in the Congo, and that an arrangement with Britain and Germany could open the way to a comprehensive redrawing of frontiers in west Africa, and perhaps attenuate 'l'action hostile de l'Allemagne au Maroc'.[10] It was the possibility of just such a Franco-German arrangement that caused Bertie to fear for the future of Britain's African possessions.

But if Bertie continued to concern himself with the direct threat which Germany could pose to Britain's position in Africa, he also remained apprehensive about the impact on French opinion of any indication of an improvement in Anglo-German relations. In his annual report for 1909 he pointed out that the French feared that Britain might come to an agreement with Germany behind their backs and in a sense detrimental to their interests. 'I do not say that the minister for foreign affairs apprehends this', he noted, 'but German agents put this fact constantly before those with whom they come into contact in France and from time to time it produces a

---

[7] Minute by Grey on Bertie to Grey, 23 Jan. 1907, *ibid.* Grey to Bertie, 19 April 1907, F.O.371/254, despt.13(Africa).
[8] Minute by Grey enclosed in Tyrrell to Bertie, 16 Dec. 1907, B.P., A, F.O.800/160.
[9] Bertie to Tyrrell, 25 Nov. 1907, and enclosed memo., *ibid.*
[10] *D.D.F.2.*, XI, no.217. Pichon was also contemplating a colonial bargain with Belgium, and but for Paul Cambon's opposition might well have gone back on previous French assurances about participation in a conference on the Congo. *D.D.F.2.*, XI, nos.202 and 205.

momentary effect.' There would, he thought, be no objection in France to a *rapprochement* between Great Britain and Germany so long as it aimed at the removal of outstanding difficulties. Only if Grey were to attempt an understanding with Germany on general policy did Bertie fear that criticism of the *entente* would become popular in France.[11] Bertie need hardly have worried, for much as Grey may have sympathized with the idea of achieving a better relationship with Germany, he was emphatic in his view that it must be one 'which will not imperil those which we have with France and Russia'. An *entente* with Germany would, Grey thought, 'serve to establish German hegemony in Europe and would not last long after it had served that purpose'.[12] Moreover, progress towards an Anglo-German *rapprochement* was confounded by British fears with regard to Germany's naval policy, and the German insistence that an agreement on naval arms limitation must either follow, or form part of, a general political accord. Thus while von Bethmann Hollweg, Bülow's successor as chancellor, could offer no more than a reduction in the *tempo* of Germany's existing naval programme, he required a pledge that Britain would stand aside if Germany were attacked by one or more powers. As Grey and his officials were well aware, this might be interpreted as a promise of British neutrality in the event of a Franco-German war, and in November 1909 the discussions which had commenced with the new chancellor were allowed to lapse.[13]

In France Pichon showed every confidence in the explanations offered to him by Grey with regard to Anglo-German *pourparlers*, and he appears to have harboured no illusions about the chances of their success.[14] After discussions with the foreign minister on 7 October 1909, Bertie observed to Grey that from his manner he had gathered that 'he does not think that the Germans mean business except to endeavour to humbug us'.[15] Only in November, when there were references in the German press to the advantages to be derived from a naval agreement with England, did Pichon begin to exhibit any signs of nervousness. Reports from Brussels of a possible Anglo-German arangement affecting the Congo, and a favourable reference to relations with Germany in a speech by Asquith, added to Pichon's

---

[11] Annual Report for France, 1909, F.O.371/898.
[12] *B.D.*, VI, no.195. Minute by Grey on Goschen to Grey, 16 April 1909, F.O.371/673, despt.141.
[13] Robbins, *Sir Edward Grey*, pp.204–7. C.J. Lowe and M.L. Dockrill, *The Mirage of Power. British Foreign Policy, 1902–1922* (3vols., London, 1972), I, pp.29–37.
[14] Bertie to Grey, 1 Sept. 1909, Grey MSS., F.O.800/51. Bertie to Grey, 9 Sept. 1909, F.O.371/695, *private*. *B.D.*, VI, no.206.
[15] Bertie to Grey, 7 Oct. 1909, F.O.371/675, *private*.

concern.[16] But after an appeal to London, Bertie was able to reassure Pichon with regard to Britain's attitude towards the Congo, and on 20 November he repeated to him Grey's promise to consult with the French government if negotiations with Germany went beyond 'general assurances of goodwill'.[17] What, however, disturbed both Bertie and Pichon more than the course of Anglo-German relations was the progress made in the following year towards an accord between Russia and Germany in the Middle East. German complaints in February and March 1910 over the terms attached to a joint Anglo-Russian loan to Persia led Bertie to wonder whether Izvolsky might, through weakness, be drawn into an understanding with Germany. And he urged Pichon, who was to lunch with Izvolsky on 13 March, to advise the Russian to be 'very firm' in dealing with Berlin.[18]

Events in the autumn of 1910 would seem to have offered some justification for Bertie's suspicions. On 4 and 5 November the German and Russian emperors met at Potsdam in the company of Bethmann Hollweg, von Kiderlen-Waechter, the new German state secretary, and Sergei Sazonov, who was soon to succeed Izvolsky as Russian foreign minister. There they arrived at a general understanding on their political and commercial interests in Persia and the Baghdad railway, the details of which were to be worked out later by Sazonov and the German ambassador at St Petersburg.[19] Bertie assumed that the Potsdam meeting had been little more than a repeat performance of what had occurred two years before at Buchlau. After learning that Bethmann Hollweg had allowed Sazonov to think that Britain was about to settle with Germany on the Baghdad railway, he wrote to Nicolson, who had recently replaced Hardinge at the Foreign Office: 'Sazonov has been *roulé* by the Bethmann-Hollweg-Kiderlen-Wächter combination as was Isvolsky by Aehrenthal.'[20]

---

[16] Bertie to Grey, 11 Nov. 1909, Grey MSS., F.O.800/51. À Court-Repington to Grey, 23 Nov. 1909, Grey MSS., F.O.800/110. After a favourable reception given to the German colonial secretary in London in November 1909 Paul Cambon wrote to reassure Pichon that the vital interests of Britain and Germany were directly opposed. He concluded 'for the moment it is impossible to foresee a true *rapprochement* between the two countries'. *D.D.F.2.* XII, no.366.
[17] Grey to Bertie, 16 Nov. 1909; Bertie to Grey, 20 Nov. 1909; Grey Mss., F.O.800/51.
[18] F. Kazemzadeh, *Russia and Britain in Persia, 1864 – 1914. A Study in Imperialism* (New Haven, Conn., 1968), pp.549 – 51. *B.D.*, VI, no.338. Bertie to Grey, 13 April 1910, B.P., A, F.O.800/177.
[19] Thobie, *Intérêts et impérialisme*, p.647. *B.D.*, X, pt. 1, no.613. Bertie and Pichon agreed to pool their information on the subject of the Potsdam meeting. Bertie to Pichon, 18 Nov. 1910, Pichon MSS., 4395. *D.D.F.2.*, XIII, no.122.
[20] *B.D.*, X, pt.1, nos.611, 615 and 616.

The Russians were probably less the unwilling victims of German diplomacy than Bertie imagined. But the efforts made by Grey in February and March 1911 to find the basis for an agreement with Berlin led Bertie to question whether Britain too might, as he saw it, be out-manoeuvred by the Germans. In a letter to Hardinge, who had become Viceroy to India, he wrote on 16 March 1911: 'I hope that the anxiety of a portion of the Cabinet to please Germany will not lead to our being *roulés* as the Russians have been. The whole object of the Germans is to sow discord between us and the Russians and between the French and us. It is a renewal of the old Bismarckian game.'[21] To Nicolson Bertie reiterated his view that Britain had better continue to outbuild Germany in warships. 'Our hope', he observed on 15 March, 'must be that heavy taxation will sooner be felt and resented in Germany than in the United Kingdom.' There was, he considered, some chance of this hope being fulfilled, since the cost of armaments in the latter country fell 'almost entirely on the non grumbling classes'.[22]

Bertie presented much the same message to Baron Ferdinand von Stumm, a former German diplomat whom he met in June 1911 at Bagnoles-de-l'Orne. While he conceded that an all-round reduction in expenditure on armaments would be welcome, he dismissed the proponents of a naval agreement in England as a 'very noisy party'. They had not, he contended, so far suggested how practically a reduction in armaments was to be arranged with Germany 'in view of the facts — so long as they remained facts — that the people of England are determined to maintain naval supremacy'. In this situation Bertie could see no room for agreement. He was certain, he told Stumm, of one thing: that no state in Europe had hitherto succeeded in having the strongest army and most powerful navy, and it was doubtful whether any country, no matter how rich, could bear the strain. Bertie had in any case strong doubts as to what would be the outcome of a naval agreement with Germany, even if it could be achieved. It might, he thought, positively worsen the situation, since, as Germany would not observe its terms in either letter or spirit, it would generate more ill-will than already existed between the two countries. Clearly in Bertie's estimate there was little that Grey could do through diplomacy to improve relations with Germany.

We ought [he observed to Nicolson] to be thankful that Germany annexed Alsace & Lorraine as that act made a combination between Germany and France against us impossible . . . Our

[21] Bertie to Hardinge, 16 March 1911, Hardinge MSS., 92.
[22] Bertie to Nicolson, 15 March 1911, B.P., B, F.O.800/186.

reconciliation and Entente with France have saved us from the danger of a French attack if we have war with Germany and there is now no probability of an Anglo-French war to give to Germany her opportunity to attack us.[23]

Whatever other benefits his friends in London might reckon the *entente* to bestow upon Britain, this for Bertie remained its principal advantage.

In spite of Bertie's readiness to volunteer his advice on how the Foreign Office should manage Britain's relations with Germany, he appears to have exercised relatively little influence upon Grey's efforts to reduce tension in Europe. The foreign secretary was resolved to do nothing that would risk upsetting the *entente* with France, and he appears not to have paid any great attention to the fears expressed by Bertie about German colonial expansion. Bertie's role in the exchanges which took place between the British and German governments on the question of naval armaments and other related topics was in the main confined to explaining Grey's policies to the Quai d'Orsay, and reporting and predicting French reactions to London. But during 1910 Bertie had the opportunity to combat personally what the Foreign Office and Britain's service chiefs regarded as an attempt by the Germans to secure international acceptance of legal principles which would suit Germany's purposes in a naval war with Britain. The occasion was provided by the international aerial navigation conference which, at the instigation of the French government, assembled in Paris on 18 May 1910.[24]

At a time when rapid advances were being made in the construction and design of aeroplanes and dirigible balloons, this conference responded to a need felt by some of the continental governments for a code of air law which would regularize international flight in Europe, and minimize the risks of a chance crossing of a frontier by a pioneer aviator giving rise to a political incident. A good deal of academic attention had already been paid to the question of how laws might be devised which would satisfy the desire of governments to safeguard state security and to protect the lives and property of their citizens, without thereby stifling the development of the new technology. Yet by 1910 jurists were still divided between

---

[23] Bertie to Nicolson, 23 June 1911, B.P., A, F.O.800/171.
[24] The origins and work of the conference are considered in more detail in K.A. Hamilton, The Air in Entente Diplomacy: Great Britain and the International Aerial Navigation Conference of 1910', *International History Review*, III(1981), 169–200; and J.C. Cooper, 'The Air Navigation Conference, Paris 1910', in I.A. Vlasič (ed.), *Explorations in Aerospace Law* (Montreal, 1968), pp.106–7.

those who contended that the air, like the high seas, should be free to all, and those who believed that states possessed sovereignty over their superincumbent air space. The conference had not, however, been expected by the British government to deal with the legal status of the air.[25] A questionnaire which the Quai d'Orsay had circulated in 1909 in anticipation of the conference had referred only to technical issues, such as the distinction between private and public aircraft, their nationality, identification marks and signals, and the rules governing the departure and landing of aircraft.[26] And although the French government also insisted that the conference should itself determine the breadth of its discussions, Louis Renault, the eminent jurist and professor of international law who was appointed to lead the French delegation, recommended in his opening address that the delegates should avoid becoming too involved in the discussion of abstract rights.[27] Indeed, both the French and German delegations proposed in written *exposés* that the conference should consider the usage rather than the status of air space.[28]

The British delegates, who were led by Rear-Admiral Sir Douglas Gamble, were, none the less, surprised by the nature of the problems with which they were confronted. Inexperienced in the art of diplomacy and unaided by a legal expert, they had to reckon with the determined efforts of the French and German delegates to secure an agreement on rules which would provide aviators with the right to fly over, ascend from and descend in, the territories of signatory states.[29] To this end the Germans proposed that contracting states should agree that such restrictions as they might impose upon aviation should apply equally to aircraft of their own nationals and those of other signatories: the assumption being that no state would wish to apply such measures of restraint upon aviation, the first effect of which would be to paralyze the development of its own aerial fleet.[30] This was opposed by the British delegates. It was contrary to the recommendation of an inter-departmental committee, which had been established under the auspices of the Home Office to consider

---

[25] An invaluable summary of the state of thought current in 1910 on the subject of air law is to be found in H.D. Hazeltine, *The Law of the Air. Three lectures delivered in the University of London at the Request of the Faculty of Laws* (London, 1911).
[26] *Questions à soumettre a la conférence internationale* enclosed in Daeschner to Grey, 16 Aug. 1909, F.O.368/292.
[27] *Conférence internationale de navigation aérienne, Paris, 18 mai-28 juin, 1910. Procès verbaux des séances et annexes* (Paris, 1910), pp.25 – 6.
[28] *Ibid*, pp.239 – 44.
[29] Minute by Crowe on Home Office to Foreign Office, 3 May 1910, F.O.368/405.
[30] *Conférence internationale de navigation aérienne, Paris, 18 mai – 19 juin 1910. Exposé des vues des puissances d'après les memorandums addressés au gouvernement français* (Paris, 1909), pp.93 – 104. *Procès-verbaux*, p.264.

the French questionnaire, that no regulation should be framed that might limit the right of any state 'to prescribe the conditions under which the air above its territories should be navigated'.[31] Besides which, as the British delegation asserted in a memorandum of 27 May, on the eve of a war a government might well wish to discriminate against foreign aircraft in order to protect its mobilization measures against foreign observation.[32] But Johannes Kriege, the senior German delegate, was reluctant to give way. Only under pressure from Renault, with whom he had worked on several previous occasions, was he finally persuaded to support a new draft formula. It maintained the principle of the equal treatment of domestic and foreign aircraft, but allowed states both to ignore it in 'extraordinary circumstances', and to establish areas over which they might prohibit flight, so long as intervals of sufficient extent were provided to permit the passage of aircraft to the sea and frontiers of other states.[33]

This formula came close to meeting the requirements which had been set by the Committee of Imperial Defence for an agreement on the admission of foreign aircraft, and had it not been for the intervention of the Foreign Office, it might have been accepted by the British delegation.[34] But Grey's officials, who had taken little interest in the proceedings at Paris, were deeply disturbed to learn from the Home Office on 20 June of the pressure which Kriege had been applying to gain the acceptance of his views, and of the extent to which the conference had strayed beyond the purely technical sphere.[35] Moreover, their fears were confirmed by the news that the drafting commission of the conference had before it proposals concerning the granting of extraterritorial rights to military aricraft.[36] During the next few days the Foreign Office assumed responsibility for directing the British delegates; at its request Gamble secured the adjournment of the conference for a week; and Hardinge sought the

---

[31] *Interim Report of the British Delegates to the International Conference on Aerial Navigation*, 12 July 1910, F.O.368/405. *Report of the Inter-Departmental Committee with reference to the International Conference on Aerial Navigation*, enclosed in Home Office to Foreign Office, 14 Oct. F.O.368/292.
[32] *Interim Report*, pp.7 – 8. *Procès-verbaux*, pp.269 – 72.
[33] Gamble to Troup, 21 June 1910, F.O.368/405. *Interim Report*, pp.12 – 13 and 20 – 1.
[34] Minutes of the 100th meeting of the C.I.D., 14 June 1910, CAB.38/16/8.
[35] Byrne to Law, 15 June 1910; Butler to Law, 17 June 1910, and minutes by Law and Crowe; Gamble to Law, 20 June 1910, and minutes by Law and Gamble; F.O.368/405. Bertie to Grey, 19 June 1910, F.O.368/405, despt.180c(ommercial), and minute by Law.
[36] Gamble to Troup, 21 June 1910; Troup to Law, 22 June 1910; Carnegie to Grey, 22 June 1910; undated note by Craigie; F.O.368/405.

advice of the secretary of the defence committee, Sir Charles Ottley.[37] The latter in a defence committee paper of 23 July, which was probably inspired by his assistant, Captain Maurice Hankey, claimed to perceive an underlying strategic motive in Kriege's diplomacy. He argued that the Germans were probably hoping to compensate for their relative inferiority in cruisers suitable for scouting by utilizing the superiority which they had already attained in the development of dirigible balloons. They would, Ottley suggested, like to survey from the air the sea lanes around Britain and the entrances to the Baltic, and the direct routes to these areas lay across Belgium, the Netherlands and Denmark. Yet, he maintained, if these countries were to adhere to a convention such as Kriege desired, they would surrender their right to discriminate against the passage of foreign civilian aircraft over their territory. In an Anglo-German war German airships might thus be able to manoeuvre freely above them, and German aeroplanes land and refuel on their territory. True, the proposed rules on the admission of foreign aircraft were not intended to apply to military machines, but in Ottley's estimation this would not hinder private aircraft from being used for naval reconnaissance. Furthermore, he explained, it would be difficult for a weak power to resist the movement of privateer airships of a strong power if its hands were tied by an international convention.[38]

The German naval authorities seem to have attached less importance to the dirigible balloon than Ottley and his colleagues had surmised. Despite the much published achievements of German airships, Tirpitz preferred to allocate his limited funds to the building of the German battle fleet, and not until April 1912 did he place the navy's first order for one of von Zeppelin's craft.[39] The Foreign Office, nevertheless, accepted Ottley's analysis of Germany's intentions, and at its behest Gamble succeeded in persuading the reluctant representatives of the Quai d'Orsay to accept a further adjournment of the conference until 29 November.[40] Consultations began with the service departments, and after a rigorous reexamination of the work of the conference, it was decided to seek the exclusion from the

---

[37] Minutes by Hardinge and Law on Bertie to Grey, 22 June 1910, F.O.368/405. Grey to Bertie, 23 June 1910, F.O.368/405, tel.11c.
[38] *The Strategical Aspect of Certain Proposals before the International Conference on Aerial Navigation*, 23 June 1910, F.O.368/405. Lord Hankey, *Supreme Command, 1914–1918* (2 vols., London, 1961), I, p.112.
[39] D.H. Robinson, *The Zeppelin in Combat. A History of the German Naval Airship Division, 1912–1918* (London, 1962), pp.12–31.
[40] Minutes of the Standing Sub-Committee of the C.I.D., 25 June 1910, CAB.38/19/60. Bertie to Grey, 28 June 1910, F.O.368/405, tel.17c. Grey to Bertie, 28 June 1910, F.O.368/405, tel.15c. Bertie to Grey, 29 June 1910, F.O.368/405, tel.18c.

proposed convention of chapters iii and vi: sections which dealt respectively with the admission of foreign aircraft and the rights of public aircraft. At this experimental stage in the development of aviation, pronounced a Foreign Office memorandum of 29 July, it would be premature for any country to 'fetter its sovereign right to make such regulations as may be necessary for its own security or for the proper discharge of its duties as a neutral'.[41]

Grey and his senior advisers hoped to attract support for their case from as many governments as possible. They were, however, above all concerned about winning the sympathy of France, and of the smaller powers of northern Europe, access to whose air space might afford Germany a valuable advantage in a naval war with Britain.[42] Yet none of these countries was to prove readily amenable to British arguments. France posed a particularly difficult problem. The French and German governments had both desired to regulate flight above their common frontier; their delegates had maintained similar positions at the opening of the conference; and Renault had gone far towards committing himself to the compromise formula that Kriege had accepted. Now after the adjournment of the conference, Renault's colleagues were reluctant to do anything that might discredit his work, especially if France were thereby to earn Germany's displeasure. Confident in the successes achieved by French aviators, the functionaries of the Quai d'Orsay were far more ready to endorse a broad agreement on the admission of foreign aircraft than their counterparts in London.[43] But the impression left in the Foreign Office by reports from the conference was that Renault had been 'by degrees . . . won over by the principal Delegate of Germany to a bold and far reaching scheme'. Armed with a carefully prepared draft convention, Kriege had appeared to brush aside all opposition to his proposals before the delegates of other countries had time to 'realize their import or opportunity to organize resistance to them'. And, according to Grey, Renault had acted as his 'willing and

---

[41] *The Strategical Aspects of the International Conference on Aerial Navigation. Appendix ii. Proceedings of the C.I.D. with reference to the International Conference on Aerial Navigation, 1910*, CAB.38/19/60. A rough draft of this paper, dated 1 July 1910, was forwarded to the Home Office. Langley to Home Office, 8 July 1910, H.O.45/10572. S.W. Roskill (ed.), *Documents Relating to the Naval Air Service, vol.i, 1908 – 1918* (The Navy Record Society, London, 1969), pp. 14 – 18 and 21 – 3. Memo. enclosed in Grey to Bertie, 29 July 1910, F.O.368/405, despt.153c.

[42] Grey to Bertie, 20 July 1910, F.O.368/405, despt.150c. Grey to Bertie, 29 July 1910, F.O.368/405, tel.18c.

[43] Carnegie to Grey, 23 July 1910, F.O.368/405, despt.221c. Bertie to Grey, 19 Sept.1910, F.O.368/405, *private*. According to a British military report the French army possessed some thirty aeroplanes in the summer of 1910. But as a result of the successes achieved by these in the French army manoeuvres in September the number

able auxiliary' in complete independence of the French military and naval delegates 'combating their arguments, and even going so far as to check them in debate'.[44] Little account was taken in London of the extent to which French jurists had previously opposed the notion of state sovereignty in the air, and the extent to which the Germans had found it expedient initially to adopt what were essentially French formulae. Nevertheless, it was on the basis of this assessment of what had been accomplished at Paris that Bertie, whose principal contribution to the conference had so far been the official reception which he had provided for Gamble and his colleagues, was required to persuade the French of the error of their ways.

Pichon's absence from Paris during August and much of September did not facilitate an early settlement of Anglo-French differences over the draft aerial convention. Unable to make direct representations to the foreign minister, Bertie tried instead to impress his government's views upon Fallières and Louis, who although now ambassador at St Petersburg had returned temporarily to the Quai d'Orsay to replace his successor, Edmond Bapst.[45] But once tackled on the subject, neither Pichon, nor General Brun, the French minister for war, seemed unsympathetic to the British case. At Pichon's instigation, it was agreed that there should be a meeting between some of the British delegates and Renault, and on 14 October Pichon assured Bertie that France would not separate herself from Britain on the matter of the conference.[46] Bertie was, however, far from optimistic about the prospect of reaching an understanding with the French. The impression left upon him by Louis was that the French were so intoxicated by their own aerial achievements that any experts sent to Paris would not succeed in persuading them that the German proposals were dangerous.[47] There were in any event still those in Whitehall who doubted the wisdom of Britain adopting a 'purely negative position' on the admission of foreign aircraft.[48] For

---

had been doubled by the end of the year. *Aeronautical Reports for 1910*, AIR 1/7 AHB.6/77/3.

[44] Minute by Law on Mallet to Law, 11 Oct. 1910, F.O.368/406. Grey to Bertie, 3 Nov. 1910, F.O.368/406, despt.211c.

[45] Bapst was not a success as *directeur politique*, and by April 1910 the Cambon brothers were already conspiring to have him transferred to Brussels and Georges Louis brought back to the Quai d'Orsay. P. Cambon to de Margerie, 21 April 1910, de Margerie MSS. (Ministère des Affaires Étrangères). Bertie to Grey, 7 and 11 Aug. 1910, F.O.368/405, despts. 236c. and 238c.

[46] Bertie to Grey, 15 Sept. 1910, F.O.368/406, despt.268c. Bertie to Grey, 19 Sept. 1910, F.O.368/406, *private*. Bertie to Grey, 13 and 14 Oct. 1910, F.O.368/406, despts.296c. and 300c.

[47] Bertie to Grey, 19 Sept. 1910, *ibid.*

[48] Butler to Foreign Office, 18 Oct. 1910, F.O.368/406.

one thing Renault seemed likely to offer stiff resistance to the emasculation of the draft convention, and for another there was little advantage to be had from Britain alone refusing to accede to chapters iii and vi. Work was therefore begun in the Foreign Office on the preparation of a set of alternative instructions to which the British delegates might revert.[49] These, as eventually modified by the standing sub-committee of the Committee of Imperial Defence, provided for the amendment rather than the omission of the disputed chapters. A new formula was drafted, which, though it obliged states to permit the circulation of aircraft of other signatories above their territories, accorded to the state the right to regulate and prohibit such aviation 'si bon lui semble', and all reference to military aircraft acquiring extraterritorial rights was excluded from chapter vi.[50]

The Foreign Office anticipated that those responsible for France's defence and foreign policies would in the end be prepared to give priority to the strategic needs of her *entente* partners. Bertie, who in October was appointed to succeed Gamble as head of the British delegation, was accordingly instructed to press the French government to send high ranking officers to the meeting of delegates, to promote an early exchange to views between the British and French military and naval representatives, and to try to win the support of the French ministers for war and marine.[51] Pichon appears, however, to have made no effort either to enlighten his colleagues about the work of the conference or to influence Renault.[52] Thus when the meeting of the delegates did take place on 7 November at the British embassy Renault alone represented the Quai d'Orsay, and the officers who accompanied him took no part in the ensuing discussion. The senior French delegate was left free to adopt what Bertie subsequently described as a 'very personal attitude' in defending the compromise which he had arranged with Kriege. He rejected the British case against chapters iii and vi, and insisted on the need of the continental powers for an agreement on the admission of foreign

---

[49] *Memo. on letter of October 18, 1910 from British Delegates to the Aerial Navagation Conference*, 26 Oct. 1910, F.O.368/406.
[50] Minutes of a meeting the Standing Sub-Committee of the C.I.D., 31 Oct. 1910. CAB.38/60/17. Nicolson to Grey, 3 Nov. 1910, and minute by Grey; Grey to the British delegates, 3 Nov. 1910; F.O.368/406.
[51] *Ibid.* Grey to Bertie, 5 Oct. 1910, B.P., A, F.O.800/174. Grey to Bertie, 14 Oct. 1910, F.O.368/406, despt.200c Grey to Bertie, 3 Nov. 1910, F.O.368/406, tel.26c.
[52] Bertie to Grey, 2 Nov. 1910, F.O.368/406, tel.30c. Bertie to Grey, 7 Nov. 1910, F.O.368/406, despt.325c. Bertie to Grey, 10 Nov. 1910, enclosed in Bertie to Nicolson, 11 Nov. 1910, F.O.368/407, *private.*

aircraft. If the conference were wrecked, he predicted, another would be held at Berlin which would not be so congenial to the British.[53]

Renault, in defending the draft convention, confined himself to speaking in his capacity as president of the conference: a position which he threatened to resign if the British proposals were pressed. This resulted in what Hankey, who was present at the interview, later described as one of the most amusing diplomatic conversations that he was ever to witness. Indeed, much to the pleasure of the other participants in the meeting of delegates, Bertie proceeded to chaff Renault over whether he was addressing a representative of the Quai d'Orsay, or a distinguished lawyer who 'could not persuade himself to abandon the infant to which he had given birth'? Bertie's raillery evidently embarrassed Renault. He had received no instructions from the Quai d'Orsay, and he was not even able to inform Bertie of Pichon's views on the Foreign Office memorandum of 29 July which had been communicated to him. But Bertie assumed from the countenances of the French military and naval representatives at the meeting that they were not always in sympathy with Renault.[54] Moreover, both Brun and Admiral Lapeyrère, the minister for marine, with whom Bertie subsequently had talks, were reluctant to proceed with the draft convention. Even Pichon, who expressed some concern over what might be the German reaction to a change of course by France, reassured Bertie on 10 November that the French government 'would proceed in accord with His Majesty's Government'.[55] It was, however, apparent that there had thus far been no consultations between the Quai d'Orsay and the service ministries on this matter, and Bertie was disturbed to learn that after the passage of three days Pichon had still not been informed of what had passed between himself and Renault. In these circumstances Bertie not only urged Pichon to discuss Britain's objections to the draft convention with Brun and Lapeyrère, but also took him to task for what he called the 'subterranean conduct of the Quai d'Orsay officials'.[56]

Pichon's reply seemed only to confirm the ambassador's suspicions that French policy towards the conference was being manipulated by Renault and his associates within the foreign ministry. After admitting that French officials were inclined to try to make their own views prevail over those of their ministers, Pichon revealed that Gavarry, the *directeur* with responsibility for the conference, had recently brought for his signature papers whose contents contradicted

[53] Bertie to Grey, 7 Nov. 1910, F.O.368/406, despt.326c. Hankey, I, pp.112–13.
[54] *Ibid*.
[55] Bertie to Grey, 10 Nov. 1910, F.O.368/406. tel.38c. and despt.330c.
[56] Bertie to Nicolson, 11 Nov. 1910, and enclosure, F.O.368/406.

the assurances that he had personally given to Bertie with regard to France's position. Such insubordination, Bertie boasted, 'would never be admitted in England, or even attempted'.[57] But Bertie was himself allowed considerable leeway in the handling of the British case. Indeed, the grim persistence with which he tried to gain French acceptance for all Britain's requirements was not always appreciated in London. Dutch objections that in the absence of fixed rules governing the admission of foreign aircraft, a small neutral country would 'in time of tension or war be exposed to pressure from neighbouring states', led some in the Foreign Office to conclude that on these grounds Britain was more likely to secure support from the minor powers by retreating to the alternative proposals contained in Grey's instructions.[58] The Danes expressed similar doubts to those of the Dutch, and discussions between the British military and naval delegates at Paris and representatives of the French army and navy general staffs revealed that while the latter were not enamoured of the draft convention, they were reluctant to countenance the wholesale abandonment of two chapters.[59] Bertie, however, consistently rejected what he termed 'a retreat before a fight from our first entrenchment to the second lines'. His object was, he claimed, to ascertain from the French government what concessions Britain might have to make to receive its support, and to find out how far other states concurred in the Foreign Office's memorandum of 29 July.[60]

Grey deferred to Bertie's judgement. His diplomacy had, after all, so far seemed to be successful. With his encouragement consultations were proceeding between Pichon, the service ministries and Renault, and Britain's naval delegate had received an assurance from Lapeyrère that he was fully in accord with British views.[61] Bertie, it seemed to Algernon Law, the senior clerk with charge of the commercial department, was 'making an excellent Permanent Under Secretary to the French Foreign Office'.[62] Grey, who was lavish in his praise of Bertie's conduct, went even further. 'You seem', he wrote to Bertie on 19 November, 'to be taking to some extent, and very successfully, the place of Pichon as French Minister for Foreign

[57] *Ibid.*
[58] Acton to Grey, 9 Nov. 1910, F.O.368/406, and minutes by Craigie and Law.
[59] Vaughan to Grey, 23 Nov. 1910, F.O.368/406, despt.68c. Enclosures in Bertie to Grey, 18 Nov. 1910, F.O.368/406, despt.341c. Enclosures in Bertie to Grey, 22 Nov. 1910, F.O.368/407, despt.345c.
[60] Bertie to Grey, 12 Nov. 1910, F.O.368/407, tel.40c. Bertie to Grey, 22 Nov. 1910, F.O.368/407, despt.348c. Bertie to Nicolson, 17 Nov. 1910, F.O.368/407.
[61] Minutes by Grey on Bertie to Nicolson, 12 and 17 Nov. 1910, F.O.368/407.
[62] Minute by Law on Bertie to Grey, 10 Nov. 1910, F.O.368/406, despt.330c.

Affairs in this business.'⁶³ But Bertie was less certain of his achievements. He had to admit on 16 November that Pichon was in a 'wobbly state'. Thus, while he indicated to Bertie that he and his colleagues at the ministries of war and marine were seeking to devise some means of meeting British wishes without upsetting the whole conference, he also protested that it would be very difficult for the French government to run counter to what had already been decided. 'He wants', Bertie complained to Grey, 'to act with us, which will be acting in the interests of France, and to do so without offending Germany.' To overcome Pichon's hesitations, he proposed that Britain should persuade as many governments as possible to make objections at once to the Quai d'Orsay.⁶⁴

It is probable that Bertie underestimated the practical value that the French attached to achieving an international accord on the admission of foreign aircraft. He was too inclined to accept the view, given some credence by the reports of the British delegates at the conference, that Renault, 'a university Professor full of law and nothing else', had failed to recognize the true interests of France and her friends and had been inveigled by Kriege into accepting his nefarious scheme. Nevertheless, Bertie was under no misconception about how few governments had 'fully realized the dangers of the German programme'.⁶⁵ Only Bulgaria, Portugal, Serbia, Spain and Turkey, had by 20 November promised their support to Britain. And despite Bertie's energetic canvassing of the diplomatic corps in Paris, no government besides that of Britain had formally communicated to Pichon its objections to the draft convention. The Foreign Office felt that Belgium and Norway were generally favourable to its views, but they, like Denmark, the Netherlands and Sweden seemed reluctant to risk compromising their neutrality in any tussle between the great powers. Moreover, while the Russian and Swiss representatives at Paris indicated their support for Britain, their governments hesitated to commit themselves to any specific course.⁶⁶ In the meantime the Austro-Hungarian government, whose senior delegate at the conference had on occasions adopted a similar stance to the British, was preparing to work with its German ally.⁶⁷

---

⁶³ Grey to Bertie, 19 Nov. 1910, Grey MSS., F.O.800/52.
⁶⁴ Bertie to Grey, 16 Nov. 1910, *ibid.* to Grey, 18 Nov. 1910, F.O.368/407, despt.341c.
⁶⁵ Bertie to Nicolson, 17 Nov. 1910, F.O.368407.
⁶⁶ *Aerial Navigation Conference: Memo. showing present results of communs, of H.M.G.'s views to various Govts.* with annotation by Craigie, F.O.368/406.
⁶⁷ Bertie to Grey, 8 Jan. 1911, F.O.368/527, despt.7c.

All Bertie's diplomacy and the feverish attempts of the British government to whip up support from the other powers were based upon the assumption that the conference was soon going to reassemble. That prospect, however, diminished steadily during the course of November. On the 16th Pichon proposed to Bertie that the reconvention of the conference should be delayed for a few weeks so as to give him more time for consultations. Bertie suspected that the foreign minister was seeking an adjournment *sine die*.[68] Three weeks before Bertie had learnt from the Swiss minister at Paris that Pichon favoured this, and there was mounting evidence of opposition within the Quai d'Orsay to any recall of the conference.[69] Apparently grieved at the likelihood of their being forced to abandon their former position, Renault's friends could see little utility in proceeding with the affair.[70] None of this was entirely welcome from the British point of view. A postponement of the conference might have ensured that Renault would be employed elsewhere when it reassembled. Its abandonment, however, threatened to leave Britain saddled with the odium of having obstructed its work, and to permit Germany the opportunity to negotiate bilateral accords with its neighbours. Some of Grey's officials were in any case beginning to wonder whether an accord on the admission of foreign aircraft should be delayed much longer. There was thus no enthusiasm in the Foreign Office for a suggestion which Pichon, prompted thereto by Bertie, made for the reconvening of the conference simply to discuss those parts of the draft convention which were less in dispute than chapters iii and vi. In the opinion of one clerk in the commercial department there would be little left to settle which did not relate to the admission of foreign aircraft, and the French government could best save its face by trying to reconcile Anglo-German differences.[71] Similar advice was proffered by Eyre Crowe, who in February 1911 had the opportunity to discuss the conference with Renault during a session of the international court at the Hague. He proposed that Grey should stay his hand for a while to see whether an understanding between Britain, France and Germany might be practicable.[72]

---

[68] Bertie to Grey, 16 Nov. 1910, F.O.368/407, tel.45c Bertie to Grey, 1 Dec. 1910, F.O.368/407, despt.366c.
[69] Bertie to Gey, 5 Nov. 1910, F.O.368/406, tel.33c.
[70] Bertie to Grey, 4 Dec. 1910, F.O.368/407, tel.54c. Bertie to Nicolson, 5 Dec. 1910, F.O.368/407. Bertie to Grey, 8 Jan. 1911, F.O.368/527, despt.7c.
[71] Bertie to Grey, 11 Jan. 1911, F.O.368/527, despt.14c. and minutes by Craigie and Davidson. Minute by Craigie on de Salis to Grey, 29 Dec. 1910, F.O.368/408, despt.173c.
[72] Minute by Crowe on Bertie to Grey, 15 March 1911, F.O.368/528, despt.67c.

Grey agreed that if the conference project were to be revived, Britain had better see if a tripartite preliminary agreement could not be concluded.[73] But Bertie, who had anticipated that Renault would try to 'win over' Crowe, was wholly opposed to such a course. It would, he protested, offend other states who had been persuaded to accept the British point of view. Britain's case, he insisted, was already supported by a 'goodly array of states', and Germany would not 'want to face the music of a conference'.[74] Indeed, much to the distress of Crowe, who feared lest the ambassador's animosity towards a 'valuable and trusted public servant' should adversely affect Anglo-French relations, Bertie persisted in delivering dire warnings to Pichon's successors against the influence of Renault in aerial matters.[75] Nevertheless, Bertie's success in helping to frustrate the aspirations of Renault and his associates contrasted well with the somewhat modest achievements of British diplomacy elsewhere. True, Britain could in the event of the reassembly of the conference hope to count upon the support of a majority of the powers. But of the smaller states of northern Europe only Norway had committed itself to the British cause.[76] The Netherlands, Denmark and Sweden all seemed likely to support the draft convention, and the Belgian government, after ten months of prevarication, announced in May 1911 that its study of the question had been 'provisionally suspended'.[77]

The apparent timidity of the smaller European powers did not augur well for the future. If they were not prepared to oppose Germany at the conference, then in the absence of any formal international accord on the rights and duties of neutrals in the air, might they not acquiesce in the passage of German aircraft over their territories in time of war. Moreover, the failure of the conference to achieve agreement on a convention still left the continental powers with the problem of dealing with cross border flights in time of peace. The unplanned landing of a German military aeroplane and a Zeppelin airship in France in April 1913 led to the reopening of negotiations between Kriege and Renault for a Franco-German accord. As a result notes were exchanged at Berlin on 26 July 1913 between Jules Cambon and the German state secretary establishing the conditions under which the aircraft of French and German

---

[73] Grey to Bertie, 4 April 1911, Grey MSS., F.O.800/52.
[74] Bertie to Grey, 9 April 1911, *ibid.*
[75] Bertie to Grey, 8 March 1911, F.O.368/527, despt.57c. Bertie to Grey, 15 March 1911, F.O.368/528, despt.67c, and minutes by Crowe, Langley, Nicolson, and Grey.
[76] Bertie to Grey, 29 Dec. 1910, F.O.368/408, despt.396c.
[77] A. Hardinge to Grey, 14 Feb. 1911, F.O.368/527, despt.12c.

nationals might fly over each other's countries.⁷⁸ By then the British military and naval authorites had themselves already arrived at the conclusion that Britain's participation in an agreement on the admission of foreign aircraft was acceptable, so long as states retained the right to discriminate between domestic and foreign aircraft.⁷⁹ Indeed, had Bertie been prepared to adopt a more flexible attitude, and had he been less obsessed with defeating the efforts of Kriege and Renault to achieve an agreement, it might have been possible to complete the draft convention in 1911. As it was international agreement on a code of air law was delayed until the Paris peace conference of 1919. Not that this delay was without its advantages. By 1919 governments had a much better understanding of the value of aircraft not only in war but also in peacetime, and the participation of the United States in the conference ensured that the Paris air convention gave a clear recognition to the principle of state sovereignty in the air.⁸⁰

Bertie for his part seems genuinely to have believed that he had, through his efforts, helped to save the French government from committing itself to a project designed in Berlin with a view to exploiting Germany's superiority in airship development.⁸¹ Yet the discussions in which he had been involved since the adjournment of the conference had also served to reinforce his prejudices with regard to the senior functionaries of the Quai d'Orsay. Thus during the autumn of 1910 he found cause to suspect not only Renault, but Gavarry, Louis and the Cambon brothers of trying to thwart the will of the foreign minister. At the same time Bapst had appeared to be both ineffective and ignorant of what was going on in his department.⁸² Pichon himself had denounced Gavarry as a 'very stupid fellow', and the news that the latter had been spreading false reports about the future of the conference had been regarded with some dismay in London.⁸³ 'The French Foreign Office', Law minuted, 'is an Augean stable. They shd. turn the Seine through it.'⁸⁴ Bertie had less Herculean feats in mind, and confined himself to recommending to Pichon that Gavarry should 'have his head

---

⁷⁸ J. Cambon to Pichon, 14 April 1913, J. Cambon MSS., 16. J.C. Cooper, 'State Sovereignty in Space: Developments 1910-1914', Vlasic, pp.126-34.
⁷⁹ *Report of a Sub-Committee of the C.I.D. Inquiry regarding the Regulation of International Aerial Traffic*, 17 July 1913, CAB.38/24/27.
⁸⁰ J.C. Cooper, *The Right to Fly* (New York, 1947), pp.29-30.
⁸¹ Bertie to Grey, 24 Nov. 1910, Grey MSS., F.O.800/52. Bertie to Nicolson, 27 Nov. 1910, F.O.368/407.
⁸² Bertie to Nicolson, 10 and 11 Nov. 1910, F.O.368/407.
⁸³ Bertie to Nicolson, 2 Dec. 1910, F.O.368/407.
⁸⁴ Minute by Law on Bertie to Grey, 4 Dec. 1910, F.O.368/407, tel.54c.

washed'.[85] But criticisms such as those which Bertie levelled against some of the permanent staff of the foreign ministry came from the ambassador of a power friendly to France. The Germans could more easily afford to dispense with diplomatic niceties in their dealings with the Quai d'Orsay. When in 1911 they too grew weary of the methods employed by French diplomats, they had recourse to measures which seemed to bring Europe to the verge of war.

---

[85] Bertie to Nicolson, 5 Dec. 1910, F.O.368/407.

9
Agadir

For Bertie, 1911 was above all else, the year of the Agadir crisis, the year in which a quarrel over Morocco once more threatened to involve Britain in a war with Germany as an ally of France. Yet neither at the beginning of 1911, nor at its end, did the Anglo-French *entente* appear to be in particularly good shape. Pichon may have felt able to assure the chamber of deputies on 12 January that France's *entente* with England had never been 'more complete', and there was not a single question upon which the two powers had not agreed to pursue a common policy, but others viewed France's international position with less optimism.[1] Thus, while Bertie questioned the wisdom of Pichon's attempt to 'gloss over' Sazonov's dealings at Potsdam,[2] Tardieu bemoaned the 'sterility' of France's foreign combinations. In a leading article which appeared in *Le Temps* on 31 January Tardieu, who had of late adopted a distinctly hostile attitude towards Pichon's handling of foreign affairs, complained that the British and French governments had proved incapable of persuading their financiers to cooperate in the Near and Middle East, and that since Clemenceau's resignation the Anglo-French military conversations had languished. 'The Triple Alliance which went in for action, was', he concluded, 'confronted only by the Triple Entente which slumbered. That Entente gave neither diplomatically nor militarily the results of which it was capable.'[3]

Tardieu's criticisms were, in so far as they applied to the *entente cordiale*, not ill-founded. The same might also be said of the comments which were made upon them by Eyre Crowe. In a minute, in which he came as close as any of Grey's officials had so far come to offering an adequate definition of the *entente*, he noted:

> The fundamental fact of course is that the Entente is not an alliance. For purposes of ultimate emergencies it may be found to

---

[1] *The Times*, 13 Jan. 1911, p.5.
[2] *B.D.*, X, pt.1, no.655. In the wake of the meeting between the German and Russian emperors at Potsdam Pichon had thought it necessary to sound an optimistic note for the sake of France's alliance with Russia and *entente* with England. Pichon to P. Cambon, 29 Jan. 1911, P. Cambon MSS., 12.
[3] Enclosures in Bertie to Grey, 31 Jan. 1911, F.O.371/1117, despt.58.

have no substance at all. For an Entente is nothing more than a frame of mind, a view of general policy which is shared by governments of two countries, but which may be, or become, so vague as to lose all content.[4]

Bertie, for his part, contented himself with suggesting that the reason for Tardieu's attacks upon Pichon was to be found in Briand's having struck his name off the ministry of the interior's list of recipients of secret service money. 'He is, or was, poor, &', Bertie explained to Nicolson, 'he had, or has, an expensive actress in tow.'[5] But Bertie was also aware that Tardieu's connexion with two commercial ventures might provide an explanation for his conduct. He had been employed to act as a lawyer on behalf of the *N'Goko Sangha* company, a French firm with large territorial concessions in the French Congo, which was seeking compensation from the French government as its price for entry into a consortium with a German firm operating in the Cameroons, and he had been engaged to promote an Anglo-French project, which aimed at the construction of a railway link between Homs and the Baghdad railway. While, however, Pichon had not given to Tardieu the support that he had hoped for with regard to the former scheme, Bompard, who had succeeded Constans at Constantinople, had opposed the involvement of British capital in a Syrian railway.[6]

The failure of the Homs-Baghdad railway project was itself symptomatic of that malaise in the *entente* of which Tardieu complained. Since October 1910 Bertie had again been trying to facilitate the formation of an Anglo-French financial combination in Turkey.[7] To this end Grey had given his backing to a proposal made by Cassel for the merger of the *National Bank* with the *Ottoman Bank* in such a way as to reestablish a strong British element in the latter institution.[8] But Pichon and his officials continued to regard Cassel and his bank as inimical to France's position in the Near East, and although the directors of the *Ottoman Bank* might have welcomed the opportunity to rid themselves of a troublesome competitor, they were reluctant to contemplate anything less than the complete absorption

---

[4] Minute by Crowe on *ibid.*
[5] Bertie to Nicolson, 6 April 1911, Nicolson MSS., F.O.800/348.
[6] E. Binion, *Defeated Leaders. The Political Fate of Caillaux, Jouvenel and Tardieu* (New York, 1960), pp.218–32. Shorrock, pp.150–1. Memo. by Grahame (undated) 1911, B.P., A, F.O.800/166. Bertie to Grey, 3 March 1913, B.P., A, F.O.800/167.
[7] K.A. Hamilton, 'Great Britain and France, 1905–1911', Hinsley, p.129.
[8] Hardinge to Cassel, 19 Sept. 1910, F.O.371/993.

of the *National Bank*.⁹ A thorough-going understanding with the French at Constantinople thus seemed only likely to succeed at the cost of subordinating the interests of British bankers and would-be concessionaires to those of their French counterparts. The threat of unfettered British competition in Turkey might, perhaps, have induced the *Ottoman Bank* to accept the collaboration of British capital on equal terms, but Grey was unwilling to foster such rivalry.¹⁰ His concern about French feelings was rarely reciprocated by the Quai d'Orsay. In Morocco, for instance, its support for the association of French and German capital was accompanied by a neglect of British treaty rights that caused Crowe to suggest in March 1911 that the time had come to warn Paul Cambon that this 'vicious policy' of doing deals with Germany, while trading on British friendship, would 'lead to the estrangement of the two countries if persisted in'.¹¹ The *entente* may, as Nicolson informed Cassel, have been the 'bedrock' of Britain's foreign policy, but during the first quarter of 1911 fissures were clearly visible.¹²

Pichon could hardly afford to be complacent about the state of Anglo-French relations. Tardieu's article, and the denunciation of the use of the term 'Triple Entente' in the Liberal press in England, were used by his opponents to attack his policies in the senate.¹³ The British general election of December 1910, and the return of a government committed to parliamentary reform and other radical measures, had also generated some nervousness in Paris. During January both Briand and Pichon spoke to Bertie about the possibility of Britain's influence on the continent being eroded as the result of domestic dissension, and other French politicians, including Delcassé, subsequently used similar language.¹⁴ Moreover, following an inquiry by Izvolsky, who had recently been appointed Russian ambassador at Paris, about the state of the Anglo-French military

---

⁹ Bompard to Cruppi, 5 April 1911, enclosed in Bompard to P. Cambon, 5 April 1911, P. Cambon MSS., 12. Memo. by Révoil (undated), Révoil MSS. (Ministère des Affaires Étrangères), 4.
¹⁰ Babington Smith to Nicolson, 7 Oct. 1910, F.O.371/993. Lowther to Nicolson, 11 Oct. 1910, Nicolson MSS., F.O.800/334.
¹¹ *B.D.*, VII, no.192.
¹² Memo. by Nicolson, 4 Oct. 1910, F.O.371/993. Nicolson to Bertie, 5 Oct. 1911, Nicolson MSS., F.O.800/344.
¹³ *Un Livre Noir. Diplomatie d'avant-guerre d'après les documents des archives russes. Novembre 1910-Juillet 1914*, preface by René Marchand (2 vols., Paris, 1922-1923), I, pp.37-8. *Annales du Sénat. Débats Parlementaires, session ordinaire de 1911, séance du 2 fév. 1911*, vol.LXXIX, pt.1 (Paris, 1911), p.122.
¹⁴ P. Rowland, *The Last Liberal Governments* (2 vols., London, 1968 and 1971), I, pp.279-341. In January 1910 Bertie had warned Hardinge about French anxiety over the political situation in Britain. Bertie to Hardinge, 12 Jan. 1910; Bertie to Grey, 18 Jan. and 2 Feb. 1911; B.P., A, F.O.800/166.

conversations, the council of ministers decided on 17 February to take up this matter with the British. Bertie thought Frenchmen feared Britain's utility to France might be impaired if Asquith's cabinet were replaced by another Liberal one with an inclination towards coming to terms with Germany.[15] But there was also the danger, which Nicolson apprehended, that the political situations in Britain and in France, which had recently suffered from a wave of industrial unrest, would lead the Russians to lean 'towards the more conservative and apparently stabler central powers'.[16] Indeed, when at the end of February a dramatic decline in its parliamentary majority led to the fall of Briand's government, Paul Cambon wrote to Pichon to warn him that unless his successor were a man of experience whose word carried some weight 'la Triple Entente risque de s'éffriter'.[17]

Jean Cruppi, who was appointed minister for foreign affairs in the government of Ernest Monis, possessed neither of the qualities desired by Cambon. A lawyer by profession, his only experience of diplomacy had been gathered during the tariff negotiations which he had undertaken as Clemenceau's minister of commerce. But the new government, which was dependent for its support in the chamber upon an unstable combination of the left and centre, did contain some strong political figures. Caillaux, whose main political concern was with the introduction of an income tax, again became minister of finance; Berteaux, who had been minister for war in the cabinets of Combes and Rouvier, and who was one of the chief links between the radical majority and the socialists, returned to his former post; and Delcassé was appointed minister of marine. With the exception of the latter, whom he would have preferred to have seen at the Quai d'Orsay, Bertie had not previously had close contact with any of the new ministers. Those whom he received at the embassy on 3 and 4 March gave him the now customary assurances of loyalty to the *entente*.[18] Not many weeks were, however, to elapse before Cruppi was to challenge Bertie on the exact nature of the Anglo-French relationship.

Cruppi's enquiry was prompted by Grey's declaration in the Commons on 30 March that the extent of Britain's commitment to France was that 'expressed or implied in the Anglo-French convention'. The statement, which was made in answer to a question about

[15] *D.D.F.2.*, XIII, no.152.
[16] Nicolson to Hardinge, 2 March 1911, Hardinge MSS., 92.
[17] Cambon, II, pp.311–12.
[18] *B.D.*, VI, no.443. *Livre Noir*, I, pp.42–4. D.E. Sumler, 'Domestic Influences on the Nationalist Revival in France, 1909–1914', *French Historical Studies*, VI (1969–70), 520–1. Bertie had expected that Pichon would remain foreign minister.

whether Britain was under any obligation to assist France with troops in a war, had been so contrived as to avoid giving the impression that the accord of 1904 might not 'be construed to have larger consequences than its strict letter'.[19] But Cruppi was unimpressed by such verbal niceties. Worried about the possible impact of Grey's words upon parliamentary opinion in France, he protested to Bertie that he would have preferred that there should have remained a suspicion that an understanding did exist for 'possible eventualities'.[20] Bertie could offer little comfort to him. When on 5 April he brought to the ambassador the text of a statement that he intended to make in the senate, Bertie objected to it containing the assurance that both powers would remain friendly and united in all eventualities, and would give 'le moment venu une forme précise à leur entente'. The effect of such language, Nicolson commented, would have been to give the impression that something was impending and that the two governments had come to a definite understanding.[21]

Bertie suspected that the line which Cruppi was taking on this matter was not his own, but that of the Quai d'Orsay instilled in him by Maurice Herbette, his forceful *chef de cabinet*. Cruppi, Bertie thought, had been led to believe that there was an inclination in Britain towards Germany.[22] It is also possible that Cruppi's proposed statement had been intended to impress upon a wider European audience the strength of France's diplomatic position. Jules Cambon, who at the end of March joined his brother, Paul, in Paris for consultations with Cruppi, had already warned the latter that the German government might be drawn by an increasingly nationalistic press into a confrontation with France. His views were reinforced by those of his military *attaché*, who in his reports to Berteaux drew attention to the attempts of the government and of the bourgeois parties in Germany to contain the growth of socialism by emphasizing the need to defend *Deutschtum* against its external enemies.[23] Monis had spoken in a similar sense to Bertie during his first official meeting with him on 4 March. Anticipating Fritz Fischer by half a century, he had told Bertie that the German government might with

---

Bertie to Grey, 25 Feb. 1911, B.P., A, F.O.800/166. Grey to Bertie, 16 March 1911, Grey MSS., F.O.800/52.
[19] *B.D.*, VII, nos.198 and 206.
[20] *Ibid.* no.205.
[21] *Ibid.* nos.200 and 202. Grey congratulated Bertie for having acted on his own initiative. Grey to Bertie, 8 April 1911, B.P., A, F.O.800/166.
[22] *B.D.*, VII, no.205.
[23] D.D.F.2. XIII, nos.179, 180 and 204. Bapst to J. Cambon, 9 March 1911, J. Cambon MSS., 14.

the object of staving off domestic discontent 'agitate foreign questions', and then be 'pushed by the Press, the military party and public opinion to take up an uncompromising attitude in some matter not of itself important'.[24] Given these apprehensions, it was not perhaps surprising that France's military and political leaders should have sought fresh guarantees from England. The initiative was taken by General Foch, who was then commandant of the French staff college. On 8 April he told Colonel Fairholme, Bertie's military *attaché*, that there was a need for a military understanding with regard to the action to be taken by the British and French armies in a war with Germany, and for a political agreement which would state exactly what the two governments were prepared to concede and resist in the many questions of the moment.[25]

The views expressed by Foch were in Bertie's opinion those held by officers and many political people in France. Cruppi himself put it to Bertie on 12 April that in view of the present political situation in Europe 'it behoved the French and British Governments to carry matters further as regards possible cooperation in certain eventualities than had hitherto been done'. What Cruppi desired, Bertie noted, was not a formal convention, but an understanding which would define what joint action the two powers would take in case they had to cooperate in a conflict. He had, Bertie observed to Grey, probably not delved very deeply into the subject of the military conversations, and had raised the question 'theoretically' rather than 'practically'.[26] Yet although Grey expected to be 'asked something', and chose this occasion to inform Asquith officially of the military conversations, over a month was to pass before Cruppi returned to this subject.[27] The troubles which were already stirring in Morocco had by that time taken on a new significance.

During Pichon's tenure at the Quai d'Orsay the practitioners of France's Moroccan policies had successfully circumvented many of the restrictions that the Algeciras act had imposed upon them. They had penetrated the administrative institutions of the empire, had attempted to assume a sort of economic patronage over its development, and had used their military mission at Fez to begin the work of reorganizing the sultan's army. French troops had also continued their established practice of extending their control over the frontier districts of Morocco, and on the pretext of restoring order

---

[24] *B.D.*, VI, no.443.
[25] *Ibid*, no.460.
[26] *B.D.*, VII, no.207. Bertie to Grey, 13 April 1911, B.P., A, F.O.800/166.
[27] Grey of Fallodon, I, p.94.

had occupied Casablanca and much of the rich Shawia region.[28] Pichon had nonetheless been able to exercise some restraint over those diplomats and soldiers who had favoured the pursuit of more adventurous courses. Conscious of the international complications that might otherwise have arisen, he had neither intervened to prevent the deposition of the Sultan Abdul Aziz, nor had he agreed to the proposal of his successor, Mulai Hafid, to place his dynasty under French protection. He had likewise refused to grant the request of General Moinier, the French officer commanding at Casablanca, for permission to take punitive action against the Zaer tribesmen who lived beyond the boundaries of the Shawia.[29] Time, Pichon assumed, was working in France's favour, and so long as the military men did nothing foolish, her position in Morocco would grow stronger.[30]

This evolutionary approach was fatally compromised by the change of government in France, and the outbreak in the spring of 1911 of a widespread tribal revolt against the authority of Mulai Hafid.[31] Monis's cabinet, with its leaning towards the socialists, was, as Bertie later explained to Grey, 'bitterly opposed in many quarters', had 'powerful interests hostile to it', and would be vehemently attacked if it left the sultan to his fate.[32] In such circumstances Cruppi was disinclined to ignore the appeals for action which came from officers like Moinier, and diplomats such as Eugène Regnault, the French minister at Tangier. Moreover, the menace which the Moorish rebels appeared to pose to the European community at Fez provided the French with a seemingly adequate motive for sending a military expedition to defend the sultan.[33]

No French government could contemplate such a course without considering the possible reactions of other European powers. It was especially necessary to take account of Spain, in theory France's partner in the future governance of Morocco, whose forces had lately

[28] The history of the economic, military, and political penetration of Morocco by the French is examined in great detail in Allain, *Agadir 1911*, pp.9–250. The same author's conclusions are summarised in his biographical study, *Joseph Caillaux. Vol.I. Le Défi victorieux, 1863–1914* (Paris, 1978), pp.372–6. See also: Barlow, pp.169–206; and G. Barraclough, *From Agadir to Armageddon. Anatomy of a Crisis* (London, 1982), pp.86–93.
[29] Allain, *Agadir*, pp.242–54.
[30] *D.D.F.2*, XIII, no.131. Pichon to P. Cambon, 29 Jan. 1911, P. Cambon MSS., 12.
[31] Allain, *Agadir*, pp.255–77.
[32] Bertie to Grey, 24 April 1911, F.O.371/1154. despt.184.
[33] Allain, *Agadir*, pp.268–74. Cruppi may also have been influenced by some of the younger officials of the Quai d'Orsay who had already been very critical of Jules Cambon's efforts to improve Franco-German relations. J.F.V. Keiger, *France and the Origins of the First World War* (London, 1983), pp.33–5.

been engaged in costly campaigns against the tribesmen of the Rif.[34] But the Spaniards had long since begun to suspect that French ambitions extended to the whole of Morocco, and that the French would eventually drain the secret Franco-Spanish agreement of October 1904 of all of its meaning. Their fears were not unjustified. Both at the French legation at Tangier and at the Quai d'Orsay Spain was regarded as a nuisance, whose untimely and misconceived interventions in Morocco could jeopardize France's own position there. Indeed, so hostile had been the views expressed by Regnault about Spain that Paul Cambon had cautioned Pichon in November 1910 against opinions, which, he claimed, were inspired by 'l'idée fausse que nous pourrons un jour ou l'autre remanier sur nos engagements avec les Espagnols'.[35] A fortnight later Geoffray, who was now French ambassador at Madrid, and who, along with Paul and Jules Cambon, favoured a more conciliatory attitude towards Spain, told de Bunsen that 'it had been almost forgotten that France had recognized the existence of a Spanish sphere of influence at all'.[36] Aggrieved at the French disregard of their aspirations, the Spaniards sought release from the provision of the 1904 agreement which required them to seek prior French approval before resorting to military action in their sphere. All, however, that Cruppi could hold out to them was the prospect of fresh talks upon Morocco.[37]

British diplomats tended to regard the French as having acted in a rather tactless fashion in their handling of the Spaniards. The French had, after all, shown scant respect for British interests in Morocco,[38] and the idea of a march on Fez, such as Paul Cambon suggested to Nicolson on 4 April, was not greeted with any enthusiasm in London. Nicolson thought that it might only 'precipitate a general catastrophe', and that if the French were determined to keep the sultan on his throne, 'what was intended merely as a temporary measure to meet an urgent need might develop into a more permanent and far-reaching proceeding'. Yet there was no question of the British government retreating from its obligations. 'What the French contemplate doing is not wise', minuted Grey, 'but we cannot under our agreement interfere.' For the moment he acquiesced in the

---

[34] Allain, *Agadir*, pp.302 – 3.
[35] *Ibid.* pp.303 – 5. Note by Regnault, 26 Oct. 1910, with annotations by Paul Cambon, Pichon MSS (M.A.E.), Maroc 2.
[36] De Bunsen to Nicolson, 25 Nov. 1910, Nicolson MSS., F.O.800/334.
[37] Allain, *Agadir*, pp.305 – 9.
[38] Hardinge to Lister, 3 May 1910; Hardinge to de Bunsen, 5 May 1910; Hardinge MSS., 21. Minutes to Villiers and Crowe on Villa Urrutia to Grey, 20 March 1911, F.O.371/1153, tel.49. Nicolson to Lister, 5 April 1911, Nicolson MSS., F.O.800/341.

prospect of this new and possibly final assault upon Morocco's independence.[39]

Bertie was fully alive to the implications of the French becoming further entangled in the interior of Morocco, and on 8 and 12 April he reminded Cruppi that the Germans might try to profit from this situation.[40] He thought that they would seize the opportunity to secure something for themselves, that they would declare the Algeciras act invalid, and that they would occupy one or two Moroccan ports, including Mogador.[41] Nevertheless, he seemed quite ready to believe that the decision sanctioned by the French council of ministers on 22 April to despatch Moinier and an expeditionary column to Fez resulted from a genuine desire on its part to cope with the problems posed by an anti-foreign movement in Morocco.[42] He also accepted at face value Cruppi's claims that the Germans were meddling at Madrid, and that Perez Caballero, the Spanish ambassador at Paris, was intriguing with his German colleague. Bertie had, in any case, little liking for the former minister of state, whom he described to de Bunsen as looking like a 'garçon coiffeur'. 'He is', Bertie continued, 'cassant and not very intelligent and very anti-French.'[43] He had already warned Perez Caballero of the possible ill-effects of a proposal which had emanated from Madrid for the publication of the Franco-Spanish agreement of 1904. That, he judged, would simply invite German criticism. And he advised Perez Caballero against looking to Germany for support. He explained that it was not 'customary for the Germans to do things gratis', that they had been credited with a longing for something on the Atlantic coast of Morocco, and that Spain had 'some nice little islands' which but for her agreements with Britain and France would not be so secure.[44] There remained, however, the possibility, which Cruppi apprehended, and Bertie took seriously, of the Germans taking advantage of Spain's exasperation in order to reopen the whole Moroccan question.[45]

[39] *B.D.*, VII, nos.202, 209 and 221. Nicolson to Grey, 4 April 1911, and minute by Grey, F.O.371/1154. Nicolson to Bertie, 11 May 1911, B.P., A, F.O.800/180.
[40] *B.D.*, VII, nos.204 and 207.
[41] G.A. Schreiner (ed.), *Entente Diplomacy and the World. Matrix of the History of Europe* (London, 1921), p.582.
[42] Bertie to Grey, 24 April 1911, F.O.37/1154, despt.184. *B.D.*, VII, no.220. Bertie to Grey, 27 April 1911, Grey MSS., F.O.800/52. Bertie to de Bunsen, 20 May 1911, B.P., A, F.O.800/179.
[43] Bertie to de Bunsen, 13 and 20 May 1911, B.P., A, F.O.800/179.
[44] Bertie to Nicolson, 5 April 1911, B.P., A, F.O.800/160.
[45] *B.D.*, VII, nos.224 and 233. Bertie to Grey, 7 and 11 May 1911, B.P., A, F.O.800/179. Bertie to Grey, 11 May 1911, F.O.371/1159, tel.55. J. Cambon to Delcassé, 4 Oct. 1911, J. Cambon MSS., 15.

AGADIR

Events would seem to have proved that Bertie was right in predicting that Germany 'would demand her price for non-intervention' in Morocco.[46] But in truth he displayed only a limited understanding of the factors that were to determine Kiderlen-Waechter's response to the latest French initiative. The domestic problems of Wilhelmine Germany, and more particularly the government's desire to weld together the various segments of a fragmented society, may, as suggested by some German historians, have played a large part in leading Bethmann Hollweg and Kiderlen-Waechter to pursue a vigorous foreign policy.[47] In the final analysis, however, Kiderlen-Waechter's diplomacy in the spring and summer of 1911 seems to have been motivated by a desire to stand up for Germany's rights and interests in an imperial dispute. Despite its critics, the Franco-German agreement of February 1909 had, as the British knew to their cost, yielded some positive results. Yet observers on both sides of the Vosges had found good cause to wonder whether Franco-German economic cooperation in Morocco could in the end be reconciled with the achievement of a French protectorate.[48] That the French might be tempted to use their political influence to check the German economic penetration of Morocco became apparent when, much to the distress of Jules Cambon, Cruppi first rejected a draft Franco-German agreement on railway construction, and then challenged Germany's right to discuss such an arrangement with the sultan.[49] Moreover, Monis's government also risked German ill-will when by refusing to compensate the *N'Goko-Sangha* company it halted progress towards the achievement of the proposed Franco-German consortium in the Congo.[50] Keenly aware of both nationalist opinion at home and his country's prestige abroad, Kiderlen-Waechter began to consider the liquidation of the 1909 accord. He warned Jules Cambon on 28 April that an indefinitely

---

[46] Bertie to de Bunsen, 13 May 1911, B.P., A, F.O.800/179.
[47] Fritz Fischer, *War of Illusions. German Policies from 1911 to 1914* (London, 1975), especially pp.71–81. V.R. Berghahn, *Germany and the Approach of War in 1914* (London, 1973), pp.85–103. Stafford Mortimer, 'Commercial Interests and German Diplomacy in the Agadir Crisis', *Historical Journal* X (1967), 440–56.
[48] Allain, *Agadir*, pp.233–50. Emily Oncken, *Panthersrung nach Agadir. Die Deutsche Politik während der Zweiten Marokkokrise 1911* (Düsseldorf, 1981), pp.22–45 and 94–5.
[49] Allain, *Agadir*, pp.279–90. D.D.F.2., XIII, no.177. In the spring Jules Cambon had been optimistic about the prospects for Franco-German co-operation. J. Cambon to Cruppi, 7 March and 16 July 1911, J. Cambon MSS., 14. J. Cambon to P. Cambon. 12 March 1911, J. Cambon MSS., 15.
[50] Allain, *Caillaux*, pp.354–6.

prolonged occupation of Fez would mean the end of the Algeciras act, and that Germany would 'resume her entire liberty of action'.[51]

It was against this background that Cruppi turned to Bertie for fresh assurances of British friendship and support. Not only did the situation in Morocco seem likely to give rise to problems with Germany, but recent gains by German concession-seekers in Turkey threatened to impinge upon France's Syrian preserve. It was also feared in Paris that Britain might follow Russia in settling with Germany upon the Baghdad railway.[52] Even if this were not to occur, there was in Cruppi's estimation still the danger that England's 'unfortunate internal difficulties' would lead the Germans to consider her a 'quantité négligéable'.[53] Apparently upset by Germany's successes, Cruppi tried to reinvigorate the *entente cordiale*, and to achieve an accord between Britain and France 'to keep Russia in line with them'.[54] He told Bertie on 13 May that the only way to combat German predominance at Constantinople was through an Anglo-French understanding for joint action in Turkish affairs, and that only if the *entente* between Britain, France and Russia were more 'active and evident' could the danger of Germany menacing the peace of Europe be averted. This allowed Bertie the chance to complain to Cruppi about the difficulties that he had previously encountered in trying to promote cooperation between British and French financial institutions. Nevertheless, on the next day he wrote to ask Nicolson if the Foreign Office could not utilize Cruppi's mood in order to secure some kind of Anglo-French combination which would enable Britain and France to make a stand against Germany's growing influence over the Porte.[55]

It also seemed to Bertie that the French were once more hankering after 'something more visible to Germany and useful to France than the existing Entente'. Again he assumed that they did not feel sure that they could rely upon the understanding with England if Germany became threatening or bluffed. Indeed, after six years in Paris his views on this issue had hardly altered. He thus explained to Nicolson that while a want of confidence on the part of the French was useful to England as security against their 'committing imprudences' in their dealings with the Germans, they might 'if hard pressed give us away in a question important to British and not to French

---

[51] Allain, *Agadir*, pp.312–17. *B.D.*, VII, nos.227 and 232. Kiderlen-Waechter to J. Cambon, 7 April 1911, J. Cambon MSS., 15.
[52] Shorrock, p.153. Poidevin, pp.624–5. *B.D.*, X, pt. 2, no.28. *D.D.F.2*, XIII, no.248.
[53] Bertie to Nicolson, 14 May 1911, B.P., A, F.O.800/180.
[54] Bertie to Grey, 28 May 1911, B.P., A, F.O.800/177.
[55] Bertie to Nicolson, 14 May 1911, B.P., A, F.O.800/180.

interests'. Evidently, as yet uncertain as to what arrangements might have been made as a result of the Anglo-French staff talks, he proposed that everthing naval and military should be 'arranged unoffically to meet the contingency of British and French forces *having to act together*'.[56] It is probable that Bertie was, as Count Szécsen, the Austrian ambassador surmised, worried lest the French should attempt to purchase German disinterest in Morocco with the offer of a Moroccan port.[57] But although his letter to Nicolson gave rise to some discussion between Asquith and Grey over the possibility of extending the *entente*, the only positive response from London to Cruppi's appeal was that Bertie was instructed to tell him that the British government shared France's wish 'for a financial and general understanding between the two powers respecting Turkish affairs'.[58] And when Grey met with Metternich on 18 May he went no further than to remind him with respect to Morocco that 'some of us were bound by Treaty engagements which would of course come into operation if difficulties arose'.[59]

The arrival just three days later of the French relief column at Fez provoked no immediate counter-move on the part of the Germans, but the Spaniards continued to clamour for a free hand in their sphere of influence. In the hope of discouraging the latter from resorting to unilateral action and from appealing to Germany for assistance, Grey tried to persuade the French to make concessions to Madrid. Bertie sympathized with his efforts. When, however, on 8 June the Spaniards took matters into their own hands and sent troops to their northern zone, occupying first Larache and then El Ksar, the fortress town on the route between Tangier and Fez, Bertie began to question the wisdom of urging further conciliation upon the French.[60] He was thus far from pleased to learn that Grey had said, in reply to a request from Paul Cambon for British cooperation at Madrid, that he dared not press Spain hard for she might then be thrown into Germany's arms. To Nicolson Bertie wrote on 21 June:

> I fear that unless by energetic language we restrain the Spaniards who of necessity must be amenable to our indications and keep them to their engagements we shall lead the French to the conclusion that we are so much afraid of Germany that we would

---

[56] *Ibid.*
[57] Bertie had known Szécsen when he was Austro-Hungarian ambassador to the Vatican. *B.D.*, VII, no.236. *Österreich-Ungarns Aussenpolitik von der Bosnischen Krise 1908 zum Kriegsausbruch 1914* (hereafter cited as Ö-U), III, no.2529.
[58] *B.D.*, VII, no.275. Grey to Bertie, 25 May 1911, F.O.371/1240, despt.516.
[59] *B.D.*, VII, no.278.
[60] Allain, *Agadir*, pp.309–12. *B.D.*, VII, nos.285, 292, 293, 307 and 311.

submit to a Franco-German arrangement concerning Morocco outside the Spanish sphere of the secret Agreement.[61]

There was never any doubt in Bertie's mind that the Spaniards must eventually receive their due on Morocco's Mediterranean littoral. But he considered it equally important that Britain should not appear to disinterest herself in the remainder of the country, and thereby permit the Germans to obtain a foothold on the Atlantic coast.

Unlike Grey, who seems already to have concluded that the French would have to proceed with a partition of Morocco in which there would be 'some difficult and rough waters to negotiate & some price to be paid', Bertie continued to believe that Cruppi felt able to fulfill his promises to withdraw from Fez and to keep within the Algeciras act. Bertie had, however, to admit that French colonialists would not like Cruppi to attain this end.[62] He was also aware that Cruppi's days at the Quai d'Orsay were probably numbered. On 21 May a monoplane had plunged into a group of official guests at the opening of the Paris to Madrid air race at Issy-les-Moulineaux, killing Berteaux, and seriously injuring Monis.[63] Unable to provide effective leadership, Monis was finally forced out of office after his government was defeated in the chamber on 23 June. Within a week Caillaux formed a new and more broadly based administration which looked both to the radical majority and the moderate republicans for support. Bertie had by then placed his embassy in the charge of his councillor, Lancelot Carnegie, and left Paris for a holiday at Bagnoles-de-l'Orne. He felt under no compunction to return to the capital to meet the new ministers. They were, he noted, 'a very mixed group', and he did not think them 'likely to row together long'.[64]

George Grahame, his first secretary and one of his most trusted colleagues, was no more favourably impressed by the new men. In a letter to Tyrrell he described Caillaux as ' "très fat", full of personal vanity and jaunty as a cock sparrow', and he predicted that the premier's 'abnormal vanity' would lead him into 'unwise courses'.[65] Caillaux was indeed excessively confident of his own ability, and he possessed a penchant for backstairs diplomacy which was to earn him

---

[61] Bertie to Nicolson, 21 June 1911, B.P., A, F.O.800/179.
[62] B.D., VII, nos.307 and 314. Minute by Grey on Nicolson to Grey, 6 June 1911, F.O.371/1155. Bertie to GRey, 14 June 1911, B.P., A, F.O.800/160. Bertie to de Bunsen, 20 May 1911, B.P., A, F.O.800/179.
[63] Bertie to Nicolson, 21 May 1911, Nicolson MSS., F.O.800/348. Bertie to Grey, 22 May 1911, F.O.371/1118, despt.223.
[64] Bertie to Nicolson, 28 June 1911, Nicolson MSS., F.O.800/349.
[65] Grahame to Tyrrell, 28 June 1911, Grey MSS., F.O.800/52.

the ill-will of the *bureaux* of the foreign ministry. Yet for the moment only his association with Egyptian finance, and the possibility that he might champion the cause of the French colony at Cairo caused Bertie to anticipate any difficulty with Caillaux.[66] He was more doubtful about the appointment of Justin de Selves as foreign minister. A former prefect of the Seine, he was, according to Bertie, a 'charming man & easy to get on with & sensible'. But where foreign affairs were concerned, he was just as inexperienced as Cruppi had been, and Bertie was perturbed lest this should give the staff of the Quai d'Orsay a 'fresh start in its policy of obstruction in the settlement of questions except on their terms'.[67] His concern was shared by Paul Cambon, who, like his brother, was increasingly unhappy about the lack of foresight and prudence displayed by the bureaucracy in Paris. 'Il a toute la fougue et l'intransigéance de la jeunesse', he observed to Cruppi, 'il s'imagine qu'on peut obtenir des résultats en faisant la grosse voix et il confond l'energie avec la brutalité.'[68] In the summer of 1911 observers in England and France were to level much the same criticism at the Wilhelmstrasse.

Ever since March 1911 Kiderlen-Waechter had had in mind the idea of sending a warship to a Moroccan port as a means of inducing the French to negotiate a settlement with Germany which would replace the obsolescent accord of 1909. A memorandum outlining such a course of action received the reluctant approval of the emperor on 5 May, and its implementation was made ever more likely by the cavalier fashion in which the French seemed ready to disregard the interests of other powers in Morocco. Even such hopes for a colonial bargain as Caillaux had encouraged were dashed when on 7 June the French government rejected a project for the construction by a Franco-German group of a railway between the Cameroons and the Congo river. A fortnight later Jules Cambon, who met with Kiderlen-Waechter at Bad Kissingen, still had nothing concrete to offer to the Germans by way of compensation. Yet by then German preparations for a minimum display of force were already far advanced. The government in Berlin, like that in Paris, claimed the right to protect the lives and property of its subjects, and on 1 July the *Panther*, a gunboat of the imperial navy, anchored off Agadir, the

---

[66] Bertie to Nicolson, 28 June 1911, B.P., A, F.O.800/166. Caillaux was the president of the *Crédit Foncier Égyptien*. Binion, p.31.
[67] Bertie to Nicolson, 28 June 1911, B.P., A, F.O.800/166. Bertie to Grey, 9 July 1914, F.O.146/4381, despt.338
[68] *D.D.F.2*, XIII, no.370.

most southerly port of Morocco.[69] Four days later it was replaced by a larger vessel, the *Berlin*, which did not finally leave Moroccan waters until the following November.

The *Panthersprung*, coming as it did after a long period during which the Germans had appeared to acquiesce in the French conquest of Morocco, was widely regarded in France as a fresh manifestation of German brutality and undiplomacy. But Bertie, who remained at Bagnoles-de-l'Orne until 8 July, would probably have been more surprised if the Germans had failed to react to the latest developments in Morocco. He, like Cruppi, had held the Germans responsible for having 'launched the Spaniards on a dispute with France', and despite the absence of any 'active objection' from them to the French advance on Fez, he had forecasted that if an opportune moment should arrive they would 'ask for payment'.[70] Moreover, the Germans by their action seemed only to confirm Bertie's original suspicions about what their price would be. 'As was to be expected', he wrote to Nicolson on 2 July, 'the German Govt. had pegged out a claim on the Atlantic coast of Morocco notwithstanding Germany's self-denying agreement with France.'[71] This view was shared by Grahame. He thought that the Germans 'must have had an eye on Agadir for a considerable time', and that they might by degrees make it into a 'Moorish Kiao-chow'. Claims in the French press that the Germans were trying to hurry up France to negotiate and to offer compensation elsewhere, he dismissed as mistaken. 'I fancy', he wrote to Tyrrell, 'that Agadir is much more valuable to the Germans than any rectification of an African colonial frontier, and if they really can stick to it, its acquisition, even in a veiled form would be a great feather in Herr von Kiderlen's cap.'[72]

The conviction that the Germans were set upon establishing themselves on the Moroccan coast coloured much of Bertie's thinking during the early stages of the ensuing crisis. In this context both he and Grahame foresaw the possibility of differences arising between Britain and France, for although Grey had once seemed ready to envisage a German presence on Morocco's Atlantic coast, they continued to assume that this would be contrary to Britain's strategic

---

[69] Allain, *Agadir*, pp.319 – 41; *Caillaux*, pp.378 – 9. Jules Cambon also felt that his previous warnings to the Quai d'Orsay about the importance of negotiating with Germany had been vindicated by the German action. 'En realité', he observed, 'l'incident d'Agadir n'a pu surprendre que les gens qui, dans les lettres qu'ils recoivent, ne veulent lire que celles qui leur plaisent.' J. Cambon to Cruppi. 16 July 1911, J. Cambon MSS., 14.
[70] Bertie to de Bunsen, 20 May 1911, F.O.371/1118, despt.223.
[71] Bertie to Nicolson, 2 July 1911, B.P., F.O.800/171.
[72] Grahame to Tyrrell, 5 July 1911, Grey MSS., F.O.800/52.

interests. Indeed, the news that de Selves had departed with Fallières on a state visit to the Netherlands was taken by Grahame as a sign that the French had not taken the new situation 'au tragique', and as confirmation of his belief that they dreaded a 'real row' with Germany and would confine themselves to recrimination.

> Besides [Grahame noted] the French feel that they have no very strong arguments to use against the German action, for in all their Moroccan enterprises they have invoked the natural right of a country to protect its nationals, and under that plea, they have played fast and loose with the spirit of the Act of Algeciras — witness their occupation of the whole of the Shawia district and parts far inside the Moroccan frontier on the east, not to mention the marchings and counter marchings of General Moinier in the heart of the country. French policy in Morocco has been itself such a tissue of sophisms and hypocrisies that the French have little to say now to Spain and Germany. All three have slipped through the too wide meshes of the Act of Algeciras on the plea of the natural right of a country to take measures to protect its subjects.

Even the French colonial party, Grahame thought, would after a fit of indignation recognize that the Agadir affair was a blessing in disguise from the point of view of their desires, for, he concluded, 'if Germany dips her finger in the sauce she will have less right to object to the pie being cut into by France'.[73] It seems unlikely that Bertie would have endorsed this frank and even-handed analysis of the situation. But he too thought that if hard pressed the French might be prepared to allow Germany a Moroccan port. Then, he predicted, the French would cast upon the British government the 'entire odium' of opposing Germany's objectives.[74]

The Germans were far less interested in Morocco's Atlantic coast than Bertie imagined them to be. Both he and Grahame were also wrong in their estimation of the positions that the British and French governments would adopt. Like Bertie, Grey and his colleagues considered that the object of the *Panthersprung* was to stake out a German territorial claim. Their first concern was not, however, with excluding the Germans from Morocco, but with dispelling any illusion that Britain would not have to be reckoned with in the making of any new Moroccan settlement. To that end the cabinet agreed on 4 July that Metternich should be warned that Britain must be party to any negotiations. The cabinet also decided, probably with

[73] *Ibid.*
[74] *B.D.*, VII, no.372.

a view to encouraging the French to accept a compromise, that Paul Cambon should be informed that it might be impossible to return to the *status quo ante* in Morocco, and that it might therefore be necessary to give 'a more definite recognition than before to German interests' there.[75] Consultations with the Admiralty had helped convince Grey that there was no point on Morocco's western coastline that might easily be turned into a naval base, that from the point of view of Britain's interests it was not necessary to prevent Germany from having a port there, and that Britain could always rely on her superior naval strength to prevent its fortification. In these circumstances Grey felt that Britain could be reconciled to Germany's acquisition of a non-fortified establishment on Morocco's Atlantic coast.[76]

This was not the attitude which either the French government or public expected the British to adopt. On the contrary, it was generally believed in Paris that the British could be counted upon 'to prevent Germany from obtaining an undue advantage on the Atlantic coastline'.[77] And although Caillaux, who in de Selves's absence was in temporary charge of the Quai d'Orsay, refused to sanction the sending of a French warship to either Agadir or Mogador, he was eager that Germany should not be given even the glimpse of acquiring anything in Morocco.[78] Grey declined, however, Paul Cambon's request that he should 'lay it down as absolutely impossible that Germany should obtain a territorial sphere' in Morocco, and would go no further on 6 July than to tell the French ambassador of his preference that Germany should be compensated elsewhere.[79] Bertie was therefore acting in a sense entirely contrary to the views expressed by Grey when on the morning of 11 July he warned de Selves that the British government would never consent to the establishment of Germany on the Moroccan coast. Yet there seems little reason to disbelieve his subsequent explanation that he had not received Grey's report of his conversation with Cambon until the evening of the 11th. He could surely have gained no advantage by encouraging de Selves to believe other than what Cambon had already learned in London.[80]

---

[75] *Ibid.*, nos.347 and 356. Asquith to George V, 4 July 1911, Asquith MSS., 6 M.L. Dockrill, 'British Policy during the Agadir Crisis of 1911', Hinsley, pp.274–5.
[76] *B.D.*, VII, nos.368 and 375.
[77] *Ibid.* no361.
[78] Allain, *Agadir*, pp.351–2.
[79] *B.D.*, VII, no.363.
[80] *Ibid*, nos.369 and 372.

Bertie, nevertheless, wasted no time in informing Grey of the error of his strategy. In a despatch of 12 July he warned the foreign secretary that the Germans might, despite assurances to the contrary, make preparations at a Moroccan port to convert it at short notice and at a favourable opportunity, into a fortified base. He cited the example of the Russian fortification of the Black Sea port of Batoum in 1886: a violation of the Berlin treaty of 1878 against which only the British had protested. German assurances, he observed to Nicolson, would last just so long as it suited them. Besides which, if the French were to learn that Britain was prepared to give way to Germany, he predicted, 'we shall help throw them into the Teuton embrace'.[81] Nicolson was not unsympathetic to Bertie's views, but doubted if the Germans could be persuaded to abandon Agadir even with offers of substantial compensation elsewhere.[82] This Bertie refuted. Under the impression that the Germans had asserted themselves because they reckoned that Britain would not stand by France, he was confident that if Grey joined with the French in refusing to accept a German presence in Morocco, the Germans would do no more than 'bluster'.[83]

Grey did not wholly reject Bertie's argument. Personally, he felt that it would be 'undesirable' to let Germany into Morocco, and a settlement that did not let her in 'would be infinitely preferable'. He, nevertheless, insisted in a private letter to Bertie of 12 July that he could not 'let the French place upon us the whole burden of keeping Germany out of Morocco at all costs'. Discouraging though Grey's attitude must have been to Bertie, he did not desist from pressing for more resolute opposition by the government to the 'brigand-like proceedings of the Germans'. He had found de Selves to be 'very much taken aback' by what Grey had said to Cambon, and he feared that if the Germans were to learn that Britain had no unalterable objections to their having a commercial port, they might 'squeeze the French'.[84] That the French might in any case settle with the Germans on terms injurious to British interests was a possibility that had not been ignored in London. On 10 July Nicolson had indicated to Bertie that he was perturbed by the failure of the French to respond promptly to a request from Grey for consultations on the resolution of the dispute.[85] And although it soon emerged that the Germans were looking for compensation in the Congo in return for allowing the

---

[81] *Ibid*, no.376.
[82] *Ibid*, nos.375 and 386.
[83] *Ibid*, no.376.
[84] *Ibid*, no.375.
[85] Nicolson to Bertie, 10 July 1911, B.P., A., F.O.800/171.

French to establish their protectorate over Morocco, Crowe objected to German claims that the participation of third parties in the Franco-German discussions was not required. Britain was, he maintained, directly concerned with the international position of Morocco.[86] In this context Grey's officials were, as they had been since the Algeciras conference, particularly sensitive about any economic deals that might be arranged between the French and Germans.[87] Bertie had warned de Selves on 11 July that 'considerable irritation had been caused in British as well as German commercial quarters by the avidity of French financiers who desired to keep everthing for themselves'. His language was approved by Grey, Nicolson and Crowe. Indeed, the latter thought that the time had come to warn the French that they should have more regard for British rights and interests in Morocco.[88]

During his interview with de Selves on 11 July Bertie also attempted to dispel the foreign minister's impression, derived from Paul Cambon, that the British government would have no objection to France meeting whatever might be Germany's requirements in the Congo.[89] These in the first instance seemed unlikely to amount to anything more than a request for the adjustment of colonial frontiers. But on the morning of 17 July Bertie was summoned to the Quai d'Orsay to learn from de Selves that Kiderlen-Waechter had proposed that France should, in return for securing a free hand in Morocco and a strip of territory in the Cameroons, cede to Germany the whole of the French Congo from the Sangha river to the Atlantic. Neither de Selves nor Paul Cambon, who was present at this meeting, made any reference to the fact that the state-secretary had included amongst his proposals an offer to cede Togoland to France. Their intention was, as Bertie admitted to Grey, to give 'prominence to the injury which such a cession as the Germans asked for would do to British interests as well as those of France'. This did not, however, prevent Bertie from adding to Cambon's warning that German ambitions extended to Belgian, Portuguese and Spanish territories in the region, a reminder to Grey of the reversionary claims staked out by Germany in 1898. He still considered that her real aim was a

---

[86] *B.D.*, VII, no.383.
[87] Minutes by Villiers, Crowe, and Langley, on Goschen to Grey, 10 July 1911, F.O.371/1164, tel.47. Minutes by Crowe and Langley on Bertie to Grey, 14 July 1911, F.O.371/1164, tel.99. Cambon, II, pp.328 – 29.
[88] Bertie to Grey, 11 July 1911, F.O.371/1155, tel.55, and minutes by Crowe, Nicolson, and Grey.
[89] *D.D.F.2*, XIV, no.369.

presence on the Moroccan coast, and that her 'excessive requirements' were intended to reconcile the French to its achievement.[90]

Nicolson agreed with Bertie's interpretation of Germany's ambitions. But for Nicolson, as also for Crowe, the details of German proposals were less important than the challenge which they posed to French prestige, and therefore to the *entente* and the balance of power in Europe. The conditions demanded by Germany were, Crowe reasoned, such as a country having an independent policy could not possibly accept, and since the 'defeat of France' was a matter vital to Britain, the 'dominant question' was whether she was prepared to fight by the side of France if necessary. Nicolson even went so far as to forecast that if France were compelled to surrender to Germany's demands 'German hegemony would be solidly established, with all its consequences immediate and prospective'. While, however, Grey agreed that the answer which he must give to de Selves's communication would be 'critical', he was not overawed by the rhetoric of his advisers. His own desire was to bring about a compromise settlement by encouraging the French to make counter-proposals, and persuading the Germans to moderate their demands. He wished to make it clear to the German government that Britain would have to be taken into account, and to that end he suggested he should propose to the Germans the summoning of an international conference on Morocco, with the intimation that in the event of their rejecting this idea Britain would take steps to protect her interests.[91]

Such a course could hardly be said to have responded to Nicolson's appeal for a 'united front' with France. Nevertheless, it was strenuously and successfully resisted by those of Grey's radical colleagues who feared the consequences of his diplomacy. At a cabinet meeting on 19 July Lord Loreburn, the lord chancellor, reasoned that Britain's direct interests in the matter were small, and that as a result of Grey's proposed communication Britain might find herself drifting towards war.[92] But Grey still proceeded to inform Bertie that Britain might propose a conference if the Franco-German negotiations broke down, and he asked whether France would in all circumstances exclude a settlement which gave Germany a foothold in Morocco. He also reemphasized that Britain could not make the admission of Germany into Morocco an unconditional *casus belli*. This was not the attitude which de Selves had expected the British to adopt, and his reply to the summary of Grey's views with which Bertie supplied him on 20 July was, in Nicolson's words, 'somewhat

---

[90] *B.D.*, VII, nos.391 and 392. Cambon, II, pp.329–331.
[91] *B.D.*, VII, no.392.
[92] Fry, pp.234–5. Asquith to George V, 19 July 1911, Asquith MSS., 6.

stiff in tone'. After pointing out that the negotiations with Germany had not yet broken down, and that according to all appearances they would last for some time to come, de Selves went on to remind Bertie of Britain's obligations to France. He did not rule out the possibility of a conference, but he did reject the idea of it considering a concession to Germany in Morocco.[93]

In the meanwhile Grey sent Bertie both a private letter in which he elaborated on his ideas, and instructions to use as much of its substance as he thought 'discreet in conversation'. He stated that he was prepared to give the French diplomatic support, but that Britain could only go to war for the defence of British interests and not to 'put the Algeciras Act aside and put France in virtual possession of Morocco'. While an attempt by Germany to humiliate France might, he admitted, affect British interests so seriously that it would have to be resisted, he thought that there was no case for that at present. The French, he observed, had 'drifted into difficulties without knowing which way they really wanted to go', and their action in Morocco he considered only 'less wrong technically' than that of Germany and Spain. If Britain were to make a move to try to turn the Germans out of Agadir, Grey feared that he would find himself in one of two false positions: Germany might propose to deal with Britain alone over Morocco, which would mean betraying France; or Britain might be led into a war with Germany, which would mean fighting solely to put France into control of Morocco. The best solution in his opinion remained a Franco-German deal on the Congo, and the next best a tripartite partition of Morocco by France, Germany and Spain. If France could not accept either of these solutions, there might, he concluded, be nothing for it but a return to the '*status quo* of Algeciras: a cumbrous troublesome and temporary expedient'. Grey also made it clear to Bertie that he was not concerned about who owned tropical territory that Britain did not want for herself, and that neither she, nor France, could justly augment their possessions in Africa without Germany gaining 'some substantial addition to her share'. Indeed, in a separate telegram he suggested to Bertie that the preemptive rights that France claimed to have in the Belgian Congo might form part of a Franco-German bargain.[94]

Little if any of this was to Bertie's liking. 'It is very shortsighted', he protested to Crowe, 'for us to show our fear of Germany and our anxiety to get the French to give away what they so much want to keep.' It might end, he thought, in the French drawing the conclusion

[93] *B.D.*, VII, nos.396, 399, 401 and 403. Nicolson to Goschen, 24 July 1911, Nicolson MSS., F.O.800/394.
[94] *B.D.*, VII, nos.404 and 405. Grey to Bertie, 20 July 1911, B.P., A, F.O.800/166.

that Britain was of no use to them, with the inevitable result that they might make terms with Germany which though 'some of those who direct the counsels of the Empire may now think harmless, may hereafter prove very harmful to us'. He preferred therefore to take advantage of the discretion which had been left to him and not to frighten de Selves by imparting to him Grey's views in full. Crowe, who was 'ashamed as well as angry' at the line which the cabinet was taking, had already requested Bertie on Nicolson's behalf not to make any reference to Grey's suggestion concerning the Belgian Congo, except in a separate telegram or despatch. Worried lest the Germans should hear of it and make things 'hot' for Britain at Brussels, they were anxious that any reference to it should be kept out of the Foreign Office print. Bertie promised not to give them away.[95] As he subsequently explained to Grey, he considered it better for Britain's relations with France that whatever concessions might be necessary to prevent a conflict should be in compliance with either Germany's demands, or France's offers.[96]

Bertie did not, however, withhold from indicating to de Selves the advantages to be had from France pursuing the sort of course that Grey had advocated. There was no question of his simply pocketing Grey's instructions. Speaking in a private and unofficial capacity, he pointed out to de Selves on the morning of 21 July that if there were a conference the Germans would probably not be satisfied with a French undertaking to withdraw by a specific date, and that it might be impossible to return to the *status quo* of Algeciras. With the aid of an atlas he also tried to demonstrate to de Selves his own understanding of Germany's territorial ambitions in central Africa. Germany, he predicted, would never quietly acquiesce in the French exercising their right of preemption upon the Belgian Congo, which, he maintained, neither the British nor the Germans had recognized. He thus enumerated the difficulties which would arise from reverting to a conference, and gently encouraged the French to seek a settlement in the Congo.[97] Nevertheless, some of his worst fears were confirmed when that evening Caillaux raised with him the subject of his communication of the previous day to de Selves. Any suggestion by the British government that France should admit Germany to a territorial position in Morocco would, he warned Bertie, be inconsistent with the agreement of 1904. Without Britain's backing, he claimed, the French might have to make great concessions to keep

---

[95] Bertie to Crowe, 21 July 1911, B.P., A, F.O.800/171. Crowe to Bertie, 20 July 1911, B.P., A, F.O.800/160.
[96] *B.D.*, VII, no.407.
[97] *Ibid.*

Germany out of Morocco, and the consequent feeling of resentment in France at being 'deserted' would, he added, be 'deep and lasting'.[98]

Grey had no intention of abandoning France. He had to reckon with opposition within the cabinet to Britain's deeper involvement in the crisis. But he personally shared with the senior officials of his department a desire to give to the French such support as would prevent them from falling under the 'virtual control' of Germany and their estrangement from England. Otherwise, he feared the break-up of the *ententes*, the reemergence of the old troubles with Russia in Asia, and German ascendancy in Europe.[99] Grey was also irritated by the failure of the Germans to respond to his statement to Metternich of 4 July, and anxious lest Germany, through ignorance of Britain's intentions, should commit herself to a course from which she could not withdraw. On 21 July the cabinet agreed that he should warn Metternich that seventeen days had elapsed without any notice being taken of Britain's position, and that while the British government wished the Franco-German negotiations on the Congo well 'it must be clearly understood that we should recognise no settlement of Morocco in which we had not a voice'.[100] That same day Lloyd George publicly stated in his Mansion House speech that it was 'intolerable' that Britain should be treated as if she were of no account 'when her interests were vitally affected'. This declaration by a minister who had previously seemed sympathetic to the idea of improved Anglo-German relations was assumed in Berlin to be a warning to Germany.[101] It was even suggested that the speech had been inspired by Bertie, who, it was claimed, had used a visit which he had made to London in July to misrepresent Germany's position.[102] In fact, however, Bertie, whose presence in London had been requested by Grey, did not travel to England until 23 July, and by then he was less concerned about impressing upon the Germans the need to take Britain into account, than with reassuring the French that Britain was not wavering in her loyalty to the *entente*.[103]

In Nicolson, whom he met shortly after his arrival in London, Bertie no doubt found a sympathetic colleague. The permanent

---

[98] *Ibid*, no.408.
[99] T. Wilson (ed.), *The Political Diaries of C.P. Scott, 1911–1928* (New York, 1970), p.51.
[100] *B.D.*, VII, no.399. Asquith to George V, 21 July 1911, Asquith MSS., 6.
[101] Fry, pp.136–9.
[102] Extract from *Neue Freie Presse* enclosed in Russel to Crowe, 25 Nov. 1911, F.O.371/1128.
[103] Grey to Bertie, 20 July 1911, B.P., A, F.O.800/166. Bertie to Grey, 21 July 1911, Grey MSS., F.O.800/52.

under-secretary had been reluctant to press the French on the issue of a concession to Germany in Morocco, and on 21 July he had advised Grey to discuss the present situation with Bertie and Paul Cambon, and 'not to enter into any discussions with France as to the scope and interpretation of the 1904 agreement, which might assume a controversial character'.[104] Bertie's own view of that arrangement was that while it did not bind Britain to give France more than diplomatic support, such support had little meaning unless it had something behind it. This he argued in a memorandum which he prepared for interviews which he was to have on the 25th with Grey, Asquith and Lloyd George. There was little that was new in this document: Bertie for the most part confined himself to reiterating opinions which he had previously expressed to Grey and others in the Foreign Office. But for once he did stress the potential value of France as Britain's ally in a war with Germany. Even if Britain were able to defeat Germany at sea, he reasoned, it would still be necessary to exert pressure on her on land in order to 'bring her to her knees', and he cited a remark by Clemenceau that 'Trafalgar only prepared for Waterloo'.

This was an argument which Bertie probably felt would appeal to ministers who had of late been so much concerned with Britain's escalating naval expenditure. But he also pointed out that the French government would find it difficult to obtain parliamentary sanction for the territorial cessions that the Germans were demanding, and that if the Germans were to increase their forces at Agadir, or were to land men for a stay, the French might suggest that British, French and Spanish forces should do likewise. If on the other hand the French were forced to submit to Germany, he maintained that Britain's 'turn would come next', and she might then have to reckon not just with France's indifference, but her hostility. 'We should', he concluded, 'be in splendid isolation which nowadays would be highly dangerous.' The course which he recommended was therefore that the British government should simply require to be kept fully informed, and that the French should be told to let it know when they required Britain's diplomatic support.[105]

Tyrrell had hoped that Bertie would 'carry the day' against the 'Powers that be', whom he thought were still under the impression that Germany could be placated with small concessions.[106] Unfortunately, however, there are apart from Bertie's memorandum, no

---

[104] *B.D.*, VII, no.409. Nicolson to Goschen, 24 July 1911, Nicolson MSS., F.O.800/349.
[105] Memo. by Bertie, 25 July 1911, B.P., A, F.O.800/160.
[106] Lowe and Dockrill, III, p.434.

records of the conversations which he was to have with Grey, Asquith and Lloyd George. Moreover, although Paul Cambon subsequently described Bertie's visit as having been very effective, it is difficult to see in what sense he meant this. Perhaps Cambon was impressed by an assurance given to him by Grey on 25 July that he shared his opinion that 'si la situation prenait une tournure pouvant nous inspirer des appréhensions il serait nécessaire de nous entendre et de prévoir toutes les eventualités'.[107] This after all was the sort of statement that in 1905 had allowed Cambon to think in terms of a forthcoming offer of an alliance. But in so far as Bertie had endeavoured to restrain Grey from advising the French to make concessions to the Germans, he had been singularly unsuccessful: a fact which became apparent when during the following week the negotiations at Berlin seemed set to enter a more critical phase.

The Franco-German negotiations, which had in effect commenced on 9 July, were concerned primarily with determining the extent of the territory which the French would concede to Germany in the Congo basin, in return for territorial accessions elsewhere in west and equatorial Africa, and the lifting of German opposition to the establishment of a French protectorate over Morocco.[108] For his part Kiderlen-Waechter had not only to reckon with the possibility of France having the assistance of Britain and Russia in the event of a European war, but also with the efforts of the emperor and Bethmann Hollweg to exercise a moderating influence upon his diplomacy, and the demands of a nationalist press for the defence of German interests in Morocco. He was, nevertheless, fortunate in having as his interlocutor Jules Cambon, a diplomat who fully appreciated the potential value of Morocco for France's north African empire, and who was prepared to urge the authorities in Paris to be generous in their offers of compensation.[109] But neither de Selves, nor those senior officials of the Quai d'Orsay, like Herbette and Bapst, on whom he relied for advice, were inclined to favour a colonial arrangement with Germany such as might involve large territorial exchanges.[110] Only Caillaux, with whom Jules Cambon corresponded, appeared ready to adopt a more flexible approach towards a Franco-German accord. During the last week of July, without the foreknowledge of de Selves and through the agency of a business friend, Hyacinthe Fondère, he held out to the German embassy at Paris the prospect of an

---

[107] *D.D.F.2*, XIV, nos. 102 and 112.
[108] Allain, *Agadir*, pp.385 – 418.
[109] *D.D.F.2*, XIV, no.99. Oncken, pp.167 – 73.
[110] Allain, *Caillaux*, pp.387 – 8. *D.D.F.2*, XIV, nos.53 and 117, and pp.749 – 53.

agreement which might embrace Morocco, the Congo, the Baghdad railway, Ottoman finance and the settlement of all outstanding Franco-German differences.[111] In the meantime Kiderlen-Waechter, who was justly angered at the way in which Lloyd George's speech had limited his room for manoeuvre, adopted an uncompromising stance, and on 28 July practically rejected the meagre offers of the Quai d'Orsay for an adjustment of the frontiers between the Cameroons and France's adjacent possessions.[112]

The news from Berlin left de Selves in what Bertie described as a 'very agitated state'. But Bertie had to discourage his hopes that Britain might, in the event of the Germans increasing their presence at Agadir, agree to join with France and Spain in sending warships there, and he impressed upon de Selves the importance of the negotiations being broken off by the German rather than the French government. If the Germans were to reject France's final offer, then Bertie recommended Jules Cambon should state that he would have to refer to Paris for instructions, so as to give the French time to inform Britain and allow Grey to propose a conference before the issue of a German ultimatum.[113] This procedure was favoured by both Paul Cambon and Nicolson, and de Selves followed up the suggestion with instructions to Berlin on very similar lines.[114] While, however, Grey was prepared to seek the cabinet's approval for the summoning, if necessary, of a conference, he would not go beyond this in defining his intentions, and he continued to urge magnanimity upon the French. He told Paul Cambon on 1 August that future German expansion in Africa could be met if the Portuguese colonies, or the Belgian Congo, were offered up for sale.[115]

According to Grey, Britain was only interested in small portions of the Belgian Congo which adjoined her existing possessions. He showed a similar lack of concern for other parts of this region when at the beginning of August Kiderlen-Waechter abandoned his original proposals and sought instead an arrangement which would have provided Germany with territorial access to the Congo river. Thus, in spite of a warning from Paul Cambon that it might be possible to offer Germany compensation which would extend her influence to the

---

[111] Allain, *Caillaux*, pp.382–3; *Agadir*, pp.360–3.
[112] D.D.F.2, XIV, no.120. *B.D.*, VII, no.438. Bertie to Grey, 31 July 1911, B.P., A, F.O.800/160. Oncken, p.291.
[113] *B.D.*, VII, nos.440 and 441. Already in the initial stages of the crisis the British cabinet had rejected the idea of sending a British warship to Moroccan waters. Dockrill, p.274.
[114] D.D.F.2, XIV, nos.126 and 127. Cambon, II, pp.336–8.
[115] *B.D.*, VII, nos.433, 434, and 449. Cambon, II, pp.338–9. Grey to Goschen, 1 Aug. 1911, F.O.371/1163, despt.184. Haldane to Spender, 27 Aug. 1911, Spender MSS., add. MS. 46390.

confines of the Bahr-el-Ghazal, Grey did not feel that he could object. He informed Mallet on 5 August that he did not think it mattered whether Germany or France were Britain's neighbours in Africa. 'It is', he added, 'no doubt preferable to have the weaker power as neighbour, but we cannot press the preference to the embarrassment of the negotiations between France and Germany.'[116] A somewhat different attitude was assumed by Crowe. Evidently disturbed by the prospect of an augmentation of German territory in the direction of the Sudan, he minuted on a telegram from Bertie, which gave details of the latest French proposals, that it was a pity the ambassador had offered no comment. 'He is so fully cognizant', Crowe observed, 'of the complicated history of the partitioning of Africa in recent years that his opinion on the effects of such an arrangement would have been particularly useful.'[117] Grey's theorizing about the future of the Belgian and Potuguese colonies had, however, already provoked Bertie into writing a rejoinder in which he made clear in no uncertain terms his views on any redrawing of the map of Africa.

In a private letter to Nicolson of 6 August Bertie wrote that he could understand the government's wish to divert the German 'land hunger' from Britain's possessions, and he appreciated the 'anxiety that France should on the present occasion give morsels to keep away the wolf from an attack on the fold in which we should have to be the shepherd dogs'. But he considered Grey's suggestions concerning France's preemptive rights and the Belgian Congo to be a mistake. The French, he claimed, would suspect 'that we hope that if we persuade them to make over some of those rights to Germany we may ourselves have a deal with her'. Likewise, he deprecated any attempt to encourage the liquidation of the Portuguese empire in Africa, which, he feared, would lead to the alienation of Portugal from Britain. While he conceded that it was unfortunate for Germany that she had 'arrived late for the feast of spoils in Asia, Africa and America'. he could see no advantage for Britain in Germany acquiring 'an African Empire extending over an enormous portion of that continent from sea to sea'. 'If', he concluded, 'she can get to the Upper waters of the Congo she will become a neighbour of small potentates who at her instigation and with her assistance might give us trouble in the Egyptian Soudan.'[118]

Faced with Grey's readiness to accept Germany's aggrandizement in Africa, Bertie may have been led to encourage the French to resist Kiderlen-Waechter's more ambitious schemes. This at least was what

[116] *D.D.F.2*, XIV, nos.126, 127, 134. *B.D.*, VII, nos.451, 458, 459 and 461.
[117] *B.D.*, VII, no.460.
[118] *Ibid*, no.464.

Caillaux asserted in his memoirs. He claimed that Bertie had warned him that England would allow Germany to take all the colonies she desired so long as they were French ones; that he had pressed upon him the impossibility of France ceding a colony to Germany; and that he had accused the Liberal government of being small-minded and incapable of seeing beyond the end of their noses.[119] Some exaggeration must, however, be allowed for on Caillaux's part. Relations between the two men were soured in the autumn of 1911 by an unhappy disagreement, and the black portrait which Caillaux painted of Bertie in his books, *Agadir* and *Mes Mémoires*, probably reflects the grudge that he continued to feel against the ambassador. Besides which, *Mes Mémoires* was completed after Caillaux had read the pungent criticisms made of him by Bertie both in his published diary and those of his letters which appeared in the *British Documents on the Origins of the War*. His contention that Bertie was complacent about the prospect of a European war, and that Bertie counted upon him 'pour mettre le feu aux poudres', were part and parcel of an attempt by Caillaux to defend his own diplomacy.[120]

Nevertheless, Caillaux was not alone in commenting upon the immoderate tone of Bertie's language. In a letter of 28 September the German ambassador complained of the 'inflammatory activity' of Bertie against Germany. He admitted, however, that Bertie expressed himself in a 'jovial witty tone which lapsed easily into the grotesque', that only a diminishing number of people took him seriously, and that he was not a 'dangerous opponent'.[121] In any case, while it is true that Bertie saw advantage for Britain in the continuing friction between France and Germany, he had no interest in helping to foment a European war. He hoped rather that Germany's ambitions in Africa might be curbed by the maintenance of a common front by Britain and France. When in mid-August it seemed possible that the Germans might attempt to consolidate their position in Morocco, Bertie gave no encouragement to Caillaux's proposal that if they increased their naval force at Agadir, the French should send ships to Saffi and Mogador. Doubtless aware of the problems that it would create for Grey in the cabinet, he warned de Selves on 22 August against giving colour to the assertion of the German press that France was taking possession of Morocco without justification. It

---

[119] Caillaux, *Mes Mémoires*, II, pp.137-8.
[120] J. Caillaux, *Agadir, ma politique extérieure* (Paris, 1919), pp.138-9.
[121] *G.P.*, XXIX, no.10651. It was also alleged in the German press that Bertie had done everthing imaginable to induce the French to put forward unacceptable demands. Extract from the *Deutsche Tageszeitung* in Goschen to Grey, 5 Nov. 1911, F.O.371/1161, despt.365.

was most important, he added, that 'France should not give an opening to the accusation of bringing on a conflict'.[122]

Despite the hope, entertained by Jules Cambon at the beginning of August, that there was scope for a Franco-German bargain, his negotiations with Kiderlen-Waechter made only slow progress. Part of the problem lay with de Selves, who, very much under the influence of his department, was reluctant to accept those German demands which would have separated the Gabon from France's remaining possessions in equatorial Africa.[123] The French were, however, provided with the opportunity to assess their position and reformulate their objectives by Kiderlen-Waechter's decision to go on leave during the last fortnight of August. The Cambon brothers and Barrère travelled to Paris, and as a result of their consultations with Caillaux and de Selves it was decided to concede to Germany access to the Congo via a narrow strip of territory between the Ubangi and Sangha rivers. But Jules Cambon also became aware that Caillaux and de Selves were far from united in their handling of the crisis. Relations between them were strained as a result of the Quai d'Orsay's discovery from decyphered German telegrams of the contact established by Caillaux with the German embassy. Besides which, the premier's continued use of his own intermediaries, and his endeavours to secure for himself and his cabinet colleagues a greater say in directing French diplomacy, further alienated the permanent officials of the foreign ministry.[124]

Before the end of August Bertie appears to have been quite ignorant of Caillaux's unofficial dealings with the Germans. De Selves indicated to Bertie on 25 August that Caillaux might have established his own contact with the German ambassador, and from a 'financial friend' Bertie learned that Schoen had for some time been trying to communicate with Caillaux with 'the notion that he might be easier to deal with than M. de Selves'.[125] Bertie did not, however, delve deeper into this matter, and it was not until the autumn, when Caillaux's conduct became a subject of public debate, that Bertie obtained any real understanding of the conflict between the premier and the Quai d'Orsay. In retrospect the intervention of Caillaux in the Franco-German negotiations appears to have been wise and perhaps necessary at a time when France could not afford to be confident either of her military strength, or of the assistance which

[122] *B.D.*, VII, nos.498, 510, 512 and 515.
[123] Allain, *Agadir*, pp.400–3 and 411–12.
[124] *D.D.F.2*, XIV, pp.753-60. Binion, p.41.
[125] *B.D.*, VII, no.517.

she might receive from potential allies. Moreover, as Jules Cambon was later to observe, the Fondère affair had its place, 'mais une place secondaire', in determining the outcome of the confrontation.[126] Of more significance was the support which Caillaux gave to the Cambon brothers in combatting the niggardly attitude of the Quai d'Orsay towards colonial concessions to Germany.[127]

Jules Cambon was none the less far from satisfied with the instructions which he took back with him to Berlin on 30 August. He was annoyed at the insistence of de Selves and Herbette on obtaining Kiderlen-Waechter's agreement to a project which contained detailed provisions for the establishment of a French protectorate in Morocco, and which seemed likely to give rise to endless wrangling. He also felt that France could still afford to offer Germany more in compensation. On 1 September he complained to Goschen, who had succeeded Lascelles at Berlin, that the French government did not seem to realize 'the *enormous* advantage of a free hand in Morocco', nor that they must 'pay *handsomely* for it'. He thought that de Selves needed stiffening against his advisers, and begged that Grey should require Bertie to press upon Caillaux and de Selves the wisdom of making more generous territorial offers to Germany. Bertie, Jules Cambon observed, 'would heartily enjoy giving such advice "et catégoriquement" ', and coming directly from Grey it would have, he claimed, a more considerable effect than if it were to go through his brother Paul.[128]

Grey agreed with Jules Cambon. He considered it 'sheer unreason' to make the issue of peace or war dependent upon whether or not the Germans received a triangle of territory between the Sangha, Alima and Weso rivers. And on 4 September he wrote to explain what had passed at Berlin to Bertie, and to warn him that the extent to which British support would be forthcoming if trouble were ahead 'must depend upon it being clear that France had no reasonable and honourable way of avoiding it'. He would be glad, he informed Bertie, if he would take any moment that he considered opportune to

---

[126] Allain, *Caillaux*, pp.387–401. J. Cambon to Mermeix, 12 Feb. 1912, J. Cambon MSS., 15.
[127] In September Jules Cambon complained to Goschen that the 'French Gov't and Press were so much in the hands of Colonial financiers that he could not answer what w'd be done'. C. Howard, *Diary*, pp.244–5. Guiot to J. Cambon, 5 Oct. 1911, J. Cambon MSS., 14. Allain, *Caillaux*, p.382 and 187–9. *D.D.F.2*, XIV, nos.456 and 461. Cambon, II, pp.334–48.
[128] *D.D.F.2*, XIV, p.760. *B.D.*, VII, no.526. Goschen to Nicolson, 1 Sept. 1911, F.O.800/350.

explain his views to the French leaders.[129] Jules Cambon had, however, misjudged Bertie's personality. Far from relishing the idea of intervening with de Selves, Bertie dismissed the French ambassador's idea as a 'foolish one'. He certainly had no wish to place himself in the position of Izvolsky, whose recent efforts to persuade the French to offer more to the Germans had been resented in Paris. In any case he suspected Jules Cambon had either had his advice turned down, or had been afraid of giving it lest it be rejected. There might, Bertie surmised, be parliamentary or other objections of which Jules Cambon was unaware, and if the French public were to learn that its government had been subjected to British pressure to make concessions, Britain would have to bear the odium of having urged such sacrifices upon France. He therefore insisted that before acting on Grey's instructions, he must first ascertain the reasons behind the latest French stand. Indeed, after learning from de Selves on 7 September that he thought that the Germans were trying to humiliate France with their demands, Bertie limited himself to asking whether the French would consider further concessions if Germany threatened war.[130]

This satisfied Nicolson, who had all along hoped that Bertie would set aside Grey's instructions.[131] Even Grey was prepared to credit Bertie with having acted with 'wise discretion'. He, nevertheless, reemphasized to Bertie that public support for a British intervention in a continental war would depend upon it being clear that Germany had forced it upon France.[132] For this reason he also favoured an idea, which was conveyed to the Foreign Office by G. Paish, a joint editor of *The Statist*, that President Taft of the United States should offer his arbitration to France and Germany. In a letter to Bertie of 8 September he admitted that although he did not think the time right to mention arbitration to the French, 'before we go to extremes, if extremes are to come, I shall have to suggest this'.[133] Bertie's response was wholly predictable. Quite apart from the complications which he foresaw arising over the settlement of the terms of arbitration, he

---

[129] On 5 September Grey himself asked Paul Cambon if France could not give to Germany the triangle of territory for which she was asking.*B.D.*, VII, no.352. Grey to Bertie, 5 and 6 Sept. 1911, B.P., A, F.O.800/160.
[130] Bertie to Nicolson, 12 Sept. 1911, B.P., A, F.O.800/160. *B.D.*, VII, nos.503 and 504.
[131] Nicolson to Goschen, 12 Sept. 1911, Nicolson MSS., F.O.800/350. Nicolson to Bertie, 21 Sept. 1911, B.P., A, F.O.800/182. *B.D.*, VII, no.544.
[132] Grey to Bertie, 8 Sept. 1911, B.P., A, F.O.800/171. Grey to Bertie, 8 Sept. 1911, tel., Grey MSS., F.O.800/52.
[133] Drummond to Bertie, 6 Sept. 1911, B.P., A, F.O.800/182. Grey to Bertie, 8 Sept. 1911, B.P., A, F.O.800/171. *B.D.*, VII, no.544.

thought that the French were unlikely to accept such a proposal unless it were accompanied by a warning that they would otherwise forfeit British support. Then, he feared, Britain would become a scapegoat for what was almost certain to be regarded by the French as an unsatisfactory settlement.[134] Nicolson considered Bertie's argument quite convincing, and Grey found much force in what he had to say. Grey had thought that if the Germans were to refuse arbitration, and the French were to accept it, this would give the latter a moral advantage and the certainty of 'very material [British] support to France if war followed'. He finally agreed, however, that if the Franco-German negotiations broke down, he would propose a conference and not mention arbitration.[135]

Neither of these two procedures was to prove necessary. The negotiations at Berlin looked once more as if they would founder when on 7 September Kiderlen-Waechter put forward a set of counter-proposals, which, if accepted, would have inhibited progress towards a French protectorate in Morocco and have provided for a thirty per cent participation by German firms in railway construction there.[136] Faced, however, with a panic on the Berlin stock exchange, itself in part induced by a withdrawal of French funds from Germany, and with the prospect of having to risk a war for which the navy was unprepared and at a time when Austria was at best lukewarm in its support, Kiderlen-Waechter was ready to accept a compromise.[137] On 19 September he and Jules Cambon succeeded in working out the basis of an agreement on Morocco, and although its premature release to the French press hampered further progress, they were able to initial an accord within a month.[138] Further difficulties arose when the Quai d'Orsay began to have second thoughts about accepting a 'coupure' through the middle Congo. Nevertheless, an understanding was eventually arrived at which provided the Germans with territorial links with the Congo and Ubangi rivers. This and the agreement on Morocco were embodied in a treaty signed at Frankfurt on 4 November 1911.[139]

Bertie was well satisfied at Kiderlen-Waechter having, as Jules Cambon had put it, climbed down in the Franco-German quarrel. 'I understand', he wrote to Nicolson on 19 September, 'the Germans

[134] Bertie to Grey, 17 Sept, 1911, B.P., A, F.O.800/182.
[135] Nicolson to Bertie, 21 Sept. 1911, Nicolson MSS., F.O.800/350. *B.D.*, VII, no.561.
[136] *B.D.*, VII, nos.537, 538 and 545.
[137] Allain, *Agadir*, pp.365 – 7. Poidevin, pp.630 – 5. Fischer, pp.54 – 8.
[138] J. Cambon to Delcassé, 4 Oct. 1911, Delcassé MSS., 16. Faramond to Delcassé, 4 Oct. 1911, Delcassé MSS., 10.
[139] Tabouis, pp.220 – 30.

have spent money in setting up their machinery to become rich, but
they have not enough to run it properly and get what they require
from France & England.' Yet despite this rather primitive, although
not wholly inaccurate, assessment of Germany's financial weakness,
Bertie still reckoned her to be a threat to the peace of Europe. In
retrospect he saw the crisis as the result of a German miscalculation of
the likely British and French reactions to Germany's raising of the
Moroccan question. That he felt to be evident in her resort to 'such a
"geste" as the Agadir coup'. Moreover, Kiderlen-Waechter's retreat
from his original demands seemed very much to Bertie like a victory
for common resistance to German pretensions. The Emperor
William and Bethman Hollweg had, he imagined, been astonished to
realize that France would certainly have Russian aid and most
probably British assistance, and they had not judged the moment
propitious for a war with France. He thought that they would await
instead a more favourable occasion.

It is [Bertie ruminated] not a pleasant prospect, an armed truce
waiting for the moment when the German Government may think
that the time has come to realise their dreams. They have pretty
well disclosed what their aims are. Meanwhile they will set about
improving their artillery & getting up aviation *and* building more
ships.

There was, however, in Bertie's estimation one ray of hope: the
German character. Luckily, he thought, the German was an
'awkward fellow', who spoiled his game by 'maladresse and brutality,
and by lies and misrepresentantion which must be discovered'.[140]

Bertie must also have been relieved that the *entente* had survived the
crisis of the summer. During July and August he had striven to avoid
a situation in which the French might be given just cause to doubt the
value of their understanding with England. And if he had not been
able to offer Caillaux any encouragement when he, like Clemenceau,
had complained to him of the small size of the British army, he had
done his best to avoid giving the impression that Britain was urging
any specific concessions on the French.[141] His desire to ensure that
Grey remained firm in his support of France may, however, have
blinded him to the differences then prevailing amongst French policy-
makers. Indeed, the lack of insight which he sometimes exhibited in
his reporting on developments in Paris could have done nothing to
alleviate the suspicions of some of Grey's more radical colleagues that

---

[140] Bertie to Nicolson, 19 Sept. 1911, B.P., A, F.O.800/171.
[141] Bertie to Grey, 3 Aug. 1911, B.P., A, F.O.800/166.

the French government had not been as frank as it should have been in its dealings with the British. This was to be of no small significance at a time when Morocco, having ceased to divide France from Germany, was about to revert to being a problem of Anglo-French relations.

10

The partition of Morocco

'The result of the Morocco affair of 1911', minuted one Foreign Office clerk in December 1911, 'is that the "entente cordiale" is stronger than ever.'[1] But the settlement of the Agadir crisis also allowed Grey's critics to proclaim that the terms of the original *entente* of 1904 had been fulfilled. The British government had assisted France in overcoming German resistance to her designs upon Morocco, and it was henceforth free to adopt new lines of policy in Europe.[2] The argument found an echo in France where Gabriel Hanotaux, Delcassé's immediate predecessor at the Quai d'Orsay and a politician not noted for his Anglophilia, maintained that the Moroccan accords of 1904 now possessed no more than 'un intérêt local et en quelque sorte, secondaire'.[3] This was substantially correct. France's agreements with Britain and Spain had, however, been drafted with a view to protecting and reconciling interests which the latter powers still regarded as nationally and strategically important. The same arrangements also denied to France that liberty of action in Morocco which she was popularly supposed to have purchased with sacrifices in the Congo, and, as Bertie was soon to discover, they could generate almost as much acrimony as cordiality in relations between the *entente* partners. Thus the interpretation and implementation of the engagements that Delcassé had undertaken towards Britain and Spain in Morocco were to involve Bertie and his successors in long and sometimes unseemly squabbling with the French.

The officials of the Quai d'Orsay and France's representatives in Morocco had already found cause to regret the obligations imposed upon them by the Franco-Spanish convention of 3 October 1904.[4] Yet that agreement had complemented the Anglo-French *entente*, and its terms, which remained unpublished until November 1911, had been formally communicated to the Foreign Office. Spain had

---

[1] Minute by G.H. Villiers on Bertie to Grey, 21 Dec. 1911, F.O.371/1170, despt.615.
[2] *Les Documents Diplomatiques Français, 3e série* (hereafter cited as *D.D.F.*), I, no.210.
[3] G. Hanotaux, *La Politique de l'Équilibre, 1907–1911* (Paris, 1912), p.431.
[4] Allain, *Agadir*, pp.303 and 415–16. Un diplomate, *Paul Cambon. ambassadeur de France (1843–1924)* (Paris, 1937), pp.252–3.

thereby been accorded a northern and a southern sphere of influence in Morocco, both of which were in effect to be administered by her in the event of a collapse of the sultan's authority. That in the north comprised a band of territory extending westwards from the mouth of the Moulouya river to a point on Morocco's Atlantic coast, and that in the south lay adjacent to Ifni, Spanish claims to which were specifically recognized by France, and Spain's colony of Rio de Oro. Article ix of the convention also stipulated that Tangier was to keep the 'special character' which the presence of the diplomatic corps and its municipal and sanitary institutions had given it: a provision which the British government assumed to mean that the city would be placed under international supervision.[5]

These arrangements, the *entente cordiale*, and the notes exchanged with Spain in May 1907, were regarded in London as having met the principal strategic requirements of Britain in the western Mediterranean. Bertie, nevertheless, still considered that there was room for improvement, and in September 1911 he tried to persuade Grey to seek an extension of the area covered by the non-fortification provisions of the Anglo-French agreement of 1904. Recalling the attempts that Lansdowne had once made to secure French assurances on the non-fortification of the whole of the Atlantic coast of Morocco, he suggested to Grey on 28 September that the government should take advantage of recent French proposals for an exchange of territory in west Africa in order to obtain such an undertaking from France. He also recommended that the French be reminded of the notes of 1907, and that the British government should intimate to them that it would consider the fortification of any port on the Moroccan coast as constituting a material change in the *status quo* and of the relative positions of Britain, France and Spain.[6] These proposals were, however, greeted with little enthusiasm in the Foreign Office. Nicolson, who thought that the two issues of a territorial exchange and a non-fortification agreement should be dealt with separately, wrote to Bertie on 5 October that it was too early to deal with this matter, and that it should be raised when Britain's concurrence in the Franco-German agreement was requested. A protest from Bertie that if they waited until then they would have no

---

[5] *B.D.*, VII, pp.826–829.
[6] The French wished to acquire a portion of northern Nigeria in order to achieve a more direct link between their territories in north-west Africa and what remained of their possessions in the Congo basin. Bertie to Grey, 19 Sept. 1911, F.O.367/227, despt.415 (Africa) and *private*. *B.D.*, VII, nos.485, 487, 488, 558, 567 and 581.

means of putting pressure upon France went unheeded.⁷ But the validity of his argument was soon to become apparent, for on 3 November both the Admiralty and the War Office informed Grey of the desirability of securing from the French a pledge not to fortify the Moroccan coast south of the Sebou river. By then Grey found it impolitic to attach such a condition to the recognition of a French protectorate over Morocco.⁸

The French were less careful of the letter of the 1904 accords. Circumstances had, after all, changed in the past seven years. Not only had the French had to provide the Germans with territorial compensation, but they had also to reckon with the Algeciras act which had accorded the sultan international recognition of both his sovereignty and the integrity of his empire. This raised the awkward constitutional problem of defining the relationship between the sultan, on whom the French intended to impose their protection, and the Spaniards in their zones of influence. The situation was further complicated by the likelihood of their being public and parliamentary opposition in France, if, after having 'paid' Germany, the French government had to accept Spain's acquisition of the Rif and its adjacent lands. There were those who were prepared to argue that Spain by acting independently of France had forfeited the rights she had obtained in 1904. And within the Quai d'Orsay, where it was assumed that Spain would be incapable of establishing an effective administration in Morocco, there were several senior officials who hoped to place severe restrictions upon the Spaniards. These included Herbette, who did much to hamper Jules Cambon's work at Berlin, and Regnault, who was on extended leave in Paris. Their views were opposed by the Cambon brothers and Geoffray, who, though they anticipated some concessions from Spain, feared that by pursuing too acquisitive a course France would simply push the Spaniards into an alignment with Germany and upset relations with Britain.⁹

The efforts of the Spanish government to have some say in the settlement of the Morocco question had been frustrated during the summer of 1911 by French diplomacy. Talks which had commenced in May between the Spanish minister of state and the British and French ambassadors at Madrid had been suspended after the

---

⁷ *B.D.*, VII, nos.567 and 582. Nicolson to Bertie, 29 Sept. 1911, B.P., A, F.O.800/160.

⁸ *B.D.*, VII, nos.619, 620, 683 and 687. War Office to F.O., 3 Nov. 1911, F.O.371/1167.

⁹ *D.D.F.2*, XIV, nos.164, 293 and 364. De Bunsen to wife, 4 Aug. 1911, de Bunsen MSS., MB/I/mm. Geoffray to de Selves, 7 and 13 Sept. 1911, N.S. Maroc 98, tels.235 and 239. J. Cambon to Delcassé, 30 Oct. 1911, Delcassé MSS., 2. Cambon, II, p.344. Bertie to Grey, 19 Sept. 1911, F.O.371/1161, despt.521. De Bunsen to Nicolson, 11 and 25 Nov. 1911, Nicolson MSS., F.O.800/344.

occupation of Larache and El Ksar, and the Spaniards had been excluded from the proceedings at Berlin. Not until August did de Selves, who steadfastly refused to open negotiations with the Spaniards before the conclusion of a Franco-German agreement, yield to Geoffray's plea to give the Spaniards 'un os à ronger'.[10] On 16 August Herbette sent to Geoffray a draft Franco-Spanish convention, which foresaw Spain acquiring a position in her northern zone similar to that which Austria-Hungary had possessed in Bosnia after 1878. But anxious to safeguard French communications with Fez, the Quai d'Orsay also demanded the neutralization of a part of the Spanish zone stretching southwards from Tangier.[11] After a protest from Geoffray against this cutting in two of the northern zone, de Selves forwarded another draft to Madrid. This document, which had not been submitted to the council of ministers, and which was not intended for communication to the Spanish government, substantially augmented Spain's administrative rights in the north of Morocco, but omitted any reference to a Spanish presence in the south. Indeed, de Selves contemplated the exclusion of the Spaniards from their projected southern zone, and the abandonment of their claims upon Ifni, in return for the sultan's absolute cession to them of an area near their *presidio* of Melilla.[12] Given, however, the evident reluctance of the Spanish authorities to contemplate such losses, and opposition within the foreign ministry to any new accord with Spain, de Selves decided to press the matter no further.[13]

Bertie, who received a copy of this draft convention on 30 August had some doubts about France's intention with regard to Tangier and Spain's southern zone. But in London the project was favourably regarded.[14] While Grey was unwilling to take a definite line about Ifni until matters were settled between France and Germany, he considered the draft an 'honest attempt to remove Spanish grievances'. Spain would, he thought, have to give France some 'reasonable compensation' if owing to French concessions to Germany, the Algeciras powers disinterested themselves in Morocco. And despite fears expressed by the Spaniards about French designs upon their spheres, Nicolson still felt able to write to Goschen on 26 September that there was no indication that there was any intention on the part of the

---

[10] *D.D.F.2*, XIV, nos.153, 155, 156, 164 and 194.
[11] *Ibid*, nos.183 and 195.
[12] *Ibid*, nos.219, 220, 229 and 248.
[13] *Ibid*, nos.231, 244, 245, 246, 261, 265 and 275.
[14] *B.D.*, VII, no.525.

French to disavow their treaty engagements with Spain.[15] Nevertheless, Paul Cambon, who probably perceived what was afoot within the Quai d'Orsay, had already thought it necessary to remind de Selves that in negotiating the convention of 1904 Spain had in effect paid France for her prospective position in Morocco, and was not therefore obliged to make any further concession. England, he contended, had in a certain measure guaranteed the execution of the Franco-Spanish agreement, and although she would not oppose French pretensions she would not press Spain to agree to them.[16]

Indications that the French might require something more than 'reasonable compensation' from Spain began to reach the Foreign Office at the end of September. In a letter of the 27th de Bunsen informed Nicolson of Geoffray's apprehension that de Selves might withdraw his draft convention. There were, according to Geoffray, 'strong influences' at work in Paris which were very hostile towards Spain, and these elements, 'the Étiennes, Regnaults, Herbettes etc.', might gain the upper hand.[17] De Bunsen's letter was disturbing, and on 4 October Grey warned Paul Cambon of the importance which British opinion attached to the safeguarding of Spain's rights.[18] On the next day Nicolson informed Bertie of the news from Madrid, and explained to him his own fears that the French were trying to 'drive too hard a bargain with Spain'. There was, he thought, a danger that the colonial party might succeed in France, and that a rupture of discussions with Spain might throw the latter on to the side of Germany.[19] Bertie felt able to assure Nicolson that he did not believe that de Selves was personally inclined towards being hard on Spain.[20] But the ambassador's confidence in the good intentions of de Selves was not shared by George Grahame. In minutes of 7 and 8 October he drew Bertie's attention to the fact that de Selves's project omitted any reference to the diplomatic body at Tangier. From this and his knowledge of Herbette's previous proposal for a neutral zone, he deduced that the French intended that Spain should be excluded from the neighbourhood of Tangier, and that the sultan's authority there should lapse in France's favour. The establishment of a protectorate would, he reasoned, mean that the diplomatic body would disappear, the French would be able to station troops in the city, and could, if it

---

[15] *Ibid*, nos.530, 543 and 569. Nicolson to Goschen, 26 Sept. 1911, Nicolson MSS., F.O.800/351.
[16] *D.D.F.2*, XIV, nos.273 and 293. Cambon, II, pp.344–5 and 355–6.
[17] De Bunsen to Nicolson, 27 Sept. 1911, Nicolson MSS., F.O.800/351.
[18] *D.D.F.2*, XIV, no.404.
[19] Nicolson to Bertie, 5 Oct. 1911, B.P., A, F.O.800/160.
[20] Bertie to Nicolson, 7 Oct. 1911, B.P., A, F.O.800/179.

were not for their treaty obligations, turn it into a naval base as they had done at Bizerta.[21]

Bertie disagreed with his colleagues's conclusions, but he considered them sufficiently important to be transmitted to Nicolson. In a covering note he observed that as Herbette's project had been dropped it was of no concern to Britain. The French might desire to have a free passage 'through' Tangier for their officers and supplies, but, Bertie added, he could find nothing in de Selves's proposals that could be twisted into giving authority for the French to station troops there.[22] This drew a rejoinder from Grahame. On 10 October he reminded Bertie that the French text spoke of officers passing 'from' Tangier. If it were intended that Tangier should be engulfed in the Spanish zone, then, he contended, the relevant article would have been expected to mention France's right to land officers and supplies. From the existing draft it might be assumed that they were already there. The French, Grahame suspected, were probably keeping the issue of Tangier's administration vague and in the background, and when other matters were disposed of, and they were *tête-à-tête* with the Spaniards, they would claim that it had been intended to leave it under the control of Fez. Bertie remained unconvinced by this argument.[23] He should have known better, for subsequent developments were to demonstrate that the fears expressed by Geoffray and Grahame were not without foundation.

It seems evident that by mid-September de Selves had begun to have second thoughts about his projected agreement with Spain. The hostility of the Spanish press towards France caused a good deal of irritation in Paris, and reports that the Spaniards were conspiring with the Germans, and that they were preparing to send an expedition to Ifni, did not endear Caillaux's government to their cause.[24] Then early in October the veteran Spanish liberal statesman, Segismondo Moret, suggested to Geoffray that instead of sharing a protectorate with France, Spain should receive the outright cession of a narrow strip of territory between Tetuan and the Moulouya. It may be, as de Bunsen surmised, that Moret was simply trying to discredit the existing administration at Madrid. But the idea of Spain being offered an absolute cession of territory was not a new one. It had

---

[21] Minutes by Grahame, 7 and 8 Oct. 1911, F.O.146/4229.
[22] Memo. by Bertie, 9 Oct. 1911, F.O.146/4229. Bertie to Nicolson, 9 Oct. 1911, F.O.371/1167, *private*.
[23] Minutes by Grahame and Bertie, 10 Oct. 1911, F.O.146/4229.
[24] Geoffray to de Selves, 14 Sept. 1911, N.S. Maroc 98, despt. 223. De Selves to Geoffray, 24 Sept. 1911, N.S. Maroc 98. Guiot to J. Cambon, 5 Oct. 1911, J.

occurred to Herbette, and Regnault now proceeded to draft a new accord which incorporated terms similar to those recommended by Moret.[25] This, the so-called 'projet Regnault', would, if accepted, have left the Spaniards with little more than the hinterland of their *presidios*, and would have allowed the French to control the strategically important triangle of territory extending from Larache and El Ksar to the east of Tangier.[26] De Selves, although not wholly averse to demanding substantial compensation from Spain, appears to have been sceptical about this scheme. Nevertheless, it was readily embraced by Caillaux, and at his behest de Selves had Regnault deliver his project to Bertie on 19 October.[27]

There was never any doubt in Bertie's mind that Britain would not be able to agree to France, a first class naval power, replacing Spain on Morocco's Atlantic seaboard, and he said as much to Regnault on 21 October.[28] Grahame was also quick to point out the dangers inherent in a project which would leave Tangier and its environs completely encircled within the French sphere. In London Crowe found it impossible not to agree with Bertie's conclusions. The latest French proposals, he minuted, would 'falsify one of the most important features of the agreements of 1904'.[29] But Bertie, who in accordance with previously made plans travelled to England on 22 October, found that Caillaux had already sent his own emissary to London, who had represented to Asquith that the French government had adopted Regnault's project and intended to impress it upon the Spaniards.[30] Not that either Asquith or Grey were prepared to countenance this course. Grey showed little sympathy towards the Spanish ambassador when he complained of recent French conduct, but he informed Paul Cambon on 30 October that once France's negotiations with Germany were concluded, Britain would not be able to support France in any negotiations with Spain unless they were based upon the 1904 agreements. Britain, he observed, was a party to those arrangements, and to treat them as if they did not exist would be to 'drag the *Entente* in the mud, and would have the most

Cambon MSS., 14. Caillaux, *Mes Mémoires*, II, pp.180–2. *D.D.F.2*, XIV, nos.183 and 229.
[25] Geoffray to De Selves, 6 and 13 Oct. 1911, N.S. Maroc 98, despts.247 and 253. *B.D.*, VII, no.594.
[26] De Selves to Geoffray, 18 Oct. 1911, N.S. Maroc 98, tel.400. *Projet d'accord Hispano-Marocain*, 20 Oct. 1911, N.S. Maroc 98.
[27] *B.D.*, VII, no.593. Bertie to Nicolson, 19 Oct. 1911, Nicolson MSS., F.O.800/351. Cambon, II, pp.355–6. Bertie to Nicolson, 1 Feb. 1912, F.O.371/1406, *private*.
[28] *B.D.*, VII, no.598.
[29] Minute by Grahame on de Bunsen to Grey, 19 Oct. 1911, F.O.146/4229.
[30] Nicolson to Hardinge, 2 NOv. 1911, Nicolson MSS., F.O.800/351. *B.D.*, VII, no.599.

disastrous effect on public opinion here'.[31] Asquith was equally firm. He told Caillaux's representative that the British government could not possibly support any 'hectoring or bullying attitude towards Spain', and when on 1 November Bertie returned to Paris, he did so armed with instructions to speak 'very strongly' on this point to Caillaux and de Selves.[32]

This Bertie did when on 2 November he had an interview with de Selves. The new project, he explained, could hardly recommend itself to the foreign minister since it 'contained elements of danger to the foreign policy of France if the Entente was intended to continue its task of preserving peace whilst protecting the solid interests of France and England'. He therefore advised de Selves to return to the draft which he had proposed in August, and to seek compensation for France in Spain's southern zone. De Selves appeared to be quite amenable to Bertie's arguments. He agreed that without British concurrence the new project must be dropped, and he tried to lay the blame for it upon Regnault and Caillaux. He also went on to complain of his treatment by the latter, and in particular of the way in which Caillaux had resorted to the use of unofficial agents in his dealings with Berlin and London. If it were not for the crisis through which France was passing, he would not, he told Bertie, remain at the foreign ministry.[33]

Bertie was to receive adequate proof of de Selves's declining influence when he met Caillaux, next day, 3 November. Then, despite de Selves's assurances and a promise to prepare Caillaux for his meeting with the ambassador, Bertie found the French premier far from ready to adopt a more conciliatory approach towards Spain. Instead, Caillaux complained of Spain's conduct, claimed that France would be justified in denouncing the Franco-Spanish agreement of 1904, and expressed doubts about the value of southern Morocco and the readiness of the Spaniards to part with it. France, he insisted, must have a railway communication between Tangier and Fez which would be free from Spanish interference. In response, Bertie again appealed to the need to maintain the friendship of Spain, and he pointed to the 'magnificent domain' which France, 'thanks to the support of England', would possess in Morocco. 'Why', he asked Caillaux 'was he bent on offending Spain and public opinion in

---

[31] *B.D.*, VII, nos.605 and 611.
[32] *Ibid*, no.611. Nicolson to Hardinge, 2 Nov. 1911; Nicolson to de Bunsen, 1 Nov. 1911, Nicolson MSS., F.O.800/351.
[33] Bertie to Grey, 2 Nov. 1911, B.P., A, F.O.800/179. There is no copy of this letter in Grey's correspondence, but there is a minute by Grey which evidently belongs with

England by making exaggerated claims?' Caillaux was unmoved. He warned Bertie that if the British government supported Spain in failing to satisfy to France's claims: 'French public opinion would be greatly irritated and there would be a danger of France and England falling out.' When Bertie protested that he did not suppose that the French would be foolish enough to quarrel with England on account of what compensation should be given to France, Caillaux explained that 'it might not be a quarrel but that there would not be the same good-will to England in all parts of the world and on all questions as now'.[34]

As both he and Caillaux were to be guests of Fallières at a shooting party at Rambouillet on 4 November, Bertie had a second opportunity to tackle Caillaux on the subject of the Spanish zones. But Bertie's hopes that a night's reflection would change Caillaux's mind were not to be fulfilled. When on the morning of the 4th the two men met at the railway station before their departure from Paris, Caillaux told Bertie that he had been confirmed in his views. He maintained that representations had been made to him by prominent men of all parties that France must have Larache and El Ksar, and that any change of policy would not be acceptable to the French parliament. In response to Bertie's protest that in view of the 1904 accords he could not fight Spain in order to gain possession of her zone, Caillaux retorted that there were other ways of getting Spain out. This Bertie assumed to mean that France might stir up rebellion against the Spaniards in Morocco and against their government at Madrid: an interpretation which would seem to have been substantiated by remarks which Caillaux was reported to have made to Coudurier de Chasaigne, the London correspondent of *Le Figaro*, to the effect that if Spain did not yield to France's demands, he would foment a revolution that would bring down the Spanish monarchy.[35] Caillaux would have known from the *Sûreté Générale* of the activities of Spanish dissidents on French soil, and both the Quai d'Orsay and the general staff of the army regarded the encouragement of insurrection as one means of dealing with a hostile Spain.[36]

---

it. 'Sir F. Bertie', Grey noted, 'handled the subject very well and effectively as usual.' Minute by Grey, Grey MSS., F.O.800/52. *B.D.*, VII, no.614.

[34] *B.D.*, VII, no.618. 'Was France', Caillaux asked Bertie, 'to submit to having her calves bitten by a wretched little dog such as Spain?' Bertie to Grey, 3 Nov. 1911, B.P., A, F.O.800/179.

[35] Bertie to Grey, 4 Nov. 1911, *ibid.* George Suarez, *Briand. Sa Vie son oeuvre, avec son journal et des nombreuses documents interdits* (6 vols., Paris 1938–52), II, pp.364–5.

[36] See the reports from the *Sûrete Générale* in N.S. Espagne 10. *Attitude probable de l'Espagne en cas de guerre franco-allemande*, departmental note (photocopy of partially destroyed manuscript, undated, but probably drafted in September/October 1911),

Caillaux also reproached Bertie for his constant references to the 1904 accords, which he claimed had been broken by the Spaniards and were not applicable to the changed circumstances. But these, Bertie insisted, were the basis of the position that France occupied in Morocco, and he repeated his warning to Caillaux that the British government could neither support negotiations with Madrid on any other grounds, nor consent to its interests being affected in the way proposed by Regnault. Then, Caillaux observed, 'friendship with England would cost dear to France if her legitimate aspirations were to be opposed by England'. He made light of Bertie's assertion that the French government must have known what France's legitimate aspirations were in 1904, and launched himself into a diatribe on the extent of the sacrifices which France had been compelled to make in the Congo on account of Britain's military weakness. Had 200,000 British troops been available to support France, he would, he claimed, have rejected Germany's demands. 'It was a question', he said, of whether France 'could not have come to more satisfactory terms with Germany without the entente on the Morocco and other questions.' If it had not been for her understanding with England, France, he suggested, 'could long ago have come to terms with Germany'. Nothing could have been more out of keeping with Bertie's assessment of the preceeding crisis than this. And in defence of the *entente* and British policy, he asked Caillaux if 'it might not be something like the mouse making friends with the cat'? He told him that he thought that the safety of France from German attack had been due to Germany's fear of the British fleet, and that if there had been a war 150,000 troops might have been furnished by Britain. These Caillaux thought would have been inadequate, and he claimed that France's coastline could have been defended against German attack by mines and submarines.[37]

No French minister had previously spoken to Bertie about the *entente* in quite so frank a fashion. In two days Caillaux had not only questioned its value, but had also challenged its legal basis, and had seemed ready to risk its future for the sake of French claims upon what once had been promised to Spain. His language, Nicolson observed, was one of the 'strangest admissions' that he had ever heard from a French statesman.[38] Caillaux had, however, appeared to

---

N.S. Espagne 65. P.G. Halpern, *The Mediterranean Naval Situation, 1908–1914* (Cambridge, Mass., 1971), p.285. On Caillaux's threats to stir up a revolution in Spain, see also: Roger de Fleurieu, *Joseph Caillaux au cours d'un demi-siècle de notre histoire* (Paris, 1951), p.127.
[37] Bertie to Grey, 4 Nov. 1911, B.P., A, F.O.800/179.
[38] Nicolson to Goschen, 7 Nov. 1911, Nicolson MSS., F.O.800/351.

soften during his second conversation with Bertie, and when the ambassador asked him whether he thought that it would be to France's advantage if the *entente* ceased to exist, he denied that he had meant that. He explained that he simply thought that 'it was being made to work to the disadvantage of French interests'. Bertie's own belief was that Caillaux, feeling that his own political existence would soon be at stake, wished to make 'great gains' at Spain's expense.[39] The stand taken by Bertie was approved and endorsed by Grey.[40] But from London the situation looked grave, for, as Crowe noted, Caillaux appeared to be not unwilling to contemplate a situation in which the *entente* 'would no longer play any part.[41] Tyrrell suspected that Caillaux, 'like Rouvier', was 'in the hands of la haute finance', who would not rest until the *entente* was 'smashed'.[42] And Grey appeared to have this prospect in mind when on 6 November he wrote to warn Bertie that Britain could 'have nothing to do with a line that...[was]...mean and dishonourable', and had got to 'keep France straight in this matter, or part company with her'.[43]

Bertie was, nevertheless, confident that Caillaux and his colleagues were not united in desiring to effect a drastic revision of the Franco-Spanish agreement. Fallières, whom de Selves had briefed on Bertie's previous representations, told Bertie at Rambouillet that he thought that any discussions with Spain should be based upon the 1904 accords, and he promised to use his influence with the cabinet.[44] Crowe even suggested that Bertie might be advised to approach Delcassé, who as minister of marine ought to carry some weight in the government. Bertie's own inclination seems, however, to have been to leave to de Selves and Fallières the task of persuading Caillaux to drop his support for the 'projet Regnault'. He felt that if Caillaux were denied British assistance at Madrid, he would 'reconsider his position,[45] and he professed to frown upon the efforts of Perez Caballero to influence French politicians and journalists in a sense favourable to Spain. Bertie had in the past made every effort to avoid being drawn into interviews with representatives of the press, and when on 8 November he met Perez Caballero, an 'indiscreet and

[39] Cambon, II, pp.352-4. Bertie to Grey, 4 Nov. 1911, B.P., A, F.O.800/179.
[40] *B.D.*, VII, no.631.
[41] *Ibid*, no.627.
[42] 'Surely', Tyrrell concluded, 'Delcassé won't see his work smashed by a creature like Caillaux! nor Clemenceau'! Tyrrell to Bertie, 6 Nov. 1911, B.P., A, Add. MS. 63027.
[43] Grey added to this warning the qualification: 'I wish of all things to avoid the latter alternative, but we can only do so by carrying the former. This we shall carry.' *B.D.*, VII, no.631.
[44] Bertie to Grey, 4 and 6 Nov. 1911, B.P., A, F.O.800/179.
[45] *B.D.*, VII, no.627.

vain-glorious talker', he delivered to him a homily on the proper conduct of anbassadors. He pointed out that interviews with journalists and with prominent politicians who were not members of the government caused irritation, and in the existing circumstances did no good. Furthermore, he explained.

> If I happened to meet such persons I should not hesitate to express my opinions in conversation if the questions at issue were broached & I thought that I should do good in so doing, but I should not do anything to give cause for suspicion that I was trying to influence persons in Parliament against the views attributed to the French Govt.[46]

This was all very virtuous, but only ten days later Bertie was openly charged by Caillaux with having meddled in French politics behind his back. The occasion for this confrontation was provided by a gala performance at the Paris opera house in honour of the king of Serbia. During the interval, Bertie, along with other members of the diplomatic corps, was due to be presented to the royal visitors. But on his entry into the ante-room of the presidential box, he was hailed by Caillaux, who was standing by the buffet, as 'Monsieur l'Ambassadeur, l'homme terrible'. When Bertie sought an explanation for this address, Caillaux accused him of having waged a campaign against him. He warned Bertie: 'Prenez garde, c'est très dangereux'.[47] These charges were repeated by Caillaux in his memoirs, where he also stated that Bertie had misrepresented their conversations, twisted and exaggerated his language, and banded his words about in Paris, so as to give a false impression of his policy. He confessed that he himself had dealt Bertie 'un ou deux coups de boutoir', but these, he maintained, were in response to the ambassador's continual provocation. Perhaps this was the case. Caillaux later admitted that he felt uneasy in Bertie's presence, and he may well have over-reacted to the protestations of a diplomat who was not noted for his reticence.[48] It is also possible that Bertie may not invariably have sent full accounts to London of what he had said to Caillaux. Yet he had no good reason for wishing to mislead Grey with regard to Caillaux's intentions.

The situation was different in Paris. There Bertie may have hoped to mobilize opposition to the 'projet Regnault' by representing

---

[46] Bertie to Grey, 9 Nov. 1911, B.P., A, F.O.800/179. Perez Caballero was suspected by Caillaux of bribing the Paris press to campaign against the French government's Moroccan policy. Suarez, II, pp.363 – 4.
[47] Bertie to Grey, 19 Nov. 1911, F.O.800/179.
[48] Caillaux, *Mes Mémoires*, II, pp.135 and 192.

Caillaux's support for it as a menace to the *entente*. Thus, although he strenuously denied having intrigued against Caillaux, he admitted to Grey that he had discussed the Morocco question with several French politicians. These included Baron Denys Cochin, a prominent member of the foreign affairs commission of the chamber, whom he met at a shooting party on 15 November, and Cruppi, de Selves, Delcassé, Pichon and Alexandre Ribot, who were all at a presidential dinner on the 16th. Bertie insisted that he had allowed the politicians to seek him out, and that in reply to their questions, he had explained his government's desire that France should respect the treaty rights of Britain and Spain.[49] Nevertheless, Caillaux was to continue to believe otherwise, and he was to recall in his memoirs that as a result of Bertie's activities the rumour had been spread in Paris that he had warned the British ambassador: 'Nous avons les amitiés de réchange'.[50] This claim received some support in the reminiscences of Raymond Poincaré, Caillaux's immediate successor as president of the council. According to information which he attributed to de Selves, Bertie had told the latter that Caillaux had said to him: 'Après tout les alliances et les amitiés sont choses que l'on peut modifier.'[51] But this and other accounts of what Caillaux was supposed to have said to Bertie may simply have resulted from the efforts made by his political opponents to discredit him. De Selves and his staff at the Quai d'Orsay were still smarting over Caillaux's intrusion into the negotiations with the Germans, and the government's determination to press ahead with a programme of fiscal and social reform had alienated some of its former supporters and done nothing to satisfy its critics on the right. They were just as prepared to attack Caillaux for his foreign as for his domestic policy.[52]

Caillaux also displayed a striking lack of caution in his handling of this matter, and he may well have wanted to give the impression that he was taking a strong line with London and Madrid. He thus reverted to an old French refrain in informing one journalist that he had no wish to be 'le gendarme de l'Angleterre en Europe', and he was recorded as having said to Paul Cambon that he did not give a damn about either England or Spain.[53] Charles Benoist, a deputy to

---

[49] Bertie to Grey, 19 Nov. 1911, F.O.800/179.
[50] Caillaux, *Mes Mémoires*, II, pp.192–3.
[51] Raymond Poincaré, *Au service de la France. Neuf années de souvenirs* (10 vols., Paris, 1925–33), I, pp.148–50.
[52] On Caillaux's political position and the domestic opposition to his policies, see: F. Seager, 'Joseph Caillaux as Premier, 1911–1912: the Dilemma of a Liberal Reformer', *French Historical Studies*, XI (1979), 239–57; and Sumler, 'Domestic Influences', 521–3.
[53] Suarez, II, p.363. Gabriel Hanotaux, *Carnets (1907–1925)* (Paris, 1982), p.64.

whom he boasted of how he had treated Bertie, noted that if he had said only half that which he claimed, he would have been fit to lock up there and then.[54] But at the beginning of November Caillaux had probably hoped to capitalize upon what was then widely regarded as a French success in the Agadir crisis in order to rally public support behind his government. There had even seemed to be a possibility that the Belgian and British governments might be prepared to negotiate understandings with France which would allow him to present French cessions to Germany as part of a general rearrangement of colonial possessions in Africa.[55] Only with the publication in *Le Matin* on 8 November of the terms of the 1904 agreement with Spain was it revealed that France was to be denied the Mediterranean coastline of Morocco, and only then did a mood of popular elation turn to one of disappointment and recrimination.[56] It may therefore have suited Caillaux's purpose to emphasize how he was seeking to overcome the opposition of Britain and Spain to the fulfilment of France's ambitions. His opponents likewise seized upon reports of what he had said to Bertie and of his alleged threats to foment a revolution in Spain as evidence of his desire to effect a radical and dangerous change in France's foreign relations. Within two months he was denounced in the French press for having conspired with the Germans, and for having been prepared to forfeit the *entente* with England.[57] This required no 'papotages' from the British embassy, for as Geoffray observed to Bertie on 1 December, Caillaux's strident voice and the locality in which he had made his remonstrance was hardly conducive to secrecy. Some people, Bertie supposed, had 'probably heard very little and reported a good deal and the story had been amplified and used by his [Caillaux's] political opponents to damage him'.[58]

---

[54] Charles Benoist, *Souvenirs* (3 vols, Paris, 1932–1934), III, p.167. Pichon subsequently told Bertie that de Selves had spoken to several people about Bertie's conversation with Caillaux. Bertie to Grey, 8 Dec. 1911, B.P., A, F.O.800/166.
[55] This would seem to have been the purpose of a speech which Caillaux made to his constituents at Saint-Calais on 5 November. *Revue des Deux Mondes*, 15 Nov. 1911, VI, pp.473–4. De Selves to P. Cambon, 19 Sept. 1911, N.S. Grande-Bretagne 24, despt.749. Jacques Willequet, *Le Congo Belge et la Weltpolitik (1894–1914)* (Brussels, 1962), pp.291–3.
[56] Carroll, *French Public Opinion*, pp.248–50.
[57] J-D. Bredin, *Joseph Caillaux* (Paris, 1980), p.104. Allain, *Caillaux*, pp.386–7. *Le Gaulois*, 26 Nov. 1911, p.1; 2 Dec. 1911, p.1. *La République Française*, 6 Dec. 1911, p.1. *Journal des Débats*, 13 Dec. 1911, p.2.
[58] This was also the view of *The Times* correspondent in Paris. Saunders to Wickham Steed, 12 Dec. 1913, Saunders MSS. (*The Times* archives). Bertie to Grey, 2 Dec. 1911, B.P., A, F.O.800/179. Bertie to Grey, 29 Dec. 1911, B.P., A, F.O.800/165.

One such tale was that put about by Ramondou, Fallières's secretary-general, who recalled that he had heard Caillaux tell Bertie at Rambouillet: 'Après tout il faut que l'Entente Cordiale me profite, que j'y trouve mon intérêt; sinon, je me tournera d'un autre côté, je ne suis pas embarrassé.'[59] As Bertie maintained that he had no conversation with Caillaux about Anglo-French relations during the shoot at Rambouillet, this story was probably meant to refer to the words which the two men exchanged at the railway station on 4 November.[60] If this were the case, then the statement attributed by Ramondou to Caillaux, with its explicit threat to abandon the *entente*, went some way beyond that which Bertie had reported to the Foreign Office. Other garbled accounts of Caillaux's disagreement with Bertie eventually found their way across the channel, and on 7 December the *Daily Mail* protested that 'certain remarks' made by Caillaux to the British ambassador at Paris were 'inexcusable on the part of the responsible political chief of a great country', and had given rise to the suspicion that he might be preparing a 'dangerous change in the direction of France's foreign policy'.[61] These suspicions were reinforced by the revelations about Caillaux's unofficial diplomacy which accompanied the passage of the Franco-German treaty through the senate. Clemenceau claimed that Caillaux and his financier friends had all along been seeking an accommodation with Germany,[62] and in January 1912 the *Journal des Débats*, a moderate republican newspaper which had begun to attack the government in October for its progressive social policies, alleged that ever since March Caillaux had been surreptitiously engaged in the pursuit of a Franco-German understanding.[63]

There is in fact little reason to suppose that Caillaux, either as finance minister, or as premier, had wanted to realign France with Germany. His rather tardy support during the spring of 1911 for the merger of French and German railway interests in the Congo had barely met the requirements set by Jules Cambon for a Franco-German *détente*, and his subsequent conduct had been governed by the need to find a satisfactory solution to the Morocco question. Nevertheless, Crowe, who was promoted in January 1912 to the rank

---

[59] Suarex, II, pp.365-6.
[60] Bertie to Grey, 8 and 29 Dec. 1911, B.P., A, F.O.800/166. Allain is almost certainly mistaken in stating that it was after a luncheon at Rambouillet on 3 December that Caillaux said to Bertie: 'Vous savez que si nous ne pouvons pas compter sur vous, nous chercherons d'autres amis et nous n'aurons pas de peine à en trouver.' *Caillaux*, p.386.
[61] *Daily Mail*, 7 Dec. 1911, p.7. *Vanity Fair*, 13 Dec. 1911, p.745; 20 Dec. 1911, p.777.
[62] Bertie to Tyrrell, 1 Jan. 1912, B.P., A, F.O.800/165.
[63] *Journal des Débats*, 12 Jan. 1912, p.1.

of assistant under-secretary, wasted no time in seeking to demonstrate a consistency between the press revelations about Caillaux's past contacts with the Germans and his more recent dealings with Bertie. Caillaux's 'practical avowal' that he did not see any advantage in the *entente* could, Crowe concluded, 'only be explained and justified if France were prepared to enter the orbit of the Triple Alliance'.[64] Others in England who were more concerned with the performance of Grey than that of Caillaux, found in the news from Paris fresh evidence to support their contention that during the Agadir crisis Britain had, as the *Manchester Guardian* declared, been 'more French than the French'.[65] Bertie's much publicized row with Caillaux was not, however, without some advantage from the British point of view. Faced with the opposition of all those who professed to fear for the future of the *entente*, Caillaux modified his stance. At the opera house he had indicated his readiness to retreat from the 'projet Regnault' if the British government could suggest something else, and from a luncheon with Cruppi on 20 November, during which the latter made what in other circumstances would have passed as a routine reference to the value of the *entente*, Bertie gathered the impression that Caillaux, 'thinking that he had indulged in too much fireworks', was using his friend and colleague to tender an olive branch.[66] Caillaux also sought personally to assure Bertie of his goodwill towards England when, eleven days later at a dinner arranged by Cruppi at the *Restaurant Voisin*, he tried in conversation with the ambassador 'to explain away without explaining his past attitude & present policy as regards Spain & the Entente'.[67]

Bertie's handling of Caillaux won him praise from Crowe and Nicolson.[68] His diplomacy may also have been in part responsible for Caillaux's decision to establish an inter-departmental committee under the chairmanship of Regnault to consider alternatives to the latter's project.[69] One of its proposals foresaw the excising from the Spanish sphere of a special railway zone between Tangier and El Ksar, which would be administered by a khalifa and policed by a

---

[64] B.D., VII, pp.821–6.
[65] Auswärtiges Amt, *Belgische Aktenstücke, 1905–1914* (Berlin n.d.), np.87. The *Manchester Guardian*, 12 Jan. 1912, p.6.
[66] Bertie to Grey, 20 Nov. 1911, B.P., A, F.O.800/179. Bertie to Grey, 26 Nov. 1911, B.P., A, F.O.800/160. Bertie to Grey, 20 Nov. 1911, F.O.371/1168, *private*. Bertie to Grey 23 Nov. 1911, Grey MSS., F.O.800/52. B.D., VII, no.716.
[67] Bertie to Grey, 2 Dec. 1911, F.O.800/179. B.D., VII, no.781.
[68] B.D., VII, nos. 685, 686, 692, 693, 703, 705 and 716. Nicolson to Stanfordham, 22 and 29 Nov. 1911, Nicolson MSS., F.O.800/352. Nicolson to Bertie, 7 Dec. 1911, B.P., A, F.O.800/165.
[69] *Textes elaborés par la commission chargé d'étudier le régime politique de la région septentrionale du Maroc*, 27 Nov. 1911, N.S.Maroc 99.

French-commanded force.⁷⁰ Another idea which was *en l'air* was for restricting the Spanish presence on the Atlantic side of their northern zone to the coastal periphery. Both these schemes were evidently intended to meet British objections to France replacing Spain on the Moroccan seaboard. Their effect would, however, have been to remove the Spanish buffer between Tangier and the French sphere which would otherwise have resulted from the application of the 1904 accords. It is possible that de Selves appreciated that this would be unpalatable to the British government. On 20 November he intimated to Bertie that although the British would soon be receiving the latest French proposals, he did not concur in them and would be neither surprised nor disappointed if they were rejected.⁷¹ But during the next few days and with the assistance of Fallières and Delcassé de Selves succeeded in winning his colleagues' support for a fresh approach to Spain. He thus envisaged an arrangement whereby Spain would retain most of her northern zone and Ifni, and France would receive territorial advantages in the Loukkos region of the north and in Spain's southern zone. A high commissioner (khalifa) would be appointed by the sultan to handle relations with the Spanish authorities, Tangier would be internationalized, and the French, in cooperation with the Spaniards, would construct a railway between Tangier and Fez which would be placed under the management of a company with the power 'to take measures for the security of the line'.⁷²

These proposals, the general purport of which were contained in an *avant-projet* which Bertie received on 30 November, appeared to offer a satisfactory basis for negotiations between Paris and Madrid. But the British still found cause to suspect French intentions with regard to the governance of Tangier.⁷³ Grahame returned to this in a memorandum which he drafted for Bertie on 28 November. He pointed out that the sultan was soon to become a French puppet, and that the 'projet Regnault' had provided for the administration of Tangier 'sous le souverainté du Sultan par une municipalité ayant un caractère international', of which the sultan's delegate would of right be president. This, Grahame argued, would leave the door open to a French military intervention, and, he forecasted, the French would

---

⁷⁰ *B.D.*, VII, no.716.
⁷¹ Bertie to Grey, 20 Nov. 1911, B.P., A, F.O.800/179.
⁷² *D.D.F.2*, I, nos. 271, 277 and 287. *B.D.*, VII, no.716. Bertie to Grey, 16 Nov. 1911, B.P., A, F.O.800/160. On the subsequent history of the Tangier–Fez railway see: J-C. Allain, 'La négociation circulaire: le dialogue franco-espagnol sur le trace du chemin de fer de Tanger à Fes', *Revue d'histoire diplomatique* (1984), 289–302.
⁷³ *B.D.*, VII, no.725. Bertie to Grey, 2 Dec. 1911, F.O.800/179. Bertie to Grey, 30 Nov. 1911; Bertie to Nicolson, 1 Dec. 1911; B.P., A, F.O.800/160.

use the vague terminology of the declaration to eventually establish themselves there. Indeed, in a statement which could well have been used to justify the course which the Germans had pursued in the summer, he contended:

> If France be not rigidly bound down by a written text of the clearest nature, it is highly probable that, in the future, we may find it exceedingly difficult to deal with some policy of slow and cautious encroachment on the part of France with respect to Tangier. The French are such past masters in the art of putting forward 'des arguments juridiques' to cover their actions that a power objecting to them has either to give up the attempt to check them or to proceed to some move which brings France up short such as 'le coup d'Agadir'.
> It would be a curious change of roles, if in the future England had to send a warship to a Moroccan port in order to stop proceedings at Tangier of which H.M. Government disapproved.[74]

Some credence was lent to Grahame's predictions both by French meddling in the existing administration of Tangier, and by the importance which the 'inspired' French press appeared to attach to the place.[75] Moreover, an annex to the *avant-projet*, which was communicated to Bertie on 1 December, seemed to demonstrate that the French were determined to have a privileged position there.[76] In consequence, Bertie was instructed on the 11th to reject the terms proposed by the French on the grounds that they did not provide for the 'real internationalisation' of Tangier.[77]

By then it was clear to Bertie that Caillaux's administration was unlikely to last for long. Pichon had said as much, and on 8 December Bertie wrote to Grey that this was the 'general opinion'. He added that the word had 'gone round to declare that Caillaux . . . [was] . . . not mad enough to be locked up, but sufficiently so to be set aside as a public danger in matters political'.[78] For the sake of public appearances, Bertie was still prepared to exchange visits with

---

[74] Memo. by Grahame, 28 Nov. 1911, F.O.146/4229.
[75] Lister to Grey, 26 Nov. 1911, F.O.371/1169, despt.342, and minute by Crowe. Lister to Grey, 27 Nov. 1911, F.O.371/1169, tel.156. Lister to Grey, 27 Nov. 1911, F.O.371/1169, *private*. B.D., VII, no.716.
[76] B.D., VII, no.725. Bertie to Grey, 2 Dec. 1911, B.P., A, F.O. 800/179. Bertie to Grey, 30 Nov. and 2 Dec. 1911, B.P., A, F.O.800/160. Minute by Grahame on draft Franco-Spanish convention, 30 Nov. 1911, B.P., A, F.O.800/160.
[77] Memo. by Crowe, 3 Dec. 1911, F.O.371/1169. B.D., VII, no.753.
[78] Bertie to Grey, 4 Dec. 1911, B.P., A, F.O.800/179. Bertie to Grey, 8 Dec. 1911, B.P., A, F.O.800/165.

him, and on 21 December he assured Caillaux that he had not been in the least offended by his language, and that he had always allowed for differences of temperament between the Latin and Anglo-Saxon races.[79] Nevertheless, rumours about Caillaux's personal diplomacy continued to circulate in Paris, and although the chamber of deputies sanctioned the Franco-German treaty, its submission to the senate allowed nationalists and moderate republicans alike to launch a new assault upon the government. Party manoeuvres and personal rivalries doubtless accounted for a good deal of the criticism to which Caillaux was subjected.[80] 'The opponents of the Ministry', Bertie noted on 31 December, 'seem to be bent on discovering some point which will afford ground for damaging it in the eyes of public opinion.'[81] But it was the handling of the treaty by a senate commission and Clemenceau's probing into the differences between de Selves and Caillaux, which eventually led to the resignation of the former, and, following Caillaux's failure to reconstruct his cabinet, to the government's collapse on 11 January 1912.[82]

Bertie was relieved by this turn of events. He had considered Caillaux to be 'an uncertain and dangerous element', who was all too ready in moments of impetuosity to push aside any obstacles in the way of his designs.[83] For his part, Caillaux was to come to regard Bertie as a hindrance to his regaining the premiership. His suspicions may have been encouraged by Poincaré, who, as president of the republic, claimed in the autumn of 1913 that he could not entrust Caillaux with the formation of a government because of the ill-effects it would have upon relations with England and Spain.[84] Poincaré's decision was, however, also affected by domestic issues, and more especially the stance adopted by Caillaux on the three years army service law.[85] In any event, Bertie had felt able to assure Poincaré in January 1912 that he thought Caillaux had been *au fond* for the *entente*, and he later maintained that his personal relations with him had

---

[79] Bertie to Grey, 29 Dec. 1911, B.P., A, F.O.800/165.
[80] *B.D.*, VII, no.766. Bertie to Grey, 27 Dec. 1911, F.O.371/1170, despt.620. Bertie to Grey, 12 Jan. 1912, F.O.371/1365, despt.28.
[81] Bertie to Grey, 31 Dec. 1911, F.O.371/1402. despt.632.
[82] Seager, 254–7.
[83] Bertie to Nicolson, 18 Jan. 1912, B.P., A, F.O.800/160. Bertie to Grey, 28 Jan. 1912, B.P., A, F.O.800/165.
[84] According to one account Caillaux, shortly after his appointment as minister of finance in December 1913, deliveratly turned his back on Bertie at an Elysée reception. De Fleuriau to de Margerie, 6 Jan. 1914, de Margerie MSS. *G.P.*, XXXIX, no.15664. Bertie to Grey, 10 Dec. 1913; Memos. by Bertie, 20 Nov. 1913 and 23 Feb. 1914; B.P., A, F.O.800/166.
[85] Gerd Krumeich, *Armaments and Politics in France on the Eve of the First World War* (Leamington Spa, 1984), pp.144–6.

'always been good even when his conduct in regard to England and the Entente was foolish and imprudent'.[86] Of Caillaux, Bertie wrote in January 1912: 'He is very able and resourceful but very impulsive and unreliable. A very good minister of finance but a bad Prime Minister. He is very agreeable.'[87] This was Bertie at his most charitable.

Poincaré, who on 14 January 1912 formed a new government with a distinctly more conservative orientation than its predecessor, seemed to Grahame to be a 'very decent sort of man'.[88] He certainly appeared to do all that he could to dissipate the ill-effects of Caillaux's 'wild talk', and Bertie had no difficulty in persuading him to transmit to Grey in writing his assurances of fidelity to the *entente*.[89] But the change of government in France did not augur well for the settlement of Anglo-French differences over Morocco. On 5 January Bertie had written to Grey that a new foreign minister might not be 'so pliable as Selves', and his colleagues might wish to show that they were more careful of France's interests.[90] There was also the danger, which Bertie was unable to neglect, that a change of government would allow the permanent officials of the Quai d'Orsay to reassert their influence. This seemed all the more likely when Poincaré, who had no previous experience of foreign affairs, decided to act both as president of the council and as foreign minister. As Geoffray pointed out to Bertie on 26 January, Poincaré would have too much to do to be able to go into questions relating to foreign affairs in any detail.[91] Besides which, Bertie doubted the trustworthiness of Paléologue[92], whom Poincaré appointed to replace Bapst, and the continued presence of Regnault in Paris hardly appeared conducive to an early arrangement with Spain. Grahame rightly feared that Regnault would be all for 'bullying' Spain, and for leaving the door open for future harassment in her zone and encroachments in Tangier. 'A French Cabinet', Grahame warned Tyrrell, 'is such a feeble thing when permanent officials in league with the "colonials" are secretly against its policy.'[93]

---

[86] Bertie to Grey, 22 Jan. 1912, B.P., A, F.O.800/165.
[87] Bertie to Kitchener, 12 Feb. 1912, B.P., B, F.O.800/187.
[88] Grahame to Tyrrell, 23 Jan. 1912, Grey MSS., F.O.800/53.
[89] Bertie to Grey, 22 Jan. 1912; Bertie to Nicolson, 1 Feb. 1912; B.P., A, F.O.800/165. Nicolson to Grey, 15 Jan. 1912, tel., Grey MSS., F.O.800/94. Grey replied to Poincaré's assurances with a private letter. Poincaré I, pp.151–2.
[90] Bertie to Grey, 5 Jan. 1912, B.P., A, F.O.800/179.
[91] Bertie to Nicolson, 18 Jan. 1912, B.P., A., F.O.800/160. Bertie to Nicolson 26 Jan. 1912, B.P., A, F.O.800/265.
[92] Bertie to Grey, 26 Jan. 1912, F.O.371/1366, despt.57.
[93] Grahame to Tyrrell, 23 Jan. 1912, Grey MSS., F.O.800/53.

Bertie shared Grahame's concern, and without instructions from Grey he tried to explain to Poincaré on 31 January the dangers involved in Regnault attempting to regain lost ground. Yet, despite assurances from Poincaré that he was 'sincerely anxious to avoid hurting Spanish susceptibilities' and that he accepted 'in principle' the internationalization of Tangier,[94] he was prepared to make new and extensive territorial demands upon the Spaniards. Indeed, it was not until November 1912, and then only after Spain had conceded to France the whole of the fertile valley of the Ouergha, that a Franco-Spanish convention was completed.[95] Where Tangier was concerned progress towards an agreement was even slower, and by the end of the summer of 1912 the British and French governments were at odds on all the important points relating to the establishment of an international municipality. An attempt by Crowe, who had already decided that the French were behaving in Morocco 'as badly as ever the Germans did', [95] to overcome this *impasse* by using Bertie's supposed influence with Poincaré proved of no avail. Poincaré was intent upon securing the presidency of the republic, and on 6 January 1913 Bertie warned Nicolson that he did not think any negotiations with the Quai d'Orsay would succeed if it meant the French having to give way.[97] Only in November 1913 were the British and French governments able to reach a tentative agreement on Tangier, and they had then to await the adherence of Spain. As a result no final agreement was reached by the outbreak of the first world war, and it was December 1923 before a convention on Tangier was formally concluded.[98]

Throughout these negotiations the British government persisted in declining to give formal recognition to the French protectorate in Morocco until its requirements for the internationalization of Tangier were met. The French in their turn protested that all that they wished to establish was a viable administration, and they complained over what appeared to be Britain's obstructive tactics. Paul Cambon did not believe that France was wholly blameless in this situation. 'Nous avons', he confessed in July 1914, 'essayé de ruser et de nous constituer une situation privilegiée à Tanger.' It was not in

---

[94] Bertie to Nicolson, 1 Feb. 912, B.P., A, F.O.800/165.
[95] De Bunsen to Grey, 27 Nov. 1912, F.O.371/1400, tel.114.
[96] Minute by Crowe on Rennie to Grey, 17 Sept. 1912, F.O.371/1410, tel.93.
[97] Nicolson to Bertie, 26 Sept. 1912; Grey to Bertie, 18 Nov. 1912; Crowe to Bertie, 18 Nov. 1912; B.P., A, F.O.800/160. Bertie to Nicolson, 6 Jan. 1913, and minute by Crowe, Nicolson MSS., F.O.800/363.
[98] Note for the president of the council, 16 April 1914, N.S. Grande-Bretagne 22. G.H. Stuart, *The International City of Tangier* (2nd edition, Stanford, 1955), pp.59–90. *Documents on British Foreign Policy*, 1919–1939, series 1A, I, pp.851–3.

his opinion the least of the follies that France had committed in the Moroccan affair.[99] Nicolson had, however, felt able in April 1912 to describe the Anglo-French differences over Morocco as 'more or less minor matters'.[100] This was a fair judgement for after Caillaux's abandonment of the 'projet Regnault', the future of Morocco could hardly be regarded as an issue which was likely to threaten the existence of the *entente*. Yet there was some irony in the fact that a mutual agreement over the fate of the Shereefian empire had been one of the principal components of the Anglo-French understanding on 8 April 1904. Moreover, during a period when Anglo-French relations were to be blighted by the persistence of what were essentially colonial disputes, Grey was to find it easier to cooperate with the Germans on just such issues. During 1912 Grey and his colleagues endeavoured to better their relations with Germany, and it was this, rather than Britain's failure to reach an accommodation with France on matters imperial, which was to give Bertie the most cause for concern.

---

[99] *D.D.F.3*, X, no.528.
[100] Nicolson to Hardinge, 18 April 1912, Nicolson MSS., F.O.800/355.

11

The clarification of the entente

Relations between Britain and France may have been marred during the autumn of 1911 by their squabbling over Morocco. Yet the Agadir crisis also gave a fresh impetus to the Anglo-French staff talks and prompted Britain's defence chiefs to reexamine their war plans and future strategy. One result of their considerations was a victory for those senior army officers who favoured British military intervention on the continent, in the event of a war with Germany, over their colleagues in the Admiralty who preferred to rely upon a naval blockade and coastal raids.[1] Another consequence was that the military conversations with the French were for the first time brought before the whole cabinet. And, under pressure from the radicals within the government, Grey, Asquith and Haldane had eventually to agree to a formula which stated that no staff talks could commit Britain to military or naval intervention, and that such communications, if they related 'to concerted action by land or sea, should not be entered into without the previous approval of the Cabinet'.[2] During that autumn the foreign secretary also had to reckon with considerable criticism from those amongst his fellow Liberals who believed that Britain had adopted an unduly provocative stance towards Germany during the recent crisis.[3] It was partly to satisfy these critics, and partly because he seems genuinely to have desired to overcome those difficulties separating Britain from Germany, that

---

[1] Willamson, pp.167-204. D'Ombrain, pp.100-7. M. Howard, *The Continental Commitment. The Dilemma of British Defence Policy in the Era of Two World Wars* (London, 1972), pp.45-6. On the implications of the Anglo-French staff talks and British military planning for Britain's strategic position see: K.M. Wilson, 'To the western front: British war plans and the "military entente" with France before the first world war'. *British Journal of International Studies*, III,(1977), 151-68.
[2] R. Jenkins, *Asquith. Portrait of a Man and an Era* (London, 1964), pp.242-4.
[3] Robbins, pp.344-357. H.S. Weinroth, 'The British Radicals and the Balance of Power, 1902-1914', *Historical Journal*, XIII(1970), 677. J.A. Murray, 'Foreign Policy Debated. Sir Edward Grey and his critics, 1911-1912', in L.P. Wallace and W.C. Askew (eds.), *Power, Public Opinion and Diplomacy. Essays in Honor of Eber Malcolm Carroll by his Former Students* (Durham, N.C., 1959), pp.140-71.

Grey attempted once more to place Anglo-German relations on a 'less unfavourable basis'.[4]

That a fresh British approach to Berlin was likely to receive a favourable reception in Germany must already have been evident to Bertie from a conversation which he had with von Stumm in mid-December. The latter, who had spent the best part of six weeks at Paris, used a farewell visit to the British embassy to discuss with Bertie the poor state of Anglo-German relations. He spoke of the desirability of a naval arrangement and suggested that Britain might care to make some concession to Germany in the colonial sphere. 'Could not', he asked, 'some prominent public man visit Berlin and talk with the German Government so as to bring about some arrangement?' But Bertie had little sympathy for what he, perhaps correctly, regarded as an attempt by the German emperor to elicit from Grey a proposal which the Germans might accept or reject at their convenience. He certainly did not think that the ill-will felt in Germany towards Britain should cause Grey to take any new initiative. 'We could', he told von Stumm, 'at present remain indifferent to the unreasonable feeling against us for we considered ourselves safe from German invasion.' If the Germans were determined to contest the supremacy of the seas with England, they would, he claimed, have to continue to reckon with unsatisfactory relations with her.[5] When, therefore, Bertie learned from London that Grey was prepared to consider both an Anglo-German naval agreement and an early partition of the Portuguese colonies, he was anything but pleased. On 12 January, at a time when he still felt able to rejoice that Grey had not been 'tempted by Metternich's satanic invitation' to look down upon the Portuguese colonies as a means of 'satisfying German land hunger', he addressed to the foreign secretary a long homily on the evils of German imperialism in Africa. Any attempt to facilitate the German aquisition of territories which were not British would, he considered, be attributed by Germany to fear and a desire to keep her away from Britain's own possessions.[6] Grey had, however, already told Metternich in December that the British government did not intend to prevent German territories from extending from east to west, across Africa. Indeed, only the existence of the Anglo-Portuguese alliance, which Salisbury had

---

[4] Grey to Roosevelt, 25 Dec. 1911, Grey MSS., F.O.800/110. Nicolson to Hardinge, 1 Feb. 1912, Nicolson MSS., F.O.800/353. A.J.A. Morris, *Radicalism against War 1906–1914* (London, 1972), pp.303–13.
[5] *B.D.*, X, pt.2, no.265.
[6] *Ibid*, no.268.

reaffirmed in October 1899, seems to have restrained Grey from advocating the dismemberment of Portugal's empire.[7]

Bertie was as ever opposed to any arrangement that might lead to an extension of Germany's colonial possessions in Africa. Besides which, he was attached to the ancient treaties with Portugal, and he could see no gain in alienating a power whose ports might one day be useful to Britain in a naval war. Similarly, he also feared that an agreement with Germany over the future of the Belgian Congo would simply have the effect of driving Belgium into friendship with the German 'mammon of unrighteousness', and adversely affect Britain's relations with France.[8] To Tyrrell he wrote on 26 January that he was against giving anything to Germany 'unless in return not for words or even so-called deeds, but for solid territorial advantage to England'.[9] Britain, he cautioned von Stumm on 11 February, had 'no spare Heligolands which the British government would be prepared to present to Germany as gifts', and she 'could not give away the goods of others'.[10] Such arguments seem not to have impressed Grey. Anglo-German discussions on the revision of the 1898 agreement on Portugal's colonies, which had commenced in the autumn of 1911, continued, and led eventually to the initialling of a new convention in October 1913.[11] Moreover, following further indications that the Germans would welcome a visit from a senior British politician, Haldane was despatched to Berlin on 7 February, ostensibly with a view to dealing with the 'business of a University Committee', but primarily with the object of engaging in a 'very frank exchange of views about naval expenditure and other things'.[12]

The government's wish to satisfy what Tyrrell termed 'a curious hankering . . . to "talk" to Germany' came in for a good deal of criticism from Grey's senior advisers.[13] Angered by the Haldane mission, Nicolson was led on 8 February to 'discharge his soul' to Bertie. He could see no reason why Britain should abandon the 'excellent position' which she had obtained, and he feared the effects that the initiative might have upon relations with France and

---

[7] *Ibid*, nos.266 and 267. The origins of the Anglo-German negotiations on the Portuguese colonies are examined in R.T.B. Langhorne, 'Anglo-German Negotiations concerning the future of the Portuguese Colonies, 1911 – 1914', *Historical Journal*, XVI(1973), 361 – 87. See also: J.D. Vincent-Smith, 'Anglo-German Negotiations over the Portuguese Colonies in Africa, 1911-1914', *Historical Journal*, XVII(1974), 620 – 9.
[8] *B.D.*, X, pt.2, no.268.
[9] Bertie to Tyrrell, 26 Jan. 1912, B.P., B, F.O.800/187.
[10] *B.D.*, VI, no.508.
[11] Langhorne, 'Portuguese Colonies'.
[12] *B.D.*, VI, no.499. S.E. Koss, *Lord Haldane, Scapegoat for Liberalism* (London, 1969), pp.71 – 81.
[13] Tyrrell to Bertie, 5 Feb. 1912, B.P. (British Library).

THE CLARIFICATION OF THE ENTENTE

Russia.[14] Bertie was similarly pessimistic about the visit. It was no more, he thought, than a 'foolish move intended . . . to satisfy the Grey-must-go radicals'. The Germans, he believed, would not be prepared to abandon their naval programme, and could not anyway be trusted to respect the spirit of an undertaking to Britain. The 'more dignified course' remained for Bertie that which he had recommended so many times before, that Britain should go on 'in increasing ratio to construct against the German building programme'.[15] And while he did not think that Poincaré and those of his ministry who were in his confidence would doubt Britain's good intentions, he was of the opinion that suspicion would be created amongst many prominent political people in France. Following a now familiar pattern, he warned Grey on 16 February that the French press and public were very suspicious about the results of the Haldane mission, and if Britain made concessions to Germany for practically no reason at all, it would be surmised that there was some secret agreement to Britain's advantage.[16] Grey really had no need for such reminders, for he had no intention of sacrificing the well-being of the *entente* for the sake of improved relations with Germany. He was quite prepared to assure the Germans that Britain did not intend to support an aggressive policy towards them, but he was insistent that the government must keep its hands free to maintain its existing relationship with France. At the same time he tried to reassure the French of England's loyalty to the *entente*, and of the government's readiness to keep them *au courant* of the discussions with Berlin.[17] Indeed, Paul Cambon seems to have been less worried by Grey's attitude towards Germany, than by the possibility of criticism of British policies in the French parliament having an ill-effect upon opinion in Britain.[18]

Like Bertie, Paul Cambon thought that the interests of Britain and Germany were too opposed to permit an agreement between them.[19] In a sense the two diplomats were right for Haldane's conversations in Berlin did not result in any definite arrangement. Both sides did, however, have the chance to explore the grounds for some kind of understanding.[20] Thus, although the publication on the eve of Haldane's visit of a new German navy bill appeared to leave little

---

[14] Nicolson to Bertie, 8 Feb. 1912, B.P., A, F.O.800/272.
[15] *B.D.*, VI, no.509.
[16] Memo. by Bertie, 16 Feb. 1912, B.P., A, F.O.800/171.
[17] *B.D.*, VI, nos. 498 and 499. *D.D.F.3*, I, no.628.
[18] *D.D.F.3*, I, no.629.
[19] *Ibid*.
[20] Sommers, pp.253–68.

scope for the achievement of a binding accord on the limitation of naval expenditure, there did emerge the prospect of an agreement affecting British and German imperial and extra-European interests, and the possibility of an exchange of political assurances on future policies. As the basis for a general imperial settlement the Germans suggested that Britain might cede to them Zanzibar and Pemba, and her reversionary claims on the strip of territory accorded to her in Angola by the 1898 agreement. Germany could then cede to Britain her right to participate on equal terms with other powers in any railway concession that might be acquired between Baghdad and the Persian gulf, and renounce her reversionary claims upon the Portuguese portion of the island of Timor. It was also proposed that in Persia Britain might promise to Germany a share in any railway concession she might obtain there in return for German diplomatic support in the gulf. But of more significance to those who hoped for the achievement of a genuine Anglo-German *rapprochement* was Bethmann Hollweg's suggestion that the two governments should pledge themselves to 'benevolent neutrality' in the event of either being involved in a war.[21]

After learning from Grey of such progress as had been made as a result of Haldane's visit, Bertie left Paris for London. There he found the government to be in a 'hesitating state'. He thought Churchill, who in October had succeeded Reginald McKenna at the Admiralty, was 'against tying our hands'; Lord Loreburn, the lord chancellor, Lewis Harcourt, the colonial secretary, and 'some others' favoured an Anglo-German agreement; and Grey was 'wavering'. For his own part Bertie could see nothing to his liking in Bethmann Hollweg's proposals for a colonial understanding as described to him by Nicolson on 16 February. When he saw Grey on that same day he protested that it would be a 'gratuitous sacrifice to *give* Germany Zanzibar and Pemba', especially as the Germans had failed to respect their previous undertakings on the sultanate. He likewise opposed the cession of Britain's reversionary claims in Angola for, as he explained, it had been intended to use the strip of territory concerned to link Rhodesia to the Atlantic. On the other hand, he considered worthless German offers to surrender their reversionary claims on Timor, and to hand over their rights on the projected Baghdad to Basra railway. The Dutch government had already made clear that it possessed preemptive rights to Portuguese Timor, and the Porte, Bertie pointed out to Grey, would have to consent to any transfer of Germany's rights in Mesopotamia. Bertie also impressed upon Lloyd

---

[21] *B.D.*, VI, nos.506 and 510.

George, whom he met at the Commons on 19 February, that while a cession of territory to Germany would be permanent, an arrangement on naval armaments might prove to be purely temporary. They had better, Bertie argued, confine themselves to seeking 'a formula of mutual assurances of good intentions'.²²

The trouble was, as Bertie knew full well, the pursuit of such a formula could complicate Britain's relations with France. Bertie was thus particularly anxious to dissuade Grey and his cabinet colleagues from saying anything to the Germans that might harm the *entente* or inhibit Britain from assisting the French in the event of a European war. There was little likelihood of the British government committing itself to the sort of benevolent neutrality that Bethmann Hollweg had suggested. But on 13 February Grey had told Paul Cambon that he was willing to assure the Germans that there was not in Britain's understandings with France and Russia 'any preparation to be aggressive towards Germany or to make an unprovoked attack upon her'. The difficulty, as Grey explained, was to find a formula that would express the British attitude correctly and reassure Germany, but still leave Britain free to go to the aid of France if she should be the victim of German aggression.²³ In Bertie's estimation Grey had little room for manoeuvre. He warned the foreign secretary on the 16th, that 'if we signed a formula binding ourselves not to join any combination to attack Germany we might tie our hands very inconveniently as regards France'. German military preparations might, Bertie speculated, lead the French to expect an imminent attack, and they might then try to secure a tactical advantage by taking the offensive and invading Germany. Such an advance would, he thought, 'with the French temperament . . . be of the highest importance as if a victory were gained by them it would infuse a spirit into the French troops which would count for much in a campaign'. In that event, Bertie wondered who would be regarded as the aggressor, and, evidently with the prospect of a divided cabinet in mind, he questioned what Britain's position would be if she had promised not to assist in an unprovoked attack upon Germany. A Franco-German quarrel, he reasoned, might be caused by Germany, who would be the aggressor even if she did not strike the first blow. To Lloyd George he offered a simpler illustration. 'If', he said, 'A spat in B's face and the latter knocked down the former the real aggressor would be A'.²⁴

---

²² Memos. by Bertie, 16 and 19 Feb. 1912, B.P., A, F.O.800/181.
²³ *B.D.*, VI, no.514. *D.D.F.3*, II, no.30.
²⁴ Memos. by Bertie, 16 and 19 Feb. 1912, B.P., A, F.O.800/181.

It would nontheless be wrong to suppose that Bertie was wholly opposed to any political arrangement with Germany. He would have been happier if the government had not embarked on the quest for one, but by mid-February he appears to have concluded that circumstances required some kind of Anglo-German accord. In response to a query from Lloyd George, he said that although it was 'chiefly the noisy section of the radicals who urged it', he thought that 'a formula of some kind had become necessary, but it should be of very general and anodyne character'. It had, he considered, better be carefully worded because the Germans could not be trusted for any longer than it suited their intentions. The French, he admitted, were 'equally slippery', but, he maintained, the essential difference between the Germans and the French was that while the latter's interests were not the same as Britain's, those of the former were in opposition to them.[25] 'No Foreign Govt.', he told the king, '— the French not excepted — adhered as we do to the spirit as well as the letter of agreements when they work out injuriously to them or contrary to their expectations and that might be the case in regard to any agreement with Germany.'[26]

All Bertie's campaigning in London and his warnings of the dangers inherent in unwisely worded pledges did nothing to discourage the search for a political and naval accommodation with Germany. Indeed, the formula which Grey offered to Metternich on 14 March as the basis for a mutual exchange of assurances seemed to flout the advice that Bertie had so recently offered. Grey thus proposed that England might declare that she would make no unprovoked attack upon Germany and pursue no aggressive policy towards her.[27] This, Bertie anticipated, would tie Britain's hands and diminish her value to France. In a letter to Nicolson of 28 March he repeated the arguments which he had previously put to Grey and Lloyd George, and he insisted that to be effective British aid must be immediate and not hindered by any non-aggression agreement with Germany. If it arrived too late, France's ill-fate would, he reasoned, be Britain's later on.[28] Yet even after Metternich had rejected the latest British formula, Grey still felt able to tell the German ambassador that the government would be glad to have an explanation of what the Germans desired.[29] To Bertie this meant that

[25] *Ibid.*
[26] Memo. by Bertie, 17 Feb. 1912, B.P., A, F.O.800/187.
[27] *B.D.*, VI, no.537.
[28] *Ibid.* no.556.
[29] *Ibid.* no.557.

the British government was prepared to consider a more comprehensive formula which might mean loosening Britain's ties with France. It would, he considered, be a high price to pay for the temporary advantage of perhaps restricting for a short period the construction of German warships. Besides which, if, as he believed unlikely, France and Russia were to launch an unprovoked attack upon Germany, he still thought it important that Britain should be at liberty to decide whether or not it was in her interests to participate. Bertie wrote to Nicolson on 1 April that the 'crushing of France would be a great danger to England and it would be detrimental to our interests to have our hands tied by a neutrality promise'.[30]

Equally disturbing to Bertie was the acquiescence of the French government in the continuing Anglo-German dialogue. Paul Cambon had remained confident that nothing would come of the exercise, and neither he nor Poincaré appear to have fully understood the direction in which the discussions were moving. As a result of Cambon's reporting Poincaré was left under the impression that all that Grey was contemplating was the offer of a verbal assurance to the German ambassador.[31] Moreover, although Grey informed Cambon on 22 March of the German rejection of his formula and of the difficulties which stood in the way of a British offer of conditional neutrality, he did not explain to the French ambassador that the cabinet had yet to consider a German request for what would amount to a promise of absolute neutrality. After his conversation with Grey Cambon thus felt sufficiently assured to signal to Poincaré: 'ainsi s'évanouissent les espérances ou les craintes que les esprits peu avertis avaient fondées sur la visite de Lord Haldane à Berlin'.[32] Bertie had in the meantime learnt from Grey that Cambon had 'seemed satisfied' with the latest British formula.[33] This Bertie doubted, although he conceded to Nicolson that the French ambassador would have been pleased at 'the German Government having knocked it on the head'.[34] Under the impression that Grey, whose policies he claimed no longer to understand, needed strengthening against his cabinet colleagues, he attempted to exert pressure on his government through Poincaré. The course which he adopted was of doubtful propriety. Nevertheless, on 27 March he approached Poincaré 'comme s'il n'était pas ambassadeur', and expressed his surprise at

---

[30] *Ibid.* no.563.
[31] Cambon, III, 10–15. *D.D.F.3*, II, nos.205 and 206. F. Stieve (ed.) *Der diplomatische Schriftwechsel Iswolskis, 1911–1914* (4 vols., Berlin, 1924–26), II, no.214.
[32] *B.D.*, VI, nos.550 and 552. *D.D.F.3*, II, no.244.
[33] *B.D.*, VI, nos.540 and 558.
[34] *Ibid*, no.556.

Cambon's reaction to Grey's explanations. The proposed declaration, he warned Poincaré, had been put aside for the moment, but not definitely abandoned. And Grey, he contended, was very much weakened and surrounded by supporters of an Anglo-German *rapprochement*. He explained the dangers which he feared might result from Britain agreeing to remain neutral in the event of an attack upon Germany, and he emphasized the need to prevent an accord on such a basis. 'Il est indispensible', he insisted, 'que Cambon n'ait pas l'air satisfait.' Finally, he urged Poincaré that if he were to speak with a little firmness at London, 'on hésitera à commettre la faute que je redoute'.[35]

Acting on this advice Poincaré next day told Cambon of the substance of Bertie's premonitions. It was essential, he informed him, that Britain should not engage herself to remain neutral in the event of a French attack upon Germany. A British declaration of neutrality would, he thought, only incite Germany to renew towards France 'sa tactique traditionelle de provocation'.[36] Nevertheless, since Poincaré confined his objections to the possibility of a British promise of neutrality, when on 29 March Cambon raised the subject with Grey, the latter was able simply to explain that the cabinet had already rejected the idea of an accord on conditional neutrality, and that it would therefore be difficult for them to accept the latest German request.[37] On the 30th Poincaré tried to make it clear to Cambon that what Bertie was preoccupied with was Grey's non-aggression formula.[38] But by then Cambon was on the point of leaving London for Paris where he was able to meet both Bertie and Poincaré. Bertie had evidently succeeded in rejuvenating latent French fears about the future of the *entente* for much of a long letter which Cambon wrote on 3 April to Aimé de Fleuriau, his *chargé d'affaires* in London, seemed to reflect the British ambassador's thinking. Grey's formula, it stated, was ambiguous and might delay British aid to France in the event of a Franco-German war as it would allow the Germanophile members of Asquith's cabinet to equivocate on whether or not Germany's actions could be considered provocative. Cambon suspected that the Germans might seek some modifications in Grey's formula so as to paralyze Britain's actions, and an Anglo-German agreement could, he thought, be used by the opponents of the *entente* in France to create a bad impression on public opinion.[39]

[35] *D.D.F.3*, II, no.266. Poincaré, *Au service*, I, pp.170–1.
[36] *D.D.F.3*, II, no.269.
[37] *B.D.*, VI, no.559.
[38] *D.D.F.3*, II, no.276.
[39] *Ibid*, no.295.

This last theme was taken up again by Bertie. He warned Grey in a despatch of 3 April that if his non-aggression formula became known in France, 'it would be a disagreeable surprise to the French public', and that there were always those who would seek to take advantage of the present situation to point out that England could not be relied upon. Nicolson, who received a copy of Cambon's letter to de Fleuriau on 4 April, believed that Britain was rapidly arriving at a 'very critical moment' in her relations with France. It would, he cautioned Grey, be disastrous if for the sake of the formula Britain were to risk alienating France and consequently Russia. Yet neither this, nor the appeals of Bertie and Cambon, had any real impact upon Grey's diplomacy. On Bertie's despatch of 3 April Grey minuted: 'Russia and France both deal separately with Germany and . . . it is not reasonable that tension should be permanently greater between England and Germany than between Germany and France, or Germany and Russia.' He saw no validity in Bertie's argument that Britain's freedom of action would be impeded by a promise to Germany not to engage in any unprovoked attack upon her, and he showed no intention of abandoning the talks with Germany.[40] If Germany 'attacked and forced war upon an ally or friend' of Britain, it would, he reasoned, be regarded as provocation by the British government.[41] Thus frustrated, Bertie turned once more to Poincaré and urged him to speak with energy at London, and to arm Grey against his colleagues so that he could demonstrate that it was not worth the risk of compromising the *entente* for the sake of an agreement with Germany.[42] Poincaré was ready to oblige. On 11 April he informed Cambon that he might tell Grey that a declaration such as he proposed would be interpreted in France as the voluntary abandonment of the policy that Britain had pursued since 1904. The *entente*, he observed, was not consecrated by any diplomatic act, and rested solely on the military conversations between the two general staffs. 'Tout qui déconcerterait le sentiment', he concluded, 'serait donc de nature à la detruire.'[43]

Paul Cambon had no need of Poincaré's instructions for on 10 April Metternich informed Gray that in view of the insufficiency of the British formula, Bethmann Hollweg intended to proceed with

---

[40] B.D., VI, nos.564, 566, and 567. Nicolson to Bertie, 6 April 1912, B.P., A, F.O.800/171.
[41] B.D., VI, no.569.
[42] *Ibid*, no.570. D.D.F.3, II, no.318.
[43] D.D.F.3, II, no.329.

Germany's projected naval programme.[44] This news reached Bertie on the Côte d'Azur, where he had gone to participate in the celebrations connected with the unveiling of statues at Nice and Cannes of Queen Victoria and King Edward VII. The occasion obliged Bertie, who was not much given to public speaking, to join Poincaré in eulogizing on the reigns of the dead monarchs, praising the goodly state of Anglo-French relations, and reenacting with due solemnity the rites of the *entente cordiale*.[45] In spite of the efforts of the Liberal government to better Anglo-German relations, Britain remained untrammeled by legal technicalities, and free to choose the course she would adopt if there were to be a war between the continental powers. Yet the failure of the British and German governments to achieve an accommodation was due neither to Bertie's protestations, nor to his subterfuge in Paris, but rather to the insufficiency of what either party felt able to offer to the other. Much to Bertie's distaste, the two powers were to continue to pursue colonial accords. Moreover, the French remained uneasy about what was passing between London and Berlin. After learning that Asquith had told the Commons on 30 April that relations between Britain and Germany were such that they could discuss their mutual interests frankly and amicably, Paul Cambon professed to Grey anxiety lest an agreement of a far reaching character had been concluded.[46] It seemed to Bertie that the French were like 'stags on the hill'. 'They are', he observed, 'more frightened of the danger that they wind, than of the danger they see clearly.' If Cambon could believe that Britain had signed something with Germany, what, Bertie asked Mallet, could be thought by the French who knew the British and their methods less?[47]

Amongst Grey's officials there remained a lingering feeling that the Germans would sooner or later return to the subject of a political formula with a view to separating Britain from France. This was reinforced by the news that the Wilhelmstrasse intended to transfer the Baron Marschall von Bieberstein, Germany's ambassador at

---

[44] *B.D.*, VI, no.573. Anglo-German relations and naval rivalry in this period are treated in more detail in R.T.B. Langhorne, 'The Naval Question in Anglo-German Relations, 1912 – 1914', *Historical Journal*, XIV(1971), 359 – 70.

[45] *B.D.*, VI, no.378. Poincaré, *Au service*, I, pp.190 – 205. There was a touch of irony in Bertie's presence at these celebrations for when the idea of erecting a statue of Queen Victoria was proposed by *Le Petit Niçoise* in 1908 Bertie had opposed it on the grounds that 'in the event of ill-feeling between the two countries [Britain and France], a statue of the sort proposed would be liable to disfigurement and exposed to insult'. Bertie to Grey, 21 Nov. 1908, F.O.371/456. despt.471.

[46] *B.D.*, VI, no.582.

[47] Bertie to Mallet, 12 May 1912, B.P., A, F.O.800/171.

Constantinople, to London as Metternich's successor. Nicolson feared that the appointment of this experienced and skilful diplomat would not find 'a very sturdy and united resistance on the part of the Cabinet'.[48] The choice of Marschall, Mallet thought, was an indication of the importance which the Germans attached to breaking up the *entente*, and on 10 May he asked Bertie to write to Grey to deprecate any further discussion of an Anglo-German understanding. While he believed Grey would stand firm on the subject of formulae, he told Bertie that he thought the foreign secretary would require 'constant reminders'.[49] Rather than appeal directly to Grey, Bertie decided to revert to the tactic that he had used in March and April. He thought it better, he observed to Mallet, that objections should come through him rather than from him.[50] Thus after a conversation with Poincaré on 15 May, Bertie transmitted to Grey a textual account of what he asserted were the foreign minister's fears about a renewed German attempt to obtain an agreement with Britain.[51] This, however, does not seem to have impressed Grey.[52] There was no indication, he told Cambon, that Marschall's arrival was intended to inaugurate any new departure in German policy, and he rejected Nicolson's proposal that he should assure Poincaré that 'all questions of any political formulas had been definitely and finally abandoned'. Instead, he instructed Bertie to tell the foreign minister that the British government 'were determined . . . not to adopt any line of policy which would in any way impair the intimate and friendly relations which they desire to maintain with France'. They had, he affirmed, 'no intention of entering into any political engagement with Germany which would have this effect'.[53]

Whilst Bertie had been trying to ensure that the British government remained free to choose when and whether it would assist France in a Franco-German war, developments elsewhere had helped to increase tension between the European powers he Agadir crisis had

---

[48] *D.D.F.3*, II, no.232. Nicolson to O'Beirne, 8 May 1912; Nicolson to Lowther, 13 May 1912; Nicolson MSS., F.O.800/355. Chirol to Hardinge, 7 June 1912, Hardinge MSS., 92.
[49] Mallet to Bertie, 10 May 1912, B.P., A, F.O.800/171. Mallet wrote of Marschall: 'He is the ablest and most unscrupulous of foreign diplomatists and is a statesman of the first order . . . he is being sent to make a final assault of the citadel'. Mallet to Short, 6 May 1912, Balfour MSS., Add. MS. 49747.
[50] Bertie to Mallet, 12 May 1912, B.P., A, F.O.800/171.
[51] *B.D.*, VI, no.s585 and 586. Bertie to Nicolson, 16 May 1912, B.P., A, F.O.800/171.
[52] *B.D.*, VI, no.587.
[53] *Ibid*, nos.588 and 589. Nicolson to Bertie, 23 May 1912, B.P., A, F.O.800/171. Nicolson to Hardinge, 3 June 1912, Nicolson MSS., F.O.800/357.

provided the Italians with a favourable moment to further their ambitions in the Mediterranean, and in late September they had embarked upon a war of conquest against the Turks in Tripoli. In the course of the ensuing hostilities Italy's forces occupied the Dodecanese islands, and through their arrest of two French steamers in January 1912 provoked a Franco-Italian confrontation.[54] The war also threatened to lead to renewed troubles in the Balkans, where the smaller states of the peninsula seemed set to exploit Turkey's embarrassment to their own advantage. Other great powers might then become involved in a Near Eastern crisis.[55] With such consequences in view Poincaré spoke to Bertie on 3 February of the need to be alert and prepared for possible complications. Poincaré subsequently interpreted Bertie's agreement as a suggestion that Britain and France should concert together.[56] This was wishful thinking on Poincaré's part, and the readiness of Grey and his colleagues to engage in the search for a political formula which would satisfy Berlin served in the end to high-light the nebulous nature of the *entente*. At the same time the Anglo-German talks emphasized the value of England's friendship to France. The tenacity with which the Wilhelmstrasse endeavoured to extract from the British a promise of neutrality 'clearly indicated' in the opinion of Paul Cambon 'that England was regarded as the Power which held largely the balance for or against peace'.[57] Poincaré, who had already expressed his desire that the arrangements worked out in the Anglo-French staff talks should receive 'diplomatic consecration', appears in these circumstances to have resolved to secure from Britain some written engagement which would place the Anglo-French understanding beyond question.[58] Thus on 15 April Paul Cambon, with some encouragement from Poincaré, raised with Nicolson the whole question of Britain's continuing support for France.

Cambon told Nicolson that Poincaré considered it necessary to 'take stock of the position of France and to see what outside support she could rely upon'. Grey's recent assurances, Cambon asserted, had not been 'sufficiently clear and precise to thoroughly satisfy him'.

---

[54] The most recent account of the origins and diplomacy of the Italo-Turkish war of 1911–1912 is to be found in R.J. Bosworth, *Italy, the Least of the Great Powers. Italian foreign policy before the First World War* (London, 1979), pp.127–195.
[55] R.J. Bosworth, 'Italy and the End of the Ottoman Empire', in Kent, pp.52–75.
[56] *D.D.F.3*, I, nos.603 and 605.
[57] *B.D.*, VI, no.576.
[58] Guy Pendroncini, 'Strategie et relations internationales. La séance du 9 janvier 1912 du Conseil Supérieur de la Défense Nationale', *Révue d'histoire diplomatique* (Jan.–June 1977), 151. Poincaré to P. Cambon, 23 April 1912, N.S. Grande-Bretagne 27, tel.414. J. Joffre, *The Memoirs of Marshal Joffre* (2 vols., London, 1932), I, p.52.

Moreover, while the existing Anglo-French relationship, based as it was upon a community of interest and reciprocal confidence, might be sufficient for the two governments, it was not, he claimed, enough for public opinion in France. Then, after reasserting that Lansdowne had been ready in 1905 to 'strengthen and extend' the *entente*, Cambon asked Nicolson if they could not seek a formula which would allow the French government to reassure 'les esprits inquièts ou incrédules'. And although he said nothing precise about what assurances should be given, he did suggest that declarations might be exchanged in note form. Much, however, as Nicolson would personally have liked to have seen the *entente* strengthened, he thought that the time was not right for pressing for any more precisely defined understandings. The 'German thermometer was in the ascendant', he maintained, and he discouraged Cambon from making any new proposal. He warned the French ambassador that he doubted if the cabinet would be prepared to tie their hands in any way with regard to the action that they would take in any given contingency at a time when there was much public support for bettering relations with Germany. For the moment he considered it wiser to leave matters as they were, and the only assurance that he could offer was that 's'il survient à un à-coup l'opinion forcera le Gouvernment à marcher'.[59]

If the response to Cambon's initiative was disappointing for the French, the naval question, which had proved to be one of the main obstacles to closer Anglo-German relations, was ironically to provide them with the opportunity to make a renewed attempt to extract a more formal definition of the *entente* from Britain. By December 1907 the Admiralty's concern with the development of the German navy had already led to the concentration of the preponderant might of the Royal Navy in home waters. But in the spring of 1912 the Admiralty was faced with the prospect of a further increase in Germany's naval strength, and the development by Italy and Austria-Hungary of a force of dreadnoughts, which would soon render obsolete the British fleet in the Mediterranean and place it in a precarious position in the event of a war with the Triple Alliance. To meet this challenge a reorganization of the fleets was proposed, the essence of which was outlined to the Commons by Churchill on 18 March 1912. This involved the withdrawal from Malta of the six pre-dreadnoughts then stationed there, and the formation of a new battle squadron which would be based at Gibraltar and be able to reinforce other squadrons

---

[59] *B.D.*, VI, nos.576 and 577. Nicolson to Bertie, 22 April 1912, B.P., A, F.O.800/166. *D.D.F.3*, II, no.363. Nicolson to Goschen, 23 April 1912, Nicolson MSS., F.O.800/355.

in the North Sea and the Atlantic, or reenter the Mediterranean if circumstances so dictated. As Churchill subsequently reasoned, Britain's peacetime dispositions would thus approximate to those intended for times of conflict.[60]

In planning for a future naval war neither Churchill and his advisers, nor their predecessors had neglected the part which France and the *entente* might play. The British naval war plans of 1907 and 1908 had reckoned with the possibility of obtaining aid from France in the Mediterranean.[61] Moreover, although Churchill always insisted that in the absence of either an agreement with Germany or a substantial increase in British naval expenditure, the new dispositions were the best that the navy could adopt, he also recognized that without French assistance British interests in the Mediterranean would be dangerously exposed in wartime.[62] When on 29 April Asquith instructed the Committee of Imperial Defence to enquire into the effects of the projected naval changes upon the situation in the Mediterranean and elsewhere, he also asked that they examine the 'degree of reliance to be placed on the co-operation of the French fleet'.[63] Yet before the Agadir crisis there had been no conversations between the British and French naval authorities of a kind similar to those which had proceeded between the two military staffs.[64] In 1906 Fisher had been reluctant to discuss his war plans with the French, and only in December 1908 did he indicate to the French naval *attaché* in London that in a war in which France and Britain were allies, France should concentrate her naval forces in the Mediterranean. Since, however, the French had already decided in 1906 to shift the greater part of their naval strength to the Mediterranean, Fisher's

---

[60] Williamson, pp.239–40, and 264–7.
[61] *Ibid.* The Royal Navy's manoeuvering in the North Sea in the spring of 1909 and the withdrawal then of the fleet from the Mediterranean had already led Mallet to consider the prospect of the Admiralty relying on the French to defend Britain's interests in the latter sea. He warned Grey that it would be 'rash to assume that *without an alliance* the French would come to our assistance in these circumstances'. Mallet to Grey, 11 April 1909, Grey MSS., F.O.800/93.
[62] R.S. Churchill, *Winston S. Churchill*, II, companion vol. pt.3 (London 1969), pp.1503–5.
[63] E.W. Lumby(ed.), *Policy and Operations in the Mediterranean, 1912–1914* (The Navy Record Society, London, 1970), pp.23–31.
[64] A report of the Director of Naval Intelligence of January 1908 on German naval construction had actually envisaged a possible Franco-German naval combination as a factor to be taken into account in calculating the strength of the British navy. P. Haggie. 'The Royal Navy and War Planning in the Fisher Era', *Journal of Contemporary History*, VIII(1973), 113–31. R.F. Mackay, *Fisher of Kilverstone* (Oxford 1973), pp.353–6. Williamson, pp.243–9.

remarks complemented rather than determined their actions.[65] Even when tentative discussions did begin in the summer of 1911 between the first sea lord, Sir Arthur Wilson, and representatives of the French navy, the net result was only a verbal agreement including provisions for possible cooperation in the Mediterranean.[66] It was Cambon who first drew the attention of the Foreign Office to the progress of these conversations. On 4 May 1912 he suggested to Nicolson that they should be resumed and that Britain might join France and Russia in a naval convention. He said that his government wanted Britain to look after the Channel and France's northern coasts while the French would take care of the Mediterranean.[67] Cambon was anxious that the British and French naval authorities should move quickly towards the conclusion of a convention, and in this seems to have been in agreement with Delcassé, still French minister for marine.[68] While both Grey and Churchill insisted that any such talks should await the completion of the government's consideration of the Admiralty's proposals, Nicolson was surprised and irritated by Cambon's reference to conversations about which he had not been fully informed.[69] Indeed, he and his colleagues might well have been excused for assuming that the projected naval moves were not unconnected with such talks.

Bertie was aware that conversations had taken place between British and French naval experts, but he seems only to have had a very general idea of what had been arranged. Five years before there had been talk in French naval circles about the existence of an accord with the British Admiralty. The British vice-consul at Brest had told Grey in March 1907 that the authorities there defended the concentration of the French fleet in the Mediterranean on the grounds that it had resulted from an understanding with Britain.[70] Yet in November 1908 Bertie learned from Grey that Paul Cambon had just broached the possibility of beginning informal naval

---

[65] A move during 1910 and 1911 towards the concentration of French naval forces in northern waters proved to be only a temporary expedient. Williamson, pp.232–4. P.G. Halpern, *The Mediterranean Naval Situation, 1908–1914* (Cambridge, Mass., 1971), pp.47–85.
[66] *D.D.F.2*, XIV, no.171. *D.D.F.3*, I, no.336. Williamson, pp.227–8 and 245–8.
[67] *B.D.*, X, pt.2, no.383.
[68] P. Cambon to Delcassé, 18 May 1912, Delcassé MSS., 3.
[69] *B.D.*, X, pt.2, nos.383, 384 and 389. Asquith to George V, 17 May 1912, Asquith MSS., 6.
[70] Memo. enclosed in Spencer S. Dickson to Grey, 5 May 1907, F.O.371/250. Bertie was aware of an inclination in France to look towards Britain for naval protection in the event of a war with Germany. Bertie to Grey, 18 Feb. 1909, Grey MSS., F.O.800/51.

conversations.[71] Moreover, although in February 1910 Pichon told Bertie that as a result of such talks the French navy had been assigned a duty, Captain Howard Kelly, the British naval *attaché* at Paris, was not aware of any joint planning having taken place until the autumn of 1911. Only then, after a conversation with Delcassé, during which the latter referred to the existence of a naval understanding, did Kelly ask the Admiralty what had been going on. There is no record of whether he passed on to Bertie any information that he received from London.[72]

The possibility of naval cooperation between Britain and France assumed a new significance for Bertie and the Foreign Office as a result of the Admiralty's proposals for the redeployment of the British fleets. Crowe contended that the British 'withdrawal' from the Mediterranean would lead to a diminution of Britain's influence there, and alter the whole power structure of the area to Britain's detriment. Most of the disadvantages that were thereby incurred might, he argued, be avoided if French cooperation were assured, and their fleet were in a position to beat those of Italy, Austria-Hungary and Turkey combined.[73] Yet neither Nicolson nor Bertie believed that France's help could be secured without Britain undertaking some fresh obligation towards her. Discounting the possibility of an increase in the naval budget, or an alliance with Germany, Nicolson recommended that the only other alternative was an understanding with France, which would have 'very much the character of a defensive alliance'. While he doubted if the cabinet would approve this, he thought that it offered the 'cheapest, simplest, and safest solution'. An ardent exponent of maintaining a 'free hand' where relations with Germany were concerned, Nicolson protested to Bertie 'we can hardly continue sitting on the fence very much longer and continue to give evasive and uncertain answers'.[74] Bertie was more cautious than Nicolson. He admitted that the French could hardly be expected not to make some use of Britain's 'desertion' of the Mediterranean 'as a lever to extract something tangible from us', but he did not believe that the British government would have to go as far as an alliance in order to secure their assistance. In a private letter to Nicolson of 9 May he suggested that the French might be satisfied

---

[71] *B.D.*, VI, no.106.
[72] *Ibid*, nos.331 and 333. *Journal as Naval Attaché*, pp.23–5, Howard Kelly MSS., KEL/3.
[73] *B.D.*, X, pt.2, no.386.
[74] *Ibid*, nos.384 and 385. Nicolson would have preferred to have seen the *entente* transformed into an alliance, but he admitted that in the present circumstances the British public were unlikely to accept this, and that it might anyway so alarm Germany

with an exchange of notes between the two governments which would define generally their respective and joint interests, and state that in the event of these being endangered they would consult together. The French, Bertie assumed, would be prepared to accept that the question of an alliance should be settled when hostilities seemed near. They desired, he thought, to have arranged exactly what military assistance Britain could give them, and what mutual support there should be. He concluded that Britain would have to arrange something like this 'unless we prefer to run the risk of being stranded in splendid isolation'.[75]

Neither the Admiralty's proposals, nor the idea of a closer relationship with France were generally regarded in London as offering good solutions to Britain's difficulties. In part this was because the former project was felt to be dependent upon the latter. The radicals within the cabinet opposed the naval changes which they believed would lead to a tighter association with France, and Grey would have preferred there to have been increased spending on the navy rather than break with his colleagues. Churchill's advisers also favoured this alternative to an alliance with a 'country of unstable politics with no particular sympathy towards British interests except in so far as they represent French interests as well'. Moreover, while the Conservative press were prepared to subscribe to the idea of an alliance with France, both it and the Liberal newspapers were critical of the idea of relying on a foreign power to defend British interests.[76] Even within the British embassy at Paris opinions differed over what was the wisest course for the British government to pursue. Kelly advised Bertie that if Britain were intending to leave the care of the Mediterranean to the French, there had better be an alliance.[77] But George Grahame took a very different view of the situation. On 27 May he wrote to Tyrrell deprecating the 'microbe-like' development in the British and French press of the idea of an alliance. There was no reason, he thought, for offering the French anything for the time being for they liked being 'cocks of the walk'. In peacetime, he argued, it was bad for Britain's prestige to allow another power to guard British possessions, and in wartime it did not really matter what happened in the Mediterranean as victory or defeat would be decided in the main theatre of operations. No-one really supposed

---

as to precipitate a war. Nicolson to Goschen, 7 May 1912; Nicolson to O'Beirne, 31 May 1912; Nicolson MSS., F.O.800/355.

[75] *B.D.*, X, pt.2, no.358.
[76] A.J. Marder, *From Dreadnought to Scapa Flow. The Royal Navy in the Fisher Era* (5 vols., Oxford, 1961 – 70), I, pp.288 – 91. Williamson, pp.270 – 80.
[77] Lumby, pp.58 – 60.

Austria and Italy could hold on to Malta and Cyprus after the defeat by the British of the German navy. If France were allowed to look after the Mediterranean, then Grahame insisted, it would be sufficient payment 'for her to know that her northern coasts had been made additionally secure from attack by our naval concentration in the North Sea'. He did not in any case consider that England and France would make 'un bon ménage', for, he added, it might be ' "un marriage d'amour" but such marriages usually go wrong here'.[78]

Some modifications were made in the Admiralty's plans as the result of consultations which took place on Malta at the end of May between Asquith, Churchill and Lord Kitchener, the British consul-general at Cairo. The latter's preoccupation with the defence of Egypt eventually led Churchill to agree to maintain a force of two or three battle cruisers and a cruiser squadron at Malta, and to seek an agreement with France.[79] In a memorandum of 15 June, in which he defended the new dispositions, Churchill argued that an Anglo-French combination in a war would be able to keep full control of the Mediterranean and afford all necessary protection to British and French interests there. Yet McKenna, who emerged as one of the most adept of Churchill's critics, was incorrect in his assertion that an alliance with France was an 'essential feature' of the new strategy. Although the naval war staff subsequently claimed that a reliable and effective arrangement with France was essential, Churchill clearly stated in his memorandum of the 15th that the Admiralty's measures stood by themselves. What he desired was not an alliance, but a 'defensive naval arrangement which would come into force only if the two Powers were at any time allies in a war'. Nevertheless, despite his insistence upon the sufficiency and autonomous nature of the Admiralty's provisions, Churchill still failed to overcome the opposition of his colleagues in the cabinet. After a lengthy meeting of the defence committee on 4 July he was compelled to abandon the scheme, and to accept their resolution that subject to the provision of a 'reasonable margin of superior strength' in home waters, the Admiralty 'ought to maintain available for Mediteranean purposes and based on a Mediterranean port a battle fleet equal to a one-Power Mediterranean standard, excluding France'. This declaration did not mean the abandonment of the idea of a naval arrangement with France. Implicit in it was the assumption that Britain would only find herself opposed by both Austria and Italy in the event of a war in which France would be involved. Besides which, it was evident that

[78] Grahame to Tyrrell, 27 May 1912, Grey MSS., F.O.800/53.
[79] Lumby, pp.19–20 and 22–3.

given Britain's current naval strength, she was unlikely to secure battleship parity with Austria in the Mediterranean before 1915, and that would depend upon the cabinet's readiness to sanction the necessary expenditure.[80]

Such information as the Quai d'Orsay had so far been able to obtain about the Admiralty's future plans, and the public discussion of a possible Anglo-French alliance, encouraged those responsible for France's foreign policy to think in terms of a tighter relationship with Britain.[81] Moreover, in July Delcassé gave his final approval to the plans of his war staff for the movement of the remaining French battle squadron at Brest to Toulon. This, de Saint-Seine, the French naval *attaché* in London, took care to inform Sir Francis Bridgeman, Arthur Wilson's successor as first sea lord, would make France stronger in the Mediterranean than a combination of the Austrian and Italian fleets.[82] But the resumption of talks between the French naval *attaché* and the Admiralty, and the possibility that plans might be arranged for cooperation in the Mediterranean, raised again the question of Britain's future liberty of action. Grey's colleagues were as ever opposed to Britain being drawn by some surreptitious deal into a commitment to assist France in a war, and on 16 July the cabinet resolved that it should be made plain to the French that conversations between military and naval experts would not prejudice the 'freedom of decision of either Government as to whether they should or should not co-operate in the event of a war'.[83] It was, however, quite apparent to Churchill that naval talks with the French might allow the French to claim that their fleet dispositions were dependent upon an arrangement with Britain, and that she was therefore morally obliged to defend their northern coasts against attack. And to avoid Britain becoming inveigled in such an obligation Churchill endeavoured to have it explicitly stated in any arrangement arrived at by the British and French naval authorities that the deployment of their respective fleets was independent of any conversations between them. Thus, while he recommended to de Saint-Seine that France should keep in the Mediterranean a fleet equal to that of Austria and Italy combined, he also insisted that the new dispositions which the Admiralty proposed were made in 'our own interests, and adequate in our opinion to the full protection of British trade and possessions in the Medit(erranean)'.[84]

---

[80] *Ibid*, pp.24–50 and 60–83.
[81] *D.D.F.3*, III, nos.56 and 102.
[82] *Ibid*, no.189.
[83] Asquith to George V, 16 July 1912, Asquith Mss., 6.
[84] *B.D.*, X, pt.2, no.399.

Bertie, who met Grey on 17 July, doubted whether the cabinet's decision would be readily accepted by the French. It would, he suggested, be sufficient to say that it was understood that points arranged between experts were not to be binding on the two governments 'unless they had agreed to give each other mutual armed support'. This form, he believed, would be 'more palatable to the French than the tautology of the Cabinet draft declaration'. Evidently under the misapprehension that the government were proposing to leave the defence of Britain's Mediterranean interests to France, he warned Grey that the French would require some *quid pro quo*. This, he thought, might take the form of an exchange of notes such as he had described to Nicolson in his letter of 9 May. But Grey was unenthusiastic about the idea, which he considered to be going much further than anything hitherto done, and approaching an alliance. Bertie demurred. He thought that the French required something to give them confidence in Britain, and he maintained that there need be no fear of the French 'creating a war with Germany', although they might find themselves in a position 'whence the only outcome could be war'. If Britain could not acquiesce in the defeat of France, then, he urged Grey, provision would have to be made for defending her existence, and an exchange of notes 'would be the means of communication whenever there was a danger to the interests of the two countries'. Armed support, if it were to be effective, would, he professed, have to be given at the outset of a conflict.[85]

The cabinet, as Grey anticipated, rejected Bertie's proposal for an exchange of notes. It preferred Churchill's formula, and this was reflected in a draft agreement for Anglo-French naval cooperation in the Mediterranean and the straits of Dover, which de Saint-Seine received from the Admiralty on 23 July. The details of this project were thus preceded by a declaration to the effect that the agreement would relate solely to the case where Britain and France were allies in a war, and that it would not affect the freedom of either power with regard to embarking on such a conflict. It also stated:

> It is understood that France has disposed almost the whole of her battle fleet in the Mediterranean leaving her Atlantic seaboard in the care of Flotillas.
>
> Great Britain on the other hand has concentrated her battle fleets in home waters, leaving in the Medit(erranea)n a strong containing force of battle and armoured cruisers and torpedo craft.

---

[85] Memo. by Bertie, 25 July 1912, B.P., A, F.O.800/166.

These dispositions have been made independently because they are the best which the separate interests of each country suggests, having regard to all circumstances and probabilities and they do not arise from any naval agreement or convention.

On the same day the draft agreement was delivered to the French embassy Grey gave to Bertie his personal assurance that he would not remain in the cabinet if there were any question of abandoning the *entente*. Indeed, he told Bertie that he might put this to Poincaré in defending the British government's proposal. To Bertie's protest that the cabinet could not afford to lose him, and that it would be the dissenting ministers who would have to resign, Grey replied that he would not risk breaking up the government and that he himself would go. It was an answer that must have left Bertie wondering what satisfaction the French might derive from the personal commitment of a foreign secretary who would resign rather than risk splitting the cabinet on the issue of Britain's loyalty to France. The French, Bertie warned Grey, would not long be content to protect or to join in defending British interests in the Mediterranean if they had nothing more promising than a statement that the arrangements between experts were entirely without prejudice.[86]

Just as Bertie had predicted, the French were anything but satisfied with the terms of the proposed agreement. Paul Cambon assumed that the achievement of the naval dispositions to which Churchill referred was the object rather than the basis of the project, and on 24 July he complained to Nicolson that it entailed the deployment of France's fleets in such a way as would leave her northern coasts unprotected, while 'England was free to aid France or not as she liked, and be under no obligation to do so'. It was possible, Cambon concluded, that the French naval authorities would first require to have assurances that British naval assistance would be forthcoming for the defence of France's Channel and Atlantic ports. Churchill's explanation to the French naval *attaché* that the fleet dispositions were to be arrived at quite independently by each navy was rejected by Cambon. France, he insisted to Grey, had concentrated her fleet in the Mediterranean as the result of naval conversations begun with Fisher in 1907.[87] This claim, which would seem to have been based on no more than diplomatic hearsay, seems to have puzzled Churchill.

---

[86] *Ibid. B.D.*, X, pt.2, no.400 and editorial note, p.602.
[87] *B.D.*, X, pt.2, no.401. A year before in the summer of 1911 Paul Cambon had been under the impression that *pourparlers* had commenced for an Anglo-French naval accord when Clemenceau was in office, and that an unwritten agreement had been

Nevertheless, while he admitted that he had not been aware of the extent to which the Admiralty had been committed by his predecessor, he still considered the non-commital proviso to be 'desirable and perfectly fair'. The present dispositions, he observed, 'represented the best arrangements either power could make independently', and it was not true that the French were occupying the Mediterranean to oblige Britain.[88]

On the advice of Nicolson, who thought that as a consequence of Cambon's protestations, Grey would issue him with supplementary instructions, Bertie decided to extend his stay in London.[89] There he had discussions with both the king and Cambon, and upon the former, who deprecated any question of an alliance with France, he impressed his idea of an exchange of notes.[90] But by 26 July even Nicolson and Tyrrell had come to accept that Churchill's argument was in substance correct. They told Bertie that the planned movement of the greater and most powerful portion of the French fleet to the Mediterranean was 'the unprompted decision of the French Government'. 'There was therefore', Bertie noted, 'no question of a quid pro quo being due to France in the shape of a protection for her Atlantic and Channel coasts by the British fleet in return for the protection or defence of British interests in the Mediterranean by the French fleet.'[91] And on the 28th Bertie returned to Paris without further instructions. Cambon had in the meantime suggested to Grey an arrangement similar to one previously proposed by Bertie. On 26 July he urged that if Churchill's proviso were to remain at the head of the projected naval agreement, the British and French governments should exchange notes promising that if the peace were menaced, they would communicate and converse with each other. Grey, however, maintained that there were 'great objections' to a secret exchange of notes, and declined the proposal for what he claimed were parliamentary reasons. In any case, he could see little utility in such an accord, for as he told Cambon, the two governments would of course consult with each other in a crisis.[92]

---

concluded. But de Selves had informed him that the ministry of marine did not know the results of such conversations. *D.D.F.2*, XIV, nos.175 and 176.

[88] *B.D.*, X, pt.2, no.403.
[89] Memo. by Bertie, 25 July 1912, B.P., A, F.O.800/166.
[90] Memo. by Bertie, 25 July 1912, B.P., B, F.O.800/187.
[91] Bertie learned from Tyrrell and Nicolson that Cambon had misunderstood the French naval *attaché's* reports of his interviews with Churchill. Memo. by Bertie, 27 July 1912, B.P., A, F.O.800/166.
[92] *B.D.*, X, pt.2, no.402.

THE CLARIFICATION OF THE ENTENTE

Bertie similarly found it necessary to discourage French aspirations for a more precise Anglo-French understanding. But Poincaré, whom he met on 30 July, required more than the affirmation that Bertie offered to him that so long as Grey remained foreign secretary Britain would not abandon the 'spirit of the Entente'. True Poincaré frankly admitted that the French government's decision with regard to the deployment of its fleets was 'quite spontaneous'. Nevertheless, he asserted that the decision to concentrate the French fleet in the Mediterranean 'would not have been taken if they could suppose that in the event of Germany making a descent on the Channel or Atlantic ports of France, England would not come to the assistance of France'. The object of the *entente*, he contended, was for the 'maintenance of each other and their defence against attack — unprovoked attack — and the balance of power'. If the *entente* did not mean that England would come to the aid of France in the event of a German attack on her ports, then, Poincaré observed, 'its value to France is not great'. Ostensibly, however, his chief objection to Churchill's draft arrangement was that a political resolution should not form part of an agreement between naval experts. While both governments must reserve to themselves the decision on putting such arrangements into force, their reservations, he argued, should be recorded in some other form of document. Technically, as Bertie pointed out, and Asquith agreed, Poincaré was correct. Yet Poincaré's real intention would seem to have been both to avoid adhering to any statement which would explicitly deny a connexion between the naval moves and the *entente*, and to use the British government's desire to make clear the non-commital nature of the staff talks in order to extract from it a written redefinition of Britain's position *vis-à-vis* France. Like Bertie and Paul Cambon, both of whom he had time to consult, Poincaré wanted some form of declaration which would entail conversations taking place between the British and French governments the moment that there appeared to be a danger to their interests, so that they might decide at once whether the arrangements arrived at by the experts should be put into force.[93]

By August matters had progressed some way since the Admiralty had decided to bring the British and French naval plans up to date, and Churchill had good reason to think that things had 'got off the rails'. Under the impression that the cause of all the difficulties was his proviso, he suggested that it might be redrafted in more general terms so as to read: 'Both Powers will make such dispositions of their naval strength as shall best conduce to their national interests.'

---

[93] *Ibid*, nos.404 and 405. Bertie to Tyrrell, 31 July 1912, Grey MSS., F.O.800/53.

Without referring to specific dispositions any link between the British and French naval moves would thus be avoided.[94] As, however, Bertie pointed out in a letter to Grey of 13 August, this would make no difference to Poincaré's objection to the inclusion of a non-commital declaration in an agreement between experts. Bertie thought that the French might find acceptable a naval agreement which stated that the British and French naval authorities would exchange full information as to the actual and prospective disposition of their naval strength 'which they make as best conducing to the preservation of their national interests'. The document would then proceed to deal with the best way in which the forces thus disposed could be utilized in a war in which both countries were allies. In a separate form, Bertie explained, it could be laid down that it was well understood that the naval arrangement would only come into force if and when both governments were agreed that they would act together. He also reminded Grey that Poincaré was not the first French foreign minister to have been dissatisfied with the existing conditions, and he once more claimed that the French government would like an exchange of notes as he had earlier suggested. Were such an exchange impossible, then he considered that they might accept an exchange of declarations to the effect that notwithstanding any arrangements resulting from the staff talks, the two governments remained free to determine whenever circumstances arose whether they would give each other armed support.[95]

One further point that Bertie seemed anxious to emphasize was the French contention that the redeployment of the British and French fleets would not have taken place if the two *entente* partners had not each been confident that in the area from which it was withdrawing it could count upon the other's help.[95] Indeed, it seemed as if Poincaré was determined to attribute to the *entente* a meaning which implicitly involved a British commitment to defend France and her interests. Churchill was fully aware of the dangers inherent in accepting these views and Bertie's interpretation of them. To Asquith he complained on 23 August: 'everyone must feel who knows the facts that we have all the obligations of an alliance without its advantages and above all without its precise definitions.' He refuted Poincaré's claims and insisted that if Britain had not existed the French could not have made better dispositions. Nevertheless, he was quite prepared to abandon his draft declaration. He informed the prime minister that he was not particular as to how his views should be given effect to,

---

[94] *B.D.*, X, Pt.2, no.406. Grey to Bertie, 7 Aug. 1912, B.P., A, F.O.800/166.
[95] *B.D.*, X, pt.2. no.409.
[96] *Ibid.*

and he made 'no avail' as to the document in which they were set forth.[97] This, Asquith agreed, was a matter of form on which the government might give way 'if Bertie could suggest some manner of affording this agreement of not too formal a character'.[98] Before any new formula was found with which to replace Churchill's declaration, Paul Cambon returned to the subject of a consultative agreement. Evidently he still hoped to be able to use the redeployment of France's naval forces as a bargaining counter in negotiations with Grey for on 19 September he warned him that the concentration of the French fleet in the Mediterranean would not be definitive until his government knew where it stood with England. The two governments, he proposed, should agree that in the event of either of them apprehending aggression, they would discuss the situation and together seek the means to maintain peace. In itself this seemed innocent enough. Unlike the exchange of notes that Bertie had hankered after during the spring and summer, it made no reference to any specific interests which the two powers might wish to defend, and it was, as Asquith noted, 'almost a platitude'.[99] But Grey, as at the time of the conclusion of the 1907 agreements with Spain, feared that the publication of an exchange of notes would have a 'very exciting effect in Europe', and both he and Asquith were at first reluctant to accept any arrangement that could not be communicated to parliament. Cambon, nevertheless, persisted in pressing for some written engagement, and in agreement with the prime minister, Grey finally consented to an exchange of letters with the ambassador on condition that this was sanctioned by the cabinet.[100]

In view of the cabinet's earlier rejection of Bertie's proposal for an exchange of notes, its acceptance of Cambon's formula may have seemed unlikely. And on 30 October Grey's colleagues turned it down as 'vague and open to a variety of constructions'. An exchange of notes did, however, offer to them the means for achieving an explicit agreement with the French on the non-commital nature of the military and naval conversations, and a substitute for Churchill's projected preamble. Grey was thus able with the approval of the cabinet to propose to Cambon that three points be recognized in an exchange of notes: that conversations between experts had taken place; that these did not bind their governments to action; and that in the event of a threatening situation arising the two governments

---

[97] W.S. Churchill, *The World Crisis, 1911–1918* (6 vols., London, 1923–31), I, pp.112–13. R.S. Churchill, *Churchill*, II, companion vol. pt.3, pp.1638–1639.
[98] Mallet to Grey, 23 Aug. 1912, Grey MSS., F.O.800/94.
[99] *B.D.*, X, pt.2, nos.410, 411, and 412.
[100] Grey to Bertie, 16 Oct. 1912, B.P., A, F.O.800/166.

would consult with one another. These, after further discussions, were to form the basis of letters which were exchanged by Grey and Paul Cambon on 22 and 23 November.[101] Although the naval staff talks had played a vital part in concentrating the attention of the British government on the state of the Anglo-French relationship, the only specific reference in the letters to the dispositions recently assumed by the British and French fleets was the assertion by Grey that they were not 'based upon an engagement to co-operate in war'. But in January and February 1913 three agreements were concluded between the British and French naval authorities which provided for cooperation in the straits of Dover, the English Channel and the Mediterranean. Each of these accords contained the provision that they were only to become effective in the event of the two powers being allies in a war with Germany or the Triple Alliance.[102]

In itself the exchange of notes between Grey and Cambon did little to extend the existing understanding between Britain and France. It simply clarified and committed to paper in a precise form the nature of the *entente* as it related to a possible European conflict, and the terms upon which the two countries would continue to cooperate with each other. But Poincaré could feel satisfied at the British cabinet having formally endorsed this new arrangement. Moreover, unlike the declaration which Churchill had proposed in August, neither the notes nor the non-commital provisions of the accords on future naval cooperation affirmed the autonomous nature of the dispositions assumed by the British and French navies. They merely stated that they were not the result of an alliance. In so far as the arrangements worked out in 1913 were dependent for their application upon the maintenance of the new dispositions, it might be contended that Britain had in any case thereby incurred a moral obligation to defend the northern coasts of France in the event of a continental war. The important point was, however, that nothing was contained in the notes which could be held to refute the claims made by Paul Cambon on 1 August 1914 that at Britain's request France had moved her fleet to the Mediterranean.[103] By then, of course, circumstances had changed. Faced by a cabinet which was as yet undecided as to the course which it would pursue in the event of a Franco-German war,

---

[101] Asquith to George V, 1 Oct. 1912, Asquith MSS., 6. *B.D.*, X, pt.2, nos.413, 416, and 417.
[102] The Anglo-French naval accords and the ensuing co-operation between the British and French navies are examined in Halpern, pp.105–49.
[103] H. Nicolson, *Sir Arthur Nicolson, Bart., First Lord Carnock. A Study in Old Diplomacy* (London, 1930), p.420. *D.D.F.3*, XI, no.352. *B.D.*, XI, nos.426 and 447.

THE CLARIFICATION OF THE ENTENTE

Cambon's appeal seemed to Nicolson like a 'happy inspiration'.[104] Even Churchill, who had so ardently disclaimed any such obligation during 1912, was prepared to endorse Grey's contention that Britain must defend the northern shores of France.[105]

Bertie for his part was less concerned with the ethics of the *entente* than with ensuring that in the event of a new international crisis Britain would be in a position to offer immediate and effective assistance to France. For this reason he had opposed Grey's efforts to settle with the German government on a non-aggression formula, and he had backed the idea of a consultative pact with France. Nevertheless, the notes exchanged in November 1912 were neither as comprehensive nor as precise as he would have favoured. When in June 1913 it seemed possible that the French government might once more seek to achieve some more binding arrangement with England, Bertie raised with Grey the need for an exchange of notes of 'a less vague character than the private letter to M. Cambon'.[106] The Grey-Cambon notes were indeed essentially the product of a compromise between the desire of Churchill and his colleagues to make clear the non-commital nature of the Anglo-French staff talks, and the endeavours of Poincaré and Paul Cambon to secure some more formal definition of the *entente*. Bertie did not abandon his proposal for an accord which would register the joint interests of Britain and France. But before the outbreak of war in August 1914 he was to witness no further progress towards its achievement.

---

[104] Nicolson to Hardinge, 5 Sept. 1914, Hardinge MSS., 93.
[105] Churchill, I, pp.201 – 2.
[106] Memo. by Bertie, 23 June 1913, B.P., A, F.O.800/166.

12

Sick at Heart

The Young Turk revolution of 1908 had generated high hopes amongst the European great powers for the achievement of orderly government and stability in Turkey's Balkan provinces. But the centralizing policies pursued by the empire's new masters served in the end to alienate further the disaffected christian population of Macedonia, and to stimulate rebellion in Albania. In the meantime the smaller states of the peninsula remained dissatisfied with their lot. Apprehensive lest the eventual emergence of an autonomous Albania, and the successes achieved by the Italians in the eastern Mediterranean, should militate against their interests, they prepared to fulfil their territorial ambitions. Thus, with some encouragement from the Russians, who saw in the formation of a Balkan *bloc* a means of checking what they assumed to be Austria's aspirations, first Serbia, and then Greece and Montenegro, allied themselves with Bulgaria. Finally, in October 1912, despite the efforts of the great powers to maintain peace, the Balkan allies embarked upon a war with Turkey which within six weeks reduced the Ottoman military presence in Europe to the three garrison towns of Andrianople, Janina and Scutari, and Constantinople's defensive lines at Tchatalja.[1] Turkey's defeat was of obvious concern to the major European powers. It threatened to become the prelude to an unseemly scramble by them for the Ottoman empire's possessions in Asia, and any redrawing of the map of the Balkans could well lead to a clash between Austria-Hungary and Russia in which each of the contestants would appeal to its friends and allies for assistance. The result might then be either the dissolution of the existing diplomatic alignments or a general European war.

Aware of these dangers, Grey sought to avoid any intervention or initiative in the Near East that might emphasize the prevailing great

---

[1] The problems of the Balkan peninsula and the events which preceded the outbreak of the first Balkan war are examined in: Andrew Rossos, *Russia and the Balkans. Inter-Balkan rivalries and Russian foreign policy, 1908–1914* (Toronto, 1981), pp.8–69: E. Thaden, *Russia and the Balkan Alliance of 1912* (Philadelphia, 1965). E.C. Helmreich, *The Diplomacy of the Blakan Wars* (London 1938), pp.3–145; and R.J. Crampton, *The*

power groupings. In pursuing this course he at long last found scope for cooperation with the German government, which also wished to contain the Balkan conflagration, and which saw in an Anglo-German *détente* a means of loosening Britain's ties with the Dual Alliance.[2] This new-found understanding manifested itself in late November when Grey responded favourably to a proposal from Kiderlen-Waechter that the great powers should attempt to reach agreement on their requirements for a future settlement in the Balkans through informal discussions between their ambassadors at some chosen capital. Grey suggested Paris as the *venue*: a course which would have allowed Bertie another chance to participate directly in the reordering of the Balkans. But the presence there, as ambassadors, of Bertie, Izovolsky and Tittoni, none of whom inspired much confidence in Berlin, was sufficient to cause Kiderlen-Waechter to veto the idea. He preferred that the *réunions* should take place in London 'where the ambassadors were of less pronounced views'.[3]

Bertie was probably relieved when Grey agreed to this. Of late he had taken little interest in Balkan affairs, and, according to von Schoen, Radolin's successor at Paris, Bertie was unenthusiastic about the extra work that the gatherings would involve.[4] His own domestic arrangements did not in any case make him welcome the prospect of long hours of conference diplomacy, for in the autumn of 1912 his life was disrupted by the need to shore up the rotting fabric of the embassy building. The state of the house had long been a cause of friction between Bertie and Vye Parminter, the Office of Works's incompetent and intemperate resident architect in Paris. The trouble was that while the office strove to keep within Treasury spending limits by refusing to sanction anything more than piecemeal construction and repair work, Parminter, in an effort to hold on to his appointment, set his estimates too low, and usually ended by skimping on materials and applying to new buildings money intended for maintenance.[5] In one instance, when Bertie had engaged

---

Hollow Détente. Anglo-German Relations in the Balkans, 1911–1914 (London, 1980), pp.30–54.

[2] By January 1912 Grey had indicated to Bertie his sympathy for the idea of a new Austro-Russian understanding on the Balkans such as might obviate the threat of a European conflict. Grey to Bertie, 9 Jan. 1912, B.P., A, F.O.800/161. Crampton, *Hollow Détente*, pp.55–74. See also by the same author: 'The Balkans, 1909–1914', in Hinsley, pp.256–270; and 'The Balkans as a Factor in German Foreign Policy, 1911-1914', *Slavonic and East European Review*, LX (1977), 370–390.

[3] Crampton, *Hollow Détente*, p.67. Ö-U., V, no.4854.

[4] *G.P.*, XXXIII, no.12432. Bertie also preferred London as the *venue* for the proposed conference because of Izvolsky's presence at Paris. Ö-U, V, no.4854.

[5] Bertie to Hardinge, 1 July 1909, F.O.371/897. Bertie to Earle, 19 Nov. 1912, B.P., B, F.O.800/187.

in a little personal diplomacy with the contractors in order to ensure the speedy and more satisfactory completion of work started, the Foreign Office had to intervene with the Treasury to save him from being compelled to meet the cost.[6] Then, in the summer of 1911, Bertie was only just able to restrain Parminter from covering the exterior walls of the building with stone coloured paint: an act of cultural vandalism which would, as Bertie remarked, have made the embassy 'the laughing stock of artistic Paris'.[7] A more serious problem was presented by the house's sagging timbers, which in 1912 the Office of Works decided to have replaced and strengthened. This meant that in October Bertie was again forced to seek lodgings elsewhere. The open beams and platforms which separated Bertie from his sitting room may, however, have put the ambassador in a suitable frame of mind to contemplate that other crumbling edifice, the Ottoman empire in Europe.[8]

Turkey's defeat compelled the Porte to accept an armistice in December, and although hostilities were resumed in February 1913, the ambassadors of the great powers in London continued their deliberations. The principal territorial issue which occupied their attention during the first quarter of the year concerned the establishment of an Albanian state, and the claims of Serbia and Montenegro. While the two latter powers usually enjoyed the sympathy and support of Russia, the Austrians saw in an independent Albania a means of preserving their influence in the western Balkans, and of denying to Serbia a port on the Adriatic.[9] From the beginning of the war Bertie's attitude towards the changing situation in the Near East was coloured by his distaste for what he considered to be unwarranted Russian meddling, and his personal dislike of Izvolsky, whom he suspected of using lies and bribery to further his government's interests.[10] 'Quel odieux animal!', Bertie exclaimed to Paléologue, 'C'est miracle qu'il n'ait pas encore mis le feu à l'Europe.'[11] He was also very critical of the way in which the French

---

[6] MacDonnell to F.O., 23 Feb. 1910; Langley to Treasury, 11 April 1910; George Murray to F.O., 21 April 1910; F.O.371/897. Minute by Crowe on Bertie to Grey, 11 Nov. 1910, F.O.371/897, despt.425. Hardinge to Bertie, 17 Feb. and 29 April 1910; Bertie to Hardinge, 21 Feb. 1910; B.P., B, F.O.800/186.
[7] Bertie to Nicolson, 24, 27 and 28 June 1911, B.P., B, F.O.800/186.
[8] Bertie to Nicolson, 24 Oct. and 17 Nov. 1912, B.P., B, F.O.800/187.
[9] Crampton, *Hollow Detente*, pp.75 – 96.
[10] Bertie to Grey, 3 Jan. 1911, B.P., A, F.O.800/173. Bertie to Nicolson, 15 May 1912, B.P., A, F.O.800/161. Memos. by Bertie, 19 Feb. 1912 and 27 June 1914, B.P., A, F.O.800/177. Bertie to Grey, 23 Nov. 1913, Grey MSS., F.O.800/54. *Ö-U*, VI, nos. 6584 and 7364.
[11] M. Paléologue, *Au Quai d'Orsay à la veille de la tourmente. Journal 1913 – 1914* (Paris, 1947), pp.122 – 3.

seemed ready to allow themselves to be 'dragged' about by their ally in support of what were 'often purely sentimental or unavowable Russian interests'.[12] Nevertheless, Bertie doubted if the Russians would allow themselves to become involved in a war with Austria over the aggrandizement of Serbia. He thought that Britain and France would, instead, have to witness a reenactment of the Bosnian crisis in which Russia had in the end climbed down. If Sazonov were faced with the prospect of a war with Austria backed by Germany, in which Italy and Roumania might act against Russia's Balkan *protegés*, then, he predicted in November 1912, Russia would submit.[13] He spoke in similar terms to Delcassé, who in February 1913 replaced Louis as French ambassador at St Petersburg. On 3 March he told the new ambassador that Russia would not fight, but that after calling upon Britain and France to support her claims, would leave them in the lurch.[14]

Bertie believed one of the objects of Delcassé's mission to be to put 'pressure on the Emperor and the Russian ministers to moderate their Balkanic zeal and to consult the French Government before addressing dangerous communications to foreign Governments'.[15] This may not have been far short of the truth. But Bertie probably underestimated the extent to which Poincaré, who in February was elevated to the presidency of the republic, desired to tighten the alliance between France and Russia, and to effect a fusion of the interests of the two powers in the Near East.[16] There was certainly no indication in the spring of 1912 that the French government was prepared to risk appearing to separate itself from Russia. This was evident when Grey proposed the despatch of an international naval force to the Adriatic in order to persuade the Montenegrins to abide by the decisions of the London conference, and to lift their seige of Scutari.[17] Sazonov, though he agreed to this proposal, declined to send a warship,[18] and Pichon, who returned to the Quai d'Orsay in March in the government of Louis Barthou, declined to commit a French vessel without the explicit concurrence of the Russians. Pichon may, as Grahame suggested, have been frightened by

[12] *Annual Report for France, 1912*, F.O.371/1646. Bertie was on the other hand quite sympathetic towards Austria. *B.D.*, IX, pt.2, nos.123, 156 and 280.
[13] Bertie to Nicolson, 8 Nov. 1912, B.P., A, F.O.800/161.
[14] Bertie to Grey, 6 March 1913, B.P., A, F.O.800/177.
[15] *Ibid.*
[16] René Girault, 'Les Balkans dans les relations franco-russes en 1912', *Révue historique*, CCLIII(1975), 179–84.
[17] Helmreich, pp.296–8. F.R. Bridge, *Great Britain and Austria-Hungary, 1908–1914* (London, 1972), pp.200–2. *B.D.*, IX, pt.2, nos.766 and 767.
[18] *B.D.*, IX, pt.2, no.762. Rossos, pp.128–31.

Tardieu's renewed criticism of his conduct.[19] His stance did not, however, endear him to Bertie, who on 1 April complained bitterly to Pichon about the vacillation of the Russians, and of their reluctance to pursue any course contrary to the wishes of their Balkan friends. 'Their attitude', he protested, 'was illogical and might in the case of Montenegrin difficulty bring about the conflagration which it had been the endeavour of . . . the Ambassadors to obviate.'[20]

Nicolson considered this a 'curious outburst against Russia to Russia's ally'.[21] But it was a line to which Bertie consistently adhered. When in conversation with Nicolson on 23 June the latter ventured to praise Russia's policy and to claim that Austria had caused discord in the Balkans, Bertie retorted that the Russian emperor by posing as the 'Protector of all Slavs had given unnecessary offence to the Emperor of Austria, the sovereign of millions of Slavs'.[22] Similarly, he supported Grey in his opposition to the Russian-backed claims of the Balkan allies for indemnities from the Porte, and on 13 June he pressed Pichon, whom he openly accused of being 'at times too Russian', to join Britain in making urgent representations at St Petersburg on this subject. It might, he argued, in the long run be to the advantage of Russia to weaken Turkey, but it would not benefit Britain and France if the Turks were left without the means to reorganize their administration and armed forces.[23] Having failed, however, to win French support for the British case, he took advantage of the visit of Poincaré and Pichon to London in June to urge Grey to speak strongly to them about indemnities. Worried lest the French government should be encouraged to believe that Britain would give way on this issue, he pressed to Grey to make it quite clear to France and Russia that British policy was to maintain what remained of the Ottoman empire as a going concern with proper means to be independent of Russian 'tutelage'. The alternative Russian policy was, he maintained, 'to bleed Turkey financially sufficiently so as to prevent her re-organising herself . . . in order that she may in future be at the mercy of Russia.[24]

The prospect of a radical change in the strategic balance in the eastern Mediterranean clearly bothered Bertie. He pleaded with Grey to take a firm stand against the continued Italian presence in the

---

[19] Grahame to Tyrrell, 2 April 1913, Grey MSS., F.O.800/54. Bertie to Grey, 22 Aug. 1913, B.P., A, F.O.800/177. *B.D.*, IX, pt.2, nos.771 and 780.
[20] *B.D.*, IX, pt.2 nos.772, 782. 789 and 794.
[21] *Ibid*, no.794.
[22] Memo. by Bertie, 23 June 1913, B.P., A, F.O.800/161.
[23] *B.D.*, IX, pt.2, nos.1051 and 1054. Bertie to Grey, 17 June 1913, B.P., A, F.O.800/180. Bertie to Grey, 18 Dec. 1913, B.P., A, F.O.800/166.
[24] Memo. by Bertie, 29 June 1912, B.P., A, F.O.800/180.

Dodecanese islands, which, he feared, would soon be treated as a *fait accompli*.²⁵ Moreover, he remained suspicious about Russia's intentions with regard to Constantinople and the straits. He therefore vigorously opposed a suggestion made originally by Paul Cambon to Grey in June 1912 that Russia should have a position in the Mediterranean. In his annual report for 1912, which he completed in August 1913, he pointed out that in a war in which Russia was on the side of France and England, she could make use of French and British ports. If, however, Russia were to possess a naval station of her own in the eastern Mediterranean, he thought that it would add to her 'power of injury to British interests if she were at war with us until we evicted her'. He contended:

> from an enfeebled Turkey she would probably obtain a right of way through the Bosphorous and Dardanelles, and her ships of war would come out of the Black Sea into the Mediterranean, make raids on our commerce, using the Russian naval station as a refuge and slipping back into the sea of Marmora, the gates of which at the Dardanelles would be closed against any pursuing British squadron!²⁶

The resumption of the Balkan struggle in July 1913, when, after quarrelling over the division of Macedonia, Bulgaria found herself engaged in a war with her former allies and Roumania, seemed in Bertie's eyes to provide a fresh opportunity for limiting Russia's influence. He wrote to Grey with regard to the initial Greek victories that the more territory which they could squeeze out of Bulgaria the better. 'Greece', he commented, 'will be more get-at-able than Bulgaria, and can be used as a block against a seizure of Constantinople by Bulgaria on her own account or on behalf of Russia later on.'²⁷ Similarly, he advised Grey against putting pressure on the Turks to withdraw from Adrianople. He refused to take talk of isolated Russian action against Turkey seriously, and Izvolsky's warning to Grahame on 23 July that Russia would act alone, he dismissed as bluff. Germany, he thought, was not yet ready

---

²⁵ *B.D.*, IX, pt.2, no.123. Bertie to Nicolson, 24 May 1912, Nicolson MSS., F.O.800/356. Memo. by Bertie, 25 July 1912, B.P., B, F.O.800/187. Memos. by Bertie, 29 June and 23 July 1913, B.P., A, F.O.800/180. R. Bosworth, 'Britain and Italy's acquisition of the Dodecanese, 1912–1915', *Historical Journal*, XIII(1970), 683–703.
²⁶ Bertie to Grey, 8 Sept. 1913, B.P., A, F.O.800/173. Annual Report for France, 1912, F.O.371/1646. In the previous autumn Bertie had suggested to Poincaré that the safest solution to the problem of the straits would be the establishment of a *régime* similar to that which prevailed at the Suez Canal. *B.D.*, IX, pt.2, no.143.
²⁷ Bertie to Grey, 17 July 1913, B.P., A, F.O.800/172.

for a partition of Asia Minor or a further humiliation of Turkey, and both she and Austria might, he suggested to Poincaré, place several army corps on their eastern frontiers if the Russians took separate action in Armenia. In any event, Bertie, who had known Sazonov when he was the Russian *chargé d'affaires* at the Vatican and later when he was councillor of the Russian embassy at London, did not consider him 'to be the man to come to great decisions with great risks to his country'.[28] Needless to say, in the following year Sazonov was to take decisions which were to be catastrophic for Europe and fatal for the future of imperial Russia.

Bertie's less than friendly attitude towards Russia was shared by other British officials. The presence of Russian forces in Persia and their activities there violated the letter and spirit of the 1907 convention, and of late there had been a recrudescence of Anglo-Russian rivalry elsewhere in central Asia.[29] Tyrrell, who had responded enthusiastically to the idea of improved relations with Germany, complained to Chirol on 17 April 1913 of the 'cynical selfishness' of Russia's policy in Asia. He reasoned that since Britain was 'relieved, at least for a good time to come, from the German menace', she could 'take up a somewhat firmer line with Russia without compromising the Entente'.[30] Chirol, who was worried by signs that Britain was 'drifting back into the old orbit of the Central Powers', may have had his apprehensions modified by an assurance offered by Tyrrell that no-one at the Foreign Office contemplated a change in the 'general orientation' of policy.[31] But the disparaging comments of Bertie and Tyrrell upon Russia's conduct still contrasted sharply with the views expressed by Nicolson. Perturbed lest the Germans should be seeking to draw Britain away from her 'friends', he frowned upon Bertie's complaints to Pichon about Russian diplomacy, and he urged Grey to support France and Russia in the Near East.[32] Like Bertie, Nicolson regarded the *entente* as a means both of preserving the peace of Europe and of safeguarding

---

[28] Bertie laid great stress upon the effect that any British pressure would have upon muslim opinion in India. In a conversation with Poincaré he also referred to the need for France to take account of muslim feelings in north Africa. Memos. by Bertie, 23 and 27 July 1913; Grahame to Bertie, 24 July 1913; B.P., A, F.O.800/180. *B.D.*, X, pt.1, no.900.
[29] David McLean, *Britain and Her Buffer State. The collapse of the Persian empire 1890–1914* (London, 1979), pp.75–105 and 139.
[30] Chirol to Hardinge, 18 April 1913, Hardinge MSS., 93.
[31] Chirol to Hardinge, 10 April 1913, *ibid*.
[32] Nicolson to Hardinge, 9 Jan. 1913; Nicolson to Goschen, 14 Jan. 1913; Nicolson MSS., F.O.800/362. Nicolson to Hardinge, 29 Oct. 1913, Nicolson MSS., F.O.800/370. *B.D.*, IX, pt.2, no.794.

Britain's imperial interests against an otherwise potentially hostile Dual Alliance. So important, however, did Nicolson consider the maintenance and strengthening of the understanding with Russia that he confessed to Buchanan, his successor at St Petersburg, that he was prepared to risk 'being considered an infatuated Russophile'.[33] Indeed, after his conversation with him on 23 June, Bertie noted that in Nicolson's view 'Russia can do no wrong'.[34]

Differences in their approach to Russia contributed during 1912 to a steady deterioration in relations between Tyrrell and Nicolson.[35] The latter had not been happy as permanent under-secretary. Dogged by ill-health, he had not proved an able administrator, and he had failed to establish the close working relationship with Grey which Hardinge had enjoyed. Instead, he and Grey differed over domestic as well as foreign issues, and he was compelled to witness the growing influence of Tyrrell in the formulation of foreign policy.[3] Anxious to leave London, he had begun in August 1912 to hanker after an appointment abroad. After being refused the embassies at Constantinople and Vienna, both of which became vacant in 1913, Grey promised to support him as Bertie's successor at Paris.[37] This and the intrigues connected with his proposed transfer helped to push Bertie into the ranks of Nicolson's opponents.

Foreign Office regulations specified that the appointment of head of mission should not exceed five years. Grey had, however, supported the extension of Bertie's tenure at Paris, and had agreed that he should continue there until his seventieth birthday in August 1914. The foreign secretary had also suggested that Bertie, like Monson, might stay at Paris until the end of his final year.[38] Indeed, it was when Bertie visited the Foreign Office on 22 September 1913 with a view to discussing this point with Grey that he learned of

---

[33] Nicolson to Buchanan, 22 April 1913, Nicolson MSS., F.O.800/365. Steiner, *Britain and the Origins*, p.115.
[34] Memo. by Bertie, 23 June 1913, B.P., A, F.O.800/161.
[35] Chirol to Hardinge, 18 April 1913, Hardinge MSS., 93.
[36] After a conversation with Tyrrell in December 1914 Bertie noted: 'No one man can properly do the work which Hardinge's system entailed. In Nicolson's case the result has been that he neglects what he is supposed to do and accepts without inquiry what others suggest. Under his rule the office is in a state of chaos. There is no discipline and the tail waggles the dog.' Memo. by Bertie, 19 Dec. 1914, B.P., A, F.O.800/163. Austin Lee to Bertie, 14 April 1914, B.P., B, F.O.800/188. Bertie to Tyrrell, 15 Jan 1915, B.P., B, F.O.800/189. Chirol to Hardinge, 15 Feb. and 15 March 1912; Mallet to Hardinge, 27 July 1912; Hardinge MSS., 92. Chirol to Hardinge, 20 June 1913 and 22 May 1914; Sanderson to Hardinge, 1 Jan. 1914; Hardinge MSS., 93.
[37] Nicolson to Grey, 14 Aug. 1912, Grey MSS., F.O.800/94.
[38] The Foreign Office regulations also provided that members of the diplomatic service should be retired on attaining the age of seventy. But Bertie could cite the names of several ambassadors who had remained at their posts beyond this age limit. These

Nicolson's ambition from Mallet and Tyrrell. The news did not please him. He may have hoped that Grey would invite him to stay longer at Paris, and in any case he agreed with Tyrrell's contention that Nicolson's pro-Russian bias would put him into the hands of Izvolsky. Bertie felt Paris needed an ambassador who would, if necessary, moderate French zeal for Russian aspirations, or assist them in resisting Russian exactions. 'The French ministers', he observed, 'are frequently desirous to resist pressing appeals by Russia for French support when such support would not be consistent with the permanent interests of France, and they are glad if they can say that H.M. Govt. would object.' Nicolson, he claimed, 'would be an out and out advocate at Paris and in London of Russian views'.[39]

From his talks with Mallet and Tyrrell Bertie gathered that Nicolson had been disappointed at the extension of his stay in Paris, and that he still hoped to succeed him in August or September 1914. This was important, for if Bertie were to remain at Paris until Christmas, Nicolson would by then have passed the age limit for ambassadorial appointments. Besides which, Nicolson wished to be in possession of the Paris embassy before the return from India of Hardinge, who was known also to want the post.[40] Bertie would have preferred that either de Bunsen or Hardinge should be his successor, and he grew to resent the tactics employed by Nicolson. He was particularly irritated when Nicolson, whom he dubbed the 'little blue eyed rogue', allowed out the secret of his[41] promised appointment and began to make enquiries about the furnishings of the embassy. But Grey had committed himself, and while he insisted that Bertie should complete the next year at Paris, he paid no heed to the ambassador's claim that Nicolson was unsuitable for the post. 'Grey', Bertie noted on 2 December 1913, 'is a weak man and having refused Nicolson's applications for Constantinople and Vienna could not make up his mind to make a third refusal.'[42]

---

included: Monson, Plunkett, Dufferin, Bryce and Pauncefote. Memo. by Bertie, 23 Sept. 1913; Bertie to Tyrrell, 27 Sept. 1913; B.P., B, F.O.800/187.
[39] *Ibid.*
[40] *Ibid.* Grey to Nicolson, 21 Oct. 1913; Nicolson to Grey, 21 Oct. 1913; Grey MSS., F.O.800/94. Hardinge to Nicolson, 28 April and 21 May 1913; Hardinge to Chirol, 7 July 1913; Nicolson to Hardinge, 21 May 1913; Hardinge MSS., 93.
[41] Bertie to Hardinge, 19 Feb. 1914, Hardinge MSS., 93. Bertie to Tyrrell, 18 Oct. 1913; memo. by Bertie, 2 Dec. 1913, B.P., A, F.O.800/173. Bertie to Tyrrell, 18 Oct. 1913; Tyrrell to Bertie, 22 Oct. 1913; B.P., A, F.O.800/188. Nicolson to Bertie, 13 Oct. 1913; Grey to Bertie, 20 Oct. 1913; Bertie to Grey, 25 Oct. 1913; Memo by Bertie, 18 July 1914; B.P., Add. Ms. 63033.
[42] Memo. by Bertie, 2 Dec. 1913, B.P., A, 800/173. Chirol to Hardinge, 15 April 1914, Hardinge MSS., 93. Hardinge to Nicolson, 2 July 1914, Nicolson MSS., F.O.800/375. Austin Lee to Bertie, 4 May 1914, F.O.800/188. Bertie's embassy at

Bertie had in the meantime to cope with changes in his own staff at Paris, for in November 1913 Lord Granville, the son of his former chief, replaced Lancelot Carnegie as councillor of the embassy. This choice did not please Bertie. He had previously served under Goschen at Berlin, and in spite of objections from Bertie, he and his wife insisted on bringing their German servants to Paris. But Bertie also questioned Granville's ability. 'He means well', he wrote to Tyrrell, 'but he is not an eagle and is very much under the thumb of his wife who is a stupid and obstinate woman.'[43] Furthermore, as Granville was one of the king's lords-in-waiting, Bertie had to reckon with the prospect of his being required in London when he wanted him at Paris. Bertie may even have been jealous of the position that Granville would occupy in court circles.[44] He himself never enjoyed such close relations with George V as he had known with Edward VII. King George, nevertheless, proved to be every bit as much of a problem for Bertie as his father had been when it came to arranging an official visit to France.

Such visits had in Bertie's opinion been 'much overdone' of late, and, he wrote to Grey on 8 March 1913, 'more often than not they do not serve any useful State purpose and they are a corvée to the visitor and the visited'.[45] He had, however, been distressed to learn from the king in February that he and his advisers thought that for the sake of upholding monarchical solidarity the royal couple should visit Vienna, Berlin and St Petersburg, before Paris. Bertie considered the notion, held by the king's private secretaries, that monarchies rated before republics to be absurd, and he warned the king that if he were to proceed with his proposed itinerary it would create an unfortunate impression in France, where he was already considered to be less sympathetic towards the French than his father had been.[46] As it happened Britain's domestic problems prevented the king from travelling abroad during 1912. But when in the following March the subject was raised again, George V was then able to support his case for going firstly to Berlin and Vienna with the argument that

---

Paris was formally extended to 31 December 1914 by a letter from Grey. Grey to Bertie, 25 July 1914, B.P., Add. MS 63033.

[43] Bertie to Tyrrell, 9 Sept. 1914, B.P., Add. MS. 63033.

[44] Bertie also disliked the idea that Granville's presence might be required in London in order to vote in the House of Lords. Memo. by Bertie, 8 July 1914, B.P., Add. MS. 63033. D. Kelly, *The Ruling Few or the human background to diplomacy* (London, 1952), p. 183.

[45] Bertie to Grey, 8 March 1913, B.P., A, F.O.800/166.

[46] Memo. by Bertie, 17 Feb. 1912; Bertie to Grey, 21 Feb. 1912; Bertie to Nicolson, 21 Feb. 1912; B.P., B, F.O.800/187. Memo. by Bertie, 19 Feb. 1912, B.P., A, F.O.800/171. On the king's attitude towards these visits see: Kenneth Rose, *King George V* (London, 1983), pp. 163 – 4.

Poincaré was a junior head of state and ought properly to visit London before receiving him at Paris. Grey, who would also have preferred to see the matter dropped, sought Bertie's advice about whether the French would be 'huffy' if the king went to Berlin before Paris. Indeed, he made it clear to Bertie that his own attitude towards the order in which the royal visits were to be made would depend upon the likely reaction of the French.[47]

Bertie readily admitted that 'as a matter of strict etiquette the King might await an official visit from M. Poincaré '. Yet he also thought that if a royal visit to Paris were to follow immediately after official visits to Vienna and Berlin, it 'would be too obviously an intended sop to a supposed slight to please the French public'. Instead, he recommended that the king should either withhold from going to Berlin and await a prior visit to London by Poincaré, or go to Vienna via Paris and there make a private call upon the president. The French, he warned Grey, 'are in a highly strung state owing to the intended additions to the German Army which they consider to be with the object of menacing their independence of action politically', and a visit by the king to Berlin would only aid German agents in propagating reports of an Anglo-German *rapprochement* detrimental to French interests.[48] Nevertheless, despite this advice, it was eventually settled that the king should go to Berlin for the wedding of the Duke of Cumberland's son to the Princess Victoria Louise in May, and that there should be a French presidential visit to London in June.[49] Not until April 1914 were King George and Queen Mary to favour Paris with their presence.

This official visit to France was not without its difficulties. The most serious of these concerned the role to be played by Madame Poincaré in the entertainment of the royal guests. During the septennate of Armand Fallières a section of the French aristocracy which Bertie called the 'little Duchesses Society' had found cause to criticize the participation of the president's wife in state functions.[50] Edward VII had been unenthusiastic about the prospect of Fallières being accompanied by his wife on an official visit to England in 1908, and Bertie had had to seek assurances from Clemenceau upon this matter.[51] And although some foreign sovereigns and their consorts

---

[47] Grey to Asquith, 26 Feb. 1913, Grey MSS., F.O.800/100. Grey to Bertie, 5 March 1913, B.P., A, F.O.800/166.
[48] Bertie to Grey, 8 March 1913, B.P., A, F.O.800/166.
[49] Grey to Bertie, 27 March, and 2 and 5 April, 1913; Bertie to Grey, 12 April 1913; Grey MSS., F.O.800/54.
[50] Bertie to Knollys, 17 June 1907, B.P., B, F.O.800/185.
[51] Bertie to Knollys, 23 Dec. 1907; Knollys to Bertie, 27 Dec. 1907; RA W52 79 and 81.

had been received by Madame Fallières and Madame Poincaré, the Empress of Russia had during a recent state visit to France insisted on driving everywhere with her husband. Moreover, it was at her instigation that Queen Mary at first refused to share a carriage on more than one occasion with Madame Poincaré.[52] Her stance was reinforced by her receipt of an anonymous letter from 'un fils d'une honnête française', which asserted that Madame Poincaré was a divorcee, that her former husband, a Marseilles cab driver, was still alive, and that she had been her present husband's mistress before their relationship was regularized by a civil ceremony.[53] After vigorous protests from Bertie, the queen did agree to drive with Madame Poincaré both at the entry to Paris and at a proposed military review, but she resolutely refused to accept the requirements of the French protocol that the two ladies should accompany each other on all official occasions. Bertie began to wonder if it might not be better if the queen were to remain at home, and the queen herself urged the king to abandon the visit altogether.[54] The French protocol, Frederick Ponsonby complained to Bertie, 'were like the middle class who wished to be thought gentlemen. They were always on the lookout for slights and frightened of making concessions for fear of losing their dignity'.[55] As the queen noticed, what the French were offering was quite different to the treatment that the royal couple had received in Germany where 'they had only to express the slightest wish, and this was carried out '.[56] All this reminded Bertie of Victor Emmanuel and his objections to wearing breeches. In a letter to Ponsonby he repeated the advice that he had given to the Italian protocol 'that it is the giver of a dinner who settles the menu and not the guest or guests'.[57]

Driven nearly to despair by Queeen Mary's attitude towards Madame Poincaré, Bertie complained to Tyrrell on 16 April: 'The ailment attributed to the latter lady is not catching and if it were measles one and the first contact — to which no objection is made — would suffice to infect her companion in the carriage. The other drives would not add to the danger. The ways of providence and of

---

[52] Memo by Bertie, 16–20 Feb. 1914; Bertie to Grey, 22 March 1914; Ponsonby to Bertie, 16 April 1914; B.P., B, F.O.800/188.
[53] Enclosure in Stamfordham to Bertie, 19 March 1914, B.P., B, F.O.800/188.
[54] Bertie to Stamfordham, 22 March 1914; Ponsonby to Bertie, 11 April 1914; B.P., B, F.O.800/188. Bertie to Grey, 22 March 1914, Grey MSS., F.O.800/55. Ponsonby, p.300.
[55] Ponsonby, p.300
[56] Ponsonby to Bertie, 6 April 1914, RA Geo.V M627 22.
[57] Bertie to Ponsonby, 10 April 1914, RA Geo.V M627 32. Bertie to Ponsonby, 16 April 1914, B.P., B, F.O.800/188.

Crowned Heads are inscrutable.'[58] When 'violent cyphering' between the embassy and London failed to change the queen's mind, Bertie had to persuade the French protocol to respect her wishes.[59] Nevertheless, no harm was done to the *entente*, and the visit was generally regarded as a great success. 'During my nine years and more here', Bertie subsequently wrote to Stamfordham, 'I have never known anything like the reception which the King and Queen had from every class.'[60] Rumour had it, noted Ponsonby, that Queen Mary's 'out of date hats and early Victorian gowns would become next year's fashions'![61]

But the ambassador's troubles were far from over, for after the return of the king and queen to England, Bertie found himself with a bill for over 8000 francs which had been incurred in consequence of the visit. The problem for Bertie was that of discovering who should settle this account.[62] George V had on his accession arranged with the Treasury that he, unlike his father, should not pay income tax, and that instead he should meet the cost of official visits received in London. Henceforth the king had absorbed himself in the minutiae of such expenditure, and, according to Tyrrell, it had been for reasons of economy that the royal couple had decided to accept the French government's invitation to stay at the Quai d'Orsay rather than with Bertie.[63] Nevertheless, Bertie still had to petition Buckingham palace for money to meet the cost of such entertainments as had been offered at the embassy. And not until mid-August was a cheque paid into his account, and then only after he had pleaded poverty and his inability to obtain credit because of the outbreak of war with Germany.[64]

The question of what position Britain would adopt in a Franco-German war had once more been brought to the fore by the prospect of such a conflict arising out of the situation in the Balkans. Yet while the Liberal government remained in office even those officials who, like Nicolson, favoured the conclusion of alliances with France and Russia, had to admit that such arrangements were out of the question. Grey had no wish either to split the cabinet or to break with

[58] Bertie to Tyrrell, 16 April 1914, B.P., B, F.O.800/188.
[59] Ponsonby to Hardinge, 28 April 1914, Hardinge MSS., 105.
[60] Bertie to Stamfordham, 27 April 1914, B.P., B, F.O.800/188.
[61] Ponsonby to Hardinge, 28 April 1914, Hardinge MSS., 105. The sad irony was that Queen Mary had made a great effort to obtain a gown of what she thought was the latest fashion. Ponsonby, p.301.
[62] Bertie to Ponsonby, 14 Aug. 1914, B.P. B, F.O.800/188.
[63] Memo. by Bertie, 23 June 1913, B.P., B, F.O.800/187. Memo. by Bertie, 16–20 Feb. 1914; Ponsonby to Bertie, 11 April 1914; B.P., B, F.O.800/188.
[64] Bertie to Ponsonby, 14 Aug. 1914; Ponsonby to Bertie, 19 Aug. 1914; Carrington to Bertie, 20 Aug. 1914; B.P., B, F.O.800/189.

France, and he continued to maintain that Britain's participation in a war would depend upon the circumstances in which it began and the reaction of public opinion.[65] In two cases, however, he felt reasonably certain about the course which the government would adopt. He told Sazonov on 24 September 1912 that public opinion 'would not support any aggressive war for revanche or to hem Germany in'. On the other hand, if Germany were led by her 'great . . . unprecedented strength to crush France', he did not think that Britain could stand aside.[66]

It was unlikely that any French government would have deliberately courted war with Germany for the recovery of France's lost provinces. But the settlement of the Agadir crisis was followed by a period of uneasy tension between Paris and Berlin which militated against a *détente* such as was favoured by Jules Cambon.[67] Decisions were taken to augment the sizes of the French and German armies; the understandings which had linked businessmen and financiers on both sides of the Vosges withered in a new climate of economic nationalism; and the long dormant issue of Alsace-Lorraine re-emerged as a subject of public debate.[68] In these circumstances Grey could hardly ignore the patriotic resurgence in France, which accompanied Poincaré's election as president of the republic, and the passage through parliament in the summer of 1913 of a three year army service bill.[69] The reports which he received from Paris of this nationalist revival were far from reassuring.[70] During December 1912 and January 1913 Grahame drew Tyrrell's attention to the change of tone in the French press, and the confidence felt in French armaments as a result of their performance in the Balkan struggles. 'If this feeling increases and Germany is ever in difficulty — a general strike or something of the kind — and an adventurous minister is in

---

[65] Nicolson to Goschen, 11 March 1913, Nicolson MSS., F.O.800/364. Nicolson to Buchanan, 7 April 1913; Nicolson to de Bunsen, 27 April 1914; Nicolson MSS., F.O.800/373. Memo. by Bertie, 23 June 1913, B.P., A, F.O.800/166. Grey to Harcourt, 10 and 11 Jan. 1914, Grey MSS., F.O.800/91.
[66] B.D., IX, pt.1, no.805.
[67] Keiger, pp.72 – 4. See also by the same author, 'Jules Cambon and the Franco-German Détente, 1907 – 1914', *Historical Journal*, XXVI(1983), 641 – 59.
[68] Grahame to Tyrrell, 26 Jan. 1913, Grey MSS., F.O.800/54. R. Poidevin and J. Bariéty, *Les relations franco-allemandes 1815 – 1975* (Paris 1969), pp.191 – 216.
[69] E. Weber, pp.106 – 28. Sumler, 517 – 37. B.D., IX, pt.2, no.461. Porch, pp.169 – 212. Krumeich, 00.5 – 117.
[70] Recent research has suggested that the nationalism of the revival was more limited in its geographical extent and in its social basis than was once supposed. Keiger, pp.74 – 7. J-J. Becker, *1914, comment les Français sont entrés dans la guerre* (Paris, 1977), pp.5 and 38. R. Girardet, *Le nationalisme français, 1871 – 1914* (Paris, 1966).

power', he speculated, 'France might one day surprise us all.'[71] Moreover, while Bertie continued to emphasize the pacific aspirations of the French, he too warned Grey on 3 March 1913 that in the 'present temper of the French people any incident with Germany might lead to war'. There are, he observed, 'many Frenchmen who think that war is predictable within the next two years and that it might be better for the French to have it soon. The doubt is whether the Russian Army is in a prepared state'.[72]

Bertie professed to welcome the three year service law.[73] But although he assured Paléologue that he had no doubt that in the event of a German attack upon France the British government would soon announce their support for the French, he did nothing to encourage Grey to commit Britain to such a course.[74] On 23 June 1913 he advised the foreign secretary that one reason for not offering an alliance to France was that it 'might encourage the French to be too defiant to Germany'.[75] Some nine months later he told Wickham Steed that the advantage of the *entente* was that, while it made the French more confident in their power to resist German aggression and threats, the uncertainty of Britain's military aid acted as a 'restraint on the French Government in the way of making them very prudent in confrontations with the German Government in order not to appear as aggressors or provokers'.[76] The dilemma which both he and Grey had to face was that a Franco-German confrontation might arise over a problem in which the British government had little or no interest, and over which the cabinet and public were not prepared to fight. Yet, failure to stand by France might lead to the collapse of the *entente*, the consequent weakening of Britain's global position, and with or without a war to German hegemony in Europe. Grey told the king in a letter of 9 December 1912 that 'it might become necessary for England to fight for . . . the defence of her position in Europe and for the protection of her own future and security'.[77] At a time, however, when it seemed possible that Austria and Russia might be drawn into the Balkan conflagration, he felt unable to tell Paul Cambon anything more than that the British public would be

---

[71] Grahame to Tyrrell, 5 Dec. 1912, and 26 and 29 Jan. 1913, Grey MSS., F.O.800/54.
[72] Annual Report for France, 1912, F.O.371/1646. Bertie to Grey, 3 March 1913; Grey to Bertie, 4 March 1913; B.P., A, F.O.800/166.
[73] Paléologue, *Au Quai d'Orsay*, pp.147–4.
[74] *Ibid*, pp.28–31.
[75] Memo. by Bertie, 23 June 1913, B.P., A, F.O.800/166.
[76] Memo. enclosed in Bertie to Tyrrell, 9 March 1914, B.P., A, F.O.800/176.
[77] *B.D.*, X, pt.2, no.453.

more ready to fight if war arose from Austrian aggression, rather than Serbian provocation.[78]

In Bertie's opinion the French were less concerned with the question of whether, than with that of when, Britain might provide them with armed assistance. 'All French Ministries', he explained to Wickham Steed, 'have had the conviction that in the event of war between France and Germany, England would be bound in her own interests to support France lest she be crushed.'[79] What they feared, he contended, was that there might be 'protracted discussions and valuable time lost in considering whether the casus foederis had arisen'. France might, if denied British aid in the initial stages of a conflict, suffer a crushing defeat to the detriment of England. This was a matter which Bertie took up with Grey on the eve of the visit to London in June 1913 of Poincaré and Pichon. He had derived the impression that the French were intending to use the occasion to try to obtain fresh assurances from Britain, and he evidently hoped that Grey could be persuaded to accept the idea of a more precise consultative accord. But Grey thought that anything that went beyond the notes exchanged in November 1912 would cause some resignations from the cabinet, and, despite Bertie's remonstrance that it 'contained so many members that some might be spared', he was reluctant to consider any new move in the direction of a tighter or more explicit *entente*.[80]

Since neither of the French statesmen chose to raise the subject of a new arrangement with Britain, Bertie's expectations were not fulfilled.[81] Grey's decision to accompany the king on his visit to Paris in April 1914, and the desire of the Quai d'Orsay to satisfy Russian wishes for a closer relationship with England, did, however, present him with another opportunity to seek acceptance of his idea.[82] Moreover, the intransigency displayed by the Triple Alliance powers in the Near East had led him to suppose that there would be less

---

[78] *Ibid*, no.228.
[79] Memo. enclosed in Bertie to Tyrrell, 9 March 1914, B.P., A, F.O.800/176.
[80] Memo. by Bertie, 23 June 1913, B.P., A, F.O.800/166. Nicolson to Goschen, 24 June 1913, Nicolson MSS., F.O.800/366.
[81] Bertie suspected that Paul Cambon had advised Pichon and Poincaré against raising the subject of a new arrangement. Their conversations with leading British politicians and the reception which they received from the public had, he thought, led them to concur in this advice. The visit was, however, marred by the refusal of Lewis Harcourt, the colonial secretary and one of the principal critics of the *entente* in the cabinet, to meet the French president. Memos. by Bertie, 29 June and 27 July 1913; Bertie to Grey, 25 July 1913, B.P., A, F.O.800/166. Nicolson to Buchanan, 30 June 1913, Nicolson MSS., F.O.800/366. Paléologue, *Au Quai d'Orsay*, p.159.
[82] On the origins of the Russian overture see: Schreiner, pp.712–16; Nicolson to Buchanan, 21 April 1914, Nicolson MSS., F.O.800/373; and Lieven, pp.107-8.

opposition in the cabinet to a new agreement with France. Bertie thus suggested to Paul Cambon on 21 April that the British, French, and Russian governments should exchange notes, which would define their mutual interests, and oblige them, in the event of these being menaced, to confer on their protection. This was approved both by Poincaré and by Pichon's successor, the radical, Gaston Doumergue, and it was agreed that the matter should be raised with Grey. In the belief that his proposal was more likely to be accepted if it appeared to come from the French, Bertie absented himself from the meeting which he arranged between Doumergue and Grey for the afternoon of the 23rd.[83] But he was again to be disappointed. Only at the end of their conversation did Doumergue take up with Grey the subject of a further exchange of notes, and even then his suggestion corresponded not to Bertie's idea, but to a proposal of Paléologue, who had replaced Delcassé at St Petersburg, for what amounted to an extension to Russia of the provisions of the Anglo-French arrangements of 1912. Indeed, the net outcome of this meeting was Grey's agreement to the communication of the Anglo-French notes to St Petersburg, and a subsequent decision by the British government to sanction conversations with Russia on possible naval co-operation: moves which were disturbing from the German point of view, but which had little to do with Bertie's desire for a clearer formulation of the objects of the *entente*.[84]

During his visit to London in June 1913 Bertie assured Grey that it was no longer necessary to worry about the French arriving at an accommodation with Germany. Sufficient irritation, he thought, had been caused France by the expansion of the German army to make that impossible.[85] Events would seem to suggest that Bertie was right. Nevertheless, at the close of 1913 there were signs that all was not well with the *entente*. The officials of the French foreign ministry were increasingly critical of what they considered to be a British readiness to separate themselves from France and Russia in Near and Middle Eastern affairs. Paul Cambon was sufficiently alarmed by 'le ton aigre-doux' of some of the correspondence which he received from Paris, that in December he wrote to Pierre de Margerie, who was on the point of succeeding Paléologue as *directeur politique*, of the need to shelter his minister against 'ces emballements et de ces vives

---

[83] Memo. by Bertie, 24 April 1914, B.P., A, F.O.800/166.
[84] Memo. by Bertie 27 April 1914, *ibid*. Grey to Buchanan, 7 May 1914, Grey MSS., F.O.800/74. *B.D.*, X, pt.2, nos.542 and 543. *D.D.F.3*, X, nos.29, 106, 111, and 135. Robbins, pp.283 – 5.
[85] Memo. by Bertie, 23 June 1913, B.P., A, F.O.800/166.

agitations dont le Quai d'Orsay a donne le spectacle trop souvent'. 'Le méfiance', he observed, 'semble telle au Quai d'Orsay contre l'Angleterre qu'on se laisse aller à parler d'une possibilité de rapprochment avec l'Allemagne.' Cambon wondered whether the proponents of such views might not be under the mistaken impression that they could thereby make themselves agreeable to Caillaux, who had recently returned to power as minister of finance. But whatever the case, Cambon inisisted that Grey had been loyal to the *entente* and that the foreign secretary had always kept him informed of his intentions.[86]

It was, perhaps, unfortunate that it was at this juncture that Cambon and the Quai d'Orsay first became fully cognizant of the results of the Anglo-German negotiations, which had been resumed in the spring of 1913 for the revision of their Portuguese colonies agreement. On 27 June Bertie had warned Grey that the publication of such an arrangement would be a 'very disagreeable surprise' to the French.[87] It was not, however, until 28 October, a week after the initialling of the new accord, that the Quai d'Orsay received from the French embassy at Berlin any clear indication of what was afoot.[88] Bertie himself was not acquainted with all the details of the negotiations, and it was 6 January 1914 before Paul Cambon appeared to comprehend precisely what had been subject to revision. Indeed, the initial French opposition to the agreement was based largely upon the misapprehension that Britain had accepted changes in that of 1898 which might enable the Germans to encircle the remnants of France's empire in the Congo. They thus objected to the attribution to Germany of Loanda and the Cabinda enclave, provision for which had actually been made in 1898, and to the fact that the new accord confirmed Britain's obligation to cooperate with Germany in opposing the establishment of French interests in Angola and Mozambique.[89]

In the hope of nullifying its possible impact upon France's future conduct in southern Africa, Paul Cambon advised Doumergue to

---

[86] P. Cambon to de Margerie, 25 Dec. 1913, de Margerie MSS.
[87] Memo. by Bertie, 29 June 1913, B.P., A, F.O.800/176. Memo. by Bertie, 23 July 1913, B.P., A, F.O.800/180.
[88] Although Paul Cambon had been told by Grey in February 1913 that the British and German governments were discussing the revision of the Anglo-German agreement of 1898, the French *chargé d'affaires* at London informed Pichon in October that he did not believe in the existence of such negotiations. *D.D.F.3*, VIII, nos.378, 391, and 397. *B.D.*, X, pt.2, nos.326 and 345. Bertie to Grey, 31 Oct. 1913, and minutes by Grey and Harcourt, Grey MSS., F.O.800/54.
[89] *D.D.F.3*, VIII, no.607; IX, no.35. *B.D.*, X, pt.2 nos.350 and 357. Notes Journalières, 4 and 6 Feb. 1914, Poincaré MSS., (Bibliothèque Nationale, Paris), N.A.Fr.16026.

oppose the publication of the Anglo-German accord.[90] Doumergue was ready to oblige.[91] But his cautious diplomacy tried the patience of his colleagues in the government. Caillaux, who suspected that England and Germany had long since settled on the partition of the French Congo, even suggested that Poincaré, his political opponent, should be persuaded to intervene personally with the British.[92] Poincaré needed little prompting, and in the second week of February first he, then Doumergue, complained to Bertie of the British government's failure to consult France on the negotiations, and of the deplorable effect that the accord would have upon French public opinion. Its publication would, Doumergue insisted, 'necessitate a formal protest by the French Government'. It was, however, the regret expressed by Poincaré at Britain having disinterested herself in the islands of San Thomé and Principé, that particularly impressed Bertie. The renunciation by Britain of any claim to the islands would, he warned Grey, be regarded in France as a 'gratuitous invitation' to the Germans to establish themselves in the gulf of Guinea.[93]

Poincaré's objections and further frantic appeals from Bertie against the publication of the revised agreement were quite sufficient to worry Grey. When Bertie visited London in order to arrange the details of the forthcoming royal visit to Paris, he found that Grey now hoped that German opposition to the publication of the renewed guarantee that Salisbury had given to Portugal in 1899 would lead to the abandonment of the project. And the king, whom Bertie met on 20 February, told him that there would be no publication of anything until after his visit to France, for he would not 'run the risk of the resulting hisses in the streets of Paris'.[94] It was doubtless, however, with some relief that Bertie learned that on 3 March Lichnowsky, the

---

[90] The French were under the mistaken impression that the publication of the revised Anglo-German agreement was desired by Berlin. In fact the Germans were opposed to the British wish to publish both the new arrangements and the assurances that Salisbury had given the Portuguese in 1899. *D.D.F.3*, IX, nos.171 and 326. Note for the president of the council, 10 May 1914, N.S. Grande-Bretagne 22. P. Guillen, 'Les questions coloniales dans les relations franco-allemandes à la vielle de la première guerre mondiale', *Revue Historique*, CCXLVIII (1972) 87-106. R.T.B. Langhorne, 'Great Britain and Germany, 1911 – 1914', in Hinsley, pp.311 – 12.
[91] *D.D.F.3*, IX, nos.116 and 256.
[92] Notes Journalières, 6, 10, and 14 Feb. 1914, Poincaré MSS., N.A.Fr. 16026. Poincaré, *Au Service*, IV, pp.56 – 58. Krumeich, pp.164 – 7.
[93] *B.D.*, X, pt.2, nos, 361, 362 and 364.
[94] Memo. by Bertie, 16 – 20 Feb. 1914, b.P., B, F.O.800/188. Memo by Bertie, 23 Feb. 1914, B.P., A, F.O.800/176. Nicolson to Goschen, 24 Feb. 1914, Nicolson MSS., F.O.800/372. Nicolson to Hardinge, 25 Feb. 1914, Hardinge MSS., 93.

German ambassador in London, had proposed, and Grey had agreed, that the matter should be dropped.[95]

It is evident from Bertie's comments upon the negotiations for the revision of the 1898 agreement that he still regarded Germany as basically acquisitive and potentially mischievous. 'The German Government', he noted in August 1913, 'keep questions simmering in the pot alongside the fire, ready at any moment to put it on and boil up for use when thought advisable.'[96] Moreover, reports such as that from an Austrian source which Walter Behrens passed on to him in November 1913, according to which Germany was planning to invade France within a year, were far from reassuring.[97] He was, however, less inclined than he had once been to credit Germany with hostile intentions towards England. The absence of any major crisis in Anglo-German relations, and the scope for cooperation which the affairs of the Balkans had presented to the governments in London and Berlin, may have contributed to this modification in his outlook. Yet more important would seem to have been his assumption that Germany's ambitions had been, and were being, successfully contained.[98]

Peace between the great powers was in Bertie's estimation the result of their mutual recognition of the prevailing balance of forces in Europe. Thus, when in June 1913 the king informed him that the Russian emperor had recently described the Anglo-Russian understanding as the best guarantee of peace, Bertie retorted that 'the best guarantee of peace between the great powers is that they are all afraid of each other'.[99] Fear of a British naval intervention had in his opinion restrained Germany from resorting to war in 1911, and Russia's apprehension about German military might had, he considered, caused her to adopt a more cautious policy in the Near East. For similar reasons he did not share the concern felt by Grey over the publication in the press of reports of the opening of

---

[95] *B.D.*, X, pt.2, no.368. Tyrrell to Bertie, 4 and 5 March 1914, B.P., A, F.O.800/176. Poincaré, *Au Service*, IV, pp.69–70.
[96] Annual Report for France, 1912, F.O.371/1646.
[97] Behrens had received this information from a source close to Berchtold. Bertie to Nicolson, 20 Nov. 1913, B.P., A, F.O.800/171.
[98] This would seem to be implied by Bertie in a remark made part in jest to Paléologue in December 1913. Of the German emperor he observed: 'C'est un grand cabotin, qui malgré ses vantardises mésure parfaitement tout ce qu'il risquerait dans une guerre contre nous trois [France, Great Britain and Russia]. . .Et puis il ne veut pas que nous lui coulions sa belle Flotte.' Paléologue, *Au Quai d'Orsay*, p.247.
[99] Memo. by Bertie, 23 June 1913, B.P., B, F.O.800/187. Tyrrell appears to have held a similar view of the international situation. To Hardinge Chirol wrote in April

conversations between the British and Russian naval staffs. Grey, who was worried lest these revelations should undermine the improvement which had so recently been effected in Anglo-German relations, tended to think that either Izvolsky or Poincaré was responsible for the leakage. But Bertie, who met Grey on 25 June 1914, maintained that it was an advantage 'that while England's position would be one of freedom from actual engagement, the impression should exist in Germany that in the event of conflict between Germany and Russia and France acting in alliance a British Fleet would give active aid to Russia'. When Grey protested that Britain was now on good terms with Germany, and that he wished to avoid a revival of friction with her, Bertie ventured to remind him that the German government might once more simply be seeking a pretext for obtaining money from the Reichstag for the expansion of the imperial navy. Nevertheless, he admitted that:

> whereas formerly the German Government had aggressive intentions under the impression that Russia was not prepared and not willing to come to the aid of France unconditionally, that France was in a weak position and that England would stand aloof, they are now genuinely alarmed at the military preparations in Russia, the prospective increase in her military forces and particularly at the intended construction at the instance of the French Government with French money of strategic railways to converge on the German frontiers.[100]

Already in November 1913 Bertie had informed Grey that the French government had made its consent to a new loan to Russia dependent upon a third of it being applied to such railways. But Bertie still doubted if Russia had either the men or the organization capable of making 'an attacking campaign against Germany and Austria'.[101] What he seems to have considered a more disturbing prospect was that of the Germans taking further measures to protect

---

1913 that Tyrrell seemed to think 'that we can now snap our fingers both at the Triple Alliance and at Russia'. Chirol to Hardinge, 10 April 1910, Hardinge MSS., 93.
[100] Memo. by Bertie, 27 June 1914, B.P., A, F.O.800/171. Bertie to Grey, 28 June 1914, B.P., A, F.O.800/177. On the revelation to the Germans of information regarding the projected Anglo-Russian naval conversations see: M. Ekstein, 'Sir Edward Grey and Imperial Germany in 1914', *Journal of Contemporary History* VI(1971), 1921 – 31; and Steiner, *Britain and the Origins*, pp.121 – 2.
[101] Bertie to Grey, 24 and 28 Nov. 1913, B.P., A, F.O.800/177. Memo. by Bertie, 24 April 1914, Bertie's doubts about Russia's military strength were probably based upon a report which he received in the previous summer from Edmond de Rothschild that de Witte, the former Russian finance minister, had said that Russia dare not go to war

themselves in the east, and their thereby upsetting the military balance in the west. They might, as Grey himself later suggested to Bertie, further augment their armed forces, or decide upon an early war with Russia. In either case Bertie assumed that the French were bound to be affected, and while he considered that they were unlikely to want to risk the calamities of even a successful war, he calculated that in the long run they would not be able to compete with the German military budget. 'This might', he wrote in a memorandum of 27 June 1914, 'make the French desperate and an incident might bring about a conflict.'[102] That the events of the following afternoon at Sarajevo might constitute such an 'incident' seems not to have occurred to Bertie.

The assassination of the Archduke Francis Ferdinand and his wife did not at first give Bertie any serious cause for alarm.[103] True, he did not share the opinion of some in Paris that it would make for peace as a firebrand had been removed. He did, however, find it quite expedient at the beginning of July to complain to the Austrian ambassador at Paris about Russia's conduct in Persia and of the danger which it posed to British interests.[104] Shortly afterwards he left France for a fortnight's leave in England. There the attitude assumed by Grey gave him no reason to suppose that a war crisis was imminent. On the contrary, where foreign affairs were concerned, Grey still seems to have been upset about the effects upon Germany of reports of an Anglo-Russian naval agreement. On 16 July he told Bertie that he had assured Lichnowsky that the military and naval conversations between Britain, France and Russia, had 'not impaired England's liberty of action', and that she was 'quite free from any binding engagements'. Germany, he explained in terms which seemed to reflect what Bertie had previously said to him, had once 'feigned alarm at the encircling policy freely attributed to H.M. Government under the inspiration of King Edward', but she was 'now really frightened at the growing strength of the Russian Army'. Grey also referred to the possibility of Germany bringing on 'a conflict with Russia at an early date' before the increases in the Russian army had had their full effect, and before the completion of the strategic railways which were being constructed in Poland. Yet, neither he nor Bertie made any reference to such a preemptive war

---

because of the internal state of the country and the military unpreparedness of its army. Memo. by Bertie, 23 July 1913, B.P., A, F.O.800/180.
[102] Memo. by Bertie, 27 June 1914, B.P., A, F.O.800/171. Memo. by Bertie, 16 July 1914, B.P., A, F.O.800/171.
[103] Mersey, p.323.
[104] Ö-U., VIII, no.10048.

resulting from an Austro-Serbian quarrel.[105] Even after his return to Paris on 20 July Bertie still felt able to propose to Tyrrell that since defects had been discovered in the embassy's chimney flues and urgent repairs were necessary, he might proceed to Martigny on 16 July in order to commence a cure that he had been planning to take there.[106]

Grey, whom government business had kept in London since April, was sensitive to the ambassador's plight. 'It must', he minuted, 'depend upon the European situation, if there is no acute and dangerous crisis Sir F. Bertie must of course avoid the soot.'[107] Yet such a crisis seemed to be made inevitable by the ultimatum which the Austrians delivered to Serbia on 23 July, for while the government in Vienna was determined to contain the Slav threat to its integrity, that in St Petersburg was in no mood to disinterest itself in the chastisement of its Balkan *protégé*. Bertie therefore decided to remain at Paris whence, despite his unruffled appearance, he viewed the ensuing developments in central and eastern Europe with a mixture of alarm and incredulity.[108] As in 1912 and 1913 he felt some sympathy for the Austrians, who, he assumed, would not have addressed such stringent terms to Belgrade unless they had proof of the complicity of Serbian officials in the murder of the archduke.[109] He urged Grey, who set great store on Austria-Hungary and Russia being restrained by Britain and the other great powers, that if he were to convene meetings at London with the French, German, and Italian ambassadors, he should call them 'consultations' for the Austrians would resent the appearance of being 'treated as a Balkan Minor State'.[110] Moreover, while he suspected that the 'Military party' at Berlin might regard the present moment as right for striking at Russia, he did not think that the German emperor and his government wanted war.[111] Nor for that matter did he agree with the suggestions made in *L'Echo de Paris* that they had been accessories before the fact to the Austrian ultimatum. 'If they had been', he somewhat naively observed, 'the German Emperor would not have been away yachting.'[112] And although he felt able to assure Szécsen

---

[105] Memo. by Bertie, 16 July 1914, B.P., A, F.O.800/171.
[106] Bertie to Tyrrell, 22 July 1914, Grey MSS., F.O.800/55.
[107] Minute by Grey on *ibid.* Tyrrell to Bertie, 24 July 1914, B.P., Add. MS.63033.
[108] H. Adam, *Paris sees it through. A Diary, 1914–1919* (London, 1919), p.20.
[109] Gordon Lennox, I, p.1. *B.D.*, XI, no.98. On Anglo-Austrian relations during the war crisis of 1914 see: F.R. Bridge, 'The British Declaration of War on Austria-Hungary in 1914', *Slavonic and East European Review*, XLVII(1969), 401–22.
[110] *B.D.*, XI, no.192.
[111] Gordon Lennox, I, p.2.
[112] *B.D.*, XI, nos.123 and 192.

on 24 July that Russia would not make war, there was little doubt in his mind that the peace of Europe was dependent upon the course which the government at St Petersburg might choose to pursue.[113]

On 27 July, by which date the Austrians and the Russians had begun to prepare for a possible resort to force, Bertie recorded in his diary: 'I cannot believe in war unless Russia wants it.' 'If', he observed, 'the Emperor of Russia adheres to the absurd and obsolete claim that she is protectress of all Slav states, however bad their conduct, war is probable.' The danger which he clearly perceived was that a Franco-German war might thus materialize in circumstances which were hardly conducive to British participation.[114] Serbia was not in Bertie's opinion an issue upon which Britain ought to fight, and on 25 July he warned Bienvenu-Martin, who during the absence on a state visit to Russia of Poincaré and the new foreign minister, René Viviani, was deputizing for the latter, that public opinion in England would not sanction a war in support of Russia if she 'picked' a quarrel with Austria over the Austro-Serbian dispute. The situation was not one which Bertie relished. 'It is', he reasoned, 'a pity that the quarrel is not one to interest us at the beginning *if there is to be a European conflict*, for our aid would then be of greatest value, but later on it will earn no gratitude and might be of little use to France.'[115]

Bertie hoped that a general European war might be avoided if the French were to hold their Russian allies in check, and he recommended to Grey that he should encourage the French to act in this sense. He thought that public opinion in France would not be in favour of backing Russia if she quarrelled with Austria, and that the French government would probably advise the Russians to moderate any 'excessive zeal' which they might display to protect Serbia.[116] In this respect Bertie seems neither to have appreciated the depth of Poincaré's devotion to the Franco-Russian alliance, nor to have understood his resolve to ensure that the French government should not seem to have separated itself from Russia. He was, however, perturbed by the way in which the efforts of the German ambassador at Paris to localize the Austro-Serbian quarrel were being used by a section of the French press to demonstrate that Austria and Germany were using the murders at Sarajevo as an excuse for humiliating the triple *entente*. *L'Echo de Paris*, which Bertie suspected of being in close touch with the Russian embassy, was, he thought, trying to make it

---

[113] *Ö-U.*, VIII, no.10679.
[114] Gordon Lennox, I, pp.1–2.
[115] *Ibid*, pp.2–3. *B.D.*, XI, no.129. René Viviani was like his predecessor, Doumergue, both president of the council and minister for foreign affairs.
[116] *B.D.*, XI, nos.134 and 192.

appear that Schoen had given the Quai d'Orsay to understand that unless France kept out of the dispute Germany would deal with her and that there would be a European conflagration. If the French public were convinced that the Germans were trying to keep France quiet, then Bertie feared it would cause great indignation in Paris and the 'task of those interested in stimulating French public opinion to range itself decidedly on the side of Russia would have been facilitated'.[117]

Schoen's efforts to allay growing press criticism of Germany in France, and his desire to give the impression that he was working in unity with the French government, thus gained Bertie's approval and support. At the same time Bertie was critical of the functionaries of the Quai d'Orsay, whom he considered to be insufficiently *coulant* with his German colleague.[118] It was perhaps unfortunate that in the absence of de Margerie, who had accompanied Viviani to Russia, the senior official at the foreign ministry was the *directeur politique adjoint*, Philippe Berthelot, a man for whom Bertie shared the contempt felt by Clemenceau and whom two years later he was to describe to Grey as being 'of anti-British sentiment, without judgement, but of pushing and intriguing nature'.[119] The Quai d'Orsay's refusal to meet Schoen's wishes by issuing a *communiqué* describing a recent meeting with Bienvenu-Martin as 'very friendly', and indicating 'solidarity' between the powers, led Bertie to propose to Grey that Britain should urge the French to publish such a notice. But his advice was opposed by Nicolson and Crowe. The latter rightly concluded that the Germans were trying to keep the other great powers out of the dispute, and that the French were apprehensive lest any declaration of solidarity be expected by the Germans to undermine the Franco-Russian alliance.[120] With this Grey seems to have agreed, and he informed Bertie on 28 July that he could not press the French to risk separating themselves from Russia.[121]

---

[117] *Ibid*, nos. 123 and 193. Carroll, pp.293–4.
[118] B.D., XI, no.92.
[119] It is not clear why Bertie had such a low opinion of Berthelot. But the view that Berthelot was anti-British was apparently widely held in Paris. It is possible that Bertie may have been influenced by the fact that Berthelot kept on good terms with Caillaux. Bertie to Grey, 14 Feb. 1916, B.P., A, F.O.800/168. Note by Gregory, 25 March 1916, Grey MSS., F.O.800/96. A. Bréal, *Philippe Berthelot* (Paris, 1937), pp.109, 152 and 172–3. Auffray, pp.251–2.
[120] B.D., XI, no.184. Bréal, pp.117–18. Bertie's conduct stands in stark contrast to that of Paul Cambon, who thought it necessary to enlighten the British public in a sense favourable to France and Russia, and who later confessed that during the crisis his embassy had 'fait la presse anglaise'. P. Cambon to Delcassé, 22 Dec. 1914, N.S. (Guerre 1914–18) Grande-Bretagne 534.
[121] B.D., XI, no.204.

Grey was not, however, in a position to prevent Bertie from giving vent to his fears about the possibility of a general European war in a peculiarly unguarded fashion. On the morning of 28 July, on which day Austria-Hungary declared war on Serbia, Szécsen informed his government that Bertie had told him that the active intervention of Russia would lead France and Germany to take part. 'England', Bertie had added, 'would look on, but would have to intervene if France were threatened with destruction.'[122] Unfortunately Szécsen's telegram does not reveal the context in which this statement was made. It may be that Bertie had simply tried to explain to his Austrian colleague the awkward position in which the British cabinet was likely to find itself, and that he had sought to warn him that a successful German invasion of France would mean Britain's involvement in the conflict. But whatever the case, Szécsen's report was regarded in Vienna as sufficiently important to be communicated to the German ambassador there.[123] Indeed, the statement coming as it did from a diplomat who had long been regarded in Berlin as hostile towards Germany, could have done nothing to discourage Bethmann Hollweg's efforts to keep Britain neutral. It may also help to explain the declaration which Bethmann Hollweg made to Goschen on the evening of the 29th that a Russian attack on Austria might involve Germany in a war with the Dual Alliance, but that Germany did not contemplate crushing France, and that she was ready to give every assurance if Britain remained neutral that she 'aimed at no territorial acquisition at the expense of France' in Europe.[124]

That Bertie was prepared to speak so freely to Szécsen was an indication of the cordial relations then prevailing between the two diplomats. By contrast, Bertie had viewed with trepidation the return of Izvolsky from St Petersburg, where he had been for a presidential visit. And after learning from Granville that Izvolsky had told him at a dinner on 27 July that he believed war to be inevitable, Bertie noted that the Russian ambassador would do 'a good deal of mischief in fomenting a war spirit here'. Yet, according to Izvolsky, a war would be the fault of England. If she 'had at once declared her solidarity with Russia and France, and her intention to fight if necessary, Germany and Austria', he insisted to Granville, 'would have hesitated.'[125] The question of what position Britain should adopt in

---

[122] Ö-U., VIII, no.10906.
[123] K. Kautsky (ed.), *Die Deutschen Dokumente zum Kriegsausbruch, 1914* (4 vols., Berlin, 1922), II, no.329.
[124] B.D., XI, no.291.
[125] *Ibid*, no.216. Gordon Lennox, I, pp.2–3. Bertie subsequently told Bienvenu-Martin that if Izvolsky's language represented the views of his government, 'it was not

the event of France being drawn by her alliance with Russia into a war with Germany was one which had to be answered by Grey, his cabinet colleagues, and parliament. It was not an issue which Bertie played any decisive role in helping to resolve. When on the evening of 30 July Poincaré, who had returned to Paris on the previous day, suggested to him that there would be no war if Grey were to announce that in the event of a Franco-German conflict resulting from differences between Austria and Serbia, Britain would come to the aid of France, Bertie responded by simply endeavouring to explain the problems faced by the British government in making such an announcement.[126] According to Poincaré's account of this conversation, Bertie also told him that he thought as he did.[127] Nevertheless, there is no other evidence to suggest that Bertie believed the time to be right for a public statement on Britain's intentions, and he certainly did not press the idea on Grey. Although he informed the foreign secretary that the feeling in Paris was that Germany would not dare risk a war with Britain for fear of a naval blockade, he also warned him of the dangers of declaring Britain *solidaire* with France. 'If we give an assurance of armed assistance to France and Russia now, Russia', he observed, 'would become exacting and France would follow in her wake.' The French, he complained, 'instead of putting pressure on the Russian Government to moderate their zeal expect us to give the Germans to understand that we mean fighting if war break out'.[128] The view held in the embassy on 30 July was put succinctly by Bertie's commercial *attaché*, Austin Lee, in a letter to his wife. 'The French', he wrote, 'say that *we* can prevent war by declaring our solidarité with France and Russia. We say that it rests with Russia not to mobilize & provoke Austria & Germany.'[129]

In London Grey offered no solace to the French. He informed Paul Cambon on 31 July that although he had told the German ambassador that in the event of a Franco-German war Britain would be drawn in, he could give him no pledge of support.[130] The Austro-

---

promising for the preservation of peace'. Bertie to Grey, 28 July 1914, B.P., Add. MS. 63033.
[126] B.D., XI, nos.318 and 373.
[127] Poincaré, *Au service*, IV, p.417.
[128] B.D., XI, no.320. Advice such as Bertie offered may well have reinforced Grey's own inclination towards relying upon Germany to restrain Austria-Hungary. See: M. Ekstein, 'Some Notes on Sir Edward Grey's Policy in July 1914', *Historical Journal*, XV(1972), 321–24.
[129] Austin Lee to wife, 30 July 1914, Austin Lee MSS., Add. MS. 46766.
[130] B.D., XI, nos.352, 367, and 447. Nevertheless, Grey's warning to Lichnowsky seems to have helped reassure Poincaré with regard to England's intentions. Notes Journalières, 1 and 2 Aug. 1914, Poincaré MSS., N.A.Fr. 16027.

Serbian quarrel remained, as Bertie noted that day in his diary, a 'bad subject on which to make a declaration of solidarity with France'. But Russia's mobilization, the military preparations made in France and Germany, and the enquiry made by Schoen of Viviani as to what France's position would be in a Russo-German war, had by the evening of 31 July left Bertie very pessimistic about the prospects for maintaining peace in Europe. In these circumstances he was anxious that Britain should be able to come to the assistance of France at the beginning of a conflict. Moreover, once war between Germany and Russia had begun on 1 August, and German troops had entered Luxemburg, Bertie began to show genuine concern over the possibility of Britain's appearing to desert France in her hour of need. So serious did he judge the situation that he had the main gates of the embassy closed in case French demonstrations of friendship should turn to those of opprobrium. 'I have', he observed in his diary on 2 August, 'been feeling so sick at heart and ashamed, that "Perfide Albion" should really become applicable.'[131]

German military plans required the defeat of the French as a prelude to an offensive against Russia, and on the next day, the 3rd, hostilities commenced between France and Germany. But, in spite of his personal feelings, the only encouragement which Bertie gave to Grey to commit Britain to the support of France was contained in an appeal not to Britain's honour, but to her interest in the outcome of the war. This he made in a brief private note of 3 August which he wrote after learning that Grey had on the 2nd assured Paul Cambon that the Royal Navy would protect the northern coasts of France, but had deprecated the sending of a British army to the continent. Bertie explained to Grey that he was not surprised by the government's decision not to send a military force to France, but, he observed: 'I think that it would be of advantage to us to give naval aid in the war, for it would bring it to an end sooner by starving Germany and it would give us a *locus standi* to determine the conditions of peace.'[132] If France were victorious, then, he reasoned in his diary, she would not be under an obligation to Britain, and 'could not be expected to consider our interests when making peace with Germany'.[133]

Bertie's argument was similar to the one which he had so frequently used in the past: Britain must either support France or see her eventually settle with Germany on terms disadvantageous to British interests. Nevertheless, the absence of any pressure on Bertie's part for the despatch of an army to France was surprising in

---

[131] Gordon Lennox, I, pp.6–9.
[132] *B.D.*, XI, nos.487 and 566.
[133] Gordon Lennox, I, p.10.

view of his previous efforts to maintain a diplomatic framework which would allow Britain to supply aid in the early stages of a conflict with Germany. Even more surprising is the fact that on the morning of 4 August Bertie refused to sanction a telegram to Grey in which Colonel Yarde-Buller, his military *attaché*, emphasized the importance of sending an expeditionary force to France. 'It had', Bertie observed, 'been decided for good reasons not to send such a force in present circumstances and the telegram . . . would serve no useful purpose'.[134] Such conduct can perhaps be explained by Bertie's recognition of the fact that Grey would find it easier to persuade his cabinet colleagues to agree to Britain allying with France if the idea of sending a military expedition to the continent were put aside, and by the faith which he himself had in the efficacy of a strategy of naval blockade.[135] Moreover, once war had begun between the great powers Bertie's primary concern was with ensuring Britain's participation on the side of France, rather than with determining the nature of the assistance that Britain might render to her *entente* partner.

Bertie was relieved by the German invasion of Belgium, which, he predicted, would 'rouse the wrath of the British Lion'. By then Germany's conduct, and more especially Schoen's enquiry of Viviani on 31 July, her violation of Luxemburg's neutrality, and the demands made upon Belgium for the free passage of German troops, had led him to reinterpret the course of recent events. 'Germany', he commented on 4 August, 'was determined to have war, and tried all she knew to lure us into abstention from the struggle.'[136] In contrast to his earlier criticisms of Russian policy towards the Balkan states, he now attributed the war to 'Hohenzollern ambition and the fears of the Habsburgs that their Slav subjects would fall away from them'. Not that he could find much to rejoice about in a conflict which he estimated would not soon be over. It might, he ruminated, provide Britain with the opportunity to share in smashing the power of the Hohenzollerns, who had been 'a curse to the world for just fifty years, when they began with poor little Denmark'. But if he now blamed Germany for the war, he did not forget that other forces also menaced British interests. On 7 August he added in his diary a cautious but prophetic note with regard to German military power. May 'it come

---

[134] Bertie to Tyrrell, 4 Aug. 1914, B.P., A, F.O.800/166.
[135] On the cabinet's initial attitude towards the idea of sending an expeditionary force to France see: C. Hazlehurst, *Politicians at War, July 1914 to May 1915. A prologue to the triumph of Lloyd George* (London, 1971), pp.86–91.
[136] Gordon Lennox, I, p.10.

to an end', he observed, 'and not be replaced by that of another Power such as Russia'![137]

Bertie's stance during the final week of July 1914 contrasted strangely with that which he had adopted during the two Moroccan crises. Far from castigating Germany for bringing the great powers to the brink of war, he seems initially to have underestimated the extent of the German government's involvement in the development of the Austro-Serbian dispute.[138] Unlike Crowe and Nicolson, he refrained from making frantic appeals to Grey to range Britain alongside France and Russia, and he instead chose to emphasize the dangers involved in allowing the Russians to believe that they could rely on British support.[139] He had even advised Grey to intervene with the Quai d'Orsay in order to persuade the French to be more accommodating in their dealings with the German ambassador. Indeed, Luigi Albertini suggested in his study of the origins of the first world war that the inexperienced Bienvenu-Martin was under Bertie's influence, and that in default of better advice, he failed to shatter the 'German illusion that they could save the peace while sacrificing Serbia and humiliating the other Great Powers'.[140] This would seem to exaggerate Bertie's role at Paris, and to overlook such advice as Berthelot may have offered to his minister. The course recommended by Bertie was in any case quite in line with the views which he had frequently expressed on Russian diplomacy in the Balkans. He had no sympathy with Serbian aspirations, and their fate was not in his opinion a matter vital to the interests of Britain, France, or Russia. Yet, he had no doubt about the importance for Britain of maintaining the continental equilibrium, and of the need to ensure for her a voice in any future peace settlement. In the final analysis these interests could, according to Bertie's reckoning, only be secured through her participation in the war against Germany.

---

[137] *Ibid*, pp.12–15.
[138] See, for instance: Fischer, *War of Illusions*, pp.421–84.
[139] B.D., XI, nos.369 and 446. Nicolson to Hardinge, 5 Sept. 1914, Hardinge MSS., 93. Steiner, *The Foreign Office*, pp.154–64.
[140] L. Albertini, *The Origins of the War of 1914* (3 vols., London, 1952–7), II, p.400.

13

Quelle fin de carrière

The war crisis of 1914 had denied Bertie his cure at Martigny. The outbreak of hostilities deprived him of the opportunity for any further leave that summer. Other pleasures had also to be foregone. The French measures of mobilization, besides disrupting commerce and public services in Paris, robbed the embassy of its under-butler and footmen, and threatened the *Ritz*, much frequented by Bertie, with closure.[1] On the morning of 3 August Bertie found himself with neither milk for his coffee, nor *The Times* for his erudition.[2] For nearly a week he had to rely upon the less than satisfactory columns of the Paris edition of the *Daily Mail* for news about political changes in England.[3] As the doyen of the *corps diplomatique*, an office which had passed to Bertie after Khevenhüller's departure in 1910, he had also to deal with the Austrian ambassador's complaints about the difficulties he had encountered in securing provisions from local tradesmen and over the treatment of Austro-Hungarian subjects in France. But such problems were bound to be of a temporary nature. Von Schoen left for Germany on the evening of 3 August, and on the 11th, twenty-four hours before the official announcement of a state of war between France and Austria-Hungary, Count Szecsen was taken by special train to the Italian frontier.[4] Four days later Bertie went to the Gare du Nord to greet Sir John French, the commander-in-chief of the British Expeditionary Force, who, along with his staff, was to be lodged at the embassy in rooms which had only recently been 'dismantled for work on the chimney flues'. Such work, Bertie lamented, 'must be postponed until after the war or when things are quieter and workmen can be obtained'.[5] In the meantime grand strategy and the menace posed by the advance of the German armies

---

[1] Gordon Lennox, I, pp.8–9
[2] *B.D.*, XI, no.659.
[3] Gordon Lennox, I, p.13.
[4] Bertie to Grey, 13 and 14 Aug. 1914, F.O.146/4382, despts.411 and 414. Freiherr von Schoen, *The Memoirs of an Ambassador* (London, 1922), p.208.
[5] Bertie to Nicolson, 14 Aug. 1914, B.P., Add. MS 63033. Bertie to Grey, 15 Aug. 1914, B.P., A, F.O.800/166. Gordon Lennox, I, p.17.

took precedence over ambassadorial comfort and the danger of a sudden descent of soot.

The British government's decision to send four divisions to France, and the conversion of the Anglo-French *entente* into a military alliance had no immediate impact upon Bertie's role as ambassador. He had exercised relatively little influence upon Grey and his colleagues during the last days of peace, and for the remainder of August he readily accepted the subordination of his diplomacy to what he understood to be the requirements of war. His knowledge of the military operations was in any case scanty, and based in the first place mainly upon rumour and tales of travellers in the war zone. Nevertheless, Bertie was not alone in his ignorance, for in the wake of Sir John French's retreat from Mons, it was to the embassy that the Foreign Office appealed for information. In a telegram of 26 August Bertie was told that the War Office was, and Sir John appeared to be, in the dark with regard to the intentions of the French commander, Joffre. All this, Grey explained, was 'very embarrassing' since they were unable to form any appreciation of the general situation and its prospects, and their 'bearing on the future disposition and use of British forces'.[6]

Bertie communicated Grey's message to Delcassé, who, as a result of a recent reshuffle in the French government, had returned to his former post at the Quai d'Orsay. Besides promising Bertie that Joffre would be instructed to keep Sir John French informed, the new foreign minister maintained that he was confident that the advancing Germany army would be held back from Paris. 'He says', Bertie added in his report to Grey, 'that no profession of faith in regard to England is required from him'. Bertie did not, however, share Delcassé's confidence with regard to the military situation. Nor for that matter did he believe Delcassé when he assured him on the next day, the 28th, that there was no question of removing the seat of government from Paris. Bertie had learnt on 'pretty good authority' that the question of a move to Bordeaux in the event of the Germans breaking through the Franco-British lines was under consideration.[7] When on 30 August he heard that there was fighting going on near Compiègne he began to burn confidential papers and to make preparations for an early evacuation of the embassy. And Granville's German servants, who had already become a matter of acute embarrassment to Bertie were, with the consent of the Swiss minister

---

[6] Grey to Bertie, 26 Aug. 1914, B.P., A, F.O.800/166.
[7] Bertie to Grey, 27 and 28 Aug. 1914, *ibid.* Gordon Lennox, I, p.23.

and the connivance of Maurice Herbette, smuggled out of France in the guise of citizens of Switzerland.[8]

The British government was far less bothered by the prospect of the removal of the embassy to Bordeaux than by the threat of Sir John French to withdraw his army to the west of Paris. Worried by Sir John's apparent loss of nerve and the evident disharmony between the British and French commanders, Lord Kitchener, who had assumed the mantle of secretary of state for war, decided to see the situation for himself. He thus hurried to France and arrived at the British embassy on the afternoon of 1 September for a conference with French, Viviani and Alexandre Millerand, the French minister for war.[9] It was after this meeting that Sir John sought and secured Bertie's support for his opposition to Kitchener's plan personally to inspect the British lines. Bertie impressed upon Kitchener the view that such a visit would have a most unfortunate effect upon French military and public opinion, and would give the impression that Sir John French had not given satisfaction to his government, and that British troops were to blame for the recent French reverse. At first Kitchener demurred, but after Bertie had telegraphed to Grey to seek instructions, he appeared to acquiesce in the ambassador's advice. On the next day he returned to England without a visit to the front.[10]

Shortly after informing London of his conversation with Kitchener, Bertie received a salient reminder of the proximity of the fighting. A German aeroplane passed over the embassy house, and the explosion of a bomb was heard from the direction of the Place de la Concorde.[11] Nonetheless, Bertie was probably as much saddened as relieved by the official notice which he received at 1.30p.m. on the 2nd that the government and diplomatic body were to leave Paris that night.[12] He was already convinced that the war would be a long one. In any event there seemed to be little chance of it being over before his impending retirement in December. When, therefore, after an afternoon spent in supervising the packing and the sealing up of archives, he finally left the Faubourg St Honoré for the Gare d'Orsay, he did so under the impression that not only was he risking

---

[8] Bertie to Grey, 31 Aug. 1914, F.O.371/1983, tel.284. Gordon Lennox, I, p.24. Bertie to Tyrrell, 9 sept. 1914, B.P., Add. MS. 63033.
[9] G.H. Cassar, *Kitchener: architect of victory* (London, 1977), pp.233-40.
[10] Memo. by Bertie (undated) 1914: Bertie to French, 10 May and 22 June 1919: B.P., Add. MS. 63051. Bertie to Grey, 1 Sept. 1914, tel., Grey MSS., F.O.800/56A. Gordon Lennox, I, pp.25 – 6.
[11] Gordon Lennox, *ibid*.
[12] Bertie to Grey, 2 and 7 Sept. F.O.371/1983, tel.308 and despt.453. Bertie had been informed 'fortuitously & confidentially' of the impending move to Bordeaux on the evening of 1 September. Bertie to Rosebery, 2 Sept. 1914, Rosebery MSS., 10124.

QUELLE FIN DE CARRIÈRE

the loss of his goods and chattels, but also that he was unlikely ever again to be ambassador at Paris.[13] Quelle fin de carrière', he remarked to the Spanish ambassador. Fifty-one years in the service of his country seemed about to be concluded with a major war and a hasty flight before the enemy.[14]

Appearances can be deceptive. The journey to Bordeaux was in fact a slow and tedious one. It took the train fourteen hours, twice the usual time, to reach its destination. Once there all was confusion. Nobody knew where they were to be lodged, and in the heat of a late summer's day the representatives of powers great and small were forced to struggle for motor cars and waggons for their luggage. But Bordeaux had its compensations. The house, for instance, which was placed at Bertie's disposal, was one of the best in town. The property of Georges Guestier, a partner in an old established firm of wine merchants, it was furnished and decorated in the style of the eighteenth century. And although it was not large enough to accommodate all of Bertie's staff, its library provided adequate space for a chancery, and a large laundry ironing room on the second floor served as an office for the military and naval *attachés*.[15] Life at Bordeaux was also a good deal more relaxed than it had been of late in Paris. A strange medley of soldiers, financiers, journalists, actresses and their companions, and some society people, had joined ministers, their officials, and the diplomats in the *mouvement* to the south. Their presence, and the apparent indifference of the Borderlais to the plight of France, made the town appear more like a centre for military manoeuvres than the seat of government of a country at war.[16]

Le Chapon Fin, a restaurant celebrated for its cuisine, became the popular place of rendezvous for the exiles from Paris. For a while, until he succeeded in recapturing his cook, who had fled from Paris to Les Landes, Bertie breakfasted and dined there.[17] He also took the opportunity to savour the other delights of the region. During September he and Grahame visited the cellars of Edmond de

---

[13] Boni de Castellane, p.186. Bertie to Grey, 7 Sept. 1914, *ibid*. Gordon Lennox, I, pp.26–27.
[14] Villa Urrutia to Bertie, 13 Sept. 1914, B.P., Add. MS. 63033.
[15] Gordon Lennox, I, p.27. Austin Lee to wife, 4 Sept. 1914, Austin Lee MSS., Add. MS. 46766. Bertie to Grey, 7 and 15 Sept. 1914, F.O.371/1983, despts. 453 and 461. Bertie to Tyrrell, 13 Sept. 1914, Grey MSS., F.O.800/56A.
[16] Bertie to Grey, 8 Sept. 1914, B.P., A, F.O.800/166. Grahame to Tyrrell, 23 Sept. 1914, Grey MSS., F.O.800/56A. Gordon Lennox, I, p.31.
[17] Bertie to Tyrrell, 13 Sept. 1914; Grahame to Tyrrell, 23 Sept. 1914, Grey MSS., F.O.800/56A.

Rothschild at the Chateau Lafite, and sampled the wines of *Messrs. Barton et Guestier* at a dinner given by their landlord's brother.[18] On another occasion Bertie was able to converse with the enemy, when, after a boat trip down the Garonne, he met German soldiers imprisoned in the Vauban fortress at Balaye.[19] Neither Bertie nor his staff had, however, retired to a life of easy living in the south. The need to make arrangements with the French authorities for the reinforcement, transportation and provisioning of the British forces in France meant that the business of the embassy steadily increased.[20] By the end of October the embassy had become what Grahame termed a 'very "hot corner" ', registering fifty-seven papers on one 'normal' day.[21] Admittedly, in spite of his regular morning visits to the ministries, Bertie rarely saw ministers, and he soon found cause to complain of the inefficiency of the *bureaux* in the handling of his enquiries.[22] Nevertheless, he was not in a position to contemplate following the example of Izvolsky, who had taken up the occupancy of the Château Margaux in the Médoc district some twenty miles from town.[23]

Amongst the several problems which beset Bertie at Bordeaux was that of the state of Britain's representation at Paris. He had decided to take with him all his diplomatic staff, and had left the embassy house in the care of Cuthbertson, the archivist, a chancery servant and an English porter. The latter had been instructed to direct any British subjects requiring assistance to apply to the British consulate-general, so long as it remained open, and after that to the United States embassy or consulate-general.[24] At the same time Bertie had required Graham, the acting British consul-general, to stay with his staff at Paris until there was a danger of either of communications with the coast being cut, or of a German entry into the capital. Graham had evidently made other plans, or at any rate interpreted Bertie's instructions more literally than was intended, for on the morning of 3 September, just eight hours after the ambassador's departure, Graham had left for London.[25] As a result British subjects arriving in Paris were forced to seek assistance from the American consular and diplomatic staff there: a situation which according to the

---

[18] Gordon Lennox, I, pp.35, 40–1, and 45.
[19] *Ibid*, pp.38–9.
[20] Grey to Bertie, 7 and 15 Sept. 1914, tels., Grey MSS., F.O.800/56A.
[21] Grahame to Tyrrell, 31 Oct. 1914, Grey MSS., F.O.800/56A.
[22] Bertie to Grey, 27 Sept. 1914, B.P., Add. MS. 63034.
[23] Grahame to Tyrrell, 23 Sept. 1914, Grey MSS., F.O.800/56A. Gordon Lennox, I, p.27.
[24] Bertie to Grey, 7 Sept. 1914, F.O.371/1983, despt.453.
[25] Bertie to Herrick, 5 Oct. 1914, B.O., A, F.O.800/166.

embassy chaplain created *'a very bad impression'*.[26] Once Bertie learned of this state of affairs, he hastened to urge the Foreign Office to replace Graham, whose 'cowardly conduct' he attributed in part to his family being of Greek origin, and of his therefore being 'not quite of British blood'.[27] Little notice was, however, at first taken of Bertie's plea, and not until October, when Austin Lee returned to Paris, was Britain's consulate general there put in any kind of order.[28]

Bertie never received a satisfactory explanation of the conduct of the acting consul-general.[29] But this was only one of a number of minor issues on which Bertie found himself at odds with the Foreign Office in the autumn of 1914. Another resulted from the unusually generous offer of the Treasury to pay members of the embassy staff twenty to thirty shillings a day, depending on whether or not they had rent to pay, to cover the extra expenses that they might incur as a result of their move to Bordeaux.[30] Bertie objected to this on the grounds that since his staff were not incurring any additional costs this was an unnecessary charge upon the public purse. He recommended that the Treasury should instead set aside a sum to cover the cost of a gift of plate for the Frenchmen who had provided two houses rent free for the British embassy at Bordeaux; that thirty pounds should be paid directly as rent for a third house which it had become necessary to acquire; and that before their return to Paris a bonus should be paid to his staff 'according to their respective merits for the very hard work they will have done'. In Eyre Crowe's opinion, this was 'one of Sir F. Bertie's typical moves to annoy his staff'. Nicolson thought that 'a "bonus according to Merit" would be invidious and difficult to adjust', and in the end it was decided to accept the Treasury's proposals.[31] There was perhaps some justice in the claims of Crowe and Nicolson. But in fairness to Bertie it should be added that some members of his staff had actually had their costs reduced as a result of the move to Bordeaux.[32] Moreover, Bertie made every effort to secure adequate recompense for Cuthbertson, who whilst in charge of the chancery at Paris was

---

[26] Bertie to Tyrrell, 28 Sept. 1914, B.P., Add. MS 63034. Grey to Bertie, 30 Sept. 1914, tel., B.P., A, F.O.800/166.
[27] Bertie to Grey, 30 Sept. 1914, tel., *ibid*. Bertie to Herrick, 5 Oct. 1914, B.P., A, F.O.800/166. Bertie to Tyrrell, 3 Oct. 1914, Grey MSS., F.O.800/56A.
[28] Bertie to Grey, 3 Oct. 1914, tel., Grey MSS., F.O.800/56A. Austin Lee to Bertie, 6 Oct. 1914, B.P., A, F.O.800/q66.
[29] Bertie to Nicolson, 9 Oct. 1914, B.P., Add. MS. 63034. Austin Lee to Bertie, 4 Nov. 1914, B.P., Add. MS. 63035.
[30] Crowe to Bertie, 9 Oct. 1914, F.O.371/1983, despt.607.
[31] Bertie to Crowe, 17 Oct. 1914, and minutes by Crowe and Nicolson, F.O.371/1983.
[32] Bertie to Crowe, 4 Nov. 1914, F.O.371/1983.

unable to return home for his meals, and in consequence compelled to eat at extra expense in restaurants.[33]

Whilst Bertie engaged in skirmishes with the Foreign Office, speculation commenced in the French press and in political circles at Bordeaux about the possible return of the government to Paris.[34] It had originally been assumed that this would only take place when, as Bertie put it, the Germans were 'on the run without visible possibility of return to the neighbourhood of Paris'.[35] But in September it had been anticipated that Joffre would soon mount an offensive which would drive the Germans out of France.[36] Indeed, at the end of October Delcassé was still talking as if this would take place within the next few weeks. Poincaré and those on the left of the French cabinet were, however, anxious to return to Paris before the end of the year. Money bills had to be voted, and the chambers were constitutionally bound to meet on the second Tuesday in January.[37] Thus, despite the opposition of Briand, Delcassé and Millerand, the council of ministers decided on 4 December in favour of returning. Bertie thought this a 'foolish decision'. The Germans were still close to Compiègne, and he agreed with Delcassé that the presence of the government at Paris could only encourage them to renew their efforts to take the city, especially at a time when the Russian military effort was faltering in the east.[38]

Even before the French government made up its mind to return to Paris, Bertie had begun to toy with the idea of paying a personal visit there. His intention had been to make arrangements for the removal of his furniture to England.[39] But this was to prove unnecessary. As Bertie subsequently learned from Tyrrell, Grey had decided in September to extend his embassy at Paris, and on 22 November he finally sent a letter to Bordeaux to request him to 'stay on and see the war through'. It would, Grey observed, 'be a pity and also a loss to the public service if you did not return to Paris when the war is successfully advanced and be there to participate in its successful

---

[33] Bertie to Tilley, 17 Nov. 1914, F.O.371/1983. Tilley to Bertie, 25 Nov. 1914; Bertie to Tilley, 29 Nov. 1914; B.P., B, F.O.800/188.
[34] Gordon Lennox, I, p.57.
[35] Bertie to Tilley, 16 Nov. 1914, F.O.371/1983.
[36] Gordon Lennox, I, pp.28 and 39.
[37] Bertie to Grey, 29 Oct. 1914, B.P., A, F.O.800/166. Bertie to Grey, 19 Nov. 1914, Grey MSS., F.O.800/56A.
[38] Bertie to Grey, 7 Nov. 1914, Frey MSS., F.O.800/56A. Bertie to GRey, 14 Nov. 1914, B.P., A, F.O.800/161. Bertie to Grey, 5 Dec. 1914, B.P., A, F.O.800/166. Gordon Lennox, I, pp.65 and 74–5.
[39] Bertie to Tyrrell, 25 Nov. 1914, tel., B.P., Add. MS. 63035.

QUELLE FIN DE CARRIÈRE

conclusion'.⁴⁰ Bertie was only too pleased to accept this offer for which he soon had the opportunity to thank Grey personally, for on 16 December, just four days after the return of the embassy to Paris, he travelled to London.⁴¹ There he met among others Asquith, Grey, Kitchener and Tyrrell, and on 18 December he had an audience with the king.⁴² The latter expressed the opinion that as Bertie was to remain at Paris, he expected that he would hope the war would 'last a long time'. Bertie imagined that this was 'H.M.'s idea of being "funny" '. Apparently it was not Bertie's.⁴³

The king had more to offer Bertie than his humour. In the following June, on the recommendation of Asquith and Grey, he conferred on Bertie the dignity of a barony of the United Kingdom.⁴⁴ Anxious to keep his name and at the same time to maintain a distinction between himself and any heir to the earldom of Lindsey, which was held by another branch of his family, Bertie chose as his title the style of Lord Bertie of Thame, after the estate and manor that he had inherited from his father.⁴⁵ What, however, he had not reckoned with was a claim from the Home Office for £330 as a fee for the peerage. He protested to the prime minister that as the honour was one given for services rendered to the state, he was inclined to think that he ought not to have to pay for it.⁴⁶ Asquith agreed, and eventually the chancellor of the exchequer was persuaded to remit the sum.⁴⁷ Not for the first time, Bertie's bluster triumphed over public parsimony.

Bertie was grateful to Grey for the prolongation of his embassy.⁴⁸ Yet his confidence in Grey's handling of Britain's wartime diplomacy soon began to wane. On one issue, the future *régime* of the straits between the Black Sea and the Aegean, Bertie found himself completely at odds with the foreign secretary. The latter with a view in the first instance to ensuring Russia's effective cooperation in the war effort against Germany, and later with the object of diverting her

---

⁴⁰ Tyrrell to Bertie, 27 Nov. 1914, B.P., A, F.O.800/166. Memo. by Bertie, 19 Dec. 1914, B.P., A, F.O.800/163.
⁴¹ Bertie to Grey, 16 Dec. 1914, B.P., A, F.O.800/166.
⁴² Memo. by Bertie, 18 Dec. 1914, B.P., A, F.O.800/177. Memo. by Bertie, 19 Dec. 1914, B.P., A, F.O.800/163.
⁴³ Memo. by Bertie, 19 Dec. 1914, B.P., B, F.O.800/288.
⁴⁴ Scott-Gatty to Bertie, 3 June 1915; Bertie to Asquith, 4 June 1915; Bertie to Asquith, 4 June 1915; B.P., B, F.O.800/189. Bertie to Grey, 7 June 1915, Grey MSS., F.O.800/57. Gordon Lennox, I, p.179.
⁴⁵ Bertie to College of Arms, 15 June 1915, B.P., B, F.O.800/189.
⁴⁶ Bertie to Asquith, 23 Aug. 1915, *ibid.*
⁴⁷ Asquith to Bertie, 27 Aug. 1915, *ibid.*
⁴⁸ Bertie to Grey, 7 Dec. 1914, B.P., A, F.O.800/166.

ambitions away from central and eastern Europe, had since Turkey's entry into the war on the side of the enemy indicated his readiness to acquiesce in the eventual dismemberment of the Ottoman empire.[49] Thus encouraged to think in terms of acquiring access for their warships to the Mediterranean, the Russians formulated their claims. And on 4 March 1915, a fortnight after the commencement of the Anglo-French bombardment of the Dardanelles forts, Sazonov formally requested British and French acceptance of the eventual cession to Russia of Constantinople, the western shores of the straits up to the Enos-Midea line, the Asiatic shore of the Bosphorus, the islands of the sea of Marmora, and Imbros and Tenedos.[50]

Bertie was horrified by Sazonov's pretensions.[51] As in 1908 he was wholly opposed to Russia obtaining a privileged position which would permit her warships to enter the Mediterranean, but leave her free to prohibit or restrict the passage of other navies through the straits. Instead, he favoured the internationalization of the waterway, the demolition of the shore forts, and the establishment of Constantinople as a free city. He thought that if the British and French governments succeeded in occupying the Gallipoli peninsula, they should continue to hold it until the Russians came to a 'reasonable condition of mind', and were ready to sign a peace which would not aggrieve Italy and the Balkan states and 'expose us to grave disadvantage in the event of a war with Russia'.[52] But all Bertie's endeavours to counter Delcassé's inclination towards yielding to Russian pressure were in vain for Grey had already decided to give way.[53] Anxious to discover the views of the French government on the Russian proposals and to ensure that Britain should not appear to be the main obstacle to their acceptance, and reluctant to make any pronouncement before consulting the cabinet and the leaders of the opposition, Grey

---

[49] M.G. Ekstein, 'Russia, Constantinople and the Straits, 1914–1915', Hinsley, pp.423–34. On this controversial issue see also: C.J. Smith, 'Great Britain and the 1914–1915 Straits Agreement with Russia: the British Promise of November 1914', *American Historical Review*, LXX (1965), 1015–34; and K. Neilson, *Strategy and Supply. The Anglo-Russian Alliance, 1914–1917* (London, 1984), pp.49–50 and 72–3.
[50] Buchanan to Grey, 4 March 1915, tel., B.P., A, F.O.800/177.
[51] Bertie to Grey, 14 Feb. 1915, *ibid*.
[52] Memo. by Bertie, 18 Dec. 1914, B.P., A, F.O.800/166. Bertie to Grey, 7 and 10 March 1915, B.P., A, F.O.800/177. Bertie had already suggested to Delcassé on 12 November 1914 that the Suez canal system should be adopted for the straits along with the removal of the fortifications of the Dardanelles and Bosphorous. Bertie to Grey, 12 Nov. 1914, B.P., A, F.O.800/177.
[53] It was Bertie's belief that during his visit to St. Petersburg in 1912 Poincaré had 'made some foolish promises about the Straits and that Delcassé when Ambassador at St. Petersburg went still further in the foolishness'. Bertie was also under the impression that Izvolsky had put pressure upon Delcassé by threatening to reveal his

deliberately refrained from giving Bertie any indication of his thinking on this matter.[54] Bertie was thus astonished to learn at midnight on 10 March that the British government had decided to agree to all Sazonov's claims, subject to the successful prosecution of the war and his acceptance of British and French desiderata in the remainder of the region.[55]

The government's decision preceded a similar move by the French and left Bertie with no room for manoeuvre. Nevertheless, during the next two years he was to continue to harp on the 'folly' of according to Russia what Grey himself termed 'the greatest prize of the whole war'.[56] As a result of this 'disastrous consequence of a competition for Russian favour', Russia would, Bertie later claimed, be a 'Mediterranean Power with an impregnable base'.[57] There seemed in any case to be few immediate advantages to be derived by Britain and France from their promise to Russia. Sazonov was obdurate in opposing Greek participation in the Dardanelles campaign, and reluctant to sanction such territorial offers as seemed likely to tempt the other Balkan neutrals and Italy to enter the war on the side of the *entente* powers. 'Our concessions to Russian sentiment', Bertie complained, 'do not bear the refreshing fruit of counter concessions. It is like drawing wisdom teeth out of Sazonov's obstinate jaw.'[58] The spectacle of the British government seeking to purchase the support of other powers with 'offers all round of goods that did not belong to England and her allies' was not in any event one which Bertie found particularly edifying. By the autumn of 1915 he had reached the conclusion that Grey was 'played out and unable to come to any virile decision . . . pushed this way and that and . . . in continual fear of being deserted by Russia or of offending Russian susceptibilities'.[59] Yet, despite these criticisms of Grey and his objections to the aims and methods of Russian diplomacy, Bertie did not lose sight of what he believed to be the greater threat posed by Germany's expansive ambitions. He never shared the view held by some that Britain and

---

promises. Bertie to Grey, 10 March 1915, B.P., A, F.O.800/177. Bertie to Grey, 21 Sept. 1916, B.P., A, F.O.800/178.
[54] Grey to Bertie, 15 March 1915, B.P., A, F.O.800/177. Ekstein, 'Russia, Constantinople and the Straits', p.433.
[55] Grey to Bertie, 10 March 1915, tel., B.P., A, F.O.800/177.
[56] Grey to Bertie, 11 March 1915, tel., with annotations by Bertie, *ibid*. On the French reactions to the British move see: G.H. Cassar, *The French and the Dardanelles. A study of failure in the conduct of war* (London, 1971), pp.100 – 03; and Andrew and Kanya-Forstner, *France Overseas*, pp.72 – 4.
[57] Bertie to Hardinge, 10 Oct. 1916, B.P., A, F.O.800/178.
[58] Bertie to Asquith, 5 April 1915, B.P., A, F.O.800/162. Bertie to Drummond, 7 April 1915, B.P., A, F.O.800/177.
[59] Memo. by Bertie, 24 Oct. 1915, B.P., A, F.O.800/167.

France would in the future have to look towards Germany to help them counter Russian hegemony in Europe.[60] On the contrary, the war only tended to confirm Bertie in his long held suspicions about Germany's intentions, and it nurtured in his mind a deep distaste for all things German. 'I feel', he wrote in May 1915 after receiving a report of an alleged German atrocity, 'that I myself would, if I could, kill every combatant German that I might meet'.[61]

At an early stage in the conflict Bertie concluded that German hatred of Britain was 'intense and undying', and that it was therefore essential to achieve a military victory that would permit the *entente* powers to deprive the Germans of any power to injure them for as long a period as possible.[62] There was never any doubt in his opinion that Germany must be brought to her knees and destroyed as a world power. Anything less than this would, he feared, 'only be a halting truce, with war to begin again in a few years'.[63] For Bertie there could therefore be no question of handing back to Germany those colonial possessions that had already been occupied by the forces of the British empire and of France. Nor in his view could there be any return to the pre-war territorial *status quo* in Europe. France would require the return of Alsace-Lorraine, and Britain, he insisted, should demand the retro-cession of Heligoland. But although he shared what he assumed to be French hopes for the disintegration of the Wilhelmine Reich and the suppression of Prussian supremacy, he evidently had doubts about the practicability of the victorious allies maintaining such a settlement.[54] If after the war the German-speaking provinces of Austria desired union with Germany, then, he thought, no treaty could prevent it. 'Prussia', he predicted in August 1916, 'would break her engagement if she undertook one and nobody would be likely to go to war to enforce a Treaty prohibiting fusion.'[65]

Bertie's aversion to the idea of a compromise peace in part explains his opposition to American efforts to bring an end to the European war. In this respect, however, Bertie was also influenced by

---

[60] Nicolson was distressed to hear it said in circles that should have been better informed that in some years time Britain would be fighting Russia 'in order to preserve the balance of power'. Nevertheless, Paul Cambon thought it necessary to warn Delcassé that England might hesitate over lending a hand to the establishment of a sort of Slav hegemony in eastern Europe. Nicolson to Buchanan, 8 Jan. 1915, Nicolson MSS., F.O.800/377. P. Cambon to Delcassé, 15 Nov. 1915, Delcassé MSS., 3. Gordon Lennox, I, p.49.
[61] Gordon Lennox, I, p.166.
[62] *Ibid*, pp.148 – 9.
[63] *Ibid*, p.67, and II, p.11. Memo. by Bertie, 10 Aug. 1916, B.P., A, F.O.800/171.
[64] Memo. by Bertie, 18 Dec. 1914, B.P., A, F.O.800/166. Gordon Lennox, I, p.366, and II, pp.40 – 1.
[65] Memo. by Bertie, 17 Aug. 1916, B.P., B, F.O.800/190.

Washington's protests about British blockade policy: protests which drew from Bertie's pen a stream of rancorous comments on Wilsonian moralizing and the self-interest of American traders and cotton growers.[66] 'They are', he wrote in his diary on 15 November 1915, 'a rotten lot of psalm-singing, profit mongering humbugs.'[67] He viewed the visits to Europe of Woodrow Wilson's friend and adviser, Colonel House, with only slightly less contempt. House, whom he first met at Paris in March 1915, did not impress him, and he resented the notion of an American diplomatic expedition to promote a mediated settlement.[68] But the Americans could not be excluded from European affairs, and neither the British nor the French government could afford to ignore their pleas. In January and February 1916 House once more visited Europe, this time with proposals for the summoning of a peace conference by Wilson, and with the assurance that if Germany rejected the idea, or refused to accept what the president thought were reasonable terms, the United States would probably enter the war on the side of Britain and France.[69] Bertie doubted if the Americans would be prepared to participate in the conflict, and he feared that if they did this would be of little advantage to the *entente* powers. The United States could, he argued, only make a small contribution to the military effort of the allies, but would still require a voice in the making of a future peace.[70] In his opinion, House, 'that sheep-faced and fox-minded gentleman', was out on an 'electioneering mission' which would permit Wilson to pose in the forthcoming presidential election as 'the arbiter of the destinies of Europe' while at the same time obtaining great advantages for America.[71] Grey had similar suspicions about the purpose of House's mission. Nevertheless, he liked House and thought him 'genuinely friendly'. And although he held that there could be no talk of mediation if the allied military and naval authorities were confident of victory, he thought that such an

---

[66] Bertie to O'Beirne, 25 Jan. 1916, B.P., A, F.O.800/181. Gordon Lennox, I, pp.202 – 3.
[67] Gordon Lennox, I, p.267.
[68] *Ibis.*, pp.130 and 144 – 5. French reactions to House's diplomacy are considered in Yves-Henri Nouailhat, *France et États-Unis, aout 1914 – avril 1917* (Paris, 1979), pp.137 – 48. See also: David Stevenson, 'French War Aims and the American Challenge, 1914 – 18', *Historical Journal*, XXII(1979), 877 – 94.
[69] House's initiative and his relations with Grey are surveyed in C.M. Mason, 'Anglo-American Relations: Mediation and "Permanent Peace" ', in Hinsley, pp.466 – 87. Memos. by Grey, 22 and 28 Feb. 1916; memo. by Bertie, 26 Feb. 1916; B.P., A, F.O.800/181.
[70] Memo. by Bertie, 10 April 1916, B.P., A, F.O.800/181. Gordon Lennox, I, p.63.
[71] Bertie to Grey, 2 March 1916, B.P., A, F.O.800/181.

intervention might be of value if the war were reduced to a stalemate.[72]

Grey's apparent readiness to consort with House caused Bertie to have fresh misgivings about his handling of affairs. During April 1916, at a time when it seemed possible that the foreign secretary might be forced to resign to save his failing eyesight, Bertie told Lord Curzon, the lord privy seal, that he feared that Grey's weakened health had 'increased the pacifism in his nature'.[73] Bertie was inclined to label as a pacifist almost anybody who was prepared to give consideration to the idea of a compromise peace. His application of the term to Grey was therefore as much a measure of his disenchantment with his diplomacy as a condemnation of its ends. Not that Grey had many illusions about the prospects for a mediated settlement. When during the second week of August 1916 Bertie was again in London, Grey explained to him that he was reluctant to risk alienating American opinion by an outright rejection of an offer of mediation. Nevertheless, he maintained that if Germany were to request the United States to mediate, he would have to consult Britain's allies before responding to any proposals for an armistice. Given the likely requirements of the French, and the promises that Britain and France had made to Italy and were about to make to Roumania, such a condition seemed, as Bertie recognised, likely to preclude a settlement based on anything less than the military defeat of the central powers. Yet the fact that Grey considered it necessary to humour Wilson was itself anathema to Bertie. Grey, he noted, 'had been inoculated with the Colonel House virus'.[74]

It was with a view to administering an antidote to halt the spread of this virus that Bertie sought to dispel such doubts as Grey had about the readiness of the French to wage another winter campaign, and to impress his views on other members of the British government. Thus, after discussing the matter with Hardinge, who had returned in June 1916 to his former post at the Foreign Office, Bertie harangued Asquith, Balfour, Curzon and Lloyd George on the evils of mediation.[75] The French, he continued, were determined to fight *jusqu'au bout* not just in order to secure the return of their lost provinces, but to crush Germany so as to prevent a renewal of the war

---

[72] Mason, 'Anglo-American Relations', p.477. Memo. by Bertie, 17 Feb. 1916; Grey to Bertie, 5 March 1916; B.P., A, F.O.800/181.
[73] Memo. by Bertie, 12 April 1916, B.P., A, F.O.800/175. Gordon Lennox, II, pp.11–13.
[74] Memo. by Bertie, 11 Aug. 1916, B.P., A, F.O.800/171.
[75] Memo. by Bertie, 10 Aug. 1916, *ibid*. Memo. by Bertie, 15 Aug. 1916, B.P., A, F.O.800/175. Memo. by Bertie, 17 Aug. 1916, B.P., A, F.O.800/176. Memo. by Bertie, 6 Oct. 1916, B.P., A, F.O.800/181.

after a 'lame peace'. If, as he expected, the Americans were to make another offer of mediation, he thought that they should be advised to tell the Germans to address themselves simultaneously to each of the *entente* allies, stating the terms on which they would be prepared to treat. This, he subsequently explained to Hardinge, would obviate the spectre of Grey acting as an intermediary between the United States and Britain's allies and a 'wordy controversy' with Washington. All four ministers sympathized with these views.[76] Moreover, much to Bertie's delight, at the end of September Lloyd George gave his so-called 'knock-out-blow' interview to an American journalist, in which he denounced any possibility of a negotiated peace.[77]

A report from Hardinge of Grey's irritation at Lloyd George's interview was taken by Bertie as further evidence that he was 'at heart a pacifist'. 'I think', he wrote to Hardinge on 16 October, 'that he is what the Americans term a "sick man".'[78] And when two months later Asquith's government fell, Bertie showed few signs of remorse over the departure from the Foreign Office of the man who had been his 'chief' for all but eleven months of his embassy at Paris. He explained to Hardinge on 16 December:

> I like Grey very much but he is 'au fond', a pacifist. I am sure that he felt acutely the Boche accusations that he could have prevented the war and that he has wondered to himself whether he did those things which he ought to have done. I think that doubts haunted him. I also think that he was bamboozled by 'Colonel' House, President Wilson's friend and Electoral Agent and that he was too much inclined towards American mediation, and if he had remained in Office might have been ready to make peace on terms which would be only a truce with a war to begin in a few years when perhaps we would not have with us our present allies.[79]

This was by Bertie's standards a considered and not wholly unsympathetic verdict upon Grey's recent conduct. But Bertie's reference to the foreign secretary having been 'bamboozled' by

---

[76] *Ibid*. Bertie to Hardinge, 24 Aug. 1916, Grey MSS., F.O.800/59. Gordon Lennox, II, pp.10 – 13. In his assessment of the French government's attitude towards a compromise peace Bertie was not mistaken. 'We feel', Briand wrote on 28 May 1916, 'that the conclusive defeat of Germany's militarism and ambition to dominate is a matter of life and death for France, and the sole guarantee of the future liberty of the world.' D. Stevenson, *French War Aims Against Germany* (Oxford, 1982), p.15.
[77] Bertie to R. Cecil, 4 Oct. 1916, B.P., A, F.O.800/181. Gordon Lennox, II, pp.34 – 5. M.G. Fry, pp.232 – 4.
[78] Hardinge to Bertie, 10 Oct. 1916, Hardinge MSS., 26. Bertie to Hardinge, 16 Oct. 1916, B.P., A, F.O.800/178.
[79] Bertie to Hardinge, 16 Dec. 1916, B.P., A, F.O.800/263.

House was patently unfair. Grey may have had his doubts about the prospect of the *entente* powers achieving a decisive military victory, but he also felt that a compromise peace would achieve nothing without a change of heart in Germany. And, as he made known to Hardinge, he had no intention of being used as 'a stalking horse for President Wilson to approach the allies'.[80] In any event there was surely more sense in trying to keep open the options of American mediation than in rejecting it out of hand. Bertie had told Grey in August 1916 that if the 'British lion . . . were to show his teeth President Wilson would stop the tail-twisting'.[81] Such swashbuckling language was fine, but took little account either of Britain's increasing dependence on transatlantic trade and finance, or of the value of the United States as a sympathetic mediator and potential ally. As with much of what Bertie found to write about Grey's shortcomings, it betrayed a certain reluctance on his part to adjust his thinking to meet the circumstances of war. It was a fault that others had already detected, and which was not to be ignored by his new masters in Whitehall.

[80] Minute by Grey on Bertie to Hardinge, 24 Aug. 1916, Grey MSS., F.O.800/59.
[81] Memo. by Bertie, 11 Aug. 1916, B.P., A, F.O.800/171.

14

The end of an embassy

Bertie welcomed the formation of Lloyd George's coalition government. It meant for him the disappearance of the so-called 'pacifists' from office, and the appointment as prime minister of a politician whom he had recently described as 'an appropriate personification of the fighting determination of the British people'.[1] He had only two causes for regret. One was the removal from government of Asquith, whom he personally liked.[2] The other was the appointment of Balfour rather than Curzon as Grey's successor. Past experience caused Bertie to fear that Balfour would be indolent in office.[3] He was, he observed to Hardinge, 'charming and most attractive, wonderfully nimble minded, but a philosopher and not vigorous in health'.[4] But the new foreign secretary was an old friend, and in January 1917 Bertie thought it right to explain to him that in future he would address him in 'official private letters' as 'Balfour' rather than 'Arthur'. 'For letters which go on to others', he added, 'it has a better appearance.'[5] Propriety in such matters still counted for much with Bertie. It counted for less with those who had just assumed the reins of power in England.

Lloyd George's 'small but strong Cabinet' would, Bertie hoped, prove a more effective instrument for directing grand strategy than the war committee that Asquith had assembled.[6] Bertie was, however, to derive no personal advantage from the prime minister's penchant for administrative innovation. With the advent of total war the conduct of Britain's foreign policy had ceased to be the preserve of the Foreign Office and its representatives abroad. Of this Bertie was keenly aware. 'I think', he had warned Hardinge in June 1916, 'that you will find that the Foreign Office is in a great part a "pass on"

---

[1] Gordon Lennox, II, p.65.
[2] *Ibid*, pp.75 and 80. Bertie had known Balfour for many years. Indeed, the two men had both been members of the British delegation at the Berlin congress of 1878. Max Egremont, *Balfour. A Life of Arthur James Balfour* (London, 1980), p.45.
[3] Memo. by Bertie, 12 April 1916, B.P., A, F.O.800/175. Bertie to Hardinge, 11 Dec. 1916, Hardinge MSS., 28. Gordon Lennox, II, p.79.
[4] Bertie to Hardinge, 16 Dec. 1916, B.P., A, F.O.800/163.
[5] Bertie to Balfour, 3 Jan. 1917, B.P., A, F.O.800/177.
[6] Gordon Lennox, II, pp.76–7.

Department viz. it issues instructions at the instance of other offices often without considering whether such instructions are advisable or feasible and sometimes in ignorance seemingly of what has already been said and done by some other Departments of the Foreign Office.'[7] His own diplomacy had been impinged upon by the agents not only of the service departments, but also by representatives of those ministries that were responsible for munitions, transport and economy. Ministers, observers, and experts, real and supposed, had flocked to France, and allied committees and military missions had multiplied at Paris. Bertie had protested at the unannounced arrival of members of the government, and had poured scorn upon the activities and reports of 'busybodies' and 'fly-gulpers' from across the channel.[8] Nevertheless, he had found his authority increasingly challenged by those who claimed to have a better understanding than himself of French politics and policies. In this respect matters were not improved by the change of government in England. The new prime minister had little or no respect for established channels of communication, and was more inclined than his predecessor to try his hand at personal diplomacy. Weakened by illness and old age, Bertie was during his last twelve months at Paris to fight his own war of attrition in a valiant but futile attempt to maintain his hold upon the embassy at Paris.

Of all those Englishmen whom the war attracted to France the one who was to trouble Bertie most was the ubiquitous Lord Esher. A courtier, and a friend of leading politicians and statesmen, Esher had played a peculiar extra-constitutional role during the ten years that had preceded the outbreak of the first world war. He had contributed to the re-organization of the British military machine, participated in the discussions of the defence committee and chaired its sub-committees, and advised Edward VII and George V on the exercise of their prerogative. An enthusiastic supporter of the understanding with France, he had been in part responsible for instigating the Anglo-French military conversations in December 1905.[9] Yet his mentality and methods were essentially those of a backstairs

---

[7] Bertie to Hardinge, 25 June 1916, Hardinge MSS., 22. Roberta M. Warman, 'The Erosion of Foreign Office Influence in the Making of Foreign Policy, 1916–1918', *Historical Journal* XV(1972), 133–59.

[8] Bertie to Grey, 17 Oct. and 30 Nov. 1915, B.P., A, F.O.800/167. Bertie to Grey, 30 Jan. 1916, B.P., B, F.O.800/190. Bertie to Nicolson, 5 Feb. 1916, B.P., A, F.O.800/175. Memo. by Bertie, 14 March 1916, B.P., A, F.O.800/173. Bertie to Grey, 24 May 1916, Grey MSS., F.O.800/59. Derby to Lloyd George, 30 Sept. 1916, Lloyd George MSS. (House of Lords Record Office), E/1/2/2.

[9] On Esher's role in British politics and military planning see: P. Fraser, *Lord Esher. A Political Biography* (London, 1973).

intriguer. He declined appointment to high office and made a virtue out of not allowing himself to be entrammelled by the bureaucracy of state. Esher, Balfour told Bertie, was 'like a mole, he reached everywhere underground'.[10] It is hardly surprising therefore that his presence at Paris during much of the war should have roused the suspicions of an ambassador who had long been wedded to official practices and clearly defined procedures.

'Esher came, in fancy khaki to ask for facilities for a mission which he says has been entrusted to him by the Prime Minister', reads the entry in Bertie's diary for 12 February 1915.[11] The outfit in question was the uniform of a general staff officer, and the so-called mission was to collect materials with which to write an account of the war operations from a strategical point of view. As the honorary colonel of a British regiment and a sub-commissioner of the British Red Cross at Paris, Esher was no doubt entitled to his khaki. But his proposed study of the war was never completed, and in the first place seems to have served as no more than a cover under which to secure access to the French ministry for war.[12] In fact Esher had already visited France during the previous autumn when he had tried to improve relations between Kitchener and French. Now during the winter of 1915 Kitchener sought to use Esher's services as an intermediary between the War Office, Millerand and the French army headquarters at Chantilly.[13]

Kitchener had originally hoped that Yarde-Buller would be a direct link between himself and Joffre, and in September 1914 he had requested him to go to Joffre's headquarters.[14] This had done little for the allied war effort for Yarde-Buller failed to win Joffre's confidence, and in the meanwhile Bertie was deprived of the services of his military *attaché*.[15] Not until May 1915 was Colonel Herman Le Roy-Lewis appointed with the title of assistant military *attaché*, and only in January 1916 did he formally succeed Yarde-Buller.[16] In the absence of a unified command, there was in these conditions probably scope for someone with Esher's talents and experience to act as a sort of superior liaison officer at Paris. And had Esher's duties been explicitly defined, and had he been prepared to limit his activities to

---

[10] Memo. by Bertie, 15 Aug. 1916, B.P., A, F.O.800/175.
[11] Gordon Lennox I, p.111.
[12] Memo. by Bertie, 10 April 1916, B.P., B, F.O.800/190. Fraser, p.272.
[13] Bertie to Hardinge, 24 Aug. 1916, B.P., B, F.O.800/190. Fraser, pp.266–72.
[14] Bertie to Grey, 6 Sept. 1914, tel., Grey MSS., F.O.800/56A.
[15] Bertie to Hardinge, 24 Aug. 1916, B.P., B, F.O.800/190.
[16] Gordon Lennox, I, pp.167 and 283. Le Roy-Lewis was originally appointed on the recommendation of Lord Murray of Elibank. War Office to Foreign Office, 10 May 1915, F.O.371/2359.

dealing with strictly military matters, Bertie might have had no just cause for complaint. Esher preferred, however, to maintain a free hand. 'I am not going to put myself out', he informed his son, 'Nor am I going to "regularise" my position, which means that someone can give me orders — I never have.'[17] He thus felt himself free to promote a scheme for an allied war council, and to prime French, his successor, Sir Douglas Haig, and various friends and associates in England with political information. Moreover, to the confusion of French ministers and officials, he represented himself as a spokesman for Kitchener and as a repository of wisdom on British politics and strategy.[18]

Relations between Bertie and Esher were at first quite cordial. Bertie furnished him with a letter of introduction to Millerand's *chef de cabinet*, and entertained him at the embassy. In his turn Esher supplied the ambassador with snippets of military information.[19] But as time passed Bertie began to tire of Esher's efforts to make his presence felt at Paris. The 'Dog-at-the-Fair', as Bertie labelled his latest *bête noir*, was all too prone to self-advertisement to meet with the ambassador's approval. Much to Bertie's amusement, his visiting card ostentatiously proclaimed: 'Colonel, Vicomte Esher, Membre du Comité de Défense Impériale, Président de la Force Territoriale de Londres, et Lt. Gouverneur du Chateau de Windsor'.[20] Yet Bertie could hardly afford to ignore such an illustrious worthy. Esher had too many friends in high places. Moreover, there was a risk that Esher might compromise Bertie's own efforts to maintain the impression in London that the majority of Frenchmen were resolved to see the war through to a victorious conclusion.[21] Like other observers from across the Channel, Esher was inclined to bouts of

---

[17] Brett and Esher (eds.), *Journals and Letters*, II, p.215.
[18] Lord Northcliffe, the owner of *The Times*, also wondered what Esher was up to in Paris. In a letter to the editor of *The Times* he described Esher as occupying 'some queer position here which nobody understands', and as being 'mixed up with some very queer Jews, but . . . really . . . only a busybody'. Northcliffe to Robinson, 8 Aug. 1916, Northcliffe MSS. (*The Times* archives). Bertie to Stamfordham, 24 Aug. 1916; Bertie to Hardinge, 28 Aug. 1916; B.P., B, F.O.800/190. G. Gallieni, *Les carnets de Gallieni* (Paris, 1932), pp.188 and 209.
[19] Gordon Lennox, I, pp.116, 121 – 2, 128, 130, and 132. Bertie to Brett, 12 Feb. 1915; Esher to Bertie, 16 April, 15 May, and 6 July 1915; B.P., A, F.O.800/167.
[20] Bertie to Stamfordham, 7 Feb. and 10 May 1916, B.P., B, F.O.800/190. Bertie to Hardinge, 20 July 1916, Hardinge MSS., 23.
[21] One of Bertie's constant refrains was that the French were resolved to 'aller jusqu'au bout'. See for example: Memo by Bertie, 14 April 1916, B.P., A, F.O.800/165.

pessimism, a tendency which Bertie attributed to his drawing his information from 'tainted sources'.[22]

In a conversation which he had with Balfour shortly after the formation of a new French government under Briand in October 1915, Bertie warned him against believing tales brought from France by British 'croaking travellers' such as Esher. 'They listened', he claimed, 'to the pessimism of adherents of Caillaux & Co., and some Society old women, male and female, who hate the present regime in France and are influenced by Vatican views.'[23] There is little evidence to suggest that Esher had any very close contact with Caillaux's friends in what Bertie termed the 'Rue de Valois gang'. Nevertheless, the news which reached Bertie during the summer of 1916 that Esher had had the temerity to suggest that the French could not hold out beyond the autumn, and that if they did not succeed in holding the enemy at Verdun they would make peace with Germany, was quite sufficient for Bertie to tar him with the same brush as he usually applied to Caillaux. The latter, who claimed to have the support of 150 deputies, was alleged to favour an early settlement with Germany. And although Bertie discounted the chances of Caillaux — 'a dangerous lunatic' — ever regaining office, he was clearly anxious lest any credence should be given to his opinions in England as a result of Esher spreading 'rubbishy information'.[24] At the same time he was perturbed that such talk might have reverberations in France and lead the French to doubt Britain's resolve to fight for a 'really victorious finish'.[25]

There was also in Bertie's opinion a danger that the French public might grow to resent the presence in France of British military personnel who were 'disposed to treat the country as if it belonged to them'.[26] It was his desire to avoid such a development that helps to explain his attitude towards the conduct of Jefferson Cohn, one of

---

[22] Writing to Kitchener in the spring of 1915 Esher had forecasted: 'If the French fail to get Douai there will come more or less rapidly a reaction among civilians and *women* in favour of peace even what they call here une paix boiteuse.' Esher to Kitchener, 20 June 1915, Kitchener MSS., 30/57/59. Bertie to Stamfordham, 18 Aug. 1916, B.P., B, F.O.800/190. Gordon Lennox, I, p.185.
[23] Memo. by Bertie, 30 Oct. 1915, B.P., A, F.O.800/177. Briand himself took over the foreign ministry, and he appointed Jules Cambon as secretary general. Granville to Grey, 30 Oct. 1915, F.O.371/2356, despt.409. Bertie to Grey, 7 Nov. 1915, B.P., A, F.O.800/167.
[24] Bertie to Grey, 4 Aug. 1915, B.P., A, F.O.800/181. Bertie to Crewe, 12 Dec. 1915, B.P., A, F.O.800/167. Memo. by Bertie, 5 Aug. 1916, B.P., B, F.O.800/190. Memo. by Bertie, 15 Aug. 1916, B.P., A, F.O.800/175. Bertie to Grey, 20 May 1916; Bertie to Hardinge, 24 Aug. 1916; Grey MSS., F.O.800/59. Gordon Lennox, I, pp.72–3.
[25] Bertie to Grey, 30 Nov. 1915, B.P., A, F.O.800/167.
[26] Bertie to Stamfordham, 25 Jan. 1916, B.P., A, F.O.800/268.

Esher's associates with the Red Cross in Paris. Besides being a wealthy American, Cohn was the son-in-law of the populist politician, Horatio Bottomley.[27] He had during the early stages of the war offered to the British Red Cross in France, first his services, and then his villa. But before the latter could be accepted, stories about his pre-war connexions with the German imperial family brought him under the surveillance of the security service of Joffre's headquarters. In September 1915 they recommended that his movements should be restricted, and despite the fact that a summary investigation by the counter-espionage service of the ministry of the interior could 'cast no slur on the honorability of Mr Cohn', Bertie secured from Haig a promise that he would not permit Cohn to enter the British army zone unless he heard from the embassy that the French objections had been dropped.[28] With the aid, however, of a financial contribution to *l'Événement*, Cohn enlisted the support of its proprietor, the radical ex-premier, Combes, whom Briand had included in his government. In June 1916 Combes visited the British army headquarters, informed Haig that the French government had nothing against Cohn, and requested that he should be allowed to circulate 'like any other well-conducted civilian'. This Haig agreed to without any further consultation with Bertie.

It is probable that Cohn was innocent of any dealings with the enemy. The French authorities never supplied Bertie with any solid evidence against him, and after 1915 they seem to have taken little interest in his case. Nevertheless, Bertie was annoyed at Haig's action. Combes had acted without instructions from his colleagues, and the embassy had received no official communication from either Briand or any of the officials of the Quai d'Orsay.[29] Subsequent enquiries from Bertie produced from Joffre a statement to the effect that nothing had been found against Cohn. But Bertie continued to insist that Cohn was still under suspicion, and that the previously expressed wishes of the French security services should be respected. As Briand agreed, there could be no doubt about 'the absolute correctness' of Bertie's part in this affair.[30] Given, however, the ambiguity of the official French position and the tenacity with which

---

[27] J. Symons, *Horatio Bottomley* (London, 1955), p.135.
[28] Briand to Bertie, 26 July 1916, and Bertie to Derby, 16 Feb. 1917, enclosed in Bertie to Hardinge, 18 Feb. 1917, Hardinge MSS., 29.
[29] Bertie to Derby, 16 Feb. 1917, *ibid.* Memo. by Bertie, 16 Aug. 1916, B.P., A, F.O.800/175. Bertie to Hardinge, 23 Feb. 1917, B.P., B, F.O.800/191. Bertie to Hardinge, 3 March 1917, Hardinge MSS., 30.
[30] Briand to Bertie, 26 July 1916, and 12 Feb. 1917, enclosed in Bertie to Hardinge, 18 Feb. 1917,Hardinge MSS., 29. Bertie to Hardinge, 27 July 1916, Hardinge MSS., 23.

Bertie sought to ensure Cohn's exclusion from the war zone, it is hardly surprising that Cohn should have come to regard himself as the victim of a malicious campaign led by the British ambassador. Indeed, so angered was Cohn that he threatened, perhaps with the encouragement of Bottomley who was something of a specialist in such matters, to take legal proceedings against Bertie.[31]

Within the Red Cross organization at Paris Cohn had several friends who were prepared to defend his name. Amongst these were Lord Michelham, the Jewish financier, and Sir Arthur Sloggett, the director general of the Royal Army Medical Corps.[32] Yet, for Bertie the whole business was also connected with his relations with Esher. Bertie suspected that Esher had assisted Cohn, and that Esher's son Major Brett, had as Assistant Provost Marshal at Paris been responsible for issuing Cohn with such travel permits as had enabled him to avoid the surveillance of the French security services.[33] Although Esher denied having any interest in Cohn, Bertie's attitude towards the latter did provide him with material for attacking the conduct of the embassy.[34] This was particularly galling to Bertie since he had hoped that with the death of Kitchener in June 1916 Esher's irregular employment by the War Office would cease. But by then Esher had already become a medium of communication between Sir William Robertson, the Chief of the Imperial General Staff, and the French war ministry, and Asquith, who for a short period took over Kitchener's duties at the War Office, favoured his continuing his work in France. Moreover, Haig, despite subsequent protestations of his friendship for Bertie, had, after complaining of the inefficacy of the latter in securing information from the French government of its military intentions, asked Esher to become his 'ambassador in Paris until the end of the war'. Bertie nevertheless, made use of a visit to London in mid-August to launch an assault on Esher's position. In conversations with Grey, Hardinge, Balfour, Stamfordham, Lloyd George and Asquith, he emphasized the trouble caused by Esher's presence at Paris. His duties as a sub-commissioner of the Red Cross were, Bertie told Asquith, incompatible with his being charged with any mission by the government, and he had, Bertie claimed, been 'chiefly responsible for the Cohn affair'. Finally, after having gained from the prime minister a commitment to write to Esher to tell him to restrict his activities to carrying messages between the British and

[31] Austin Lee to de Bunsen, 4 April 1917, de Bunsen MSS., MB/IV/d.
[32] Bertie to Hardinge, 18 Sept. 1916, B.O., B, F.O.800/190. Bertie to Hardinge, 23 Nov. 1916, Hardinge MSS., 27.
[33] Bertie to Hardinge, 27 July 1916, Hardinge MSS., 23.
[34] Memo. by Bertie, 5 Aug. 1916, B.P., B, F.O.800/190.

French military authorities, Bertie returned to Paris 'filled', in the words of Le Roy-Lewis, 'with the sacred fire of Esher hunting'.[35]

Bertie would have been wiser to have chosen a less elusive quarry. Henceforth Esher avoided the embassy, and concentrated his efforts upon impressing on military men and politicians the value of the services that he could offer to them. On one occasion in September he made what seems to have been a conciliatory gesture towards Bertie and suggested to a mutual acquaintance that he might persuade Cohn to abstain from legal action. But Bertie would have no truck with such an approach, and he continued to lace his correspondence with malevolent comments on the doings of 'the Dog'.[36] The latter was not, however, to be shifted from his chosen haunts. Nor for that matter were his duties made any clearer by those whom he professed to serve. Lord Robert Cecil, the parliamentary under-secretary of state for foreign affairs, told the Commons in October 1916 that Esher 'had no definite military or diplomatic appointment', but that 'he was charged from time to time with particular tasks of a military character'.[37] Hardinge felt that this would 'go some way towards confining him to his kennel'.[38] Bertie thought otherwise. He reckoned that the government's statement did not go far enough for, according to his knowledge, Esher had no 'military, diplomatic or political appointment or mission in France'.[39] Nevertheless, he evidently hoped that events would destroy Esher's credibility. The mobbing of Caillaux and his wife at Vichy seemed to demonstrate that there was little likelihood of his forming a government, and by November 1916 the early peace predicted by Esher appeared as remote as ever. Esher, Bertie wrote to Hardinge, 'is looked upon as a false prophet. What would be his fate if he were amongst his Semitic relations'?[40]

False prophet Esher may have been, but he was none the less adept at promoting the interests of his followers. In December Bertie was astonished to learn that Cohn, with the backing of Esher's friend, Sloggett, had been granted an honorary captaincy in the British army.[41] The British military authorities, Bertie thought, had

---

[35] Memo. by Bertie, 11 Aug. 1916, B.P., A, F.O.800/171. Memos. by Bertie, 15, 16, and 17 Aug. 1916, B.P., A, F.O.800/175. Bertie to Stamfordham, 18 Aug. 1916, B.P., B, F.O.800/190. Le Roy-Lewis to Lloyd George, Lloyd George MSS., E/3/14/5.
[36] Bertie to Hardinge, 28 Aug. 1916, B.P., B, F.O.800/190.
[37] Bertie to Hardinge, 6 Nov. 1916, *ibid.*
[38] Hardinge to Bertie, 8 Nov. 1916, B.P., A, F.O.800/167.
[39] Bertie to Hardinge, 6 Nov. 1916, B.P., B, F.O.800/190.
[40] Bertie to Hardinge, 24 Aug. and 19 Nov. 1916, B.P., F.O.800/190.
[41] Bertie to Hardinge, 8 Dec. 1916, Hardinge MSS., 28. Bertie to Briand, 10 Jan. 1917, B.P. B, F.O.800/191.

completely ignored the feelings of the French. Yet his plea that either Cohn should be withdrawn from France, or deprived of his captaincy, was rejected by Lord Derby, Lloyd George's secretary of state for war. He insisted that Haig was satisfied with what had happened, and that in any case Cohn had been exonerated by previous French statements.[42] Accustomed to having his views treated with more deference in Whitehall, Bertie was upset by the War Office's refusal to heed his advice. 'It would', he objected to Derby, 'be strange if I were not a better judge than Sir Douglas Haig and his advisers of the views of the French Government as communicated by them to me particularly when expressed to me in French.'[43] But such protests were in vain. They were also impolitic. In criticizing Haig and his friends in the War Office Bertie risked weakening his own standing in London at a time when Esher was seeking to discredit his position at Paris.

Irritated by what he considered to be the efforts of a jealous and senile septuagenerian to injure his work, Esher retaliated by drawing the attention of all and sundry to the shortcomings of Bertie's diplomacy. In June 1916 he had complained to Robertson that since all the diplomatists at Paris listened 'to each other's gossip, and to nobody else . . . their estimates of political and military events are rarely correct'.[44] Indeed, in view of this assertion there is some irony in the fact that Esher should also have chosen to criticize Bertie for his poor relations with Izvolsky and intimacy with de Gunzburg.[45] Relations between Bertie and Izvolsky had rarely been better than formal, and they took a turn for the worst when at the end of July 1916 Arthur Meyer, the editor of *Le Gaulois*, sought to commemorate the second anniversary of the outbreak of hostilities by publishing declarations by the ambassadors of France's three principle allies. Bertie declined to say anything, but permitted his letter of refusal to be printed alongside declarations by Izvolsky and Tittoni.[46] The responsibility for this rested with Meyer as the latter two had made the publication of their opinions conditional upon Bertie issuing a similar declaration. Nevertheless, so offended was Izvolsky by what

---

[42] Derby to Bertie, 6 Jan. 1917, enclosed in Bertie to Hardinge, 18 Feb. 1917; Derby to Bertie, 23 Feb. 1917, enclosed in Bertie to Hardinge, 25 Feb. 1917; Hardinge MSS., 29. Fraser, p.324. Brett and Esher, IV, pp.34 – 35.
[43] Bertie to Derby, 6 Jan. 1917, enclosed in Bertie to Hardinge, 18 Feb. 1917; Bertie to Derby, 25 Feb. 1917, Hardinge MSS., 29.
[44] Esher to Robertson, 18 June 1916, Robertson MSS. (King's College, London), I/34/4. Fraser, p.346.
[45] Fraser, pp.346 – 7.
[46] Bertie to Hardinge, 2 and 6 Aug. 1916, and enclosures, Hardinge MSS., 24. Gordon Lennox, II, pp.5 – 6.

he took to be an affront to his dignity, that several months were to pass before he deigned to speak to Bertie of anything more significant than the weather.⁴⁷ As Esher recognized, this state of affairs was hardly conducive to allied unity, and in a letter of 21 December 1916 which he drafted for, but did not send to, the prime minister, he appealed for Bertie's replacement.⁴⁸

Where Bertie's relations with de Gunzburg were concerned, matters were more complicated. In his draft letter of 21 December Esher referred to the 'notorious intimacy' between Bertie and de Gunzburg, and to the suspicions raised amongst Frenchmen by the 'paramount' influence which this financier 'of Russian-German extraction' exercised over the ambassador.⁴⁹ Moreover, Esher was able in the following month to supplement these assertions with information which he had received from Bertie's military attaché, Le Roy-Lewis. The latter had known Esher for some time, but quite why he chose to align himself against Bertie remains a matter for speculation. Howard Kelly later wrote of Bertie that he had 'an inherent dislike for all Military and Naval Attachés', and it is true that he seems to have resented the degree of autonomy which they possessed within the embassy.⁵⁰ Yet in the industrious and companionable Le Roy-Lewis Bertie had at first recognized a kindred spirit. The two men had become bosom friends. Le Roy-Lewis was given easy access to the chancery, and Bertie went out of his way to ensure that he received proper remuneration for his work.⁵¹ In his turn Le Roy-Lewis applied his business experience to tackling the problems of military transport and supply with which the embassy became involved. He was soon on intimate terms with many of the leading French politicians and officials, and in August 1916 Lloyd George agreed that he should report privately to him on the politico-military situation in France.⁵² But the energetic *attaché* soon grew dissatisfied with his status. He complained about the inadequacy of his staff, and about the difficulties presented by the multiplication of

---

⁴⁷ Bertie to Hardinge, 23 Dec. 1916, Hardinge Mss., 28.
⁴⁸ Esher to Lloyd George, 21 Dec. 1916, *War Journals*, Esher MSS. (Churchill College, Cambridge), ESHR 2/17. The substance of this letter was conveyed to Balfour's private secretary. Fraser, p.347.
⁴⁹ *Ibid*.
⁵⁰ *Journal as Naval Attaché*, pp.5–6. Howard Kelly MSS., KEL/5. Bertie probably regarded Le Roy-Lewis as an improvement upon Yarde-Buller whom he could not bear. C. à Court Repington, *The First World War, 1914–1918* (2 vols., London, 1920), I, p.166.
⁵¹ Austin Lee to de Bunsen, 4 April 1917, de Bunsen MSS., MB/IV/d. Bertie to Grey, 20 May 1915, B.P. Add. MS.63037. Bertie to Nicolson, 17 June 1915, F.O.371/2359.
⁵² Mersey, p.283. Le Roy-Lewis to Lloyd George, 18 Aug. 1916, Lloyd George MSS., E/3/14/4.

British military missions at Paris. The latter problem could, he thought, be remedied by the appointment of a general officer as a 'Military Commissioner' with the task of supervising and synthesising 'this heterogenous collection of services'.[53]

Le Roy-Lewis received support for his plan from Lord Murray of Elibank, the former Liberal chief whip who was in Paris on business, and together they proposed it to Esher on 21 January 1917. Esher was sympathetic. He recognized that Le Roy-Lewis might himself be appointed military commissioner, that this would secure his promotion, and that it would free him from Bertie's control. But after Haig's initial rejection of the scheme, Le Roy-Lewis offered Esher another explanation for his wish to separate himself from the embassy. He confided to Esher that he was perturbed lest his personal integrity should be compromised. De Gunzburg's estranged wife had, Le Roy-Lewis related, confirmed to him a story which he had heard elsewhere to the effect that de Gunzburg had offered to Bertie the chairmanship of the *Central Mining Company* with a salary of £5000 per annum.[54] He also subsequently told Esher that Bertie had taken a considerable interest in a War Office investigation into the value of bored shells, a contract for the manufacture of which de Gunzburg had tried to obtain; that with Bertie's backing de Gunzburg had successfully negotiated a deal for the supply of aero-engines to the British armed forces; that Bertie had given to de Gunzburg the transcripts of certain German radio messages which had been forwarded to the embassy; and that de Gunzburg had acted on Caillaux's behalf in the negotiations with Berlin in 1911 and was still on intimate terms with the former premier, who at the time was propagating the cause of peace in Italy.[55]

Clearly these accusations would appear to have stood on their head those which Bertie had previously made against Esher. Apart, however, from the claim that de Gunzburg had once acted as an intermediary between the governments in Paris and Berlin, there is little evidence to support Le Roy-Lewis's assertions. Bertie may, for instance, have been offered the chairmanship of de Gunzburg's company, and with retirement in view the ambassador might well

---

[53] Memo. by Le Roy-Lewis, 19 Jan. 1917, *War Journals*, Esher MSS., ESHR 2/8.
[54] Note by Esher, 21 Jan. 1917; Esher to Robertson, 24 Jan. 1017; Esher to Haig, 25 Jan. 1917; memo. by Esher, 3 Feb. 1917; *War Journals*, Esher MSS., 2/18. At Esher's request Murray of Elibank had written to Asquith in November 1916 to propose the appointment of Le Roy-Lewis to the secretariat of his war council. Elibank to Asquith, 29 Nov. 1916, Elibank MSS. (National Library of Scotland), 8804.
[55] Memo. by Esher, 11 Feb. 1917, *War Journals*, Esher MSS., ESHR 2/18. Memo. by Bertie, 28 Feb. – 2 June 1917, B.P., B, F.O.800/191. Hardinge to Bertie, 19 March 1917, Hardinge MSS., 30. Hardinge to Bertie, 29 April 1917, Hardinge MSS., 31.

have been tempted to take up the appointment. But there is no hint in Bertie's correspondence of such an offer having been made, or of its having been accepted. Moreover, Bertie's own notes indicate that his connexion with the aero-engine contract was a very tenuous one, since the negotiations were conducted between a representative of the British aviation committee at Paris and a Spanish company for which de Gunzburg acted as agent. Only after the contract had been settled did Bertie learn from his naval *attaché* of de Gunzburg's involvement.[56] There is, on the other hand, no good reason for disbelieving Le Roy-Lewis's claim that Bertie had admitted to communicating embassy papers to his friend. The documents in question related to material that the Germans already had in their possession, and seem to have been primarily concerned with Russia. And since de Gunzburg kept the embassy supplied with detailed reports from his correspondents at Petrograd of events in Russia, it was perhaps not unnatural that Bertie should have reciprocated with information which may have been of interest to him. Nevertheless, such conduct, and the frequent visits to the embassy by de Gunzburg, whom Esher believed to be under police surveillance, did leave Bertie exposed to criticism.

It was possible that Le Roy-Lewis was, as Esher believed, genuinely worried about becoming implicated in a scandal, and he may have been anxious lest de Gunzburg were a security risk.[57] This would explain his apparently deliberate withholding of information from Bertie during the spring of 1917. Yet it has to be remembered that Le Roy-Lewis was trying to improve his position in the military hierarchy in Paris, and, in so far as he hoped to achieve this with Esher's help, he had an interest in blackening Bertie's reputation. Besides which, Murray, who on 4 February wrote to Lloyd George to advise him to turn Le Roy-Lewis 'into a General Officer and give him an adequate staff', had his own reasons for finding fault with Bertie's friendship with de Gunzburg.[58] Shortly before the outbreak of war Murray had gone to Paris, with the blessing of the Foreign Office, as a representative of the engineering firm of *S. Pearson and Son* in order to seek a concession for oil drilling rights in Algeria. Bertie had tried to help him, and had introduced him to de Gunzburg. But Murray had quarrelled with the latter, and although Bertie later claimed that he had held aloof from their squabbles, it is probable

---

[56] Memo. by Bertie, 22 June 1917, B.P., B, F.O.800/191.
[57] Memo. by Esher, 3 Feb. 1917, *War Journals*, Esher MSS., 2/18.
[58] Elibank to Lloyd George, 4 Feb. 1917, Elibank MSS., 8804.

that Murray, who made only slow progress in promoting his scheme, suspected Bertie of siding with de Gunzburg.[59] In any event, Le Roy-Lewis's allegations and Murray's frustration, offered Esher an opportunity to strike back at Bertie.

Esher made sure that Haig was aware of the dangers involved in the intimacy between Bertie and de Gunzburg, and soon tales of the baron's influence reached England. Alarmed at this threat to the good name of his colleague, Hardinge wrote to Bertie on 2 March that he had heard him 'strongly criticized by others for seeing Gunzburg so much, and having him so often to the Embassy', and that these stories were 'making some impression'. He recommended that Bertie should either 'see less of that gentleman, or perhaps not at all'.[60] Bertie, who came swiftly to the defence of his friend and friendship, assured Hardinge that he would check wiether de Gunzburg was under any suspicion at the Quai d'Orsay. Unfortunately, he was prevented from proceeding with this enquiry by what he termed 'congestion of the lungs'.[61] His doctor called it pneumonia.[62]

Since his appointment to Paris Bertie had suffered very little from illness. Eczema and psoriasis, which had rendered his body like a 'boiled lobster', had led him to take a cure at La Bourboule in the summer of 1910, and influenza and rheumatism of 'gouty origin' had occasionally kept him in bed.[63] Yet he had maintained his strength and stamina, and he took a pride in what he liked to think of as his youthful appearance. He continued to work late into the night and to take long walks in the faubourgs and the Bois de Boulogne. The arctic cold of the winter of 1917 and the shortage of fuel for heating was, however, to be more than either Bertie or his colleagues could stand. Bronchitis and influenza took their toll of his staff, and early in March, after attending a concert at the Sorbonne, Bertie was forced to call in his doctor. With the aid of the latter, 'a good constitution and youth', Bertie seemed set to make a speedy recovery. But his refusal to take sufficient rest, and his determination to keep

---

[59] Bertie to Hardinge, 31 March 1917, B.P., A, F.O.800/169. J.A. Spender, *Weatman Pearson, First Viscount Cowdray, 1856–1927* (London, 1930), p.211.
[60] Hardinge to Bertie, 9 March 1917, B.P., B, F.O.800/191.
[61] Bertie took Hardinge's advice and avoided seeing de Gunzburg. Bertie to Hardinge, 12 March and 15 April 1917, B.P., B, F.O.800/191.
[62] Grahame to Drummond, 12 March 1917, B.P., A, F.O.800/169. Gordon Lennox, II, p.114.
[63] Bertie to Hardinge, 9 July 1910, B.P., B, F.O.800/186. Bertie to Hardinge, 16 Oct. 1916, B.P., A, F.O.800/178. Gordon Lennox, II, p.46.

up his correspondence, soon led to a relapse, and in the end he was lucky to escape with less than six weeks confinement to his bed.[64]

The onset of Bertie's illness coincided with a political crisis in France which ended in the fall of Briand's government and the appointment on 19 March of the seventy-five year old Alexandre Ribot as president of the council.[65] Bertie regretted this change. During the last eighteen months he had more than once found cause to criticize Briand for his laziness, and the way in which he had allowed affairs at the Quai d'Orsay to fall increasingly into the hands of his *chef de cabinet*, 'that skunk M. Berthelot'.[66] Yet his personal relations with Briand had generally been good, and by 1917 he had reached the conclusion that the *entente* could not benefit from his replacement.[67] In the event Ribot's government was composed very largely of radicals and radical socialists, and one of its leading figures, the minister for war, Paul Painlevé, had recently contributed articles to *L'Événement*, with which newspaper Michelham and Cohn had had connexions.[68] None of this seemed likely to endear Bertie to the new administration. Moreover, Briand's resignation came at an opportune moment for the ambassador's opponents. With Bertie incapacitated by pneumonia, Esher and Le Roy-Lewis felt free to impress on Painlevé the value of a change in Britain's representation at Paris.[69]

In fairness to his critics it must be said that at this stage in the war Bertie's conduct left something to be desired. When, for instance, Murray returned to France at the end of March with the object of furthering his company's project, he found Bertie reluctant to help him in securing an interview with Ribot. Bertie doubted the value of Murray's lobbying and newspaper cultivation at Paris. Besides which, matters were complicated by the efforts of *Pearsons* to overcome French parliamentary opposition to a British concession in Algeria by forming a company with a majority French shareholding. While, however, Bertie's recommendation that the embassy should simply seek through the Quai d'Orsay the consent of Ribot to a meeting between Murray and the minister for public works was no

---

[64] Bertie to Hardinge, 4 Feb. 1917; Bertie to Balfour, 19 March 1917; Grahame to Russell, 20 March 1917; B.P., A, F.O.800/169.
[65] Grahame to Balfour, 20 March 1917, F.O.371/2934, despt.128.
[66] Bertie to Grey, 10 March 1916, Grey MSS., F.O.800/59. Bertie to Hardinge, 24 and 28 Sept. 1916, B.P., A, F.O.800/181. On Berthelot's influence on Briand see: J. Laroche, *Au Quai d'Orsay avec Briand et Poincaré* (Paris, 1957), pp.30 – 1.
[67] Gordon Lennox, II, p.116.
[68] Grahame to Russell, 20 March 1917; Bertie to Hardinge, 9 April 1917; B.P., A, F.O.800/169.
[69] Bertie to Hardinge, 9 April 1917, B.P., B, F.O.800/191.

THE END OF AN EMBASSY

doubt diplomatically correct, it was politically inept.[70] Murray had too much influence in London to be trifled with in this fashion. He had won the backing of the Board of Trade and the Admiralty, and in the City his project was seen as a test case for future Anglo-French economic relations.[71] Moreover, given Lloyd George's lack of respect for professional diplomacy, Balfour was only too well aware of the dangers of exposing the Foreign Office and the embassy to criticism, and he advised Bertie that if Murray were persuaded that he could not achieve his ends except through an interview with Ribot, it 'would be well to arrange matters'.[72] Bertie was obliged to comply. Nevertheless, the damage had been done. Murray suspected that Bertie was hostile to his firm, and on 2 April he wrote to Grahame to withdraw his request for embassy support.[73]

Murray may have been prompted to take this course by Esher, who subsequently took the oil drilling project under his protection. For his part, Bertie thought that Murray, whom he renamed 'Oily Bank', Esher and Le Roy-Lewis, were responsible for spreading a rumour in Paris that even if he, Bertie, were to recover his health, he was unlikely to be of any more use, and was therefore to be replaced by a 'big wig' from London.[74] There seems to have been little substance in this tale, which probably owed much to Esher's wishful thinking. During a brief stay in Paris on 20 April Lloyd George ridiculed Esher's pretensions and assured Bertie that he had never been consulted on the subject of his replacement. Bertie, who made every effort to demonstrate that he was 'still alive and all there', left a favourable impression on the prime minister.[75] Nevertheless, while he was at Paris, Lloyd George also found time to lunch with Esher at the Hotel Crillon: a gesture which provided Esher with the opening he required.[76] In the following week Lloyd George received the first of several letters containing thinly veiled attacks upon the British embassy.[77]

Esher mixed flattery with reason. Writing in the wake of the failure of the Nivelle offensive, and at a time when the allies appeared to be

---

[70] Bertie to Hardinge, 31 March 1917, B.P., A, F.O.800/169. Gordon Lennox, II, p.118.
[71] Elibank to Bertie, 20 and 28 March 1917, B.P., A, F.O.800/169.
[72] Balfour to Bertie, 3 April 1917, tel., B.P., B, F.O.800/91. Warman, p.142.
[73] Elibank to Grahame, 2 and 8 April 1917; Memo. by Grahame, 8 April 1917; B.P., B, F.O.800/191. Gordon Lennox, II, p.132.
[74] Memo. by Bertie, 28 Feb. – 2 June 1917; Bertie to Hardinge, 24 May 1917; B.P., B, F.O.800/191. Bertie to Hardinge, 25 June 1917, Hardinge MSS., 33.
[75] Memo. by Bertie, 28 Feb. – 2 June 1917, *ibid*. Hardinge to Bertie, 27 April 1917, B.P., A, F.O.800/169. Gordon Lennox, II, p.122.
[76] Memo. by Bertie, 21 April 1917, B.P., B, F.O.800/191.
[77] Esher to Lloyd George, 25 April 1917, Lloyd George MSS., F/16/1/6.

losing direction in their pursuit of the war, Esher urged the prime minister in a letter of 25 April 'to catch the French a bit tighter by the head'. They, he claimed, had no statesman of their own who could do this, and Lloyd George should use his popularity and prestige in France in order to take command: 'Cannot you [he continued] send here someone who possesses your full confidence who can keep you personally in touch with the people who matter? . . . You are badly served, indifferently informed and not represented at all. This is not a satisfactory state of affairs, at the moment of gravest crisis.'[78] In January 1917 Esher had sought to persuade Robertson to use his influence with the prime minister to secure the appointment of either Curzon or Lord Milner, both of whom were members of the war cabinet, to Paris 'as Ambassador Extraordinary, *and as a Member of the Cabinet*'.[79] This was the sort of solution he continued to favour to what he regarded as the problem of Britain's representation at Paris. He also apparently hoped that Le Roy-Lewis would benefit from any such diplomatic reshuffle.[80]

Relations between Bertie and his military *attaché* had in the meantime become so strained that the two men were hardly on speaking terms.[81] Neither seems to have been prepared to trust the other, and Bertie complained bitterly to Hardinge that Le Roy-Lewis was withholding from him political and politico-military information which he supplied to London.[82] Of yet more concern to Bertie were the efforts of Le Roy-Lewis to obtain for himself the rank of brigadier general and the supervision of all British military offices at Paris. By the spring this plan also involved a proposal for the appointment of Major Edward Spiers as a liaison officer at the French ministry for war with the title of assistant military *attaché*. This Bertie found most objectionable since it implied an expansion of Le Roy-Lewis's authority, and the establishment of a connexion between the embassy and an officer over whom the ambassador would have no effective control.[83] From the point of view of the War Office neither the title nor the appointment seemed unreasonable. Robertson maintained

---

[78] *Ibid.*
[79] Esher to Robertson, 9 Jan. 1917, *War Journals*, Esher MSS., ESHR 2/7.
[80] Esher to Haig, 15 April 1917, *War Journals*, Esher MSS., ESHR 2/18.
[81] Memo. by Bertie, 28 Feb. – 2 June 1917; Bertie to Hardinge, 9 April 1917; B.P., B, F.O.800/191. Bertie to Hardinge, 13 and 15 April 1917; Hardinge to Bertie, 17 April 1917; Hardinge MSS., 31.
[82] Bertie to Hardinge, 22 April 1917, B.P., B, F.o.800/191. Bertie to Hardinge, B.P., A, F.O.800/175.
[83] Memo. by Bertie, 28 Feb. – 2 June 1917; Bertie to Hardinge, 2 and 5 May 1917; B.P., 1917; Cecil to Bertie, 19 May 1917, tel.; B.P., A, F.O.800/175.

that it was only intended that in matters of discipline and general supervision he should look to Le Roy-Lewis, and that a similar system worked perfectly well at Petrograd. He was, nevertheless, prepared to accept the severance of any formal ties between the embassy and Spiers if the secretary of state approved.[84]

Derby, who was in Paris on 21 May, accepted the validity of Bertie's case. But by then Derby was also convinced that Bertie would have to go.[85] Ever since the beginning of May he and Lloyd George had been subject to increasing pressure from Esher, who seems to have been determined to exploit the differences between the ambassador and his military *attaché* to effect the removal of the former. In a brief note of 6 May he advised Lloyd George to send Bertie on leave for four months, to instal a *changé d'affaires* at the embassy, and to appoint a war commissioner to the French government responsible to himself, the prime minister.[86] Then, three days later in a letter to Derby, which he wanted the latter to discuss with Lloyd George, he elaborated upon the substance of his complaints. In a style that was no less abrasive than that customarily employed by Bertie, he claimed that the ambassador and his staff were ill-informed, that they were out of touch with French parliamentarians, that they were unacquainted with any of the owners, or directors, of the great French newspapers, and that they belittled Lloyd George 'just as they besmirched Asquith'. He urged the government to take the 'surgeon's knife' to this 'gangrene', to separate war work from the normal business of the embassy and to appoint a secretariat at Paris under Le Roy-Lewis 'responsible to 10 Downing Street and charged with all business affecting the war'.[87] At the same time he sought to explain to the prime minister that the prevailing differences between Bertie and Le Roy-Lewis were not the fault of the military *attaché*. 'He', Esher wrote to Lloyd George, 'has

---

[84] Robertson had for some time desired to have a more direct line of communication between the French war ministry and the War Office than had previously existed. Robertson to Esher, 21 Feb. and 15 March 1917; Robertson to H. Wilson, 17 April 1917; Robertson MSS., I/34/15a, 17a and 24a. Memo. by Bertie (undated) 1916, B.P., A, F.O.800/168 (Fr/16/63). Hardinge to Bertie, 15 May 1917, B.P., A, F.O.800/175. Robertson to Hardinge, 17 May 1917, enclosed in Hardinge to Bertie, 21 May 1917, B.P., B, F.O.800/191.
[85] Bertie to Cecil, 21 May 1917, B.P., A, F.O.800/175. Derby to Lloyd George, 19 May 1917, Lloyd George MSS., F/14/4/44. The appointment of Spiers as assistant military *attaché* was cancelled in June 1917. He was instead designated General Liaison Officer. D.M.O. to Foreign Office, 19 June 1917, F.O.371/2937.
[86] Esher to Lloyd George, 6 May 1917, Lloyd George MSS., F/16/1/8. Esher to Elibank, 7 May 1917, Elibank MSS., 8804.
[87] Esher to Derby, 9 May 1917, Lloyd George MSS., F/14/4/41.

been loyal, too, to the Ambassador throughout very trying times. But to senile vanity there are not limitations.'[88]

There was an element of truth in Esher's indictment of Bertie's diplomacy. Bertie had always been more inclined to rely on the information of a small group of friends, journalists and confidants, than upon the gossip of the Palais Bourbon, and he had never attempted to cultivate good relations with the magnates of the Paris press. 'I have', he had noted some five years before, 'always successfully refused to have any relations with the Press.'[89] Moreover, Bertie remained above all else a Foreign Office man. He possessed neither the will nor a sufficient grasp of military matters to play anything more than a strictly diplomatic role.[90] Wedded to the traditions of pre-war diplomacy, he continued to insist on forms and procedures that Esher and his ilk found cumbersome and irrelevant to the prosecution of the war. In the past his colleagues had learnt to live with his tantrums, and to respect his requirements. But in the spring of 1917, when the war was entering one of its most critical phases, it must have seemed extraordinary to the British generals in France and the War Office in London that Bertie could have afforded to devote so much of his time and energy to a private feud with his military *attaché*.

Already irritated by the trouble which Bertie had stirred up over Cohn's honorary captaincy, Derby was impressed by Esher's case. He even went so far as to suggest that Esher himself might replace Bertie and take Henry Wilson, who was then liaison officer at the French headquarters, as his military *attaché*. Esher was unenthusiastic about the idea.[91] He did, however, explain to Wilson on 21 May the conditions under which he would be prepared to accept the post. These included the appointment of a second ambassador in the person of Le Roy-Lewis, who would be solely responsible for handling civil matters, while he, Esher, would take over the military work with Wilson as his chief expert adviser.[92] Ten days later Esher wrote to Lloyd George to propose a slightly different version of this scheme. In this he made no reference to his own future, but again urged the separation of the 'ordinary "peace" business of the Embassy from "War" work'. He recommended the establishment at Paris of a 'war committee' or 'mission' into which 'could be drawn

---

[88] Esher to Lloyd George, 9 May 1917, Lloyd George MSS., F/16/1/9.
[89] Bertie to Ponsonby, 31 March 1910, B.P., B, F.O.800/187. Adam to Robinson, 11 June 1917, and enclosure, Adam MSS. (*The Times* archives).
[90] Haig noted in February 1916 after a conversation with Bertie: 'The Ambassador seemed to be to be quite out of touch with what was happening in the military world'. R. Blake (ed.), *The Private Papers of Douglas Haig* (London, 1952), p.135.
[91] Fraser, p.364.
[92] C.E. Callwell, *Field Marshall Sir Henry Wilson* (2 vols., London, 1927), I, p.355.

the liaison between the *two* War Councils, through Leroy Lewis and Spiers, and between the armies by means of Henry Wilson, but coordinated and concentrated in Paris'. The proposal was a bold and imaginitive one, which Esher thought could provide the basis for closer collaboration between those responsible for overall strategy. But Esher also hoped that it would enable the prime minister to exert his personal authority in France where, he feared, the 'Governing forces' were 'losing all control'. 'We are', he predicted, 'on the high road to a peace such as no one ever dreamed of, arranged over the heads of statesmen, parliaments and armies.'[93]

Poincaré's *année troublée* did, indeed, witness more unrest in France than in any period of the war. There were violent strikes, and after the failure of the Nivelle offensive the French army was afflicted by a series of mutinies whose effects continued to be felt for another nine months. Rising prices and the seemingly futile manner in which the war was being fought probably had more to do with these protests than the spread of any revolutionary doctrine. Nevertheless, both strikers and mutineers drew some of their inspiration from the upheavals in Russia. The wisdom of continuing the war was questioned, and revelations from Petrograd about the hitherto secret accord on the straits and a Franco-Russian agreement of February 1916, which provided for the separation of the left bank of the Rhine from Germany, raised doubts about the justice of the allied cause. The idea of a negotiated peace gained in popularity, and in May French socialists agreed to send representatives to an international socialist conference at Stockholm, where it was anticipated they would be able to talk of peace with their German comrades. Ribot's rejection of their request for passports, and the state of the army, became in June and July the subjects of secret sessions of the chamber of deputies, and these marked the beginning of a prolonged political crisis.[94]

Bertie viewed the rising tide of political and social discontent in France far more dispassionately than did Esher.[95] 'There is', he wrote to Balfour on 2 June, 'a general feeling of unrest and discontent. The

---

[93] Esher to Lloyd George, 31 May 1917, Lloyd George MSS., F./16/1/13.
[94] Watson, *Clemenceau*, pp.258–65. J-B. Duroselle, *La France et les Français, 1914–1920*(Paris, 1972), pp.174–92. On the mutinies see: G. Pedroncini, *Les Mutineries de 1917*(Paris, 1967), and *Les Mutineries des Armées Francaises* (Paris, 1980). The strikes are examined in J-J. Becker, *Les Francais dans la Grande Guerre* (Paris, 1980), pp.192–220. The most recent treatment of the Franco-Russian agreement of February 1916 is in Stevenson, *French War Aims*, pp.51–6 and 67–71.
[95] Esher was predicting at the end of May 1917 that the Russian revolutionary doctrine would spread over Europe just as the French revolutionary doctrine had done a century before. Esher to Robertson, 31 May 1917, Robertson MSS., I/21/68a.

moral of the French troops is not universally what it was.'[96] Yet until the end of June Bertie appears to have had no inkling of the extent to which the French army had been disabled by mutiny and disaffection.[97] The French military authorities were in fact remarkably successful in keeping the whole affair a secret. Moreover, where military matters were concerned, Bertie was largely dependent upon Le Roy-Lewis, who had taken to telegraphing reports on the situation at the front to the War Office by a non-ambassadorial channel. Aware of this, and encouraged thereto by Hardinge, Bertie eventually treated Le Roy-Lewis to a thorough dressing down for his failure to keep him informed. 'I was', Bertie subsequently noted, 'very calm with him and gave him no opportunity to be impertinent, but he looked daggers.'[98] The treatment yielded some results. On 23 May Le Roy-Lewis, now 'aux petits soins', brought him an invitation to an entertainment being offered by a visiting British guards band at the Trocadero, and on the next day he brought promises of 'political information'.[99]

Bertie, who was recovering from a stomach ailment, did not attend the concert.[100] Nevertheless, on the afternoon of 25 May he had the pleasure of entertaining some of the muscians in the embassy garden. The weather was fine, the guardsmen thirsty and Bertie, who had laid on some three hundred large bottles of *Bass*, evidently enjoyed the occasion.[101] All, however, was far from well. Only the day before Ribot had informed the French war committee that Lloyd George was intent on Bertie's recall, and the matter was again raised when a few days later the French premier visited London.[102] Asquith, Esher and Austen Chamberlain, the secretary of state for India, were all mentioned as possible candidates for the post.[103] The king, who was also consulted, protested to Lloyd George that Hardinge had already practically been promised the succession to Bertie.[104] But there was considerable opposition to the idea of replacing Bertie by another career diplomat. According to Henry Norman, a Liberal member of

---

[96] Bertie to Balfour, 2 June 1917, F.O.371/2938, despt.261.
[97] Gordon Lennox, II, pp.140–141.
[98] Hardinge to Bertie, 2 May 1917, B.P., A, F.O.800/175. Bertie to Hardinge, 19 May 1917, B.P., B, F.O.800/191.
[99] Bertie to Hardinge, 24 May 1917, B.P., B, F.O.800/191.
[100] *Ibid*.
[101] Gordon Lennox, II, p.131.
[102] Poincaré. *Au service*, IX, p.146.
[103] Memo. by Bertie, 28 Feb. – 2 June 1917; Athelstan Johnson to Bertie, 2 June 1917; B.P., B, F.O.800/191. Norman to Lloyd George, 18 June 1917, Lloyd George MSS., F/41/6/5.
[104] Stamfordham to Lloyd George, 30 May 1917, Lloyd George MSS., F/29/1/42. Gordon Lennox, II, p.134.

parliament and representative of the Ministry of Munitions at Paris, who had for some time been urging Lloyd George to effect a change at the embassy, Ribot and Painlevé had objected to Hardinge's candidature. Norman thought a better choice would be Le Roy-Lewis. 'In the very difficult Anglo-French relations that are coming', he observed to Lloyd George, 'his intimate knowledge, his friendship with the chief men, his tact and his perfect understanding of the French, would be of inestimable value.'[105]

Bertie was not oblivious to such pressures as were being applied to secure his removal. On 31 May Paul Cambon, who had travelled from London to Paris with Ribot, visited Bertie to warn him that in England Esher's intriguing against him was having some effect. He indicated that Painlevé was sympathetic towards Esher and Le Roy-Lewis, and pressed Bertie to speak with Lloyd George, who, he claimed, was 'impulsive' and often acted on 'outside influence'.[106] Two days later Athelstan Johnson, who after seven years absence from Paris had returned as a temporary secretary in May 1916, wrote from London to urge Bertie 'to come over here as soon as possible'. In the meantime the ambassador's opponents had triumphed again, for on 21 May Cohn's services were rewarded with the legion of honour. Worried lest his previous advice should thus be discredited, Bertie sought explanation from the foreign ministry. Jules Cambon, who now held the position of secretary-general at the Quai d'Orsay, assured him that Ribot would not sanction the award.[107] Matters had, however, already progressed too far, and in the end Cohn received his decoration, and for the time being Bertie retained his embassy.[108]

In spite of the advice of his friends, Bertie did not hurry home to England. He decided instead to stay for a few days with Lady Algernon Gordon Lennox at Boulogne, where he remained until on 6 June he joined Paul Cambon on the ferry for Folkestone.[109] Many assumed that this journey would mark the end of his official career. His arrival in London was followed by reports in the British press of his impending retirement, and in anticipation of this Geoffrey Robinson, the editor of *The Times*, instructed George Adam, the paper's correspondent at Paris, to prepare an appreciation of Bertie's life and work. But Adam's panegyric was not to be required. Bertie

---

[105] Norman to Lloyd George, 31 May 1917, Lloyd George MSS., F/41/6/1. J. Turner, *Lloyd George's Secretariat* (Cambridge, 1980), p.70.
[106] Memo. by Bertie, 28 Feb. – 2 June 1917, B.P., B, F.O.800/191.
[107] *Ibid*. Athelstan Johnson to Bertie, 2 June 1917, B.P., B, F.O.800/191.
[108] Memo. by Bertie, 22 June 1917, B.P., B, F.O.800/191.
[109] Austin Lee to de Bunsen, 18 June 1917, de Bunsen MSS., MB/IV/b. Gordon Lennox, II, pp.135 – 4.

had no intention of resigning, and was far from despondent about defending his position.[110] The king, who received him on 7 June, assured him of his support, and neither Curzon, nor Balfour, who was in any case not privy to the prime minister's intentions, gave him any cause for concern. From other friends he received messages of support, and even an aged and somnolent Alfred de Rothschild awoke to urge him not to resign.[111] Bertie also had an ally in Printing House square. Wickham Steed was convinced that Bertie was about to fall victim to a conspiracy being hatched by Esher, Michelham and Cohn, and that his removal would give encouragement to Caillaux and his friends.[112] He therefore took advantage of the absence of Robinson and Northcliffe from London, and inserted in the leader columns of *The Times* of 12 June a spirited defence of Bertie's diplomacy. 'Few greater mistakes', the article claimed, 'could be made at this critical juncture of the war than to remove from the Paris Embassy a distinguished public servant with such a record as that of LORD BERTIE'.[113]

Curzon subsequently told Bertie that such praise as *The Times* had offered him was 'none too great'.[114] Lloyd George thought otherwise. He was far from pleased with the way in which the affair had developed, and according to Hardinge, there was a 'tremendous row in the "Times" office raised by the PM'.[115] Adam and Robinson were equally indignant at Steed's conduct. Both thought that Bertie had been 'really past his work for some time', and that he ought to be replaced. In Adam's opinion Bertie's 'cussedness of temperament . . . [had] ended in creating complete chaos at the Embassy itself'. Indeed, in view of this and the absence of any effective control over the various overlapping and quarrelling British missions at Paris, he, like Esher, favoured putting the embassy in commission and

---

[110] Austin Lee to de Bunsen, 18 June 1917, *ibid.* Adam to Robinson, 11 June 1917, Adam MSS. Norman to Lloyd George, 12 June 1917, Lloyd George MSS., F/41/6/4. Phipps to Bertie. 13 June 1917; Howard to Bertie, 13 June 1917; B.P., B, F.O.800/191. Gordon Lennox, II, pp.133 – 6.

[111] *Ibid.* Hardinge to Chirol, 21 June 1917, Hardinge MSS., 33.

[112] Wickham Steed to Adam, 14 June 1917, Adam MSS. Wickham Steed seems to have been only too ready to accept that there was a Jewish plot against Bertie. Wickham Steed to Brock, 26 July 1917, Wickham Steed MSS.

[113] Austin Lee to de Bunsen, 18 June 1917, de Bunsen MSS., MB/IV/b. *Official Diary*, 12 June 1917, *The Times* MSS. (*The Times* archives). *The Times*, 12 June 1917, p.7. On relations between Northcliffe and Lloyd George during the war see: J.M. McEwen, 'Northcliffe and Lloyd George at War, 1914-1918', *Historical Journal*, XXIV(1981), 651 – 72.

[114] Gordon Lennox, II, p.138.

[115] Hardinge, *Old Diplomacy*, p.214. Hardinge to Chirol, 21 June 1917, Hardinge MSS., 33.

appointing Le Roy-Lewis as high commissioner. Not that either he or his editor had any sympathy with Caillaux and the 'international Jews' who were generally supposed to be plotting against Bertie. Robinson personally thought such tales were exaggerated, and in any case he did not consider that the existence of an intrigue necessarily made Bertie 'an ideal Ambassador'.[116]

Lloyd George may, however, have been reluctant to risk appearing to give way to pressure from pacifist financiers and other disreputable people. The extent and quality of the support which Bertie was able to rally in his favour may also have led him to delay taking any decision on the future of the embassy. *The Times* article certainly did much to boost Bertie's confidence, and although he returned to Paris on 22 June without having seen the prime minister, there seemed to be no reason why the latter should not be persuaded to adopt a more sympathetic attitude towards him. Athelstan Johnson, for instance, suggested that 'as a weather cock' Lloyd George could 'easily be brought round'.[117] At Paris too there was room for manoeuvre and Johnson secured for Bertie the assistance of his friend, the arms dealer, Basil Zaharoff, who agreed to intercede with Ribot on the ambassador's behalf.[118] At the same time Joseph Reinach, Dreyfus's defender (an odd recruit indeed to the cause of this supposed victim of international Jewry), volunteered to republish *The Times* article in *Le Figaro*, and Paul Cambon successfully impressed on Ribot the value of retaining Bertie in France. It was, nevertheless, still assumed by some in London that Ribot wanted Bertie's recall. And despite their disappointment at having failed to obtain the immediate removal of Bertie, Esher and his friends soon renewed their efforts to achieve this end.[119]

Bertie's opponents seemed set to profit from the publication of the report of the Mesopotamia Commission whose criticisms of the conduct of the vice-regal government opened up the prospect of

---

[116] Austin Lee to de Bunsen, 18 June 1917, de Bunsen MSS., MB/IV/b. Robinson to Adam, 13 June 1917; Robinson to Northcliffe, 22 June 1917, Dawson MSS. (*The Times* archives). Adam to Robinson, 11 June 1917; Adam to Wickham Steed, 17 June 1917; Adam to Robinson, 17 June 1917; Adam MSS. Bertie was himself not slow to claim that Caillaux and 'some pacifist financiers, chiefly Jews' were working for his recall. Poincaré, *Au service*, IX, p.176. Bertie to Balfour, 16 June 1916, B.P., B, F.O.800/191.
[117] Athelstan Johnson to Bertie, 20 June 1917, B.P., B, F.O.800/191.
[118] Basil Zaharoff was the chief shareholder of *Vickers Maxim*. Memo. by Bertie, 22 June 1917, B.P., B, F.O.800/191.
[119] Reinach to Bertie, 22 June 1917; memo. by Bertie, 24 June 1917; B.P., B, F.O.800/191. Cambon, III, pp.185–6. Gordon Lennox, II, p.141.

Hardinge being squeezed out of the Foreign Office.[120] The king, whom Bertie met at Abbeville on 10 July, assured him that he might consider the prime minister's 'proposal' for his withdrawal as dropped.[121] But when Lloyd George visited Paris towards the end of the month for an inter-allied conference, he lunched with Esher and studiously avoided the embassy and its staff. Not until two minutes before his departure by train did he have any conversation with Bertie. Even then his language was obtuse. Taking Bertie by the arm, he told him: 'We nearly had to ask you to take charge at the F.O. in Hardinge's place for he ought to have gone.' All that Bertie could manage in reply was the protest that while he was not too old to be an ambassador, he was too old to be permanent under-secretary. 'There would', he explained, 'be too much confinement and too little exercise.'[122]

One member of Bertie's staff was getting more exercise than was good for him. Not long after his return from London Bertie learned that his military *attaché* had been conducting an affair with Mlle de Salvette, the divorced wife of a German-American businessman and mistress of the French pretender, the Duc d'Orléans. The couple who were known to the gossip mongers of the *faubourgs* as 'Le Roi et la Reine', had taken rooms at the Hotel de Trianon at Versailles. But the *ménage à deux* was discovered by Mrs Le Roy-Lewis, and a little later Mlle de Salvette returned to the arms of her former lover. In consequence, the apparently repentant and 'much worn' colonel sought leave to go with his wife to take the cleansing waters of Mont-Doré. Bertie was delighted with the scandal, but indignant that Le Roy-Lewis intended to seek permission to take with him to the Auvergne the motor car and chauffeur with which he had been supplied by the ministry of war. No amount of 'washing', Bertie noted, would 'cure him of his love of intrigue'.[123] And when, despite his sins, the French government decided to present Le Roy-Lewis with the *Croix de Guerre avec Palmes*, Bertie immediately petitioned the Admiralty for some equivalent decoration for Captain Acton, his industrious naval *attaché*.[124] Powerless to punish the wicked, Bertie sought to reward the righteous.

---

[120] For a thorough examination of this issue see: J.D. Goold, 'Lord Hardinge and the Mesopotamia Inquiry, 1914 – 1917', *Historical Journal*, XIX(1976), 919 – 45. See also: Busch, *Hardinge*, pp.265 – 74.
[121] Memo. by Bertie, 11 July 1917, B.P., A, F.O.800/175.
[122] Memo by Bertie, 23 – 28 Aug. 1917, B.P., A, F.O.800/169. Gordon Lennox, II, p.16.
[123] Memo. by Bertie, 23 June 1917, B.P., B, F.O.800/191. Bertie to Hardinge, 25 June 1917, Hardinge MSS., 33.
[124] Bertie to Stamfordham, 25 Aug. 1917; Bertie to Admiral Hall, 27 Aug. 1917; B.P., B, F.O.800/191.

While Bertie was making good the defences of his embassy, Haig was preparing for his offensive against the German lines in Flanders. The two campaigns were not entirely unconnected. That which Bertie waged against Esher was more than just a matter of personal enmity. At stake was the whole issue of the role of the embassy in the coordination of the allied war effort. Esher's contention remained that the British government ought to have at Paris someone who was more closely in touch with, and who could therefore better represent, the views of the war cabinet.[125] There was much force in Esher's argument. As a result of the increasing frequency of inter-allied conferences at a prime ministerial level the main function of the embassy as a channel of communication had been sensibly diminished. Moreover, although Bertie believed himself to be best placed to provide the government in London with a full and accurate understanding of the political situation in France, he had not of late shown any urgency in supplying the Foreign Office with such information.[126] There is also evidence to suggest that he was all too ready to seek in French politics and society only that which he wished to find. Shocked during his visit to London in June by the extent to which it was generally believed that Caillaux and his 'pacifist friends' would regain office, Bertie sought assurances from Clemenceau and Poincaré. Both of these erstwhile opponents of Caillaux were ready to oblige and to confirm Bertie in his conviction that Caillaux, despite the strength of the radical socialists in the chamber, would remain in the political wilderness.[127]

Bertie was also reluctant to give such representations as were made to him on the low morale of the French army the attention that they deserved. On 29 June Walter Behrens spoke to him about the depressed condition of French troops and the 'deplorable effect' that the excesses of the Russian revolution had had upon them.[128] Three days later he supplied the ambassador with a report drafted by Abel Ferry, the *rapporteur* of the army commission of the chamber, which drew attention to the mutinous state of the army and urged the French government to negotiate with the British for a more equitable distribution of allied forces in France. A copy of this was promptly

---

[125] Esher to Elibank, 11 Aug. 1917, Elibank MSS., 8804.
[126] Athelstan Johnson had suggested to Bertie in June that a 'long despatch which would be read as having been written by yourself giving a résumé of French political events would . . . be rather opportune'. Athelstan Johnson to Bertie, 2 June 1917, B.P., B, F.O.800/191.
[127] Bertie to Balfour, 26 June 1917, B.P., A, F.O.800/169. Bertie to Balfour, 29 June 1917, F.O.371/2934, tel.626. Bertie to Balfour, 7 July 1917, F.O.371/2934, despt. 343. Gordon Lennox, II, p.140.
[128] Memo. by Bertie, 29 June 1917, B.P., A, F.O.800/169.

sent by Bertie to Balfour with the intimation that it showed 'what may be asked of us'.[129] Bertie refused, however, to discuss military matters with a deputation from the chamber on the grounds that he could not appear to act behind the back of the French government. For similar reasons he advised the Comtesse de Greffulhe, who feared that the French government would not dare inform the British of the true state of the French army, against giving Ferry and his colleague, Albert Favre, letters of introduction to Balfour and Curzon. He was prepared to listen to her claims that if British forces did not relieve the exhausted French troops there would be disturbances and revolution. But he maintained that any communications on this subject should be made through proper channels.[130] Besides which, on 14 July he accepted without protest a denial from Painlevé, a politician for whom he had little respect, a denial that there had been any mutinies at all. 'He', Bertie noted, 'is for fighting to a finish.'

His meeting with Painlevé allowed Bertie the occasion once more to refer to the 'peace propaganda of financiers, mostly Jews or of Hebrew origin, and others who think only of money making'.[131] He might have spoken in other terms if he had known that Painlevé had under his consideration a paper by a *sous-chef* of his *cabinet* which recommended that since neither side could achieve a decisive victory, and since Europe was threatened by economic ruin and social revolution, France should seek a compromise peace.[132] But Bertie did not probe beneath the tales that reached him about conditions at the front. His own estimation of the situation there was probably close to that which he gave to the Labour leader and minister, Arthur Henderson, when he visited Paris at the end of July for discussions with the French socialists on their attitude towards the proposed Stockholm conference. In reply to a statement by Henderson that the French army could not go through another winter campaign, Bertie asserted that after the Nivelle offensive, there 'had been great discontent and some mutiny', but since then the morale of the troops had greatly improved.[133] Admittedly, Bertie was unlikely to want to

---

[129] Bertie to Balfour, 2 July 1917, B.P., Add. MS.63047. Memo. by Bertie, 4 July 1917, B.P., A, F.O.800/169.
[130] Memo. by Bertie, 5 July 1917, B.P., A, F.O.800/169. Bertie to Balfour, 3 July 1917, F.O.371/2938, tel.637. Bertie to Balfour, 8 July 1917, F.O.371/2934, despt. 344. Gordon Lennox, II, pp.148 – 50.
[131] Gordon Lennox, II, pp.152 – 3.
[132] *Étude sur les conditions d'une Paix Française*, Cdt. Herscher, 12 July 1917, Painlevé MSS. (Archives Nationales, Paris), 313 AP, 129, dossier 1.
[133] Bertie to Balfour, 29 July 1917, tel., B.P. A, F.O.800/169. Arthur Henderson was a member of Lloyd George's war cabinet until he resigned after quarrelling with the prime minister over British representation at the Stockholm conference. V.H. Rothwell, *British War Aims and Peace Diplomacy, 1914 – 1918* (London, 1971), p.98.

appear pessimistic to one to whom Lloyd George had asked him to give 'good and calming advice'.[134] This was, however, about as far as Bertie ever committed himself on the subject of the mutinies. He did not in any case regard it as part of his duty to make assessments on the military situation. 'I suppose', he wrote to Balfour on 29 July, 'that reliable information in regard to the morale of French soldiers reaches HMG from the British mission at French GHQ and other sources military.'[135]

Hardinge thought that more was required from Bertie. On 31 July he wrote to urge him to make 'immediate and discreet enquiries in unofficial as well as official quarters as to the general attitude in France towards the continued prolongation of the war, and, in particular to the prospect of another winter campaign', and to write the result 'fully and frankly' in a private letter. With this Hardinge hoped to counter reports of British travellers of war weariness in France, and to destroy in its embryo stage the idea which had recently been raised in a 'responsible quarter' of the need for an early peace. Since Bertie was already on the way to London when he received this letter at Boulogne, there was no opportunity for him to attempt any immediate soundings of French politicians.[136] He did not in any event respond to Hardinge's request, and it was 12 September before he sent in an official despatch to Balfour a report on the state of French morale.[137] Bertie's apparent lassitude may in part have been due to a warning which he had received from Athelstan Johnson that in 'these days private letters to Hardinge and Cecil from a political point of view count for very little'.[138] Added to which his stay in London offered him ample opportunity to impress on members of the government his own view that if after the present offensive the British extended their front and showed no signs of yielding to the pacifists, the French would hold on through the winter until the Americans, who had entered the war in April, arrived in sufficient numbers to count militarily.[139] And when he returned to Paris on 22 August Bertie was straightway confronted with a political crisis that commenced with the arrest and death of Almereyda, the editor of the defeatest *Bonnet Rouge*, and the hounding from office of Malvy, the radical minister of the interior, and ended with Ribot's resignation on

---

[134] Memo. by Bertie, 23–28 Aug. 1917, B.P., A, F.O.800/169.
[135] Bertie to Balfour, 29 July 1917, *ibid.*
[136] Hardinge to Bertie, 31 July 1917, Hardinge MSS., 33. Grahame to Bertie, 5 Aug. 1917, B.P., Add. MS.63047.
[137] Bertie to Balfour, 12 Sept. 1917, F.O.371/2934, despt.413.
[138] Athelstan Johnson to Bertie, 2 June 1917, B.P., B, F.O.800/191.
[139] Gordon Lennox II, pp.164–9.

11 September and the formation of a new government under Painlevé.[140] There is, however, evidence of a certain coolness at this time in Bertie's relations with Hardinge. The latter had, despite Bertie's presence in London for over a fortnight, made no effort to see him, and on 27 August sent Bertie a somewhat sharply worded reminder that he had not yet received a reply to his letter of 31 July.[141] Hurt perhaps by this treatment, Bertie withheld from writing to his friend until well into September.[142]

Not that Bertie had anything new to say on matters French. In his despatch of 12 September he simply repeated his conviction that the great majority of French people were confident of the ultimate victory of Britain and France, and that they were prepared to go through another winter campaign. To this he added his now customary diatribe against pacifists and prophets of doom. But, he warned Balfour:

> If . . . there be signs of flinching on our part, we cannot expect the French not to do likewise, . . . There are in Paris as in London Pacifists by profession, Pacifists by conviction, Pacifists by convenience, and Pacifists by the prospect of money-making when Peace comes, and the International Financiers with no particular country for which to feel patriotism. A good deal of harm is done by those who may best be described as British Casuals who during a more or less short stay are caught by Pacifist spiders always on the look out for easy prey. These casuals are well stuffed with the belief that France cannot continue the war beyond the autumn, the French troops being in a condition bordering on mutiny will not face another winter campaign; that unless there be peace before then there will be serious disturbances in France and perhaps a revolution at Paris.

Bertie readily admitted that as a result of the failure of the Nivelle offensive, there had been 'great disappointment and discouragement throughout France', but he claimed that this 'neurasthenic mood' had since been replaced by a 'determined feeling'. There was in his opinion no reason for altering the estimate which he had made in the previous February of the likely requirements of the French at a future peace conference. These included, besides the evacuation and

---

[140] It is interesting to note that Jefferson Cohn lost no time in seeking to win Painlevé's friendship. J.D. Cohn to Painlevé, (probably Sept. 1917), Painlevé MSS., 313 AP 126. Watson, *Clemenceau*, pp.261–5.
[141] Hardinge to Bertie, 27 Aug. 1917, B.P., A, F.O.800/169.
[142] Hardinge to Bertie, 11 Sept. 1917, B.P., A, F.O.800/175.

rehabilitation of Belgium and northern France, guarantees against future aggression, the retrocession of Alsace-Lorraine, a light rectification in France's favour of the frontier with Luxemburg, the remaining portion of which would be ceded to Belgium, the valley of the Saar, and the payment by Germany of a war indemnity.[143]

In the event of Germany's total defeat, Bertie thought the French would expand their *desiderata*, and that the public in France would demand the establishment of a buffer state on the left bank of the Rhine.[144] There was nothing novel about these conclusions. Bertie was aware that Briand had sought Russian support for such aspirations, and he knew that Paul Cambon had informed Balfour on 2 July of French ambitions in the Rhineland.[145] But Bertie was wary about engaging in discussions on the future terms of peace. Despite his insistence on the determination of the majority of Frenchmen to fight *jusqu'au bout*, he could not ignore the absence of agreement between French politicians on the proper *buts de guerre*. Albert Thomas, the socialist leader and minister for munitions in the governments of Briand and Ribot, went so far in June as to advocate a plebiscite for the inhabitants of Alsace-Lorraine in order to determine their political future.[146] Yet more disturbing, however, from Bertie's point of view, were those who seemed ready to advocate a separate peace with Germany. On 3 March he had warned Hardinge that he had information that Caillaux, Combes, Malvy and Charles Humbert, the proprietor of *Le Journal*, were seeking a settlement which would give Alsace-Lorraine to France and leave Britain in the lurch.[147] Even Briand, whom Bertie suspected of moving towards a reconciliation with Caillaux, sought permission in September from the government for a meeting in Switzerland with von der Lancken, a diplomat attached to the German forces of occupation in Belgium.[148]

Neither Poincaré nor Ribot were prepared to sanction Briand's mission. Not that the terms which Briand thought the Germans prepared to offer were unattractive. They included provision for the retrocession of Alsace-Lorraine and the evacuation of Belgium. But Briand appears to have been misled by his intermediaries, and Ribot

---

[143] Bertie to Balfour, 12 Sept. 1917, F.O.371/2934, despt.413.
[144] *Ibid.*
[145] Bertie to Balfour, 4 June 1917, F.O.371/2937, tel.513. Balfour to Bertie, 2 July 1917, F.O.371/2937, despt.483.
[146] Bertie to Balfour, 12 Sept. 1917, F.O.371/2934, despt. 413.
[147] Bertie to Hardinge, 3 March 1917, Hardinge MSS., 30.
[148] Bertie to Balfour, 23 Sept. 1917, B.P., A, F.O.800/169. Rothwell, pp.105–8. W.B. Fest, 'British War Aims and German Peace Feelers during the First World War (December 1916– November 1918)', *Historical Journal* XV(1972), 300–1.

suspected a trap that might embroil France with her allies. Indeed, so perturbed did Ribot seem with regard to reports of peace manoeuvres that Bertie wrote privately to Lloyd George on 24 September to urge him to make a public declaration on France's right to the restitution of Alsace-Lorraine without a plebiscite. 'If', he noted in his diary, 'we do not back up the French in this matter we cannot expect them to "stick it" for us in matters which we regard as a capital condition for ourselves.'[149] It nevertheless took pressure from Painlevé, who met Lloyd George on 25 September and subsequently visited England, to squeeze from the prime minister the declaration of 11 October that Britain would stand by France until 'she redeems her oppressed children from the degradation of a foreign yoke'.[150]

It was because he wished to see allied unity maintained that Bertie also opposed the suggestion that was first made by the Russians in July for a conference to formulate a programme of allied war aims. A conference of that kind would, he feared, reveal differences between the *entente* powers which Germany would attempt to exploit.[151] For similar reasons he frowned on such efforts as were made during 1917 to detach Austria-Hungary from her alliance with Germany. Unlike Esher, he thought their end unrealistic and the exercise fraught with danger, for it could lead to squabbles with those allies whose support had been purchased with promises of Austrian territory. A satisfactory peace was in his opinion only to be obtained by the military defeat of Germany. There would, he observed on 23 September, 'be no peace on earth until it is "Deutschland unter Alles," and for that we *must* go on fighting to a finish'.[152]

That finish must have seemed as far off as ever in the autumn of 1917. During the last days of October Haig's offensive ground to a halt; the Petrograd soviet prepared to seize power in Russia; and Austro-German forces broke through the Italian lines at Caporetto and precipitated the most spectacular rout of the war. At Paris Painlevé seemed incapable of providing either leadership or political stability, and allegations of treason multiplied. To the *Bonnet Rouge* affair were added the cases of Turmel, Bolo Pasha and Humbert, all of whom were accused of having received German money. And

---

[149] Stevenson, *French War Aims*, pp.89 – 90. Bertie to Balfour, 24 Sept. 1917; Bertie to Lloyd George, 24 Sept. 1917; B.P., A, F.O.800/169. Rumbold to Bertie, 12 Sept. 1917, B.P., A, F.O.800/161.
[150] Stevenson, *ibid*, p.83.
[151] Bertie to Balfour, 22 July 1917, B.P., A, F.O.800/178. Gordon Lennox II, pp.158 – 9.
[152] Gordon Lennox, II, pp.170, 189, and 191. The Austro-Hungarian peace manoeuvres are considered in Z.A.B. Zeman, *A Diplomatic History of the First World War* (London, 1971), pp.121 – 61.

THE END OF AN EMBASSY

Caillaux, who had once provided funds for the *Bonnet Rouge*, also came under suspicion.[153] Denied the support of the socialists, who objected to Ribot's continued presence at the Quai d'Orsay, and sniped at by Clemenceau, who demanded a thorough investigation of the 'scandals', Painlevé's government tottered from one crisis to another. On 23 October Painlevé resigned in order to reconstitute his cabinet, but the replacement of Ribot by Barthou did nothing to satisfy his opponents of the left.[154] Despairing of this state of affairs, Bertie began to speculate on the prospects for a military *coup d'état*. If the French armies were successful in the field, then, he thought, 'a *Corps d'Armée* might march back on Paris and suppress the present lot of authorities'. 'Nobody', he added, 'would be any the worse, and the good public and the country would be all the better off for a change of administration.'[155]

The one politician whom Bertie felt might have the audacity to summon the troops to Paris was Clemenceau.[156] Ever since August he had seemed to be the obvious choice for the presidency of the council.[157] But Bertie feared that there was too much ill-feeling between Clemenceau and Poincaré to permit this, and he doubted whether any government formed by Clemenceau would last long.[158] He had, Bertie wrote to Balfour, 'so many personal enemies . . . that any ministry formed by him would not last any useful time'.[159] On both these counts Bertie was, however, to be proved wrong. By mid-October Poincaré had reconciled himself to the fact that there was little chance of forming a strong government without Clemenceau, and the administration which he headed after the fall of Painlevé on 13 November was to retain power for another two years.[160] Bertie welcomed Clemenceau's return to office. Clemenceau, he opined, was 'not a man to dally with peace manoeuvres', and he was devoted to maintenance of the alliance with England.[161] Moreover, this change of government seemed advantageous to Bertie from a personal point of view, for there was no chance of Esher or his friends being able to influence Clemenceau in a sense contrary to Bertie's interests. It was therefore ironic that Clemenceau's appointment

---

[153] Watson, *Clemenceau*, pp.265–9.
[154] Bertie to Balfour, 24 Oct. 1917, B.P., A, F.O.800/169.
[155] Gordon Lennox, II, p.209.
[156] Bertie to Lloyd George, 14 Nov. 1917, B.P., A, F.O.800/169.
[157] Gordon Lennox, II, p.172.
[158] Bertie to Balfour, 25 Aug. 1917, B.P., A, F.O.800/169.
[159] Bertie to Balfour, 29 Oct. 1917, *ibid.*
[160] Watson, *Clemenceau*, pp.268–72.
[161] Bertie to Balfour, 11 Oct. 1917, B.P., A, F.O.800/272. Bertie to Lloyd George, 15 Nov. 1917, B.P., A, F.O.800/169.

should have coincided with a fresh upset in Bertie's relations with Lloyd George.

One of Painlevé's last acts before his resignation was to meet the British and Italian premiers at Rapallo. There on 7 November he formally accepted Lloyd George's proposal for the establishment of a supreme inter-allied war council: a body which was to be composed of the political leaders of the allies and assisted by a permanent advisory general staff at Versailles. This long overdue reform in the direction of the war aimed at centralizing and coordinating the allied command structure. It also seemed likely to by-pass Robertson and the army council in London, and appeared to pose a direct challenge to their authority. With this in mind Lloyd George made every effort to secure a favourable press in London.[162] But, despite the assurances offered by Franklin-Bouillon, Painlevé's minister for propaganda, that the scheme would be warmly welcomed in France, the French press offered a distinctly cool reception to the Rapallo accord. Having been led to expect the appointment of a commander-in-chief with overall control of the allied armies, there was some disappointment in France at the creation of yet another inter-allied committee. Gustav Hervé in *Le Victoire* put the point clearly when he bemoaned placing the armies under a 'Soviet of irresponsible generals' instead of under a generalissimo backed by a large general staff.[163]

Bertie did not share Hervé's apprehensions. He personally thought that the creation of a supreme war council was inevitable since while the British and French military authorities had in theory been agreed, they had in practice not always acted up to their understanding. Haig had, for example, made great difficulties in carrying out the agreed prolongation of the British front in France.[164] Nevertheless, Bertie thought it necessary to report by telegram the substance of Hervé's article, and since Lloyd George was in Paris, he also communicated his message to him on the afternoon of the 12th. This was a mistake for Bertie had failed to take into account either the prime minister's vanity, or his sensitivity to criticism in the press. Indeed so incensed was Lloyd George by the ambassador's report, that he protested to him that it did not in the least represent the opinion of the French and Italian press which were 'overwhelmingly favourable to the creation

---

[162] J. Marlowe, *Milner. Apostle of Empire* (London, 1976), p.285.
[163] Bertie to Balfour, 11 Nov. 1917, tel.1230, Balfour MSS., F.O.800/199. Bertie to Balfour, 12 Nov. 1917, B.P., A, F.O.800/169. Athelstan Johnson to J.T. Davies, 14 Nov. 1917, Lloyd George MSS., F/51/4/56.
[164] Bertie to J.T. Davies, 14 Nov. 1917, B.P., A, F.O.800/169.

THE END OF AN EMBASSY

of this Council'.¹⁶⁵ Furthermore, he threatened to bring the matter before the war cabinet.¹⁶⁶ In this course he was no doubt encouraged by Esher, who took the opportunity offered by a meeting with Lloyd George on the evening of the 12th to once more impress upon him the inadequacies of the government's representation at Paris. The creation of the supreme war council had, he claimed, made it all the more necessary to have an ambassador who was a member of the war cabinet, and who would 'dominate French politics'. He advised Lloyd George to send Milner to Paris 'to give stability where there is none', and to ensure that Henry Wilson, the newly appointed British military representative at Versailles, would get 'information'.¹⁶⁷

Bertie was justly irritated by Lloyd George's reaction to his telegram, news of which he received from John Davies, the prime minister's private secretary. 'The Government', he later wrote to Hardinge, '*ought* to be glad to know the criticisms of the Press.'¹⁶⁸ He wasted no time, however, in writing a long private letter to Lloyd George. In this he attempted to explain more fully the feelings of the French, and he hailed a recent speech by Lloyd George in which he had condemned the absence of true allied military collaboration as a 'tremendous success for all classes for it said what no French minister would dare say'. This and further explanatory telegrams sufficed to enable Hardinge and his colleagues to quell Lloyd George's indignation.¹⁶⁹ Nevertheless, the episode had done Bertie no good. Apart from some attacks made upon him by Bottomley in his weekly rag, *John Bull*, the question of his recall had been dormant since the summer.¹⁷⁰ But the issue was now being reopened. In a letter to Lloyd George of 3 December Esher repeated his appeal for the appointment of Milner in Bertie's place. Paris, he wrote, was 'the nerve centre of the war', and the prime minister should transfer all the diplomatic activities of the government there.¹⁷¹

Lloyd George was not inclined to follow this advice. He had no wish to lose Milner's services in London, and since, as the prime minister's alternative on the supreme war council, he already had

---

¹⁶⁵ Lloyd George to Balfour, tel., 12 Nov. 1917, Balfour MSS., F.O.800/199. Lloyd George was again encouraged to be critical of Bertie by Esher who indicated that the ambassador had not kept London properly informed of Briand's peace manoeuvres. Esher also pressed for Milner's appointment as ambassador at Paris. Fraser, p.373.
¹⁶⁶ J.T. Davies to Bertie, 12 Nov. 1917, B.P., A, F.O.800/169. Bertie to Hardinge, 12 Nov. 1917, Hardinge MSS., 35.
¹⁶⁷ Brett and Esher, IV, pp.157–9. Fraser, p.373.
¹⁶⁸ Bertie to Hardinge, 20 Nov. 1917, Hardinge MSS., 35.
¹⁶⁹ Bertie to Lloyd George, 14 Nov. 1917; Hardinge to Bertie, 16 Nov. 1917; B.P., A, F.O.800/169.
¹⁷⁰ *John Bull*, XXII, no.590, p.7, and no.595, p.3.
¹⁷¹ Esher to Lloyd George, 3 Dec. 1917, Lloyd George MSS., F/16/1/20.

access to the French political leadership, there were few solid advantages to be had from designating him ambassador to France. Indeed, on 20 December Bonar Law, the chancellor of the exchequer, told the Commons that Bertie was not shortly to be recalled.[172] There was, however, renewed speculation in the British and French press about Bertie's future. *The Weekly Despatch* of 6 January 1918 forecasted changes in Britain's representation at Paris, Petrograd and Washington. The story was repeated in *L'Echo de Paris* and there was talk of Bertie being replaced by Lord Crewe. But Bertie was not perturbed by this gossip, and both *The Times* and *Le Temps* denied that there was any truth in the rumours of Bertie's impending retirement.[173] Events in Paris appeared in any case to be moving in the ambassador's favour, and the prospect of Caillaux being brought to trial led him to speculate about the likely embarrassment of his 'English friends'. Thus, while he supposed 'that with the cunning of the Jew the dog at the fair' would not have 'left any traces in Caillaux's booth', he delighted in the momentary discomfort of those like Esher who had once regarded Caillaux as the 'coming man'.[174] Moreover, the news that Clemenceau had refused to receive Esher, and that the head of the French protocol was trying to recover from 'Lord Eyscher' the car that had been loaned to him by the *Reserve Générale des Automobiles*, only added to his pleasure.[175]

Esher, his advice apparently ignored by Lloyd George, and his proffered assistance rejected by Clemenceau, decided to return to England. But before he left Paris he called at the embassy on 3 February to bid farewell to Le Roy-Lewis. The moment was ill-chosen for he arrived at the embassy just as Bertie was completing an interview with the military *attaché*. The events which followed were gleefully recorded by Bertie in the following extract from a letter which he subsequently addressed to Stamfordham:

> As I came out of the room with Colonel Le Roy-Lewis I ran up against an elderly gentleman in khaki with a red band to his cap. He promptly wheeled about and was off precipitately. When I got to the door in the courtyard and looked round the corner I saw that it was the Dog and he was fleeing like a hare. Captain Goldney the Assistant to the Military Attaché, who happened to be in the street

---

[172] *The Times*, 21 Dec. 1917, p.8.
[173] Extracts from *The Weekly Despatch*, 6 and 13 Jan. 1918, and *L'Echo de Paris*, 8 Jan. 1918, B.P.B, F.O.800/191. Gordon Lennox, II, pp.240–1.
[174] Bertie to Lloyd George, 11 Dec. 1917, B.P. A, F.O.800/159. Bertie to Stamfordham, 11 Dec. 1917, B.P., B, F.O.800/191.
[175] Bertie to Hardinge, 7 Dec. 1917, Hardinge MSS., 35. N. Martin to Bertie, 20 Dec. 1917, B.P., A, F.O.800/169.

outside the Embassy wondered what could be the matter for Esher was striding towards the Élysée every now and again looking furtively behind as though he was expecting to be followed . . . I went out in the automobile to see what damage had been done to Madame Henri de Breteuil's home by the German bombardment. The chauffeur turned up the Rue de l'Élysée and near the end of it I saw the Hare scuttling along. Poor thing, it was I suppose very frightened. It doubled to the left down the Avenue Gabriel making for the Place de la Concorde at the back of the Embassy Garden. I went on my way up the Champs Élysée. What a fool the dog must be to turn into a hare.[176]

But miraculous though Esher's metamorphosis may have been, it in fact afforded Bertie only a temporary respite from his troubles. As he was soon to learn, the prime minister was already preparing plans to instal a new tenant in the Faubourg St-Honoré.

Lloyd George's concern was not so much with Britain's diplomatic representation at Paris as with her army in Flanders. Ever since the previous summer he had been toying with the idea of replacing Haig and Robertson with men who shared his own more flexible approach to strategy. The problem was how to make such a change. The establishment of the supreme war council had provided the prime minister with an alternative source of military advice. The public reaction against his criticism of the generals had, however, offered him a reminder of the sympathy which they enjoyed in parliament and the press and of the need to proceed with caution. If Robertson were to be removed from his post as C.I.G.S., Haig might also go, and Derby, their friend and supporter in the government, might resign. The result could then be a major political upset. Evidently with this and, perhaps, Derby's electoral influence in mind, Lloyd George had begun to think in December 1917 in terms of easing Derby out of the War Office and replacing him with Milner. To this end he considered offering to Derby the embassy at Paris.[177] After all, Lord Reading, who in January 1918 was sent to Washington to replace Spring Rice as ambassador there, had been accorded 'special powers', and the opportunity to fulfill a similar role in France might be sufficient to tempt Derby to leave the War Office.[178] His removal

---

[176] Bertie to Stamfordham, 3 and 4 Feb. 1918, B.P., B, F.O.800/191.
[177] S. Roskill, *Hankey, Man of Secrets* (3 vols., London 1970–74), I, pp. 474–5. P. Guinn, *British Strategy and Politics 1914 to 1918* (Oxford, 1965), pp. 259–303. Hardinge, *Old Diplomacy*, pp. 226–7. Journal, 16–19 Dec. 1917, C.P. Scott MSS. (British Library), Add. MS 50904. D.R. Woodward, *Lloyd George and the Generals* (Newark, N.J., 1983), pp. 160–252.
[178] D. Judd, *Lord Reading* (London, 1982), pp. 140–2.

from the government might then be disguised in such a way as to make it appear that he was going to Paris both as a colleague and as a representative of the prime minister. Thus in mid-January 1918 Lloyd George confronted Derby with the proposal that he might go to Paris in Bertie's stead.[179]

Derby did not reject the offer. He told Lloyd George he was likely to accept, provided that his powers were clearly defined, that he was able to keep his independence, and that he was 'not called upon to be simply a mouthpiece of the Government and gagged on all those questions on which' he held 'a very strong opinion'. He was also reluctant to appear to be abandoning his friends, and after further talks on the matter with Lloyd George and Balfour, he wrote to the latter on 24 January that he could not go until he had defended 'those who have placed confidence in me and in whom I have confidence'. Nevertheless, when three weeks later a quarrel over the powers of the supreme war council led to Robertson's replacement by Henry Wilson, Derby hesitated over what course to pursue. As was generally expected, he threatened to resign, and on 16 February Lloyd George, in seeking the king's approval for the military changes, mentioned to him the possibility of Derby going to Paris. But since it seemed inevitable that Derby's departure at this stage would lead to the sort of political row that Lloyd George wanted to avoid, and since Derby was prone to prevarication, he was eventually persuaded to remain at the War Office. For the moment the prime minister could afford to bide his time and await a more favourable occasion on which to free himself from Derby.[180]

Bertie was aware of what was going on in London. Towards the end of January Clemenceau had told him that he had heard that there was an intrigue to oust him from the embassy; on 6 February Hardinge wrote to explain that Derby had been selected as a candidate for the post; and ten days later at the time of Robertson's dismissal, Stamfordham sent Bertie a warning '*to be on the look out!*'.[181] Bertie's friends were, however, reassured when Derby seemed to prefer the 'fleshpots of London' to the uncertainties of Paris. 'I think', Athelstan Johnson wrote from London on 14 March, 'everything connected with the Paris Embassy has blown over

---

[179] R.S. Churchill, *Lord Derby, 'King of Lancashire'* (London, 1959), pp.336–9.
[180] *Ibid*, pp.338–40. Hankey, I, pp.497–501. Stamfordham to J.T. Davies, 16 April 1918, Lloyd George MSS., F/29/2/14. D. Lloyd George, *War Memoirs of David Lloyd George* (6 vols., London, 1933–6), V, pp.2784–833.
[181] Hardinge to Bertie, 6 Feb. 1918, B.P., A, F.O.800/175. Bertie to Hardinge, 9 Feb. 1918; Stamfordham to Bertie, 15 Feb. 1918, B.P., B, F.O.800/191.

completely.'[182] Moreover, both Clemenceau, who had already promised Bertie his support, and Pichon spoke out very strongly in the ambassador's favour during a visit to London in March.[183] In any case it then seemed more likely that Bertie would be driven from Paris by Prussian bayonets than by Welsh wizardry.

By the spring of 1918 the outlook for the *entente* powers was bleak. To the setbacks suffered by their armies had to be added the prospect of a separate peace between Germany and the Bolsheviks in Russia. Bertie still had faith, as he put it, 'in our people and the French and Americans to stick it and ultimately to win a peace to suit *us three*'.[184] Yet where allied war aims were concerned, he had been satisfied rather than inspired by the programme outlined by Lloyd George on 5 January to the Labour conference at Caxton hall. He had some reservations about Lloyd George's reference to leaving the fate of Germany's colonies to be settled by a peace conference, but he thought the commitment sufficiently vague to enable the government to find a reason for hanging on to them.[185] Moreover, he must surely have welcomed the prime minister's declaration that the passages between the Black Sea and the Mediterranean should be 'internationalized and neutralized'. On only one issue of foreign policy did he find himself wholly at odds with Lloyd George and Balfour. That was the question of Palestine.[186]

Since Turkey's entry into the war Bertie had played only a minor role in the efforts of the British and French governments to harmonize their policies towards the Arab lands of the Ottoman empire. The terms of the Sykes-Picot agreement of January 1916 had been for, the most part settled in London, and after the formation of Lloyd George's coalition the future of the region had become a matter of peculiar personal interest to the prime minister.[187] Bertie did, however, offer consistent opposition to the notion of British or Anglo-French support for Zionist aspirations. Thus he poured scorn on the proposal made by Grey in March 1916 to win sympathy for the *entente* powers in America by offering the Jews an arrangement on Palestine.

---

[182] Hardinge to Bertie, 5 March 1918, B.P., A, F.O.800/178. Athelstan Johnson to Bertie, 14 March 1918, B.P., B, F.O.800/191.
[183] Hardinge to Bertie, 20 March 1918, B.P., A, F.O.800/169.
[184] Gordon Lennox, II, p.220.
[185] *Ibid.* pp.237 – 9, and 240 – 1. Bertie to Hardinge, 12 Jan. 1918, Hardinge MSS., 36. Zeman, pp.262 – 6.
[186] Zeman, *ibid.*
[187] Jukka Nevakivi, *Britain, France and the Arab Middle East, 1914 – 1920* (London, 1969), pp.13 – 67. Roger Adelson, *Mark Sykes. Portrait of an Amateur* (London, 1975), pp.196 – 214.

Given the treatment of their coreligionists in Russia, he did not think that the Jewish community in the United States would be influenced by promises about Palestine. Besides which, he was perturbed lest Britain should thereby risk forfeiting Arab support in the war. How, he asked Grey, would the Jews, who were not a 'combative race . . . fare against the warlike Arabs unless physically supported by Britain and France'?[188]

Bertie spoke similarly to Lloyd George when he visited the embassy in April 1917. Then, however, he was also disturbed by a recent suggestion made by Mark Sykes that Britain should in future assume a protectorate over Palestine. Bertie had very little sympathy for French pretensions in the Levant, but he warned Lloyd George of the catholic and colonialist opposition that would be raised in France against acceptance of such a proposition. The prime minister was unmoved by this appeal. The French, he insisted, would have to accept a British protectorate.[189] And six months later the war cabinet sanctioned Balfour's letter to Lord Rothschild of 2 November with its explicit declaration of support for the 'establishment in Palestine of a national home for the Jewish people'. On this occasion Bertie wisely confined to the pages of his diary his protest against a promise which he feared would do Britain no good in the Islamic world.[190] A 'Jew State in Palestine', he wrote on 1 June 1919, 'would be the gathering together of all the scum of the Jewish populations of Russia, Poland, Germany, Hungary, and what has been the Austrian Empire — which scum has been active in Bolshevist propaganda and might have to emigrate after Peace.'[191] Lacking Balfour's philosophical idealism, he considered his declaration, like Grey's concession to the Russians on the straits, as a sacrifice of Britain's interests in the Near and Middle East for the sake of uncertain and at best short term advantages.

The British government had at one time thought that a public commitment to Zionism might be a means of countering pacific tendencies amongst Russia's six million Jews.[192] But the Balfour declaration came too late to have any influence upon developments in eastern Europe, and as a result of the Bolshevik decision to sue for peace and the conclusion of the treaty of Brest-Litovsk on 3 March

---

[188] Bertie to Grey, 13 March 1916, B.P. A, F.O.800/176. Gordon Lennox, I, pp.105 – 6.
[189] Memo. by Bertie, 28 Feb. – 2 June 1917, B.P., B, F.O.800/91.
[190] Gordon Lennox, II, pp.228 – 9. The origins of the Balfour declaration are considered in detail in Isaiah Friedman, *The Question of Palestine, 1914 – 1918. British-Jewish-Arab Relations* (London, 1973), especially pp.244 – 1.
[191] Gordon Lennox, II, p.330.
[192] Friedman, pp.288 – 9.

1918 the Germans were able to concentrate more of their forces in the west. Bertie had already been made more aware of the intensity of the struggle by the commencement in January of the aerial bombardment of Paris. In March the German air raids became more frequent, and Bertie was eventually forced at the sounding of the *alerte* to retreat with coffee and newspapers to the cellars of the embassy. Not that he was averse to trying conclusions with the enemy.[193] During one raid which began while Bertie was dining with friends at the embassy, he insisted on climbing up to the roof, there to stand and beat defiantly upon a tin tray with a spoon. With such tactics Bertie may well have entertained his guests, and helped to maintain the spirits of his household. Yet he too was beginning to feel uneasy about the seriousness of the military situation.[194]

The predicted German offensive, which commenced on 21 March, exposed Paris to a new terror in the form of the shelling of the city by Big Bertha, the German army's long range cannon. This and the continuing German air-raids led many Parisians to seek refuge in the provinces. Shops and offices were closed, the railway stations congested, and there were rumours of an impending evacuation of the capital by the government and diplomatic corps. The situation was reminiscent of the first weeks of the war.[195] There was, however, considerably more cooperation between the commanders at the front than there had been in 1914. In the face of the German onslaught, Haig accepted what amounted to unity of command, and in April Foch was formally appointed commander-in-chief of the allied armies in France. It was a decision which Bertie sincerely welcomed. Past military disasters had, he maintained, 'been in great part due to false *amour propre* in refusing to allow our Army to be under a man of the country in which the war has been raging for three years, and in rejecting French aid when it was needed'.[196]

Bertie was far from well when he wrote these lines on 14 April. He had been taken ill with internal pains on the night of the 5th, and since then he had not been able to leave his bed for more than an hour and a half. His doctor was unable to offer any satisfactory remedy to the complaint, and the ambassador appeared unlikely to make a speedy recovery.[197] This and the reverses suffered by the British army

---

[193] Gordon Lennox, II, pp.252, 280, and 286–7.
[194] Gladwyn, p.175.
[195] Gordon Lennox, II, pp.282–3, and 287–90.
[196] John Terraine, *Douglas Haig. The educated soldier* (London, 1963), pp.414–25. Gordon Lennox, II, p.296.
[197] Bertie to Curzon, 27 April 1918; Bertie to Stamfordham, 28 April 1918; B.P., A, F.O.800/175. Gordon Lennox, II, pp.295–6.

in Picardy provided Lloyd George with both an opportunity and a reason for putting into effect his plan for transferring Derby to Paris. Moreover, in a letter to the prime minister of 13 April Esher launched a fresh offensive against a system which permitted the government to be represented at Paris 'by men trained in Peace, imbued with archaic ideas, and above all *irresponsible*'. Again he urged Lloyd George to send there 'any man in whom you have confidence, but of *Ministerial* rank'. If Milner could not be spared, then he thought Austen Chamberlain might do. 'Derby', he added, 'if he retained *Ministerial* rank and was accompanied by a strong staff, would be more effective in Paris than a man of greater abilities, but less "panache" '.[198] But Esher's advice probably did no more than confirm Lloyd George in the course which he had already decided to pursue. Anxious to avoid any leakage to the press, he acted swiftly. Balfour's support was gained for the political and diplomatic changes which he had outlined in February, and on 16 April Lloyd George and the foreign secretary pressed Derby to accept the embassy at Paris. Derby still had reservations. He protested that the ways of diplomacy were strange to him, and that he had never in his 'wildest moments' thought of himself as a diplomat. Nevertheless, he recognized that he had no alternative but to agree if he wished to retain some vestiges of office.[199] Whilst Derby was making up his mind, the prime minister telephoned Windsor castle to obtain the king's permission to 'announce' the new appointment the next day, 17 April. The king was in no mood to fall in wth Lloyd George's plan. Two months had passed since Lloyd George had last mentioned the possibility to him of Derby going to Paris, and the king now rightly insisted that the approval of the French government must be obtained.[200] A somewhat reluctant Hardinge was therefore sent to the French embassy to inform Paul Cambon and to impress on him the prime minister's wish for an early and positive response from his government. At 6.50 that evening Balfour despatched a telegram to Bertie to inform him of his fate.[201]

'You could not sack a kitchenmaid like that', Bertie complained to Nevile Henderson, who as a second secretary at the embassy, had the melancholy task of helping him to decypher Balfour's message.[202] He

---

[198] Esher to Lloyd George, 13 April 1918, Lloyd George MSS., F/16/1/24.
[199] Balfour to Lloyd George, 15 April 1918, Lloyd George MSS., F/3/3/7. Churchill, *Derby*, pp.349–50.
[200] Stamfordham to J.T. Davies, 16 April 1918, Lloyd George MSS., F/29/2/14. Stamfordham to Bertie, 1 May 1918, RA Geo.V. P1273 11.
[201] Hardinge, *Old Diplomacy*, pp.226–7. Balfour to Bertie, 16 April 1918, tel., B.P., A, F.O.800/175.
[202] N. Henderson, p.86.

had good reason to be annoyed. The telegram, which arrived at Paris on the morning of the 17th, was hardly the most coherent of documents. 'There are', it began, 'changes in contemplation here which will involve, among other things, the transfer of Lord Derby to Paris.' Then in an almost apologetic tone it went on to praise Bertie's work, and to explain that his 'successor' would have the advantages of a first hand knowledge of war problems. This, however, was dismissal by implication, for nowhere did the telegram explicitly state that Derby was to replace Bertie as ambassador to France.[203] The omission, which was perhaps a measure of Balfour's embarrassment at being party to the removal of an old and trusted friend, was corrected in a later telegram. In this the foreign secretary added: 'If the embassy at Paris alone had been concerned, this undue haste, which I regret, would not have been necessary.'[204]

Speed was indeed essential to the success of Lloyd George's manoeuvre. The prime minister had, however, more to reckon with than Derby's capacity for procrastination and the possible opposition of his colleagues. Bertie had in the previous spring demonstrated the reserves that he could muster in the defence of his position, and had he been fitter and his friends alerted to what was afoot, he might yet have saved his embassy. As it was, the king, who resented the summary fashion in which he was informed of the impending changes, lost no time in objecting to Bertie's dismissal. To John Davies, Stamfordham wrote on 16 April:

> The King assumes that the Prime Minister has carefully considered the wisdom and the expediency of changing his representative in Paris at this critical moment in the War, and replacing a diplomatist of Lord Bertie's vast experience, one who thoroughly understands the French language and diplomacy, besides being a personal friend of Monsieur Clemenceau, by Lord Derby who will, without any special equipment, make his debut in a new profession in this, the most important position in the diplomatic world.[205]

This was strong stuff, but it was without consequence. The king's insistence on the French government being consulted, and a refusal on the part of Cambon to telephone the news to Paris, meant that the announcement of Derby's appointment had to be delayed for twenty-

---

[203] Balfour to Bertie, 16 April 1918, Tel., B.P., A, F.O.800/175.
[204] Balfour to Bertie, 16 April 1918, tel. (Mis/18/11), B.P., A, F.O.800/175.
[205] Stamfordham to J.T. Davies, 16 April 1918, Lloyd George MSS., F/29/2/14.

four hours.²⁰⁶ Neither Clemenceau nor Pichon felt themselves able to challenge Lloyd George's decision, and to save time even assented to the change without first informing Poincaré.²⁰⁷ Other of Bertie's allies were equally impotent, and could do no more than express their grief at the manner of his dismissal. 'I am sorry and indignant,' Curzon wrote to Bertie, 'that you have been the victim of such procedure, of which you must not believe the Cabinet as a whole had the faintest cognizance.'²⁰⁸

When on the morning of 18 April Lloyd George informed the war cabinet of Derby's appointment, he was careful to pay tribute to the service at Paris of 'one of our most distinguished and able diplomatists'. But, he argued, at present 'there was not very much diplomacy required in Paris'. He claimed that experience had shown 'that what was needed was some representative who was in active touch with the views of the British Government on the innumerable questions, mainly of a military character, that were arising between the two countries'. Many such questions could, he suggested, be dealt with by one such as Derby who had a broader knowledge of the war cabinet's views than any diplomatist could possess.²⁰⁹ This explanation bore a marked resemblance to the case which Esher had repeatedly put forward for Bertie's replacement. It was, however, a lame excuse. Only a year before Lloyd George had joined Bertie in denigrating the abilities and intelligence of the secretary of state for war, and after the latter's appointment to Paris the prime minister was in no hurry to grant him the mandate he claimed.²¹⁰ Not that Derby was under any misapprehension with regard to Lloyd George's intentions. 'I am', he complained to Balfour on 22 April, 'like a fish out of water, almost homesick and quite convinced that unless you help me, as I know you will, the PM will simply have shunted me to make room for Milner by promising power he never intended to give. I wonder if he has ever spoken the truth even by accident'.²¹¹ Derby had to wait nearly a month before he received the title of head of British missions at Paris which Lloyd George had promised him. Even then, the prime minister continued to by-pass the embassy in his dealings with the French in matters relating to the

---

206 Bertie to Curzon, 27 April 1918; Stamfordham to Bertie, 1 May 1918; B.P., A, F.O.800/175.
207 Poincaré to Bertie, 18 April 1918, *ibid*. Hardinge, *Old Diplomacy*, pp.226–7.
208 Curzon to Bertie, 27 April 1918, B.P., A, F.O.800/175.
209 Minutes of a Meeting of the War Cabinet, 18 April 1918, CAB.23/6/394.
210 Memo. by Bertie, 28 Feb. – 2 June 1917, B.P., B, F.O. 800/91.
211 Derby to Balfour, 22 Aprii 1918, Balfour MSS., Add. MS. 49743. Derby to H. Wilson, 25 April 1918, Derby MSS. (Liverpool Public Library).

THE END OF AN EMBASSY

war, and Derby's mission was in the end to be remembered more for its social than its diplomatic achievements.[212]

During the next two years Derby was to make himself popular with all sections of Parisian society. His initial reception in France was, however, distinctly cool. So disgruntled was Clemenceau at being parted from his *cher ami* that at his first meeting with the new ambassador he declined to speak English, a gesture that was probably not without effect since Derby's French left much to be desired.[213] But Bertie bore no grudge against his successor. He regarded Derby as a friend, and despite their previous differences, was full of praise for the kind treatment that he received from him during his last days at the embassy. Bertie had in any case already concluded that his own ill-health would have forced him to abandon his duties. To Curzon he wrote on 27 April: 'I have no reason to complain of ceasing to be Ambassador for I am 73 and I have had a good innings and I feel that I have been of service to my Country; but the manner of my removal was rather hurried and may be described as the latest fashion.'[214] Never inclined to waste words on worthless protest, Bertie accepted his fate with as much old-fashioned courtesy as he could manage.

The news of his dismissal may have contributed to a worsening of Bertie's physical condition. On 17 April he suffered a relapse, and by the time of Derby's arrival in Paris had already been confined to bed for the best part of three weeks.[215] None of the doctors who attended him were able to offer a satisfactory diagnosis of his ailment. One leading French surgeon suggested that it was due to an intestinal 'stoppage', but after Bertie had been X-rayed, he and other stomach specialists agreed that the malady was 'one for medical and not surgical treatment'.[216] Unable to take any nourishment other than a little milk often mixed with Vichy water or bouillon, Bertie steadily lost weight, and was far from well when on 6 May he was removed from the embassy to the Hotel Crillon.[217] In the meantine his

---

[212] R.A. Barlow, *Lord Derby and the Paris Embassy* (M.Sc.Econ. dissertation, University College of Wales, Aberystwyth, 1976), pp.38 – 9 and 71 – 2.
[213] Derby confessed to Bertie 'though I can understand it, I cannot talk French'. Derby to Bertie, 17 April 1918, B.P., A, F.O.800/175. Bertie to Hardinge, 20 April 1918, Hardinge MSS., 37.
[214] Bertie to Curzon, 27 April 1918; Bertie to George V, 1 May 1918, B.P., A, F.O.800/175.
[215] Derby to Balfour, 22 April 1918, Balfour MSS., Add. MS.49743. Gordon Lennox,II, p.296.
[216] Bertie to Queen Alexandra, 2 May 1918, B.P., Add. MS. 62012. Bertie to George V, 1 May 1918, B.P., A, F.O.800/175.
[217] Derby to Balfour, 1 May 1918, Balfour MSS., Add. MS. 49743. Grahame to Hardinge, 8 May 1918, Hardinge MSS., 37.

thoughts strayed to what had been happier days in Rome. 'I should', he wrote to Barrère on 7 May, 'like to go back to the time when you and I were good colleagues together. We should be much younger.'[218] But some of his friends doubted if he would ever leave Paris alive.[219] They need not have despaired. Bertie had a sturdy frame, and in June he recovered sufficiently to make the journey by train and hospital ship to England, where in a nursing home he gradually overcame the debilitating effects of his illness.[220]

Bertie eventually settled in London, and in October 1918 was made a viscount. He naturally rejoiced at the successes achieved by the allied armies in the late summer and autumn of 1918, and he hoped that the victors would not hesitate in imposing draconian peace terms on Germany. A negotiated settlement based on Wilson's fourteen points would, he thought, inevitably lead to another war.[221] France's need for compensation and security could, he assumed, only be obtained by the 'annihilation of the German military machine and spirit and the occupation of German territory, the reinstatement of Belgium so far as humanly possible, the addition to that country of Luxemburg, and the exclusion of Germany from any territory west of the Rhine.'[222] He also derived satisfaction from the descent of Russia into civil war. 'There is no longer a Russia', he noted in his diary on 8 December 1918, it 'is broken up, and the Imperial and Religious Idol which kept together the several races of the Orthodox faith is gone.' Provided that independence and statehood were secured for the peoples on Russia's flank, Bertie thought that the remainder might 'hang and stew in their own juice'. He could see no advantage in trying either to accommodate the Bolsheviks or to resuscitate imperial Russia. The only future he could see for 'old Russia in Europe' was that of a landlocked country with way leave to the Black Sea and the Baltic.[223] It was a prospect that was particularly pleasing to one who had long been accustomed to regarding Russia as Britain's principal rival in central Asia and the Far East.

News from Paris of the work of the peace conference was not, however, always to Bertie's liking. Thus while he was glad to learn that restrictions were to be placed upon Germany's armaments, and

---

[218] Bertie to Barrère, 7 May 1918, Barrère MSS. (Ministère des Affaires Étrangères).
[219] Derby to Balfour, 24 May 1918, Balfour MSS., Add. MS. 49743. Derby to Stamfordham, 25 May 1918, R.A. Geo.V P1273 12. Hardinge to Grahame, 6 June 1918, Hardinge MSS., 38.
[220] Grahame to Hardinge, 8 June 1918; Hardinge to Grahame, 22 June 1918; Hardinge MSS., 38.
[221] Gordon Lennox, II, pp.303–6.
[222] *Ibid.* p.302.
[223] *Ibid*, pp.310–11, and 323.

that no fortifications were to be permitted in the Rhineland, he had doubts about how these terms were to be enforced. He had little faith in the idea of a League of Nations, and he questioned the value of the proposed Anglo-American guarantee of France. As in 1912 he foresaw difficulties in the way of deciding what was aggression, and in the event of a future conflict he thought the United States would lose precious time before taking action in defence of France.[224] But what disturbed Bertie more than these arrangements was Lloyd George's readiness to adopt a more lenient attitude towards the Germans than the French. The opposition put up by the prime minister in March 1919 to the inclusion of Danzig in Poland caused Bertie to fulminate against attempts to make political frontiers conform with race and religion. 'We are', he noted, 'dealing with a people who cannot be tamed by kindness, and to endeavour to reconcile them to being beaten in war we are to alienate our Ally France.'[225] Yet in the end Bertie gave qualified approval to the Versailles treaty. 'The Peace Treaty', he commented, 'might have been worse and ought to have been better.'[226]

Such doubts as Bertie had about the durability of the European peace seem not to have stopped him celebrating it. On 19 July, at the invitation of Paul Cambon, he watched the victory parade from above the porch of the French embassy at Albert gate. 'Altogether', he recorded, 'the *défilé* was a fine sight, and I am glad to have seen it.'[227] It was, indeed, to be one of the last public reviews that Bertie was to witness, for not long afterwards he was again taken ill. This time the decision was taken to risk an operation. But surgery proved of no avail, and on 26 September 1919, just six weeks after his seventy-fifth birthday, Lord Bertie died.[228] Three days later his coffin was transported by motor hearse from London to the railway station at Thame. It was there transferred to an Oxfordshire farm wagon for a procession which recalled Bertie's links with a rural England from which he had long since departed. Thus, in accordance with his wishes, six of his estate workers, duly attired in white smocks, acted as his bearers. In their company the wagon was drawn by two powerful black shire horses to Thame parish church, where during a service conducted by his younger brother, Bertie was finally laid to rest in the chancel wall.[229] His earthly mission was complete, he had now but to await the judgement of heaven and of history.

---

[224] *Ibid*, pp.320, and 328–33.
[225] *Ibid*, p.324.
[226] *Ibid*, p.333.
[227] *Ibid*, p.334.
[228] *The Times*, 29 Sept. 1919, p.1.
[229] *The Times*, 1 Oct. 1919, p.2.

15

Conclusion

Bertie left a formidable impression upon the minds of his contemporaries. 'A big landmark and a tower of strength in time of trouble disappears with Lord Bertie's recall', observed one member of the embassy staff in a letter of 20 April 1918.[1] Forty years later Vansittart wrote of Bertie that he was 'not only a great ambassador . . . but *the* very last of the great ambassadors'.[2] Even Esher, who at the time of Bertie's dismissal condemned him as 'an ambassador of the old pre-war type' who had 'failed to maintain the prestige and authority of England', could be generous in his praise of his erstwhile opponent.[3] 'He was', Esher later recorded, 'in many respects an excellent Ambassador, the representative among British diplomats of a class long since passed away.'[4] By contrast Caillaux found in the pages of Bertie's published diary fresh support for the unfavourable opinion that he had already formed of the ambassador. Bertie's conversational powers may, as Esher was to suggest, have been matured in the 'far distant atmosphere of Holland House and Strawberry Hill', and they may have appealed to some Frenchmen, but in Caillaux's estimation Bertie possessed the soul of an English country squire who had never left his hole, and a mind firmly closed to any elevated conception of foreign policy. 'L'Angleterre, les intérêts de l'Angleterre petitement mesurés, vus par le gros bout de la lorgnette, voila', noted Caillaux, 'ce qui limitait son horizon.'[5]

There was some substance in Caillaux's charge. Bertie's views on international affairs were empirical and pragmatic, his judgements on specific issues peremptory and absolute. He thought almost entirely in terms of a European state system composed of great and small powers, each of which had clearly definable and recognizable interests. Only rarely did he offer any detailed consideration of domestic political, economic or social factors, and their relevance to

---

[1] Extract from a letter from H.M. Embassy at Paris, 20 April 1918, to be shown by Hankey to Lloyd George, Lloyd George MSS., F29/2/16.
[2] Vansittart, p.53.
[3] Esher to Stamfordham, 19 April 1918, R.A. Geo.V Q724 105.
[4] Esher, *Kitchener*, p.96.
[5] *Ibid*. Caillaux, *Mes Memoires*, II, pp.134–7.

CONCLUSION

foreign policy. Such theorizing as he engaged in was usually confined to speculation about the possible effect of one diplomatic move upon another and about the advantages or disadvantages involved in adopting a particular stance. There is, for instance, nothing in Bertie's papers that might be fairly compared with that broad, if not wholly accurate, survey of Britain's relations with France and Germany which Crowe offered in his memorandum of January 1907. Bertie seems to have preferred to concern himself with the more immediate matters at hand, and in this respect his perspective, conditioned as it was by the forty years which he had spent in dealing with the routine business of the Foreign Office, was essentially that of a *Realpolitiker* of the Bismarckian era. 'The gratitude of a nation', he noted in May 1901, 'is an ephemeral product. No nation believes that another nation does a kindness except for its own advantage.'[6] Narrowly state-centred in his outlook, Bertie was both before, and more especially during, the first world war, to denegrate the cosmopolitanism of princes and financiers, and to denounce the internationalism of socialists and liberal idealists. '*Professional* Diplomacy', he reflected in April 1919, 'has shown little foresight and committed great blunders, but how about the amateurs who are negotiating, such as Wilson, House, Lloyd George, Smuts and others with their so-called ideals — self-determination, League of Nations, moderation in terms to be exacted from Germany — dubbed statesmanship!'[7] Experience had in any case taught him to regard politicians with suspicion. Their 'trade' he considered a dishonest one, and their ideas he believed to be 'fogged by the vision of electoral urns'.[8] Such indeed was his attachment to the national interest writ small that by the last years of the war Bertie, the loyal servant of liberal England, was to exhibit in his condemnation of those who appeared to favour a compromise peace a disturbing inclination towards authoritarianism and a rough and ready anti-semitism.

Bertie denied that he had any strong political convictions, and in so far as party politics were concerned there is little reason to doubt his word.[9] During the spring of 1910 he castigated Asquith's cabinet as 'vacillating, inconsistent, dishonest, and reckless', in its handling of the constitutional crisis.[10] But references to English politics are few

---

[6] Memo. by Bertie, 21 May 1901, F.O.17/1505. Bertie was in many ways a good example of what Professor J.A.S. Grenville has described as a tendency for Britain 'to follow increasingly a neo-Bismarckian *Realpolitik*' in the Edwardian period. Donald Read (ed.), *Edwardian England* (London, 1982), p.178.
[7] Gordon Lennox, II, p.325.
[8] *Ibid*, p.302.
[9] *Ibid*.
[10] Bertie to Hardinge, 3 March 1910, B.P., A, F.O.800/174.

and far between in Bertie's correspondence. There was never any doubt in Bertie's mind about the *Primat der Aussenpolitik*, and the political complexions of the governments which he represented were usually only of interest to him in so far as they might affect either his personal position or relations with foreign powers. Bertie also maintained that he had no bias in his attitude towards Britain's continental neighbours.[11] 'I am pro-British', he protested to Caillaux when the latter offered him a discourse on his vision of a new Europe.[12] And Bertie would not seem to have found in any trait of national character or culture a reason for preferring Frenchmen to say Germans or Russians. He treated most foreigners with caution, and he placed his trust in few of them. Yet, by the time of his appointment to Rome he was regarded by his colleagues as a Germanophobe, and after the conclusion of the Anglo-French *entente* he readily adopted the view that Germany constituted the greatest immediate threat to Britain's position in the world.[13]

To some extent Bertie's attitude towards Germany at the turn of the century reflected a disenchantment then prevalent in some circles in London with a power, which, although it posed as a friend, acted towards Britain in a manner indistinguishable from that of her older rivals. The continued expansion of Germany's overseas commerce, and the decision of her leaders to combine a *Weltmacht-* and a *Flottenpolitik*, were also peculiarly pertinent in a period in which Bertie was becoming increasingly critical of the failure of the British government to show a firm resolve in defending British interests. 'The mistake which we generally make', he complained to Cranborne in May 1903, 'is by sonorous platitudes or evasion of the question at issue or silence, to encourage Foreign Powers to encroach on our interests.'[14] On the other hand, Salisbury's defence of Britain's position in the Sudan had seemed to yield benefits, and had helped to ease the way towards a reconciliation with France on Egypt and Morocco. Likewise in the Far East, if the Anglo-Japanese alliance did not deter the Russians from their meddling in Korea, Japan's military and naval victories did check the growth of Russian influence in the region, and may have made an accommodation with Britain more acceptable to the authorities in St Petersburg. Bertie welcomed both the understanding with France and that with Russia. But he saw neither a basis nor a need for a similar arrangement with Germany. This was due to several factors. For one thing in his

[11] *B.D.*, X, pt.2, no.265.
[12] Caillaux, *Mes Memoires*.
[13] Cranborne to Bertie, 12 April 1903, B.P., A, F.O.800/181.
[14] Bertie to Cranborne, 11 May 1903, Cecil MSS., S(4) 52/80.

CONCLUSION

opinion any new colonial bargain with Germany seemed almost bound to be one-sided. Thus a division of Portugal's colonies, such as was foreseen in the agreement of 1898 and the draft accord of 1913, could only be achieved at the expense of Britain's ally. Further, he thought that a politico-naval agreement would in the end tie Britain's hands, and leave Germany free to continue, albeit perhaps at a slower *tempo*, with the construction of her high seas fleet. 'I cannot believe', he wrote to Nicolson in March 1911, 'that by a paper agreement the fundamentally opposing interests of the British and German peoples can be reconciled.'[15] Just as it had been necessary to convince the French and the Russians of Britain's determination to uphold her position in Africa and Asia, so Bertie considered it essential to persuade the Germans that Britain had no intention of abandoning her two-power naval standard.

Bertie's view of what policies the British government should pursue was also modified by the changes which he perceived in the European balance of power. Wary of the dangers involved in the possible emergence of a continental coalition, he had in 1903 favoured the adoption by Britain of such courses as would encourage differences between France and Germany and leave Britain free to play the part of *tertius gaudens*. He was thus not wholly displeased by the Franco-German quarrel over Morocco. But Russia's defeat in the Far East and the preoccupation of her government with a serious domestic crisis threatened to leave the Germans free to impose their will upon France, and thereby to upset the recently achieved Anglo-French understanding. It required no great feat of imagination by Bertie for him to recognize that the Wilhelmstrasse might seek to draw advantage from these developments. His notion of a continental equilibrium may have been simplistic. It may also have been divorced from the strategic realities of the day. He was not, however, a party to what Keith Wilson has referred to as the 'invention' by the British of a German menace.[16] Nor was he inclined to attribute Napoleonic ambitions to the Germans. What he feared was that Germany might regain that diplomatic preeminence amongst the great powers that she had known in Bismarck's time, and that she would then be able to pose a powerful challenge to Britain's global position. Given the conduct of William II and Bülow during 1905, and the continued expansion of the German navy, it was hardly odd that he should have thought along these lines.

---

[15] Bertie to Nicolson, 11 May 1911, B.P., B, F.O.800/186.
[16] K.M. Wilson, *Policy of the Entente*, pp.100 – 20.

It was with the object of ensuring that the Germans should not be able to undermine the *entente cordiale* that Bertie urged first Lansdowne, and then Grey, to back France, and although before the outbreak of war in 1914 he was never to advocate Britain's formal entry into a continental alliance, he constantly insisted upon the importance of maintaining French confidence in Britain. He also thought that through association with France Britain could limit the expansion of German influence in the extra-European world. Support for French policies in Morocco was therefore for him both a matter of fulfilling an obligation, and a means of denying an Atlantic port to Germany. The consequent containment of Germany carried with it the corresponding danger of a war arising from the too rigid opposition by Britain to the attainment by her of a global status commensurate with her economic and military strength. Bertie had, however, no desire as some commentators alleged to promote an Anglo-German conflict. He told von Stumm in December 1911 that his recent bellicosity 'had been limited to the feeling . . . that Lord Palmerston would have thought it preferable to bring matters to a head rather than to sit still and submit to increasing expenditure of vast sums to maintain the supremacy of England at sea'. But times, he admitted, had changed: wars were no longer as cheap as they had once been, and it had become more necessary to take public opinion into account.[17] He expressed himself in similar terms to Lloyd George in February 1912 when the latter suggested to him that in the previous year the French 'had thrown away the finest opportunity they had ever had or were likely to have again to try conclusions with Germany'. The only battle that Bertie could foresee was 'one of money' over whether Britain or Germany could afford to outbuild the other in warships.[18]

Throughout his embassy at Paris Bertie found in Germany, and the aspirations which he ascribed to her one of the principal reasons for seeking to maintain the Anglo-French understanding. Nevertheless, he did not regard that relationship as a fixed and permanent feature of the international system, and he rarely lost sight of the fact that France and Russia remained imperial rivals of Britain, and that they might one day have to be reckoned with as enemies. It was because of this that in the autumn of 1911 he did all that he could to support Grey's efforts to ensure that the French should not secure a foothold on the northern coastline of Morocco. It was for similar reasons that he regarded as errors both Grey's promise to support

---

[17] *B.D.*, X, pt.2, no.265.
[18] Memo. by Bertie, 19 Feb. 1912, B.P., A, F.O.800/171.

CONCLUSION

Russian claims to Constantinople and the straits, and his subsequent acceptance of the eventual French presence on the coastal littoral of Syria. The acquisition by France of Alexandretta was, he warned Balfour, 'likely to be a danger to us'.[19]

Where these last two decisions were concerned, Bertie had clearly not been able to make his views prevail in London. Yet in the past his logic had not been without its impact. Grey, who was foreign secretary for eleven of the thirteen years that Bertie was at Paris, willingly praised his work and his opinions. Indeed, in December 1911 Nicolson assured Bertie that he knew of no other ambassador who occupied a higher position in respect of the trust placed in him by the government.[20] It would, however, be difficult to try to assess the degree of influence that Bertie had upon Grey, or for that matter to select any one occasion on which his advice might be said to have been decisive. Many of the views which he expressed on Britain's relations with France and Germany were not dissimilar to those held by other officials who were in closer and more continuous contact with the foreign secretary. Moreover, there were occasions before 1915 when Bertie was clearly in disagreement with policies being pursued by Grey. The latter was, for example, prepared to adopt a more conciliatory approach towards Germany than Bertie would have favoured. Since, however, Grey was generally ready to subordinate improved relations with Germany to the maintenance of the *entente* with France, and since concessions to Germany in almost any part of the globe could be portrayed by Bertie as injurious to French interests, the courses preferred by Bertie and the ends achieved by Grey often coincided.

Grey probably attached more value to Bertie's tactical judgement on the day to day management of affairs at Paris than to his advice on the broad lines of policy. He was certainly prepared to concede to him wide discretion in his dealings with the Quai d'Orsay. Bertie also drew strength from the fact that during most of the time that he was at Paris he enjoyed the confidence of those politicians and senior officials who were responsible for framing France's foreign policy. They found reassurance in his attachment to England's friendship with France, and confirmation of their own prejudices and presumptions in his distrust of Germany. He thus became closely identified with the *entente cordiale*, and it is not without significance that Caillaux, the one French head of government who dared to indicate to Bertie that France might derive better value from a different diplomatic

[19] Memo. by Bertie, 14 April 1916, B.P., A, F.O.800/175.
[20] Nicolson to Bertie, 7 Dec. 1911, B.P., B, F.O.800/186.

orientation, was to emerge as one of his harshest critics. Relative political stability in England denied to Bertie the sort of opportunities that Paul Cambon knew for enlightening inexperienced ministers on the modalities of *entente* diplomacy. Nevertheless, while the Anglo-French understanding remained no more than what Crowe had defined as a 'frame of mind' and a 'view of general policy', it was obviously of importance to its supporters in London that they should have at Paris an ambassador who commanded the respect of leading Frenchmen.[21] This is not to say that relations between Britain and France would necessarily have evolved in any different fashion in the years between 1905 and 1914 if Bertie's post had been occupied by, for instance, Lascelles or Nicolson. Developments elsewhere were to play a very large part in shaping the relationship. Indeed, if the bonds which linked the two countries were tightened in this period it was due more to the diplomatic ineptitude of the authorities in the Wilhelmstrasse, than to the skills exercised by Bertie in the Faubourg St-Honoré.

The outbreak of the first world war and the transformation of the *entente* into a military alliance at first placed new demands upon Bertie's time and energy. Both at Bordeaux and at Paris he had to deal with questions which related to the logistics and the economics of military collaboration. But the war led not only to the subordination of diplomacy to grand strategy, but also to the creation of new channels of communication between the British and French governments. Ministers were increasingly ready to cross the Channel for meetings with their opposite numbers, and the presence of British troops in France and the proximity of the front to Paris, led to the creation there of a variety of British agencies and military institutions. Had Bertie had the will to do so, he might perhaps have been able to establish his authority over these missions, and he might thereby have provided the coordination between them that was so often lacking. As it was Bertie had little understanding of military matters, and he showed no desire to involve himself in what he regarded as the province of the generals.[22] Esher, who recognized the problems resulting from the new situation, was thus able to create for himself an unofficial and undefined role at Paris. It was natural that Bertie should have resented Esher's pretensions. Yet it was ludicrous that he should have become so obsessed with the activities of Esher

---

[21] Minute by Crowe on Bertie to Grey, 31 Jan. 1911, F.O.371/1117, swapr.58.
[22] There is also evidence to suggest that Bertie was in any case reluctant to take on new tasks. See for instance Izvolsky's comments in *Die Internationalen Beziehungen im Zeitalter des Imperialismus. Dokumente aus den Archiven der Zarischen und der Provisorischen Regierung*, VIII/2, p.622, n2.

CONCLUSION

and a nonentity like Cohn. A wiser man would have been able to put aside such personal enmities in time of crisis. Moreover, Bertie did not redeem the circumstances in which he found himself by his continued neglect of the social duties of an ambassador. There was much sense in the claim made by à Court Repington in August 1917 that a 'great *diplomat de carrière*' was no longer needed at Paris, and that the embassy 'ought to be and might be made a centre of social and political life in Paris, and that what was needed was a *grand seigneur* who knew how to do things properly and had the wherewithal to do them'. The fact that British ministers visiting Paris rarely frequented the embassy and that Lloyd George preferred to lodge elsewhere did nothing for the prestige of the ambassador.[23] Too set in his ways, too forthright in his manner, Bertie displayed no enthusiasm for the requirements of prime ministerial diplomacy.

Bertie was not the only British ambassador to incur the wrath of those who felt that the traditions of pre-1914 diplomacy were unsuited to the demands of modern war. Buchanan at Petrograd, Spring Rice at Washington, and Rennell Rodd at Rome, were all subjected to similar criticism. But it should not be overlooked that Bertie had already exhibited serious shortcomings as an intermediary in time of peace. Of him Grey wrote in 1924 that he could 'express dissent by an ironical question even more forcibly than by a direct negative'. 'He could say things', Grey observed 'that were crisp even to the point of brusqueness, and yet make the person to whom he said them feel that he was well disposed and a friend.'[24] Unfortunately, this was not invariably the case. Even one as sympathetic towards him as Vansittart considered him 'unnecessarily rude at times'.[25] His colleagues at the Foreign Office, and some of his staff at Rome and Paris, may have eventually accustomed themselves to his language, but those who knew him less well found it difficult to do so. George Murray, an official of the Treasury who had been the victim of a bout of Bertie's grousing, complained to Grey in April 1908 about the ambassador's use of the ' "curative" argument', which entitled you 'to use language which does not mean what you say if you can assume at the same time that the person addressed is sufficiently instructed to know that you don't mean it'.[26] And although Bertie's bullying tactics may on occasions have served to keep Pichon and his functionaries up to their commitments, they had a very different effect upon a more sensitive creature like Caillaux. What Grey termed an 'ironical

---

[23] à Court-Repington, *The First World War*, II, pp.24–5.
[24] Gordon Lennox, I, p.IX.
[25] Vansittart, p.54.
[26] G. Murray to Grey, 20 April 1908, Grey MSS., F.O.800/101.

395

question' was regarded by him as a 'sneer', and had Caillaux's political position been less precarious in the autumn of 1911 Bertie's confrontation with him might have done great harm to the *entente*.[27] True, the differences between the British and French governments over the Spanish zone in Morocco were real enough, and Bertie's quarrel with Caillaux was not wholly of his making, but a less robust approach to the problem might have more easily achieved the desired solution. Bertie was too ready to allow a supposed slight or wrong word to blight his judgement of an interlocutor, and too disposed to respond in terms which seemed more likely to provoke than to appease.

The frankness with which Bertie was prepared to speak his mind was a quality which some admired, and it probably helped to earn him Clemenceau's respect. Yet given the divisions and tensions which prevailed between the European powers in the years that preceded the first world war it is not difficult to realize why Bertie's blustering about German policies and intentions was mistaken for bellicosity in Berlin. Moreover, the zeal with which Bertie gave voice to his opinions may have contributed as in 1905 to French misunderstanding of Britain's standpoint. It may also have led French governments to pursue courses that they might otherwise have neglected. In 1912 Bertie encouraged Poincaré to oppose more vigorously the efforts of the Liberal government to achieve an agreement with Germany on a political formula, and two years later he suggested to Doumergue the basis of a consultative accord that he might propose to Grey. Nevertheless, there is no conclusive evidence with which to demonstrate that before 1914 he did not endeavour to accurately interpret the wishes of Lansdowne and of Grey in his official dealings with the Quai d'Orsay. If sometimes the advice which he offered to the French went far beyond the letter of the instructions that he had received, it was not so much because he sought to misrepresent his masters as to influence them.

Bertie was never content simply to act the part of chief spokesman for the Foreign Office at Paris. From the embassy he poured out his thoughts in private letters and memoranda on a variety of issues, some of which had only a tenuous connexion with Anglo-French relations. He could after all draw upon a long experience of dealing with the administration of foreign affairs. His career spanned more than half a century of British diplomacy. It had begun in the era of Palmerston, it ended in the age of Lloyd George. Within the Foreign Office he had striven to make his voice heard, he had championed the

---

[27] Caillaux, *Mes Memoires*, II, p.134.

CONCLUSION

cause of some of the younger men of the diplomatic service, and he had posed as an advocate of reform. Yet as an ambassador his bureaucratic strictures were resented by his staff, and after nine years at Paris he found it difficult to adjust his methods to the conditions of war and eventually fell victim to the intrigues of those who claimed to perceive a need for change. Moreover, although older diplomatic practices were to survive the advent of the 'New Diplomacy', Bertie would have been a misfit in the post-war world. When Derby arrived at the embassy in 1918 he found every paper there neatly folded into four, docketed on the outside, tide with pink tape, and filed in one of four or five series': a system which dated back to the middle years of the nineteenth century.[28] In this sense at least Hardinge was perhaps correct in his assertion that Bertie 'was the last of the old school of diplomats'.[29]

---

[28] G. Rendel, *The Sword and the Olive. Recollections of Diplomacy and the Foreign Service* (London, 1957), p.43.
[29] Mersey, p.312.

Bibliography

Primary Sources

Department, embassy and cabinet archives
Public Record Office (P.R.O.), Kew
Foreign Office papers:
General correspondence before 1906 in the series
F.O.1 Abyssinia
F.O.2 Africa
F.O.17 China
F.O.27 France
F.O.45 Italy
F.O.46 Japan
F.O.63 Portugal
F.O.64 Germany (Prussia)
F.O.65 Russia
F.O.69 Siam
F.O.72 Spain
F.O.99 Morocco

Correspondence for the period 1906–1918 contained in the series
F.O.367 Africa
F.O.368 Commercial
F.O.371 Political

The papers of the British embassy at Paris contained in F.O.146

Confidential Print in F.O.185 and F.O.425

The papers of the Chief Clerk's Department in F.O.366

Memoranda on Political and Other Questions by Mr F.L. Bertie, 1874–1875, in F.O.97/452

Records and papers of the British cabinet and the Committee of Imperial Defence contained in the series
CAB.37 cabinet papers
CAB.38 papers of the Committee of Imperial Defence
CAB.41 cabinet minutes

BIBLIOGRAPHY

CAB.23 war cabinet minutes

Air Ministry records:
The papers assembled by the Air Historical Branch in the series AIR 1/7.

Home Office records:
Registered papers in H.O.45.

Foreign and Commonwealth Office Library, London
F.O. General Librarian's Department. Correspondence and Memoranda, 1845 – 1905

Archives du Ministère des Affaires Étrangères (M.A.E.), Paris
The commercial and political correspondence of the French foreign ministry contained in the Nouvelle Série (N.S.) and Guerre
Crète
Espagne
Éthiopie
Grande-Bretagne
Maroc
Turquie

Private papers
George ADAM MSS., *The Times* archives, London
Herbert Henry ASQUITH MSS., Bodleian Library, Oxford
Madeleine AUSTIN LEE MSS., British Library (B.L.), London
Arthur James BALFOUR MSS., B.L. and P.R.O.
Camille BARRÈRE MSS., M.A.E.
BERTIE MSS., (family and estate papers), Bodleian Library
Francis L. BERTIE MSS., B.L. and P.R.O.*
Robert de BILLY MSS., M.A.E.
Wilfrid Scawen BLUNT MSS., Fitzwilliam Library, Cambridge
BRADFER-LAWRENCE MSS., (the papers of Reginald LISTER), Yorkshire Archaeological Society, Leeds
Maurice de BUNSEN MSS., Mill Down, Hampshire
Jules CAMBON MSS., M.A.E.
Paul CAMBON MSS., M.A.E.
Henry CAMPBELL-BANNERMAN MSS., B.L.
CECIL MSS., (the papers of the 4th Marquis of SALISBURY), Hatfield House, Hertfordshire
Joseph CHAMBERLAIN MSS., University of Birmingham
Valentine CHIROL MSS., *The Times* archives
Lord CROMER MSS., P.R.O.

Geoffrey DAWSON (originally ROBINSON) MSS., *The Times* archives
Theophile DELCASSÉ MSS., M.A.E.
Lord DERBY MSS., Liverpool Record Office
Murray of ELIBANK MSS., National Library of Scotland (N.L.S.), Edinburgh
Lord ESHER MSS., Churchill College, Cambridge
Lord GRANVILLE MSS., P.R.O.
Edward GREY MSS., P.R.O.
Lord HALDANE MSS., N.L.S.
Lord HANKEY MSS., Churchill College, Cambridge
Charles HARDINGE MSS., University Library, Cambridge
William Howard KELLY MSS., National Maritime Museum, Greenwich
Lord KITCHENER MSS., P.R.O.
Lord LANSDOWNE MSS., P.R.O.
Frank LASCELLES MSS., P.R.O.
William LAVINO MSS., *The Times* archives
David LLOYD GEORGE MSS., House of Lords Record Office, London
Percy LORAINE MSS., P.R.O.
Georges LOUIS MSS., M.A.E.
Gerard LOWTHER MSS., P.R.O.
Pierre de MARGERIE MSS., M.A.E.
Edmund MONSON MSS., Bodleian Library
Robert MORIER MSS., Balliol College, Oxford
Arthur NICOLSON MSS., P.R.O.
Lord NORTHCLIFFE MSS., *The Times* archives
Paul PAINLEVÉ MSS., Archives Nationales, Paris
Eric PHIPPS MSS., Churchill College, Cambridge
Stephen PICHON MSS., M.A.E. and Bibliothèque de l'Institut de France, Paris
Raymond POINCARÉ MSS., Bibliothèque Nationale, Paris
Arthur PONSONBY MSS., Bodleian Library
Joseph REINACH MSS., Bibliothèque Nationale
Paul RÉVOIL MSS., M.A.E.
William ROBERTSON MSS., King's College, London
James Rennell RODD MSS., Bodleian Library
Lord ROSEBERY MSS., N.L.S.
ROYAL ARCHIVES, Windsor Castle
Horace RUMBOLD MSS., Bodleian Library
Lord John RUSSELL MSS., P.R.O.
Lord SALISBURY MSS., Hatfield House

John S. SANDARS MSS., Bodleian Library
Thomas SANDERSON MSS., P.R.O.
George SAUNDERS MSS., *The Times* archives
Charles SCOTT MSS., B.L.
C.P. SCOTT MSS., B.L.
John A. SPENDER MSS., B.L.
Cecil SPRING RICE MSS., Churchill College
Lord TENTERDEN MSS., P.R.O.
THE TIMES MSS. (Official Diary and Foreign Department's Letter Books), *The Times* archives
Henry WICKHAM STEED MSS., *The Times* archives

*NOTE ON THE BERTIE PAPERS. As indicated above there are three collections of Bertie papers. That in the Bodleian library consists of family and estate papers and has been of only marginal value in the preparation of this work. The collection in the P.R.O. is divided into two series: A, which consists of typed copies of Bertie's correspondence and memoranda; and B, which contains mainly hand-written correspondence relating to matters of a more personal nature than that in series A. The collection in the British Library was purchased from the Pierpont Morgan Library in New York in 1980. For the most part it consists of the originals of those papers contained in series A of the P.R.O. collection. There are, however, in the British Library set a number of letters concerning Bertie's career prospects and his relations with his staff and Edward VII, no copies of which are to be found in the P.R.O.

Published Primary Sources

Austria-Hungary.
Österreich-Urgarns Aussenpolitik von der Bosnischen Krise 1908 bis zum Kriegsausbruch 1914. Diplomatische Aktenstücke des Österreichisch-Ungarischen Ministeriums des Äussern, compiled and edited by L. Bittner, A.F. Pribram, H. Srbik, and H. Uebersberger (7 vol., Vienna, 1930)

Belgium
Belgische Aktenstücke 1905 – 1914. Berichter des Belgischen Vertreter in Berlin, London und Paris an den Minister des Äusseren in Brüssel (Auswärtiges Amt, Berlin)

France

Documents diplomatiques français, 1871 – 1914, Ministère des Affaires Étrangères, commission de publication des documents relatifs aux origines de la guerre de 1914 (3 series, Paris, 1929 – 57)
Conférence internationale de navigation aérienne. Paris, 18 mai – 28 juin 1910. Exposés des vues des puissances d'après les memorandums adressés au gouvernement français (Paris, 1910)
Conférence internationale de navigation aérienne, Paris, 18 mai-28 juin, 1910. Procès-verbaux des séances et annexes (Paris, 1910)
Annales du Sénat. Débats Parlementaires, session ordinaire de 1911, vol. LXXIX (Paris, 1911)

Germany

Die deutschen Dokumente zum Kriegsausbruch 1914, colpiled and edited by K. Kautsky, M. Montgelas, and W. Schülking (4 vols., Berlin 1922)
Die grosse Politik der europäischen Kabinette, 1871 – 1914, edited by J. Lepsius, A. Mendelssohn Bartholdy, and F. Thimme (40 vols., Berlin, 1922 – 7)

Great Britain

British and Foreign State Papers, vol. XCIX, edited by R.W. Brant and W. Maycock (London, 1910)
British Documents on the Origins of the War, 1898 – 1914, edited by G.P. Gooch and H.W. Temperley (11 vols., London 1926 – 38)
Documents on British Foreign Policy, 1919 – 1939, series 1A, vol. I, edited by W.N. Medlicott, D. Dakin, and M.E. Lambert (London, 1966)
Documents Relating to the Naval Air Service, i: 1908 – 1918, edited by S.W. Roskill (London, 1969)
Policy and Operations in the Mediterranean, 1912 – 1914, edited by E.W.R. Lumby (London, 1970)

The Netherlands

Bescheiden Betreffende Buitenlandse Politiek van Nederland, 1848 – 1919, 3rd period, vol. II, edited by C. Smit (The Hague, 1958)

Russia

Entente Diplomacy and the World. Matrix of the History of Europe, 1909 – 1914, translated by B. de Siebert and edited by G.A. Schreiner (London, 1921)
Un livre noir: diplomatie d'avant guerre d'après les documents des Archives russes: novembre 1910 – juillet 1914, edited by R. Marchand (2 vols., Paris, 1922 – 3)

BIBLIOGRAPHY

Die Internationalen Beziehungen im Zeitalter des Imperialismus. Dokumente aus den Archiven der Zarischen und der Provisorischen Regierung, edited by O. Hoetzch (11 vols., Berlin, 1931 – 6)

Secondary Sources

Memoirs and published personal correspondence and diaries

Adam, H.P., *Paris sees it through. A Diary, 1914 – 1919* (London, 1919)
Antrobus, G.P., *King's Messenger. Memories of a Silver Greyhound* (London, 1941)
Asquith, H.H., *The Genesis of the War* (London, 1923)
―――― *Memories and Reflections, 1852 – 1927* (2 vols., London, 1928)
Barclay, T., *Thirty Years: Anglo-French Reminiscences, 1876 – 1906* (London, 1914)
Baring, M., *The Puppet Show of Memory* (London, 1930)
Benoist, C., *Souvenirs* (3 vols., Paris, 1932 – 4)
Blake, R.(ed.), *The Private Papers of Douglas Haig, 1914 – 1918* (London, 1952)
Blanche, J.E., *Portraits of a Lifetime. The Late Victorian Era. The Edwardian Pagent. 1870 – 1914* (London, 1937)
Blunt, S.W., *My Diaries, being a personal narrative of events, 1888 – 1914* (2 vols., 1919 and 1920)
Bompard, M., *Mon Ambassade en Russie, 1903 – 1908* (Paris, 1937)
Brett, M.V. and Esher, Oliver, Viscount, *Journals and Letters of Reginald, Viscount Esher* (4 vols., London, 1934 – 8)
Brock, M. and E.(eds.), *H.H. Asquith. Letters to Venetia Stanley* (Oxford, 1982)
Bruce, H.J., *Silken Dalliance* (London, 1946)
Bülow, Prince von, *Memoirs* (English trans., 4 vols., London, 1931 – 2)
Cadogan, E., *Before the Deluge. Memories and Reflections, 1880 – 1914* (London, 1961)
Caillaux, J., *Agadir: ma politique extérieure* (Paris, 1919)
―――― *Mes Mémoires* (3 vols., Paris, 1942 – 7)
Cambon, H.(ed.), *Paul Cambon. Correspondance, 1870 – 1924* (3 vols., Paris, 1940 – 4)
Castellane, Boni de, *L'art d'être pauvre* (Paris, 1925)
Charles-Roux, F., *Souvenirs diplomatiques d'un âge révolu* (Paris, 1956)
Chirol, V., *Fifty Years in a Changing World* (London, 1927)
Chklaver, G.(ed.), *Au service de la Russie. Alexandre Isvolsky, correspondance diplomatique, 1906 – 1911* (Paris, 1937)

Churchill, W.S., *The World Crisis, 1911–1918* (6 vols., London, 1923–31)

Combarieu, A., *Sept ans à l'Élysée avec le Président Émile Loubet. De l'affaire Dreyfus à la conférence d'Algeciras, 1899–1906* (Paris, 1932)

Corbett, V., *Reminiscences, autobiographical and diplomatic* (London, 1927)

David, E(ed.), *Inside Asquith's Cabinet. From the Diaries of Charles Hobhouse* (London, 1977)

Eckhardstein, Baron von, *Ten Years at the Court of St. James, 1895–1905* (English trans., London 1921)

Ferry, A., *Les carnets secrets d'Abel Ferry, 1914–1918* (Paris, 1957)

Fitzroy, A., *Memoirs* (2 vols., London, 1925)

Foch, F., *Mémoires pour servir à l'histoire de la guerre de 1914–1918* (2 vols., Paris, 1931)

Fortescue, S., *Looking Back* (London, 1920)

Gallieni, G.(ed.), *Les carnets de Gallieni* (Paris, 1932)

Gérard, A., *Mémoires d'Auguste Gérard* (Paris, 1928)

Gordon Lennox, Lady Algernon (ed.), *The Diary of Lord Bertie of Thame, 1914–1918* (2 vols., London, 1924)

Gower, G. Leveson, *Years of Content, 1858–1886* (London, 1940)

────── *Years of Endeavour, 1886–1907* (London, 1942)

Grey of Fallodon, Viscount, *Twenty-five Years, 1892–1916* (2 vols., London, 1925)

Gwynn, S.(ed.), *The Letters and Friendships of Sir Cecil Spring Rice* (2 vols., London 1929)

Hankey, M., *Supreme Command* (2 vols., London, 1961)

Hanotaux, G., *Carnets (1907–1925)* (Paris, 1982)

Hardinge of Penshurst, Lord, *Old Diplomacy* (London, 1947)

Henderson, N., *Water Under the Bridges* (London, 1945)

Hertslet, E., *Recollections of the Old Foreign Office* (London, 1901)

Homberg, O., *Les Coulisses de l'histoire. Souvenirs, 1898–1922* (Paris, 1938)

Howard, C.H.D. (ed.), *The Diary of Edward Goschen, 1900–1914* (London, 1980)

Howard, E., *Theatre of Life* (2 vols., London, 1935)

Joffre, J.J.C., *The Memoirs of Marshal Joffre* (English trans., 2 vols., London, 1932)

Kelly, D., *The Ruling Few, or the human background to diplomacy* (London, 1952)

Lancken, Baron von der, *Mémoires* (French trans., Paris, 1932)

Laroche, J., *Quinze ans à Rome avec Camille Barrère (1898–1913)* (Paris, 1948)

────── *Au Quai d'Orsay avec Briand et Poincaré* (Paris, 1957)

Lister, B.(ed.), *Emma, Lady Ribblesdale. Letters and Diaries* (London, 1930)
Lloyd George, D., *War Memoirs of David Lloyd George* (6 vols., London, 1933 – 6)
Louis, G., *Les carnets de Georges Louis* (2 vols., Paris, 1926)
Marder, A.J.(ed.), *Fear God and dread Nought. The Correspondence of Admiral of the Fleet Lord Fisher of Kilverstone* (3 vols., London, 1952 – 9)
Meath, Reginald, 12th Earl of, *Memories of the Nineteenth Century* (London, 1923)
Mersey, Viscount, *A Picture of Life, 1872 – 1940* (London, 1941)
Messimy, A., *Mes Souvenirs* (Paris, 1937)
Mordacq, J.J.H., *Le Ministère Clemenceau. Journal d'un témoin* (4 vols., Paris, 1930 – 1)
Murray, A., *Master and Brother* (London, 1945)
Norman, P., *In the way of understanding* (Godalming, 1982)
Paléologue, M., *La Russie des Tsars pendant la Grande Guerre* (3 vols., Paris, 1921 – 2.
——— *The Turning Point. Three Critical years, 1904 – 1906* (English trans., London, 1935)
——— *Au Quai d'Orsay à la veille de la tourmente. Journal 1913 – 1914* (Paris, 1947)
Poincaré, R., *Au service de la France. Neuf Années de souvenirs* (10 vols., Paris, 1926 – 33)
Ponsonby, F., *Recollections of Three Reigns* (London, 1951)
Rattigan, F., *Diversions of a Diplomat* (London, 1924)
Redesdale, Lord, *Memories* (2 vols., London, 1915)
Rendel, G., *The Sword and the Olive, Recollections of Diplomacy and the Foreign Service* (London, 1957)
Rennell Rodd, J., *Social and Diplomatic Memories* (3 vols., London, 1922 – 5)
Repington C. à Court-, *The First World War, 1914 – 1918* (2 vols., London 1920)
——— *After the War. A Diary* (London, 1922)
Ribot, A., *Lettres à un ami. Souvenirs de ma vie politique* (Paris, 1924)
——— *Journal d'Alexandre Ribot et correspondances inedites, 1914 – 1922* (Paris, 1936)
Rich, N. and Fischer, M.H. (eds.), *The Holstein Papers* (4 vols., Cambridge, 1963)
Riddell, Lord, *Lord Riddell's War Diary, 1914 – 1918* (London, 1933)
Saint-Aulaire, Comte de, *Confessions d'un vieux diplomate* (Paris, 1953)
Sazonov, S.D., *Fateful Years, 1909 – 1916* (London, 1928)
Schoen, Freiherr von, *The Memoirs of an Ambassador* (English trans.,

London, 1922)
Seymour, C.M.(ed.), *The Intimate Papers of Colonel House* (4 vols., London, 1926 – 8)
Stieve, F.(ed.), *Der diplomatische Schriftwechsel Iswolskis, 1911 – 1914* (4 vols., Berlin, 1924 – 1926)
Thierry, A., *L'Angleterre au temps de Paul Cambon* (Paris, 1961)
Tilley, J., *London to Tokyo* (London, 1942)
Vansittart, Lord, *The Mist Procession. The autiobiography of Lord Vansittart* (London, 1958)
Whyte, F.(ed.), *Letters of Prince von Bülow* (London, 1930)
Wickham Steed, H., *Through Thirty Years, 1892 – 1922* (2 vols., London, 1925)
Wilson, T.(ed.), *The Political Diaries of C.P. Scott, 1911 – 1928* (London, 1970
Wolff, T., *The Eve of 1914* (English trans., London 1936)

Monographs, essay collections and works of reference.
Adelson, R., *Mark Sykes. Portrait of an Amateur* (London, 1975)
Ahmad, F., *The Young Turks. The Committee of Union and Progress in Turkish Politics, 1908 – 1914* (Oxford, 1969)
Albertini, L., *The Origins of the War of 1914* (English trans., 3 vols., London, 1952 – 7)
Allain, J-C., *Agadir 1911. Une crise impérialiste en Europe pour la conquête de Maroc* (Paris, 1976)
——— *Joseph Caillaux* (2 vols., Paris, 1978 and 1981)
Anderson, E.N., *The Moroccan Crisis, 1904 – 1906* (chicago, 1930)
Anderson, R.D., *France, 1870 – 1914. Politics and Society* (London, 1977)
Andrew, C.M., *Théophile Delcassé and the Making of the Entente Cordiale. A Reappraisal of French Foreign Policy, 1898 – 1905* (London, 1968)
——— and Kayna-Forstner, A.S., *France Overseas. The Great War and the Climax of French Imperial Expansion* (London, 1981)
Auffray, B., *Pierre de Margerie (1861 – 1942) et la vie diplomatique de son temps* (Paris, 1976)
Barlow, I.C., *The Agadir Crisis* (Chapel Hill, N.C., 1940)
Barlow, R.A., *Lord Derby and the Paris Embassy* (M.Sc.Econ. dissertation, University College of Wales, Aberystwyth, 1976)
Barraclough, G., *From Agadir to Armageddon. Anatomy of a Crisis* (London, 1982)
Becker, J-J., *1914, comment les Français sont entrés dans la guerre* (Paris, 1977)
——— *Les Français dans la Grande Guerre* (Paris, 1980)

BIBLIOGRAPHY

Berghahn, V.R., *Germany and the Approach of War in 1914* (London, 1947)
Bertie, Lady Georgina, *Five Generations of a Loyal House. Part I. Containing the lives of Richard Bertie, and his son Peregrine, Lord Willoughby* (London, 1845)
Binion, R., *Defeated Leaders. The Political Fate of Caillaux, Jouvenel, and Tardieu* (New York, 1960)
Bosworth, R.J.B., *Italy, the least of the Great Powers, Italian Poreign Policy before the First World War* (Cambridge, 1979)
—— *Italy and the Approach of the First World War* (London, 1983)
Bourne, K., *The Foreign Policy of Victorian England, 1830 – 1902* (Oxford, 1970)
Bouvier, J. and Girault, R.(eds.), *L'impérialisme français d'avant 1914* (Paris, 1976)
Bréal, A., *Philippe Berthelot* (Paris, 1937)
Bridge, F.R., *From Sadowa to Sarajevo. The foreign policy of Austria-Hungary, 1866 – 1914* (London, 1972)
—— *Great Britain and Austria-Hungary, 1908 – 1914* (London, 1972)
Brook-Sheperd, G., *Uncle of Europe. The Social and Diplomatic Life of Edward VII* (London, 1975)
Bruun, G., *Clemenceau* 0Cambridge, Mass., 1943)
Busch, B.C., *Britain and the Persian Gulf, 1894 – 1914* (Berkely, 1967)
—— *Hardinge of Penshurst. A Study in Old Diplomacy* (Hamden, 1980)
Callwell, C.W., *Field-Marshal Sir Henry Wilson* (2 vols., London, 1927)
Carr, R., *Spain, 1808 – 1975* (2nd edn., Oxford, 1982)
Carroll, E.M., *French Public Opinion and Foreign Affairs, 1870 – 1914* (London, 1931)
—— *Germany and the Great Powers, 1866 – 1914. A Study in Public Opinion and Foreign Policy* (New York, 1938)
Cassar, G.H., *The French and the Dardanelles. A study of failure in the conduct of war* (London, 1971)
—— *Kitchener: architect of victory* (London, 1977)
Centre National de la Recherche Scientifique, Editions du, *Les affaires étrangères et le corps diplomatique* (2 vols., Paris, 1984)
Chastenet de Gastaing, J.A., *Une époque pathétique. La France de Monsieur Fallières* (Paris, 1949)
—— *Histoire de la Troisième République* (6 vols., Paris, 1952 – 63)
Churchill, R.S., *Lord Derby, 'King of Lancashire'* (London, 1959)
—— and subsequently Gilbert, M., *Winston Churchill, 1874 – 1965* (6 vols., London, 1966 – 83)
Christienne, C. and Lissarrague, P., *Histoire de l'aviation militaire française* (Paris, 1980)

Cohen, S.A., *British Policy in Mesopotamia, 1903–1914* (London, 1976)
Cooke, J.J., *New French Imperialism, 1880–1910. The Third Republic and Colonial Expansion* (Newton Abbot, 1973)
Cookey, S.J.S., *Great Britain and the Congo Question, 1885–1914* (London, 1968)
Cooper, J.C., *The Right to Fly* (New York, 1947)
Crampton, R.J., *The Hollow Détente. Anglo-German Relations in the Balkans, 1911–1914* (London, 1980)
Dakin, D., *The Unification of Greece, 1830–1923* (London, 1972)
Dansette, A., *Histoire des Présidents de la République* (Paris, 1953)
Davis, H.W.C. and Weaver, J.R.H.(eds.), *Dictionary of National Biography* (Oxford, 1927)
Digeon, C., *La Crise Allemande de la Pensée française (1870–1914)* (Paris, 1959)
Un Diplomate (pseud. H. Cambon), *Paul Cambon, ambassadeur de France* (Paris, 1957)
Driault, E. and Lhéritier, M., *Histoire diplomatique de la Grèce de 1821 à nos jours* (5 vols., Paris, 1925–6)
Dugdale, E.T.S., *Maurice de Bunsen. Diplomat and Friend* (London, 1934)
Duroselle, J-B., *La France et les Français, 1900–1914* (Paris, 1972)
—— *La France et les Français, 1914–1920* (Paris, 1972)
Egremont, M., *Balfour. A Life of Arthur James Balfour* (London, 1980)
Esher, Viscount Reginald, *The Tragedy of Lord Kitchener* (London, 1921)
Eubank, K., *Paul Cambon. Master Diplomatist* (Norman, Oklahoma, 1960)
Farrar, M.M., *Conflict and Compromise. The Strategy, Politics and Diplomacy of the French Blockade, 1914–1918* (The Hague, 1974)
Felstead, S.T., *Horatio Bottomley. A Biography of an Outstanding Personality* (London, 1936)
Feis, H., *Europe the World's Banker, 1870–1914* (New Haven, Conn., 1930)
Fischer, F., *Germany's Aims in the First World War* (English trans., London, 1967)
—— *War of Illusions. German Policies from 1911 to 1914* (English trans., London, 1973)
Fleurieu, R. de, *Joseph Caillaux au cours d'un demi-siècle de notre histoire* (Paris, 1951)
Fraser, P., *Lord Esher. A Political Biography* (London, 1973)
Friedman, I., *The Question of Palestine, 1914–1918. British-Jewish-Arab Relations* (London, 1973)

Fry, M.., *Lloyd George and Foreign Policy. Vol i. The Education of a Statesman* (London, 1977)
Ganiage, J., *L'expansion coloniale de la France sous la Troisième République, 1871 – 1914* (Paris, 1968)
Geiss, I., *German Foreign Policy, 1871 – 1914* (London, 1976)
Gifford, P. and Louis, W.R. (eds.), *Britain and Germany in Africa. Imperial Rivalry and Colonial Rule* (London, 1967)
────── *France and Britain in Africa. Imperial Rivalry and Colonial Rule* (London, 1971)
Gilbert, M., *Sir Horace Rumbold. Portrait of a Diplomat, 1869 – 1941* (London, 1973)
Gillard, D., *The Struggle for Asia, 1828 – 1914. A study in British and Russian imperialism* (London, 1977)
Girardet, R., *Le nationalisme français, 1871 – 1914* (Paris, 1966)
────── *L'idée coloniale en France de 1871 à 1962* (Paris, 1972)
Girault, R., *Emprunts russes et investissements français en Russie, 1887 – 1914: recherches sur l'investissement international* (Paris, 1973)
Gladwyn, C., *The Paris Embassy* (London, 1976)
Gollin, A., *No Longer an Island. Britain and the Wright Brothers, 1902 – 1909* (London, 1984)
Gooch, G.P., *Before the War. Studies in Diplomacy and Statecraft* (2 vols., London, 1936 and 1938)
Gooch, S., *The Plans of War. The General Staff and British Military Strategy, c.1900 – 1916* (London, 1974)
Gosses, F., *The Management of British Foreign Policy before the First World War, especially the period 1880 – 1914* (English trans, London, 1948)
Goudswaard, J.M., *Some Aspects of the End of Britain's 'Splendid Isolation', 1898 – 1904* (Rotterdam, 1952)
Grenville, J.A.S., *Lord Salisbury and Foreign Policy. The close of the Nineteenth Century* (London, 1964)
Guillen, P., *L'Allemagne et le Maroc de 1870 à 1905* (Paris, 1967)
Guinn, P., *British Strategy and Politics, 1914 to 1918* (Oxford, 1965)
Halpern, P.G., *The Mediterranean Naval Situation, 1908 – 1914* (Cambridge, Mass., 1971)
Hammond, J.L., *C.P. Scott of the Manchester Guardian* (London, 1934)
Hanotaux, G., *La Politique de l'Équilibre, 1907 – 1911* (Paris, 1912)
Hazeltine, H.D., *The Law of the Air. Three Lectures delivered in the University of London at the Request of the Faculty of Laws* (London, 1911)
Hazlehurst, C., *Politicians at War, July 1914 to May 1915. A prologue to the triumph of Lloyd George* (London, 1971)
Heller, J., *British Policy towards the Ottoman Empire, 1908 – 1914* (London, 1983)

Helmreich, E.C., *The Diplomacy of the Balkan Wars* (Cambridge, Mass., 1938)
Her Majesty's Stationary Office, *P.R.O. Handbooks No. 13. The Records of the Foreign Office, 1782 – 1939* (London, 1969)
Higham, R., *The British Rigid Airship, 1908 – 1931. A Study in Weapons Policy* (London, 1961)
Hinsley, F.H. (ed.), *British Foreign Policy under Sir Edward Grey* (Cambridge, 1977)
Holmes, R., *The Little Field Marshal. Sir John French* (London, 1981)
Howard, C.H.D., *Splendid Isolation* (London, 1967).
—— *Britain and the Casus Belli, 1822 – 1902* (London, 1974)
Howard, J.E., *Parliament and Foreign Policy in France* (London, 1948)
Howard, M., *The Continental Commitment. The Dilemma of British Defence Policy in the Era of Two World Wars* (London, 1972)
Jarausch, K., *The Enigmatic Chancellor. Bethmann Hollweg and the Hubris of Imperial Germany* (New Haven, Conn., 1973)
Jenkins, R., *Asquith. Portrait of a Man and an Era* (London, 1964)
Jeshurun, C., *The Conflict for Siam. A Study in Diplomatic Rivalry* (Kuala Lumpa, 1977)
Joll, J., *1914. The Unspoken Assumptions* (London, 1968)
—— *The Origins of the First World War* (London, 1984)
Jones, N., *The Origins of Strategic Bombing. A Study of the Development of British Air Strategic Thought and Practice up to 1918* (London, 1973)
Jones, R.A., *The Nineteenth Century Foreign Office. An Administrative History* (London, 1971)
—— *The British Diplomatic Service, 1815 – 1914* (Ontario, 1983)
Judd, D., *Lord Reading* (London, 1982)
Judet, E., *Georges Louis* (Paris, 1925)
Kazemzadeh, F., *Russia and Britain in Persia, 1864 – 1914. A Study in Imperialism* (New Haven, Conn., 1968)
Keiger, J.F.V., *France and the Origins of the First World War* (London, 1983)
Kennedy, A.L., *Old Diplomacy and New, 1876 – 1922* (London, 1923)
Kennedy, P.M., *The Rise of Anglo-German Antagonism, 1860 – 1914* (London, 1982)
Kent, M.(ed.), *The Great Powers and the End of the Ottoman Empire* (London, 1984)
Koch, H.W.(ed.), *The Origins of the First World War* (London, 1972)
Koss, S.E., *Lord Haldane. Scapegoat for Liberalism* (London, 1969)
—— *Asquith* (London, 1976)
Krumeich, G., *Armaments and Politics in France on the Eve of the First World War The Introduction of Three Years Conscription, 1913 – 1914* (Leamington Spa, 1984)

Lambi, I.N., *The Navy and German Power Politics, 1862–1914* (London, 1984)
Langer, W.L., *The Diplomacy of Imperialism* (2nd edn., New York, 1951)
Langhorne, R., *The Collapse of the Concert of Europe. International Politics, 1890–1914* (London, 1981)
Larkin, M., *Church and State after the Dreyfus Affair. The Separation Issue in France* (London, 1974)
Lauren, P.G., *Diplomats and Bureaucrats. The First Institutional Responses to Twentieth Century Diplomacy in France and Germany* (Stanford, 1976)
Lee, D.E., *Europe's Crucial Years. The diplomatic background to World War I* (Hanover, N.H., 1974)
Lee, S., *King Edward VII, a biography* (2 vols., London, 1925)
Lee, S. (ed.), *The Dictionary of National Biography, vol.XLI* (London, 1895)
Lieven, D.C.B., *Russia and the Origins of the First World War* (London, 1983)
Lindberg, F., *Scandinavia in Great Power Politics, 1905–1908* (Stockholm, 1958)
Longford, E., *A Pilgrimage of Passion. The Life of Wilfrid Scawen Blunt* (New York, 1980)
Louis, W.R., *Ruanda-Urundi, 1884–1919* (Oxford, 1963)
—— *Great Britain and Germany's Lost Colonies, 1914–1919* (Oxford, 1967)
Lowe, C.J., *Salisbury and the Mediterranean* (London, 1965)
The Reluctant Imperialists. British Foreign Policy, 1878–1902 (2 vols., London, 1967)
Lowe, C.J. and Dockrill, M.L., *The Mirage of Power. British Foreign Policy, 1902–1922* (3 vols., London, 1972)
Lowe, C.J. and Marzari, F., *Italian Foreign Policy, 1870–1940* (London, 1975)
Lowe, P., *Britain in the Far East. A survey from 1819* (London, 1981)
Luntinen, P., *The Baltic Question, 1903–1908* (Helsinki, 1975)
McKercher, B.J.C. and Moss, D.W.(eds.), *Shadow and Substance in British Foreign Policy, 1895–1939. Memorial Essays Honouring C.J. Lowe* (Edmonton, Alberta, 1984)
McKay, R.F., *Fisher of Kilverstone* (Oxford, 1973)
—— *Balfour. Intellectual Statesman* (Oxford, 1985)
McLean, D., *Britain and Her Buffer-State. The Collapse of the Persian Empire, 1890–1914* (London, 1979)
Magnus, P., *King Edward the Seventh* (London, 1964)
Marcus, H.G., *The Life and Times of Menelik II. Ethiopia, 1844–1913* (Oxford, 1975)

Marder, A.J., *The Anatomy of British Sea Power. A History of British Naval Policy in the pre-Dreadnought Era, 1880 – 1905* (New York, 1940)
——— *From Dreadnought to Scapa Flow. The Royal Navy in the Fisher Era* (5 vols., Oxford, 1961 – 70)
Marlowe, J., *Milner. Apostle of Empire* (London, 1976)
Martin, R.G., *Lady Randolph Churchill, a biography, 1854 – 1895* (London, 1969)
Matthew, C.G., *The Liberal Imperialists. The ideas and policies of a post-Gladstonian élite* (Oxford, 1973)
May, E.R.(ed.), *Knowing One's Enemies. Intelligence Assessment before the two world wars* (Princeton, 1984)
Mayeur, J-M. and Reberioux, M., *The Third Republic from its Origins to the Great War, 1871 – 1914* (Cambridge, 1984)
Mermeix (Terrail, G., pseud.), *La chronique de l'an 1911* (Paris, 1912)
Miquel, P., *Poincaré* (Paris, 1961)
Monger, G.W., *The End of Isolation. British Foreign Policy, 1900 – 1907* (London, 1963)
Morris, A.J.A., *Radicalism against War, 1906 – 1914* (London, 1972)
——— *The Scaremongers. The Advocacy of War and Rearmament, 1896 – 1914* (London, 1984)
Morrow, J.H., *Building German Airpower, 1909 – 1914* (Knoxville, 1976)
Moses, J.A. and Kennedy, P.M.(eds.), *Germany in the Pacific and the Far East, 1870 – 1914* (St. Lucia, Queensland, 1977)
Neale, R.G., *Britain and American Imperialism, 1898 – 1900* (Brisbane, 1965)
Neilson, K., *Strategy and Supply. The Anglo-Russian Alliance, 1914 – 1917* (London, 1984)
Nevakivi, J., *Britain, France and the Arab Middle East, 1914 – 1920* (London, 1969)
Newton, Lord, *Lord Lansdowne, a biography* (London, 1929)
Nicolson, H., *Sir Arthur Nicolson, Bart., First Lord Carnock. A Study in Old Diplomacy* (London, 1930)
——— *King George V. His Life and Reign* (London, 1952)
Nish, I., *The Anglo-Japanese Alliance. The Diplomacy of Two Island Empires, 1894 – 1907* (London, 1966)
——— *The Origins of the Russo-Japanese war* (London, 1985)
Nouailhat, Y-H., *France et États-Unis, août 1914 – avril 1917* (Paris, 1979)
Ombrain, N, d', *War Machinery and High Policy. Defence Administration in Peacetime Britain, 1902 – 1914* (Oxford, 1973)
Oncken, E., *Panthersprung nach Agadir. Die deutsche Politik während der*

Zweiten Marokkokrise, 1911 (Düsseldorf, 1981)
Palmer, A., *The Chancellries of Europe* (London, 1983)
Parsons, F.V., *The Origins of the Morocco Question, 1880–1800* (London, 1976)
Pearl, C., *Morrison of Peking* (London, 1967)
Pedroncini, G., *Les Mutineries de 1917* (Paris, 1967)
────── *Les Négociations secretes pendant la Première Guerre Mondiale* (Paris, 1969)
────── *Les Mutineries des Armees Francaises* (Paris, 1980)
Pingaud, A., *Histoire Diplomatique de la France pendant la Grande Guerre* (3 vols., Paris, 1938–40)
Platt, D.C.M., *Finance, Trade, and Politics in British Foreign Policy, 1815–1914* (Oxford, 1968)
Poidevin, R., *Les relations économiques et financières entre la France et l'Allemagne de 1898 à 1914* (Paris, 1969)
Poidevin, R. and Bariéty, J., *Les relations franco-allemandes, 1815–1975* (Paris, 1977)
Porch, D., *The March to the Marne. The French Army, 1871–1914* (Cambridge, 1981)
Porter, A.N., *The Origins of the South African War. Joseph Chamberlain and the Diplomacy of Imperialsim* (Manchester, 1980)
Porter, C.W., *The Career of Théophile Delcassé* (Philadelphia, 1936)
Raulff, H., *Zwischen Machtpolitik und Imperialismus. Die deutsche Frankreichpolitik, 1904–1905* (Düsseldorf, 1976)
Read, D.(ed.), *Edwardian England* (London, 1982)
Rich, N., *Friedrich von Holstein. Politics and Diplomacy in the Era of Bismarck and Wilhelm II* (2 vols., Cambridge, 1965)
Ritter, G., *The Sword and the Scepter. The problem of Militarism in Germany* (English trans., 4 vols., Coral Gables, Florida, 1969–71)
Robbins, K., *Sir Edward Grey. A biography of Lord Grey of Fallodon* (London, 1971)
────── *The First World War* (Oxford, 1984)
Robinson, D.H., *The Zeppelin in Combat. A History of the German Naval Airship Division, 1912–1918* (London, 1962)
────── *Giants in the Sky. A History of the Rigid Airship* (London, 1973)
Röhl, J.C.G. and Sombart, N.(eds.), *Kaiser Wilhelm II. New Interpretations* (Cambridge, 1982)
Rolo, P.J.V., *Entente Cordiale. The Origins and Negotiation of the Anglo-French Agreements of 8 April 1904* (London, 1969)
Roper, A., *La convention internationale du 13 octobre 1919 pourtant la réglementation de la navigation aérienne. Son origine — son application — son avenir* (Paris, 1930)
Rose, K., *King George V* (London, 1983)

Roskill, S., *Hankey, Man of Secrets* (3 vols., London, 1970 – 4)
Rossos, A., *Russia and the Balkans. Inter-Balkan Rivalries and Russia's Foreign Policy* (Toronto, 1981)
Rothwell, V.H., *British War Aims and Peace Diplomacy, 1914 – 1918* (Oxford, 1971)
Rowland, P., *The Last Liberal Governments* (2 vols., London, 1968 and 1971)
—— *Lloyd George* (London, 1975)
Schmitt, B.E., *The Coming of the War, 1914* (2 vols., New York, 1930)
—— *The Triple Alliance and the Triple Entente* (New York, 1947)
Schuman, F.L., *War and Diplomacy in the French Republic* (London, 1931)
Shankland, P., *The Death of an Editor. The Caillaux Drama* (London, 1981)
Shorrock, W.I., *French Imperialism in the Middle East. The failure of policy in Syria and Lebanon, 1900 – 1914* (London, 1976)
Sommer, D., *Haldane of Cloan. His Life and Times, 1856 – 1928* (London, 1960)
Spender, J.A., *The Life of the Right Honourable Sir Henry Campbell-Bannerman* (2 vols., London, 1923)
—— *Weatman Pearson, First Viscount Cowdray, 1856 – 1927* (London, 1930)
Steinberg, Z., *Yesterday's Deterrent. Tirpitz and the Brith of the German Battle Fleet* (London, 1965)
Steiner, Z., *The Foreign Office and Foreign Policy, 1898 – 1914* (Cambridge, 1969)
—— *Britain and the Origins of the First World War* (London, 1977)
Stevenson, D., *French War Aims against Germany, 1914 – 1919* (Oxford, 1982)
Stuart, G.H., *The International City of Tangier* (2nd edn., Stanford, 1955)
Suarez G., *Briand: sa vie — son oeuvre* (6 vols., Paris, 1938 – 1952)
Symons, J., *Horatio Bottomley* (London, 1955)
Tabouis, G., *Jules Cambon* (English trans., 1938)
Tardieu, A., *Le Mystère d'Agadir* (Paris, 1912)
Taylor, A.J.P., *The Struggle for Mastery in Europe* (Oxford, 1954)
—— *English History, 1914 – 1945* (Oxford, 1965)
Terraine, J., *Douglas Haig. The educated soldier* (London, 1963)
Thaden, E., *Russia and the Balkan Alliance of 1912* (University Park Pa., 1965)
Thobie, J., *Intérêts et impérialisme français dans l'Empire Ottoman (1895 – 1914)* (Paris, 1977)
Tilley, J. and Gaselee, S., *The Foreign Office* (London, 1935)

BIBLIOGRAPHY

Trevelyan, G.M., *Grey of Fallodon, being the life of Sir Edward Grey* (London, 1937)

Turner, J., *Lloyd George's Secretariat* (Cambridge, 1980)

Turner, L.C.F., *The Origins of the World War* (London, 1970)

Vlasic, I.A.(ed.), *Explorations in Aerospace Law* (Montreal, 1968)

Waites, N.(ed.), *Troubled Neighbours. Franco-British Relations in the Twentieth Century* (London, 1971)

Walker, P.B., *Early Aviation at Farnborough* (2 vols., London, 1971 and 1974)

Waterfield, G., *Professional Diplomat. Sir Percy Loraine of Kirkharle Bt., 1880–1961* (London, 1973)

Watson, D.R., *Georges Clemenceau. A Political Biography* (London, 1974)

Weaver, B.J.R.H., *The Dictionary of National Biography. Twentieth Century, 1922–1930* (London, 1933)

Weber, E., *The Nationalist Revival in France, 1905–1914* (Berkley, 1959)

Willequet, J., *Le Congo Belge et la Weltpolotik (1894–1914)* (Brussels, 1962)

Williamson, S.R., *The Politics of Grand Strategy. Britain and France Prepare for War, 1904–1914* (Cambridge, Mass., 1969)

Willson, B., *The Paris embassy. A Narrative of Franco-British Diplomatic Relations, 1814–1920* (London, 1927)

Wilson, J., *C-B. A Life of Sir Henry Campbell-Bannerman* (London, 1973)

Wilson, K.M., *The Role and Influence of the Professional Advisers to the Foreign Office on the Making of British Foreign Policy from December 1905 to August 1914* (D.Phil. thesis, University of Oxford, 1972)

——— *The Policy of the Entente. Essays on the Determinants of British Foreign Policy, 1904–1914* (Cambridge, 1984)

Wolf, J.B., *The Diplomatic History of the Bagdad Railway* (Columbia, 1936)

Woodward, D.R., *Lloyd George and the Generals* (Newark, N.J., 1983)

Woodward, E.L., *Great Britain and the German Navy* (Oxford, 1935)

——— *Great Britain and the War of 1914–1918* (London, 1967)

Wright, G., *Raymond Poincaré and the French Presidency* (Stanford, 1942)

Young, H.F., *Prince Lichnowsky and the Great War* (Athens, Georgia, 1977)

Young, L.K., *British Policy in China, 1895–1902* (Oxford, 1970)

Zeldin, T., *France, 1848–1945* (2 vols., Oxford, 1973 and 1977)

Zeman, Z.A.B., *A Diplomatic History of the First World War* (London, 1971)

Articles and contributions.

Abrams, L. and Miller, D.J., 'Who were the French Colonialists? A reassessment of the Parti Colonial, 1890 – 1914', *Historical Journal*, XIX,(1976)

Allain, J-C., 'La Négociation circulaire: le dialogue franco-espagnol sur le trace de chemin de fer de Tanger à Fes', *Revue d'histoire diplomatique* (1984)

Andrew, C.M., 'German World Policy and the Reshaping of the Dual Alliance', *Journal of Contemporary History*, II(1966)

────── 'France and the Making of the Entente Cordiale', *Historical Journal*, X(1967)

────── 'Déchiffrement et diplomatie: le cabinet noir du Quai d'Orsay sous la Troisième République', *Relations Internationales*, III (1976)

────── 'The French Colonialist Movement during the Third Republic: the Unofficial Mind of Imperialism', *Transactions of the Royal Historical Society*, 5th ser., XXVI(1976)

Andrew, C.M. and Kanya-Forstner, A.S., 'The *Groupe Colonial* in the French Chamber of Deputies, 1892 – 1932', *Historical Journal*, XVII(1974)

────── 'The French Colonial Party and French Colonial War Aims, 1914 – 1918', *Historical Journal*, XVII(1974)

────── 'The French "Colonial Party": Its compositions, Aims and Influence, 1885 – 1914', in Cairns, J.C.(ed.), *Contemporary France: Illusion, Conflict and Regeneration* (New York, 1978)

Baumont, M., 'Le Prince Radolin', in *Mélanges Pierre Renouvin. Études d'histoire des relations Internationales* (Paris, 1966)

Bestuzhev, I.V., 'Russian foreign policy, February-June, 1914', *Journal of Contemporary History*, I(1966)

Blesdoe, G.B., 'Spanish Foreign Policy, 1898 – 1936', in Cortada, J.W.(ed.) *Spain in the Twentieth Century World. Essays on Spanish Diplomacy, 1898 – 1975* (London, 1980)

Bosworth, R.J.B., 'Britain and Italy's Acquisition of the Dodecanese, 1912 – 1915', *Historical Journal*, XIII(1970)

Bovykin, V.I., 'The Franco-Russian Alliance', *History*, IXIV(1979)

Bridge, F.R., 'The British Declaration of War on Austria-Hungary in 1914', *Slavonic and East European Review*, XLVII(1969)

────── 'Izvolsky, Aehrenthal, and the End of the Austro-Russian Entente, 1906 – 8', *Mitteilungen des österreichischen Staatsarchivs*, XXIX(1976)

Butterfield, H., 'Sir Edward Grey in July 1914', *Historical Studies* (1965)

Cairns, J.C., 'International Politics and the Military Mind: the Case of the French Republic, 1911 – 1914', *Journal of Modern History*, XXV(1953)

BIBLIOGRAPHY

Chandler, J.A., 'Spain and Her Moroccan Protectorate, 1898 – 1927', *Journal of Contemporary History*, X(1975)

Collins, D.N., 'The Franco-Russian Alliance and Russian Railways', *Historical Journal*, XVI(1973)

Cooper, M.B., 'British Policy in the Blakans, 1908 – 1909', *Historical Journal*, VII(1964)

Cosgrove, R.A., 'A Note on Lloyd George's Speech at the Mansion House, 21 July 1911', *Historical Journal*, XII(1969)

Crampton, R.J., 'The Decline of the Concert of Europe in the Balkans, 1913 – 1914', *Slavonic and East European Review*, LII(1974)

——— 'The Balkans as a Factor in German Foreign Policy, 1911 – 1914', *Slavonic and East European Review*, LV(1974)

Dockrill, M.L., 'David Lloyd George and Foreign Policy before 1914', in Taylor, A.J.P.(ed.), *Lloyd George. Twelve Essays* (London, 1971)

Dutton, D.J., 'The Balkan Campaign and French War Aims in the Great War', *English Historical Review*, XCIV(2979)

Edwards, E.W., 'The Japanese Alliance and the Anglo-French Agreement of 1904', *History*, XLII(1957)

——— 'The Franco-German Agreement on Morocco, 1909', *English Historical Review*, LXXXI(1966)

——— 'The Prime Minister and Foreign Policy: The Balfour Government 1902 – 1905', in Hearder, H. and Loyn, H.R. (eds.), *British Government and Administration. Studies Presented to S.B. Chimes* (Cardiff, 1974)

Ekstein, M., 'Sir Edward Grey and Imperial Germany in 1914', *Journal of Comtemporary History*, IV(1971)

'Some Notes on Sir Edward Grey's Policy in July 1914', *Historical Journal*, XV(1972)

Fest, W.B., 'British War Aims and German Peace Feelers during the First World War (December 1916 – November 1918)', *Historical Journal*, XV(1972)

French, D., 'The Edwardian Crisis and the Origins of the First World War', *International History Review*, IV (1982)

Ganiage, J., 'Les affaires de Crète (1895 – 1899)', *Revue d'histoire diplomatique* (1974)

Girault, R., 'Les Balkans dans les relations franco-russes en 1912', *Revue historique* CCLIII (1975)

Gollin, A., 'The Wright brothers and the British authorities, 1902 – 1909'. *English Historical Review*, XCV (1980)

Goold, J.D., 'Lord Hardinge and the Mesopotamia Inquiry, 1914 – 1917', *Historical Journal*, XIX (1976)

Gordon, M.R., 'Domestic Conflict and the Origins of the First World War: The British and German Cases', *Journal of Modern*

History, XXXVI (1974)

Grenville, J.A.S., 'Lansdowne's Abortive Project of 12 March 1901 for a Secret Agreement with Germany', *Bulletin of the Institute of Historical Research*, XXVII (1954)

'Foreign Policy and the Coming of the War', in Read, D.(ed.), *Edwardian England* (London, 1982)

Grupp, P., 'Eugène Étienne et la tentative de rapprochement franco-allemand en 1907', *Cahiers d'Etudes africaines*, LVIII (1975)

Guillen, P., 'Les accords coloniaux franco-anglais de 1904 et la naissance de l'entente cordiale', *Revue d'histoire diplomatique* (1968)

────── 'Les questions coloniales dans les relations franco-allemandes à la veille de la première guerre mondiale', *Revue historique*, CCXLVIII (1972)

Haggie, P., 'The Royal Navy and War Planning in the Fisher Era', *Journal of Contemporary History*, VIII (1973)

Hamilton, K.A., 'An attempt to form an Anglo-French "Industrial Entente"', *Middle Eastern Studies*, XI (1975)

────── 'The Air in Entente Diplomacy: Great Britain and the International Aerial Navigation Conference of 1910', *International History Review* III (1981)

Hargreaves, J.D., 'The Origins of the Anglo-French Military Conversations in 1905', *History*, XXXVI (1951)

────── 'Lord Salisbury, British Isolation and the Yangtse Valley, June – September 1900', *Bulletin of the Institute of Historical Research*, XXX (1957)

Hatton, P.H.S., 'The First World War: Britain and Germany in 1914. The July Crisis and War Aims', *Past and Present*, LXXXVI (1967)

────── 'Harcourt and Solf. The Search for an Anglo-German Understanding through Africa, 1912-1914', *European Studies Review* I (1971)

Howard, C.H.D., 'Splendid Isolation', *History*, XLVII (1962)

────── 'The Policy of Isolation', *Historical Journal*, X (1967)

Johnson, D., 'French War Aims and the Crisis of the Third Republic', in Hunt, B. and Preston, A.(eds.), *War Aims and Strategic Policy in the Great War* (London, 1977)

Jones, R.B., 'Anglo-French Negotiations, 1907: A memorandum by Sir Arthur Milner', *Bulletin of the Institute of Historical Research*, XXXI (1958)

Keiger, J., 'Jules Cambon and the Franco-German Détente, 1907 – 1914', *Historical Journal*, XXVI (1983)

Kennedy, P.M., 'Imperial Cable Communications and Strategy, 1870 – 1914', *English Historical Review*, LXXXVI (1971)

────── 'German Weltpolitik and the Alliance Negotiations with England, 1897–1900', *Journal of Modern History*, XLV (1973)
────── 'The Development of German Naval Operations Plans Against England, 1896–1914', *English Historical Review*, LXXXIX (1974)
Kent, M., 'Agent of Empire? The National Bank of Turkey and British Foreign Policy', *Historical Journal*, XVIII (1975)
Kernek, S., 'The British Government's reaction to President Wilson's 'Peace Note of December 1916', *Historical Journal*, XIII (1970)
Koch, H.W., 'The Anglo-German Alliance Negotiations: Missed Opportunity or Myth?', *History*, LIV (1969)
Krumeich, G., 'Raymond Poincaré et l'affaire du "Figaro"', *Revue historique*, CCLXIV (1980)
Langhorne, R., 'The Naval Question in Anglo-German Relations, 1912–1914', *Historical Journal*, XIV (1970)
────── 'Anglo-German Negotiations concerning the future of the Portuguese Colonies, 1911–1914', *Historical Journal*, XVI (1973)
Lee, H.I., 'Mediterranean Strategy and Anglo-French Relations, 1908–1912', *Mariner's Mirror*, LVII (1971)
────── 'The Grey-Cambon Exchange of 22 November 1912: A Note on the Documents', *Bulletin of the Institute of Historical Research*, XLVI (1973)
Long, J., 'Franco-Russian Relations during the Russo-Japanese War', *Slavonic and East European Review*, LII (1974)
McDermott, J., 'The revolution in British military thinking from the Boer war to the Moroccan crisis', *Canadian Journal of History*, IX (1974)
MacDonald, J.F., 'Jules CAMBON et la menace de l'impérialisme americain (1898–1899)', *Revue d'histoire diplomatique* (1972)
McEwen, J.M., 'Northcliffe and Lloyd George at War, 1914–1918', *Historical Journal*, XXIV (1981)
Mcgeoch, L.A., 'British Foreign Policy and the Spanish corollary to the Anglo-French Agreement of 1904', in Barker, N. and Brown, M.L. (eds.), *Diplomacy in an Age of Nationalism. Essays in Honor of Lynn Marschall Case* (The Hague, 1971)
Marcus, H.G., 'A Preliminary History of the Tripartite Treaty of December 13, 1906', *Journal of Ethiopian Studies*, II (1964)
────── 'The Rodd Mission of 1897', *Journal of Ethiopian Studies*, III (1965)
Monger, G.W., 'The End of Isolation; Britain, Germany and Japan 1900–1902', *Transactions of the Royal Historical Society*, 5th ser., XIII (1963)
Morgan, K.O., 'Lloyd George's Premiership. A Study in "Prime

Ministerial Government''', *Historical Journal*, XIII (1970)

Mortimer, J.S., 'Commercial Interests and German Diplomacy in the Agadir Crisis', *Historical Journal*, X (1967)

Muret, P., 'La politique personelle de Rouvier et la chute de Delcassé (31 mars – 6 juin 1905), *Revue d'histoire de la Guerre Mondiale*, XVII (1939)

Murray, J.A., 'Foreign Policy Debated: Sir Edward Grey and his Critics, 1911 – 1912', in Askew, W.C. and Wallace, L.P.(eds), *Public Opinion and Diplomacy. Essays in Honor of E.M. Carroll* (Durham, N.C., 1959)

Pendroncini, G., 'Strategie et relations internationales. La séance du 9 janvier 1912 de Conseil Supérieur de la Défense Nationale', *Revue d'histoire diplomatique* (1977)

Picquart, A., 'Le commerce des armes à Djibouti de 1888 à 1914', *Revue française d'Histoire d'Outre-Mer*, LVIII (1971)

Poidevin, R., 'Weltpolitik allemande et capitaux français (1898 – 1914)', in Geiss, I. and Wendt, B.J..(eds.), *Deutschland in der Weltpolitik des 19 and 20 Jahrhunderts* (Düsseldorf, 1973)

Porch, D., 'The French Army and the Spirit of the Offensive, 1900-1914', in Bond, B. and Roy, I. (eds.), *War and Society. A Yearbook of Military History* (London, 1975)

Ram, K.V., 'The British Government, Finance Capitalists and the French Jibuti-Addis Abbaba Railway, 1898 – 1915', *Journal of Imperial and Commonwealth History*, IX (1981)

Renouvin, P., 'La politique française en juillet 1914 d'après les Documents diplomatiques français', *Revue d'histoire de la Guerre Mondiale*, XV (1937).

—— 'Les but de guerre du governement français, 1914 – 1918', *Revue historique*, CCXXXV (1966)

Robbins, K., 'Sir Edward Grey and the British Empire', *Journal of Imperial and Commonwealth History*, I (1972 – 1973)

Seager, F., 'Joseph Caillaux as Premier, 1911 – 1912. The Dilemma of a Liberal Reformer', *French Historical Studies*, XI (1979)

Shorrock, W.I., 'The Origins of the French Mandate in Syria and Lebanon: The Railroad Question, 1901 – 1914', *International Journal of Middle East Studies*, I (1970)

Silberstein, G.E., 'Germany, France and the Casablanca incident, 1908 – 1909; an investigation of a forgotten crisis', *Canadian Journal of History*, XI (1976)

Smith, C.J., 'Great Britain and the 1914 – 1915 Straits Agreement with Russia: the British Promise of November 1914', *American Historical Review*, LXX (1965)

Soutou, G-H, 'La France et les marches de l'Est, 1914-1918', *Revue historique*, CCLX (1978)

Steiner, Z., 'Great Britain and the Creation of the Anglo-Japanese Alliance', *Journal of Modern History*, XXXI (1959)
—— 'The Last Years of the Old Foreign Office, 1898 – 1905', *Historical Journal*, VI(1963)
—— 'Grey, Hardinge and the Foreign Office, 1906 – 1910', *Historical Journal*, X(1967)
—— 'Foreign Office Views, Germany and the Great War', In Bullen, R.J., Pogge von Strandmann, H., and Polonsky A.B.(eds), *Ideas and Politics. Aspects of European History, 1880 – 1950* (London, 1984)
—— and Cromwell, V., 'The Foreign Office before 1914: A Study in Resistance', in Sutherland, G.(ed.), *Studies in the Growth of Nineteenth Century Government* (London, 1972)
Stevenson, D., 'French War Aims and the American Challenge, 1914 – 18', *Historical Journal*, XXII (1979)
Sumler, D.E., 'Domestic Influences on the Nationalist Revival in France, 1909 – 1914', *French Historical Studies* VI (1970)
Sweet, D.W.., 'The Baltic in British Diplomacy before the first World War', *Historical Journal*, XIII (1970)
Thobie, J., 'Finance et Politique: le refus en France de l'emprunt Ottoman de 1910', *Revue historique*, CCXXXIX (1968)
Vincent-Smith, J.D., 'Anglo-German Negotiations over the Portuguese Colonies in Africa, 1911 – 1914', *Historical Journal*, XVII (1974)
Warman, R.M., 'The Erosion of Foreign Office Influence in the Making of Foreign Policy, 1916 – 1918', *Historical Journal*, XV (1972)
Watson, D.R., 'The Making of French Foreign Policy during the First Clemenceau Ministry, 1906 – 1909', *English Historical Review*, LXXXVI (1971)
Watt, D.C., 'The First Moroccan Crisis', in Roberts, J.M.(ed.), *Europe in the Twentieth Century* (4 vols., London, 1970 – 1)
Williams, B., 'The Strategic Background to the Anglo-Russian Entente of August 1907', *Historical Journal*, IX (1966)
—— 'The Revolution of 1905 and Russian Foreign Policy', in Abramsky, C.(ed.), *Essays in Honour of E.H. Carr* (London, 1974)
Wilson, K.M., 'The Agadir Crisis, the Mansion House Speech and the Double-Edgeness of Agreements', *Historical Journal*, XV (1972)
—— 'The War Office, Churchill and the Belgian Option: August to December 1911' *Bulletin of the Institute of Historical Research*, L (1977)
—— 'The Opposition and the Crisis in the Liberal Cabinet over Foreign Policy in November 1911', *International History Review*, III (1981)

────── 'British Power in the European Balance, 1906–1914', Dilks, D.(ed.), *Retreat from Power. Studies in Britain's Foreign Policy of the Twentieth Century* (2 vols., London, 1981)

────── 'The cabinet Diary of J.A. Pease, 24 July to 5 August 1914', *Proceedings of the Leeds Philosophical and Literary Society*, XIX (1983)

────── 'Sir Eyre Crowe on the Origins of the Crowe Memorandum of 1 January 1907', *Bulletin of the Institute of Historical Research*, LVI (1983)

────── 'The Foreign Office and the "Education" of Public Opinion before the First World War', *Historical Journal*, XXVI (1983)

────── 'The Question of Anti-Germanism at the British Foreign Office before the First World War', *Canadian Journal of History*, XVIII (1983)

────── 'Imperial Interests and the British Decision for war, 1914: the Defence of India in Central Asia', *Review of International Studies*, X (1984)

────── 'To the Western Front: British war plans and the "military entente" with France before the first world war', *British Journal of International Studies*, III (1977)

Wilson, T., 'Britain's "Moral Commitment" to France in August 1914', *History*, LXIV (1979)

Winzen, P., 'Prince Bülow's *Weltmachtpolitik*', *Australian Journal of Politics and History*, XXII (1976)

Newspapers
The Daily Mail
The Daily Telegraph
L'Echo de Paris
Le Gaulois
John Bull
Journal des Débats
La République Française
Revue des Deux Mondes
The Spectator
Le Temps
The Times
Vanity Fair

Index

Abdul Aziz, sultan of Morocco, 69-72, 81, 90, 94, 118, 159, 161
Abingdon, Elizabeth Lavinia, countess of, 4
Abingdon, James Bertie, 1st earl of, 3
Abingdon, Montagu Bertie, 6th earl of, 3-5
Abyssinia: Anglo-Italian discussions on, 40, 47-50, 55-7; France and Jibuti-Addis-Ababa railway, 47, 55, 57, 74-5, 119, 162; negotiations for tripartite accord on, 55, 63, 74-5, 85, 88, 118-21; threat of German intervention in, 74-5, 119
Acton, Fitzmaurice, Captain, 366
Adam, George, 363-4; criticisms of Bertie's conduct, 364-5
Aehrenthal, Alois, Baron Lexa von, 173-4, 198
Aerial navigation, international conference (1910), 200-13; adjournment of, 202-3; Franco-German cooperation at, 204-5; international convention on (1919), 212
Agadir, arrival of *Panther* at, 227-8. *See also* Morocco
Aland islands convention (1856), Russian desire for abrogation, 142-3, 144n, 146
Albert, king of Saxony (1873-1902), 6
Albert I, prince of Monaco, 112, 113n, 159
Alexandra, queen of Great Britain and Ireland, 34, 41, 155, 157

Alfonso XIII, king of Spain, 70, 93, 127-8, 134-6
Algeciras: conference at, 103-4, 108-18; act of, 118, 224, 226, 229, 234
Alington, Henry Gerard Sturt, 1st Baron, 34
Almereyda, Eugène Bonaventure, arrest of (1917), 369
Anderson, Sir Percy, 6
Andrássy, Julius, count von, 5-6
Asquith, Herbert Henry, 1st earl of Oxford and Asquith, 53, 177, 197, 217, 225, 237-8, 270, 340, 389; and Mediterranean naval situation, 284, 288, 294; Anglo-French exchange of notes (1912), 293, 295; Bertie's peerage, 335; resignation, 343; relations with Esher, 349; succession to Bertie, 362
Athelstan Johnson, Wilfrid, 97; and intrigues against Bertie, 363, 365, 369, 378-9
Auboyneau, Gaston, 151, 168-9
Austria-Hungary, 18, 33, 63; supposed Pan-German designs upon, 58; proposals of at Algeciras, 112-17; Mediterranean naval strength of, 283; war crisis (1914), 320-8 *passim. See also* Balkan wars, Bosnia and Herzegovina

Baghdad railway, *see* Ottoman empire
Balfour, Arthur James, 1st earl of, 20, 23, 36-7, 43, 53, 58, 61, 85,

134, 340, 347, 357, 364, 370, 378; and support for France, 76, 78; appointed foreign secretary, 343; his opinion of Esher, 345, 349; declaration (1917), 380; and Bertie's recall, 382-3
Balkan wars (1912-13), diplomacy of, 282, 298-302
Baltic and North Sea agreements (1907-8), 141-7
Bapst, Edmond, 205, 238, 267
Barclay, Sir Thomas, 153-4
Bardac, M., 170
Baring, Maurice, 12
Barrère, Camille, 39, 46, 57, 67, 84, 87-8, 110n, 119, 138, 141n, 143, 162, 242, 386; efforts to draw Italy away from Triple Alliance, 48, 59
Barrington, Sir Eric, 53, 62
Barry, Ernest, 171-2
Barthou, Louis, 301, 373
Behrens, Walter, 110, 317, 367
Beit, Alfred, 96
Benckendorff, Count Alexander, 140, 176
Benoist, Charles, criticism of Caillaux, 260-1
Berger, Commandant, 151
Berlin, congress of (1878), 5-6, 173-4, 343n
Berteaux, Maurice, 217-18, 226
Berthelot, Philippe, 196, 322, 327, 356
Bertie, Lady Feodorowna née Wellesley (1840-1920), 9-10, 34n, 48, 52
Bertie of Thame, Francis Leveson, 1st Viscount
chronology: birth and lineage, 3-4; clerk in F.O., 4-7; assistant under-secretary, 6, 18; married, 9-10; knighted, 35; appointed ambassador, Rome, 36-9; boredom at Rome, 51-2, 60; seeks Paris embassy, 52-4; temporary return to F.O., 60-3; appointed to Paris, 60-1, 63-5;
extension of embassy, 305-6, 334-5; doyen of *corps diplomatique*, 328; removal to Bordeaux, 329-34; raised to peerage, 335; contracts pneumonia, 355-6; rumours of recall, 357, 362-6, 375-9; onset of prolonged illness, 381-2; dismissal, 382-5; made a viscount, 386; death and burial, 387
character: appearance, 9; industry, 7; temperament, 7-10, 395-6; bureaucratic methods, 54, 65, 397; unsociability, 109-10, 157, 395; pragmatism, 388-9; shortcomings as intermediary, 395-6; influence, 393-7
proposes: Anglo-French notes defining interests, 286-7, 290, 313-14; Anglo-Italian accord on Abyssinia, 49; offer to France of 'reinsurance à la Bismarck', 67-8; closer Anglo-French understanding, 87, 100; arbitration on Morocco (1905), 94-5; guarantee of Spanish possessions, 92-3, 132-5, 137; fresh assurances to France, 106, 224-5; modification of 1904 agreement on Morocco, 249-50
relations with: Balfour, 343, 383; de Bunsen, 14, 65-6; Caillaux, 241, 255-67, 393-6; Clemenceau, 126, 178-81, 192, 373; Derby, 351, 359, 385; Edward VII, 34-7, 44-5, 60-1, 98-9, 110-12, 155-7; Esher, 344-7, 349-51, 357-8, 376-7, 394-5; George V, 307-10, 364; G. Grahame, 226; Grey, 101-3, 340-1, 393; de Gunzburg, 170, 352-5; Hardinge, 13-14, 34-5, 61, 101, 121-4, 369-70; Izvolsky, 140-1, 173-5, 300, 323, 351-2; Knollys, 52-3; Lansdowne, 35-6; Le Roy-Lewis, 352-5, 358-9, 362, 366; Lister, 66, 157; Lloyd George, 357, 366, 374-5; Mallet, 14; Nicolson, 302, 305-6; press,

424

351-2, 359-60, 363-4; Rodd, 7, 39, 52, 54; Sanderson, 10-16, 35-7, 61; Spring Rice, 12-14; Tyrrell, 14

rôle in: promoting Anglo-Japanese alliance, 24-8, 31; negotiating accord on Abyssinia, 47-52, 55-7, 63, 75, 118-21; Morocco crisis (1905), 70-90, 94-100; downfall of Delcassé, 86-7, 90; promoting Anglo-French 'industrial entente', 167-72, 184-8, 192-3, 215-16, 224-5; Near Eastern crisis (1908-9), 177-83; aerial navigation conference (1910) 205-13; Agadir crisis, 228-47; settlement of Morocco question, 248-69; bringing about Anglo-French exchange of notes (1912) 282-97; war crisis (1914), 319-27

views upon: Anglo-French colonial squabbles after 1904, 161-5; Anglo-French staff talks, 105, 219, 224-5; Anglo-German relations, 16-33, 46, 58, 61-2, 103, 121-2, 194-9, 271-81; Anglo-Italian relations, 40; Austrian proposals at Algeciras, 114-17; balance of power in Europe, 30, 32, 46, 68, 125, 317-19; diplomacy, 60, 389; *entente cordiale* (1904), 46, 56, 58-9, 217-18; Far East, 18-19, 21, 24-5, 67-8; Fashoda crisis (1898) 23, 32; F.O. reform and functions, 13-15, 343-4; Franco-German relations, 20, 29, 83-4, 87, 96-8, 122-3, 147-52, 158-61, 191-3, 199-200, 224-5, 226, 235, 312-14, 319; Franco-Italian relations, 48-9, 59-60; French character and susceptibilities, 21, 69, 98-9, 117, 157-9, 189, 273, 275, 279; French foreign ministry, 207-8, 211-13, 227, 322; French wartime morale, 347, 361-2, 367-70, 373; German ambitions and diplomacy, 18-22, 23-4, 26, 28-32, 58, 61-2, 71-2, 75, 77, 84-5, 87, 98-9, 105-6, 107, 130, 194-5, 222-4, 228-35, 237, 240-1, 245-7, 317-27, 390-2; Italians, 50, 56; Italy and the Mediterranean agreements (1907), 138-9; Japanese victories over Russia, 68; ministerial and municipal visits to Paris, 109-10, 152-5, 344; Palestine, 379-80; Paris peace settlement (1919), 386-7; Poincaré's government (1912), 267-8; politicians, 389-90; Portugal and her colonies, 19-21, 195, 232, 240, 271-2, 316-17; Russia and her territorial designs, 23, 25-7, 31, 68, 99, 142, 176-7, 300-4, 321, 335-7, 386; Russo-German relations, 20, 29, 58, 61-2, 141-7, 198-9, 318; Salisbury's diplomacy, 22-3; Spanish diplomacy and Morocco, 32, 221-2, 225-6, 228, 251-68; U.S. mediation, 338-42; war aims and peace diplomacy, 338, 370-2

Bethmann Hollweg, Theobald von, 197-8, 223, 238, 246; and pursuit of Anglo-German agreement (1912), 274-5, 279; war crisis (1914), 323

Béthune, duc de, 64

Betzold, Wilhelm, 84, 98

Bienvenu-Martin, Jean-Baptiste, 321-2, 327

Bigge, Arthur John, Baron Stamfordham, 20-1, 310, 349, 376, 378, 383

Bismarck, Otto, prince von, 17-18, 123, 148

Block, Sir Adam, 151, 166-7, 183

Blunt, Wilfrid Scawen, 10n

Boer war (1899-1902), 23-4, 30, 32

Bolo, Paul-Marie (Bolo Pasha), 372

Bompard, Louis Maurice, 139, 142, 144n, 215

Bonar Law, Andrew, 276

Bordeaux, as wartime seat of government, 331-4
Borghese, Princess Pauline, 64
Bosnia and Herzegovina, annexation of (1908), 172-3
Bottomley, Horatio, 348-9, 375
Bourgeois, Léon, 114-17, 122, 127, 129; apprehensions over Abyssinian agreement, 119-21
Bourke, Robert, Lord Connemara, 5
Brest-Litovsk, treaty of (1918), 380-1
Breteuil, Henri, marquise de, 87, 377
Brett, Maurice, Major, 349
Briand, Aristide, 192, 215-17, 334; and French war aims, 341n, 371; forms government (1915), 347; and Cohn affair, 348; resigns, 356; and peace diplomacy, 371, 375n
Bridgeman, Sir Francis, Admiral, 289
Bridgeman, Sir Reginald, 14
Brun, Jean-Jules, General, 205-7, 209
Brussels sugar convention (1902), 158-9
Buchanan, Sir George, 305, 395
Bulgaria, independence of, 173-4
Bülow, Bernhard, prince von, 25, 59-60, 70, 83, 95-6, 98-9, 112, 159-60, 194, 391; conversation with Bertie (1899), 18, 20, 22-3
Bunsen, Sir Maurice de, 14, 65-6, 84, 131, 134-5, 221-2, 252-3; possible successor to Bertie, 306

Cadogan, George Henry, 5th earl of, 60
Caillaux, Joseph, 169, 185, 187, 212, 217, 227, 230, 235-6, 246, 253; poor opinion of Bertie, 7, 9, 241, 388, 393-5; criticizes British conduct in Turkey, 188; use of unofficial intermediaries (1911), 238-9, 242-3; disparages value of *entente*, 257-8; unconciliatory approach towards Spain, 254-8; quarrels with Bertie, 259-66; returns to finance ministry (1913), 315; suspects British intentions in Congo, 316; wartime politics and pacifism, 347, 350, 364, 367, 371, 373, 376
Cambon, Jules, 84, 93, 146, 205, 221, 227, 250; and Mediterranean agreements (1907), 130-8, 147; and value of *entente cordiale*, 148; favours better Franco-German relations, 159-60, 190, 223; warns of possible confrontation with Germany (1911), 218; negotiates with Kiderlen-Waechter (1911), 227, 238-9, 242-5; supports *détente* with Germany, 311; secretary-general at Quai d'Orsay, 347n, 363
Cambon, Pierre-Paul, 49, 56, 67, 72, 74, 84, 88, 90, 94-6, 106, 113, 116-19, 121, 162, 184, 191-2, 195-6, 198n, 205, 212, 216, 225, 230-2, 238-9, 242-3, 244n, 260, 312, 313n; criticizes F.O.'s handling of press (1904), 62-3; anticipates offer of British alliance, 86, 88-9; seeks clarification of *entente* (1905), 82; complains of German intrigues, 85-6; and appointment of Grey, 102-3; seeks pledge of British armed assistance, 104-5, 107-8; helps promote Mediterranean agreements (1907), 131-2, 134, 136-8; apprehensive about future of *entente* (1911), 217-18; criticizes French policy towards Spain, 221; criticizes Quai d'Orsay, 227; and partition of Morocco, 250, 252, 254, 268-9; and prospects for Anglo-German accord (1912), 273, 275, 278-81; seeks clarification of *entente* (1912), 284, 292, 295-7; and naval cooperation with Britain, 285,

291-2, 296; and possible Russian Mediterranean base, 303; and Anglo-German agreement on Portugal's colonies, 315-16; claims to manage British press (1914), 322n; opposes Bertie's recall, 363, 365, 382-3; and French war aims, 371; celebrates victory with Bertie, 387

Campbell, Sir Francis, 34-5

Campbell-Bannerman, Sir Henry, 101-2, 108, 116, 130, 135, 154; misunderstanding with Clemenceau (1907), 152-3

Carnegie, Sir Lancelot, 187-8, 226, 307

Casablanca deserters affair (1908), 161

Cassel, Sir Ernest, 172, 184-6, 215-16

Cecil of Chelwood, Edgar Algernon Robert, Viscount, 369; defines Esher's position at Paris, 350

Central Mining Company, 353

Chamberlain, Sir Austen, possible successor to Bertie, 362, 382

Chamberlain, Joseph, 19, 24, 53, 101

Chasaigne, Coudurier de, 256

China: intervention of great powers in, 19-20, 24-6; and Anglo-French railway loan, 188-9

Chirol, Sir Ignatius Valentine, 32-3, 39, 60, 63, 167, 188, 304

Churchill, Lady Randolph (*née* Jennie Jerome), 10n

Churchill, Sir Winston Spencer, 10n, 274; wish to visit Paris, 154-5; and naval redeployment (1912-13), 283-4, 287-9, 291-7

Clarke, George, Baron Sydenham of Combe, 104, 133

Clemenceau, Georges, 114-16, 140, 142, 150, 158, 160, 169-70, 174-5, 185, 190-1, 214, 217, 237, 246, 258n, 308, 322, 396; values British friendship, 125-7; and Mediterranean agreements (1907), 136-7; hostility towards Russo-German accord (1907-8), 144-7; complains of British military weakness, 149, 152-4; philhellenism and Cretan question, 178-83; criticisms of British policy in Turkey, 188-91; resigns (1909), 192; attitude towards Caillaux, 262, 266; reassures Bertie on French domestic situation (1917), 367; returns to power, 373-4; declines to receive Esher, 376; and Bertie's recall, 378-9, 383-5

Cochin, Baron Denys, 260

Cohn, Jefferson Davis, Hon. Captain: position in France, 348-51, 356, 364, 370n, 395; receives legion of honour, 363

Colebrooke, Lady Alexandra, 157

Combarieu, Abel, 88n, 110n

Combes, Émile, 65, 90, 217, 348, 371

Congo: Anglo-Congolese agreement (1894), 18, 195; German aspirations in, 29, 231-5, 238-40, 243, 272; transfer of Free State to Belgian sovereignty, 195-6; French pre-emptive 'rights' upon Free State territory, 195-6, 235; Franco-German agreement on, 245

Constans, Jean Antoine Ernest, 150-1, 182, 215

Constantinople, Anglo-French purchase of quays company shares, 167

Courcel, Alphonse, baron de, 83, 87

Cowley, Henry Wellesley, 1st earl of, 3, 9, 10n

Crete, international reaction to proclamation of union with Greece (1908), 177-83

Crewe, Robert Ashburton, marquis of, suggested successor to Bertie, 376

Cromer, Evelyn Baring, 1st earl of, 55
Crowe, Sir Eyre, 109n, 113, 148, 240, 254, 322, 327, 389, 394; and armed assistance to France (1906), 107; memorandum (1907), 125, 130; dissatisfaction with French conduct overseas, 162-3, 216, 232, 268; supports Renault, 210-11; defines *entente*, 214-15; response to Agadir, 233-5; doubts about Caillaux, 258-60; supports closer Anglo-French cooperation, 286; criticizes Bertie's treatment of his staff, 333
Crozier, Philippe Marius, 116-17
Cruppi, Jean, 217, 220-3, 226, 228, 260, 263; and Anglo-French *entente*, 218-19, 224-5
Cumberland, Ernest, duke of, marriage of son, 308
Currie, Sir Philip, 11, 24n, 35, 38, 41, 54, 65
Curzon of Kedleston, George Nathaniel, Marquis, 340, 343, 358, 368; and Bertie's recall, 384
Cuthbertson, William Darling, 332-4

Davies, John Thomas, 375, 383
Delcassé, Théophile, 57, 60, 62, 65-75, 78-83, 126, 160, 182n, 216, 248, 258, 260, 264; desires improved Anglo-Russian relations, 67-8; criticism of, 75-6; offers resignation (1905), 76-7; political intrigues against, 84-5, 87, 89, 94, 100; opposes French participation in Baghdad railway, 150; minister of marine, 217; and Anglo-French naval cooperation, 285-6, 289; appointed to St Petersburg, 301; wartime foreign minister, 329, 334, 336
Denmark, possible neutralization of, 141-3
Derby, Edward Stanley, 17th earl of: and Cohn affair, 351; relations with Esher, 359-60; offered Paris embassy, 377-8; succeeds Bertie (1918), 382-5, 397
Deschanel, Paul, 76
Deutsche Bank, 150
Disraeli, Benjamin, 1st earl of Beaconsfield, 5, 167
Dogger bank incident (1904), 62, 67
Doumergue, Gaston, 314, 316, 396
Doumer, Paul, 68
Dual Alliance, see France, relations with Russia
Dupuy, Jean, 96, 192

Eastern Telegraph Company, 128-31
Eckhardstein, Hermann, baron von, 82-3
Edward VII, king of Great Britain and Ireland (1901-10), 1, 28, 34-7, 51, 65, 98-9, 101, 124, 140-1, 154; supports Bertie's ambitions, 36-7, 52, 60-1, 63, 121; visits to: Italy (1903) 40-6; France (1903) 45-6, (1905) 73, 82-3, (1906) 110-12, (1907) 155-7, (1908) 157, (1909) 191; Spain (1907) 136-8; attitude towards presidential wives, 308
Egerton, Sir Edwin, 36, 122, 180
Egypt, 6, 18, 46, 49, 56, 58, 60, 63, 69, 162-3
Elibank, Alexander, 11th Baron Murray of, 353; and Algerian oil-drilling rights, 354-7
Ellis, Arthur, 38
Esher, Reginald Baliol Brett, 1st Viscount, 53; rôle in wartime Paris, 344-55, 356-65, 373, 376; criticizes Bertie, 351-2, 388; views on British representation at Paris, 358-61, 367, 375, 382, 384; leaves Paris, 376-7
Étienne, Eugène, 75, 88, 116, 252; visits Kiel (1907), 159-60

Fairholme, William Ernest, Colonel, 219

Fallières, Armand, 111, 154, 173, 205, 229, 256, 264; reassures Bertie regarding treatment of Spain (1911), 258; and wife and official visits, 308-9
Favre, Albert, 368
Feltern und Guilleaume, 128-9, 131
Ferry, Abel, 367-8
Ferry, Jules, 148
Fife, Alexander Duff, 6th earl of, 6
Fisher, Sir John Arbuthnot, Admiral, 77-8, 81, 284-5, 291
Fleuriau, Aimé de, 278-9
Foch, Ferdinand, General, 219, 381
Fondère, Hyacinthe, 238-9, 243
Ford, Sir Francis Clare, 39
France: relations with Russia, 18, 66-8, 84, 141-7, 173-5, 190-1, 214, 216-17, 300-2, 304-6, 314, 321-2, 337; *entente cordiale* of 1904, 23, 55-8, 60, 69, 248; domestic politics in peacetime, 65, 114-15, 152, 217, 261-2, 310-13; prospects for understanding with Germany, 147-52, 158-60, 189-93, 199-200, 262-3, 311; pursuit of 'industrial *entente*' with Britain, 167-72, 183-9, 192-3, 215-16, 224-5; war aims, 338, 341n, 370-2; mutinies and internal crises (1917), 361-2, 367-70
Francis Ferdinand, archduke of Austria-Hungary, assassination of, 319
Francis Joseph, emperor of Austria and king of Hungary (1848-1916), 42
Franklin-Bouillon, Henri, 374
French, Sir John, Field Marshal, 328-30, 345-6

Gamble, Sir Douglas, Rear-admiral, 201-2, 206
Gavarry, Napoléon Ernest Camille, 207-8, 212
Geoffray, Léon, 72, 75, 145, 221; favours conciliation of Spain, 250-3, 267; verdict on Caillaux, 261
George I, king of the Hellenes, 179-80, 182
George V, king of Great Britain and Ireland (1910-36), 276, 294, 312, 317, 335, 378; visit to Paris (1914), 307-10, 316; supports Bertie's remaining at Paris, 364, 366; and Bertie's recall, 382-3
Germany: and *Weltpolitik*, 18; seizure of Kiaochow, 18-19, 21; agreements with Britain, 19-20, 25, 195, 271-2, 274, 315-17; prospects for alliance with Britain, 24-6, 28-31; Moroccan policy, 29, 69-71, 100, 109, 112, 223-4, 227-33; naval policy and rivalry with Britain, 98, 194, 197, 199-200, 203, 279-80, 283
Gibraltar, security of, 91-3, 132-6, 147
Giolitti, Giovanni, 50
Gladstone, William Ewart, 11, 18
Godley, John Arthur, 1st Baron Kilbracken, 61
Goldney, Captain, 376
Gordon-Lennox, Lady Algernon, 9, 363
Gorst, Sir John Eldon, 103n, 162-3
Goschen, Sir Edward, 154, 243, 251
Gosselin, Sir Martin, 6, 34-5
Graham, Constantine, and wartime consulate-general, 332-3
Grahame, Sir George Dixon, 226, 228-9, 302-3, 331-2; suspects French intentions at Tangier, 252-3, 254, 264-5, 267-8; deprecates idea of Anglo-French alliance, 287-8; and 'nationalist revival' in France, 311-12
Granville, Granville George Leveson-Gower, 2nd Earl, 11, 18
Granville, Granville George Leveson-Gower, 3rd Earl, appointed to Paris, 307, 323, 329-30

Great Britain: Foreign Office
administration of policy and
reform, 5-6, 11-15, 343-4, 357,
369; Admiralty and naval
strategy, 33, 135-6, 176, 230,
250, 283-89; domestic politics,
101, 216, 224; cabinet and
Anglo-French staff talks, 270,
289-91, 295-6
Greece, *see* Crete
Greffulhe, comtesse de, 368
Grey of Fallodon, Edward,
Viscount, 11, 122-4, 127, 132-4,
136, 140-3, 145-6, 152-4, 158,
174, 184, 187, 190, 200, 202,
204, 210-11, 246, 249-50, 302,
349, 392, 396; and Anglo-French
entente, 102-5, 107-8, 111-12, 137-
8, 161-4, 191-2, 217-18, 221-5,
291; possibility of Franco-German
war, 104-9, 244-5, 279, 311-13;
staff talks with France, 104-9,
219, 270, 285, 287-9, 290-1;
Germany's Morocco policy, 106,
113-15, 229-34, 236-8; French
diplomacy at Algeciras, 113-18;
tripartite agreement on
Abyssinia, 119-21; high opinion
of Bertie, 124, 181, 208-9, 256,
393, 395; German transatlantic
cable, 129-31, 135; Spain in
Morocco, 133, 225-6, 251-2, 254;
cooperation with France in
Turkey, 167, 171, 216; Russia
and the straits, 176-7, 303, 335-7;
Germany in central Africa, 195-
6, 234-5, 239-40, 243-4, 271,
315-17; desire for improved
relations with Germany, 270-1,
273-81; opposition to his
diplomacy, 270-1, 276-7; Anglo-
French exchange of notes (1912),
292, 294-7, 313-14; cooperation
with Germany over Balkans, 298-
9; extension of Bertie's tenure,
306-7, 334-5; naval accord with
Russia, 317-19; wartime
diplomacy, 329, 335-42, 379-80

Guestier, Georges, 331-2
Gunzburg, Baron Jacques de, 170-
1, 184; and plots against Bertie,
352-5

Haig, Douglas, 1st earl, Field-
Marshal, 346, 353, 360n, 367,
374, 377, 381; and Cohn affair,
348, 351; relations with Esher,
349
Haldane of Cloan, Richard
Burdon, Viscount, 103n, 104,
270; visits Germany (1906), 122-
3; mission (1912), 272-4, 277
Hamilton, Lord George, 37
Hankey, Sir Maurice, 203, 207
Hanotaux, Gabriel, 248
Harcourt, Lewis, 1st Viscount,
274, 313n
Hardinge of Penshurst, Charles,
Baron, 56, 98-9, 104n, 105, 108,
113, 123-4, 127, 133, 136-7, 139-
40, 144-8, 153, 157, 162, 167,
172, 175-6, 179, 182n, 183, 202-
3; career, 13-14, 36, 52-3, 61,
101-2, 198-9, 305-6; friendship
with Edward VII, 34;
accompanies king to Italy, 40,
44-5, 62; favours improved
relations with Germany, 121-2;
cooperation with France in
Turkey, 168, 184-7; praises
Bertie's diplomacy, 175; possible
successor to Bertie, 306, 362-3;
wartime permanent under-
secretary, 340-4, 349, 366-7; and
Esher, 350; warns Bertie of
critics, 355; requests information
on French morale, 369-70; quells
Lloyd George's indignation, 375;
and Bertie's recall, 382; view of
Bertie, 397
Harrington, Sir John Lane, 55
Harris, Walter, 71
Hatzfeldt, Paul, count von, 19-20,
24, 60, 72
Henderson, Arthur, 368-9

Henderson, Sir Nevile Meyrick, 382
Henry, Arsène, 131, 168n, 169-70
Herbette, Maurice, 218, 238, 243, 250-4
Hervé, Gustav, 374
Holstein, Friedrich, baron von, 70-1, 75, 96, 99, 105, 109, 112
House, Edward Mandell, Colonel, 339-40
Howard, Sir Esme, 8, 44
Huguet, Victor Jacques-Marie, Major, 104
Humbert, Charles, 371-2

Ignatieff, Count Nicholas Pavlovitch, 141
Imperial Ottoman Bank, 150-1, 166-71, 183, 186, 189, 215-16
Italy, desires cooperation with Britain, 38-40, 63; improved relations with France, 59; and Mediterranean agreements (1907), 138-9; war with Turkey, 282, 298, 303-4; naval strength, 283. *See also* Abyssinia.
Izvolsky, Alexandre Petrovitch, 139, 244, 300, 303, 332, 351-2; desires to avoid provoking Germany, 139-42; pursues Baltic accord, 142-7; Buchlau meeting and subsequent diplomacy, 173-7, 179, 198; enquires about staff talks, 216; and war crisis (1914), 323

Japan: allies with Britain, 24-8, 31; and war with Russia, 53, 61-2, 66-8, 90-1, 99
Jaurès, Jean, 76
Joffre, Joseph, General, 329, 334-5, 348
Johnstone, Sir Alan, 66
Judet, Ernest, 156

Kelly, William Archibald Howard, Captain, 8-9, 286-7, 352

Khevenhüller-Metsch, Rudolf, count zu, 76, 173, 328
Kiderlen-Waechter, Alfred von, 198, 223-4, 227-8, 232, 238-40, 242, 245-6, 299
Kimberley, John Wodehouse, 1st earl of, 18
Kitchener, Herbert, 1st earl of Khartoum, 23, 288, 330, 335, 345
Knollys, Francis, 1st Viscount, 28, 41, 54, 157; assists Bertie and Hardinge, 36-7, 52-3
Kriege, Dr Johannes, 202-4, 206, 209, 211-12

Lagarde, Léonce, 56
Lancken-Wakenitz, Oskar von der, 371
Lansdowne, Henry Charles, 5th marquis of, 24-9, 31, 34-5, 39-40, 43, 45, 48-50, 52-3, 55-6, 59-61, 64, 66-7, 74-6, 85, 92-7, 102-4, 132-3, 135, 249, 392, 396; reluctant to lose Bertie from F.O., 36; reactions to William II's Tangier visit, 73; offers support to France (1905), 85-6, 88-9; and Delcassé's fall, 89-91, 97, 100
Lapeyrère, Boué de, Vice-admiral, 206-9
Lascelles, Sir Frank Cavendish, 23, 32-3, 36-7, 53, 62, 103, 105, 122, 243, 394
Lavino, William, 63, 90n, 100, 187
Law, Algernon: praises Bertie, 208; denigrates Quai d'Orsay, 213
Lee, Sir Henry Austin, 60, 324, 333
Leo XIII, Pope, meeting with Edward VII (1903), 41-5, 63
Le Roy-Lewis, Herman, Colonel, 345, 350, 366, 376; seeks to enhance position, 352-3, 358-60, 365; intrigues against Bertie, 353-

4, 356-7, 362; possible successor to Bertie, 363
Lichnowsky, Karl Max, prince von, 316-17
Lister, Reginald, 66, 75, 77n, 104n, 116-17, 144-7, 149, 157, 168-9, 189-90; suggests extension of *entente*, 97, 100
Lloyd George, David, 155, 237-8, 274-5, 276, 340, 349, 389; Mansion House speech (1911), 236, 239; 'knock-out blow' interview (1916), 341; forms government, 343-4; acquaintance with Le Roy-Lewis, 352; and Esher, 357-61; and future of Paris embassy, 362-3, 365; suggests Bertie as permanent under-secretary, 366; sympathy for French claims to Alsace-Lorraine, 372; reacts against press criticism, 377-8; war aims and diplomacy, 379-80; replaces Bertie by Derby, 382-5; and peace settlement (1919), 387
Loreburn, Robert Reid, Earl, 233, 274
Loubet, Émile, 59-60, 65, 73, 82, 111
Louis, Georges, 115, 146, 159, 173, 182, 205, 212, 301

McKenna, Reginald, 274, 288
Madrid convention (1880), 75, 94
Mallet, Sir Louis du Pan, 14, 33, 60, 62, 65, 73-5, 77, 87, 90, 101, 103, 104n, 111, 121-2, 141, 151, 153, 155, 167, 240; desires tighter relationship with France, 57-8, 81, 85, 105; and financial cooperation with France, 168, 171-2, 186; appointment of Marschall von Bieberstein, 281; and naval agreement with France, 284n
Malvy, Jean-Louis, 369, 371
Marchand, Jean Baptiste, Captain, 23

Margerie, Pierre Jacquin de, 314, 322
Marschall von Bieberstein, Adolf, Baron, 280-1
Mary, queen of Great Britain and Ireland, visit to Paris (1914), 309-10
Maura, Antonio, 135
Mediterranean agreements: (1887), 18, 40; (1907), *see* Spain
Menelik II, emperor (negus) of Ethiopia, 47, 49, 74, 119
Merry del Val, Cardinal Raphaël, 44
Metternich zur Gracht, Paul Count Wolff, 60, 90, 104-5, 108-9, 225, 229, 236, 271, 276-7, 279
Meyer, Arthur, 351
Michelham, Herbert Stern, 1st Baron, 349, 356, 364
Millerand, Alexandre, 152, 192, 330, 334, 345
Milner, Alfred, Viscount, 358, 375, 377, 382, 384
Moinier, General, 220, 222, 229
Monis, Ernest, 217, 219-20, 223, 226
Monson, Sir Edmund, 52-3, 61, 64, 305
Monts, Anton, count von, 77
Moret, Segismundo, 253
Morin, Enrico Constantino, Vice-admiral, 38-9, 42, 48-50
Morocco: Anglo-French *entente* on, 46, 56-7, 69; German challenge to French designs on, 69-73, 75-100, 103-9, 112-18; Franco-Spanish agreement (1904), 69, 91, 221, 248-9, 261, 269; Franco-German accord (1909), 189-93, 223, 227; French policy and the Agadir crisis, 219-45; Franco-Spanish differences (1911-12), 220-3, 226, 229-30, 235-6; internationalization of Tangier, 252-3, 264-5. *See also* Germany, Spain

Morrison, George, opinion of Bertie, 24
Mühlberg, Otto von, 26n, 98
Mulai Hafid, sultan of Morocco, 161, 220, 223
Murat, Joachim, prince de, 95
Murray, Sir George, 395
Muscat, Anglo-French dispute over arms trading, 162-5

National Bank of Turkey, 183-6, 215-16
Netherlands, supposed German designs upon, 29, 33, 58, 87
Newfoundland fisheries, Anglo-French differences over, 162-3
N'Goko Sangha company, 215, 223
Nicholas II, emperor of Russia, meetings with William II, 98, 142-3, 198
Nicolson, Arthur, 1st Baron Carnock, 36, 92-3, 128, 131-2, 145, 165, 198-9, 217, 224-5, 228, 231-2, 237, 239-40, 244-6, 249-50, 257, 268, 322, 327, 391, 393-4; rôle at Algeciras, 112-17; pro-Russian views, 139-40, 176, 302, 304-6; deprecates march on Fez (1911), 221; attitude towards *coup d'Agadir*, 233-4; partition of Morocco, 251-2; praises Bertie, 264, 393; Anglo-German relations (1912), 272, 274, 276; French desire for tighter understanding, 282-3, 286-7, 310; succession to Bertie, 305-6; bonuses for embassy staff, 333
Norfolk, Henry Fitzalan-Howard, 15th duke of, 41-4
Norman, Henry, urges Bertie's recall, 362-3
Northcliffe, Alfred Harmsworth, Viscount, 346n, 364
Norway, relations with the great powers, 141-3. *See also* Baltic and North Sea agreements

O'Conor, Sir Nicholas, 60

Orléans, Philip, duc d', 366
Ottley, Sir Charles Langdale, Rear-Admiral, 203
Ottoman empire: and Macedonian problem, 39, 59, 66-7; Baghdad railway, 149-51, 162, 198, 215, 224, 239, 274; British interests and investment in, 166-193 *passim*; Young Turk revolution, 172-3, 183, 298. *See also*, Balkan wars, Bosnia and Herzegovina, Crete
Ottoman Society, 171, 185-6

Painlevé, Paul-Prudent, 356, 363, 368, 370, 372-4
Paish, Sir George, 244
Paléologue, Georges-Maurice, 77, 83, 267, 300, 312, 314
Palmerston, John Henry Temple, Lord, 392, 396
Paris: status of British embassy, 3, 52; state of embassy building, 64, 299-300, 320, 328-9; evacuation of, 329-31; German bombardment of, 381
Parminter, Vye, 299-300
Pauncefote, Sir Julian, 6, 306n
S. Pearson and Son, 354, 356
Pérez Caballero y Ferrer, Juan, 131, 134, 222; Bertie's advice to, 258-9
Phipps, Sir Eric, 1
Pichon, Stephen, 127, 129-30, 134, 136-8, 141, 143-4, 148, 150-1, 156, 160, 162-4, 169, 173-5, 178-9, 181-3, 186-8, 194n, 196, 212, 214, 216-17, 221, 260, 265, 395; and Franco-German agreement (1909), 189-91; remains foreign minister (1909), 192; concern over Anglo-German relations, 197-8; appears to work with Britain at aviation conference, 205-10; reluctant to act independently of Russia, 301-2; visits London, 313; and Bertie's recall, 384

Poincaré, Raymond, 23, 260, 311, 324, 367, 371, 373, 384, 396; opposition to Caillaux, 266; forms government, 267-8; and Haldane mission, 273, 277-81; seeks clarification of *entente*, 282, 293-4; wishes to work with Russia in Balkans, 301, 321; and state visits (1913-4), 308-10, 313-14; protests over Portuguese colonies agreement (1914), 316

Poincaré, Mme. Raymond, and royal visit (1914), 308-10

Puklewsky-Kozlell, M.P., 140

Ponsonby, Sir Frederick, 10, 156

Portugal: and colonial empire in international relations, 19-21, 29, 232, 239-40, 272-2, 274, 315; celebration of peninsular war, 158

Prinetti di Merate, Giulio, 38-40, 50

Radolin, Hugo, prince von, 17, 65, 84, 94, 112, 152, 159-60; conversation with Edward VII (1905) 82-3; reported quarrel with Bertie, 95-6

Radowitz, Joseph Maria, count von, 92, 115-16, 129

Radziwill, princess Marie (*née* de Castellane), 38

Ramondou, M., 262

Rampolla, Cardinal Mariano del Tindaro, 44-5

Rapallo, allied accord (1917) and public reaction to, 374

Rattigan, William Frank, 12

Reading, Rufus Isaacs, 1st marquis of, 377

Regnault, Eugène Louis, 220-1, 250, 252, 267-8; his '*projet*', 254-5, 257-9, 263, 269

Reinach, Joseph, 112n, 365

Renault, Louis, 201-2, 204-8, 210-12,

Repington, Charles à Court, opinion on Paris embassy (1917), 395

Révoil, Paul, 113-17, 127

Ribot, Alexandre, 260, 362-3, 365, 372-3, 356, 369-70

Robertson, Sir William, Field-Marshal, 349, 351, 358-9, 374, 377-8

Robinson (Dawson from 1917), Geoffrey, 363-5

Rodd, James Rennell 1st Baron, 7, 9, 38-40, 44, 48, 52, 54-5, 65-6, 157, 395

Rodd, Lady Lilias, 54

Rome: British embassy building at, 38; quality of ambassadors there, 38-9

Rosebery, Archibald Philip Primrose, 5th earl of, 6, 12, 14, 16, 33, 35, 39, 53

Rothschild, Alfred de, urges Bertie not to resign, 364

Rothschild, Edmond de, 318n, 331-2

Rothschild, Lionel Walter, 2nd Baron, 380

Rouvier, Pierre-Maurice, 65, 75-6, 90, 103-5, 111-15, 150, 217, 258; seeks understanding with Germany (1905), 83-4, 90, 94-6, 98; opposes Delcassé, 88-9

Rumbold, Sir Horace, 12

Russell, Lord John, 4-5

Russia: involvement in China and Korea, 23, 25; agreements with Britain (1907), 139, 176; policy towards Germany and Baltic states, 139-47; demands regarding Constantinople and the straits, 175-7, 335-8; rôle in Balkan conflicts (1912-13), 298, 300-4; recrudescence of friction with Britain in Asia, 304-5. *See also* Bosnia and Herzegovina, Japan

Rycote, Henry, Baron Norreys of, 3

Saint-René Taillandier, Georges, 69

Saint-Seine, Captain Legoux de, 289, 291
Salisbury, James Edward Cecil, 4th marquis of (as Lord Cranborne parliamentary undersecretary of state for foreign affairs, 1900-03), 45-6, 51, 390
Salisbury, Robert Arthur Cecil, 3rd marquis of, 5, 12, 19, 24, 31, 33, 36, 40, 72, 91, 272, 316, 390; opinion of Bertie, 6, 13
Salvette, Mlle., de, 366
Sandars, John Satterfield, 77, 85
Sanderson, Thomas Henry, Baron, 11-12, 16, 23-24, 25n, 33-7, 60-3, 92, 95, 101, 103; attitude towards F.O. reform, 12-15; doubts Bertie's suitability for Rome, 37; suspects German intentions in Morocco, 72
Sarrien, Jean, 114, 149
Saunders, George, 187-8
Sazonov, Sergei Dimitrievitch, 198, 214, 301, 311, 336-7; Bertie's estimate of, 304
Schoen, Wilhelm, baron von, 190, 242, 299, 325, 327-8; views on Bertie (1911), 241; efforts to localize conflict (1914), 321
Scott, Sir Charles Stewart, 52
Selves, Justin de, 227, 229-35, 238, 241-4, 251-4, 258; resents Caillaux's conduct, 255, 260; withdraws 'projet Regnault', 264
Sloggett, Sir Arthur, 349, 351
Smuts, Jan Christian, 389
Société des Agents de Change, 168
Société Générale, 185
Société Mirabaud, 169-70
Somaliland, Anglo-Italian cooperation in, 40, 47-8
South American Cable Company, 126
Soveral, Louis, marquis de, 35
Spain: British offers of guarantee to, 91-3; German investment and involvement in, 92-3, 128, 131, 134; and Mediterranean agreements (1907), 127-39, 147, 249; occupation of Larache and El Ksar, 225, 251. See also Gibraltar and Morocco
Spiers (Spears), Edward, Major, 358-9, 361
Spring Rice, Sir Cecil, 12-13, 16, 32-3, 52, 58, 62, 377, 395
Stanford, Sir Charles Villiers, 8-9
Steed, Henry Wickham, 154, 312-13; defence of Bertie in *The Times*, 364
Stonor, Monsignor Edmund, 42, 44
Stuebel, Dr Oskar Wilhelm, 25-6, 60
Stuers, A.L.E., Ridder, de, 95n
Stumm, Ferdinand, Baron von, 17, 199, 271-2
Sweden, relations with great powers, 142-3, 146
Sykes, Sir Mark, 379-80
Széczen von Temerin, Nicholas, Count, 225, 319-21, 323, 328

Taft, William Howard, 244
Talbot, Lord Edmund, 42
Tardieu, André, 149, 151, 215, 302; criticizes 'sterility' of *entente*, 214
Tattenbach, count von, 75
Tenterden of Hendon, Charles Abbot, 3rd Baron, 5, 11
Thame, John, Lord Williams of, 3
Thomas, Albert, 371
Tirpitz, Alfred von, Admiral, 70, 203
Tittoni, Tommaso 50-1, 58-9, 63, 121, 179-80, 351
Transvaal, relations with Britain, 18-21. See also Boer war
Tschirschky und Bögendorff, Heinrich von, 121
Turmel, L. 372
Tyrrell, William George, Baron, 14, 103n, 111, 121, 135, 155, 175-6, 188-9, 228, 237, 258, 267, 320, 334-5; dissatisfied with

Haldane mission, 272; and naval cooperation with France, 292; criticizes Russia, 304-6; and royal visit to Paris (1914), 310

United States of America, 32-3, 71, 212; wartime diplomacy of, 338-42

Vansittart, Robert, Baron, views on Bertie, 7, 9, 388, 395
Vere, Sir Arthur, 167-8, 172, 184, 186-7
Verneuil, M. de, 168-71, 185-6, 188
Victor Emmanuel III, king of Italy, 38, 40, 40-2, 48, 51, 309
Victoria Eugenia, princess of Battenberg, 128n
Victoria Louise, princess of Prussia, 308
Villa-Urrutia, Wenceslao Ramírez de, 93, 133, 135
Villiers, Sir Francis Hyde, 6, 14, 101

Villiers, Gerald Hyde, 248
Viviani, René, 321, 325, 330

Waddington, William Henry, 5
Walpole, Sir Horace, 13
William II, German emperor and king of Prussia, 21-2, 33, 41-2, 45, 62, 68, 70, 77, 81-2, 96-9, 110-11, 121, 142, 148, 159-60, 182, 194, 198, 227, 238, 246, 271, 320, 391; visit to Tangier (1905), 70, 73-5
Wilson, Sir Arthur, Admiral, 285, 289
Wilson, Sir Henry, General, 360, 375, 378
Wilson, Woodrow, 339-42, 389

Yarde-Buller, Sir Henry, Brigadier-General, 326, 345

Zaharoff, Sir Basil, 365
Zanardelli, Giuseppe, 38-9, 41, 50
Zeppelin, Ferdinand, count von, airships of, 203